GRAPHICS
GEMS

GRAPHICS GEMS

edited by

ANDREW S. GLASSNER

Xerox Palo Alto Research Center
Palo Alto, California

ACADEMIC PRESS, INC.
Harcourt Brace Jovanovich, Publishers
Boston   San Diego   New York
London   Sydney   Tokyo   Toronto

Parts of the Gem "Rotation tools," by Michael Pique, were adapted from his
paper "Semantics of Interactive Rotations," *Proceedings of the 1986 Workshop on Interactive 3D Graphics* (Chapel Hill, NC, October 23–24, 1986), ACM,
New York, 1987, pp. 259–269. Reproduced with permission.

An earlier version of the Gem "A Simple Method for Color Quantization:
Octree Quantization," by Michael Gervautz and Werner Purgathofer, as well as
the figures on the back cover of this book, originally appeared in their
paper, "A Simple Method for Color Quantization: Octree Quantization," in
New Trends in Computer Graphics: Proceedings of CG International '88,
Nadia Magnenat-Thalmann and Daniel Thalmann, eds. Heidelberg: Springer-Verlag,
1988. Reproduced with permission.

ACADEMIC PRESS, INC.
1250 Sixth Avenue, San Diego, CA 92101

United Kingdom Edition published by
ACADEMIC PRESS LIMITED
24-28 Oval Road, London NW1 7DX

Library of Congress Cataloging-in-Publication Data

Graphics gems/edited by Andrew S. Glassner.
    p. cm.
   Includes bibliographical references.
   ISBN 0-12-286165-5 (alk. paper)
    1. Computer graphics. 2. Microcomputers—Programming.
 I. Glassner, Andrew S.
 T385.G697 1990
 006.6—dc20   90-496
                                  CIP

Printed in the United States of America
90 91 92 93   9 8 7 6 5 4 3 2 1

To the spirits of creativity and sharing that imagine new inventions and urge their communication

About the Cover

The cover picture was designed and produced by Thad Beier at Pacific Data Images. The book inspired the picture, although there are only 74 gems on the cover and over 100 in the book. There are four gem shapes repeated many times in many colors. The bag is modeled after the bag a certain Scotch comes in. While the picture was created over a two-month period, it of course came down to the last minute to get it created, so it was ray-traced on 18 Silicon Graphics workstations in about an hour and a half. The text behind the gems and the title is from the animation script that places the gems and the ray-tracing program that created the picture from that script.

Thad Beier
Pacific Data Images

◆

When Andrew showed us the image designed for the cover of Graphics Gems and asked if we were interested in digitally converting it to printable form, we said "What a wonderful image! It's going to be tricky, but it will be fun." It was both. The image colors were designed with respect to a color monitor, producing red, green, and blue pixels. For printing, we needed to convert these pixels to cyan, magenta, yellow and black color separations.

Whether colors are defined for a printer or a monitor, they can be defined with respect to a device-independent standard based on the *Commission Internationale de l'Éclairage* (CIE) standards for color measurement. Given such a definition, we can define the *gamut*, or set of all possible colors that can be reproduced by each device. Colors outside of the device gamut cannot be reproduced. The figure shows a plot of the monitor, printer and image gamuts overlaid. It is easy to see that the monitor and image gamuts are much larger than the printer gamut, and that the image nearly fills the monitor gamut. To make the best reproduction of the picture, we had to squeeze the image colors into the printer gamut in a way that maintained the appearance of the image. We did this with a piecewise, non-linear 3D transformation that collapsed the monitor gamut into the printer gamut. The constraints on this transformation were that colors should move radially towards the lightness axis of the color space (preserves hue and lightness at the cost of saturation) and that colors outside of the gamut should move more than colors inside the gamut (preserves overall saturation).

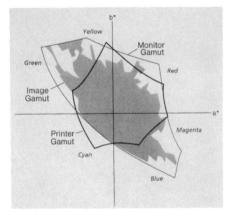

Finding the best transformation is still a research problem. The image was particularly challenging because it filled the monitor gamut, so we had to compress in all directions at once. The texture on the bag and the sparkle of the gems were very sensitive to variations in the transformation; many attempts produced dull, plastic looking gems or an untextured bag, even though the absolute color fidelity was better than the one chosen for final reproduction (proving there is much more to good color reproduction than the colors).

Maureen Stone and Bill Wallace
Xerox Palo Alto Research Center

CONTENTS

Italic page numbers refer to location of corresponding C implementation.

I
2D GEOMETRY

2
2D RENDERING

3
IMAGE PROCESSING

4
FRAME BUFFER TECHNIQUES

5
3D GEOMETRY

6
3D RENDERING

7
RAY TRACING

8
NUMERICAL AND PROGRAMMING
TECHNIQUES

9
MATRIX TECHNIQUES

10
MODELING AND TRANSFORMATIONS

11
CURVES AND SURFACES

APPENDIX 1:
C UTILITIES

APPENDIX 2:
C IMPLEMENTATIONS

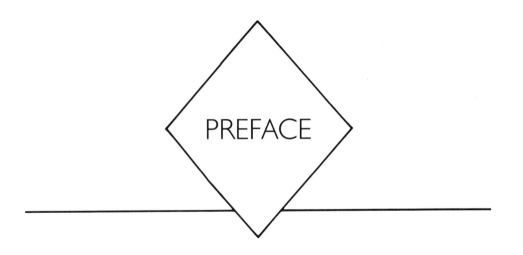

PREFACE

Welcome to *Graphics Gems*: a collection of algorithms, programs, and mathematical techniques for the computer graphics programmer.

I have wanted a book like this for a long time. I have written tens of thousands of lines of computer graphics code in the last few years, and I know that much of it could have been better. I even knew that when I wrote it. But often I didn't have the time to find the best data structure or design the most elegant or robust algorithm. Sometimes I only realized how to do something well after doing it the wrong way first.

As time went on I found myself sharing my experiences and tricks with friends and colleagues, who offered their insights in return. Though we were trading our hard-earned lessons with each other, there was no more general or public forum where we could document these ideas permanently. And I sometimes wondered what insights I was missing simply because I couldn't talk with everyone in the field.

Thus *Graphics Gems* was born. This book was created for the working graphics programmer. Its production concludes one turn of a cycle of discovery, documentation, editing, publishing, and reading, which will lead to new discoveries. The articles in this book are not research papers. The formal publication process in journals and conferences works well for disseminating the architecture of large, new ideas. Rather, this book focuses on the nuts-and-bolts of programming and implementation, supplying the details often left out of technical papers.

How This Book Came to Be

In the spring of 1989 I decided that there was probably enough informal (and unpublished) community wisdom in the graphics field that we could put together a "little book" of clever ideas. The book's title was inspired by Jon Bentley's excellent *Programming Pearls* column published in the *Communications of the ACM*. At Siggraph '89 in Boston I handed out the first call for contributions, which was followed up at other conferences and in graphics publications. I asked for tools that belong in a graphics programmer's toolbox, yet don't appear in the standard literature.

I expected about 25 or 30 contributions; by the deadline in January 1990 over 110 Gems had been submitted. As contributions arrived I let the scope of the book grow slightly, and accepted a few short tutorials. I accepted these longer pieces because they were in tune with the philosophy of the book, presenting useful information not easily accessible in the current literature.

Most of the contributions went through at least one revision step after submission. I have attempted to make the book consistent in presentation by asking everyone to use a uniform mathematical notation and pseudo-code. I hope that most of the Gems in this book are accessible to most readers.

I originally planned to include a set of appendices providing source code in various programming languages. But, except for one short assembly-language routine, all the code submitted was in C! Thus there is one substantial appendix containing C implementations of many Gems. This source code is public domain—it is yours to use, study, modify, and share. By the time you read this, all the code in the appendix should be available on many of the popular networks, so you need not type it in yourself.

I would like to thank my employer, the Xerox Corporation, for its support of this project as part of my work in the Electronic Documents Lab at its Palo Alto Research Center (PARC).

It gives me great pleasure to offer you a book that I have always wanted to have myself. Through the efforts of over 50 contributors, you are holding many valuable nuggets of knowledge and craft earned by experience over many years. We hope that you will find these Gems useful in your work, enhancing your programs and extending your reach.

Enjoy!

Andrew S. Glassner
February, 1990
Palo Alto, California

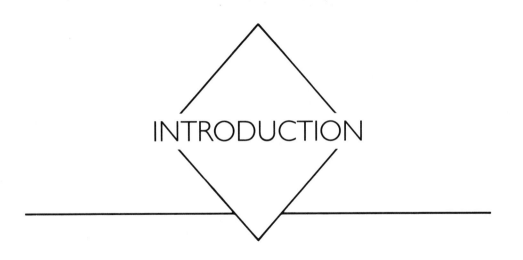

INTRODUCTION

This introduction is designed to help you get the most our of this book. I will discuss some aspects of the book's structure, and then summarize the mathematical notation and the pseudo-code used in many of the Gems.

Some of the Gems originally submitted to this book presented different solutions to the same problem. I've included some of these multiple approaches when I felt they demonstrated interesting alternatives that were useful either for their practical differences or educational value. Some Gems place a high premium on speed; others emphasize algorithmic clarity. Similarly, some Gems take slightly different views of the same problem: For example, there are many ways to draw a line, but your needs are quite different for thick lines, thin lines, anti-aliased lines, and so on.

I have indicated connections between Gems in this book in two ways. When related Gems are all in the same chapter, I have grouped them together and written a short summary that appears at the start of the group. If you refer to one of the Gems in such a group you should at least take a look at the others. When related Gems are not sequential I have included a listing of other relevant Gems under the heading "See also" at the end of the Gem. The "See also" lists are not exhaustive, but they should point you in the right directions.

To make the most of the connections in this book, I suggest you skim briefly all the Gems once. I sometimes find that I can apply an algorithm in a setting completely different from the one for which it was originally designed; knowing what the book contains will help you make these leaps of interpretation.

All of the references are collected together into a single bibliography. Each reference entry contains back-pointers to all the Gems that reference it. You may draw further connections between Gems by following these pointers.

Except for some of the tutorials, most Gems do not provide the background mathematics for their discussions. Usually this math does not go beyond 3-dimensional vector geometry; you can find good summaries of this topic in Kindle, or in virtually any modern textbook on introductory calculus and analytic geometry, such as Flanders. Many graphics programmers have a copy of Beyer on their shelves; this standard reference work distills many important mathematical results into a form that is easy to access.

Some Gems use matrix techniques for geometric transformations. These techniques are described in detail in the standard graphics texts. Our convention is that points are represented by row vectors, and are transformed by post-multiplication with a matrix. You must be careful when transferring the results in this volume to other systems, for they may use a different convention. For example, the PHIGS standard and the Doré rendering system use pre-multiplication of column vectors. You can make the switch between conventions simply by transposing the transformation matrix.

Most of the Gems assume that you are familiar with most of the fundamental material of computer graphics. If you find that you're left behind somewhere, you may wish to consult the classic standard texts, Newman and Foley, or one of the more modern textbooks that have appeared recently; some of these references are listed in the bibliography.

Beyer, W. B. *CRC Standard Mathematical Tables*, CRC Press, Inc., Boca Raton, Florida. (Updated yearly.)

Flanders, H. and Price, J. (1978). *Calculus with Analytic Geometry.* Academic Press, New York.

Foley, J., and van Dam, A. *Fundamentals of Interactive Computer Graphics*, Addison-Wesley, Reading, MA.

Kindle, J. H. (1950). *Plane and Solid Analytic Geometry, Schaum's Outline Series.* McGraw-Hill, New York.

Newman, W. M., and Sproull, R. F. (1979). *Principles of Interactive Computer Graphics, 2nd edition.* McGraw-Hill, New York.

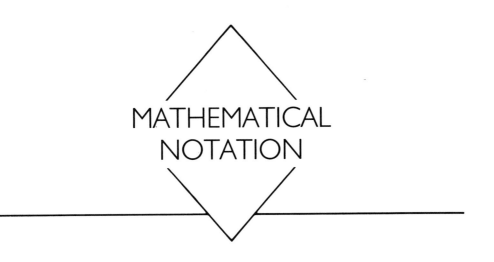

MATHEMATICAL NOTATION

Geometric Objects

0	the number 0, the zero vector, the point $(0, 0)$, the point $(0, 0, 0)$
a, b, c	real numbers (lower-case italics)
P, Q	points (upper-case italics)
l, m	lines (lower-case bold)
A, B	vectors (upper-case bold) (components A_i)
M	matrix (upper-case bold)
θ, φ	angles (lower-case greek)

Derived Objects

$\mathbf{A}^{\perp}$	the vector perpendicular to **A** (valid only in 2D, where $\mathbf{A}^{\perp} = (-A_y, A_x)$)
$\mathbf{M}^{-1}$	the inverse of matrix **M**
$\mathbf{M}^{\mathrm{T}}$	the transpose of matrix **M**
$\mathbf{M}^{*}$	the adjoint of matrix **M** $\left(\mathbf{M}^{-1} = \dfrac{\mathbf{M}^{*}}{\det(\mathbf{M})} \right)$
$\|\mathbf{M}\|$	determinant of **M**
$\det(\mathbf{M})$	same as above
$\mathbf{M}_{i,j}$	element from row i, column j of matrix **M** (top-left is $(0, 0)$)
$\mathbf{M}_{i,}$	all of row i of matrix **M**

$\mathbf{M}_{,j}$ all of column j of matrix $\mathbf{M}$
$\triangle\,ABC$ triangle formed by points A, B, C
$\angle\,ABC$ angle formed by points A, B, C with vertex at B

Basic Operators

$+, -, /, *$ standard math operators
$\cdot$ the dot (or inner or scalar) product
$\times$ the cross (or outer or vector) product

Basic Expressions and Functions

$\lfloor x \rfloor$ floor of x (largest integer not greater than x)
$\lceil x \rceil$ ceiling of x (smallest integer not smaller than x)
$a|b$ modulo arithmetic; remainder of $a \div b$
$a \bmod b$ same as above
$B_i^n(t)$ Bernstein polynomial $= \binom{n}{i} t^i (1-t)^{n-i}, \; i = 0 \cdots n$

$\binom{n}{i}$ binomial coefficient $\dfrac{n!}{(n-i)!\,i!}$

PSEUDO-CODE

Declarations (not required)

name: TYPE ← initialValue;

examples:
π:**real** ← 3.14159;
v: **array** [0..3] **of integer** ← [0, 1, 2, 3];

Primitive Data Types

array [lowerBound..upperBound] **of** TYPE;
boolean
char
integer
real
double
point
vector

matrix3
>   *equivalent to:*
>   *matrix3: record [array [0..2] of array [0..2] of real;];*
>   *example: m: Matrix3 ← [[1.0, 2.0, 3.0], [4.0, 5.0, 6.0], [7.0, 8.0, 9.0]];*
>   *m[2][1] is 8.0*
>   *m[0][2] ← 3.3;   assigns 3.3 to upper-right corner of matrix*

matrix4

> *equivalent to:*
> *matrix4: record [array [0..3] of array [0..3] of real;];*
> *example: m: Matrix4 ← [*
> > *[1.0, 2.0, 3.0, 4.0],*
> > *[5.0, 6.0, 7.0, 8.0],*
> > *[9.0, 10.0, 11.0, 12.0],*
> > *[13.0, 14.0, 15.0, 16.0]];*
> *m[3][1] is 14.0*
> *m[0][3] ← 3.3;*   *assigns 3.3 to upper-right corner of matrix*

Records (Structures)

Record definition:

Box: **record** [
> left, right, top, bottom: **integer**;
>];

newBox: Box ← **new**[Box];
> *dynamically allocate a new instance of Box and return a pointer to it*

newBox.left ← 10;
> *this same notation is appropriate whether newBox is a pointer or structure*

Arrays

v: **array** [0..3] **of integer** ← [0, 1, 2, 3]; *v is a four-element array of integers*

v[2] ← 5;   *assign to third element of v*

Comments

A comment may appear anywhere – it is indicated by italics

Blocks

begin
Statement;
Statement;
. . .
end;

Conditionals and Selections

if Test
    then Statement;
    [**else** Statement];   *else clause is optional*

result = **select** Item **from**
    instance: Statement;
    endcase: Statement;

Flow Control

for ControlVariable: Type ← InitialExpr, NextExpr **do**
    Statement;
    endloop;

until Test **do**
    Statement;
    endloop;

while Test **do**
    Statement;
    endloop;

loop; *go directly to the next endloop*

exit; *go directly to the first statement after the next endloop*

return[value]   *return value as the result of this function call*

Logical Connectives

or, and, not, xor

Bitwise Operators

bit-or, bit-and, bit-xor

Relations

=, ≠, >, ≥, <, ≤

Assignment Symbol

←

(note: the test for equality is =)

Available Functions

These functions are defined on all data types

min(a, b)	*returns minimum of a and b*
max(a, b)	*returns maximum of a and b*
abs(a)	*returns absolute value of a*
sin(x)	*sin(x)*
cos(x)	*cos(x)*
tan(x)	*tan(x)*
arctan(y)	*arctan(y)*
arctan2(y, x)	*arctan(y / x), defined for all values of x and y*
arcsin(y)	*arcsin(y)*
arccos(y)	*arccos(y)*
rshift(x, b)	*shift x right b bits*
lshift(x, b)	*shift x left b bits*
swap(a, b)	*swap a and b*

lerp(α, l, h)   *linear interpolation: $((1 - \alpha)*l) + (\alpha*h) = l + (\alpha*(h - l))$*

clamp(v, l, h)   *return l if $v < l$, else h if $v > h$, else v: $min(h, max(l, v))$*

floor(x) or $\lfloor x \rfloor$ *round x towards 0 to first integer*

ceiling(x) or $\lceil x \rceil$ *round x away from 0 to first integer*

round(x)   *round x to nearest integer, if frac(x) = .5, round towards 0*

frac(x)   *fractional part of x*

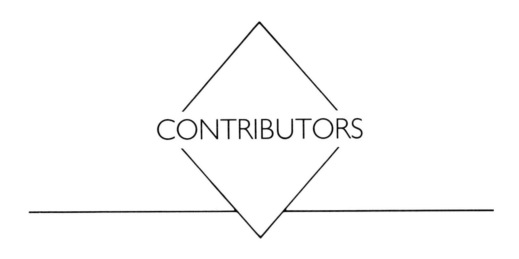

CONTRIBUTORS

Numbers in parentheses indicate pages on which authors' Gems begin.

James Arvo (335, 548), *Apollo Systems Division of Hewlett-Packard, 330 Billerica Road, Chelmsford, Massachusetts 01824*

Didier Badouel (390), *IRISA/INRIA, Campus Universitaire de Beaulieu, 35042 Rennes Cédex, France*

Paul D. Bame (321), *Hewlett-Packard, P.O. Box 617, Colorado Springs, Colorado 80901-0617*

Jules Bloomenthal (567), *Xerox PARC, 3333 Coyote Hill Road, Palo Alto, California 94304*

Richard Carling (470), *13 Overlook Drive, Bedford, Massachusetts 01730*

Steve Cunningham (516), *Department of Computer Science, California State University, Stanislaus, Turlock, California 95380*

Joseph M. Cychosz (64, 476), *Purdue University CADLAB, Potter Engineering Center, West Lafayette, Indiana 47907*

Robert Dawson (424), *Dalhousie University, 1179 Tower Road, Halifax, Nova Scotia B3H 2Y7, Canada*

Ken Fishkin (278, 448), *Pixar, Inc., 3240 Kerner Boulevard, San Rafael, California 94901*

Michael Gervautz (287), *Technische Universität Wien, Institut fur Praktische Informatik, Karlsplatz 13/180, A-1040 Wien, Austria*

Andrew S. Glassner (3, 13, 215, 257, 297, 364, 366, 376, 438, 562, 575) *Xerox PARC, 3333 Coyote Hill Road, Palo Alto, California 94304*

Ronald Goldman (20, 304, 305, 472, 587, 604), *Department of Computer Science, University of Waterloo, Waterloo, Ontario N2L 3G1, Canada*

Julian Gomez (585), *MacroMind, Inc., 410 Townsend St., Suite 408, San Francisco, California 94107*

Ned Greene (485), *Apple Computer, Inc., 20705 Valley Green Drive, MS 60-W, Cupertino, California 95014*

Mark Hall (552, 558), *Computer Science Department, Rice University, P.O. Box 1892, Houston, Texas 77251-1892*

Stephen Hawley (176), *13 Catherine Lane #2, Morristown, New Jersey 07960*

Paul S. Heckbert (61, 84, 87, 99, 246, 265, 275), *1415 Arch Street, Berkeley, California 94708*

D. G. Hook (416), *Department of Engineering Computer Resources, Faculty of Engineering, The University of Melbourne, Melbourne, Australia*

Jeff Hultquist (346, 388, 462), *Mailstop T-045-1, NASA Ames Research Center, Moffett Field, California 94035*

Paul Lalonde (424), *Dalhousie University, 1179 Tower Road, Halifax, Nova Scotia B3H 2Y7, Canada*

Greg Lee (129), *Weitek Corporation, 1060 East Arques Avenue, Sunnyvale, California 94086*

Mark Lee (348), *Amoco Production Company, Tulsa Research Center, P.O. Box 3385, Tulsa, Oklahoma 74102*

Patrick-Gilles Maillot (498), *Sun Microsystems, Inc., Desktop and Graphics Development Organization, 2550 Garcia Avenue, MS 21-04, Mountain View, California 94043*

P. R. McAree (416), *Department of Engineering Computer Resources, Faculty of Engineering, The University of Melbourne, Melbourne, Australia*

Claudio Montani (327), *Istituto di Elaborazione dell'Informazione, Consiglio Nazionale delle Ricerche, Via Santa Maria 46, 56100 Pisa, Italy*

Jack C. Morrison (76), *5654 South Jackpine Road, Evergreen, Colorado 80439*

Mike Morton (221), *P.O. Box 11299, Honolulu, Hawaii 96828*

John Olsen (166), *Hewlett-Packard, Mail Stop 73, 3404 E. Harmony Road, Fort Collins, Colorado 80525*

Alan W. Paeth (18, 49, 57, 171, 179, 219, 233, 249, 307, 427), *Computer Graphics Laboratory, Department of Computer Science, University of Waterloo, Waterloo, Ontario N2L 3G1, Canada*

Mark J. Pavicic (144), *Department of Computer Science, North Dakota State University, 300 Minard Hall, SU Station, P.O. Box 5075, Fargo, North Dakota 58105-5075*

Andrew Pearce (397), *Alias Research, Inc., 110 Richmond Street East #550, Toronto, Ontario M5C 1P1, Canada*

Mike Penk (129), *525 South East 15th Street, Apartment #2, Portland, Oregon 97214*

Michael E. Pique (465), *Research Institute of Scripps Clinic, MB-5, 10666 North Torrey Pines Road, La Jolla, California 92037*

Werner Purgathofer (287), *Technische Universität Wien, Institut fur Praktische Informatik, Karlsplatz 13 / 180, A-1040 Wien, Austria*

Eric Raible (464), *1591 Ensenada Drive, Campbell, California 95008*

Richard Rasala (579), *Northeastern University, 117 Cullinane Hall, Boston, Massachusetts 02115*

Jack Ritter (107, 301, 385, 432, 440), *Versatec, Inc., MS 1-7, 2710 Walsh Avenue, P.O. Box 58091, Santa Clara, California 95052-8091*

Philip J. Schneider (408, 607, 612), *University of Geneva, CUI 12 rue du Lac, Geneva CH–1207, Switzerland*

Dale Schumacher (196, 270), *399 Beacon Avenue, St. Paul, Minnesota 55104-3527*

Jochen Schwarze (404), *ISA GmbH, Azenberstrasse 35, 7000 Stuttgart 1, Federal Republic of Germany*

Roberto Scopigno (327), *Istituto di Elaborazione dell'Informazione, Consiglio Nazionale delle Ricerche, Via Santa Maria 46, 56100 Pisa, Italy*

Clifford A. Shaffer (51, 443), *Department of Computer Science, Virginia Technical University, Blacksburg, Virginia 24061*

Andrew Shapira (29), *ECSE Department, Rensselaer Polytechnic Institute, Troy, New York, 12180*

Ken Shoemake (442), *Xerox PARC, 3333 Coyote Hill Road, Palo Alto, California 94304*

Hans J. W. Spoelder (121), *Physics Applied Computer Science, Faculty of Physics and Astronomy, Vrije Universiteit, De Boelelaan 1081, 1081 HV Amsterdam, The Netherlands*

Kelvin Thompson (38, 40, 43, 47, 105, 210, 361, 434, 435, 453, 456, 460), *903 Romeria #204, Austin, Texas 78757-3435*

Greg Turk (24), *Department of Computer Science, Sitterson Hall, UNC-Chapel Hill, Chapel Hill, North Carolina 27599-3175*

Ken Turkowski (147, 494, 522, 539), *Apple Computer, Inc., 20705 Valley Green Drive, MS 60-W, Cupertino, California 95014*

Fons H. Ullings (121), *Physics Applied Computer Science, Faculty of Physics and Astronomy, Vrije Universiteit, De Boelelaan 1081, 1081 HV Amsterdam, The Netherlands*

Bill Wallace (285), *101 Earl Grey Road, Toronto, Ontario M4J 3L6, Canada*

Bob Wallis (92, 114, 129, 533, 594), *Weitek Corporation, 1060 East Arques Avenue, Sunnyvale, California 94086*

Andrew Woo (394, 395), *Alias Research, Inc., 110 Richmond Street East, Toronto, Ontario M5C 1P1, Canada*

Brian Wyvill (101, 343, 436), *University of Calgary, Computer Science Department, 2500 University Drive N.W., Calgary, Alberta T2N 1N4, Canada*

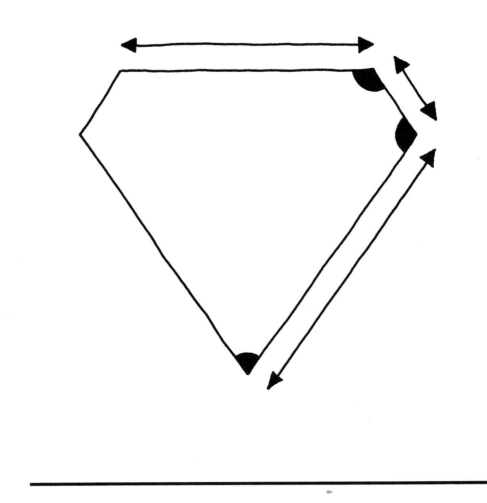

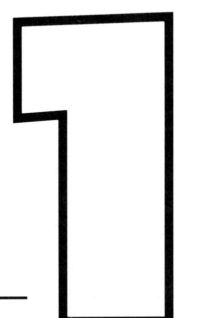

2D GEOMETRY

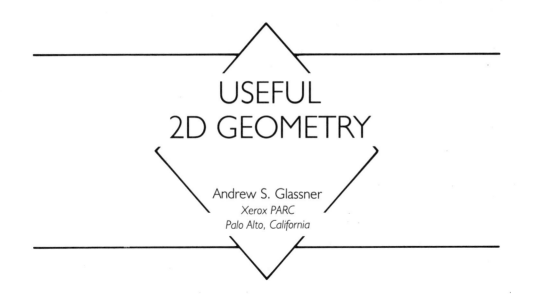

USEFUL
2D GEOMETRY

Andrew S. Glassner
Xerox PARC
Palo Alto, California

Many of the formulae in this section are 2D specializations of a more general solution. Why don't we bother giving the multidimensional solution in its full generality? There are at least two good reasons that the equations in this section are mostly valid only in 2D: they either produce a unique answer, or they require less computation. These advantages are usually related to the facts that in 2D Euclidean geometry, nonparallel lines intersect and there is exactly one line perpendicular to a given line.

Some of these formulae are valid in higher dimensions, and are repeated in the Gem on *Useful 3D Geometry* without much change in the notation. Others are generalized in that Gem, when appropriate.

I will use a programmer's notation to express the formulae. This allows us to express some computations in terms of previous results. I use the prefix V2 to distinguish the techniques for 2D vector geometry in this section from techniques with similar names in the 3D section. In this section the dot (or inner or scalar) product of two vectors $\mathbf{A}$ and $\mathbf{B}$ will be written $\mathbf{A} \cdot \mathbf{B}$; this may be translated for implementation as V2 Dot$(\mathbf{A}, \mathbf{B})$. I will sometimes treat points as vectors; this will be allowed with the understanding that a point P will represent a vector $\mathbf{P}$ with tail at the origin and head at P; thus, the coordinate descriptions of both entities will have the same values.

```
Record Line: [
        implicit: N, c;      Points P satisfy N · P + c = 0 (see Fig. 1a)
        explicit: U, V;      Points P satisfy P = U + Vt for some scalar t (see
                             Fig. 1b)
        normalized: BOOL ← FALSE   True if and only if |N| = |V| = 1
        ]
```

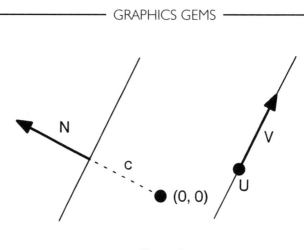

Figure 1.

Line structures of this form will be represented in italic (e.g., *l, m*).

Record Circle: [
    center: *C*;
    radius: *r*
    ]

Circles of this form will be represented by capital roman letters (e.g., A, B) (*see Fig.* 2).

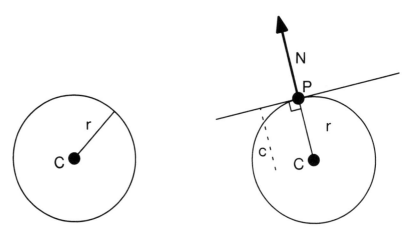

Figure 2.

Figure 3.

$A \leftarrow$ V2 Normalize (A)

$$A \leftarrow \frac{A}{\text{V2 Length}(A)}$$

$d \leftarrow$ V2 Dot(A, B)

$$d \leftarrow A_x B_x + A_y B_y$$

$l \leftarrow$ V2 Implicit to Explicit (l)

$l_U \leftarrow$ V2 Point on Line (l) Nearest the Origin

$l_V \leftarrow$ V2 Perpendicular(V2 Reflect (l_N))

$l \leftarrow$ V2 Explicit to Implicit(l)

$l_N \leftarrow$ V2 Perpendicular(l_V)

$l_c \leftarrow l_N \cdot l_U$

$l \leftarrow$ V2 Line Tangent to a Circle (C) at a Point (P) (*see Fig. 3*)

$l_N \leftarrow P - C_C$

$l_c \leftarrow -(l_N \cdot P)$

$N \leftarrow$ V2 Perpendicular(V) (*see Fig. 4*)

$N \leftarrow (-V_x, V_y)$

$N \leftarrow$ V2 Reflect(V) (*see Fig. 5*)

$N \leftarrow (-V_y, -V_x)$

$d \leftarrow$ V2 Length (A)

$d \leftarrow \sqrt{A \cdot A}$

$P1, P2 \leftarrow$ V2 Intersection of a Circle (C) and a Line (l) (*see Fig. 6*)

$G \leftarrow l_U - C_C$

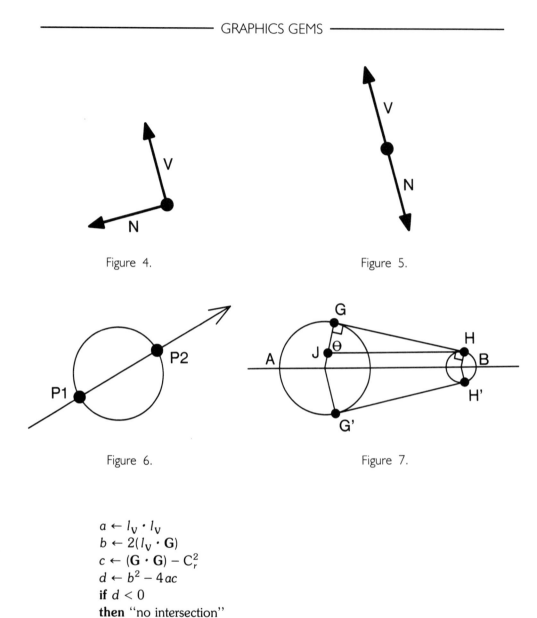

Figure 4.

Figure 5.

Figure 6.

Figure 7.

$$a \leftarrow l_v \cdot l_v$$
$$b \leftarrow 2(l_v \cdot \mathbf{G})$$
$$c \leftarrow (\mathbf{G} \cdot \mathbf{G}) - C_r^2$$
$$d \leftarrow b^2 - 4ac$$
if $d < 0$
then "no intersection"
else
$$P1 \leftarrow (-b + \sqrt{d})/2a$$
$$P2 \leftarrow (-b - \sqrt{d})/2a$$

V2 Lines Tangent to Two Circles Meeting Outside
$l, m \leftarrow$ V2 Lines Tangent to Two Circles (A, B) Meeting Outside (*see Fig. 7*)
To make life easier, we label circles A and B so that $A_r \geq B_r$

We assume that A_C is the origin, and B_C is on the X axis.
We build a line parallel to the X axis through H; it intersects line $A_C G$ at
point J. Thus by construction, $|JG| = A_r - B_r$

Note from the figure that $\cos\theta = \dfrac{|JG|}{|JH|}$.

$\theta \leftarrow \arccos\left(\dfrac{A_r - B_r}{A_C - B_C}\right)$

$G \leftarrow A_C + A_r(\cos\theta, \sin\theta)$
$G' \leftarrow A_C + A_r(\cos-\theta, \sin-\theta)$
$H \leftarrow B_C + B_r(\cos\theta, \sin\theta)$
$H' \leftarrow B_C + B_r(\cos-\theta, \sin-\theta)$
$l \leftarrow$ V2 Line through 2 Points(G, H)
$m \leftarrow$ V2 Line through 2 Points(G', H')

V2 Lines Tangent to Two Circles Meeting Inside

$l, m \leftarrow$ V2 Lines Tangent to Two Circles (A, B) Meeting Inside (*see Fig. 8*)

From similar triangles, observe that $\dfrac{A_r}{x} = \dfrac{B_r}{d - x}$.

d is the distance between the centers: $d \leftarrow B_C - A_C$.

$x \leftarrow (B_C - A_C)\left(\dfrac{A_r}{A_r + B_r}\right)$

$M \leftarrow A_C + x$

Observe from the figure that $\cos\theta = \dfrac{A_r}{x}$.

$\theta \leftarrow \arccos\left(\dfrac{A_r}{x}\right)$

$G \leftarrow (A_r\cos\theta, A_r\sin\theta) + A_C$
$H \leftarrow (B_r\cos\theta, B_r\sin\theta) + B_C$
$l \leftarrow$ V2 Line through 2 Points (G, M)
$m \leftarrow$ V2 Line through 2 Points (H, M)

V2 Lines Tangent to Circle and Perpendicular to Line

$l, m \leftarrow$ V2 Lines Tangent to Circle (C) and Perpendicular to Line (k) (*see Fig. 9*)

$P \leftarrow C_C + C_r k_V$
$Q \leftarrow C_C - C_r k_V$
$l_N \leftarrow m_N \leftarrow k_V$
$l_c \leftarrow -(l_N \cdot P)$

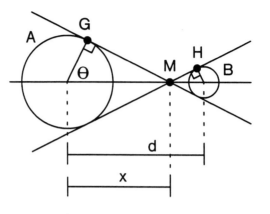

Figure 8.

$$m_c \leftarrow -(l_N \cdot Q)$$
$$l \leftarrow \text{V2 Implicit to Explicit}(l)$$
$$m \leftarrow \text{V2 Implicit to Explicit}(m)$$

Point on Circle Nearest Point

$$Q \leftarrow \text{Point on Circle (C) Nearest Point } (P) \ (\textit{see Fig. 10})$$
$$Q \leftarrow C_C + C_r * \text{V2 Normalize}(P - C_C)$$

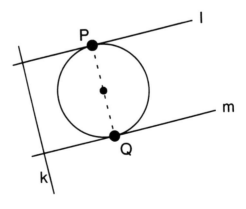

Figure 9.

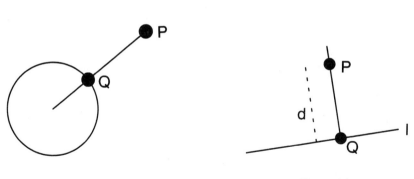

Figure 10.

Figure 11.

V2 Line Through Two Points

$l \leftarrow$ V2 Line Through Two Points (A, B)
  $l_U \leftarrow A$
  $l_V \leftarrow$ V2 Normalize$(B - A)$
  $l \leftarrow$ V2 Explicit to Implicit(l)

V2 Normalize

$l \leftarrow$ V2 Normalize(l)
  $l_c \leftarrow l_c /$V2 Length (l_N)
  $l_N \leftarrow$ V2 Normalize(l_N)
  $l_V \leftarrow$ V2 Normalize(l_V)
  $l_{normalized} \leftarrow$ TRUE

V2 Distance from Point to Line

$d \leftarrow$ V2 Distance from Point (P) to Line (l) *(see Fig. 11)*
  $Q \leftarrow$ V2 Point on Line (l) Nearest to Point(P)
  $d \leftarrow$ V2 Distance between Point (P) to Point (Q)

V2 Point on Line Nearest Origin

$P \leftarrow$ V2 Point on Line (l) Nearest the Origin
  $d \leftarrow$ V2 Point on Line (l) Nearest Point (0)

V2 Point on Line Nearest Point

$Q \leftarrow$ V2 Point on Line (l) Nearest Point (P)
  For notational convenience in this discussion, we write $\mathbf{N}$ for l_N and c for l_c.
  Observation 1: Since Q is on l, then $(\mathbf{N} \cdot Q) + c = 0$.
  Observation 2: The straight line that joins P and Q is perpendicular to l, so $P = Q + q\mathbf{N}$, for some value of q. Rewrite this as $Q = P - q\mathbf{N}$.

Plug this expression for Q into the line equation, distribute the dot product, and solve for q:

$\mathbf{N} \cdot (P - q\mathbf{N}) + c = 0$

$\mathbf{N} \cdot P - q(\mathbf{N} \cdot \mathbf{N}) + c = 0$

$q = (c + \mathbf{N} \cdot P)/(\mathbf{N} \cdot \mathbf{N}).$

We now plug this value for q back into the equation in observation 2 to find Q:

$q \leftarrow l_c + (l_{\mathbf{N}} \cdot P)$

if not $l_{\text{normalized}}$

$\quad$ **then** $q \leftarrow \dfrac{q}{\text{V2 Length}(l_{\mathbf{N}})}$

$Q \leftarrow P - q l_{\mathbf{N}}.$

V2 Distance between Point and Point

$d \leftarrow$ V2 Distance between Point (P) and Point (Q)

$\quad d \leftarrow$ V2 Length$(P - Q))$

V2 Line Perpendicular to Line through Point

$m \leftarrow$ V2 Line Perpendicular to Line (l) through Point (P)

General Solution

$\quad\quad Q \leftarrow$ V2 Point on Line (l) Nearest Point (P)

$\quad\quad m \leftarrow$ V2 Line through Point (P) and Point (Q)

Direct Solutions $(\mathbf{A}^{\perp} = \bar{V}2\ Perpendicular(\mathbf{A}))$

		explicit	implicit
			INPUT
	explicit	$m_U \leftarrow P$	$m_U \leftarrow P$
		$m_V \leftarrow l_V^{\perp}$	$m_V \leftarrow l_{\mathbf{N}}$
OUTPUT			
	implicit	$m_{\mathbf{N}} \leftarrow l_V$	$m_{\mathbf{N}} \leftarrow l_{\mathbf{N}}^{\perp}$
		$m_c \leftarrow -l_V \cdot P$	$m_c \leftarrow -l_{\mathbf{N}}^{\perp} \cdot P$

V2 Cosine of Angle between Line and Line

$d \leftarrow$ V2 Cosine of Angle between Line (l) and Line (m)

$\quad d \leftarrow (l_V \cdot m_V)$

$\quad$ **if not** $l_{\text{normalize}}$ **and** $m_{\text{normalized}}$

$\quad\quad$ **then** $d \leftarrow \dfrac{d}{\text{V2 Length}(l_V)\ \text{V2 Length}(m_V)}$

V2 Point of Intersection between Line and Line

$P \leftarrow$ V2 Point of Intersection between Line (l) and Line (m)

The point P must be on both lines, so it satisfies both line equations. Write one explicitly and one implicitly: $l_N \cdot P + l_c = 0$, and $P = m_U + t m_V$. Since both are true at the same time, plug the explicit into the implicit, distribute the dot product, and solve for t:

$$l_N \cdot (m_U + t m_V) + l_c = 0$$

$$(l_N \cdot m_U) + t(l_N \cdot m_V) + l_c = 0$$

$$t = -\frac{l_c + (l_N \cdot m_U)}{l_N \cdot m_V}.$$

Now it can happen that $l_N \cdot m_V = 0$. This indicates that the two lines are parallel, and there is no intersection at all. Otherwise, we plug this value of t back into the explicit form to find the point of intersection:

$d \leftarrow l_N \cdot m_V$

  if $d = 0$

        then Error["no point of intersection"]

      else $P \leftarrow m_U - \dfrac{(l_N \cdot m_U) + l_c}{d} m_V$

V2 Parameter of Point on Line from Point to Point

$a \leftarrow$ V2 Parameter of Point (P) on Line from Point (Q) to Point (R)

$$a \leftarrow \frac{\text{V2 Distance between Point } (P) \text{ to Point } (Q)}{\text{V2 Distance between Point } (P) \text{ to Point } (Q + R)}$$

V2 Area of Polygon

$a \leftarrow$ V2 Area of Polygon (P)

polygon has n points, $P0, P1, \ldots Pn - 1$

$$a = \frac{1}{2} \sum_{i=1}^{n-1} \left(x_i y_{(i+1) \bmod n} - y_i x_{(i+1) \bmod n} \right)$$

See also Useful 3D Geometry (297); Useful Trigonometry (13)

11

TRIG SUMMARY

The following two Gems provide some relationships that may prove useful when working on trigonometry problems. The first Gem includes some relationships based on the geometry of planar triangles; for more discussion on this topic see *Triangles*. The second Gem provides simple closed-form values for the major trig functions at a number of special angles. These values can be helpful when you are doing symbolic calculations prior to writing a program.

See also Fixed-Point Trigonometry with CORDIC Iterations (494); Triangles (20)

USEFUL TRIGONOMETRY

Andrew S. Glassner
Xerox PARC
Palo Alto, California

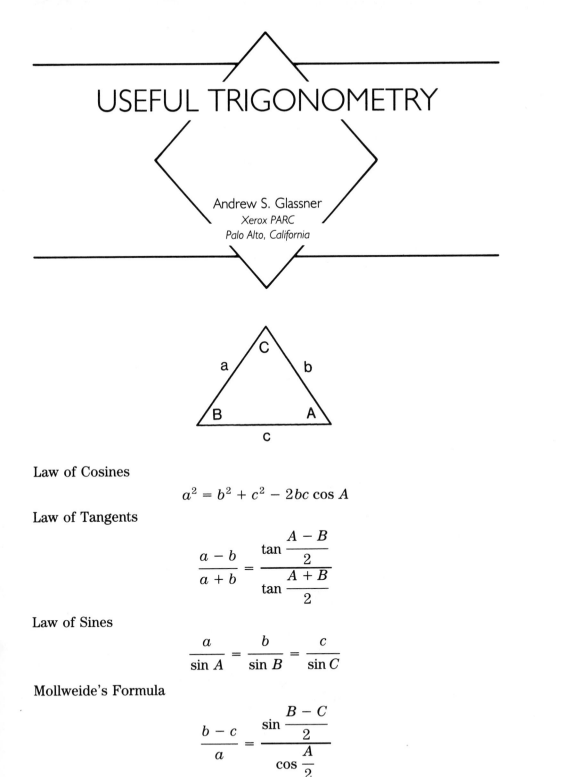

Law of Cosines

$$a^2 = b^2 + c^2 - 2bc \cos A$$

Law of Tangents

$$\frac{a-b}{a+b} = \frac{\tan \dfrac{A-B}{2}}{\tan \dfrac{A+B}{2}}$$

Law of Sines

$$\frac{a}{\sin A} = \frac{b}{\sin B} = \frac{c}{\sin C}$$

Mollweide's Formula

$$\frac{b-c}{a} = \frac{\sin \dfrac{B-C}{2}}{\cos \dfrac{A}{2}}$$

Newton's Formula

$$\frac{b + c}{a} = \frac{\cos \dfrac{B - C}{2}}{\sin \dfrac{A}{2}}$$

Inverse Trig Functions in Terms of Inverse Tangent

$$\sin^{-1}(x) = \tan^{-1}\left(\frac{x}{\sqrt{1 - x^2}}\right)$$

$$\cos^{-1}(x) = \frac{\pi}{2} - \tan^{-1}\left(\frac{x}{\sqrt{1 - x^2}}\right)$$

Functions Sums and Differences

$$\sin \alpha + \sin \beta = 2 \sin \frac{\alpha + \beta}{2} \cos \frac{\alpha - \beta}{2}$$

$$\sin \alpha - \sin \beta = 2 \cos \frac{\alpha + \beta}{2} \sin \frac{\alpha - \beta}{2}$$

$$\cos \alpha + \cos \beta = 2 \cos \frac{\alpha + \beta}{2} \cos \frac{\alpha - \beta}{2}$$

$$\cos \alpha - \cos \beta = -2 \sin \frac{\alpha + \beta}{2} \sin \frac{\alpha - \beta}{2}$$

$$\tan \alpha + \tan \beta = \frac{\sin(\alpha + \beta)}{\cos \alpha \cos \beta}$$

$$\tan \alpha - \tan \beta = \frac{\sin(\alpha - \beta)}{\cos \alpha \cos \beta}$$

DeMoivre's Theorem

$$(\cos\theta + i\sin\theta)^n = \cos n\theta + i\sin n\theta; \qquad \text{where } i = \sqrt{-1}$$

Sines and Cosines in Exponentials

$$e^{i\alpha} = \cos\alpha + i\sin\alpha; \qquad i = \sqrt{-1}$$

$$\sin\alpha = \frac{e^{i\alpha} - e^{-i\alpha}}{2i}$$

$$\cos\alpha = \frac{e^{i\alpha} + e^{-i\alpha}}{2}$$

$$\tan\alpha = -i\left(\frac{e^{i\alpha} - e^{-i\alpha}}{e^{i\alpha} + e^{-i\alpha}}\right) = -i\left(\frac{e^{2i\alpha} - 1}{e^{2i\alpha} + 1}\right)$$

Power Relations

$$\sin^2\alpha = \frac{1}{2}(1 - \cos 2\alpha)$$

$$\sin^3\alpha = \frac{1}{4}(3\sin\alpha - \sin 3\alpha)$$

$$\sin^4\alpha = \frac{1}{8}(3 - 4\cos 2\alpha + \cos 4\alpha)$$

$$\cos^2\alpha = \frac{1}{2}(1 + \cos 2\alpha)$$

$$\cos^3\alpha = \frac{1}{4}(3\cos\alpha + \cos 3\alpha)$$

$$\cos^4\alpha = \frac{1}{8}(3 + 4\cos 2\alpha + \cos 4\alpha)$$

$$\tan^2\alpha = \frac{1 - \cos 2\alpha}{1 + \cos 2\alpha}$$

Product Relations

$$\sin \alpha \sin \beta = \cos \frac{\alpha - \beta}{2} - \cos \frac{\alpha + \beta}{2}$$

$$\cos \alpha \cos \beta = \cos \frac{\alpha - \beta}{2} + \cos \frac{\alpha + \beta}{2}$$

$$\sin \alpha \cos \beta = \sin \frac{\alpha + \beta}{2} + \sin \frac{\alpha - \beta}{2}$$

Half-Angle Relations

$$\sin \frac{\alpha}{2} = \pm \sqrt{\frac{1 - \cos \alpha}{2}}$$

$$\cos \frac{\alpha}{2} = \pm \sqrt{\frac{1 + \cos \alpha}{2}}$$

$$\tan \frac{\alpha}{2} = \pm \sqrt{\frac{1 - \cos \alpha}{1 + \cos \alpha}} = \frac{1 - \cos \alpha}{\sin \alpha} = \frac{\sin \alpha}{1 + \cos \alpha}$$

Angle Sum and Difference Relations

$$\sin(\alpha + \beta) = \sin \alpha \cos \beta + \cos \alpha \sin \beta$$

$$\sin(\alpha - \beta) = \sin \alpha \cos \beta - \cos \alpha \sin \beta$$

$$\cos(\alpha + \beta) = \cos \alpha \cos \beta - \sin \alpha \sin \beta$$

$$\cos(\alpha - \beta) = \cos \alpha \cos \beta + \sin \alpha \sin \beta$$

$$\tan(\alpha + \beta) = \frac{\tan \alpha + \tan \beta}{1 - \tan \alpha \tan \beta}$$

$$\tan(\alpha - \beta) = \frac{\tan \alpha - \tan \beta}{1 + \tan \alpha \tan \beta}$$

Double-Angle Relations

$$\sin 2\alpha = 2 \sin \alpha \cos \alpha = \frac{2 \tan \alpha}{1 + \tan^2 \alpha}$$

$$\cos 2\alpha = \cos^2 \alpha - \sin^2 \alpha = 2 \cos^2 \alpha - 1 = 1 - 2 \sin^2 \alpha = \frac{1 - \tan^2 \alpha}{1 + \tan^2 \alpha}$$

$$\tan 2\alpha = \frac{2 \tan \alpha}{1 - \tan^2 \alpha}$$

Multiple-Angle Relations

$$\sin n\alpha = 2 \sin(n - 1)\alpha \cos \alpha - \sin(n - 2)\alpha$$

$$\cos n\alpha = 2 \cos(n - 1)\alpha \cos \alpha - \cos(n - 2)\alpha$$

$$\tan n\alpha = \frac{\tan(n - 1)\alpha + \tan \alpha}{1 - \tan(n - 1)\alpha \tan \alpha}$$

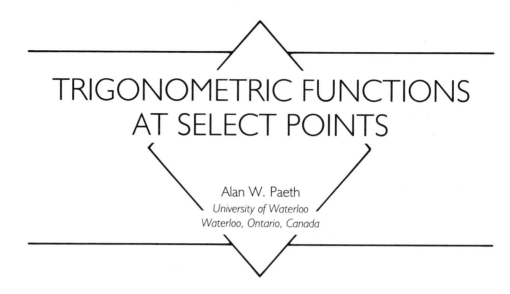

TRIGONOMETRIC FUNCTIONS AT SELECT POINTS

Alan W. Paeth
University of Waterloo
Waterloo, Ontario, Canada

Brief trigonometric tables as appearing in high-school texts usually present values of sine, cosine and tangent for a small number of arguments. Most often the values coincide with a subset of vertex locations on the regular dodecagon (a twelve-sided n-gon). This implicit choice relates to that polygon's underlying three- and four-fold symmetries, for which the related trigonometric values are easily derived.

Although trig functions have transcendental value for most arguments, other n-gons yield up coordinates expressible in simple algebraic forms. This is a consequence of Gauss's seminal work on the compass construction of the 17-gon. Generally, any n-gon is constructible if n's factors are members of the set (2 3 5 17 257 65537), in which each odd factor appears at most once. The factors are the known prime Fermat numbers of the form $2^{2^n} + 1$. (Euler found the factor 641 in $2^{32} + 1$, and no further Fermat primes have been found through $n = 20$, a number containing a third of a million digits; current research suggests that the above set is complete.) Surprisingly, $2^{32} - 1 = 4,294,967,295$—known to lovers of computer trivia as the largest unsigned thirty-two bit integer —is also the largest known constructible polygon having odd sides.

By considering the regular pentagon and octagon, a more useful table may be derived. This has value in the symbolic computation of vertex locations for these n-gons, which are commonplace. As an example, the twenty-faced icosahedron, which underlies many geodesic domes, rests heavily on the cosine for an argument of thirty-six degrees, a value that is easily represented. Here $\phi = \frac{1}{2}(\sqrt{5} + 1) \approx 1.618$ (the golden mean) with the useful properties $\phi^{-1} = \phi - 1$ and $\phi^2 = \phi + 1$. By the Fibonacci series, $\phi^{n-1} + \phi^n = \phi^{n+1}$, making a series of arbitrary powers easily

Table I.   Select Rational Trigonometric Values.

Degrees	Radians	Sine	Cosine	Tangent
0	0	0	1	0
15	$\pi/12$	$\frac{1}{2}\sqrt{2-\sqrt{3}}$	$\frac{1}{2}\sqrt{2+\sqrt{3}}$	$2-\sqrt{3}$
18	$\pi/10$	$\frac{1}{2}\phi^{-1}$	$\frac{1}{2}\sqrt{2+\phi}$	$\sqrt{1-\frac{2}{5}\sqrt{s}}$
22.5	$\pi/8$	$\frac{1}{2}\sqrt{2-\sqrt{2}}$	$\frac{1}{2}\sqrt{2+\sqrt{2}}$	$\sqrt{2}-1$
30	$\pi/6$	$\frac{1}{2}$	$\frac{1}{2}\sqrt{3}$	$\sqrt{3}/3$
36	$\pi/5$	$\frac{1}{2}\sqrt{3-\phi}$	$\frac{1}{2}\phi$	$\sqrt{5-2\sqrt{s}}$
45	$\pi/4$	$\frac{1}{2}\sqrt{2}$	$\frac{1}{2}\sqrt{2}$	1

derived from the three terms given. Values outside of the first octant may rely on the identities $\cos((\pi/2) - x) = \sin(x)$ or $\tan((\pi/2) - x) = 1/\tan(x)$. Half-angle identities using $\cos(\theta/2) = \sqrt{\frac{1}{2}(1 + \cos\theta)}$ and $\sin(\theta/2) = \sqrt{\frac{1}{2}(1 - \cos\theta)}$ allow the construction of higher order even-sided n-gons by angle bisection, though the symbolic forms quickly become awkward.

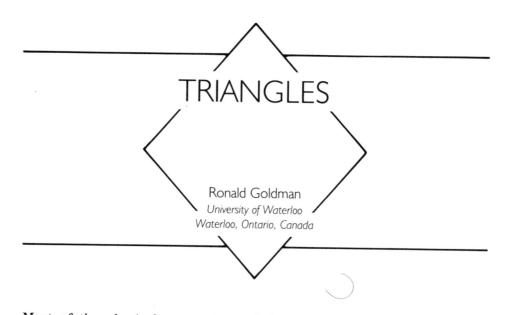

TRIANGLES

Ronald Goldman
University of Waterloo
Waterloo, Ontario, Canada

Most of the physical properties and distinguished points of a triangle $\triangle P_1P_2P_3$ can be written as simple, symmetric, closed-form expressions in the vertices P_1, P_2, P_3. We provide examples below.

Perimeter

$$\text{Perimeter}\{\triangle P_1P_2P_3\} = |P_1 - P_2| + |P_2 - P_3| + |P_3 - P_1|$$

Area

$$\text{Area}\{\triangle P_1P_2P_3\} = |P_1 \times P_2 + P_2 \times P_3 + P_3 \times P_1|/2$$

Center of Gravity (Intersection of the Medians—see Fig. 1)

$$C_G = (P_1 + P_2 + P_3)/3$$

In Radius and In Center (Intersection of the Angle Bisectors—see Fig. 2)

$$r_{\text{In}} = 2\,\text{Area}\{\triangle P_1P_2P_3\}/\text{Perimeter}\{\triangle P_1P_2P_3\}$$

$$C_{\text{In}} = \{|P_2 - P_3|P_1 + |P_3 - P_1|P_2 + |P_1 - P_2|P_3\}/\text{Perimeter}\{\triangle P_1P_2P_3\}$$

Circumradius and Circumcenter (Intersection of the Perpendicular Bisectors—see Fig. 3).

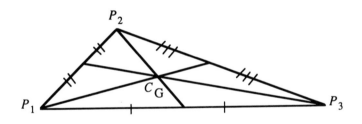

Figure 1. Center of gravity: Intersection of the medians.

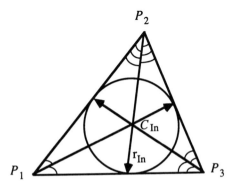

Figure 2. The in radius and in center: Intersection of the angle bisectors.

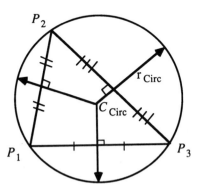

Figure 3. The circumradius and circumcenter: Intersection of the perpendicular bisectors.

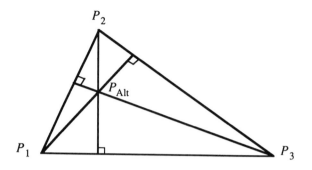

Figure 4.   Intersection of the altitudes.

First define scalars d_1, d_2, d_3 and c_1, c_2, c_3, c by setting

$$d_1 = (P_3 - P_1) \cdot (P_2 - P_1)$$

$$d_2 = (P_3 - P_2) \cdot (P_1 - P_2)$$

$$d_3 = (P_1 - P_3) \cdot (P_2 - P_3)$$

$$c_1 = d_2 d_3 \qquad c_2 = d_3 d_1 \qquad c_3 = d_1 d_2 \qquad c = c_1 + c_2 + c_3.$$

Then we can compute the circumradius and circumcenter by setting

$$r_{\text{Circ}} = 1/2 \sqrt{(d_1 + d_2)(d_2 + d_3)(d_3 + d_1)/c}$$

$$C_{\text{Circ}} = \{(c_2 + c_3)P_1 + (c_3 + c_1)P_2 + (c_1 + c_2)P_3\}/2c.$$

Intersection of the Altitudes of $\triangle P_1 P_2 P_3$ (see Fig. 4)

Let c_1, c_2, c_3, c be as above. Then

$$P_{\text{Alt}} = \{c_1 P_1 + c_2 P_2 + c_3 P_3\}/c.$$

The formulas for the intersection of the perpendicular bisectors (C_{Circ}) and the intersection of the altitudes (P_{Alt}) are related because the altitudes of the triangle $\triangle Q_1 Q_2 Q_3$ formed by the midpoints of the sides of $\triangle P_1 P_2 P_3$ are identical to the perpendicular bisectors of $\triangle P_1 P_2 P_3$ (see

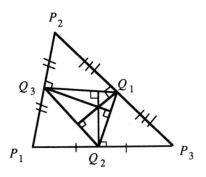

Figure 5.   Altitudes and perpendicular bisectors.

Fig. 5). That is,

$$Q_{\text{Alt}} = P_{\text{Circ}},$$

where

$$Q_k = (P_i + P_j)/2$$

$$P_k = Q_i + Q_j - Q_k,$$

and the indices i, j, k represent a permutation of the integers 1, 2, 3. Thus we can find Q_{Alt} by solving for P_1, P_2, P_3 and using the formula for the circumcenter of $\triangle P_1 P_2 P_3$. Similarly, we can find P_{Circ} by solving for Q_1, Q_2, Q_3 and using the formula for the intersection of the altitudes of $\triangle Q_1 Q_2 Q_3$.

Observe that the circumcenter and circumradius solve the problem of finding the circle through three given points P_1, P_2, P_3. Similarly, we can use the in center and in radius to solve the problem of finding the circle tangent to three given lines. To find this tangent circle, first find the pairwise intersections P_1, P_2, P_3 of the three given lines. Then simply compute the in center and in radius of $\triangle P_1 P_2 P_3$. The results are the center and the radius of the circle tangent to the original three lines.

See also Generating Random Points in Triangles (24)

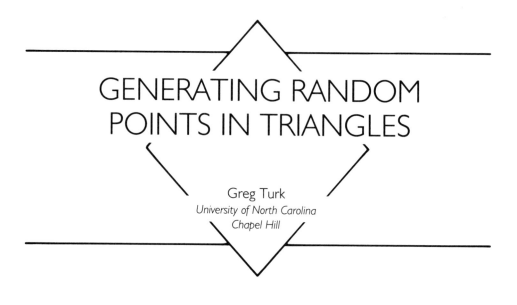

GENERATING RANDOM POINTS IN TRIANGLES

Greg Turk
University of North Carolina
Chapel Hill

Problem

Given three points A, B and C that describe a triangle, pick a random point in the triangle. When many such points are picked the distribution of the points should be uniform across the triangle.

Method 1

Let s and t be two numbers chosen from a uniform distribution of random numbers in the interval $[0, 1]$. Then the point Q given below is a random point in the triangle with vertices A, B and C.

$$a \leftarrow 1 - \sqrt{t};$$

$$b \leftarrow (1 - s)\sqrt{t};$$

$$c \leftarrow s\sqrt{t};$$

$$Q \leftarrow aA + bB + cC;$$

This amounts to having t determine a line segment parallel to BC that joins a point on AB with a point on AC, and then picking a point on this segment based on the value of s (see Fig. 1). Taking the square root of t is necessary to weight all portions of the triangle equally. The values a, b and c are the barycentric coordinates for the point in the triangle.

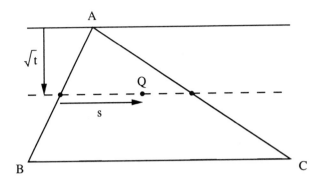

Figure 1.   Random point in polygon using method 1.

Method 2

Let s and t be random numbers in $[0, 1]$. A random point Q in the triangle is given by the following:

```
if s + t > 1 then
    begin
        s ← 1 − s;
        t ← 1 − t;
    end;


a ← 1 − s − t;
b ← s;
c ← t;


Q ← aA + bB + cC;
```

Without the "if" statement, the point Q will be a random point in the parallelogram with vertices A, B, C and $(B + C - A)$ (see Fig. 2). A point that lands in the triangle $B, C, (B + C - A)$ is moved into the triangle A, B, C by reflecting it about the center of the parallelogram.

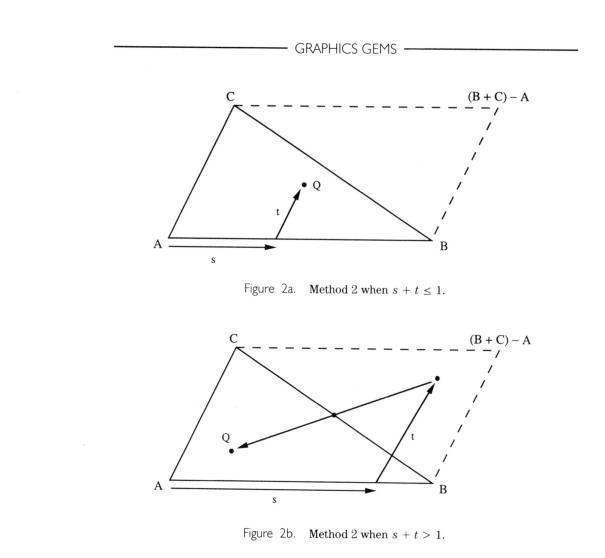

Figure 2a.   Method 2 when $s + t \leq 1$.

Figure 2b.   Method 2 when $s + t > 1$.

Generalizations

Method 1 can be extended to higher-dimensional shapes in a straightfor-ward manner. For example, a random point in a tetrahedron can be found by using three random numbers: the cube root of the first number is used to pick a triangle that is parallel to the base of the tetrahedron, and then the two remaining numbers are used to pick a random point on that triangle.

Method 2 does not gracefully generalize to higher dimensions. For picking a random point in a tetrahedron, the analog of method 2 will use three random numbers r, s and t to give a random point in a parallelepiped. This parallelepiped cannot be easily dissected into parts that are all congruent to the desired tetrahedron, so it is difficult to take points that fall outside the tetrahedron and map them back into the tetrahedron. The simplest thing to do is throw out points in the parallelepiped that are not also in the tetrahedron, and this can be accomplished by rejecting triples r, s, t when $r + s + t > 1$. As this method is extended beyond tetrahedra, a higher proportion of the random values must be rejected.

Either method can be used to pick random points in a polygon by breaking the polygon into triangles and using a random number to choose a triangle in which to pick a random point. The triangle must be selected taking into account the relative areas of the subtriangles. Given random numbers s and t in $[0, 1]$, here is how to pick a random point in a convex polygon described by the vertices $V_1, V_2, \ldots, V_n$:

```
area_sum ← 0;
    for k ← 1 to n − 2 do              find area of triangles radiating from V₁
        areaₖ ← |(V_{k+1} − V_k) × (V_{k+2} − V₁)|;    half area of triangles
        area_sum ← area_sum + areaₖ;   find total area of polygon

    endloop;
sum ← 0;
    for k ← 1 to n − 2 do              pick a triangle based on relative areas
        sum ← sum + areaₖ;             keep running area subtotal
        if sum ≥ s*area_sum then exit; see if we're within proper range

    endloop;
s ← 1 + (s * area_sum − sum / areaₖ;   map s into [0, 1]
```

pick random point in the sub-triangle with vertices V_1, V_{k+1}, V_{k+2}

$$Q \leftarrow (1 - \sqrt{t})V_1 + (1 - s)\sqrt{t}\,V_{k+1} + s\sqrt{t}\,V_{k+2};$$

The above code extends method 1 to give a mapping from the unit square $[0, 1] \times [0, 1]$ into the given polygon. This mapping is continuous, one-to-one and onto. We can use this mapping to define a Peano (area-filling) curve for a convex polygon. If we have a Peano curve that maps the interval $[0, 1]$ into $[0, 1] \times [0, 1]$, we can compose this with our mapping from above to give a mapping from $[0, 1]$ into the polygon. Method 2 does not give a one-to-one mapping from $[0, 1] \times [0, 1]$ into a triangle, so a Peano curve constructed using method 2 for mapping onto the triangles would fold on top of itself, which is probably undesirable.

Acknowledgements

Some of these ideas were worked out during conversations I had with John Airey and David Banks.

See also Triangles (20)

See Appendix 2 for C Implementation (**649**)

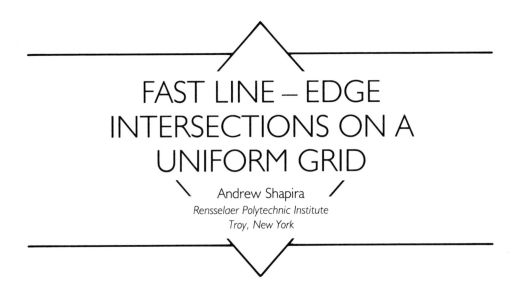

FAST LINE – EDGE INTERSECTIONS ON A UNIFORM GRID

Andrew Shapira

Rensselaer Polytechnic Institute
Troy, New York

This paper presents an algorithm that uses only integer addition and subtraction to find intersections between a uniform grid and a line segment having grid vertices as its endpoints. The output of the algorithm is a list of grid vertices and edges that intersect the line segment; the precise points of intersection are not found. The algorithm is very similar to Bresenham's algorithm for drawing line segments on a raster device. The problem is stated below.

Given: (1) A 2D uniform grid G with square cells of unit side length
(2) Two distinct vertices of G, $P = (P_x, P_y)$ and $Q = (Q_x, Q_y)$

Find: All edges and vertices of G, excluding P and Q, that intersect PQ

The solution of this problem was motivated by the need to compute visibility in a grid-based terrain. An implementation of the line-edge algorithm presented in this paper was used as a platform by a grid visibility algorithm. The resulting grid visibility data have been used for several applications, including terrain labelling, path planning, line-of-sight communication, visualization, visibility theory experiments, and object recognition in images. Other possible visibility applications include terrain orientation, terrain navigation, and representation of terrain physiography.

The terrain model mentioned above was selected because digital terrain data are often packaged in a form that matches this model. The terrain model is as follows. Each vertex in a 2D uniform grid has an integer-val-

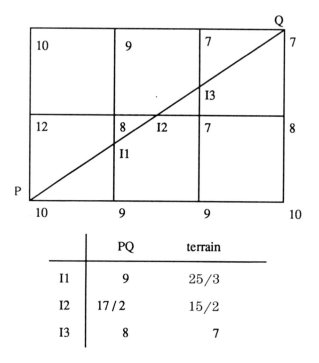

	PQ	terrain
I1	9	25/3
I2	17/2	15/2
I3	8	7

Figure 1. Determining whether or not two points are mutually visible. The upper diagram shows a terrain as seen from above, with elevations given next to each vertex. The projection of line-of-sight *PQ* intersects the grid at points I1, I2, and I3. The table shows the heights of *PQ* and the terrain at each intersection. Since the line of sight is above the terrain at all intersections, points *P* and *Q* are mutually visible.

ued elevation associated with it; each of the resulting points in 3-space is called a *data value*. Terrain elevations above grid edges are obtained by linear interpolation between the appropriate data values. The terrain above the interior of all grid cells is defined in such a way so as not to interfere with the intervisibility of data values.

Visibility within this simple terrain model approximates visibility within more complicated models such as triangulated terrain models, but is simpler to calculate (see Fig. 1). To determine whether two data points *U* and *V* are mutually visible, a test is performed everywhere that the 2D projection of *UV* intersects a grid edge or vertex. The test determines whether the line-of-sight UV is above the terrain at the point of intersection. If UV always turns out to be above the terrain, then U and V are visible. If any test shows that UV is below the terrain, then U and V are mutually invisible, and testing terminates.

This computation is very efficient. The entire visibility calculation can be done using only integer additions, subtractions, and multiplications. If desired, the calculation for many pairs of data values can easily be adapted to execute in parallel on a coarse-grained machine.

The visibility algorithm was implemented in C; intersections are generated using a slightly modified version of the line-edge intersection algorithm in this paper. On a SUN 3/60 computer running SUN Operating System 3.4 with 12 megabytes of memory, the program took roughly 11 hours of CPU time to compute the 100 million visibility pairs of a 100 by 100 terrain taken from United States Geological Survey data.

The line-edge intersection algorithm is derived below using pseudo-C. Included are two intermediate versions that use floating point. Because of rounding problems, these versions may not work on machines with finite floating point precision. They are used only to derive the final version.

First we will discuss a few miscellaneous items. We will assume for the time being that Q lies between $0°$ and $45°$ from P, inclusive. If PQ forms an angle with the x-axis that is a multiple of $45°$, then PQ will be considered to intersect the terrain only at grid vertices. In Algorithms 1–4, the symbols Δx and Δy are used as abbreviations for $(Q_x - P_x)$ and $(Q_y - P_y)$ respectively, and m denotes $(\Delta y / \Delta x)$. All variables are local and type *integer* unless otherwise indicated. The unary operator (**real**) converts its operand to type **real**. In any expression containing one or more floating point operands, all operations are performed using floating point. The value of an arbitrary variable t during loop iteration i is denoted t_i; t_0 denotes the value of t just before the first loop iteration.

To derive the first version of the algorithm, consider each point $(x, y(x))$ along PQ such that $x \in \{P_x + 1, P_x + 2, \ldots, Q_x - 1\}$, and $y(x) = P_y + m(x - P_x)$. It is apparent from Fig. 2 that if $y(x) = \lfloor y(x) \rfloor$, then PQ intersects a vertex at $(x, y(x))$. If $y(x) \neq \lfloor y(x) \rfloor$, then PQ intersects the vertical edge connecting $(x, \lfloor y(x) \rfloor)$ and $(x, \lceil y(x) \rceil)$; if, in addition, $y(x - 1) < \lfloor y(x) \rfloor$, then PQ also intersects the horizontal edge connecting $(x - 1, \lfloor y(x) \rfloor)$ and $(x, \lfloor y(x) \rfloor)$. An algorithm based on these ideas is given below.

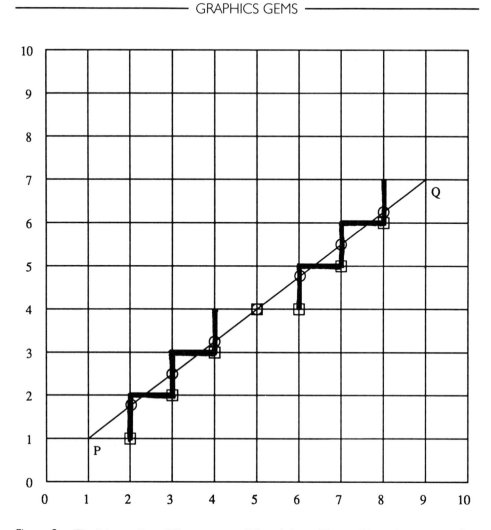

Figure 2. The intersection of line segment PQ and the uniform grid can be expressed as {up(2, 1), left(3, 2), up(3, 2), left(4, 3), up(4, 3), vertex(5, 4), up(6, 4), left(7, 5), up (7, 5), left(8, 6), up(8, 6)}. Highlighted grid edges indicate intersections with PQ. Circles indicate points traversed by Algorithm 1; squares indicate points traversed by Algorithms 2–4.

Algorithm 1

```
oy, fy: real

cx ← Pₓ + 1
oy ← P_y
while cx < Q_x do
        begin
                fy ← P_y + (cx − Pₓ)*(Δy/(real)Δx)
                if fy ≠ ⌊fy⌋ then
                        begin
                                if oy < ⌊fy⌋ then left (cx, ⌊fy⌋)
                                up (cx, ⌊fy⌋)
                        end
                else vertex (cx, ⌊fy⌋)
                oy ← fy
                cx ← cx + 1
        end
        endloop
```

Instead of traversing points (cx, fy) as in Algorithm 1, we can traverse points (cx, cy), where $cy = \lfloor fy \rfloor$, and use a new variable r that contains as its value $fy - \lfloor fy \rfloor$. The value of r can be computed inductively as follows:

$$r_0 = 0$$

$$r_i = \begin{cases} r_{i-1} + m & \text{if } r_{i-1} + m < 1 \\ r_{i-1} + m - 1 & \text{otherwise} \end{cases}$$

The intersection tests of Algorithm 1 can be rewritten as follows: at (cx_i, cy_i), PQ intersects a vertex if $r_i = 0$, an upward edge if $r_i \neq 0$, and a leftward edge if $r_i \neq 0$ and $r_{i-1} + m > 1$. The resulting algorithm is given below.

Algorithm 2

r, or, m: **real**
C: **IntPoint2**

$C_x \leftarrow P_x + 1$
$C_y \leftarrow P_y$
$r \leftarrow 0$
while $C_x < Q_x$ **do**
    begin
        or ← r
        if r + m < 1 **then** r ← r + m
        else
            begin
                r ← r + m − 1
                $C_y \leftarrow C_y + 1$
            end
        if r ≠ 0 **then**
            begin
                if or + m > 1 **then** left (C)
                up(C)
            end
        else vertex (C)
        $C_x \leftarrow C_x + 1$
    end
    endloop

All floating point operations in Algorithm 2 can be eliminated by introducing a new variable $nr = r \Delta x$. The Algorithm 2 operations on r can be expressed in terms of nr as listed below, yielding Algorithm 3.

In terms of r	In terms of nr
$r = 0$	$nr = 0$
$r + m < 1$	$nr + \Delta y < \Delta x$
$r = r + m$	$nr = nr + \Delta y$
$r = r + m - 1$	$nr = nr + \Delta y - \Delta x$

Algorithm 3

C: **IntPoint2**

$C_x \leftarrow P_x + 1$
$C_y \leftarrow P_y$
$nr \leftarrow 0$
while $C_x < Q_x$ **do**
    begin
        $onr \leftarrow nr$
        if $nr + \Delta y < \Delta x$ **then** $nr \leftarrow nr + \Delta y$
        else
            begin
                $nr \leftarrow nr + \Delta y - \Delta x$
                $C_y \leftarrow C_y + 1$
            end
        if $nr \neq 0$ **then**
            begin
                if $onr + \Delta y > \Delta x$ **then** left (C)
                up (C)
            end
        else vertex(C)
        $C_x \leftarrow C_x + 1$
    end
    endloop

Several simplifications can be made. Introducing a constant *const* = $\Delta x - \Delta y$ moves some computation out of the loop. The check for a left edge need only be made when C_y is incremented. With this check moved to its new location, it is sufficient to check for *nr* ≠ 0. This leaves *onr* unused, so it can be removed. Finally, a redundant check of *nr* can be eliminated by copying and combining **if** statements. The final version of the single-octant algorithm is given below.

Algorithm 4

C: **IntPoint2**

$C_x \leftarrow P_x + 1$
$C_y \leftarrow P_y$
nr ← 0
const ← $\Delta x - \Delta y$
while $C_x < Q_x$ **do**
    begin
        if nr < const **then**
            begin
                nr ← nr + Δy
                if nr ≠ 0 **then** up (C)
                else vertex(C)
            end
        else
            begin
                $C_y \leftarrow C_y + 1$
                nr ← nr − const
                if nr ≠ 0 **then**
                    begin
                        left (C)
                        up (C)
                    end
                else vertex (C)
            end
        $C_x \leftarrow C_x + 1$
    end
    endloop

Algorithms 1–4 assume that Q lies between 0° and 45° from P, inclusive. To handle the other eight octants without slowing down the algorithm, separate code segments are used for each octant of the plane (see Appendix).

See Appendix 2 for C Implementation (651)

ANTI-ALIASING SUMMARY

The following four Gems are useful for anti-aliasing calculations. One technique for exact anti-aliasing is to find the area of overlap between a piece of geometry to be rendered and a filter function. Often this filter is a unit-height box over a pixel, but larger, more symmetric filters (such as a Gaussian with a radius of 1.5 pixels) will usually give better results. Since such filters are radially symmetric, they have a circular footprint, and one needs to find the region of this circle occupied by the geometry; a weighting factor is then usually included to account for the changing height of the filter.

The first Gem determines the area of overlap between a circle and a half-plane. This technique may be adapted for polygon anti-aliasing by observing that a convex polygon may be represented as the intersection of a collection of half-planes. The second Gem applies this technique to thick lines. The third Gem is useful when anti-aliasing circles. The final Gem may be useful to determine whether a particular piece of geometry is a candidate for anti-aliasing in a particular situation by examining some points (for example, the vertices of a polygon).

See also Line Drawing Gems; Polygon Scan Conversion Gems; Filtering Gems; Anti-Aliasing Filters Summary (143); A Fast 2D Point-on-Line Test (49)

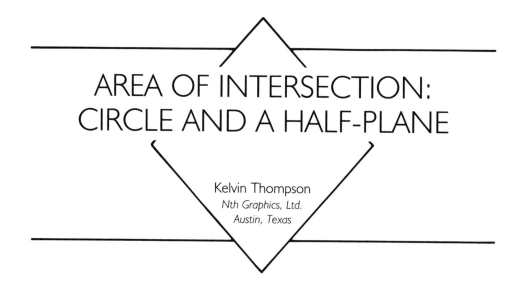

AREA OF INTERSECTION: CIRCLE AND A HALF-PLANE

Kelvin Thompson
Nth Graphics, Ltd.
Austin, Texas

Given a circle of radius r whose center is a distance d from the edge of a half-plane (see Fig. 1), the fraction of the circle that intersects the half-plane is

$$\text{cov}(d, r) = \begin{cases} d \leq r, & \dfrac{1}{2} - \dfrac{d\sqrt{r^2 - d^2}}{\pi r^2} - \dfrac{1}{\pi} \arcsin \dfrac{d}{r} \\ d \geq r, & 0 \end{cases}$$

and the area of intersection is $\pi r^2 \cdot \text{cov}(d, r)$. If the center of the circle is inside the half-plane, then the fractional coverage is $1 - \text{cov}(d, r)$ and the area $\pi r^2 \cdot (1 - \text{cov}(d, r))$.

The function $\text{cov}(d, r)$ can be useful when anti-aliasing lines and polygon edges—see Gupta and Sproull (1981) and "Area of Intersection: Circle and a Thick Line" in this volume.

Proof

We will take the integral of part of a semicircle, and then double that to get the area of intersection; the area of intersection divided by the area of the circle gives us the fractional coverage. We know the equation for a semicircle is $y = \sqrt{r^2 - x^2}$, and a table of integrals tells us

$$\int \sqrt{a^2 - u^2} \, du = \frac{u}{2}\sqrt{a^2 - u^2} + \frac{a^2}{2} \arcsin \frac{u}{a}.$$

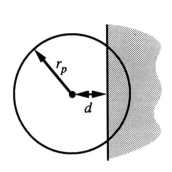

Figure 1.

To get the area of intersection with the semicircle we integrate from d to the edge of the circle, r. After a little bit of algebra this gives us

$$\int_d^r \sqrt{r^2 - x^2}\, dx = \frac{1}{2}\left[\frac{\pi}{2}r^2 - d\sqrt{r^2 - d^2} - r^2 \arcsin\frac{d}{r}\right].$$

When we double this and divide by πr^2, we get the expression for $\text{cov}(d, r)$ shown above.

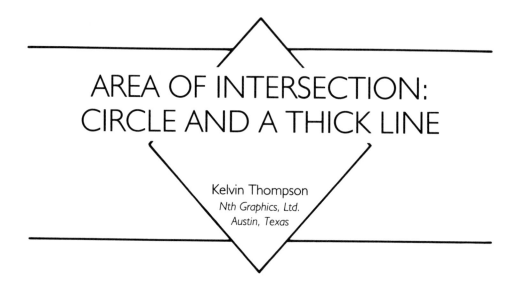

AREA OF INTERSECTION: CIRCLE AND A THICK LINE

Kelvin Thompson
Nth Graphics, Ltd.
Austin, Texas

Given a circle of radius r at a distance p from the center of a line of thickness $2w$ (see Fig. 1), the fraction of the circle that overlaps the line is defined in terms of the function $\text{cov}(d)$, which in turn is defined in terms of the coverage function found in "Area of Intersection: Circle and a Half-Plane" in this volume:

$$\text{cov}(d) \equiv \text{cov}(d, r).$$

Our use of $\text{cov}(d)$ depends on whether the line is thinner than the pixel:

For $w < r$ (the line is thinner than the pixel):

Range of p	Coverage
$0 \leq p \leq w$	$1 - \text{cov}(w - p) - \text{cov}(w + p)$
$w \leq p \leq r - w$	$\text{cov}(p - w) - \text{cov}(p + w)$
$r - w \leq p$	$\text{cov}(p - w)$

For $w \geq r$ (the line is thicker than the pixel):

Range of p	Coverage
$0 \leq p \leq w$	$1 - \text{cov}(w - p)$
$w \leq p$	$\text{cov}(p - w)$

The area of intersection is the coverage shown above multiplied by the area of the circle πr^2.

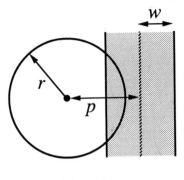

Figure 1.

Proof, by Observation of the Geometry

For skinny lines we have:

Geometry:	See Fig. 2.	See Fig. 3.
Coverage:	$1 - \text{cov}(w - p) - \text{cov}(w + p)$	$\text{cov}(p - w) - \text{cov}(p + w)$
Range:	$0 \leq p \leq w$	$w \leq p \leq r - w$

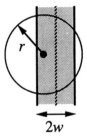

Figure 2.

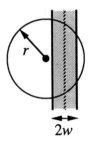

Figure 3.

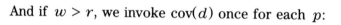

Figure 4.   Figure 5.

And if $w > r$, we invoke cov(d) once for each p:

Geometry:	See Fig. 4.	See Fig. 5.
Coverage:	$1 - \text{cov}(w - p)$	$\text{cov}(p - w)$
Range:	$0 \leq p \leq w$	$w \leq p \leq r + w$

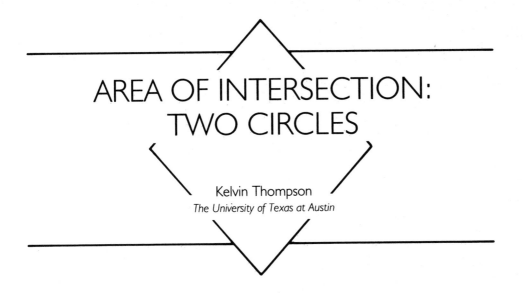

AREA OF INTERSECTION: TWO CIRCLES

Kelvin Thompson
The University of Texas at Austin

Given two filled circles (discs) with radii $r_1 \leq r_2$ whose centers are a distance d apart (see Fig. 1), and some expressions relating to this geometry,

$$x_1 \equiv \frac{d^2 + r_1^2 - r_2^2}{2d}, \qquad x_2 \equiv \frac{d^2 + r_2^2 - r_1^2}{2d}, \qquad s \equiv \frac{r_2^2 - r_1^2 - d^2}{2d}, \qquad (1)$$

$$a(x, r) \equiv \frac{1}{2}\pi r^2 - x\sqrt{r^2 - x^2} - r^2 \arcsin\left(\frac{x}{r}\right), \qquad (2)$$

then the area of intersection is given by

$o(r_1, r_2, d)$

$$\equiv \begin{cases} d \leq r_2 - r_1, & \pi r_1^2 & \text{(3a)} \\ d \geq r_2 + r_1, & 0 & \text{(3b)} \\ \text{otherwise} & \begin{cases} d^2 < r_2^2 - r_1^2, & \pi r_1^2 - a(s, r_1) + a(s + d, r_2) & \text{(3c)} \\ d^2 \geq r_2^2 - r_1^2, & a(x_1, r_1) + a(x_2, r_2). & \text{(3d)} \end{cases} \end{cases}$$

Proof

Equations 3a and 3b are obvious by inspection, since they occur when (a) disc 1 is completely inside disc 2, and (b) the two circles do not intersect. We now prove the remaining expressions in Equation 3.

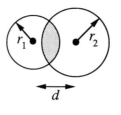

Figure 1.

First we note that the area of intersection can be split into two crescentlike shapes, where each of these shapes is the intersection between a disc and half-plane. The two regions—denoted C_1 and C_2 in Fig. 2—are always separated by the chord connecting the two points where the boundaries of the discs intersect (we call this the *shared chord*).

From "Area of Intersection: Circle and a Half-Plane" in this volume we know that the area of intersection between a disc and a half-plane is given by $a(x, r)$ in Equation 2, where x is the distance between the center of the disc and the edge of the half-plane, and r is the radius of the disc. Thus, once we know the distance between the center of each disc and the shared chord, we can determine the area of intersection. Now let us draw a triangle (see Fig. 3) whose vertices are at the centers of the two circles and at one of the endpoints of the shared chord. When $r_1^2 + d^2 = r_2^2$ the triangle is a right triangle (with r_2 the hypotenuse), and the distances x_1 and x_2 are 0 and d by inspection. However, if we hold r_1 and d constant, then as r_2 gets larger and smaller, we encounter two differing

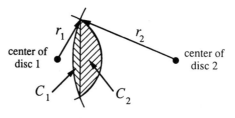

Figure 2.

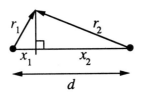

Figure 3.

geometries. When r_2^2 is less than $r_1^2 + d^2$ we get the geometry shown above, and this gives us the simultaneous equations

$$r_1^2 - x_1^2 = r_2^2 - x_2^2, \quad \text{and} \quad x_1 + x_2 = d.$$

With a little bit of algebra we get the expressions for x_1 and x_2 in Equation 1. Since x_1 and x_2 are the distances between the centers of the discs and the shared chord, we immediately get Equation 3d.

Now we let r_2 grow larger than $r_1^2 + d^2$, and we get the geometry in Fig. 4. This, in turn, gives us the relation

$$r_2^2 - (s + d)^2 = r_1^2 - s^2.$$

Again, we apply a little algebra to get the expression for s in Equation 1.

Here, however, the geometry is a little more complicated. The distance from the center of disc 2 to the shared chord is $d + s$, and the distance

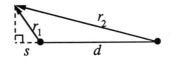

Figure 4.

45

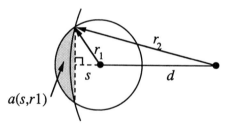

Figure 5.

from the center of disc 1 is s. However, the center of disc 1 is inside the half-plane with which we are intersecting it, so Equation 2 is not valid.

To get the correct area for C_1, we use the expression $\pi r_1^2 - a(s, r_1)$, which leads us to Equation 3c.

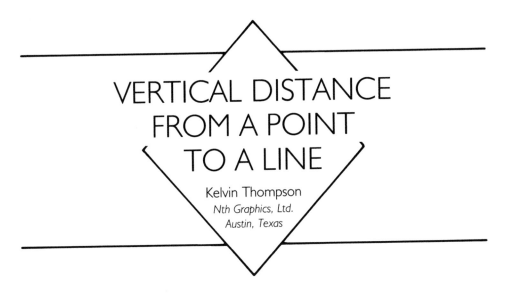

VERTICAL DISTANCE FROM A POINT TO A LINE

Kelvin Thompson
Nth Graphics, Ltd.
Austin, Texas

Given a line with slope $m = dy/dx$, and "perpendicular" and "vertical" distances p and v between a point and the line in Fig. 1, the ratio k relating p and v is

$$k = \frac{p}{v} = \sqrt{\frac{1}{1 + m^2}} \, .$$

(The "vertical" distance v is the length of the shortest vertical line segment between the point and the line.) Further, if $-1 \le m \le 1$, then $1/\sqrt{2} \le k \le 1$.

This relationship can be useful for rendering anti-aliased lines and polygon edges—see Gupta and Sproull (1981), and "Area of Intersection: Circle and Half-Plane" in this volume.

Proof

By elementary geometry, the three right triangles (two inside the third) in Fig. 2 are similar.

Figure 1.

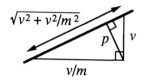

Figure 2.

Hence,

$$k = \frac{p}{v} = \frac{v/m}{\sqrt{v^2 + v^2/m^2}} = \frac{1}{m\sqrt{1 + 1/m^2}} = \sqrt{\frac{1}{1 + m^2}} .$$

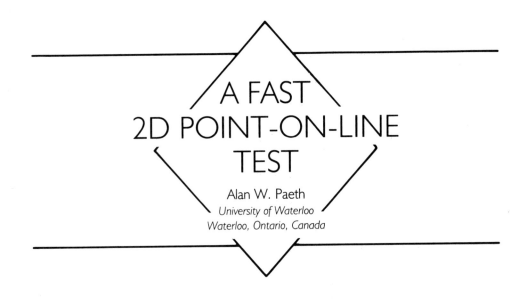

A FAST 2D POINT-ON-LINE TEST

Alan W. Paeth
University of Waterloo
Waterloo, Ontario, Canada

Introduction

Fast proximity testing between a point and a line on a two-dimensional plane finds common application, particularly in graphics editors. Unfortunately, the "first principles" perpendicular distance test requires a square-root operation to form a normalized (Euclidean) vector of unit length. This step is expensive and often unnecessary. For simple "hit/miss" selection, the distance inequality may be squared to yield a form requiring only multiplication, yielding faster code, which operates on integer variables while maintaining mathematical consistency. Substitution of an alternate vector norm reduces multiplication counts and in some cases yields a more useful proximity test. For instance, a vector rasterized using conventional DDA techniques generates a pixel set of "on" points, whose distances to the underlying vector "backbone" all fall within a common infinity-norm distance independent of line slope, though an outer, bracketing Euclidean distance may always be fitted.

The code presented below was originally written to merge chains of short vectors having similar slope into a larger constituent vector (Paeth, 1988), provided that all intermediate vertices lie along the common parent—an application for which the Euclidean norm is both slow and inappropriate. An example of test distances returned by the code appears in the comments prefacing the C source code in the appendix.

49

Pseudo-Code

Given two points P and Q and a test point T
return   0 if T is not on the (infinite) line $\overleftrightarrow{PQ}$
1 if T is on the open ray $\overrightarrow{P}$
2 if T is within the line segment $\overline{PQ}$
3 if T is on the open ray $\overrightarrow{Q}$

if ABS(($Q_y - P_y$) × ($T_x - P_x$) − ($T_y - P_y$) × ($Q_x - P_x$))
    ≥ MAX(ABS($Q_x - P_x$), ABS($Q_y - P_y$)) **return**[0];
if ($Q_x < P_x$ **and** $P_x < T_x$) **or** ($Q_y < P_y$ **and** $P_y < T_y$) **return**[1];
if ($T_x < P_x$ **and** $P_x < Q_x$) **or** ($T_y < P_y$ **and** $P_y < Q_y$) **return**[1];
if ($P_x < Q_x$ **and** $Q_x < T_x$) **or** ($P_y < Q_y$ **and** $Q_y < T_y$) **return**[3];
if ($T_x < Q_x$ **and** $Q_x < P_x$) **or** ($T_y < Q_y$ **and** $Q_y < P_y$) **return**[3];
return[2];

See also Solving the Nearest-Point-on-Curve Problem (607); A Fast Approximation to the Hypotenuse (427); Line Drawing Summary (98)

See Appendix 2 for C Implementation (654)

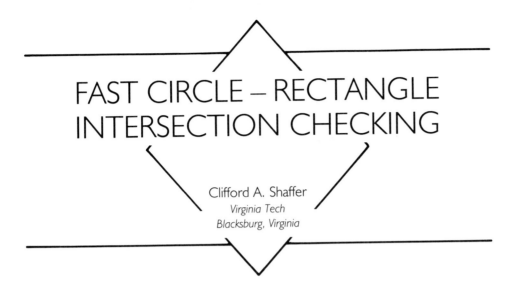

FAST CIRCLE – RECTANGLE INTERSECTION CHECKING

Clifford A. Shaffer
Virginia Tech
Blacksburg, Virginia

If you do a lot of graphics or spatial data programming, sooner or later you will want to know if a circle and a rectangle intersect, or if a sphere and a box intersect. This is even more likely if you use quadtree or octree methods. (For example, you may want to find all nodes of the tree within a certain Euclidean distance of a point). Unfortunately, this problem is not as easy to solve as it appears. The first approach that normally comes to mind is to check if any corner of the rectangle falls within the circle (using a simple distance check). Unfortunately, this approach will sometimes give false negative results. There are three anomalous cases to watch out for. First, while no corner of the rectangle may be in the circle, a chord of the circle may overlap one edge of the rectangle (see Fig. 1). Second, the rectangle might fall inside a bounding box placed around the circle, but still be outside the circle (see Fig. 2). Third, the circle might lie entirely inside the rectangle (see Fig. 3).

A fast algorithm is presented, for determining if a circle and a rectangle intersect. The 3D case can easily be derived from the 2D case; although it is a little longer, it requires only slightly more execution time. The 2D version of this algorithm requires at most five comparisons (all but one test against 0), three multiplies, five add/subtracts (four of which are for normalization) and one absolute-value function. It basically works by determining where the rectangle falls with respect to the center of the circle. There are nine possibilities in 2D (27 in 3D): the rectangle can be entirely to the NW, NE, SW, or SE of the circle's centerpoint (four cases), directly N, E, S, or W of the circle's centerpoint (four cases) or in the center (that is, containing the circle's centerpoint). The algorithm

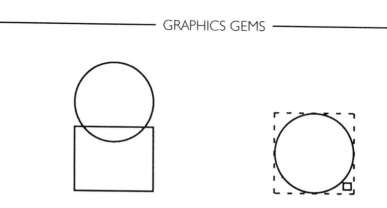

Figure 1.

Figure 2.

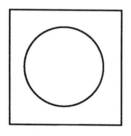

Figure 3.

enumerates these cases and determines the distance between the single closest point on the border of the rectangle and the center of the circle.

```
boolean Check_Intersect(R, C, Rad)
Return TRUE iff rectangle R intersects circle with centerpoint C and radius Rad.
begin   Comments assume origin is at lower left corner
        Translate coordinates, placing C at the origin
        R.max ← R.max − C; R.min ← R.min − C;
        if (R.max.x < 0) R to left of circle center
           then if (R.max.y < 0) R in lower left corner
                   then return (R.max.x² + R.max.y² < Rad²);
                else if (R.min.y > 0) R in upper left corner
                        then return (R.max.x² + R.min.y² < Rad²);
                     else  R due West of circle
                             return (|R.max.x| < Rad);
```

    else if (R.min.x > 0) R *to right of circle center*
      then if (R.max.y < 0) R *in lower right corner*
        then return (R.min.x^2 + R.max.y^2 < Rad^2);
        else if (R.min.y > 0) R *in upper right corner*
          then return (R.min.x^2 + R.min.y^2 < Rad^2);
        else R *due EAST of circle*
          return (R.min.x < Rad)
    else R *on circle vertical centerline*
      if (R.max.y < 0) R *due South of circle*
        then return (|R.max.y| < Rad);
        else if (R.min.y > 0) R *due North of circle*
          then return (R.min.y < Rad);
        else R *contains circle centerpoint*
          return (TRUE);
  end; *Check_intersect*

See also Fast Ray–Box Intersection (395); Spheres-to-Voxels Conversion (327); A Simple Method for Box–Sphere Intersection Testing (335); Ray Tracing (383)

See Appendix 2 for C Implementation (**656**)

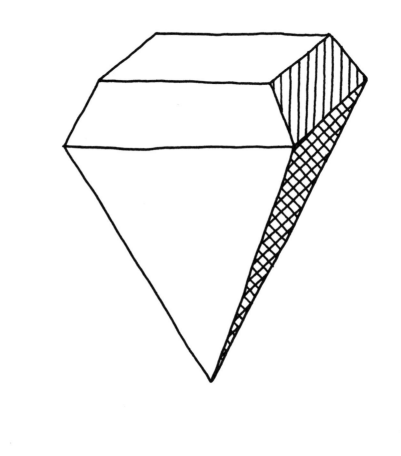

2D RENDERING

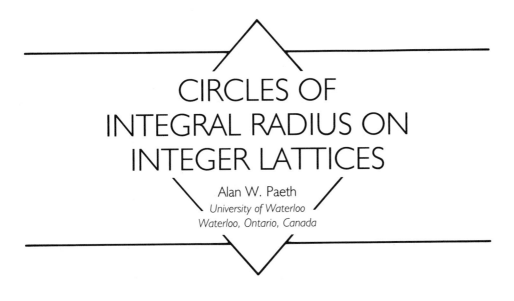

CIRCLES OF
INTEGRAL RADIUS ON
INTEGER LATTICES

Alan W. Paeth
University of Waterloo
Waterloo, Ontario, Canada

Introduction

Consider the question of drawing circles of integral radius R on an integer point lattice (i, j) so that select points on the lattice fall exactly along the circle's perimeter. This situation occurs implicitly when rendering circles of integral size on a raster display. Here the pixels represent the point lattice. The question arises explicitly when we represent a circle by an interpolating curve: a desirable control polygon places knots at locations having exact representations. When the circles are small the interpolation curve may degenerate to simple line segments, and a convex polygon of irregular edge lengths (but precise circumferential vertices) is rendered.

Sets of points (i, j) lying at a constant distance R solve the well-known Pythagorean relation $i^2 + j^2 = R^2$. What values of R yield up large sets of integral sides and what are their properties? A brute-force search of the solution space yields those triangles with hypotenuse less than one hundred. Restricting R to prime numbers assures triangles in lowest terms; the generation of additional triangles with composite, relatively prime, edge lengths is explained later:

It is unfortunate that in lowest terms the hypotenuse must be an odd length. To show this, note that an even number (of form $2n$ and congruent to $0 \bmod 2$) is congruent to $0 \bmod 4$ after squaring as $(2n)^2 = 4n^2$. Similarly, squaring an odd yields $(2n + 1)^2 = 4(n^2 + n) + 1$, leaving it congruent to $1 \bmod 4$. In particular, even/odd parity is preserved under squaring.

Parity implies that a triangle of even hypotenuse must be the sum of either two even or two odd legs. The first case is immediately discarded

Table I. Prime Pythagorean Triangles.

R	i	j
5	4	3
13	12	5
17	15	8
29	21	20
37	35	12
41	40	9
53	45	28
61	60	11
73	55	48
89	80	39
97	72	65

as it is not in lowest terms, as stated. In the remaining case, the sum of two odd legs gives a hypotenuse length congruent to $2 \bmod 4$, which cannot be represented as a perfect square. Thus, even hypotenuse lengths are ruled out for triangles in lowest terms. Worse, a hypotenuse with length a power of two can have no (odd) factors in common with either odd leg—the form is necessarily in lowest terms. Thus, no Pythagorean triangles exist whose hypotenuse length is a power of two.

By dividing edge lengths by the hypotenuse, a unit vector is formed with rational coefficients. For instance, binary floating point hardware approximates real values by using scaled rationals, in which both the implicit mantissa denominator and scaling exponent are powers of two. Thus, there exist (under radix-2 or radix-16 floating point) no values $0 < x < 1$ and $0 < y < 1$ such that $x^2 + y^2 = 1$ when evaluated in full precision. This further implies that the universal identity $\sin^2 x + \cos^2 x = 1.0$ holds only as round-off allows.

Fortunately, the situation is not as severe in base ten. By happenstance this base possesses an odd factor (5), which appears in Tab. 1 in the $(3, 4, 5)$ triangle known to the Egyptians. This allows Cartesian pairs possessing exact integral length in finite digits. For instance, scaling the above onto $(6, 8, 10)$ and dividing gives $(0.6, 0.8)$ as a unit vector. To show that there are additional points of higher precision, additional triangles are formed whose hypotenuse lengths are the product of two (possibly identical) hypotenuse values appearing in the table. This yields triangles of two types: the scaled versions of the original parents, plus additional triangles which, surprisingly, are already in lowest terms (the algebraic number theory is left as a recreation to the interested reader).

For instance, scaling $(3, 4, 5)$ by five yields two triangles of common hypotenuse: the expected $(15, 20, 25)$, found directly, plus the unexpected $(7, 24, 25)$ in lowest terms, found by searching edge lengths for $R = 25$. Similarly, the product of table entries two and three (hypotenuses of length 13 and 17) yield four integral triangles of hypotenuse 221: the originals scaled by 17 and 13, plus the additional members $(21, 220, 221)$, and $(140, 171, 221)$.

This property may be applied to generate coordinate pairs with exact decimal representation in a fixed number of digits. For any vector of length 10^D a lowest-term triangle of length 5^D exists; normalization yields a Cartesian pair of D decimal digits. Searching the set of powers (5 25 125 625 3125 15625) for edge pairs through six digits yields these unit vectors:

(0.6	0.8)
(0.28	0.96)
(0.352	0.936)
(0.5376	0.8432)
(0.07584	0.99712)
(0.658944	0.752192)

As a circle is symmetric about any line through the origin, the eight symmetry axes implicit in the Cartesian coordinate system may be used to map the point (a, b) into all eight octants, $(\pm a, \pm b)$ and $(\pm b, \pm a)$, but note that $(1, 0)$ gives rise to only three new points. Taking the first two entries above, a twenty-point polygonal approximation to a circle may be formed, in which all vertices are exact and required only two significant digits for specification. Presented in counterclockwise direction beginning on the x-axis these are as follows:

(1.0, 0.0),	(0.96, 0.28),	(0.80, 0.60),	(0.60, 0.80),	(0.28, 0.96)
(0.0, 1.0),	(−0.28, 0.96),	(−0.60, 0.80),	(−0.80, 0.60),	(−0.96, 0.28)
(−1.0, 0.0),	(−0.96, −0.28),	(−0.80, −0.60),	(−0.60, −0.80),	(−0.28, −0.96)
(0.0, −1.0),	(0.28, −0.96),	(0.60, −0.80),	(0.80, −0.60),	(0.96, −0.28)

Alternately, the method is useful in providing large triangle families with common hypotenuse lengths by choosing values rich in table factors. For instance, the easily remembered $16385 = (2^{14} + 1)$ has factors (5 29 113) all within the prime table and yields thirteen triangles with sides ranging from $(256, 16383)$ through $(11484, 11687)$. Much larger triangle sets are possible. For instance, a hypotenuse length of 27625, factored as (5 5 5 13 17) yields up thirty-one distinct triangles, making possible a polygon coincident with a circle at two hundred fifty-two rational vertices.

What can be said of a circle drawn on a conventional frame buffer? In this setting, the method provides an excellent accuracy test for any circle-drawing algorithm—for select integer radii many pixels should be always visited regardless of implementation specifics, as they lie precisely on the circle's perimeter. Two noteworthy values are $R = 325$ (seven triangles, sixty vertices in circular agreement) and $R = 1105$ (thirteen triangles, one hundred eight vertices). Searching for the edge sets is straightforward since the hypotenuse lengths are given, and may be sped using the identity $(i^2 - j^2)^2 + (2ij)^2 = (i^2 + j^2)^2$. Row n of the decimal coordinate table contains an entry $|T_n(0.6)|$. This Chebyshev polynomial may be evaluated using the recursive form $T_{n+1} = 1.2T_n - T_{n-1}$ with $T_0 = 1$ and $T_1 = 0.6$.

See also What Are the Coordinates of a Pixel? (246); Precalculating Addresses for Fast Fills, Circles, and Lines (285)

NICE NUMBERS FOR GRAPH LABELS

Paul S. Heckbert
University of California
Berkeley, California

When creating a graph by computer, it is desirable to label the x and y axes with "nice" numbers: simple decimal numbers. For example, if the data range is 105 to 543, we'd probably want to plot the range from 100 to 600 and put tick marks every 100 units (see fig. 1). Or if the data range is 2.03 to 2.17, we'd probably plot a range from 2.00 to 2.20 with a tick spacing of .05. Humans are good at choosing such "nice" numbers, but simplistic algorithms are not. The naive label-selection algorithm takes the data range and divides it into n equal intervals, but this usually results in ugly tick labels. We here describe a simple method for generating nice graph labels.

The primary observation is that the "nicest" numbers in decimal are 1, 2, and 5, and all power-of-ten multiples of these numbers. We will use only such numbers for the tick spacing, and place tick marks at multiples of the tick spacing. We choose the minimum and maximum of the graphed range in either of two ways: (a) loose: round the data minimum

naive labels:	105.00	214.50	324.00	433.50	543.00
loose labels:	100	200	300	400	500	600
tight labels:	105	200	300	400	500	543

Figure 1.

down, and the data maximum up, to compute the graph minimum and maximum, respectively, or (b) tight: use the data minimum and maximum for the graph minimum and maximum. The relative merits of these two approaches are discussed in Tufte (1983). Below is some pseudo-code for the loose method:

const ntick ← 5;   *desired number of tick marks*

loose_label: *label the data range from* min *to* max *loosely.*
   (*tight method is similar*)

procedure loose_label(min, max: **real**);
nfrac: **int;**
d: **real;**   *tick mark spacing*
graphmin, graphmax: **real;**   *graph range min and max*
range, x: **real;**
begin
   range ← nicenum(max − min, **false**);
   d ← nicenum(range / (ntick − 1), **true**);
   graphmin ← floor(min / d)*d;
   graphmax ← ceiling(max / d)*d;
   nfrac ← max(− floor(log10(d)), 0);   *number of fractional digits to show*

   for x ← graphmin **to** graphmax + .5*d **step** d **do**
      put tick mark at x, *with a numerical label showing* nfrac *fraction digits*
      endloop;
   endproc loose_label;

nicenum: *find a "nice" number approximately equal to* x.
Round the number if round = **true**, *take ceiling if* round = **false**.

function nicenum(x: **real**; round: **boolean**): **real;**
exp: **int;**   *exponent of x*
f: **real;**   *fractional part of x*
nf: **real;**   *nice, rounded fraction*
begin
   exp ← floor(log10(x));
   f ← x / expt(10., exp);   *between 1 and 10*

```
if round then
    if f < 1.5 then nf ← 1.;
    else if f < 3. then nf ← 2.;
    else if f < 7. then nf ← 5.;
    else nf ← 10.;
else
    if f ≤ 1. then nf ← 1.;
    else if f ≤ 2. then nf ← 2.;
    else if f ≤ 5. then nf ← 5.;
    else nf ← 10.;
return nf*expt(10., exp);
endfunc nicenum;
```

We assume in the above that log10(z) is log base 10 of z.

We also assume expt(a, n) = a^n for integer n. But note that the exponentiation routines in some math libraries are inexact for integer arguments, and such errors can cause the above code to fail. On early UNIX systems I found that pow(10.,2.) ≠ 100 exactly, so I wrote my own expt function by multiplying or dividing in a loop. The pow routine in current (BSD 4.3) UNIX is trustworthy, however.

See Appendix 2 for C Implementation (657)

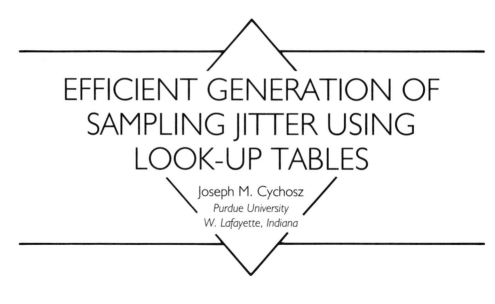

EFFICIENT GENERATION OF SAMPLING JITTER USING LOOK-UP TABLES

Joseph M. Cychosz
Purdue University
W. Lafayette, Indiana

Introduction

Presented in this paper is a method for generating sampling jitter using a limited number of random numbers. The proposed jitter function is a function of three variables, namely the sample location (x, y) and the sample number (s) for the location. Furthermore, the method will produce repeatable jitter for all x and y without requiring either the storage of a large number of random numbers, or the consistent access of x, y, and s. This paper examines the application of this jitter function to the ray-tracing algorithm.

Recent advances in the ray-tracing algorithm have used stochastic sampling techniques as a method of rendering anti-aliased images. Cook *et al.* (1984) pioneered this approach in their work on "distributed ray tracing." Other works by Cook (1983, 1986) examined the use of stochastic sampling in ray tracing from a theoretical perspective. Lee *et al.* (1985) and Dippé and Wold (1985) also examined the use of stochastic sampling in ray tracing. Kajiya (1986) in a later work used stochastic sampling as a basis for evaluating the "rendering equation." The three works by Cook, Lee, and Dippé used a jitter function to simulate Monte Carlo integration, in which random sampling points for the image plane are generated. The generated jitter is then used to perturb the sampling rays as they pass through the image plane. Cook, however, (1985, 1986) identified that the distribution of samples should approximate a Poisson disk based on Yellot's study (1983) of the distribution of cones in the retina of Rhesus monkeys.

Although it is not desirable to have a method that can produce a consistent set of sample points for each frame in an animation, it may be desirable to have a method that can produce a consistent set of sample points during the rendering of an individual frame. For example, in a scan-conversion environment using a z-buffer such as Reyes (Cook *et al.*, 1987) each polygon should be sampled with the same set of points for each pixel being processed. Without consistency, temporal artifacts may occur as the sample points move within the pixels. A basic approach to this problem would be to save all of the sample points used in the generation of an image for reuse at a later time. For a 512×512 image with 16 samples per pixel, more than eight million numbers would have to be stored. An alternative approach might be to use a congruential random-number generator to generate the sample points as each pixel is processed. Production of a consistent set of sample points would not only require that the initial seed of the random-number function be the same, but also that the pixels be accessed in a consistent manner. An optimization algorithm, such as screen space bounding, may eliminate the need to examine certain pixels, thereby disturbing the random-number sequence. Other optimization algorithms may alter the number of samples required for particular pixels. Multiprocessor implementations would experience similar problems in the generation of consistent jitter.

In ray tracing only the efficiency aspect of generating sampling jitter is of concern. Multiprocessor implementations (Dippé and Swensen, 1984; Cleary *et al.*, 1983; Nishimura *et al.*, 1983) and computationally distributed approaches (Arvo and Kirk, 1987; Arvo and Kirk, 1987 Film Show Contribution) would experience similar problems, only this time in the generation of jitter without spatial regularity.

A Jitter Function Using Look-up Tables

With stochastic sampling, the sampling locations within the area of a pixel are perturbed, or *jittered*. To implement this method of anti-aliasing, an efficient method for generating jitter is necessary. As stated earlier, the generated random numbers must be a function of both the pixel location and the sample number for that pixel. Although it is not necessary that the function have a long period (that is, the time it takes for the number sequence to repeat), it is necessary that the function not exhibit any patterns of spatial or temporal regularity with respect to the image. Shown below is an implementation of the proposed jitter function:

$$x_j = \text{URAND}(\text{mod}(x + 2y + \text{IRAND}(\text{mod}(x + s, n)), n)$$

$$y_j = \text{URAND}(\text{mod}(y + 2x + \text{IRAND}(\text{mod}(y + s + 1, n)), n),$$

where

x, y = the location of the given pixel,

s = the sample number for the given pixel,

x_j = the amount of jitter in x for the sample point,

y_j = the amount of jitter in y for the sample point,

URAND = a table of uniform random numbers,

IRAND = a table of random integers of the range 0 to n,

n = the number of elements in the random-number tables.

The jitter function uses two look-up tables. One table, URAND, simply contains a uniformly distributed set of random numbers, which may be prescaled to the size of the jitter for final use in the sampling process. The numbers in these tables may be generated using standard, random-number generation techniques, such as those found in Knuth (1981) in press (1988), or in L'Ecuyer (1988). The second table, IRAND, contains a set of integers, which is used as a *shuffle generator* to prevent the function from exhibiting any spatial patterns. Without this table, the sampling pattern generated by the function would repeat, thus causing a low-frequency artifact to appear from the resulting correlation of the sampling pattern. The $y + s + 1$ component of the equation for y-jitter is used to ensure that the x and y indices into URAND are nonequal for all values of x and y. Should they become equal, only the diagonal of the pixel will be sampled. This component can be simplified to $y + s$ by either extending IRAND to $n + 1$ elements and by repeating the first element, or by substituting two independent tables, one for x and one for y, for URAND. The latter approach is more desirable, especially if the scaling of the jitter is nonuniform in x and y.

A slightly more computationally efficient jitter function can be implemented by using a bitwise *or* operation to compute the sums $x + 2y$ and $y + 2x$. Shown below is an implementation of the jitter function using the *or* operations and independent tables for URAND:

$$x_j = \text{URANX}(\text{mod}(\text{or}(x, 2y) + \text{IRAND}(\text{mod}(x + s, n)), n)$$

$$y_j = \text{URANY}(\text{mod}(\text{or}(y, 2x) + \text{IRAND}(\text{mod}(y + s, n)), n).$$

Evaluation of the Computational Cost

If the size of the look-up tables is a power of two, then the *mod* functions can be replaced with bitwise *and* operations. Multiplications by 2 may be replaced with *shift* operations. This allows the function to be implemented fairly efficiently, requiring only four *additions*, four *indexed loads*, four *and* operations, and two *shift* operations.

Typical pseudo–random-number generators use a feedback approach, in which each number generated is used as a seed to generate the next number in the sequence. Random-number generators of this type, otherwise known as *linear congruential generators* (LCG), have the following form:

$$R_{i+1} = \text{mod}(R_i s + c, m),$$

where R_{i+1} is the next random number in the sequence, and R_i is the current seed. S, c, and m are the multiplier, and additive and modulo terms of the generator. While this method seems to be computationally simpler than the proposed approach, this computation often requires the use of either double-precision or multiple-precision integer arithmetic, thus requiring several multiplications and additions. Furthermore, this approach does not exhibit the desirable repeatability that the jitter func-

Table I.   Operational Cost Comparison for Jitter Generations.

Operation	Jitter 1	Jitter 2	LCG
multiplies	0	0	4
adds	3	2	2
indexed loads	2	2	0
ands/ors	2	3	0
shifts	1	1	0
Total	8	8	6

tions do. Table 1 compares the unweighted operational costs of the jitter-generation methods, and Table 2 compares the measured computational costs of the methods for a variety of computers. The times reported in Table 2 are the CPU times in seconds required to generate jitter for a 512 by 512 image with 16 samples per pixel. The random-number generator used was $R_{i+1} = R_i\ 1629 + 1$ modulus 1048576, with an initial seed of 98531.

Table 2.   Computational Comparison for Various CPUs.

Machine	Jitter 1	Jitter 2	LCG	Jitter 1 Inline	Jitter 2 Inline	LCG Inline	Comments
Ardent Titan	29.53	29.48	73.21	8.40	7.88	43.22	P2 16Mhz
	6.76	6.76	22.59	4.13	3.88	22.59	MIPS R2000 P3 32Mhz
Cray YMP	7.38	7.51	9.73	2.32	2.34	4.26	MIPS R3000/3010 6ns
ETA 10-P*	83.55	83.55	91.82	32.47	32.47	49.30	21ns
Gould NP1	32.30	32.75	41.33	16.80	16.98	29.47	Arithmetic Accelerator
SGI 4D/20G	19.68	19.69	37.69	10.10	10.07	32.91	12.5Mhz MIPS R2000A
Sun 3/160	92.95	89.62	367.30	63.50	63.51	248.08	16Mhz 68020, 12.5Mhz 68881
Sun 4/280	17.70	17.70	103.15	13.85	13.82	133.46	16Mhz SPARC FPU1, 32kb cache

Evaluation of the Sampling Properties

The sampling properties of the two jitter functions are evaluated using approaches similar to those used by Cook. The visual results of these tests are presented in Figs. 1 and 2. The first test (shown in the upper left of each figure), examines the sampling pattern generated by the functions. A good sampling pattern will have the points randomly distributed with very little clustering of the points. Once again, to simulate a Poisson disk distribution, the sample points should be randomly distributed with

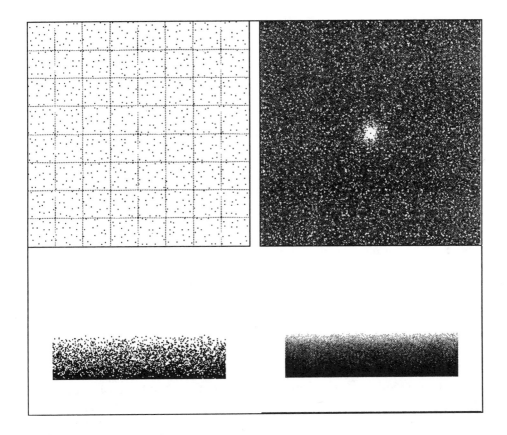

Figure 1. Jitter function 1 results. *Upper left*: sampling pattern; *upper right*: 2D FFT of the pattern; *lower left*: image of single-point/pixel sampled comb; *lower right*: image of 16-points/pixel sampled comb.

69

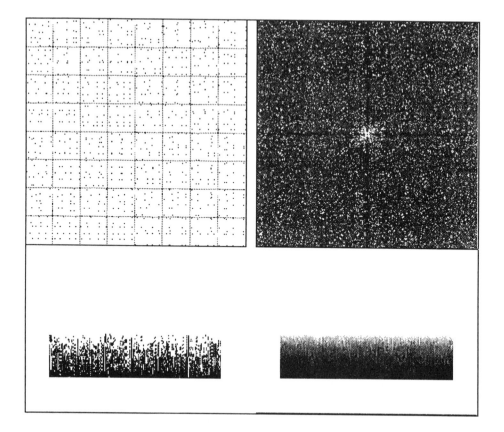

Figure 2. Jitter function 2 results. *Upper left*: sampling pattern; *upper right*: 2D FFT of the pattern, *lower left*: image of single-point/pixel-sampled comb; *lower right*: image of 16-point/pixel-sampled comb.

some minimal separation. In the test, the pixels are 8×8 with 1 sample per pixel. The 2D Fourier transform of the sample pattern is shown in the upper right of each figure. For comparison, the 2D Fourier transforms for uniformly spaced sampling and for correlated random sampling are shown in Fig. 3.

The second test examines the image resulting from the sampling of a comb of slivers, in which each sliver is 1.01 pixels wide and 50 pixels high. The results for jittered single-point sampling are shown in the lower left of Figs. 1 and 2. The lower right shows the results for jittered

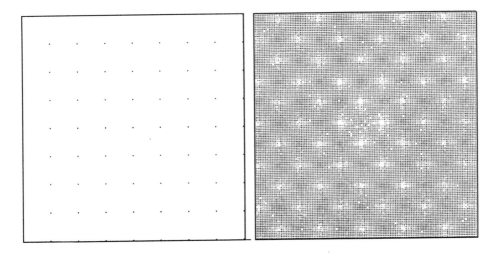

Figure 3. *Left*: 2D FFT of uniformly spaced sampling; *right*: 2D FFT of correlated sampling using 128 by 128 tiles.

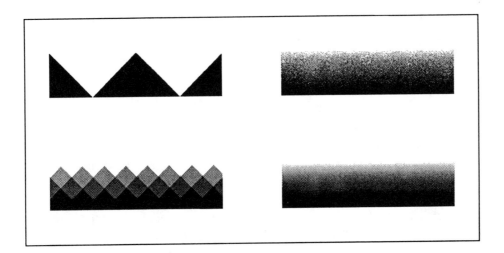

Figure 4. Comparison images. *Upper Left*: single-point/pixel uniform sampling; *lower left*: 16-point/pixel uniform sampling; *upper right*: 16-point/pixel random sampling; *lower right*: "ideal" image.

Table 3. Error Analysis Results for Single- and 16-Point Sampling.

Sampling Method	Average Error	Standard Deviation	RMS Error
Single-point sampling:			
Random	.3319	.2351	.1654
Jitter function 1	.3332	.2361	.1668
Jitter function 2	.3297	.2335	.1632
Uniformly spaced	.3313	.2347	.1648
16-point sampling:			
Random	.0774	.0657	.0103
Jitter function 1	.0787	.0651	.0104
Jitter function 2	.0804	.0701	.0114
16-point subpixel sampling:			
Random	.0519	.0427	.0045
Jitter function 1	.0533	.0440	.0048
Jitter function 2	.0544	.0439	.0049
Uniformly spaces	.0794	.0568	.0095

16-point subpixel sampling. For comparison, Fig. 4 shows results of uniformly spaced sampling for single-point and 16-point sampling, and 16-point random sampling, as well as the "ideal" image.

Table 3 compares the error of the various sampling methods for single- and 16-point sampling. The error is determined by comparing the pixel values of the resulting image for the sampling method with the pixel values of an ideal square-aperture sampled image. Both jitter functions produce error levels comparable to that of completely random sampling (that is, the jitter is generated using the LCG random-number generator presented earlier) for all three categories of sampling. Sixteen point subpixel random sampling produces the least error, followed closely by 16-point subpixel sampling using jitter functions 1 and 2.

Use of the Jitter Function in Ray Tracing

In ray tracing, the jitter function is used to perturb the direction of the sampling rays as they pass through the image plane. Other sampling rays may be jittered also, such as the rays used to sample an area light source to produce soft shadows, or the location of the eye to simulate depth of focus (Cook *et al.*, 1984). To anti-alias a given pixel located at x, y, the following equations may be used to perturb the point where the ray passes through the image plane:

$$x_s = x_c + w_x(x_j - .5)$$

$$y_s = y_c + w_y(y_j - .5),$$

where

x_s, y_s = the sampling location for the pixel,

x_c, y_c = the location of the center for the pixel,

w_x, w_y = the width and height of the pixel,

x_j, y_j = the amount of jitter (0. to 1.).

Traditional ray tracing passes the ray through the center of the pixel for single ray sampling, or through uniformly spaced points within the pixel for multiple ray sampling. To jitter a square set of regularly spaced sample points the following equations may be used:

$$w_{xs} = \frac{x_x}{\sqrt{n}}, \qquad w_{ys} = \frac{w_y}{\sqrt{n}}$$

$$x_s = x_c - \frac{w_x}{2} + w_{xs} \bmod(s - 1, \sqrt{n}) + w_{xs} x_j$$

$$y_s = y_c - \frac{w_y}{2} + w_{ys} \operatorname{floor}\left(\frac{s - 1}{\sqrt{n}}\right) + w_{ys} y_j,$$

where

s = the sample number for the pixel,

n = the number of samples per pixel (1 to n).

A final value for the pixel may be found by computing the average of the samples for the pixel (that is, applying a box filter). Other filter functions may be used by weighting the samples by the shape of the filter function.

Conclusions

Presented is a jittering method that is not only computationally efficient (shown in Tables 1 and 2), but that also produces image-sampling results comparable to random jittering (shown graphically in Figures 1, 2, and 4, and analytically in Table 3). The method can also generate reproducible jitter that is a function of pixel location and sample number. To aid in providing insight into the construction of a jitter function, two jittering methods using look-up tables are presented for comparison. Function 1 exhibits a good sampling pattern with a Poisson distribution; function 2, on the other hand, has a less desirable sampling pattern with some degree of spatial regularity.

See also Ray Tracing (383); Scan Conversion Summary (75)

See Appendix 2 for C Implementation (660)

SCAN CONVERSION SUMMARY

Scan conversion is the general technique of rendering a piece of 2D geometry into a discrete mesh. Typically in graphics we use scan conversion to render polygons, lines, alphanumeric characters, and other such image elements into a rectangular grid. Usually this grid is either a frame buffer or a piece of standard computer memory, though various other approaches are possible. (Imagine a Logo turtle carrying cans of paint, trailing paint behind it as it crawls.)

The next four Gems demonstrate some different ways to scan-convert polygons. They show some different approaches to trading off speed, simplicity, efficiency, support of anti-aliasing, and generality.

See also Anti-Aliasing Gems; Scanline Depth Gradient of a Z-Buffered Triangle (361)

FAST ANTI-ALIASING POLYGON SCAN CONVERSION

Jack C. Morrison
Evergreen, Colorado

Introduction

This algorithm scan-converts polygons into raster lines at subpixel resolution, providing some anti-aliasing benefits without the expense of polygon-to-pixel clipping or brute-force subpixel scan conversion. The resulting data may be used with depth-buffer or scanline anti-aliasing hidden-surface methods.

Background

One approach to reducing aliasing artifacts (for example, "jaggies") in computer-generated pictures is to render the image at a high resolution, then average the resulting pixel data to a lower-resolution display. Although this method requires no new algorithms, the additional memory and execution time required to prevent aliasing effectively is high.

More sophisticated anti-aliasing hidden-surface methods, such as Carpenter's *A*-Buffer (1984), typically require information about the coverage of a pixel by the polygon being rendered. The usual method for extracting this subpixel detail is to apply repeatedly a 2D clipping algorithm to clip the original polygon to the boundaries of each pixel, and compute the exact fraction of the pixel area covered by the polygon. This area is then used to scale the polygon color intensity. The *A*-Buffer method also converts the clipped polygon into a bitmask for visible surface determination within the pixel.

For smooth-shaded and textured images, a significant amount of data is maintained at each polygon vertex, including model coordinates (for texture computation), world coordinates and normal vector (for shading), and display coordinates (for pixel coverage and depth-prioritizing). All this information must be interpolated at each clipping boundary, making the pixel-clipping method expensive. Since ultimately only a single shading result is needed at each pixel, a faster approximate method is possible.

The Scan Conversion Algorithm

The following algorithm efficiently determines approximate pixel coverages from a polygon represented by its vertex coordinates. Coverage area and a subpixel bitmask can both be readily computed.

It is assumed that the polygon to be converted is convex, and that the vertices are consistently ordered (for example, clockwise). For each vertex, integer x (horizontal) and y (vertical) subpixel coordinates are computed from transformed floating point image coordinates. In fact, only the y-coordinates need be stored for each vertex; x-coordinates are referenced only once and can therefore be computed on the fly. X resolution can be increased at no cost, up to the number of bits available for an integer. Increasing y resolution requires two integers and a small time increase per subpixel y-coordinate. Powers of two are always convenient, and it seems wise to keep the two resolutions on the same order of magnitude. For clarity, the pseudo-code assumes a subpixel resolution of eight times the final rendering resolution.

In this algorithm, x and y refer to subpixel coordinates, while *pixel* and *scanline* refer to their corresponding low-resolution counterparts. Both refer to the display coordinate system (see Fig. 1). Polygon x and y coordinates are interpolated at subpixel resolution, but all other vertex information is interpolated only at display pixel resolution. To compute pixel coverage, only the left and right x-coordinates of the polygon at each y-coordinate within the current scanline need to be saved.

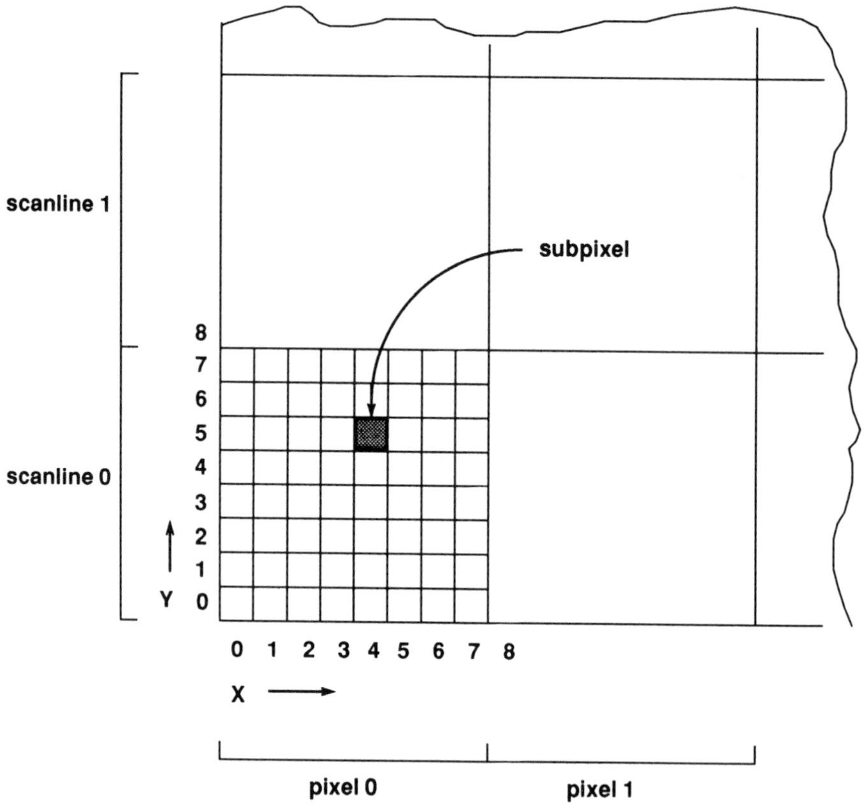

Figure 1. Subpixel display coordinates.

```
Vertex: record [              polygon vertex information
   model, world,
   normal, image: vector;    geometric information
   x, y: integer;            subpixel display coordinates
];

Vleft, VnextLeft: Vertex;        limits of current left polygon edge
Vright, VnextRight: Vertex;      limits of current right polygon edge
VscanLeft, VscanRight: Vertex;   interpolated vertices at scanline

subpixel x-coordinates of polygon within current scanline
xLeft, xRight: array [0 .. 7] of integer;
```

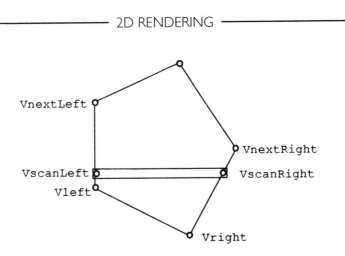

Figure 2. Polygon vertices during scan conversion.

Scan convert one polygon. For each scanline, build xLeft[ ] *and* xRight[ ]
with subpixel x edges at each of eight subpixel y's, and interpolate other
polygon vertex information once. See Fig. 2.

begin

      Vleft ← Polygon vertex V with minimum V.y;
      VnextLeft ← (Vleft + 1) **mod** numVertex;
      Vright ← Vleft;
      VnextRight ← (Vright − 1) **mod** numVertex;

      for each subpixel y covered by polygon
      for y ← Vleft.y **by** 1 **do**

          update edge data if reached next vertex
          if y = VnextLeft.y
              then begin
                  Vleft ← VnextLeft;
                  VnextLeft ← (Vleft + 1) **mod** numVertex;
                end;
         if y = VnextRight.y
             then begin
                Vright ← VnextRight;
                VnextRight ← (Vright − 1) **mod** numVertex;
              end;

79

if $y >$ VnextLeft.y **or** $y >$ VnextRight.y
 then begin last scanline
   call renderScanline(Vleft, Vright, $\frac{y}{8}$);
   return;
   end;

   interpolate subpixel x endpoints at this subpixel y
   xLeft [y **mod** 8] ← lerp(Vleft.x, VnextLeft.x at y);
   xRight[y **mod** 8] ← lerp(Vright.x, VnextRight.x at y);
   if (y **mod** 8) = 7
    then begin *end of scanline*
     VscanLeft ← lerp(Vleft, VnextLeft at y);
     VscanRight ← lerp(Vright, VnextRight at y);
     call renderScanline(VscanLeft, VscanRight, $\frac{y}{8}$);
    end;
  endloop;
 end;

Render one scanline of the polygon from the subpixel information. The shading and renderPixel procedures are beyond the scope of this Gem!

renderScanline: **procedure** (VscanLeft, VscanRight, scanLine);
begin
 for each pixel in scanline overlapped by polygon
 for pixel ← $\dfrac{\min(xLeft)}{8}$ **to** $\dfrac{\max(xRight) + 7}{8}$ **do**
  area ← computePixelCoverage(pixel);
  Vpixel ← lerp(VscanLeft, VscanRight at pixel);
  color ← $\dfrac{area}{256}$ ∗ shading(Vpixel);
  mask ← computePixelMask(pixel); *(if needed)*
  insert anti-aliased pixel data into hidden surface routine
  renderPixel(scanLine, pixel, color, mask);
  endloop;
 end;

Compute fraction of the pixel (actually, number of subpixels) covered by the polygon. See Fig. 3.

computePixelCoverage: **procedure** (pixel);
begin
       area ← 0;
       pixelLeft ← pixel * 8; *subpixel edges of pixel*
       pixelRight ← pixelLeft + 7;
       for y ← 0 **to** 7 **do**
           partialArea ← min(xRight[y], pixelRight) −
                     max(xLeft[y], pixelLeft) + 1;
           if partialArea > 0 *polygon overlaps this pixel*
               then area ← area + partialArea;
           endloop;
       return area;
       end;

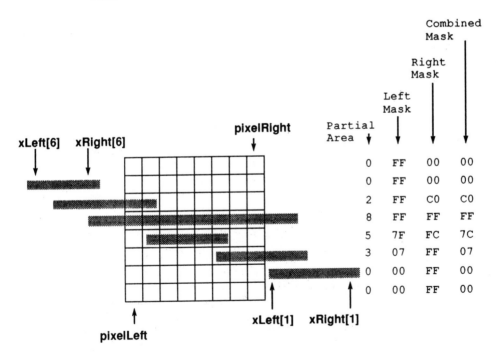

Figure 3. Example pixel coverage computation.

81

Compute subpixel bitmask indicating which parts of the pixel are covered by the polygon. Look-up tables speed up mask computation when the polygon edge occurs inside the pixel. See Fig. 3.

computePixelMask: **procedure** (pixel);

leftMaskTable: **array**[0 .. 7] **of char** ←
    [0xFF, 0x7F, 0x3F, 0x1F, 0x0F, 0x07, 0x03, 0x01];
rightMaskTable: **array**[0 .. 7] **of char** ←
    [0x80, 0xC0, 0xE0, 0xF0, 0xF8, 0xFC, 0xFE, 0xFF];

begin
    pixelLeft ← pixel ∗ 8;   *subpixel edges of pixel*
    pixelRight ← pixelLeft + 7;
    for y ← 0 **to** 7 **do**
        if xLeft[y] < pixelLeft
            then leftMask ← 0xFF;
        else if xLeft[y] > pixelRight
            then leftMask ← 0;
        else *left edge of polygon is inside pixel*
            leftMask ← leftMaskTable[xLeft[y] − pixelLeft];
        if xRight[y] > pixelRight
            then rightMask ← 0xFF;
        else if xRight[y] < pixelLeft
            then rightMask ← 0;
        else *right edge of polygon is inside pixel*
            rightMask ← rightMaskTable[xRight[y] − pixelLeft];
        mask[y] ← leftMask **bit-and** rightMask;
        endloop;
    return mask;
    end;

Implementation Notes

Care must be taken at the first and last scanline of a polygon, where some *y*-coordinates may not be covered. Setting the uncovered *xLeft*[ ] and *xRight*[ ] values to − 1 is sufficient, making sure *renderScanline* ignores such edges.

Pixel area (and bitmask) computation can be readily optimized to make use of pixel-to-pixel coherence, since most pixels within a scanline are completely covered by the polygon. One approach is to determine the maximum *xLeft*[ ] and minimum *xRight*[ ], for all subpixel y's, at the beginning of *renderScanline*. *ComputePixelCoverage* can then immediately return maximum area for pixels between these limits.

If the pixel bitmask is to be computed at coarser resolution than the area, the left and right limits should be averaged over each group of y-coordinates to compute partial bitmasks. The lookup tables can account for reducing x resolution automatically. If both bitmasks and areas are desired, they can be computed together to reduce overhead, or the area determined from the bitmask. (See Carpenter's *A*-Buffer article for tips on computing area from a bitmask.)

As described, the scan conversion algorithm is suitable for depth-buffer hidden-surface methods, where one polygon at a time is rendered. For scanline methods, where one scanline at a time is rendered (for all polygons), standard interpolation or clipping procedures can be used to extract polygon vertex data at the scanline limits, with the above algorithm used within the scanline to compute subpixel detail.

For an *RGBaZ*-style hidden-surface method, such as the one described by Duff (1985), it may be useful to interpolate *Z*-coordinates (depth) at high resolution also, so that depth at each corner of the pixel can be determined more accurately.

For related information see Catmull (1978), Crow (1977), and Sutherland (1974).

See Appendix 2 for C Implementation (**662**)

GENERIC CONVEX POLYGON SCAN CONVERSION AND CLIPPING

Paul S. Heckbert
University of California
Berkeley, California

When doing faceted shading, Gouraud shading, Phong shading, or texture mapping in a painter's or z-buffer hidden-surface algorithm, typically a small set of floating point attributes need to be interpolated across a polygon. For example, when doing z-buffered color Gouraud shading, the four attributes r, g, b, and z are used: they are initialized at each polygon vertex and interpolated at each pixel within the polygon. If linear interpolation is used for all attributes, then the code for interpolating each attribute is very similar. Maintaining separate source code for scan converting each different attribute set becomes very tedious.

I see three general techniques for reducing the code redundancy: (1) use a vertex structure with dynamic size and layout containing only the attribute set of interest; (2) use a static vertex structure that includes all attributes, and interpolate everything; and (3) use a static vertex structure but interpolate only the attributes of interest. Alternative (1) is the most space-efficient, but attribute offsets must be computed at run-time, so it is slow. Method (2) reduces access time because the fixed structure offsets allow compile-time optimization, but it is less efficient overall because unused attributes would be allocated and interpolated. Method (3) is the fastest, as offsets are fixed at compile-time, and only relevant attributes are interpolated. It uses more storage than the first method, however.

The following is C code that I have evolved over the years to perform scan conversion and clipping of generic convex, planar polygons. Use of method (3) allows a variety of attribute sets to be handled efficiently without changing the scan converter or clipper code, as those routines are device-independent and ignorant of the semantics of the attributes being interpolated. The scan converter is based on an algorithm by Frank Crow at NYIT, and the clipper is based on an implementation of Sutherland-Hodgman by Ed Catmull and Alvy Ray Smith (Sutherland and Hodgman, 1974). I rewrote and evolved the code several times at Pacific Data Images, Pixar, and UC Berkeley. I have been careful with roundoff; consequently, polygons sharing an edge abut perfectly with no gaps or overlap. Lance Williams suggested interpolation of generic attributes, and interpolation masks were inspired by Whitted and Weimer (1982). Henry Moreton suggested the texture coordinate interpolation trick involving division by sw.

The general method for using these routines is as follows: load data into the vertices, set the polygon's *mask* to indicate which attributes are in use, call the clipper, modify the vertex attributes (typically a homogeneous divide), set the polygon's *mask* to indicate which attributes are still in use, call the scan converter, supplying a callback procedure that is called by *poly_scan* at each pixel, and in the pixel routine, unload data from the interpolated point, using it to draw into a raster image.

There are four files of generic code,

poly.h	Polygon data structure.
poly.c	Utility subroutines to print polygons.
poly_scan.c	Scan convert a convex, planar polygon by uniform sampling at pixel centers.
poly_clip.c	Clip a convex, planar polygon to a screen space parallelepiped,

and two files giving simple examples of their use:

scantest.c	Gouraud shading with z-buffer using *poly_scan*.
fancytest.c	Phong shading and texture mapping using *poly_clip* and *poly_scan*.

You can change anything in the *Poly_vert* structure definition except the screen space position fields sx, sy, sz, and sw, which are required by *poly_scan* and *poly_clip*. All fields of *Poly_vert* should be doubles. Note that incorrect settings of the interpolation mask can result in meaningless attribute values or wasted compute time. For C environments that don't have the *bcopy* routine, use *#define bcopy(from, to, nbytes) memcpy(to, from, nbytes)*.

Note that linear interpolation is not correct for all attributes; it is appropriate only when the mapping between screen space x, y and the attribute is affine (linear plus a constant). Incidentally, linear interpolation for Gouraud and Phong shading on polygons with more than three sides gives results that are, in general, not rotation-invariant, so in this sense linear interpolation is not "correct" for those purposes. The errors caused by linear-interpolated Gouraud and Phong shading are invisible in most images, however, unlike the errors of linear-interpolated perspective texture coordinates, which typically cause a distracting "rubber sheet" effect. A discussion of affine and projective mappings and their efficient computation is given in Heckbert (1989).

See also Concave Polygon Scan Conversion (87)

See Appendix 2 for C Implementation (**667**)

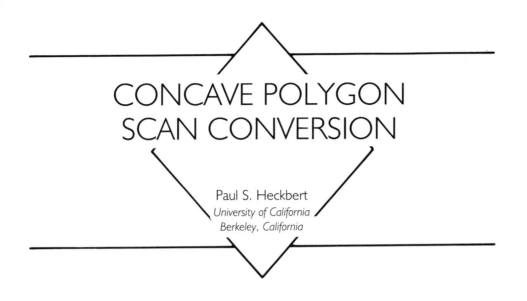

CONCAVE POLYGON SCAN CONVERSION

Paul S. Heckbert
University of California
Berkeley, California

Scan conversion of concave polygons or nonsimple polygons is more complex than scan conversion of convex polygons because each scan line can intersect the polygon in more than one interval or span of pixels. (A polygon is simple if it does not intersect itself.) When scan-converting concave polygons one must keep track of a variable-length *active edge list* of polygon edges intersecting the current scan line. This is not as difficult as it may seem. Many published algorithms for concave (or convex) polygon scan conversion employ voluminous code to handle the special cases of horizontal edges. In fact, such cases do not require special treatment if care is taken in the inequalities of the conditionals. The program resulting from this approach, listed below, is surprisingly simple. It is very similar to that of Rogers (1985), p. 76.

This program assumes the polygon is described by a single cyclic loop of points. To describe polygons with holes using this data structure, construct "bridges" joining the holes to the outer vertices. For example, if the outer polygon has vertices $p[i]$ for $0 \leq i < np$, and the inner polygon has vertices $q[i]$ for $0 \leq i < nq$, construct a single polygon consisting of the vertices: $p[0] \ldots p[np - 1]$, $p[0]$, $q[0]$, $q[0] \ldots q[nq - 1]$, $q[0]$. The two new bridge edges connect vertices $p[0]$ and $q[0]$ in both directions.

Depending on the sorting algorithm used and the shape of the polygon, the complexity of this algorithm will be between $O(n)$ and $O(n^2)$.

Figure 1. Output for a "random" 25-sided polygon.

The program follows:

concave: scan convert n-sided concave nonsimple polygon with vertices at $(pt[i].x, pt[i].y)$ *for i in* $[0..n-1]$ *within the window win by calling drawproc for each visible span of pixels.*
Polygon can be clockwise or counterclockwise.
Algorithm does uniform point sampling at pixel centers.
Inside – outside test done by Jordan's rule: a point is considered inside if an emanating ray intersects the polygon an odd number of times.
drawproc should fill in pixels from xl to xr inclusive on scanline y, e. g:

```
procedure drawproc(y, xl, xr: int);
x: int;
begin
    for x ← xl to xr do
        pixel_write(x, y, pixelvalue);
        endloop;
    endproc;
```

Note: lines enclosed in angle brackets '⟨', '⟩' should be replaced with the code described.

Point: **type** ← **record** [x, y: **real**];   *2D point*

Window: **type** ← **record** [xmin, ymin, xmax, ymax: **int**];   *inclusive window*

Spanproc: **type** ← **procedure**(y, xl, xr: **int**);

procedure concave(
    n: **int**;   *number of vertices*
    pt: **array** [0..n − 1] **of** Point;   *vertices of polygon*
    win: Window;   *screen clipping window*
    drawproc: Spanproc;   *called for each span of pixels*
    );

Edge: **type** ← **record** [*a polygon edge*
    x: **real**;   *x-coordinate of edge's intersection with current scanline*

    dx: **real**;   *change in x with respect to y*
    i: **int**;   *edge number: edge i goes from pt[i] to pt[i + 1]*

    ];
nact: **int**;   *number of active edges*
active: **array** [0..n − 1] **of** Edge;   *active edge list: edges crossing scanline y*
ind: **array** [0..n − 1] **of int**;   *list of vertex indices*
k, y0, y1, y, i, j, xl, xr: **int**;
begin *procedure concave*

    create y-sorted array of indices ind[k] into vertex list
    for k ← 0 **to** n − 1 **do**
        ind[k] ← k;
        endloop;
    ⟨sort ind by pt[ind[k]].y⟩

        nact ← 0;   *start with empty active list*
        k ← 0;   *ind[k] is next vertex to process*
        y0 ← max(win.ymin, ceiling(pt[ind[0]].y − .5));   *ymin of polygon*
        y1 ← min(win.ymax, floor(pt[ind[n − 1]].y − .5));   *ymax of polygon*

for y ← y0 **to** y1 **do**   *step through scanlines*
 scanline y is at y + .5 in continuous coordinates

 check vertices between previous scanline and current one, if any
 while k < n **and** pt[ind[k]].y ≤ y + .5 **do**
  invariant: y − .5 < pt[i].y ≤ y + .5
  i ← ind[k];
  insert or delete edges before and after vertex i (i − 1 to i, and
  i to i + 1) from active list if they cross scanline y

  j ← **if** i > 0 **then** i − 1 **else** n − 1; *vertex previous to i*
  if pt[j].y ≤ y − .5 **then**   *old edge, remove from active list*
   delete(j);
  else if pt[j].y > y + .5 **then** *new edge, add to active list*
   insert(j, y);

  j ← **if** i < n − 1 **then** i + 1 **else** 0; *vertex next after i*
  if pt[j].y ≤ y − .5 **then**   *old edge, remove from active list*
   delete(i);
  else if pt[j].y > y + .5 **then** *new edge, add to active list*
   insert(i, y);
  k ← k + 1;
  endloop;

 ⟨ *sort active edge list by active[j].x* ⟩

 draw horizontal segments for scanline y
 for j ← 0 **to** nact − 1 **step** 2 **do**
  span between j and j + 1 is inside, span from j + 1 to j + 2 is outside
  xl ← ceiling(active[j].x − .5); *left end of span*
  if xl < win.xmin **then** xl ← win.xmin;
  xr ← floor(active[j + 1].x − .5); *right end of span*
  if xr > win.xmax **then** xr ← win.xmax;
  if xl ≤ xr **then**
   drawproc(y, xl, xr);   *draw pixels in span*
  increment edge coords
  active[j].x ← active[j].x + active[j].dx;
  active[j + 1].x ← active[j + 1].x + active[j + 1].dx;
  endloop;
 endloop; *y loop*

```
procedure delete(i: int);                    remove edge i from active list
j, k: int;
begin
    for j ← 0 to nact − 1 do
        if active[j].i = i then begin       edge found
            nact ← nact − 1;
            for k ← j to nact − 1 do        shift remainder of array down
                active[k].x ← active[k + 1].x;
                active[k].dx ← active[k + 1].dx;
                active[k].i ← active[k + 1].i;
                endloop;
            return;
            end;
        endloop;

    edge not found; this can happen at win.ymin
    endproc delete;

procedure insert(i, y: int);                 append edge i to end of
                                                active list
j, p, q: int;
begin
    j ← if i < n − 1 then i + 1 else 0;
    if pt[i].y < pt[j].y then begin p ← i; q ← j; end;
    else                   begin p ← j; q ← i; end;
    initialize x position at intersection of edge with scanline y
    active[nact].dx ← (pt[q].x − pt[p].x) / (pt[q].y − pt[p].y);
    active[nact].x ← active[nact].dx*(y + .5 − pt[p].y) + pt[p].x;
    active[nact].i ← i;
    nact ← nact + 1;
    endproc insert;

endproc concave;
```

See also Generic Convex Polygon Scan Conversion and Clipping (84)

See Appendix 2 for C Implementation (681)

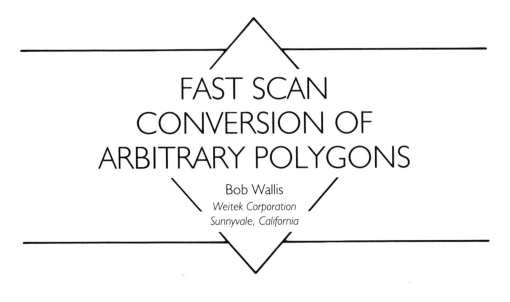

FAST SCAN CONVERSION OF ARBITRARY POLYGONS

Bob Wallis
Weitek Corporation
Sunnyvale, California

Introduction

Many of the traditional scan-conversion methods described in the literature are not well suited to implementation on RISC processors. A fast and extremely simple algorithm, which maximizes usage of machine registers but sacrifices memory to gain speed, is described.

Keeping the Registers Full

In devising algorithms for implementation on RISC processors, a major goal is minimizing the amount of load/store traffic between machine registers and memory. This is particularly true in cost-sensitive platforms employing slow external memory in which wait-state penalties are incurred. On CISC processors, which are less register oriented, this is not as much of a concern (or at least, there is less opportunity to do anything about it).

Active Edge Lists

The standard scan-conversion schemes typically fill a polygonal path by employing a data structure called an *active edge list* (Foley and Van Dam, 1982). As the scan line scrolls through the y direction, the list's edge elements are updated by adding new line segments that have just begun straddling the active scan, and by deleting lines that no longer straddle y. Each x element of the list structure contains the parameters required to produce x values for that given line segment of the polygon. By maintaining the list's elements in x sorted order, the x spans for a given y are produced directly.

A problem with this scheme is that it is difficult to take advantage of the relative speed of register-to-register operations. Each element of an active edge list corresponds to a line of a *different* slope with different DDA parameters; thus, there is a great deal of load/store thrashing involved, with a significant loss of efficiency in the normally very efficient DDA interpolator. Furthermore, there is a fair amount of sorting involved in setting things up.

The following is a description of an alternate method, which scan-converts the line segments of the polygon one at a time so that the same DDA coefficients may be kept in registers and used for the entire duration of the line segment. The price to be paid is that the method uses more memory than the active edge scheme. However, the memory requirements are quite modest for applications such as scan conversion of fonts, which are typically represented as small polygons.

The X-Transition Table

The basic concept is to eliminate explicit y-sorting and active edges altogether. A polygon is treated as just a succession of chained line segments, and each line segment is rasterized separately as the perimeter of the polygon is traversed. As with all scan-conversion algorithms, if a scan line is permitted to go directly through a vertex there are messy special cases to be dealt with, and one has to worry about half-open intervals and other ugly details. The most expedient way to deal with this problem is to avoid it by using a coordinate system that is much finer than the pixel grid—for example, eight bits of binary fraction for an x or y coordinate. On a CPU with 32 bit registers, this leaves plenty of room to the left of the decimal point. If the least significant bit of the fraction is always set to 1, this amounts to adding a tiny amount of additional roundoff error, but a scan line never hits a vertex (see "Rendering Fat Lines on a Raster Grid" in this volume).

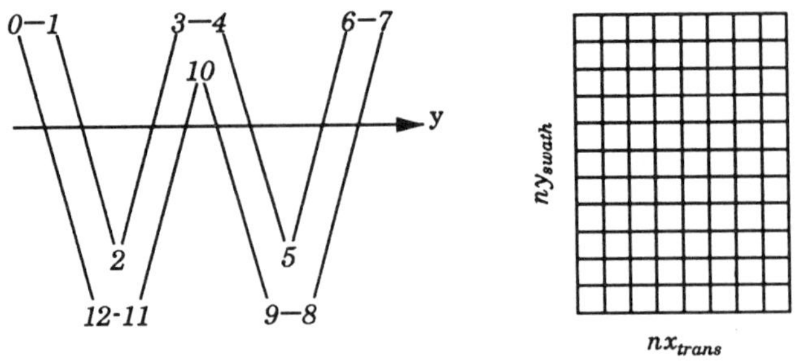

Figure 1.

Each line segment $[x1, y1] \rightarrow [x2, y2]$ is processed separately, producing an x value for every scan line that it straddles. This is done with a slightly modified Bresenham DDA that supports subpixel resolution. The x values that are produced go into a rectangular array referred to as the *transition table* for the polygon. The array is high enough in the y direction to accommodate all required scan lines for the given polygon, and wide enough in the x direction to accommodate the maximum possible number of line segments that can straddle a scan line. Consider the example in Fig. 1, which has a table 8 columns wide and 11 scan lines high. The line segments of the W polygon are scan-converted in the order 0–1, 1–2, and so on. As the DDA walks down the scan lines, each x produced is loaded into the next available column in the yth row of the table. The sign of $y2 - y1$ is also recorded in a reserved bit of the x value.

Once the table has been completed, it is a simple matter to visit each row, sort the x values, and produce interior spans to be filled for that scan line. The x-sorting required from one row of the map to the next row is highly coherent, making it advantageous to use the sort permutation required on the previous row as an initial guess on how to x-sort the current row. A very general way to determine the interior regions of the polygon is to use the signs of $y2 - y1$ to track the *winding number* transitions (Newell and Sequin, 1980) at each x intersection (see Fig. 2).

The winding number starts at zero outside the polygon and is incremented ± 1 depending on whether the line segment being crossed is rising or falling. Horizontal lines are not encountered because scans never hit vertices. In the example above, the winding number rises to 3 in the

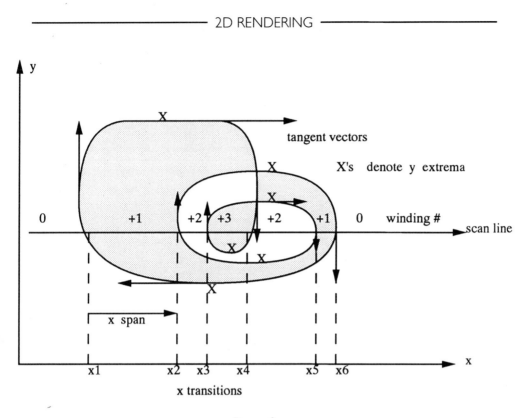

Figure 2.

innermost loop. If the sense of the polygon had been counterclockwise, the winding numbers would have been negative but nonzero in both cases. The shaded areas in the figure illustrate the standard even/odd parity rule, which declares a span to be interior whenever the least significant bit of the winding number is 1. An alternate definition, suitable for self-intersecting polygons, is to declare any span with a nonzero winding number as interior.

Y Extrema and Memory Requirements

One issue was glossed over earlier: determining how many columns should be allocated for the transition table. This should be the worst-case number of x transitions possible for any scan line (maximum number of active edges). This can be easily determined by counting the number of times that the polarity of $y2 - y1$ changes as we traverse the polygon. This count is easily obtained at the same time as the polygon's bounding box is calculated. Each of the points where the slope of y changes is a y *extrema*. These are indicated for X's in Fig. 2. It has six extrema, and thus has a maximum of six x transitions possible. The W polygon in Fig. 1 has eight extrema, so its transition table needs eight columns.

To be able to scan-convert polygons of arbitrary size and complexity, it is necessary that the algorithm be able to break polygons that are too big for the transition table into horizontal swaths, which are scan-converted separately. The amount of memory available for the table should be large enough so that most polygons can be handled without resorting to stripping.

Intersecting Polygons

A simple modification of the previous algorithm permits it to determine the intersection of two or more polygons. For example, the intersection of a W and E is shown below. The trick is to feed both polygons to the scan converter as if they were one single polygon, but to keep their winding numbers separate. For a given scan line, the x regions within which both winding numbers are nonzero are interior to both polygons. The intersection corresponds to the Boolean AND of both winding numbers, but any other logical function could be used.

Figure 3.

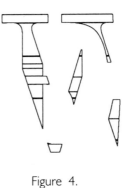

Figure 4.

Convex Decompositions

Some applications require that arbitrary polygons be fractured into convex figures, such as trapezoids. By adding a little more data to the x elements stored in the transition table, the algorithm can serve as a front end for a convex decomposer. It is necessary that the x elements "remember" which line segments they came from, so that segments with matching left and right sides from successive scan lines can be merged and grown into convex polygons. Figure 4 shows a convex decomposition of the E/W intersection.

LINE-DRAWING SUMMARY

Vector graphics remains an important application area of computer graphics. Although shaded images have much to offer, lines remain a valuable primitive for many types of images. Fast and efficient line-drawing is not a simple task, particularly if you want to avoid aliasing artifacts.

The basic line-drawing algorithm is Bresenham's algorithm, developed originally for digital plotters. The first three of the following algorithms present the basic Bresenham technique and then extend it for increased speed, or for inclusion of anti-aliasing information. The next two Gems discuss only lines thicker than one pixel, showing how to put bevels on the corners formed by two flat line ends, and how efficiently to render fat lines in a rectangular grid.

See also Anti-Aliasing Gems; Fast Spline Drawing (585); Tutorial on Forward Differencing (594)

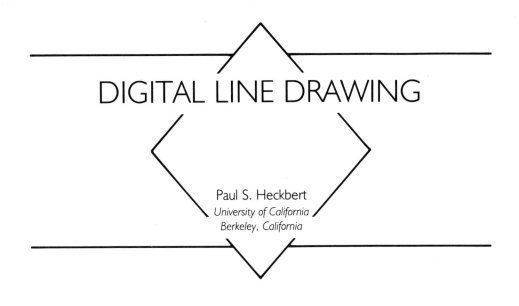

DIGITAL LINE DRAWING

Paul S. Heckbert
University of California
Berkeley, California

A digital line-drawing algorithm is one of the most basic tools in a computer graphicist's toolbox. The following is skeleton code for Bresenham's algorithm (1965). The code as listed calls a user-supplied procedure at each pixel, but for efficiency you may prefer to do inline/macro substitution for the pixel procedure.

> **digline:** *draw digital line from* ($x1$, $y1$) *to* ($x2$, $y2$),
> *calling a user-supplied procedure at each pixel.*
> *Does no clipping. Uses Bresenham's algorithm.*

```
Pixelproc: type ← procedure(x, y: int);

procedure digline(x1, y1, x2, y2: int; dotproc: Pixelproc);
d, x, y, ax, ay, sx, sy, dx, dy: int;
begin
    dx ← x2 − x1;  ax ← abs(dx)*2;  sx ← sgn(dx);
    dy ← y2 − y1;  ay ← abs(dy)*2;  sy ← sgn(dy);

    x ← x1;
    y ← y1;
```

```
        if ax > ay then begin                    x dominant
            d ← ay − ax/2;
            while true do
                dotproc(x, y);
        if x = x2 then return;
        if d ≥ 0 then begin
            y ← y + sy;
            d ← d − ax;
            end;
        x ← x + sx;
        d ← d + ay;
        endloop;
    end;
        else begin                               y dominant
            d ← ax − ay/2;
            while true do
                dotproc(x, y);
                if y = y2 then return;
                if d ≥ 0 then begin
                    x ← x + sx;
                    d ← d − ay;
                    end;
                y ← y + sy;
                d ← d + ax;
                endloop;
            end;
        endproc digline;

    function sgn(x: int): int;
    begin return if x > 0 then 1 else −1; endfunc;
```

See Appendix 2 for C Implementation (685)

100

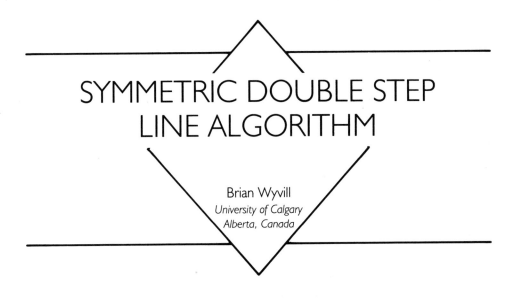

SYMMETRIC DOUBLE STEP
LINE ALGORITHM

Brian Wyvill
University of Calgary
Alberta, Canada

Line Drawing

Drawing straight lines on a raster device, such as an incremental graph plotter or frame store is an old problem. Jack Bresenham (1965) produced a simple and efficient algorithm that lent itself to hardware implementation. Bresenham's algorithm works by keeping track of the error between the actual line and the nearest pixel. This value is called a *discriminator*. The method has to find the next pixel closest to the true line. Once the direction of the line is determined, all the algorithm has to do is decide between two alternative pixels at each step. To do this the discriminator is tested to find the next pixel and then (and this is the clever bit) incremented by a constant amount ready for the next test. This basic algorithm was not greatly improved in over twenty years. Many researchers became interested in line drawing, particularly the hardware manufacturers, who relied on producing faster line drawing for comparison with their competitors. Today Bresenham's algorithm is at the heart of several fast line drawing chips.

Double Speed Bresenham's

A few years ago one of my students, Xialon Wu, approached me with an exciting new line drawing algorithm. At the time his English was bad, his claims outrageous, and I was busy. Eventually Wu developed his double step algorithm with Prof. Jon Rokne and I realized what a good idea he

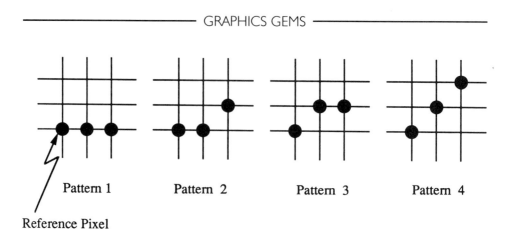

Reference Pixel

Figure 1.   Double step pixel patterns (Wu, 1987).

had had (see Wu and Rokne, 1987). Like all good ideas it is very simple: instead of using a discriminator to choose the next pixel, Wu chooses the next pattern of two pixels (see Fig. 1). Since there are four distinct patterns, how does the algorithm reduce to a simple binary decision? Let us for the moment call patterns 2 and 3 one pattern, 2(3). This could be the case on a multilevel display since both patterns could be shown as one with the center pixels at half intensity to achieve a degree of anti-aliasing. It can be shown that for lines whose slope is less than $1/2$ that pattern 4 does not occur; the choice is then between pattern 1 and 2(3). Similarly, for lines with slope greater than or equal to $1/2$, the choice is between pattern 2(3) and pattern 4 (pattern 1 cannot occur). Simply by testing the slope outside the plotting loop the algorithm reduces to a single discriminator. To distinguish between patterns 2 and 3 also turns out to be easy, requiring one more test but using the same discriminator. In this way the algorithm does only slightly more work to produce two pixels instead of one per step, virtually doubling the speed of Bresenham's original. (A similar, but much more complex algorithm also exists for quadruple step patterns (Bao and Rokne, 1990).

Using Symmetry

So impressed was I with this breakthrough that I coded the algorithm and added a small change of my own. Since lines are symmetric about the center, it makes sense to use this symmetry to plot from both ends

```
symwuline(a1, b1, a2, b2) int a1, b1, a2, b2;
drawline from a1,b1 to a2,b2
The algorithm is described for slopes between 0 and 1/2
The C version given later is generalized to all quadrants
begin
    dx ← a2 − a1;              This may be generalized to
    dy ← b2 − b1;              axis of greatest movement
    xend ← (dx − 1) / 4;
    pixelsLeft ← (dx − 1) mod 4;
    incr2 ← 4*dy − 2*dx;
    plot first two points
    setpixel(a1, b1);
    setpixel(a2, b2);
    c ← 2*dy;
    incrl ← 2*c;
    D ← incrl − dx;
    plotting loop
    for i:int ← 0, i < xend, i ← i + 1 do
        a1 ← a1 + 1;
        a2 ← a2 − 1;
        if (D < 0) then
            begin
                drawPattern1Forwards;
                drawPattern1Backwards;
                D = D + incr1;
            end;
        else begin
            if (D < c) then
                begin
                    pattern2Forwards;
                    pattern2Backwards;
                end;
            else begin
                    pattern3Forwards;
                    pattern3Backwards;
                end;
            D = D + incr2;
            end;
        endloop;
    if pixelsLeft > 0 then
        begin
            drawTwoForwardPixels;
            drawTwoBackwardPixels;
            end;
end;
```

Figure 2. Pseudo-code for symmetrical double step line algorithm.

simultaneously using half the number of steps. Wu was not pleased to see that I had doubled the speed of his algorithm overnight! It turns out that using the symmetry was not a new idea; probably Bresenham himself thought of it originally. The symmetric double step algorithm is between three and four times faster than the original Bresenham's (see Rokne *et al.*, 1990). The hardware manufacturers were not particularly interested in Wu's idea. The bottleneck (currently) in line drawing is not choosing the pixels, but getting the information to the display, the pixel write operations. Wu went on to develop a similar idea for drawing conics and Jon Rokne and Paul Bao continued with the pattern idea to produce a quadruple step version of the line algorithm. Pseudo code for lines with slopes from 0 to 1/2 is set out in Fig. 2. C code for lines of any slope is given in the appendix.

See Appendix 2 for C Implementation (686)

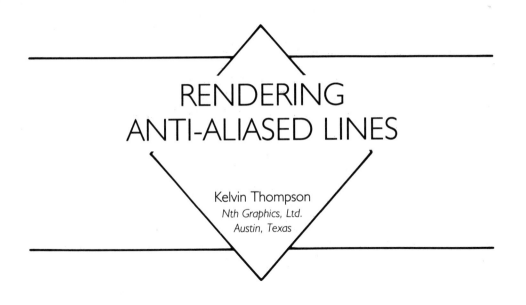

RENDERING
ANTI-ALIASED LINES

Kelvin Thompson
Nth Graphics, Ltd.
Austin, Texas

Problem

Render an anti-aliased line segment.

Solution 1

Model the line segment as having a finite thickness and set each pixel's intensity according to how much it overlaps the line. We accomplish this with an extension to the traditional Bresenham line algorithm (Bresenham, 1965). With each iteration, the usual algorithm moves by one pixel along a major axis and by zero or one pixel along a minor axis (for example, if the line's slope is in the range $[-1, 1]$, then the major axis is X and the minor is Y). To expand the algorithm we add two loops—called *orthogonal loops*—in sequence inside the traditional loop. Immediately after the traditional algorithm chooses the central pixel of the line, the first orthogonal loop examines ajacent pixels in the positive direction along the minor axis, then the second orthogonal loop examines adjacent pixels in the negative direction.

At each pixel (including the central pixel) the algorithm updates a variable that contains the distance between the center of the pixel and the middle of the thick line; this *distance variable* can be used to calculate (usually via a look-up table) how much the pixel overlaps the thick line.

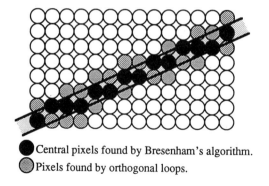

● Central pixels found by Bresenham's algorithm.
● Pixels found by orthogonal loops.

Figure 1.

Also see Gupta and Sproull (1981) for a more detailed description of the algorithm; "Vertical Distance from a Point to a Line" (in this volume) for the mapping between the "vertical" and true distances between a point at a line; "Area of Intersection: Circle and a Thick Line" (in this volume) for the overlap calculation; and subroutine *Anti_Line* for example code.

Solution 2

Render several slightly offset lines using the traditional Bresenham line algorithm, but use alpha blending with progressively smaller coverage values (for example, $1, \frac{1}{2}, \frac{1}{3}, \frac{1}{4}, \ldots$; see "Alpha Blending" in this volume). The lines should all be parallel with slightly different starting positions. You can change the subpixel starting position in Bresenham's line algorithm by adding values in the range $[0, 2 \cdot dx]$ to the initial decision variable.

See Appendix 2 for C Implementation (**690**)

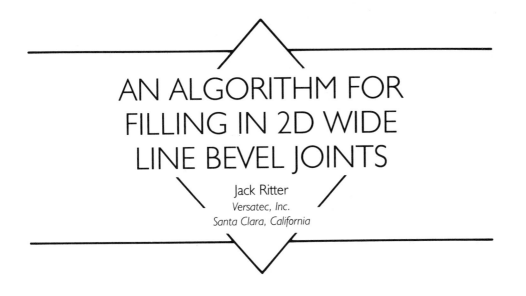

AN ALGORITHM FOR FILLING IN 2D WIDE LINE BEVEL JOINTS

Jack Ritter
Versatec, Inc.
Santa Clara, California

Typical 2D graphics packages allow for wide lines to be joined end to end, where their end center points are coincident. Bevelling fills in the triangle between the outer corners. This is an arbitrary isosceles triangle. From Fig. 1, this bevel triangle is made of the two outer points $O1$ and $O2$, and the center point C.

This algorithm is an alternative to breaking the bevel triangle into two triangles with a horizontal line, then generating both triangles, thus doing Bresenham walking along all three edges of the bevel triangle. This algorithm fills in the bevel triangle area with one nonrotated right triangle, and zero, one, or two orthogonal rectangles. The advantage is that only the outer edge is walked (as part of drawing the right triangle), and so the amount of Bresenham step calculation is reduced to about one third. The other advantage is that it won't leave "stiches" (holes) along the two interior edges, where the old method might, if the drawing of the wide line and the drawing of the triangles did not meet flush. This algorithm may be easily implemented in integer arithmetic.

The right triangle is $(O1, O2, R)$, where the outer edge $(O1, O2)$ is its hypotenuse, shown as a *dashed line* in all figures. The triangle's two interior legs are shown as *dotted* lines. Its inside 90-degree corner point will be one of the two "opposite points" to the hypotenuse. Note in Figs. 2, 3, and 4: that one opposite point is R, and the other is depicted by X. Between R and X, how do we choose the inside point? We pick the one *closest* to c. Closeness can be determined by "Manhattan distance," which is the number of blocks you would walk in a city grid to get from one point to another. Euclidian distance need not be used.

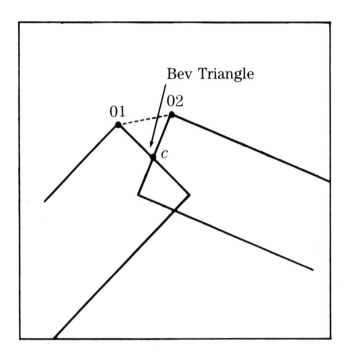

Figure 1. General Case.

Now we have two triangles: the original bevel triangle $(O1, O2, C)$, and the right triangle $(O1, O2, R)$. They share the outer edge. The situation can now be broken down into one of three states, depending on the topological relationship between these two triangles. One of the following will be the case:

case 1 (Fig. 2): C is inside the right triangle

case 2 (Fig. 3): R is inside the bevel triangle

case 3 (Fig. 4):   neither point is inside the other triangle.

For case 1, all we need draw is the right triangle. For case 2, we draw the

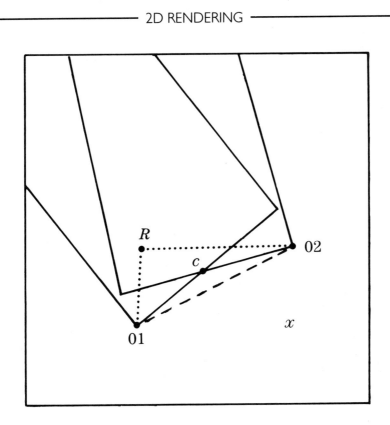

Figure 2. Case 1.

right triangle, plus the two rectangles whose diagonals are the two interior edges. For case 3, we draw the right triangle, plus a rectangle whose outer edge is the *longest leg* of the right triangle, and whose opposite edge goes through C. C can be left of, right of, below, or above this outer edge. This rectangle can be thought of as the area swept out if we "push" the outer edge up to C.

Here is the pseudo-code for this algorithm:

01 is specified as $(01x, 01y)$,

02 is specified as $(02x, 02y)$,

C is specified as (Cx, Cy),

R is specified as (Rx, Ry).

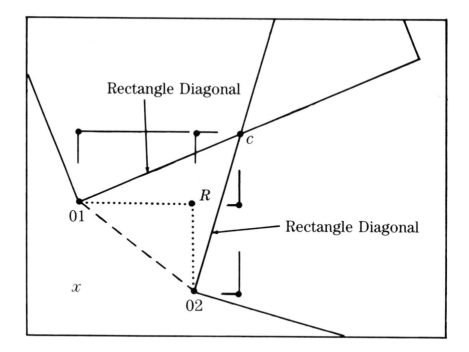

Figure 3. Case 2.

The main routine is first, and the called routines are described afterwards.

Input parameters are the 3 points 01, 02, & C
bevel_fill (01x, 01y, 02x, 02y, Cx, Cy)
{
    First Anomoly
    If all three points are collinear, the two wide lines are parallel.
    This means the bevel triangle has collapsed to nothing.
if (01, 02, and C are colinear)
            then
            return;
            end;
    Second anomoly
    If the bevel edge (01, 02) is horizontal or vertical
    (Fig. 4 comes close to being vertical), then the right
    triangle has collapsed to nothing. In this case, we simply
    draw the "push" rectangle of case 3.

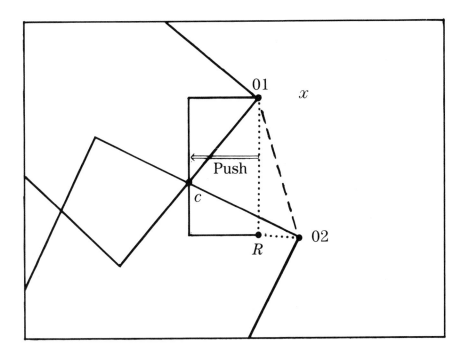

Figure 4.   Case 3.

if ((0x1 = 0x2) **or** (0y1 = 0y2))
    then
    push line (01, 02) to point C.
    emit_push_rec(01, 02, C);
    return;
    end;

    set R (eg, Rx, Ry) to 1 of the 2 hypotenuse opposite points,
    whichever one is closest to C.
    The 1st point passed to manhattan_dist is C, the 2nd is a pair of
coordinates
if (manhattan_dist(C, 01x, 02y) < manhattan_dist(C, 02x, 01y))
    then
    begin
    Rx ← 01x;
    Ry ← 02y;

```
        end;
    else
        begin
        Rx ← 02x;
        Ry ← 01y;
        end;
```

emit_right_tri(R, 01, 02); *for all 3 cases*

```
    if ( pt_in_tri(C, 01, 02, R) )
            then
```
CASE 1
C is inside the triangle (01, 02, R).
Above emitted triangle has covered the full bevel triangle.
```
            return;
            end;
    if (pt_in_tri(R, 01, 02, C))
            then
```
CASE 2
R is inside the triangle (01, 02, C).
Draw the two rectangles whose diagonals are the interior edges
(C, 01) and (C, 02).
```
        emit_diag_rec(C, 01);
        emit_diag_rec(C, 02);
        return
        end;
    else CASE 3
```
Neither point is inside the other's triangle
Draw the rectangle swept by pushing an edge perpendicularly to C.
The edge to be pushed will be the longest leg of the right triangle:
```
    if ( manhattan_dist(R, 01x, 01y) > manhattan_dist(R, 02x, 02y) )
        then emit_push_rec (R, 01, C);
        else emit_push_rec (R, 02, C);
    end of bevel_fill( )
```
Routines called from above

emitt_right_tri(P1, P2, P3)
draws the right triangle made of the three points passed, P1 is the triangle's inside point.

emit_diag_rec(P1, P2)
  draws the rectangle whose diagonal is (P1, P2).
emit_push_rec(P1, P2, P3)
  determines if P3 is left of, right of, above, or below the
  edge (P1, P2), and draws the rectangle that would be swept out if the edge
  were pushed directly to the point C.

pt_in_tri(P, T1, T2, T3)
  Returns TRUE if the point P is in the triangle (T1, T2, T3).
  This is done by comparing the signs of crossproducts:
  Here, sign_of( ) is actually the sign of the z component of the cross vector
  get winding direction of triangle:
  Let tri_wind = sign_of [(T1, T2) × (T1, T3)]
  V3Cross ((T1, T2), (T1, T3), WIND);
  tri_wind = sign_of(WIND);

  Now cross P with each side
  V3Cross ((T1, P), (T1, T3), WIND);
  sign1 ← sign_of(WIND);
  V3Cross ((T2, P), (T2, T1), WIND);
  sign2 ← sign_of(WIND);
  V3Cross((T3, P), (T3, T2), WIND);
  sign3 ← sign_of(WIND);

if   (
      sign1 = tri_wind
      and
      sign2 = tri_wind
      and
      sign3 = tri_wind
)
      then return(TRUE);
      else return(FALSE);
NOTE: all calls to pt_in_tri( ) have 01 before 02,
        for consistent winding.

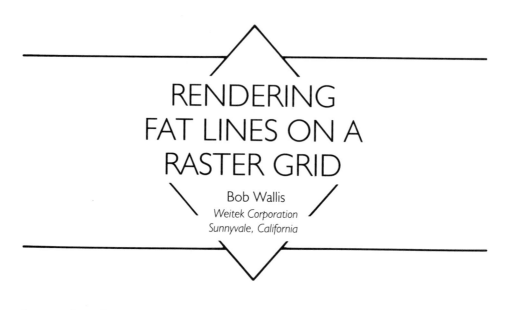

RENDERING FAT LINES ON A RASTER GRID

Bob Wallis
Weitek Corporation
Sunnyvale, California

Introduction

If multipixel wide lines are rendered improperly, unattractive beat frequencies with the raster grid may result. A practical method for producing aesthetically pleasing fat lines is presented.

The standard textbooks in computer graphics do not appear to cover algorithms for rendering multipixel wide lines on a raster grid. On devices such as laser printers, the standard skinny lines generated by the conventional Bresenham algorithm might be too narrow to be acceptable. A good method for generating uniform-looking wide is known, but the approach hasn't received the exposure that it deserves in the graphics community. It is based on the polygonal pens used by Hobby (1985).

Hobby's Polygonal Pens

Denoting pixel centers by the integer coordinates $[x, y]$, we may define the interior of a line to be those pixels that satisfy the criterion

$$-d < (ax + by + c) \le d. \tag{1}$$

This implies a line whose width in pixel space is roughly

$$w = 2d/\sqrt{a^2 + b^2}. \tag{2}$$

The problem is that the actual width can change with the phasing (c offset) of the line in pixel space. For example, using $a = -1$, $b = 3$,

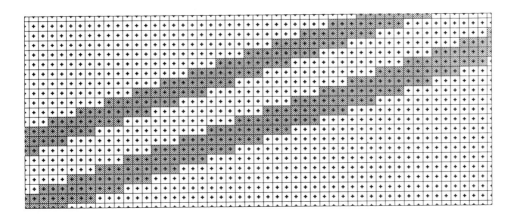

Figure 1.

$c = \{0, -20.5\}$, $d = 4.01$, we obtain different-looking lines for the two different c offsets (see Fig. 1).

Since the phasing of a line relative to the pixel grid may be random, this behavior should be avoided if possible. What is going on can be analyzed by examining the set of pixels "turned on" by Eq. 1 as we change the line equation offset c. For the time being, assume that the coefficients a, b are mutually prime, that is, they have been scaled by $1/gcd(a, b)$. Using $a = -1$, $b = 3$, $c = 0$, $d = 4$, we have the situation depicted in Fig. 2. The numbers above each pixel are the values of $ax + by + c$, which will be defined to be *class numbers* for that pixel

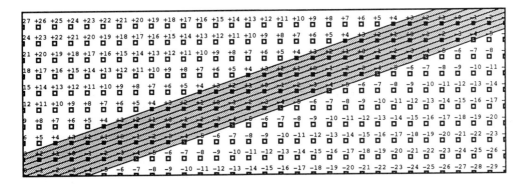

Figure 2.

(Hobby's nomenclature). The diagonal lines through the pixel centers are intended to show that all pixels having the same class number are equivalent in a sense; each class is a diagonal row of pixels, which stack together to form our fat line. Since $gcd(a, b) = 1$, pixel centers of the same class along a given diagonal line are separated by the displacement vector $[b, -a] = [3, 1]$. Each diagonal of the stack contributes a pixel density of $1/\sqrt{a^2 + b^2}$ pixels per unit length, and there are precisely d classes, so our line width expressed in Eq. 2 is indeed the average number of pixels per unit length.

Note that as we slide the interior region up and down by changing the c coefficient, the fact that we are using an open and closed interval for the permissible class numbers in Eq. 1 and an exact integer for $2d$, ensures that the number of pixels turned on in a given column doesn't behave discontinuously. If our a, b coefficients were irrational, the behavior would be similar to using rational a, b coefficients, but gradually changing the c offset. Therefore, keeping the line width invariant with c is required for uniformity.

In one dimension, the analogous question is how many integers lie in the semiopen interval of width $2W$,

$$-W < (x + c) \leq W \qquad c = arbitrary\ phase\ shift, \qquad (3a)$$

as we slide the window left or right by changing the c phasing factor? Since the phase factor is arbitrary, we can merge the W terms by using a different phase factor:

$$c' = c + W \qquad\qquad different\ phase\ factor$$

$$-c' < x \leq 2W - c' \qquad combine\ with\ Eq.\ 3a. \qquad (3b)$$

The answer can be formulated in terms of floor functions (Graham *et al.*, 1989):

$$n = \lfloor 2W - c' \rfloor - \lfloor -c' \rfloor \qquad \#\ of\ integers\ in\ interval. \qquad (4)$$

If $2W$ is an integer, it can be taken out of the floor function, reducing the value of n to

$$n = 2W + \lfloor c' \rfloor - \lfloor c' \rfloor = 2W \qquad \textit{invariant with phase.} \quad (5)$$

If $2W$ is not an integer, it cannot be taken out of the floor functions, and it will cause variations in n as we shift c.

In the 2D line drawing case, the counterpart of $2W$ is $2d$. To achieve an integer value of $2d$ for an arbitrary line, Hobby has proposed using *polygonal pens*, defined by *integer offset vectors*. Relative to the center of the polygon, the vectors need only have coefficients that are multiples of $\frac{1}{2}$. The symmetry will guarantee that the value of $2d$ is then an integer. For a line of a given slope, the value of d in Eq. 1 is obtained by dotting the vector $[a, b]$ with the integer offset vector that is closest to being normal to the line. This is easily accomplished with some *abs* and *max* functions. An example is shown in Fig. 3. The envelope may be considered the convolution of a line with a polygonal brush.

If we had formulated the line geometry using the obvious Euclidean metric for line width (a perfectly circular pen instead of a polygon with integer "diameters"), not only would the calculation of our x-spans require square roots, but the results would actually be inferior to the more efficient, integer based, polygonal pen approach.

Software Implementation

Writing efficient code to implement polygonal pen fat lines is quite straightforward. In a bitmapped environment, we would like to lay down an entire scan line (x-span) at a time as we walk up our fat line in the y direction. This requires a slight modification (described here) to the classic one-pixel-at-a-time, Bresenham DDA algorithm. Some of the tricks described fall in the category of expediencies, and thus may offend purists.

The easiest way to achieve subpixel accuracy is to use a pixel coordinate system with a binary fraction. Eight bits of pixel fraction (1/256th of a pixel) works quite well. This provides a simple way to implement floor/ceiling functions, half-open intervals, and so on. If the lsb of the

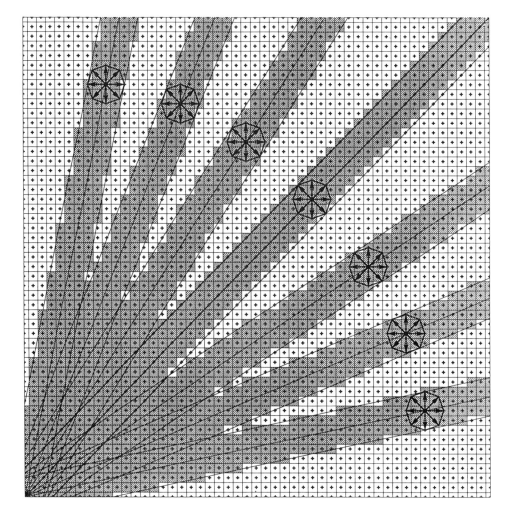

Figure 3.

fraction is always set, this prevents vertices from ever hitting an exact scan line and eliminates an entire class of ugly special cases that are usually required in scan conversion algorithms. This effectively reduces the accuracy to 1/128th of a pixel.

The basic trick in Bresenham-type linear interpolators is to express the dx/dy part as an (exact) integer part and a positive fractional part,

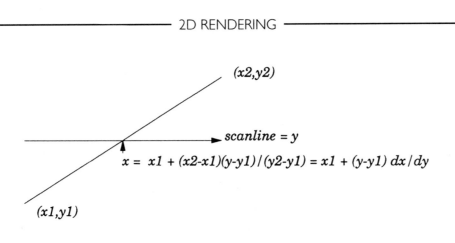

(x2,y2)

scanline = y

$x = x1 + (x2\text{-}x1)(y\text{-}y1)/(y2\text{-}y1) = x1 + (y\text{-}y1)\,dx/dy$

(x1,y1)

Figure 4.

instead of trying to approximate it by a single number. This eliminates accumulated roundoff error:

$$dx/dy = I + f \quad \text{where} \quad 0 \le f < 1 \qquad \textit{DDA increment}.$$

That is, $-7/3 = -2 - 1/3 = -3 + 2/3$ ($I = -3; f = 2/3$). Assuming $f = p/q$, we insist that

$$0 \le f < 1 \qquad \textit{fractional part}$$

$$0 \le p < q \qquad \textit{numerator}.$$

In the standard (one-pixel-at-a-time) algorithm, $I = 0$. The modified algorithm is as follows:

```
p ← p0                          init frac term
until finished do               keep 0 ≤ p ≤ q
      X ← X + I                 integer part
      p ← p + dp                bump numerator of fraction
      if (p ≥ q) then begin     overflow
            p ← p - q           restore legality of fraction
            X ← X + 1           carry into int part
      end
endloop
```

We can simplify this with the usual trick of biasing the p term so it overflows by crossing 0 instead of q. This usually saves one instruction in the inner loop.

One price to be paid for the subpixel accuracy is that the initialization of the DDA coefficients requires a divide and remainder operation. If the pixel coordinates with their binary fractions exceed 16 bits, then the intermediate product will require 64 bits.

Once the d term of Eq. 1 has been determined, using the polygonal pen, the width of the x-span is fixed. Consequently, the DDA needs to track only the left side of the line, and may determine the right side of the x-span by knowing the width. All of this can be done with exact rational arithmetic. Some additional code is required to deal with miter joints at the ends of line segments.

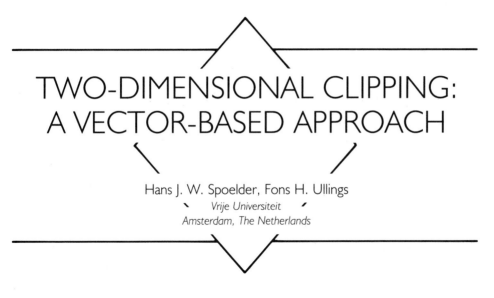

TWO-DIMENSIONAL CLIPPING: A VECTOR-BASED APPROACH

Hans J. W. Spoelder, Fons H. Ullings
Vrije Universiteit
Amsterdam, The Netherlands

Introduction

The problem we address here is the intersection of lines with polygons. Although numerous textbooks on computer graphics give partial solutions and hints (Sedgewick, 1983; Sutherland and Hodgeman, 1974; Nicholl *et al.*, 1987; Van Wyck, 1984; Cheng and Jiaan, 1986), it is hard to find a complete algorithm. The algorithm described here provides a robust solution of the problem of clipping a vector against a polygon. The same algorithm can with minor extensions be used for applications such as area shading and polygon filling.

Representation: Integers and Vectors

We will assume that the algorithms will be used for drawing graphics on some kind of graphics device with a possibly high but finite resolution. Consequently, an integer notation of the coordinates involved seems most appropriate. Since the user coordinates will generally consist of floating point quantities, they will have to be converted into integers. This can be done by multiplying the floating point quantities by a well-chosen integer constant and by rounding the result to an integer. With this, one enters the field of fixed point arithmetic. Although precautions have to be taken to ensure sufficient accuracy (and avoid overflows) no fundamental problems are involved. We summarize the most relevant features here.

Let (x_p, y_p) denote the floating point quantity to be converted and let SCALE denote the integer used for upscaling. Note that the number of "decimals" preserved is equal to $\log_{10}(\text{SCALE})$. The integer representation corresponding to (x_p, y_p) is then given by

$$iy_p = \lfloor y_p \ SCALE \rfloor$$

$$ix_p = \lfloor x_p \ SCALE \rfloor.$$

Addition and subtraction do not pose a problem. For multiplication and division a rescaling has to be performed. The correct way to perform the last two operations is

$$multiplication: \quad a = (b * c)/SCALE$$

$$division: \quad a = (b * SCALE)/c.$$

Furthermore, one should bear in mind that divisions should be avoided as much as possible. So rather than evaluating, for instance, the inequality

$$(a/b) > (c/d),$$

one should evaluate

$$a * d - c * b > 0.$$

These slight arithmetic inconveniences are more than matched by the advantages. Not only do integer operations perform faster than their floating point counterparts on almost any machine, but above all the calculations are now done in standard integer "infinite" precision.

Another fundamental decision is concerned with the representation. In the algorithm described here we will use a so-called vector notation, in which the endpoints of the line segments are specified. This implies that the line segments themselves are not digitized. Although this complicates somewhat the algorithm used, the advantage is that at every stage the resolution is merely determined by the value of *SCALE* and not by the resolution with which the vectors are digitized. This is the case in the final stage of pixel-based algorithms—for example the Post-Script stencil operation.

Some Basic Considerations

Let $\{P_i\}_{i=1}^n$ denote a set of n points $(x_{i,p}, y_{i,p})$. The polygon P is then defined by the n line segments connecting two consecutive points. Note that this implies that the contour is always closed. We will furthermore assume that no three consecutive points of the contour are colinear; this constraint can be easily accommodated. As a generalized notation for the points of the jth segment of the contour, we will use

$$P(s) = P_j + s(P_{j+1} - P_j), \qquad s \in [0, 1).$$

Note that we use a half-open interval for s to avoid double use of the endpoint of a segment. Some basic algebra suffices to determine the intersection between a line segment l and the segments of the contour (see Appendix). The problem of clipping a line segment against a polygon can now easily be solved. It involves two major steps: the calculation of the intersections of the line segment l with the polygon and the determination of the status of an arbitrary point of l. By *status* we mean in this context whether the point under investigation lies inside or outside the polygon (note that the polygon is always closed). Within the set of possible intersection of the line segment l with the contour P three different classes must be considered:

1. intersections coinciding with begin (or end) points of the line segments of the polygon (see Fig. 1).

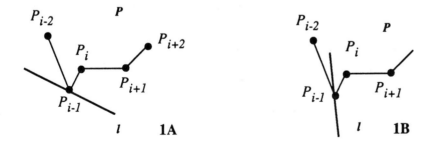

Figure 1. Two illustrations of begin points of the polygon coinciding with the line segment l.

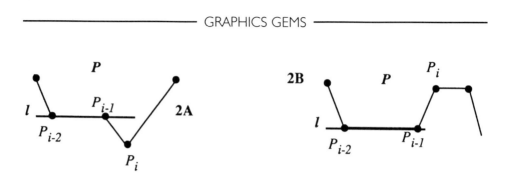

Figure 2. Two illustrations of line segments l, which (partially) coincide with the contour P.

2. line segment l, which coincides (partially) with line segments of the polygon, that is, an infinite number of intersections, (see Fig. 2).

3. intersections not belonging to 1. or 2. We will refer to these as *standard*.

It will be clear from the examples given that it does not suffice to merely calculate the possible intersection, but that additional information has to be computed and stored. One further ingredient is needed for a complete description of the algorithm. This is to determine the relative position of two points with respect to a given line segment l. Again some basic algebra suffices. Let (x_1, y_1) and (x_2, y_2) denote the endpoints of the line segment l and let P with coordinates (x_p, y_p) denote the given points. Then comparison of the slopes of line segment l with the line segment defined by one of the endpoints of l and P will result in a quantity of which the sign determines the relative position of P with respect to l. This quantity S is given by:

$$S = (x_2 - x_1)(y_p - y_1) - (y_2 - y_1)(x_p - x_1) \quad \begin{array}{l} > 0\text{: } P \text{ lies on "one" side of } l \\ = 0\text{; } P \text{ lies on } l \\ < 0\text{: } P \text{ lies on "other" side of } l \end{array}$$

Algorithm

After these basic considerations, the complete algorithm for finding the intersections can now be stated as follows:

1. Test if there is a simple intersection between line segment l and the polygon segment $P_i P_{i+1}$. If not, goto 5.

2. Test if the intersection found coincides with P_i or P_{i+1}. If not, add the intersection to the list marked *standard* and goto 8.

3. Test if the intersection is P_{i+1}. If so, goto 8.

4. Test if the polygon points P_{i-1} and P_{i+1} lie at opposite sides of l. If so, add the intersection to the list marked *standard*. Goto 8.

5. Test if the line segment l coincides with the polygon segment $P_i P_{i+1}$. If not, goto 8.

6. Test if both P_i and P_{i+1} lie on l; if not, goto 8.

7. Test if P_{i-1} and P_{i+2} lie at opposite sides of l. If so, add both points to the intersection list marked *delayed*.

8. Test if more polygon segments have to be investigated. If so, goto 1.

9. Add the begin and endpoints of l to the intersection list and sort it.

10. Scan the list for two successive points marked *delayed*. If present, remove the first point from the list and remark the second as *standard*.

If the number of intersections found is two, the segment l does not intersect the polygon (note that the endpoints of the l have been added to the list!) Otherwise the status of an arbitrary point of l has to be determined.

This can be done using the same algorithm albeit with a slight modification. The idea behind this calculation is that in going from the "inside" of the polygon to the "outside," one will encounter an odd number of intersections. Note that it is essential to have a point that lies outside the polygon. This can be found easily by first calculating the smallest rectangular box enclosing all the points of the polygon. Any point outside this box will clearly lie outside the polygon. Let (x_0, y_0) denote such a point and let (x_1, y_1) denote an arbitrary point of l. We can then determine the number of intersections k of this line segment with the polygon using steps 1 to 6 of the algorithm. The interpretation of k is not completely straightforward since it is possible that (x_1, y_1) lies on the polygon. In that case (x_1, y_1) need not be taken into account and consequently k has

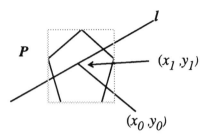

Figure 3.   Determination of the status of point (x_1, y_1). The dashed line represents the box enclosing the polygon P.

to be decreased by 1. If the resulting k is odd, (x_1, y_1) lies inside the polygon; otherwise it lies outside the polygon.

Each line segment of the intersection list, defined by two successive points of the list, can now be marked as *outside* or *inside*. If we want to clip the line segment l against the polygon, only the segments marked *outside* have to be taken into account, whereas the reverse is true for filling the polygon. It will be clear that this scheme can be recursively repeated for m polygons.

Implementation

We have implemented a clipping procedure, based on this algorithm in standard C. The polygons are stored in a linked list. Each element of this linked list holds information about a specific polygon and contains among other things an identification, a segment count, the coordinates of the smallest rectangular box enclosing the polygon, some status information, and a pointer to a circular linked list. The elements of this circular list contain the endpoints of the segments of the polygon (see Fig. 4).

Upon entering these routines, user coordinates are transformed to integer representation. During the definition of a contour, the contour is also stretched to avoid colinearity of three or more points. For clipping purposes the algorithm described in the previous section is applied recursively to the linked list of polygons. The specific actions depend on the status information of the polygon. When a line segment is clipped against a specific polygon this will result in a (new) set as line segment, which can either be plotted directly or clipped subsequently against other polygons.

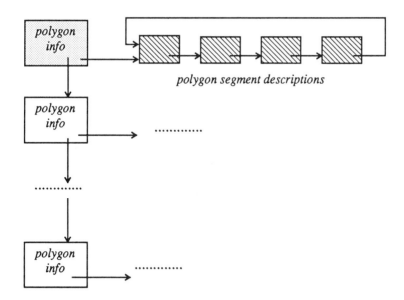

polygon segment descriptions

Figure 4.   Symbolic representation of the storage structure of the polygons.

Our implementation took approximately 500 lines of C code. Among others, the following utilities were included: definition of polygons, removal of polygons, temporarily on and off switching of polygons. *SCALE* was set to 1024. The efficiency of the algorithm was tested by clipping random generated line segments l against polygons with a variable number of segments. Using a SUN3/60 (MC68020, 20 MHz, SunOS 4.0 C-compiler) workstation we find that the average time needed to handle one segment of the polygon is approximately 125 microseconds. Consequently, for a rectangular-shaped polygon one can process about 2000 vectors per second.

Appendix: Polygon Stretching and Intersection Calculation

The problem of polygon stretching can be handled very easily. Consider the three consecutive points P_{i-1}, P_i, and P_{i+1}. Since the two line segments defined by these three points have one point in common (P_i), one needs merely to compare the slopes of the two line segments to test for colinearity. If the relation

$$(y_i - y_{i-1})(x_{i+1} - x_i) = (y_{i+1} - y_i)(x_i - x_{i-1})$$

holds, the three points are colinear. In that case it suffices to consider the segment $P_{i-1}P_{i+1}$ rather than the two segments $P_{i-1}P_i$ and P_iP_{i+1}.

The problem of intersecting the two line segments determined by the points P_iP_{i+1} and Q_iQ_{i+1}, respectively, can be solved as follows. Let

$$P(s) = P_j + s(P_{j+1} - P_j), \qquad s \in [0, 1)$$

$$Q(t) = Q_j + t(Q_{j+1} - Q_j), \qquad t \in [0, 1)$$

define the line segments under consideration. Then the quantities a, b, and c can be defined as

$$a = (x_{i+1,P} - x_{i,P})(y_{i,Q} - y_{i+1,Q}) - (x_{i,Q} - x_{i+1,Q})(y_{i+1,P} - y_{i,P})$$

$$b = (x_{i,Q} - x_{i,P})(y_{i,Q} - y_{i+1,Q}) - (x_{i,Q} - x_{i+1,Q})(y_{i,Q} - y_{i,P})$$

$$c = (x_{i+1,P} - x_{i,P})(y_{i,Q} - y_{i,P}) - (y_{i+1,P} - y_{i,P})(x_{i,Q} - x_{i,P})$$

and $s = b/a$ and $t = c/a$.

The following possibilities then exist:

$$a = 0 \quad \text{and} \quad b = 0: P_iP_{i+1} \quad \text{and} \quad Q_iQ_{i+1} \text{ coincide}$$

$$a = 0 \quad \text{and} \quad b \neq 0: P_iP_{i+1} \quad \text{and} \quad Q_iQ_{i+1} \text{ are parallel}$$

Otherwise, they intersect if $s \in [0, 1)$ and $t \in [0, 1)$, that is $c < a$ and $b < a$. Note that the proper way to evaluate s (and t) is

$$s = (b*SCALE)/a.$$

See Appendix 2 for C Implementation (**694**)

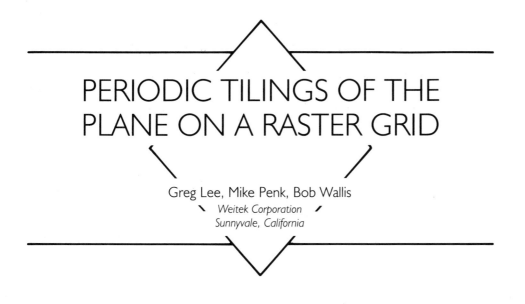

PERIODIC TILINGS OF THE PLANE ON A RASTER GRID

Greg Lee, Mike Penk, Bob Wallis
Weitek Corporation
Sunnyvale, California

Introduction

Certain results from group and number theory are ideally suited for analyzing and manipulating periodic patterns on raster grids. Conversely, periodic plane tilings may be used to illuminate some otherwise abstract mathematical concepts in a concrete manner. A general method for bit-blitting any periodic pattern into a raster grid will be derived.

Wallpaper Groups

Consider the periodic plane tesselation of Fig. 1. It is basically a jigsaw puzzle composed of identical butterflies (diseased moths?) in a hexagonal array. The standard manner in which such tilings are categorized is by examining the types of symmetries that leave the pattern invariant. Informally, this process can be thought of as overlaying an infinite translucent tracing of the pattern over the original (also extended to infinity), and examining the nature of the translations, rotations, and flips (mirror images) of the tracing that result in an exact realignment of the tracing with the underlying image. If an x, y coordinate of the plane is viewed as a complex number, the operations of flipping the tracing over, shifting it, and rotating may be modelled as compositions of complex conjugation, addition, and multiplication.

Figure 1.

If symmetry-preserving operations are combined together, the elements are found to produce yet other symmetry-preserving operations. Algebraically, the set of manipulations obey closure, possess inverses, are associative, and have an identity element. Therefore, they form a mathematical group structure. The group properties of a periodic tiling may be used as a means of classifying it. It turns out that there are exactly 17 types of these, and they are known as the plane crystallographic groups, or wallpaper groups (Burn, 1985). The first organized collection of (most of) these appears to be in the ornamental decorations used in the Granada's Alhambra cathedral, which dates back to the thirteenth century.

Consider the tiling depicted in Fig. 1. The parallelograms and boxes depict three different types of regions, each of which may be used to step and repeat a template of the pattern to form an extended region of wallpaper. The rectangular boxes are quite attractive from an implementation standpoint, since once we fill one box, we can repeat it over the plane with bit-blit operations to produce the desired tiling. The next section will describe how to do this.

The wallpaper group represented in Fig. 1 is of type p6, characterized by sixfold and threefold rotational symmetries about two different fixed points. The six-center is at the right wingtip, while the three-center is at the trailing edge of the left wing. If we take the origin of the coordinate system as one of the six-centers (the center of Fig. 1), and call the coordinate of the three-center z_3, then we can define two symmetry operators α and β as

$$\alpha: z \to z e^{j2\pi/6} \qquad \textit{sixfold rotation about } z = 0$$

$$\beta: z \to (z - z_3)e^{j2\pi/3} + z_3 \qquad \textit{threefold rotation about } z_3.$$

These two group elements are sufficient to generate the entire structure. The following will show how various combinations of these two generators may be used to extract other symmetries. There have to be pure translations lurking about in the set of symmetry operations. We can ferret one of them out by combining the α and β operators in such a way as to neutralize the rotation component, leaving only a translational residue. One way to do this is to combine two rotations of -60 degrees about $z = 0$ with one rotation of 120 degrees about z_3. The result is

$$\alpha^{-2}\beta: z \to e^{-j2\pi/3}\big[(z - z_3)e^{j2\pi/3} + z_3\big],$$

which reduces to

$$\tau: z \to z + z_3\big(e^{-j2\pi/3} - 1\big) = z - z_3\sqrt{3}\, e^{2\pi(1/12)}.$$

The τ translation vector is precisely a shift from one six-center to another. Combining α and τ yields other translations, which are just 60-degree rotations of one another. Any two adjacent translations form the legs of a fundamental parallelogram (two types of which are shown in Fig. 1). Note that each contains exactly six butterflies (if we cut and paste wrapped-around fragments together). We can step and repeat one of these parallelograms to fill the entire plane with the periodic pattern.

131

There are of course many other symmetries waiting to be discovered by combining powers of α and β. For example, a 240 rotation about z_3 followed by a -60 about 0 results in a net rotation of 180. This must be a two-center,

$$\alpha^{-1}\beta^2: z \to e^{-j2\pi/6}\big[(z - z_3)e^{j8\pi/6} + z_3\big],$$

which reduces to

$$\gamma: z \to -z + z_3(e^{-j2\pi/6} + 1),$$

which is a 180-degree rotation about the middle leading edge of the left wing. The fixed point of this two-center is located at

$$z_2 = -z_3\sqrt{3}\,e^{-j2\pi/12} \qquad two\text{-}center.$$

If we join butterflies paired together by γ and color the pairs white, gray, and black, we get Fig. 2.

Figure 2.

Figure 3.

If we produce triplets of butterflies by combining the triad produced by the β rotation, and color these distorted triangles black and white, we get Fig. 3.

Figs. 2 and 3 depict groups within groups. In the case of Fig. 3, if the triads are viewed as the basic element, the tiling is an example of wallpaper group p3. The group theoretic description of this embedding is a factor group or quotient group (Bloch, 1987; Burn, 1985). This concept proves useful in the design of color tilings that preserve the inherent symmetry of the embedding group (Coxeter *et al.*, 1987).

Tiling in Raster Grids

In this section, we are interested in devising an algorithm to tile periodic patterns efficiently into a pixel array. Clearly, there must be a way to exploit the step-and-repeat tiling suggested by the interlocking parallelograms. If we can find rectangular bricks orthogonal to the coordinates of our raster, such as those in the lower right area of Fig. 1, we could load up one copy of the brick and then step and repeat it with a bit-blit operation over whatever area of the plane we wish to cover.

It will be shown that this is always possible to do. The basic mathematical tools for doing this come from the field of number theory, which deals with the properties of integers. We have to deal with exact integers because we want a bit-blit template whose corners are aligned exactly with pixel centers. All we need is a parallelogram basis with one component that is *exactly* horizontal. Referring again to Fig. 1, note that the rectangles can be derived from the horizontal parallelograms by slicing off the triangle from the left edge of the parallelogram and gluing it to the right edge.

Assume that we start with a pair of valid basis vectors $[a, b]$ and $[c, d]$. Topologically, we treat the entire plane as if it were just one (fundamental) parallelogram cell that wraps around itself in toroidal fashion. A pixel in the plane translated by any integer combination of these basis vectors will land at the same place relative to the parallelogram cell. It is easy to show that we can transform a set of basis vectors to another set of valid basis vectors as long as we use integer weights and preserve the area of the parallelogram. We wish to do this in a fashion that will produce a new basis with an exactly horizontal component (in order to make a horizontal block, which is more suitable for bit-blitting). Denoting the new basis vectors as $[A, 0], [C, D]$,

$$[A, 0] = i[a, b] + j[c, d] \qquad \text{\textit{the new horizontal basis vector}}$$

$$[C, D] = k[a, b] + l[c, d] \qquad il - jk = 1 \rightarrow \textit{preserve area}.$$

First we want to find the smallest i and j that satisfy:

$$0 = ib + jd \qquad \text{\textit{y component of horizontal vector}}.$$

The solution is

$$i = d/g$$

$$j = -b/g$$

$$g = gcd(b, d) \qquad \text{\textit{greatest common denominator}}.$$

The remaining k, l components must satisfy:

$$1 = il - jk = (d/g)l + (b/g)k \qquad \textit{unit determinant}$$

$$g = dl + bk \qquad \textit{solve for } l, k.$$

This is exactly the problem solved by the extended version of Euclid's gcd algorithm (Knuth, 1981b), and a solution is guaranteed to exist. The final results are

$$A = ai + cj$$

$$C = ak + cl$$

$$D = bk + dl$$

You can always put $[C, D]$ in the upper half-plane and then add any integer combination of the $[A, 0]$ vector to the $[C, D]$ vector, so you can always adjust $[C, D]$ such that

$$0 \le C < A$$

$$0 < D.$$

This represents a reduced canonical representation of the lattice. That is, any two lattices that reduce to the same set of A, B, C values are equivalent. The matrices with integral weights and unit determinants that relate equivalent lattices are known as *unimodular transforms*, and form a group themselves.

As an example, consider the parallelogram lattice with basis vectors $[9, 9]$ and $[-3, 6]$. We have

$$g = gcd(b, d) = gcd(9, 6) = 3$$

$$A = ia + jc = (ad - bc)/g = 27$$

$$3 = dl + bk = 6l + 9k,$$

whose solution is $l = -1$, $k = 1$.

So the new basis is $[27, 0]$ and $[12, 3]$.

The old basis is shown in Fig. 4, overlaying a periodic array of 81 numbers arranged to show the pattern that we wish to tile by a step and

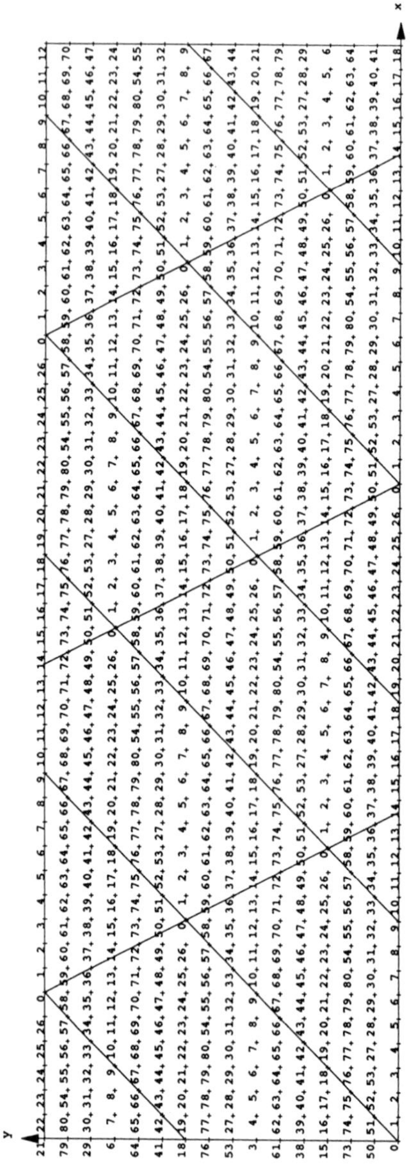

Figure 4.

repeat process. The + signs represent pixel centers. In the language of group theory, the set of pixels marked 0 is the subgroup of the plane generated by the basis vectors. All the pixels marked as 1 represent one of 81 possible cosets of the subgroup.

The same diagram with the new basis is shown in Fig. 5.

Note that in both cases the same numbers appear in the same places in each parallelogram, which is precisely what we want. Our bit-blit rectangle is 27 pixels wide by 3 pixels high, and each row of bricks should be right-shifted by 12 pixels relative to the previous row.

An alternate way to see what is happening is to view the basis vectors as the axes of a new $[u, v]$ coordinate system.

$$x = au + cv \qquad [u, v] = [1, 0] \rightarrow [x, y] = [a, b]$$

$$y = bu + dv \qquad [u, v] = [0, 1] \rightarrow [x, y] = [c, d]$$

$$M = ad - bc \qquad \textit{number of pixels in cell}$$

If we try to solve for $[u, v]$ in terms of $[x, y]$ by inverting this relationship, we seem to be faced by a division with the determinant, which would destroy the exact integer relationships we wish to maintain. However, if we scale up the $[u, v]$ coordinates so that they lie in the interval $[0, M - 1]$ instead of $[0, 1]$, and enforce wrap conditions on the boundary of our fundamental cell, we obtain

$$u = \langle dx - cy \rangle_M \qquad \textit{generators for group structure}$$

$$v = \langle -bx + ay \rangle_M \qquad \textit{of tiling pattern,}$$

where $\langle x \rangle_M$ denotes taking the least positive residue mod M.

The residue reduction ensures that an $[x, y]$ from anywhere in the plane maps to a $[u, v]$ in the interior of the fundamental cell. This dual basis is exactly equivalent to the "reciprocal lattice" used in crystallography. In the case of our example in Fig. 5, we have

$$u = \langle 3x - 12y \rangle_{81}$$

$$v = \langle 0x + 27y \rangle_{81}$$

137

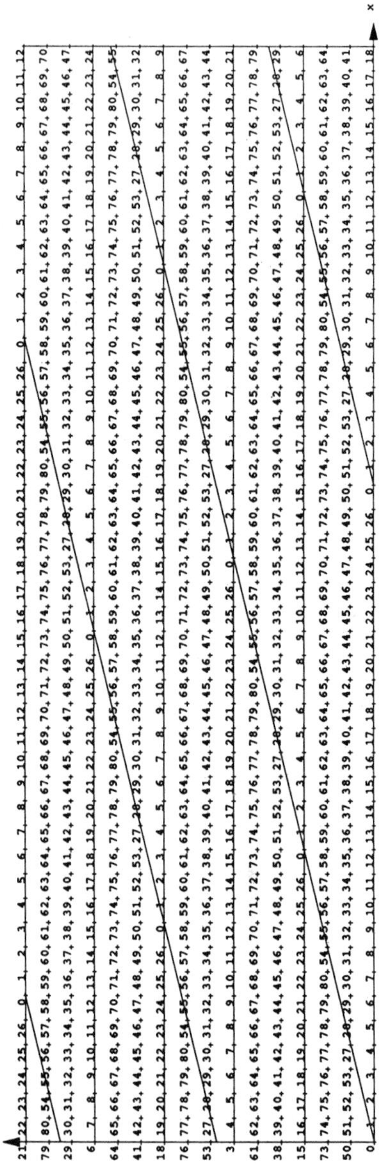

Figure 5.

If we run through all possible values of $[x, y]$, number theory tells us that u can only take on $81/\gcd(3, 12) = 27$ different values, all of which will be multiples of 3. The v component can only take on the three values $\{0, 27, 54\}$. The geometrical significance of this is that the u basis vector hits three pixel centers, and the v vector hits 27 (not including the origin). Consequently, our exact integer relationships will be maintained if we shrink the basis vectors (group generators) by 3 and 27, that is,

$$u' = u/3 = \langle x - 4y \rangle_{27} \qquad u \text{ in range } \{0, 1, \ldots 26\}$$

$$v' = v/27 = \langle y \rangle_3 \qquad v \text{ in range } \{0, 1, 2\}$$

This means that the group structure is essentially $Z_{27} \times Z_3$. One way that we can use the above to produce a 1D function that assigns a unique number to every pixel in the cell is to form a map $Z_{27} \times Z_3 \to Z_{81}$ with

$$z(x, y) = u' + 27v' = \langle x - 4y \rangle_{27} + 27\langle y \rangle_3.$$

This is exactly the function used to produce the pixel indices in Figs. 4 and 5.

The utility of the above indexing method is that we can load up all possible M elements of the cell into a linear array, and then for each $[x, y]$ in the plane, pick out the one selected by $z(x, y)$.

Another practical application of the above technique is in generating digital patterns for halftone screens that are rotated relative to the raster grid (Holladay, 1980). In this case, the pixels are usually one bit deep, and the tiling is accomplished by bit-blitting an entire rectangle.

IMAGE
PROCESSING

ANTI-ALIASING
FILTERS SUMMARY

Aliasing is a fact of life when using digital computers to represent continuous signals. One must be constantly aware of the implications of sampling and quantization, and attempt to avoid or suppress image artifacts resulting from these processes. An essential step in all algorithms that suppress or eliminate aliasing is the choice of filters used in the sampling and reconstruction processes. The search for "good" filters (according to different criteria) is an active research area.

The following Gems present some different filtering strategies, ranging from the explicit to the implicit. These filtering techniques may be adapted for use in almost any anti-aliasing technique.

See also Anti-Aliasing Summary (37); Scan Conversion Summary (75); Line-Drawing Summary (98)

CONVENIENT ANTI-ALIASING FILTERS THAT MINIMIZE "BUMPY" SAMPLING

Mark J. Pavicic
North Dakota State University
Fargo, North Dakota

A solution to the spatial aliasing problem is to convolve the image with an appropriate filter function. Two commonly used functions are the cube and the Gaussian. Advantages of the cube are that it is a simple function and it evenly weights the image plane. Uneven weighting contributes to problems such as lines that appear to have varying thickness. Advantages of the Gaussian are that it is a closer approximation to a CRT dot and it is radially symmetric. The radial symmetry makes it easy to construct a look-up table, since it is indexed by a single variable, r, which is the distance of an edge from the center of a pixel.

An ideal function would be radially symmetric and would evenly sample the image plane. A properly chosen Gaussian can come close to this ideal. Figure 1 shows how a particular Gaussian weights the square region whose corners are the centers of four pixels. The square region forms the base of the cube. The top surface results from taking the sum of four Gaussian "mountains." The partial outline of one of the Gaussian mountains is shown on the front face of the cube. This filter has the equation

$$f(r) = \alpha\left[1 - \frac{1 - \exp(-\beta r^2)}{1 - \exp(-\beta)}\right],$$

where $\alpha = 1$ and $\beta = 2.378$. It satisfies the criteria that it have a unit volume, that $f(0) = 1$, and that $f(1) = 0$. It is defined to be zero for $r > 1$. Note that $f(0) = \alpha = 1$ is not a fixed requirement. In fact, a more even weighting can be achieved if $\alpha \neq 1$. Figure 2 shows the optimal result, which occurs when $\alpha = 0.918$ and $\beta = 1.953$. The unit-volume and $f(1) = 0$ criteria are still satisfied.

An interesting alternative is the sum of a cone and a cosine. This composite function satisfies all the criteria imposed on the Gaussian in

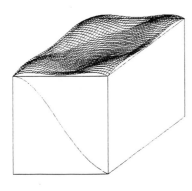

Figure 1. Unit height Gaussian.

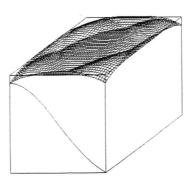

Figure 2. Optimized Gaussian.

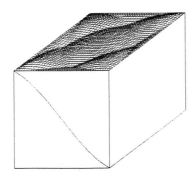

Figure 3. Cone plus cosine.

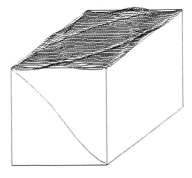

Figure 4. A tabular solution.

Fig. 1, yet samples the image plane nearly as evenly as the optimized Gaussian in Fig. 2. This filter has the equation

$$f(r) = \alpha(1 - r) + (1 - \alpha)(1 + \cos(\pi r))/2$$

for $r < 1$, where $\alpha = (1 - v2)/(v1 - v2)$, $v1 = \pi/3$, and $v2 = \pi/2 - 2/\pi$. It was used to generate Fig. 3. Note that the filters sum to 1 along the top edges of the cube.

To get a quantitative comparison of these three cases, the percentage of the volume above and below a unit height was calculated and found to be 3.25, 1.03, and 1.13 for Figs. 1, 2, and 3, respectively. Thus, these measures verify what is already evident in the figures, namely that carefully chosen filter functions can do a superior job of minimizing "bumpy" sampling while still retaining the convenient characteristic of radial symmetry.

Table I.   A Tabular Solution.

Radius	Height	Radius	Height	Radius	Height
0.000	0.98408	0.350	0.68296	0.700	0.25793
0.025	0.97480	0.375	0.65948	0.725	0.22992
0.050	0.94708	0.400	0.63234	0.750	0.20212
0.075	0.93409	0.425	0.60675	0.775	0.17534
0.100	0.91498	0.450	0.57303	0.800	0.15028
0.125	0.89570	0.475	0.54482	0.825	0.12665
0.150	0.87605	0.500	0.51341	0.850	0.10394
0.175	0.85232	0.525	0.48111	0.875	0.08269
0.200	0.83052	0.550	0.44843	0.900	0.06390
0.225	0.80723	0.575	0.41493	0.925	0.04723
0.250	0.78173	0.600	0.38189	0.950	0.03279
0.275	0.75696	0.625	0.34996	0.975	0.02462
0.300	0.73128	0.650	0.31849	1.000	0.00000
0.325	0.70686	0.675	0.28760		

At this point one might ask, "What is the optimum?" To get some idea, a table of 41 values was adjusted to minimize the volume displaced by uneven sampling. The result is shown in Fig. 4 and the values are listed in Tab. 1. The percentage volume displaced in this case is 0.43. This level of performance can also be approximated by radially symmetric filters whose shapes are described by polynomials or spline curves. As a final example, Tab. 2 lists the five control points for a nonuniform cubic *B*-spline that has a "bump factor" of 0.60.

Table 2.   Control Points.

Radius	Height
0.00	1.000
0.25	0.788
0.50	0.558
0.75	0.149
1.00	0.000

FILTERS FOR COMMON RESAMPLING TASKS

Ken Turkowski
Apple Computer
Cupertino, California

Continuous, Sampled, and Discrete Signals

Signals or functions that are *continuous* are defined at all values on an interval. When these are then *sampled*, they are defined only at a given set of points, regularly spaced or not. When the values at these sample points are then quantized to a certain number of bits, they are called *discrete*. A sampled function may or may not be discrete.

In computer graphics, we deal with all three of these representations, at least in our models of computation. A function such as $\sin(x)$ is considered continuous. A sequence of floating-point values may be considered to represent a sampled function, whereas a sequence of integers (especially 8-bit integers) represent a discrete function.

Interpolation and Decimation

Even though a signal is sampled, we may have certain rules about inferring the values between the sample points. The most common assumption made in signal processing is that the signal is bandlimited to an extent consistent with the sampling rate, that is, the values change smoothly between samples. The Sampling Theorem guarantees that a continuous signal can be reconstructed perfectly from its samples if the signal was appropriately bandlimited prior to sampling (Oppenheim and Schaeffer, 1975). Practically speaking, signals are never perfectly bandlimited, nor can we construct a perfect reconstruction filter, but we can get as close as we want in a prescribed manner.

We often want to change from one sampling rate to another. The process of representing a signal with more samples is called *interpolation*, whereas representing it with less is called *decimation*. Examples of interpolation are zooming up on an image; correcting for nonsquare pixels; and converting an image from 72 dpi to 300 dpi to feed a high-resolution output device. Applications of decimation are reducing the jaggies on an supersampled image; and correcting for nonsquare pixels.

Choices of Filters

Several types of filters are more popular than others: box, tent, Gaussian, and sinc. In Fig. 1, we show the frequency response of a few of the continuous versions of these filters. The ideal filter would have a gain of 0 dB between frequencies of 0 and 1 (the passband), and $-\infty$ beyond 1 (the stopband). The rolloff in the passband is responsible for blurriness, and the leakage in the stopband is responsible for aliasing (jaggies). One generally has to make the tradeoff between sharpness and aliasing in choosing a filter. We will be sampling some of these filters, specifically for use in interpolation and decimation ratios of integer amounts, such as 2, 3, and 4.

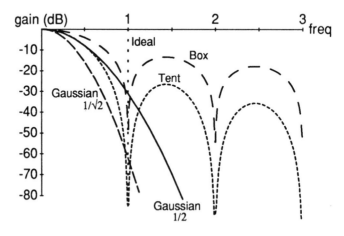

Figure 1.

Box

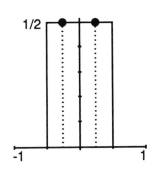

Figure 2.

The box filter for interpolation merely picks the closest value. For decimation, it is simply an average of the input samples. With an even number of samples, the filter produces an output that is situated between two input samples (half phase), whereas with an odd number, it is situated at the same location as the middle sample (zero phase). With other filters, you can select the phase of the filter, but not so for the box filter. In Fig. 2, we show the half-phase box filter for decimation by 2. Higher decimation ratio filters just have coefficients with weights that sum to 1.

Tent

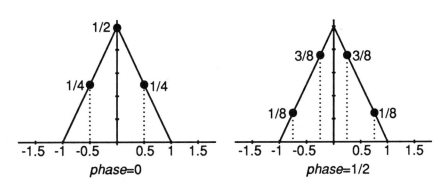

Figure 3.   Decimation by a factor of two with the tent function.

149

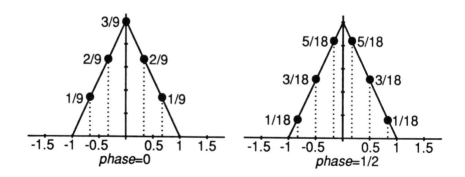

Figure 4. Decimation by a factor of three with the tent function.

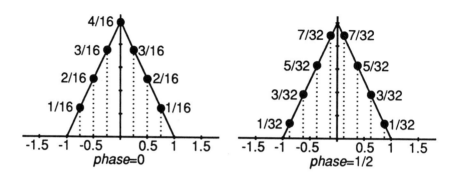

Figure 5. Decimation by a factor of four with the tent function.

The tent filter is a generalization of linear interpolation, and *is* so when interpolating. Unlike the box filter, this can accommodate arbitrary filter phases; we show the zero-phase and half-phase filter for decimation by two, three, and four (see Figs. 3, 4, and 5).

Gaussian

The Gaussian function is popular for its many elegant analytical properties; it is entirely positive, it is the limit of probability density functions, and it is its own Fourier transform. Here, we give a rationale for choosing an appropriate width, or variance, or filtering in graphics.

We choose Gaussian filters here whose variances have physical and computational significance. The first is the narrowest that we would probably ever want to use, and has a half-amplitude width of $\frac{1}{2}$, that is, it has the value $\frac{1}{2}$ at a distance $\frac{1}{2}$ from its center. Its value gets negligible $1\frac{1}{2}$ samples away from the center, so it can be considered to have a support of 3.

Energy, in general terms, is the square of the magnitude. If the eye is more linear in energy than in magnitude, then a more appropriate Gaussian might be one in which the square of the magnitude is $\frac{1}{2}$ at a distance $\frac{1}{2}$ from the center, or that the magnitude itself has a value of $1/\sqrt{2}$ at that point. This is a wider Gaussian than the first, and its magnitude doesn't become negligible until 2 samples from the center, so that it may be considered a filter with support 4.

In Fig. 1, we compare the box, tent, and these two Gaussians. The box filter captures more of the passband (freq < 1) than the others, but it also lets through more of the stopband (freq > 1). It is the leakage in the stopband that is responsible for aliasing artifacts, or "jaggies." The tent filter is 15 dB better at eliminating aliasing in the stopband, but does so at the expense of losing more features in the passband. The Gaussian $\frac{1}{2}$ filter matches the tent for a good portion of the passband, but continues to attenuate the stopband. The Gaussian $1/\sqrt{2}$ filter does an even better job at attenuating the aliases, but does so at the expense of losing additional detail in the passband.

A comparison of the tent and the narrow Gaussian in the time (space) domain will show that they look very similar, except that the Gaussian is

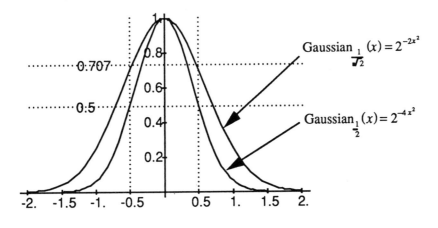

Figure 6.

smooth at the peak and the base, whereas the tent has slope discontinuities there. It is these discontinuities that cause the ringing and ineffective alias suppression in the stopband.

One of the side effects of our particular choices of Gaussian variance is that many of their coefficients at interesting locations are scaled powers of two, which makes way for faster computation. We will see this in the following filters, specialized for certain interpolation and decimation tasks.

Interpolation with the Gaussian $\frac{1}{2}$ Filter

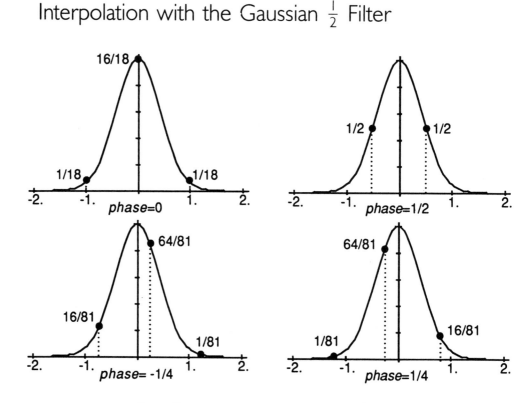

Figure 7.   Interpolation with the Gaussian $\frac{1}{2}$ filter.

In Fig. 7, we give the filter coefficients for a set of filters to interpolate between two given samples: halfway between, and a quarter of the way to either side of a sample. Notice the nice rational coefficients that are scaled powers of two.

To determine the coefficients for a filter to produce the value at any other point between two samples, we merely sample the Gaussian at a series of locations one sample apart, and normalize them so that their sum equals one. Even though the Gaussian is zero nowhere, we consider this filter's value to be negligible greater than 1.5 samples away from its center.

Decimation with the Gaussian $\frac{1}{2}$ Filter

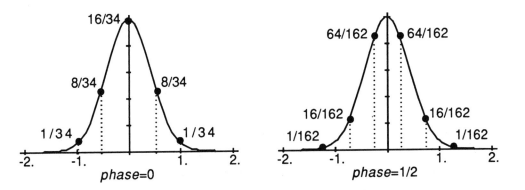

Figure 8.   Decimation by a factor of two with the Gaussian $\frac{1}{2}$ filter.

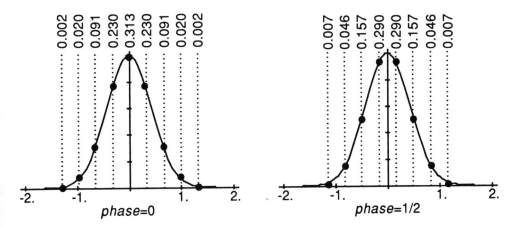

Figure 9.   Decimation by a factor of three with the Gaussian $\frac{1}{2}$ filter.

153

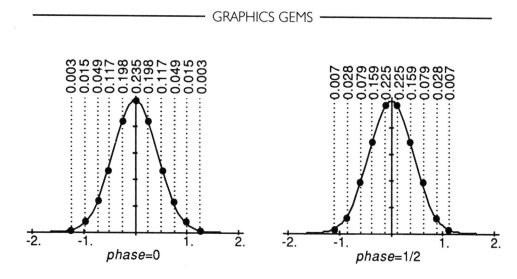

Figure 10. Decimation by a factor of four with the Gaussian $\frac{1}{2}$ filter.

Interpolation with the Gaussian $\frac{1}{\sqrt{2}}$ Filter

This wider Gaussian becomes negligible greater than two samples away from the center (see Fig. 11).

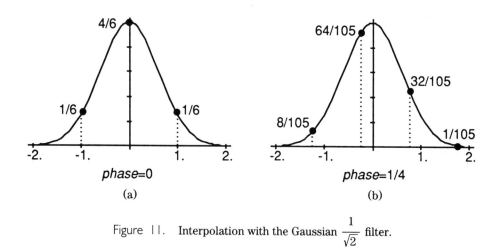

Figure 11. Interpolation with the Gaussian $\frac{1}{\sqrt{2}}$ filter.

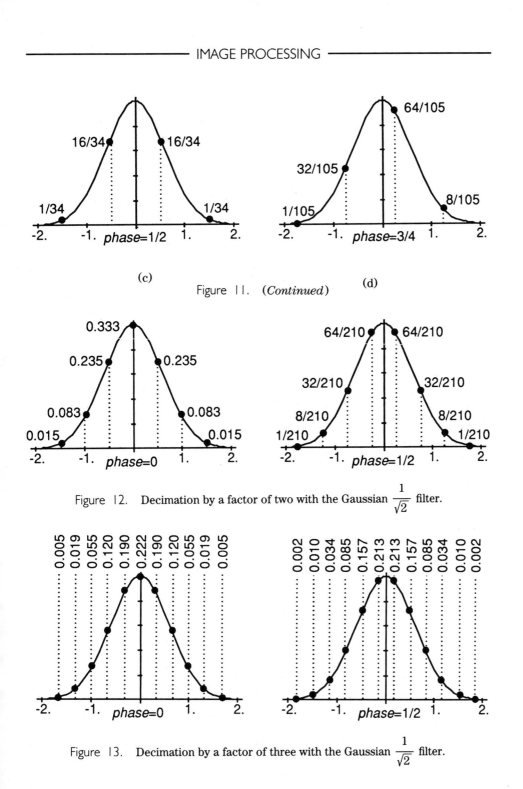

(c)

Figure 11. (*Continued*)

(d)

Figure 12. Decimation by a factor of two with the Gaussian $\dfrac{1}{\sqrt{2}}$ filter.

Figure 13. Decimation by a factor of three with the Gaussian $\dfrac{1}{\sqrt{2}}$ filter.

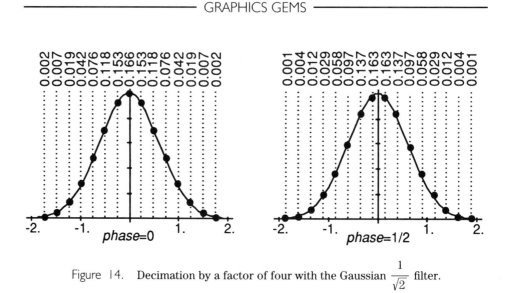

Figure 14. Decimation by a factor of four with the Gaussian $\frac{1}{\sqrt{2}}$ filter.

The Sinc Function

The sinc function (see Fig. 15) is the ideal low-pass filter (Oppenheim and Schaeffer, 1975).

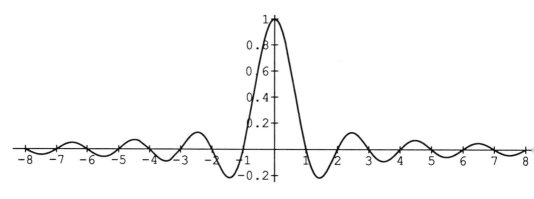

Figure 15.

The Lanczos-Windowed Sinc Functions

Since the sinc function never goes to zero but approaches it slowly, we multiply it by an appropriate windowing function. The two-lobed Lanczos-

156

windowed sinc function is one such windowed sinc function, and is defined as follows (see Fig. 16):

$$\text{Lanczos } 2(x) = \begin{cases} \dfrac{\sin(\pi x)}{\pi x} \dfrac{\sin\left(\pi \dfrac{x}{2}\right)}{\pi \dfrac{x}{2}}, & |x| < 2 \\[4mm] 0, & |x| \geq 2. \end{cases}$$

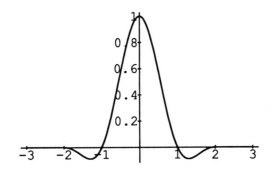

Figure 16.

The three-lobed Lanczos-windowed sinc function is defined similarly (see Fig. 17):

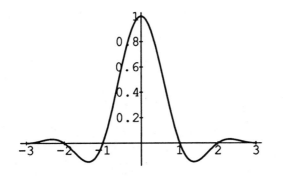

Figure 17.

$$\text{Lanczos 3}(x) = \begin{cases} \dfrac{\sin(\pi x)}{\pi x}\, \dfrac{\sin\left(\pi\dfrac{x}{3}\right)}{\pi\dfrac{x}{3}}, & |x| < 3 \\[20pt] 0, & |x| \geq 3. \end{cases}$$

The Lanczos-windowed sinc function filters have been shown to be particularly useful for graphics applications.[1] We will concern ourselves here mainly with the two-lobed version, because of its smaller kernel.

Interpolation by a Factor of Two with the Lanczos2 Sinc Function

Note that in Fig. 18, with a zero-phase filter, the contributions from other than the central pixel are zero, so that only the central pixel is used.

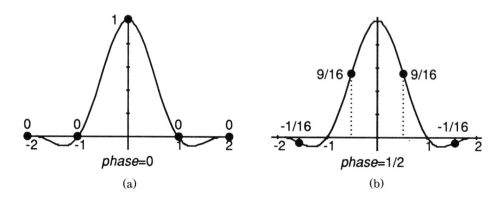

Figure 18.   Interpolation by a factor of two with the Lanczos2 sinc function

[1] Turkowski, Ken and Gabriel, Steve, 1979. Conclusions of experiments done at Ampex, comparing box, Gaussian, truncated-sinc, and several windowed-sinc filters (Bartlett, cosine, Hanning, Lanczos) for decimation and interpolation of 2-dimensional image data. The Lanczos-windowed sinc functions offered the best compromise in terms of reduction of aliasing, sharpness, and minimal ringing.

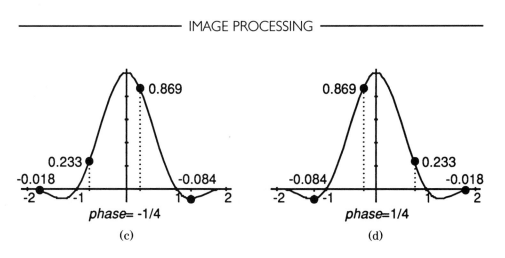

phase= -1/4

(c)

phase=1/4

(d)

Figure 18. (*Continued*)

Decimation with the Lanczos2 Sinc Function

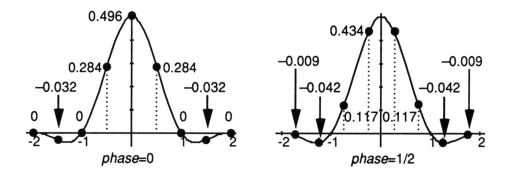

phase=0

phase=1/2

Figure 19. Decimation by a factor of two with the Lanczos2 sinc function.

The zero-phase filter (Fig. 19) has coefficients that are nearly rational. If the negative coefficients are scaled so that they are equal to -1, then the remaining coefficients are 9 and 15.7024. This inspired a search for such filters with rational coefficients. This yielded the two zero-phase filters in Fig. 20.

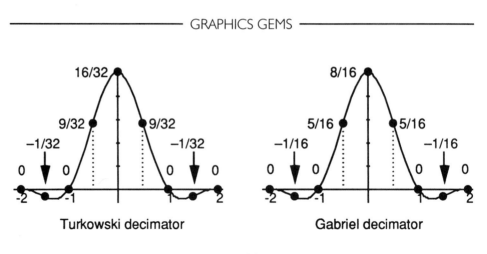

Turkowski decimator   Gabriel decimator

Figure 20.

Comparative Frequency Responses

Filters are evaluated on their ability to retain detail in the passband (sharpness is valued more than blurriness) and to eliminate aliasing in the stopband (smoothness is valued more than jagginess). The frequency response of a sampled filter is quite different than the continuous one

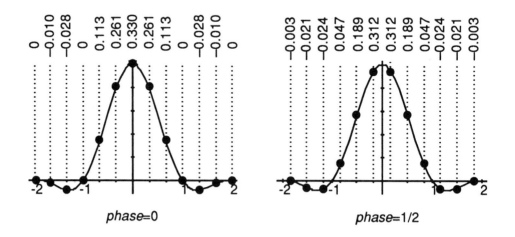

phase=0   *phase=1/2*

Figure 21.   Decimation by a factor of three with the Lanczos2 sinc function.

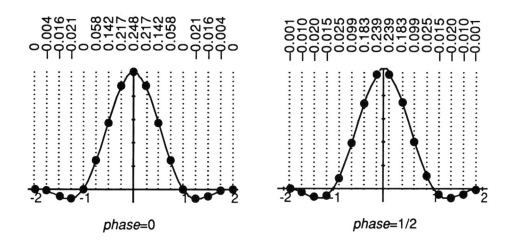

Figure 22. Decimation by a factor of four with the Lanczos2 sinc function.

By the way, one bit corresponds to about 6 dB, so that attenuation beyond 48 dB is irrelevant when working with 8-bit pixels.
from which it was derived. Instead of taking the Fourier transform as with continuous filters, we take the z-transform and sample on the unit circle.

In Figs. 23 and 24 we see that the filter derived from the Gaussian $1/2$ filter doesn't perform as well as the one derived from the tent, although we know that in the continuous case, the Gaussian is much better. What happened? We sampled the filter functions, that's what happened. In the process, we changed the characteristics of the filter. In fact, there are several continuous filters that give rise to the same sampled filters. The labels on each of the filters are actually misnomers, since the sampled filters are not the same as the continuous ones.

The box filter seems to retain a large portion of the passband, but lets through a tremendous amount of energy in the stopband, resulting in noticeable aliasing. The Lanczos filters keep more of the passband than the others (except for maybe the box), and they cut off more of the stopband (except for maybe the Gaussian $1/\sqrt{2}$), with the Lanczos3 filter coming closest to the ideal filter shape of all the filters evaluated. The Gaussian $1/\sqrt{2}$ filter is competitive with the Lanczos3 for stopband response, but does so at the expense of excessive attenuation on the passband.

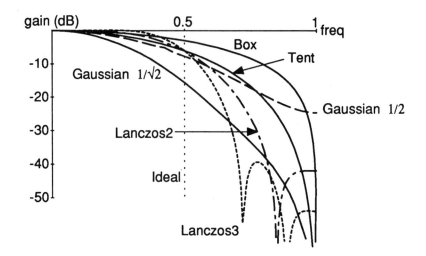

Figure 23.   Frequency response of the zero-phase filters for decimation by 2.

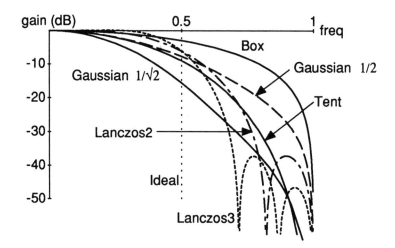

Figure 24.   Frequency response of the half-phase filters for decimation by 2.

Frequency Response of the Gaussian Filters for Several Decimation Ratios

The cutoff frequencies are 0.5 for the $\div 2$ filter, 0.333 for the $\div 3$, 0.25 for the $\div 4$. Note that the zero-phase and the half-phase filters for decimation by 2 diverge, whereas the higher-decimation filters do not.

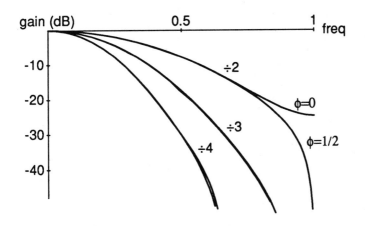

Figure 25. Frequency response of the Gaussian $\frac{1}{2}$ filter for several decimation ratios.

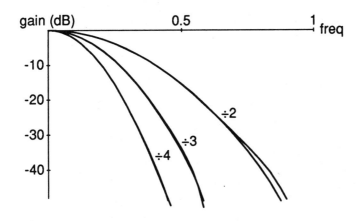

Figure 26. Frequency response of the Gaussian $\dfrac{1}{\sqrt{2}}$ filter for several decimation ratios.

163

Frequency Response of the Lanczos2 Sinc Functions

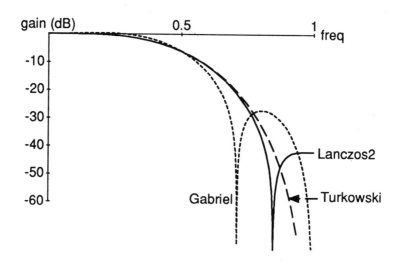

Figure 27.   Frequency response of the Lanczos2 sinc functions.

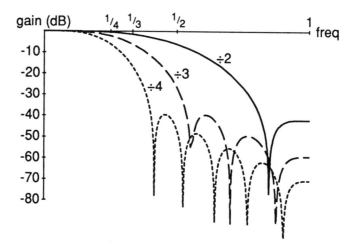

Figure 28.   Frequency response of the Lanczos2 sinc functions for several decimation ratios.

We show the responses of the decimate-by-2 filters related to the Lanczos2 filter in Fig. 27. Note that the Gabriel decimator lets more of the passband through and has a sharper cutoff in the stopband, but also bounces back in the stopband at a higher level than that of the Lanczos2. The Turkowski decimator, however, does not bounce back and eliminates more of the highest frequencies than the other two. They all have approximately the same passband response and aliasing energy, but the aliasing energy is distributed differently throughout the spectrum, so they can be considered about equivalent.

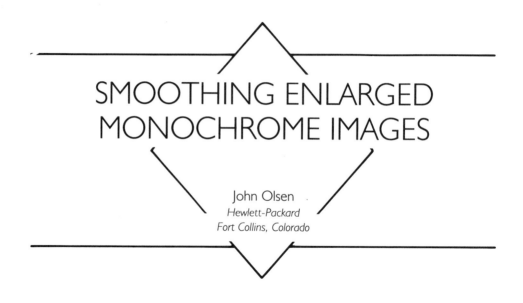

SMOOTHING ENLARGED MONOCHROME IMAGES

John Olsen
Hewlett-Packard
Fort Collins, Colorado

Typical methods of enlarging a monochrome image result in a very blocky product because of pixel replication or repeating a pixel to fill in the area added between pixels when an image is increased in size. The enlarging method that follows will preserve many of the angles that are missed by simple enlargement schemes such as pixel replication, and will generate a much more intuitive result. This method of image enlargement is especially effective on images such as circles, disks, and other continuous or smooth curves.

Only monochrome images will be discussed here because there are many complications that arise when dealing with color or grayscale images. This technique of enlarging bitmaps will not be extended to color images because there is no obvious or intuitive scheme for doing so. The difficulty arises because the result image can vary, depending on which colors are smoothed first.

The monochrome enlarging process is implemented as a search over a series of rules that govern how the enlarged pixels are filled in. These rules consist of an array of source pixels and of data indicating what additional areas are filled with the foreground color, as is seen in the rules shown in Fig. 1.

Scaling by integer multiples gives the most uniform results, but this scaling technique is equally applicable to noninteger increases in size. The code required for noninteger scaling will of course be more complex.

Each of the specified rules is to be rotated by 90-degree increments and mirrored in order to generate a complete set of eight final rules per

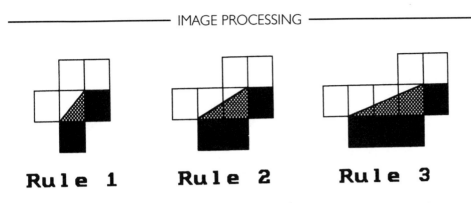

Figure 1. The rules used to create smooth monochrome enlargements.

initial rule. Fig. 2 shows how one of the rules from Fig. 1 is used to generate a set of eight rules.

By using all three rules in Fig. 1 and applying the mirroring in Fig. 2 you will obtain a set of 24 rules that will each preserve a unique angle. A simplified set of rules is obtained by using only rules 1 and 2 with their associated mirroring, and rotating to obtain a set of 16 rules. The

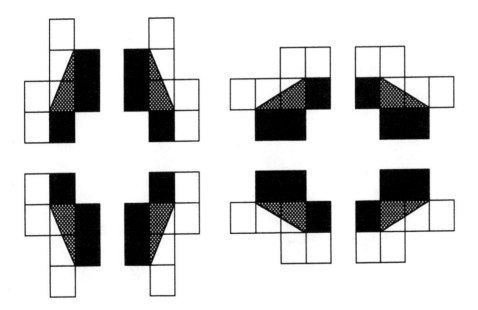

Figure 2. The original rule 2 with its rotations and reflections.

simplified set is well-behaved because the preserved angles are evenly distributed, whereas with the set of 24 the additional preserved angles tend to be close to multiples of 90 degrees.

The initial step used to create a smoothed image is to generate a blown up image, just as with pixel replication. Next, the rules are applied to the image from the most complex to the least complex, which will partially

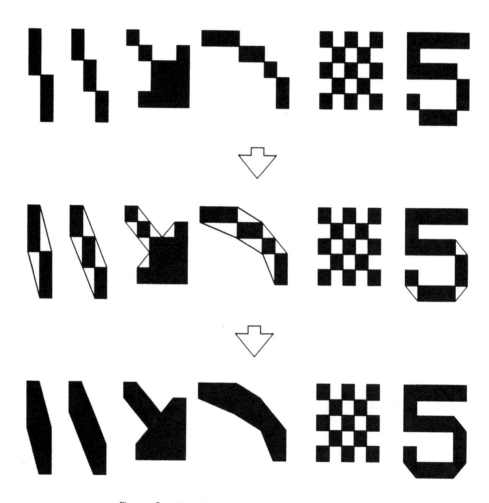

Figure 3. Results of smoothing various patterns.

fill some of the previously empty blocks within the result image. The rules need to be sequentially checked from complex to simple only until a match is found because the simpler rules will fill only a subset of the area filled by the more complex rules.

There is a definite pattern within the rules: each successive rule is a copy of the previous one, with one column added to generate the following more complex rule. This means that the process of generating rules can continue as far as you would like to take it, but it is generally not practical to go past rule 3 as specified in Fig. 1 because of the increased CPU time required for the more complex rules.

These rule sets will preserve many patterns (such as the interior and edges of checkerboards and both inside and outside square corners) instead of causing them to be smoothed in distracting or unexpected ways, yet will do a very good job of smoothing curves on objects where smoothing makes more sense. Fig. 3 shows a few typical patterns and how the smoothing algorithm will modify each.

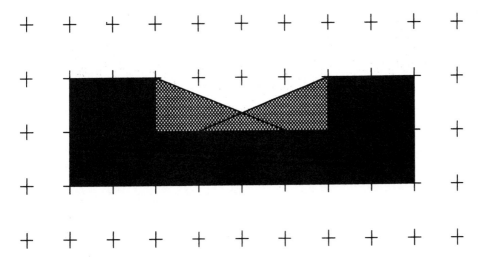

Figure 4. Smoothing causes certain areas to be filled by multiple rules.

These results are obtained by taking each of the original rules and its seven rotated and mirrored rules and comparing them to each location on the image. Wherever a match occurs, the shaded areas are filled in. Best results are obtained by skipping pixels that appear exactly at the edge of the area to be filled. This is demonstrated by doubling the scale of a simple object that uses only rule 1, and noting that horizontal and vertical edges are emphasized when the border pixels are drawn. Care must also be taken in applying the rules to generate the final output, since destination blocks of pixels can be modified by more than a single rule, as seen in Fig. 4.

Admittedly, this smoothing algorithm does not take all possible angles into consideration, but it is meant to produce a much better final result than simple scaling of bitmapped images with pixel replication. The greatest gain in using this technique is that the resulting smoothed images will always be generated in a predictable and intuitive manner.

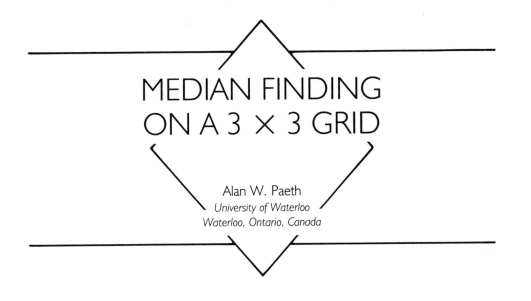

MEDIAN FINDING ON A 3 × 3 GRID

Alan W. Paeth
University of Waterloo
Waterloo, Ontario, Canada

Overview

A fast implementation for finding the median of nine elements is presented. This supports median filtering on 2D raster images—output pixels are defined as the median value contained by a corresponding 3 × 3 pixel region on the input. Filtering by this nonlinear technique removes "shot" noise, pixel dropout, and other spurious features of single pixel extent (Fig. 1) while preserving overall image quality (Huang, 1981). The technique is also attractive in that median is defined by a logical ranking of element values, not by arithmetic computation, yielding tools that operate on images of arbitrary pixel precision (Paeth, 1986a, 1986b; Paeth, 1987). Fast median evaluation is essential as operation counts on images quickly approach one million.

The median on n elements is that value having rank $\frac{1}{2}(n + 1)$, where rank is each element's relative sorted position within the array. That is, the median element is the central element on the sorted data set. The computation time for median finding is known to increase linearly with input length but the related methods are unsuitable for small arrays. Brute-force sorting performs unnecessary computation because all n elements become ranked. The approach presented here requires twenty comparisons and is close to the minimum exchange-network bound for median finding on nine elements (nineteen comparisons) and a clear win over a bubble-sort featuring early completion after sorting has ranked the first five elements (thirty comparisons).

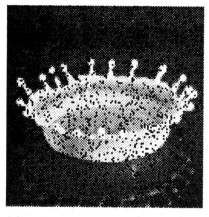

(a)   (b)

Figure 1.   Median filtering (3 × 3).

Element Exchange

Ranking of the data is achieved using simple element exchanges. This supports straight-line code implementation lacking conditional logic or subroutine calls. This approach also allows for parallel execution or reuse of partial terms for larger 2D filter kernels. Exchanging may be done in a manner reminiscent of data swapping without a temporary variable using three bit-wise exclusive OR's:

	A: a	B: b
a ← a **bit-xor** b	A: a xor b	B: b
b ← b **bit-xor** a	A: a xor b	B: b xor (a xor b) = a
a ← a **bit-xor** b	A: a xor b xor a = b,	B: a.

Subtraction behaves in a self-complementary fashion identical to **xor** because both bit complementation and arithmetic negation are their own inverses. The basic two-element exchange that underpins the entire algorithm shares the subtraction implicit in any arithmetic comparison. This reduces three program statements to two; coding as a macro removes the cost of subroutine invocation:

> *s2(a, b) – place a and b in ascending order*
> **macro** s2(a, b) **if** (z ← b − a) < 0 **then begin** a ← a + z; b ← b − z; **end**.

The *s2* sorting operator is a special case of the $minmax_k$ operation with $k = 2$. The general operation finds the overall winner and loser (elements of rank 1 and k) on a k element set. Finding the minimum and maximum on larger sets using two element comparisons may be done by way of a tournament. Here elements and comparisons are represented by players and matches (which may take place in parallel), respectively. The tournament commences by pairing off all players; in subsequent rounds only matches between remaining winners (or losers) occur. Play ends when both an all-time winner and an all-time loser have been found. For tournaments whose membership is not a power of two some players will draw byes and will (re)enter later rounds. A k-player tournament ends after completion of $\lceil\frac{1}{2}(3n - 4)\rceil$ matches. An illustration of minmax on six elements using seven comparisons is diagramed in Fig. 2, in which circles represent players and arrows represent matches with an arrowhead indicating the winner.

The median operation on a nine-element array partitions the array into three sets: a set of four elements with $rank < 5$, the median with $rank = 5$, and a set of four elements with $rank > 5$. The median may be found by placing elements pairwise into the nonmedian sets until the median remains. Any six-element subset of the nine-element input array contains an element whose rank is at least six (as when the subset happens to contain the six smallest elements of the array); conversely,

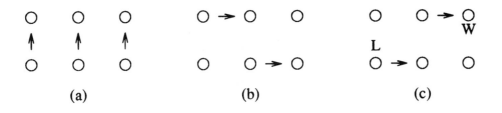

Figure 2.   Six-player min–max tournament.

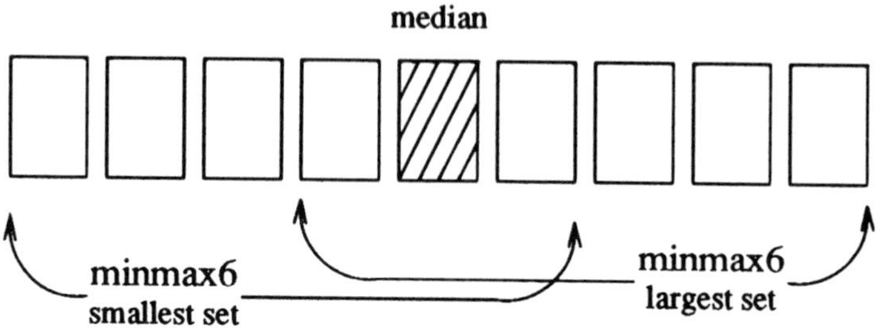

median

Figure 3. Reducing the median.

this subset contains a smallest element whose rank can be no greater than four (see Fig. 3).

These outermost two elements bracket the median and belong within the remaining two partitions: discarding them reduces the input data to seven elements. The median (rank 4) on the remaining elements is then found by finding and discarding minimum and maximum elements using a subset of four; the procedure continues through $minmax_3$. At this point, eight discard values have been partitioned and the median remains. The complete pseudo-code requires twenty comparisons and is listed here:

```
macro s2(a, b) if (z ← b − a) < 0 then begin a ← a + z; b ← b − z; end
macro mn3(a, b, c) s2(a, b); s2(a, c);
macro mx3(a, b, c) s2(b, c); s2(a, c);
macro mnmx3(a, b, c) mx3(a, b, c); s2(a, b);
macro mnmx4(a, b, c, d) s2(a, b); s2(c, d); s2(a, c); s2(b, d);
macro mnmx5(a, b, c, d, e) s2(a, b); s2(c, d); mn3(a, c, e); mx3(b, d, e);
macro mnmx6(a, b, c, d, e, f) s2(a, d); s2(b, e); s2(c, f); mn3(a, b, c,); mx3(d, e, f);

integer function median9 (v)
v:array [1..9] of integer              Subscripting from one for clarity,
   begin                               v is of type real or integer.
   mnmx6(v[1], v[2], v[3], v[4], v[5], v[6]);  Cast off two elements each time.
   mnmx5(v[2], v[3], v[4], v[5], v[7]);
   mnmx4(v[3], v[4], v[5], v[8]);
   mnmx3(v[4], v[5], v[9]);
The median is now in v[5]; v[1..4] and v[6..9] are the ranked partitions.
   return[v[5]];
   end;
```

Although the macro expansion form suggests underlying machine code with many costly indexing operations (as compared to the pointer arithmetic possible with sorting), this is not the case. Because the array size is small, most array elements can be cached in local registers. The form presented here is particularly useful because discarding of min/max pairs may commence immediately after the first six elements have been read in consecutive order; subsequent program statements drop two elements and fetch only one additional input so the number of active registers steadily declines. This suggests C code (see the Appendix) in which the "register" source code directive—which provides the compiler a list of suggested candidates for register variables—leads to further speed-ups.

For larger odd-order boxes the comparison technique is still useful. The above approach costs $1/16[3n^4 + 10n^2 - 13]$ integral comparisons for boxes of n^2 elements and odd edge length n, giving 132 comparisons for a 5×5 box. An alternate network for median on twenty-five elements (Paeth, 1990), requiring less than one hundred comparisons, is included in the C code. It has been exhaustively checked against all possible input permutations and transcribed directly from the sources. For larger sampling boxes (kernels) reuse of common elements suggests traditional median finding methods on large arrays. In the 2D spatial case, these include the use of sorted data structures in which the trailing and leading element columns are deleted and added while indexing across a scan-line.

See also Storage-free Swapping (436)

See Appendix 2 for C Implementation (711)

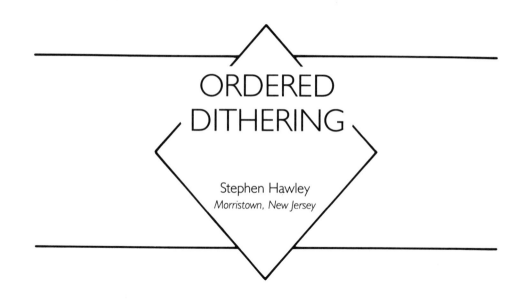

ORDERED DITHERING

Stephen Hawley
Morristown, New Jersey

Ordered dithering is a technique of reducing high-precision, two-dimensional data to a lower precision using positional information to retain as much information as possible. In the context of image processing, ordered dithering can be used to reduce multilevel grayscale images to fewer levels, or in the simple case, to black and white. This can be used to reduce the storage space of an image, while retaining a fair amount of the image contents or to display multilevel grayscale images on a black-and-white display.

Ordered dithering is a very fast, efficient technique. Dithering typically requires one comparison, one array lookup, and two modulo operations per pixel and can be implemented as a macro or inline function. In most cases, the modulo operations can be done with bit-ands.

The whole idea behind ordered dithering is to distribute evenly the expected range of gray levels throughout a matrix, which will act as a screen. A gray level is compared to a value in the matrix using the coordinates of the gray level as indices into the matrix. Gray levels that are greater than the corresponding value in the dithering matrix are filtered out as representing black. All other values represent white. This is almost exactly the same as the halftoning process used in newspapers.

The real trick is to come up with a way to design the matrix so that each gray level will produce an even pattern in the output. For example, a 50% gray level should come out as a checkerboard pattern. If we adopt a recursive definition of the matrix, we get this for free.

To start off, here's a base case for a dithering matrix for 256 gray levels:

$$\mathbf{M}_0 = [0].$$

This is the zero*th* dithering matrix. Its dimensions are 2^0 by 2^0. It contains the range from 0 to 255, but is not very useful by itself. $\mathbf{M}_1$ looks like this:

$$\mathbf{M}_1 = \begin{bmatrix} 0, & 192 \\ 128, & 64 \end{bmatrix}.$$

$\mathbf{M}_1$ is the first dithering matrix. Its dimensions are 2^1 by 2^1. It contains the range from 0 to 255, but with only four numbers. This means that $\mathbf{M}_1$ can only generate four distinct "halftone" patterns. If we use larger $\mathbf{M}$'s we'll get more patterns, and better image quality.

$\mathbf{M}_1$ can be thought of as four copies of $\mathbf{M}_0$ with constants added:

$$\mathbf{M}_1 = \begin{bmatrix} \mathbf{M}_0 + 0, & \mathbf{M}_0 + 192 \\ \mathbf{M}_0 + 128, & \mathbf{M}_0 + 64 \end{bmatrix}.$$

Similarly, $\mathbf{M}_2$ appears as follows:

$$\mathbf{M}_2 = \begin{bmatrix} 0, & 192, & 48, & 240 \\ 128, & 64, & 176, & 112 \\ 32, & 224, & 16, & 208 \\ 160, & 96, & 144, & 80 \end{bmatrix}.$$

In this case, $\mathbf{M}_2$ is just four copies of $\mathbf{M}_1$ with constants added:

$$\mathbf{M}_2 = \begin{bmatrix} \mathbf{M}_1 + 0, & \mathbf{M}_1 + 48 \\ \mathbf{M}_1 + 32, & \mathbf{M}_0 + 16 \end{bmatrix}.$$

In general, $\mathbf{M}_k$ can be defined as follows:

$$\mathbf{M}_k = \begin{bmatrix} \mathbf{M}_{k-1} + 0*2^{n-2k}, & \mathbf{M}_{k-1} + 3*2^{n-2k} \\ \mathbf{M}_{k-1} + 2*2^{n-2k}, & \mathbf{M}_{k-1} + 1*2^{n-2k} \end{bmatrix},$$

where 2^n is the upper limit of the range that is being dithered over (in the above examples, n is 8) and k such that $n \geq 2k$. Generating dithering matrices by hand is time-consuming and prone to error. It is far easier to use a program to generate them. For an example of such a program, please refer to the Appendix.

In the following example, you'll see how to reduce a multilevel image to a bilevel image. The function **reduce** loops over the entire input bitmap dithering each pixel. To stress the size-independence of the code, neither the dithering matrix nor its dimensions are specified in the pseudo-code.

```
DitherSize: integer;
DitherMatrix: array [0..DitherSize − 1] of array [0.. DitherSize − 1] of integer;
MultiMap: record [
    array [0..m] of array [0..n] of integer;
    ];
BiMap: record [
    array [0..m] of array [0..n] of boolean;
    ];
macro dither(x, y, level)
    (level > DitherMatrix[x mod DitherSize] [y mod DitherSize]);
```
This macro compares the given level to an element in the dithering matrix.
The element is located by mapping the coordinates of the pixel into the dithering matrix.

```
function reduce (in: MultiMap; out: BiMap;)
begin
  for i: integer ← 0, i ← i + 1 while i ≤ m do
    for j: integer ← 0, j ← j + 1 while j ≤ n do
        out[i][j] ← dither(i, j, in[i][j]);
```
Since the dither macro is a boolean expression, it reduces the
multilevel input to binary output.
```
        endloop;
    endloop;
end;
```

See Appendix 2 for C Implementation (713)

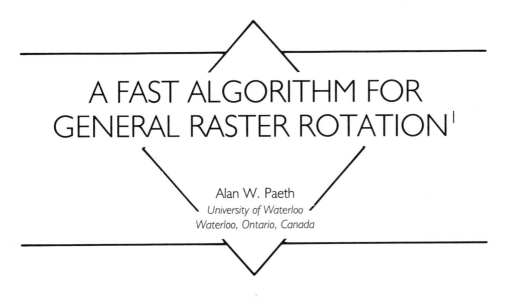

A FAST ALGORITHM FOR GENERAL RASTER ROTATION[1]

Alan W. Paeth
University of Waterloo
Waterloo, Ontario, Canada

Introduction

The rotation of a digitized raster by an arbitrary angle is an essential function for many raster manipulation systems. We derive and implement a particularly fast algorithm which rotates (with scaling invariance) rasters arbitrarily; skewing and translation of the raster is also made possible by the implementation. This operation is conceptually simple and is a good candidate for inclusion in digital paint or other interactive systems, where near real-time performance is required.

We derive a high-speed raster algorithm based on the decomposition of a 2D rotation matrix into the product of three shear matrices. Raster shearing is done on a scan-line basis, and is particularly efficient. A useful shearing approximation is to average adjacent pixels, where the blending ratios remain constant for each scan-line. Taken together, our technique (with anti-aliasing) rotates rasters faster than previous methods. The general derivation of rotation also sheds light on two common techniques: small-angle rotation using a two-pass algorithm, and three-pass 90-degree rotation. We also provide a comparative analysis of Catmull and Smith's method (1980) and a discussion of implementation strategies on frame buffer hardware.

[1]This paper revises and updates the journal article (Paeth, 1986a), which first described general raster rotation using three shearing passes. Minor errors have been corrected, the references have been augmented, and an addendum has been included, which provides additional background and application notes.

Statement of the Problem

A general 2D counterclockwise rotation of the point (x, y) onto (x', y') by angle theta is performed by multiplying the point vector (x, y) by the rotation matrix

$$M = \begin{bmatrix} \cos \theta & -\sin \theta \\ \sin \theta & \cos \theta \end{bmatrix}.$$

The matrix is orthogonal: its inverse is its transpose, rows and columns are unit vectors, and the determinant is one. To rotate a raster image, we consider mapping the unit cell with center at location (i, j) onto a new location (i', j').

The image of the input cell on the output grid is a cell with (usually) a nonintegral center, and with a rotation angle theta (θ). We adopt a "box-filter" sampling criterion, so the value of the output pixel is the sum of the intensities of the covered pixels, with each contributing pixel's intensity weighted in direct proportion to its coverage (see Fig. 1). Note that the output pixel may take intensities from as many as six input pixels. Worse, the output pixel coverage of adjacent input pixels is nonperiodic; this is directly related to the presence of irrational values in the rotation matrix. Clearly, the direct mapping of a raster by a general 2×2 matrix is computationally difficult: many intersection tests result, usually with no coherence or periodicity to speed program loops.

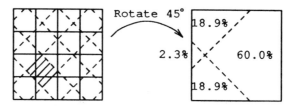

Figure 1.   Rotation by raster sampling.

Rotation through Shearing

Now consider the simplest 2×2 matrices that may operate on a raster. These are shear matrices:

$$x \text{ shear} = \begin{bmatrix} 1 & \alpha \\ 0 & 1 \end{bmatrix} \qquad y \text{ shear} = \begin{bmatrix} 1 & 0 \\ \beta & 1 \end{bmatrix}.$$

Shear matrices closely resemble the identity matrix: both have a determinant of one. They share no other properties with orthogonal matrices. To build more general matrices, we form products of shear matrices—these correspond to a sequence of shear operations on the raster. Intuitively, consecutive shearing along the same axis produces a conforming shear. This follows directly:

$$\begin{bmatrix} 1 & a \\ 0 & 1 \end{bmatrix} \begin{bmatrix} 1 & a' \\ 0 & 1 \end{bmatrix} = \begin{bmatrix} 1 & a + a' \\ 0 & 1 \end{bmatrix}.$$

Thus, shear products may be restricted to products of alternating x and y shears, without loss of generality. The product of three shears gives rise to a general 2×2 matrix in which three arbitrary elements may be specified. The fourth element will take on a value that ensures that the determinant of the matrix remains one. This "falls out" because the determinant of the product is the product of the determinants (which are always one for each shear matrix). Orthogonal 2×2 matrices also have unit determinants, and may thus be decomposed into a product of no more than three shears:

$$\begin{bmatrix} 1 & \alpha \\ 0 & 1 \end{bmatrix} \begin{bmatrix} 1 & 0 \\ \beta & 1 \end{bmatrix} \begin{bmatrix} 1 & \gamma \\ 0 & 1 \end{bmatrix} = \begin{bmatrix} \cos\theta & -\sin\theta \\ \sin\theta & \cos\theta \end{bmatrix}.$$

Solving the general equation, we have $\alpha = \gamma = (\cos\theta - 1)/\sin\theta$; $\beta = \sin\theta$. The first equation is numerically unstable near zero, but can be replaced by substituting the half-angle identity for the tangent:

$$\tan\frac{\theta}{2} = \frac{\sin\theta}{1 + \cos\theta} = \frac{1 - \cos\theta}{\sin\theta}$$

yielding $\alpha = \gamma = -\tan(\theta/2)$. Counterclockwise rotation by θ is thus the shear product:

$$\begin{bmatrix} 1 & -\tan\theta/2 \\ 0 & 1 \end{bmatrix} \begin{bmatrix} 1 & 0 \\ \sin\theta & 1 \end{bmatrix} \begin{bmatrix} 1 & -\tan\theta/2 \\ 0 & 1 \end{bmatrix}.$$

Notice that β and α have opposing signs for nonzero θ. As will be shown later, $\beta = -2\alpha/(1 + \alpha^2)$. Program code to shear and update the point (x, y) with (x', y') is then:

x *shear* y *shear*
$x' \leftarrow x - \tan(\theta/2) \times y;$ $x' \leftarrow x;$
$y' \leftarrow y;$ $y' \leftarrow y + \sin(\theta) \times x;$

When the output vector replaces the input, $x \equiv x'$ and $y \equiv y'$, so the second line of the sequence may be optimized out. Consecutive shears yield sequential program steps. Thus, a three-shear rotation is achieved by the three program statements:

$$x \leftarrow x + \alpha \times y; \qquad\qquad x \ shear \quad (1)$$

$$y \leftarrow y + \beta \times x; \qquad\qquad y \ shear \quad (2)$$

$$x \leftarrow x + \alpha \times y; \qquad\qquad x \ shear \quad (3).$$

With $\theta \approx 0$, Cohen (Newman and Sproull, 1979) uses steps (1) and (2) to generate circles by plotting points incrementally. His derivation begins by choosing α and β to approximate the conventional rotation matrix and then points out that by reassigning $x + \alpha \times y$ to the original variable x in (1), and not to a temporary value x', the determinant becomes one, and the circle eventually closes. Our analysis demonstrates formally why this is true: rewriting the variables constitutes a shear, and the sequence of shears always maintains a determinant of one. Augmenting the code with line (3) would convert the two-axis shear in a true rotation: the circle generator would then produce points rotated through a constant angle relative to the preceding point. This is important should the algorithm be used to produce circle approximations as n-gons (and not point drawings), where $\theta = 360/n$ is no longer small.

Raster Shearing

Raster shearing differs from point transformation in that we must consider the area of the unit cell that represents each pixel. Fortunately, the shear operation modifies the pixel location with respect to only one axis, so the shear can be represented by skewing pixels along each scan-line. This simplifies the intersection testing that must go on to recompute the intensity of each new output pixel.

In general, the unit square $P(i, j)$ on row i is rewritten as a unit parallelogram with side of slope $1/\alpha$ on row i, with the former displaced by $\alpha \times i$ pixel widths. This displacement is not usually integral, but remains invariant for all pixels on the ith scan-line. For illustration and

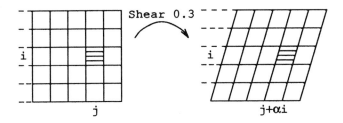

Figure 2.   Raster shearing along the x-axis.

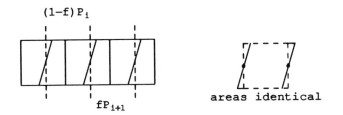

Figure 3.   The parallelogram approximation.

implementation, it is represented as the sum of an integral and a fractional part (f in Fig. 3; *skewf* on p. 187). Those pixels covered by this parallelogram are written with fractional intensities proportional to their coverage by the parallelogram. The sum of all these pixels must equal the value of the original input pixel, as they represent this input pixel after shearing.

We next approximate this parallelogram of unit area with a unit square. Placing the edges of the square through the midpoints of the parallelogram, we produce an exact approximation when the parallelogram covers two pixels, but not when it covers three. This approximation is the basis for our rotation algorithm. As we shall see, it can be implemented as a very efficient innermost pixel blending loop, thus offsetting the cost of making three shearing passes, as compared with previous techniques, which employ two less efficient (though more general) passes.

Based on this filtering strategy, we consider two approaches to rotation. First, we seek angles θ for which the filtering is exact. Second, we analyze the filter for arbitrary values of θ where the filter may not be exact.

Rational Rotation

Filtering is exact when all parallelograms overlap no more than two pixels. This will always occur when the shear offset is of length $1/n$, because a periodic cycle of n parallelograms results in which each spans exactly two pixels. Choosing this ideal filter for the first and third passes, we derive the second pass shear value. This requires the general solution of β in terms of α. Since $\alpha = -\tan(\theta/2)$, $\theta = -2\tan^{-1}\alpha$ as $\tan - x = -\tan x$. Substitution yields $\beta = \sin \alpha = -\sin(2\tan^{-1}\alpha)$; similarly $\sin - x = -\sin x$. Given a right triangle of adjacent side 1 and opposite side α it is clear that

$$\tan^{-1}\alpha = \sin^{-1}\frac{\alpha}{\sqrt{\alpha^2 + 1}} = \cos^{-1}\frac{1}{\sqrt{\alpha^2 + 1}}.$$

Also, $\sin(2\theta) = 2\sin\theta\cos\theta$. By expressing arctangent successively in terms of arcsine and arccosine, we have

$$\beta = -2\sin\left(\sin^{-1}\frac{\alpha}{\sqrt{\alpha^2+1}}\right)\cos\left(\cos^{-1}\frac{1}{\sqrt{\alpha^2+1}}\right) = \frac{-2\alpha}{1+\alpha^2}.$$

In the case at hand, we choose α in the form $\dfrac{-1}{n}$ yielding $\beta = \dfrac{2n}{1+n^2}$.

An all-integer case occurs when setting $n = 1$, which yields $\alpha = -1$, $\beta = 1$. Thus, rotations with $\theta = 90°$ are exact, a feature not possible when using the two-pass approach of Catmull-Smith. Because no fractional pixel values are generated, rotation by 90 degrees may be coded as a high-speed three pass "shuffle" for use on either software or hardware (Kornfeld, 1987).

We may consider rotation by rational values generally, as these specific forms allow "loop unrolling" for fast rotations. β pass generates small errors on a periodic basis. When α and β are small rationals of the form i/j, then the shear values (which are used as blending coefficients by our algorithm) will recur every j scan-lines. In particular, the jth scan-line will have no fractional remainder and can be "blitted" directly into the output buffer. Solving for general rational values of α and β, we find that $\alpha = -i/j$ and $\beta = 2ij/(i^2+j^2)$. These tabulated values give rise to highly efficient filters, with approximation errors minimized (see Fig. 4).

Graphically, these rotation angles are related to solutions of Pythagoras' theorem $i^2 + j^2 = k^2$ wherein the coordinates of select input pixels and matching output pixels remain integral. As an example, rotation by

α	β	θ
-1	1	90.00
$-3/4$	24/25	73.74
$-2/3$	12/13	67.38
$-1/2$	4/5	53.13
$-1/3$	3/5	36.87
$-1/4$	8/17	28.07
$-1/5$	5/13	22.62

Figure 4. Rotation by a rational shear.

$\theta = 53.13°$ maps all input pixels at coordinates $(5i, 5j)$ onto output pixels at $(3i, 4j)$ exactly. (See also "Circles of Integral Radius on Integer Lattices" beginning on page 57.)

Arbitrary Rotation

We now consider arbitrary choices of θ and then the precision of the rotation. For $\theta > 90°$, our shear parallelogram may span four pixels and the filtering rapidly breaks down. Based on the four-fold symmetry of a raster, we may restrict our attention to rotations of no more than 45 degrees, where our approximation has worst-case performance (because α and β grow monotonically with $0 \le \theta < 90°$). Here $\alpha = 1 - \sqrt{2} \approx -.4142$; and $\beta = \sqrt{2}/2 \approx .7071$. The second β pass is the most error-prone.

Probabilistically, its filter is exact 29.3% of the time. Otherwise, the parallelogram spans three pixels, and the error, as a function of fractional pixel skew, grows quadratically to a cusp, reaching its worst-case error when the parallelogram is symmetric about the output pixel. This error is $\sqrt{2}/8$ or 17.7%. However, the sampling tile shifts as the shear value changes with each scan-line, so average degradation to the sheared raster is computed by integrating over parallelograms of all possible skew. Solving the equations, we find that the worst-case shear filter approximates intensities to within 4.2% of the actual intensity. For rotations less than 45 degrees, the approximation is even closer, as the probability of

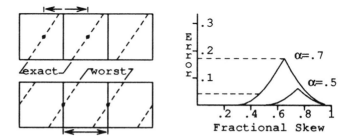

Figure 5. Approximation error.

the parallelogram spanning three pixels decreases. Where it does, the error terms are also smaller.

The nature of the error is to concentrate intensities from a center pixel, whereas the true box-filter approximation calls for contributing coverages from two neighboring pixels. Thus, the approach "peaks" the data: the nature of the degradation is not random. Further, a reasonable implementation of the filter guarantees that when any scan-line is skew-sheared by a fractional amount, the contributing intensities of each input pixel sum to 1.0—the filter parallelograms never overlap. If we consider the sum of the pixel intensities along any scan-line, this sum remains unchanged after the shear operation. Thus, the algorithm produces no visible shifts in intensity and introduces no "holes" during rotation—all pixel flux is accounted for. The only rotation artifacts discernible appear with high-frequency data (such as lines of single pixel width), and even then only after magnification. This property is shared generally with rotation and translation algorithms, which must resample such "sharp" rasters onto nonintegral pixel boundaries.

Implementation

Scan-line shearing is approximated by a blending of adjacent pixels. In the following code segment, the *pixmult* function returns a pixel scaled by a value *skewf*, where $0 \le skewf < 1$ is a constant parameter for all width passes through the innermost loop.

```
procedure xshear(shear, width, height)
begin
      for y ← 0 to height − 1 do begin
      skew ← shear × (y + 0.5);
      skewi ← floor(skew);
      skewf ← frac(skew);                    (see addenda)
      oleft ← 0;
      for x ← 0 to width − 1 do begin
          pixel ← P[width − x, y];
          left ← pixmult(pixel, skewf);   pixel = left + right
          pixel ← pixel − left + oleft;   pixel − left = right
```

```
            P[width − x + skewi, y] ← pixel;
            oleft ← left;
        endloop;
    P[skewi, y] ← oleft;
    endloop;
    end

function pixmult(pix, frac)
begin
    pix_r ← pix_r × frac
    pix_g ← pix_g × frac
    pix_b ← pix_b × frac
    end.
```

This operation is a shearing algorithm for the x-axis; it shears a raster of size (width, height) by the value present in *shear*, so the data matrix P must be of sufficient width to accommodate the shifted output data. Note that only *width* output entries are written, so the skewed output line may be written to frame buffer memory modulo the frame buffer scan-line width, thus requiring no additional memory but complicating the specification of data to the three shear passes. A virtual frame buffer implementation, which provided a notion of "margins" to active picture detail, can maintain this offset information implicitly.

A shear operation always has an axis of shear invariance (it is in fact an eigenvector). In this implementation, the axis is the pixel boundary below the final row of pixel data at a distance *height*. This gives rise to rotation about the interstices between pixel centers. To rotate rasters about pixel centers, the 0.5 half-pixel offset may be removed.

The code splits each pixel into a *left* and *right* value using one multiply per pixel; *left* and *right* always sum exactly to the original pixel value, regardless of machine rounding considerations. The output pixel is then the sum of the remainder of the lefthand pixel, plus the computed fractional value for the present (righthand) pixel. The *pixmult* function reduces to a fractional multiply or table look-up operation with monochromatic images. More generally, it may operate on an aggregate pixel, which might contain three color components or an optional coverage factor (Porter and Duff, 1984). Because read and write references to

P occur at adjacent pixel locations during the course of the innermost loop, pixel indexing can be greatly optimized.

On machines lacking hardware multiply, code to shear a large (512×512) image may build a multiply table at the beginning of each scan-line and then use table look-up to multiply. By skew symmetry, x-shearing of line $-n$ and line n are identical, save for shear direction, so one table may be used for two scan-lines, or for every 1024 pixels. With a pixel consisting of three 8-bit components, the table length is 256, and table fetches will exceed table loads by a factor of 12. Since the table can be built with one addition per (consecutive) entry, its amortized cost per look-up is low, and decreases linearly with raster size.

Many frame buffers now incorporate integer multiply hardware, often targeted to pixel blending applications (The Adage/Ikonas frame buffers at Waterloo's Computer Graphics Laboratory provide a 16-bit integer multiply in hardware). This speeds the evaluation of the pixel blending; the majority of the inner-loop overhead is in (un)packing the 24-bit RGB pixel to provide suitable input for the multiplier. Fortunately, the addition used to complete the blend may be done as a 24-bit parallel add, because the values to be summed, *left* and *right*, have been scaled by *frac* and 1-*ffrac* respectively. Thus, the blending operation is closed, and no carry can overflow from one pixel component into the next.

Finally, the shear code may more generally be used to introduce spatial translation of the raster. By introducing an output offset in the shear code, a BitBlt-style operation (Ingalls, 1978) may be included at no extra cost. In this setting, *skewi* and *skewf* would have integral and fractional offsets added to them to accommodate the lateral displacement of the raster. Displacement during data passes two and three provides arbitrary displacement on the plane, with orthogonal specification of the displacement parameters.

More generally, when the code is incorporated into a larger package, which provides arbitrary (affine) matrix operations on a raster, the composite of all intermediate image transformations are represented in one matrix. This avoids unnecessary operations to the image. Eventually, this matrix is decomposed into three operations: scaling, rotation, and shearing (plus an optional translation if a 3×3 homogeneous matrix is used). The shearing, rotation, and possible translation operations may be gathered into one three-shear operation. The scale pass prefaces the rotation if it scales to a size larger than 1 : 1; otherwise it follows the rotation. This maximizes image quality and minimizes data to the shear (and possibly rotate) routines. Other four pass scale/shear sequences are discussed in the literature (Weiman, 1989).

Comparisons

As with the Catmull-Smith approach, the algorithm may be implemented as a pipeline for real-time video transformation. Both approaches require two "rotators" to transpose the data entering and leaving the second scan-line operator, since this step requires data in column (and not row) order.

Most two-pass warps are described in terms of separable functions on x and y (Smith, 1989). By way of comparison, they may be modeled by the two-matrix transformation

$$\begin{bmatrix} x' \\ y' \end{bmatrix} = \begin{bmatrix} 1 & 0 \\ \tan \theta & \sec \theta \end{bmatrix} \begin{bmatrix} \cos \theta & -\sin \theta \\ 0 & 1 \end{bmatrix} \begin{bmatrix} x \\ y \end{bmatrix}.$$

These slightly more general matrices perform a simultaneous shear and scale along one axis, while leaving the second axis unchanged. This approach saves one data pass, but incurs the penalty of more complex scan-line sampling. Moreover, in two-pass scale-invariant rotation all pixels undergo a $\cos \theta$ minification and restoring $\sec \theta$ spatial magnification. Thus, for intermediate values represented in integer arithmetic (frame buffer pixels), there is a small penalty in roundoff error.

Finally, because sample pixels are both sheared and scaled, no pixel-to-pixel coherence of fractional sampling location exists. Thus, each pixel must be sampled at two fractional locations, doubling the number of pixel (aggregate RGB) multiplies for each pass. Hand analysis of our microcode showed that this is already the dominant operation in the pixel loop. Finally, the Catmull-Smith approach must additionally recompute the fractional sample points for each next pixel or approximate their location using fixed-point arithmetic. In our implementation, fractional sampling points are constant per scan-line, and are calculated exactly in floating point at the beginning of each line.

Compared generally to other work, our algorithm finds application where a generalized BitBlt operation is needed to perform rotation and translation efficiently. More complex pixel sampling passes may justify their added expense in allowing for generalized rotation operations, such as Krieger's modified two-pass approach (Krieger, 1984) used to perform 3D rotation with perspective transformation, useful in texture mapping.

Conclusions

The technique outlined here performs arbitrary high-speed raster rotation with anti-aliasing and optional translation. The mathematical derivation guarantees scaling invariance when rotating. The implementation strategy allows for particularly fast operation, while minimizing the approximation error. This algorithm is a powerful tool in the repertoire of digital paint and raster manipulation systems. Coupled with state-of-the-art raster scaling techniques, it can transform an input raster by an arbitrary 2×2 transformation matrix in near real time.

Addenda: History

The shear-matrix notation and associated code optization sheds light on the "register saving technique" which is now an oft-repeated bit of Computer Graphics lore. It is almost indisputable that the first implementation was MIT. An entry from "HAKMEM" (Beeler *et al.*, 1972) is excerpted here:

Item 149 (Minsky)

Here is an elegant way to draw almost circles on a point-plotting display. CIRCLE ALGORITHM:

$$\text{NEW X} = \text{OLD X} - \epsilon * \text{OLD Y}$$

$$\text{NEW Y} = \text{OLD Y} + \epsilon * \text{NEW}(!) \text{ X}$$

This makes a very round ellipse centered at the origin with its size determined by the initial point.

...The circle algorithm was invented by mistake when I tried to save one register in a display hack!

...[It is] exciting to have curves, and I was trying to get a curve display hack with minimal instructions.

The earliest use of triple shear matrices is much older. Gauss paired one spatial shear with each of the three physical processes that occur at the boundaries and interior of each element in an optical system: refraction, transfer (across the new media), refraction (Blaker, 1971). Ironically, his application was in ray tracing!

Circle Drawing

This algorithm updates the circle-drawing routine cited above. In this guise a circle of radius r located at the origin is represented by the initial point $(r, 0)$ with subsequent points formed iteratively by applying successive triple shears. This formulation yields a radius vector of demonstrably invariant length, thus assuring the creation of true circles. The previous two-pass method maintains a constant swept area between successive radii as a consequence of unit system determinant. The locus of points generated therefore describes ellipses as a consequence of two of Kepler's laws of motion: planets move along elliptical orbits and sweep out regions of constant area per unit time. Closure is thus guaranteed, albeit with a residual eccentricity. The three-pass trigonometric matrix formulation describes rotation by arbitrary constant angle. Thus, the revised algorithm may be used for the efficient construction of arbitrary n-gons in which no trigonometric functions appear within the innermost code loop.

When representing a circle as a polygon of large n the matrix product $(XYX)^n$ represents all shears constituting one complete cycle. Therefore, this product is the identity matrix and we may permute any run of $3n$ products cyclically. Also, matrix products associate, thus allowing arbitrary grouping. In particular, the product may be written as $(Y(XX))^n$. This reduces the number of shears to two by summing the off-diagonal values for the consecutive X matrices, yielding $(YX')^n$ as a valid two-pass technique for closed curve generation. By Taylor expansion we have

$$X' = 2X = -2\tan(\theta/2) = -\theta - \theta^3/12 + 0(\theta^5)$$

$$Y' = \quad Y = \quad\quad \sin(\theta) = \quad \theta - \theta^3/6 \ + 0(x^5).$$

For $\theta \approx 0$ zero we omit all but the linear terms and thus rederive Minsky's original circle generator:

$$\begin{bmatrix} 1 & -\theta \\ \theta & 1 - \theta^2 \end{bmatrix} = \begin{bmatrix} 1 & 0 \\ \theta & 1 \end{bmatrix}\begin{bmatrix} 1 & -\theta \\ 0 & 1 \end{bmatrix}.$$

Note that the coordinates for circumferential points are no longer generated explicitly, but are now implicit within the aggregate X' shear. Thus, the two-pass method yields circles with overall X shear: ellipses with major and minor axes not parallel to the Cartesian ones. The two-pass technique maintains high accuracy because it provides an approximation correct to the quadratic term while employing only linear operations.

Font Rendering

The three-pass algorithm is well-suited for the rendering of bitmapped fonts at various rotations and emphases (normal, bold, italic). Most often, glyph libraries are hand-tuned for specific sizes making a fast rotator providing anti-aliasing (but lacking scaling) an ideal choice. Raster-based character italicization is most often done using scan-line skewing (x-axis shearing) by the discrete values 0.25 or 0.2. These values correspond to a single pixel scan-line displacement occurring every fourth or fifth scan-line within the character string, respectively. When combined with rotation, this skew matrix S of arbitrary x-shear value prefaces the three-pass rotation as we wish to rotate an italic font, not the converse—the symmetry of the three-pass formula is destroyed and matrix multiplication does not commute. For the new $XYXS$ we may immediately regroup the trailing x-shears to form XYX'. The complete operation utilizes shear matrix products in their most general capacity.

Similarly, glyph emboldening is an operation that occurs prior to the first shear pass. Simple emboldening merely brightens pixel values. When made implicit to the operation of the scan-line code, emboldening increases the fractional pixel coverage value *skewf*, thereby thickening the vertical edges of the original character set. With imagination, related effects such as haloing or shadowing can also take place concurrently.

Generalized BitBlt

The entire pseudo-code algorithm can be rewritten using incremental pointer arithmetic (C-language "el = *ptr ++") as all memory reads and writes are to consecutive pixels. This is a consequence of the overall scale invariance, which means no rate differentials exist on the input and output data streams that otherwise give rise to the bottlenecking and fold-over problems of generalized warping (Wolberg and Boult, 1989). The input and output pointers may share the same 2D pixel buffer space, thus allowing *in situo* rotation with impunity: the output pointer will never overwrite an input pixel not yet visited. Frame buffer algorithms for two-pass magnification and minification that share this valuable property have recently been discussed (Heckbert, in press). A public-domain C-language implementation of *xshear* in both fixed and floating point which accommodates out-of-core rasters of arbitrary spatial and pixel dimension is present in the IM Raster Toolkit (Paeth, 1986a, 1986b, 1987).

Advanced Anti-Aliasing

Text and other objects may also be sharpened by substituting more general aliasing filters in the fractional coverage test. The present implementation blends neighboring input pixels together as a linear function of the fractional pixel distance by which the output box overlaps both inputs —the spatial *skewf* value directly drives the blending coefficients. This simple coverage sampling yields a triangular (Bartlett) filter window—the convolution of the input and output boxes. Good results are also afforded using the window created by J. von Hann (termed *Hanning* or *raised cosine*). Under this window the fractional pixel displacement along the domain [0..1) maps onto the range [0..1) in a sinusoidal fashion (Johnson, 1989). As the inner loop considers only left and right neighbors, a three-point version of the filter yields the function $y = \frac{1}{2}(1 - \cos \pi x)$, which biases the blending weight in the direction of that input pixel closest to the fractional x location (page 187), sharpening the data.

It is worth reiterating that the fractional offset (the skew between input and output pixel edges) remains constant along an entire scan-line because the algorithm is scale-invariant. Thus, the weight-adjustment computation takes place outside the innermost loop. Typically, the function is tabulated prior to the entire algorithm and is both stored and indexed in integer precision. This filtering upgrade therefore adds one table look-up per scan-line, which occurs when the assignment to *skewf* is made on the fourth line of the pseudo-code fragment. Related filters such as that by

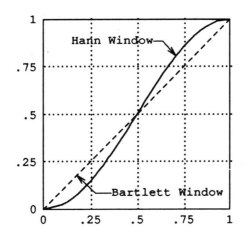

Figure 6. Filter windows.

R. W. Hamming introduce negative blending coefficients, which can complicate operation on pixel fields, which are typically treated as unsigned integers of small precision. Higher-order filters additionally require pixel sampling at more than merely adjacent pixels and rapidly increase the complexity of the inner loop.

Further Work

Data structures modeling "virtual" frame buffers (Higgins and Booth, 1986) allow the implicit representation of scan-line skew, thereby reducing storage. This has greatest benefit when rendering narrow objects such as character strings at values of $\theta \approx 45°$. General affine transformations are possible when combining rotation with rectilinear scaling. As neither method requires fractional (phase) recomputations on a per-pixel basis, highly simplified 1D filtering may be used throughout. This approach requires more than three passes, making an algorithmic test for image degradation desirable. The use of matrix products in representing spatial operations on rasters is desirable and should generally be encouraged.

USEFUL 1-TO-1
PIXEL TRANSFORMS

Dale Schumacher
St. Paul, Minnesota

Many useful kinds of image enhancements can be achieved with 1-to-1 pixel transforms. These are transforms where the new value of a pixel is strictly a function of the old value of that pixel. The digital equivalents of most photographic darkroom techniques fall into this category. This paper discusses some of the more useful 1-to-1 pixel transforms and illustrates their effect on a sample image.

In this discussion, the images are composed of monochrome grayscale pixel values with a floating point range of [0.0, 1.0]. The transforms will usually be shown as an input–output relationship graph with the original pixel value on the horizontal axis as the input, and the new pixel value on the vertical axis as the output.

The simplest transform is a null transform, where the new pixel has the same value as the old pixel. If the transform function is called $f(x)$, then the null transform is simply $f(x) = x$. The corresponding input–output graph is Fig. 1. The next simplest transform is photo-inversion, where the luminance values are reversed, similar to a photographic negative. The function for photo-inversion is $f(x) = 1.0 - x$. Figure 2 shows the input–output graph.

A quantization transform, also called posterization, is accomplished by dividing the input values into discrete ranges and assigning the same output value to all pixels in the range. The output values are usually chosen to create a stair-step effect. In the extreme case, with only two

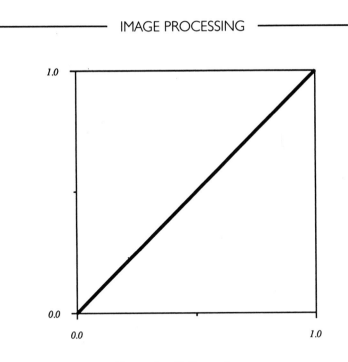

Figure 1. **Null transform.**

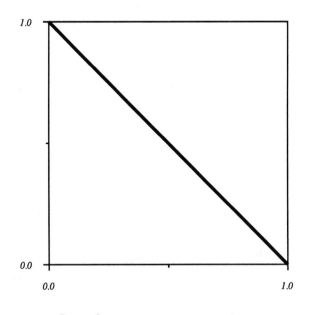

Figure 2. **Photo-inversion transform.**

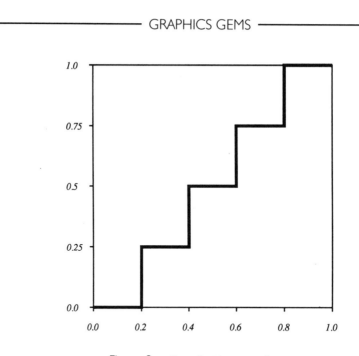

Figure 3.   Quantization transform.

ranges (above or below a certain threshold value), this results in all input values mapping to either 0.0 or 1.0. Figures 3, 4, and 5 illustrate the effect of a five-step quantization based on the transform function

$$f(x) = \begin{cases} 0.00 & 0.0 \leq x < 0.2 \\ 0.25 & 0.2 \leq x < 0.4 \\ 0.50 & 0.4 \leq x \leq 0.6 \\ 0.75 & 0.6 < x \leq 0.8 \\ 1.00 & 0.8 < x \leq 1.0 \end{cases}.$$

A contrast enhancement transform alters the slope of the transform function. Steeper slope results in greater contrast. Often, when an image has poor contrast, there is relatively little picture information at the high and/or low end of luminance range. A very useful tool for finding this clustering of information across the luminance range is a luminance histogram. This histogram shows the relative number of pixels in the image at each luminance value. Peaks on this graph indicate significant

Figure 4. Original image.

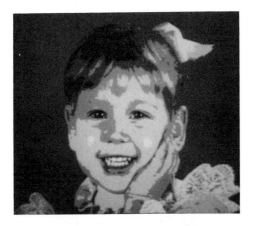

Figure 5. Transformed image.

Figure 6. Original image.

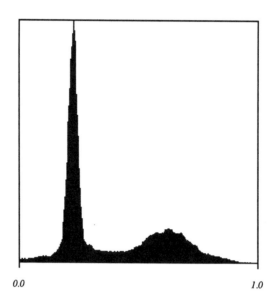

0.0   1.0

Figure 7. Original histogram.

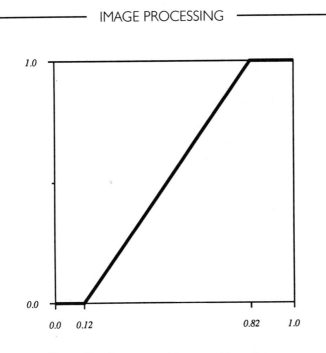

Figure 8.   Contrast enhancement transform.

numbers of pixels with nearly the same luminance. Figure 7 shows a luminance histogram for the sample image. A significant improvement in the image through increased contrast may be gained by setting all values below some lower bound to 0.0, all values above some upper bound to 1.0, and all values between the bounds to a linear ramp of values from 0.0 to 1.0. These upper and lower bounds are chosen by examining the histogram for relatively lower pixel counts near the high and low ends of the luminance range. Figure 8 shows the transform chosen, with a lower bound of 0.12 and an upper bound of 0.82. The general form of this transform function is

$$f(x) = \begin{cases} 0.0 & x \leq \text{low} \\ (x - \text{low})/(\text{high} - \text{low}) & \text{low} < x < \text{high} . \\ 1.0 & x \geq \text{high} \end{cases}$$

Figure 9 shows the transformed image, and Fig. 10 shows the histogram of the transformed image. The histogram shows that the bulk of

Figure 9.   Transformed image.

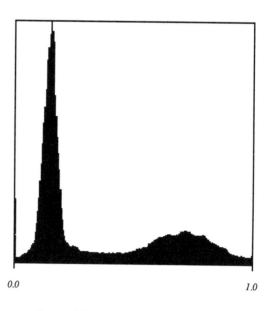

0.0   1.0

Figure 10.   Transformed histogram.

the image information is now spread more evenly across the luminance range.

The overall "brightness" of an image can be adjusted with a gamma correction transform. This is a nonlinear transform, which relates closely to the effects of the "brightness" control on a CRT or variations in exposure time in photography. The general form of the gamma correction function is

$$f(x) = x^{\text{GAMMA}}.$$

A GAMMA value of 1.0 produces a null transform. Values greater than 1.0 darken the image and values between 0.0 and 1.0 lighten the image. In the examples below, Figs. 11, 12, and 15 show a gamma correction of 0.45 and Figs. 13, 14 and 16 show a gamma correction of 2.2. Histograms of the transformed images are included to show the effect this transform has in the distribution of intensities within an image. Sometimes an output device like a CRT is described as having a gamma of 2.2. This indicates the amount of darkening that will occur when the device displays an image. To account for this, you can apply a gamma correction that is the reciprocal of the gamma of the output device to your image before it is displayed. For a device with a 2.2 gamma, the correction is 0.45.

Arbitrary 1-to-1 transforms can also create useful effects that have no photographic equivalents. Some applications, such as medical imaging, find great utility in a variety of "banding" techniques, which can be used to highlight particular image features. Two banding transforms are shown here. The first transform is a sawtooth function, which divides the input range into a series of full-range output sweeps. Each sawtooth acts as a dramatic contrast enhancement transform of the corresponding input range. This gives consistently high slope in the transform function and thus high contrast throughout the image, with a wrap-around effect from white to black at the boundary between ranges. The sawtooth transform function, in general form, looks like

$$f(x) = frac(x \times \text{ranges}).$$

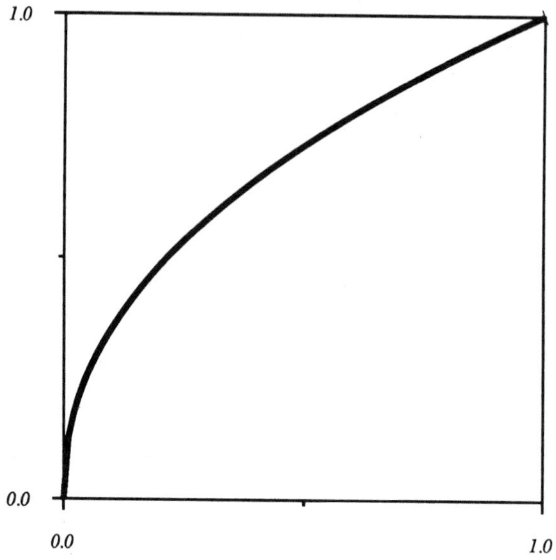

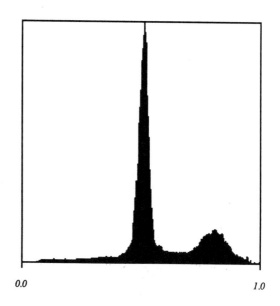

Figure 11. 0.45 gamma correction transform.

Figure 12. 0.45 gamma histogram.

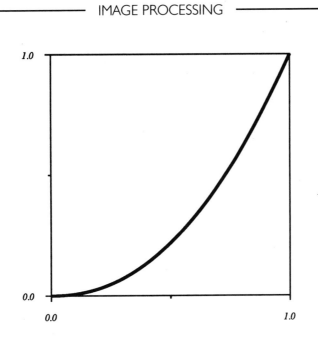

Figure 13.   2.2 gamma correction transform.

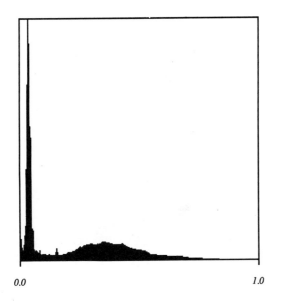

Figure 14.   2.2 gamma histogram.

Figure 15.   0.45 gamma transformed image.

Figure 16.   2.2 gamma transformed image.

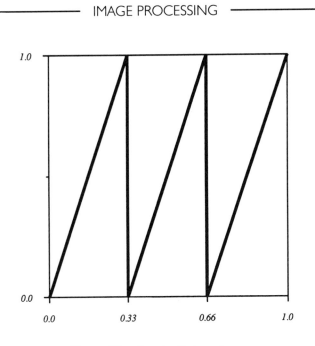

Figure 17. Saw-tooth transform.

Figure 18. Transformed image.

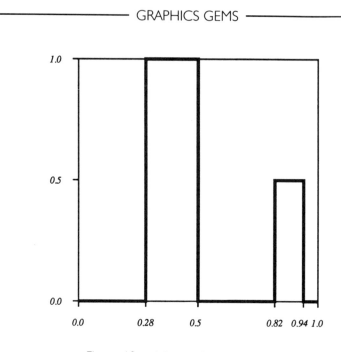

Figure 19. Arbitrary band transform.

Figure 20. Transformed image.

The second transform is an arbitrary series of graybands chosen to highlight specific input luminance ranges. This type of transform typically is defined as a look-up table (particularly if the input is actually discrete luminance values rather than a full floating point range) or a series of highlight ranges. The function shown is

$$f(x) = \begin{cases} 1.0 & 0.28 < x < 0.50 \\ 0.5 & 0.82 < x < 0.94 \\ 0.0 & \text{else.} \end{cases}$$

The use of a histogram helps identify important relationships between the image and its luminance distribution. This information can then be used to guide the application of 1-to-1 transforms for maximum improvement of the original image.

See also 1-to-1 Pixel Transforms Optimized through Color-Map Manipulation (270)

ALPHA BLENDING

Kelvin Thompson
Nth Graphics, Ltd.
Austin, Texas

Alpha blending works best when you *premultiply* color vectors with alpha channels (Porter and Duff, 1984). Specifically, it is best to represent the color (r, g, b) and coverage α with the color vector

$$(r \cdot \alpha, g \cdot \alpha, b \cdot \alpha, \alpha).$$

Some example colors using this convention are as follows:

Color	Vector
half red	$(0.5, 0, 0, 0.5)$
full black	$(0, 0, 0, 1)$
invisible	$(0, 0, 0, 0).$

Suppose we want to composite two vectors $A = (r_A, g_A, b_A, \alpha_A)$ and $B = (r_B, g_B, b_B, \alpha_B)$ into a new vector $C = (r_C, g_C, b_C, \alpha_C)$ with operator **op**, that is, $C = A$ **op** B. Then for each component color $c \in \{r, g, b, \alpha\}$, premultiplication allows us simply to write

$$c_C = c_A F_A + c_B F_B,$$

where F_A and F_B are fractions determined by the operator **op**. Table 1 lists some useful alpha operators and their associated blending fractions. The **over** operator makes a foreground image A occlude a background image B. The **in** and **out** operators allow B to act as a matte for A: A is visible only where allowed or disallowed by the alpha channel of B (the color channels of B are not used). **Atop** is sometimes useful when B

Table I. Alpha compositing operators.

Operation	Diagram	F_A	F_B	Description
clear		0	0	result is completely transparent
A		1	0	A only
B		0	1	B only
A **over** B		1	$1 - \alpha_A$	foreground A occludes background B
A **in** B		α_B	0	A within B; B acts as a matte for A; A shows only where B is visible
A **out** B		$1 - \alpha_B$	0	A outside B; not-B acts as a matte for A; A shows only where B is invisible
A **atop** B		α_B	$1 - \alpha_A$	$(A \text{ in } B) \cup (B \text{ out } A)$; B is both background and matte for A
A **xor** B		$1 - \alpha_B$	$1 - \alpha_A$	$(A \text{ out } B) \cup (B \text{ out } A)$; A and B mutually exclude one another; rarely used
A **plus** B		1	1	blend without precedence

should act as both background and matte for A. The remaining operators are useful primarily for occasional special effects.

The α component of a color vector may describe two kinds of coverage: the transparency of the color, or the fraction of the pixel that the color covers. The diagrams in Table 1 show the meanings of the operators when α represents pixel coverage.

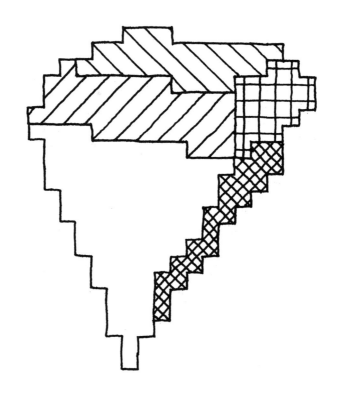

4

FRAME BUFFER TECHNIQUES

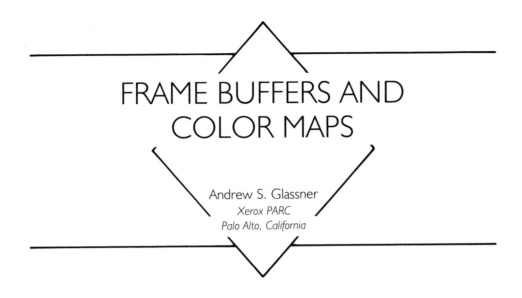

FRAME BUFFERS AND COLOR MAPS

Andrew S. Glassner
Xerox PARC
Palo Alto, California

A *frame buffer* is a piece of hardware often found in computer graphics installations. The idea behind the frame buffer is that a picture may be represented by a two-dimensional matrix of colors. This matrix is usually implemented with fast random-access memory. The RAM itself is the frame buffer, since it stores, or buffers, one frame of video information. To display this frame on a CRT, the colors in the frame buffer are read to the CRT's input circuits in synchrony with the scanning beam. Thus, as the electron guns in the tube sweep the face of the screen top-to-bottom, left-to-right, a signal is arriving that specifies the color to be displayed at each point.

In this scheme there is a one-to-one correspondence between screen locations and memory locations. Individual elements in the frame buffer are called *pixels* (a contraction of "picture element"), and since the correspondence is so strong, the associated point on the screen is usually called a pixel as well.

Typically, frame buffers organize their constituent pixels in a rectangular grid. Each pixel may therefore be identified by its address in a Cartesian coordinate system as (x, y) (see Fig. 1). Common frame buffer resolutions are 512-by-512 and 640-by-480 pixels. Frame buffers with higher resolutions are also available for applications where the displayed image will be large; for film applications one sometimes finds frame buffers as large as 4096-by-4096. The advantage of more resolution is finer control over small details in the final image. The disadvantage is increased cost, both fiscally to buy the extra hardware, and temporally in the extra computer time required to calculate the appropriate color for each pixel.

215

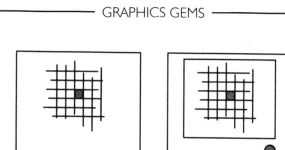

RAM   CRT

Figure 1. The shaded square indicates the same pixel in both devices.

The simplest form of pixel is a single number. The most common form of frame buffers store one 8-bit byte at a pixel (allowing one to specify a number from 0 to 255 inclusive). This number does not directly encode a color; rather, it is an index into a list of colors called the *color map*. In this example, the color map would contain 256 entries, one for each possible value stored in the pixels. Each entry in the color map is typically composed of three numbers. These indicate the red, green, and blue intensities of the color associated with that entry.

Thus, when a picture is being scanned out to a CRT, the value in the pixel about to be displayed is first fetched from the frame buffer, and then used as an index into the color map. Out of the color map come the red, green, and blue components of that color; these components are then fed directly to the color guns in the CRT (see Fig. 2).

Figure 2. The highlighted pixel in the frame buffer indicates that color number 54 should be displayed at the corresponding screen location. The color-map entry for index 54 contains the color (32, 20, 50), which is then displayed on the screen.

216

This technique allows an image to have up to 256 different colors. The contents of the color map, not the pixel itself, determine which color is associated with each of these 256 numbers. A common demonstration of color maps is to turn a day scene into a night scene by leaving the values in the pixels constant, but changing the color-map entries. For example, imagine a picture of a farmhouse with the sky overhead, and suppose the pixels in the sky region have color number 73. For the day scene, color number 73 in the color map might be a light blue, but for the night scene, color number 73 may be changed to dark blue or black. The number of the color in the image didn't change; only the description of the color to which it referred changed.

Typical color maps contain 8, 10, or 12 bits to represent each of these red, green, and blue components for each color.

A more expensive but also more powerful frame buffer may be built, which allows each pixel to represent any color at all. Rather than storing the index into a color map, each pixel directly stores the red, green, and blue components of the color at that location. Thus each pixel contains three pieces of data—as with the color map, the intensity of each of these primaries typically is represented by 8, 10, or 12 bits. Thus, such a frame buffer is typically 24, 30, or 36 bits deep at each pixel.

Often there is a color map associated with these frame buffers as well. In this arrangement, there are actually three individual color maps, one each for the red, green, and blue components of the image. When a pixel is to be displayed, its three color components are retrieved from the frame buffer. The red value is used as an index into the red color map to determine a new intensity for the red component at that point; similar look-ups are performed for green and blue (see Fig. 3). This allows one to apply overall intensity changes to the image without directly affecting the pixel values in the image. A common use of these color maps is to implement gamma-correction, which compensates for the nonlinearity of the display monitor.

Each layer of information in a frame buffer is called a *plane* (or *channel*). Thus, the first form of frame buffers discussed above has but a single plane (which is 8 bits deep), whereas frame buffers that store the red, green, and blue components at each pixel are three planes deep. A frame buffer may be constructed with an arbitrary number of planes at each pixel. Typically these other planes hold information that varies from pixel to pixel across the image, such as transparency (often called alpha),

217

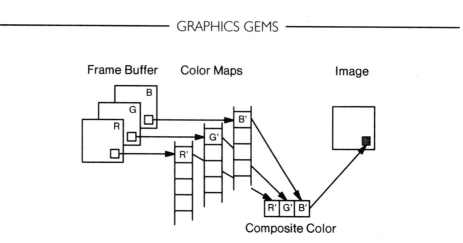

Figure 3. Each of the three color planes holds an 8-bit index into its own color map.

or depth (often called z). Rather than use a single physical frame buffer with many channels, one may use many smaller frame buffers. Sometimes one hears references to "the alpha buffer" or "the depth buffer" of an image, referring to the plane that contains that information, whether or not it is physically located in the same frame buffer that holds the color information for that image.

READING A WRITE-ONLY WRITE MASK

Alan W. Paeth
University of Waterloo
Waterloo, Ontario, Canada

Overview

On many frame buffers the current display modes are contained in hardware registers and not in read/write memory. Although a "shadow" set of outboard memory might maintain these modes (including the current pixel color and write mask) in some cases it is desirable to ascertain the hardware state directly, as it represents the "truth." The following pseudo-code recovers the current hardware write mask in a nondestructive fashion, thereby providing a useful diagnostic. The code also serves as a start-up configuration test for bit plane depth in a manner analogous to memory self-sizing as when booting an operating system. In this case the write mask is set to the known value minus one (all bit planes enabled) and the procedure is executed directly.

procedure setxy(x, y)   *set pixel location for future readpix and writepix*
integer function readpix()   *return pixel (integer) from the latest setxy() location*
procedure writepix(bits)   *write pixel (integer) to the latest setxy() location*

integer function getwritemask()
integers must contain as many bits as hardware pixels

   begin
   tmp, mask: **integer;**   *saved pixel, computed mask*
   ones, zeros: **integer;**   *two probe words*
   setxy(0, 0);   *to probe pixel at origin*
   tmp ← readpix();   *save "original" value*
   writepix(− 1);   *write all ones through unknown mask*
   ones ← readpix();   *recover ON bit planes*
   writepix(0);   *write zeros through unknown mask*
   zeros ← readpix();   *recover OFF bit planes*
   writepix(tmp);   *fully restore origin*
   mask ← ones **bit-xor** zeros;   *WRITMASK BITS TOGGLED **IFF** ENABLED*
an alternate operation is "bit-clear" i.e., "bit-and bit-invert"
   return[mask];   *return computed write mask*
   end

A DIGITAL "DISSOLVE" EFFECT

Mike Morton
Honolulu, Hawaii

Computer screens are looking more and more like movie screens—presentation and animation applications pan, zoom, and cut. Analog video hardware under software control yields the best special effects, but all-digital solutions in software can produce good results, too.

For instance, consider the problem of dissolving one image into another. In the analog world, this is easy: just mix two images, bringing the new image's intensity up while decreasing the old image's. In the digital world, color or grayscale images can be dissolved by computing a weighted average of the old and new values for each pixel, then varying the weighting from 0 to 100%, much as with analog video.

Dissolving monochrome images is a different problem—in the world of binary pixels, there are no intermediate pixel values through which to make a smooth transition. One solution is to copy the new image's pixels over the old ones in a pseudo-random order. This article presents a machine-independent technique for this, with a partial case study of an implementation for a single-monitor Macintosh. Carefully crafted assembly code, directly manipulating video memory, can dissolve quite quickly. For instance, a full-screen dissolve on a Macintosh SE takes only about three seconds.

Randomly Traversing a 2D Array

Traversing a large number of screen pixels (an array, in effect) in pseudo-random order is easier said than done. A first step is to reduce the problem by numbering each pixel, starting at zero. If you can produce the pixel numbers in random order, you can produce coordinate pairs in random order, and bring the problem from two dimensions to one.

One simple mapping from a linear random sequence to a 2D sequence is to take each sequence element N and compute N **div** $width$ and N **mod** $width$ to get the vertical and horizontal coordinates in the array. This is much like randomly scrambling integers from 0..51, then mapping them to playing-card values by computing (N **div** 13) and (N **mod** 13).

A typical method for scrambling a set of integers (such as 0..51) is to store them in an array and swap random pairs of numbers. This isn't useful when you want to shuffle a deck of a million cards. To dissolve a million-pixel screen, you need the integers 0..1,048,575 scrambled. Most applications don't have that much room, nor do they have the time to make a million swaps.

Scrambling Integers in Hardware

The software trick that avoids this is based on a simple circuit. Hardware types will recognize Fig. 1 as a "linear feedback shift register." At each cycle, selected bits are sent through an n-way XOR, the entire register is shifted left, and the result of the XOR feeds in as the new rightmost bit. (If you're a hardware-phobe, don't panic—the software version is presented below.)

For each length of register, there's at least one combination of bits to take from it that will make the register cycle through all nonzero values (zero is a "demon state"). If you interpret the contents of the register as a number, the sequence produces each of the numbers from 1 to 255 (in this example) in a fairly random manner.

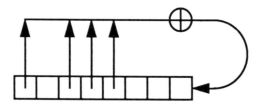

Figure 1. An 8-bit hardware sequence generator: a shift register with selected bits XORed to form the next input. In software, the corresponding mask would be 10111000 (binary).

How random is this sequence? Actually, it fails many randomness tests, but the circuit has a software analog that is easy to code and runs so fast that it's worth it. Knuth points out that the sequence of *bits* shifted out is actually quite random, although the successive numeric *values* aren't.

Scrambling Integers in Software

Although you can exactly mimic the circuit in software, a much faster algorithm is to shift the current element right (not left, as in the circuit); if a "1" bit falls out because of the shift, XOR the mask into the new element. This code fragment shows the code to advance from one element to the next:

```
reg: integer;                           current sequence element
reg ← 1;                                start in any nonzero state
...
if (reg bit-and 1) ≠ 0                   is the bottom bit set?
then reg ← rshift(reg, 1) bit-xor MASK;  yes: toss out 1 bit; XOR in mask
else reg ← rshift(reg, 1);               no: toss out 0 bit
```

For certain values of the constant MASK, executing the *if* statement in a loop will make the register take on all values from $1..2^n - 1$, for various values of n. Table 1 gives one constant (there may be more than one) for each width. (The "width" of the values produced need not be the full width of the variable storing it, of course.)

A First Attempt

With a software-based 1D sequence generator, and a way to map elements of a 1D sequence into a 2D array of pixels, you can write a dissolve algorithm. The idea is to find a "register width" for the sequence generator such that the sequence will generate at least as many elements as there are pixels. The highest-numbered elements don't map to pixels, and they are discarded. Figure 2 illustrates this approach.

The main loop maps each sequence element to a pair of coordinates, using modulo and division. Coordinates past the last row are ignored; those in bounds are copied. The loop ends when the sequence returns to

Table I. For any given bit-width w, there's usually more than one mask that produces all values from 1 to $2^w - 1$. These particular masks are chosen because they can each be packed into a byte—note that bit #w of the mask for width w is set, so each mask can be shifted down for compact storage, then shifted left until the highest "1" bit is positioned correctly. The masks are shown in 8-, 16-, and 32-bit hex only for readability.

Bit width (w)	Mask	Produces sequence values from 1 to...
2	0x03	3
3	0x06	7
4	0x0C	15
5	0x14	31
6	0x30	63
7	0x60	127
8	0xB8	255
9	0x0110	511
10	0x0240	1,023
11	0x0500	2,047
12	0x0CA0	4,095
13	0x1B00	8,191
14	0x3500	16,383
15	0x6000	32,767
16	0xB400	65,535
17	0x00012000	131,071
18	0x00020400	262,143
19	0x00072000	524,287
20	0x00090000	1,048,575
21	0x00140000	2,097,151
22	0x00300000	4,194,303
23	0x00400000	8,388,607
24	0x00D80000	16,777,215
25	0x01200000	33,554,431
26	0x03880000	67,108,863
27	0x07200000	134,217,727
28	0x09000000	268,435,455
29	0x14000000	536,870,911
30	0x32800000	1,073,741,823
31	0x48000000	2,147,483,647
32	0xA3000000	4,294,967,295

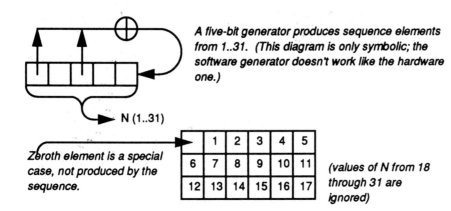

A five-bit generator produces sequence elements from 1..31. (This diagram is only symbolic; the software generator doesn't work like the hardware one.)

N (1..31)

Zeroth element is a special case, not produced by the sequence.

1	2	3	4	5
6	7	8	9	10	11
12	13	14	15	16	17

(values of N from 18 through 31 are ignored)

Figure 2.   Mapping sequence elements into an array, using the formulas:
row ← N **div** width
column ← N **mod** width.
Values of row which are ≥ height are ignored.

the original element. The function to copy a single pixel should eventually get called once for every (row, col) such that $0 \le$ row $\le$ height $- 1$, and $0 \le$ col $\le$ width $- 1$.

Listing 1

A first attempt at the dissolve algorithm. This will be improved later by eliminating the division and modulo computations in the main loop.

```
procedure dissolve1 (height, width: integer);
begin
  pixels, lastnum: integer;          # of pixels; last pixel's number
  regwidth: integer;                 "width" of sequence generator
  mask: longint;                     mask to XOR with to create sequence
  seq: unsigned longint;             1 element of sequence
  row, column: integer;             row and column numbers for a pixel

  Find the smallest "register" that produces enough pixel numbers
  pixels ← height * width;           compute # of pixels to dissolve
  lastnum ← pixels − 1;              last element (they go 0..lastnum)
  regwidth ← bitwidth (lastnum);     how wide must the register be?
  mask ← randmasks [regwidth];       which mask produces that bitwidth?
```

225

Now cycle through all sequence elements.

```
seq ← 1;                          1st element (could be any nonzero)
loop do
  begin
    row ← seq/width;              how many rows down is this pixel?
    column ← seq mod width;       and how many columns across?
    if row < height               does seq element fall in the array?
      then copy (row, column);    yes: copy the (r, c)'th pixel

    Compute the next sequence element
    if (seq bit-and 1) ≠ 0        is the low bit set?
      then seq ← rshift(seq, 1) bit-xor mask;  yes: shift, XOR
        else seq ← rshift(seq, 1);  no: just shift
  end;
  until seq = 1;                  loop till original element
  copy (0, 0);                    kludge: loop doesn't produce (0, 0)
end;                              of procedure dissolve1
```

The correct width of sequence generator is found with a function called *bitwidth*(). Given a number, this function computes how wide a "register" is needed to hold the number. Here it's used to find what width of generator is needed to produce at least as many pixel numbers as needed.

Listing 2

The bitwidth () function

```
function bitwidth (N: unsigned integer): integer;
begin
  width: integer ← 0;            initially, 0 bits needed for N
  while N ≠ 0 do                 loop till N is whittled down to 0
    N ← rshift (N, 1);          NB: N is unsigned
    width ← width + 1;           and remember how wide N is
    endloop;                     end of loop shrinking N
  return width;                  return bit positions counted
  end;                           of function bitwidth
```

Once the width has been found, the *randMasks*[] array is used to find the magic value to generate the sequence. The sequence length can be nearly twice as long as the number of pixels to copy, because the length must be a power of 2 and larger than the number of pixels. The [0] and [1] elements of the array aren't defined—the smallest generator is 2 bits wide. Again, see Table 1.

The *copy* () routine—the code to copy a pixel from the old image to the new—isn't defined here. It will depend on which hardware and graphics system you're using. We'll cover this in more detail in the case study for Macintosh, but you will almost certainly want to make *copy*() be in-line code, to save the cost of a function being called many thousands of times.

Because the sequence never produces the value 0, the dissolve function must call *copy* with $(0, 0)$ explicitly. (Sharp-eyed users watching a dissolve will notice that the top-left pixel is always the first or last to be copied.)

Faster Mapping

This method works, but it's too slow because of the division and modulo calculations. Another approach is shown in Fig. 3. Here, the bits in the sequence element are broken apart bitwise into row and column numbers. This bit operation is much faster than a division for most CPUs. (If you're lucky to have a fast divide on your favorite CPU, skip this section.)

With this method, the number of sequence elements can be almost four times the number of pixels—twice as bad as the worst case for the simpler algorithm. But generating elements is so much faster than division that the new method is still faster. In addition, since many screens have a width that is a power of 2, a full-screen fade is no slower.

The code for this faster version is shown in Listing 3. It's a lot like the original function, except for the way the sequence-to-coordinates mapping is done.

Listing 3

An improved dissolve, which breaks up the sequence element into coordinates with bit operations, not with division

```
procedure dissolve2 (height, width: integer);
begin
  rwidth, cwidth: integer;              bit width for rows, for columns
  regwidth: integer;                    "width" of sequence generator
  mask: longint;                        mask to XOR with to create sequence
  rowshift: integer;                    shift dist to get row from element
  colmask: integer;                     mask to extract column from element
  seq; unsigned longint;                1 element of sequence
  row, column: integer;                 row and column for one pixel

  Find the mask to produce all rows and columns.
  rwidth ← bitwidth (height);           how many bits needed for height?
  cwidth ← bitwidth (width);            how many bits needed for width?
  regwidth ← rwidth + cwidth;           how wide must the register be?
  mask ← randmasks [regwidth];          which mask produces that bitwidth?

  Find values to extract row and col numbers from each element.
  rowshift ← cwidth;                    dist to shift to get top bits (row)
  colmask ← lshift(1, cwidth) − 1;      mask to extract bottom bits (col)

  Now cycle through all sequence elements.
  seq ← 1;                              1st element (could be any nonzero)
  loop do
    begin
      row ← rshift(seq, rowshift);      find row number for this pixel
      column ← seq bit-and colmask;     and column number
      if (row < height)                 does element fall in the array?
        and (column < width)            ...must check row AND column
        then copy (row, column);        in bounds: copy the (r, c)'th pixel

      Compute the next sequence element.
      if (seq bit-and 1) ≠ 0            is the low bit set?
        then seq ← rshift(seq, 1) bit-xor mask; yes: shift, XOR
        else seq ← rshift(seq, 1);      no: just shift
      end;
    while seq ≠ 1;                      loop till original element
  copy (0, 0);                          kludge: element never comes up zero
  end;                                  of procedure dissolve2
```

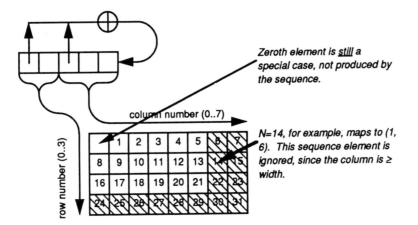

Figure 3. A revised calendar with more holidays? Not quite... This shows a faster mapping of 1D sequence elements into a 2D array, using the formulas:

row ← rshift(N, rowShift) [rowShift = 3]

column ← N **bit-and** colMask [colMask = 00111 base 2].

Coordinate pairs where row ≥ height or column ≥ width are ignored.

Case Study: Details

When you code this, here are some reminders that probably apply to most implementations:

- Don't forget the $(0, 0)th$ element of the array, as handled explicitly in Listings 1 and 3.

- The algorithm breaks down for tiny images, because the sequence generator doesn't work for small widths of registers. You should probably hand this case off to your system's graphical-copy function.

- To copy pixels quickly, you probably will not be able to use your local graphics primitives, but will have to access video memory directly, in assembly language. Be careful to check exactly how this interferes with your high-level graphics. (For instance, a Macintosh dissolve function must hide the cursor in software so as not to overwrite it in hardware.)

- I found it easiest to convert byte addresses of a bitmap to bit addresses, do all my computation in bit numbers, and convert to bytes only when it was time to access video memory. (This assumes that very large addresses on your machine won't overflow when scaled to be bit addresses.)

Case Study: Optimizations

That's all there is to it—just write a fast *copy*() function. But if you want a megapixel screen to fade in a few seconds, you have only a few microseconds per call of *copy*. Here are some hints to obtain speed approaching that of analog hardware.

Many of these hints apply only for certain inputs to the function. There are many possible combinations of optimizations. Instead of trying to code all possible combinations, it might be interesting to compile optimal dissolve code at the time of the call.

- For an actual function for a single, monochrome Macintosh screen, see Morton (1986). I don't recommend this routine for the Mac any more because it doesn't work in the brave, new world of multiple monitors or color. It's the first code I ever wrote for the 68000, so it's hardly textbook reading.

- When the pixel array is less than 64K pixels, you can store the sequence elements in 16-bit words.

- When either the width or height of the array is a power of 2, you can of course omit the respective checks for whether the coordinates are in bounds—the sequence will exactly cover the needed coordinates in that dimension. A dissolve where both the width and height are powers of 2 will be incredibly fast.

- In pseudo-code and C, there are separate checks for whether the low bit is 1 and whether the element has returned to its original value. In assembler, you can sometimes combine these, as in this 68000 code:

```
lsr.l   #1, d0        shift current element right by one
bhi.s   loopTop       if no carry out and not zero, do it again
eor.l   mask, d0      otherwise, flip magic bits...
cmp.l   mask, d0      ...but has this brought us back to the sequence start?
bne.s   loopTop       nope: loop back for more grueling fun
bra     done          go copy element (0, 0).
```

This code takes advantage of the fact that the initial shift instruction (lsr) affects the Zero condition code (based on the value after the shift) and also sets the Carry bit if a "1" bit fell out in the shift. The first branch instruction (bhi) branches if both Carry and Zero are false—just right to test for "no XOR needed, but not a zero result either."

- The sequence element can be viewed as a pair of coordinates concatenated together. Before extracting either one, you can check if the left one is in bounds by comparing the entire sequence element to the maximum value plus 1, shifted to align with the left one.

- Once the left end of the sequence element is found to be in bounds, extract and check the coordinate from the right end, before taking the time to extract the left end.

- When there's no carry, the mask isn't XORed into the next element, and you know the element has a top bit equal to zero (since it was just shifted). This means that the value at the left end of the sequence element is in bounds, and thus the "bhi.s loopTop" in the 68000 code can actually enter the loop late, after the point where the left end is checked.

- The code currently has to test the source pixel and branch to either set or clear the destination pixel. It might be faster to XOR the destination into the offscreen source, creating a bitmap that has "1" bits only where the bitmaps differ. Then the dissolve code would ignore "0" source bits and toggle the destination on "1" source bits. Finally, it would copy the destination back to the source to undo the damage done by the XOR.

- On the 68000, bytes are numbered in increasing order from left to right, while bits go the other way. Thus if you want to convert a bit number to a byte address and a bit, you need to map the bit number from 0..7 to 7..0. But if your source and destination bitmaps have both their left and right edges at byte boundaries, you can skip this mapping. A full-screen dissolve, for example, will typically be able to do this.

Further Research

I've done this technique something of a disservice by implying it's good only for copying an image over another. In general, this is a way to traverse a 2D array of nearly any size in pseudo-random order. (Or, sticking with a 1D sequence, it's the world's fastest coin-flip randomizer.) Some examples of other uses and possible variations are as follows:

- Given that the original motivation for the sequence generator comes from a hardware circuit, why not develop video-hardware support for a dissolve?

- Because the sequence generator's state can be described with a single number, it's simple to start and stop the sequence at any point, allowing partial dissolves—sort of a dithered blending.

- Graphical primitives besides copying could be supported—pixels could be ORed, ANDed, XORed, and so on. Or a repeating pattern could be used for the source instead of a source bitmap.

- Inverting the destination image (XORing from a black pattern) is especially interesting because it's an invertible process. Combining this with a partial dissolve yields very interesting results: traversing the first 50% of the pixels will yield a screen full of gray noise. Re-traversing those pixels will bring back the image.

- When images can't be placed rapidly on the screen, such as in calculating images of the Mandelbrot set, the pixels can be calculated and drawn pseudo-randomly, to present an approximate image as soon as possible. This is also useful when transmitting an image over a slow communications link.

Suggestions and comments for other applications are welcome!

See also Generating Random Integers (438); Circles of Integral Radius on Integer Lattices (57); Precalculating Addresses for Fast Fills, Circles, and Lines (285)

See Appendix 2 for C Implementation (715)

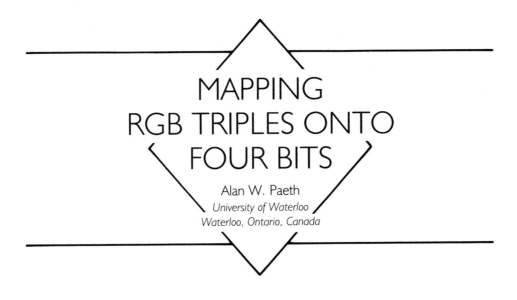

MAPPING RGB TRIPLES ONTO FOUR BITS

Alan W. Paeth
University of Waterloo
Waterloo, Ontario, Canada

Introduction

We describe a method for the efficient mapping of arbitrary triples (typically RGB color values) onto a reduced set of 14 triples. The intended use is for pixel reduction for use on four-bit frame buffers, though the technique may be used generally on any three-element vector.

Background

Many frame buffers provide the choice of displayable colors by way of color look-up table (LUT) hardware. How are representative colors chosen? Further, how can arbitrary input points (high-precision color pixels) be efficiently mapped to a nearest select point within this color cube? On systems providing a large color palette (256 or more) a specific set of color choices may be allocated based on the nature of the input data. A quantization method using this approach is well-known (Heckbert, 1982). On systems providing the minimal number of colors (eight) the choice is clear: the extreme points of the interval [0.0..1.0], must be taken separately on each of the RGB axes.

This Cartesian product yields the point set $[1/2 \pm 1/2, 1/2 \pm 1/2, 1/2 \pm 1/2]$ of primary and secondary colors, which coincides with the vertices of the unit color cube (see Fig. 1). Thus, with small look-up tables the choice of representative colors may be made *a priori*—without regard to the nature of the input data being mapped. The accompanying software procedure is straightforward (see Fig. 2). This fragment locates

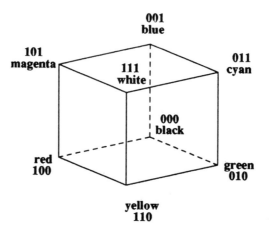

Figure 1.   Eight-point color cube.

that vertex triple $[R2, G2, B2]$ closest to the input triple $[R, G, B]$ and additionally returns a code (the vertex number), which serves as a color-map index.

Unfortunately, in the world of computer logic most low-end frame buffers provide a palette of 16 representable colors based on an underlying four-bit data path. Because any fixed color table necessarily contains the eight vertices of the bounding cube, a four-bit index leaves half of the colors unassigned. This suggests that a preselected set of suitable values might be chosen. An essential feature of a reduced color set is a distribution that shows little bias and high uniformity, while lending itself to an efficient nearest neighbor test. As the number of potential colors will

```
integer function remap8(real: R, G, B, R', G', B')
begin
    integer code;
    R' ← G' ← B' ← code ← 0;
    if (R ≥ 0.5) then begin R' ← 1.0; code ← code bit-or 1; end
    if (G ≥ 0.5) then begin G' ← 1.0; code ← code bit-or 2; end
    if (B ≥ 0.5) then begin B' ← 1.0; code ← code bit-or 4; end
    return[code];
end
```

Figure 2.   RGB onto RGB (three-bit).

234

double, an algorithm running in not more than twice the time of *remap8* is sought, with a sublinear (or logarithmic) increase in time ideal. Given the simplicity of *remap8*, a brute-force linear search for nearest neighbor is ruled out.

A Four-Bit Color Solid

A highly symmetric set of target colors is now created, making for a uniform selection set. Consider a unit cube augmented by allocating new vertices at the center of each of its six faces. This extends the color set to fourteen colors in a uniform manner, owing to the high symmetry of the cube. Enumerating the location of vertices yields the target color space. The new colors include three desaturated primaries and three secondaries of reduced intensity. These are tabulated in Fig. 3. Note that the midpoint of the cube (50% gray) does not appear.

To form a uniform solid with these color vertices, add edges from each face center to the four face vertices that bound it. This *facets* each

Code	Name	Red	Green	Blue
0000	black	0	0	0
0001	olive	$\frac{1}{2}$	$\frac{1}{2}$	0
0010	purple	$\frac{1}{2}$	0	$\frac{1}{2}$
0011	red	1	0	0
0100	aqua	0	$\frac{1}{2}$	$\frac{1}{2}$
0101	green	0	1	0
0110	blue	0	0	1
0111	(undef)	—	—	—
1000	(undef)	—	—	—
1001	yellow	1	1	0
1010	magenta	1	0	1
1011	pink	1	$\frac{1}{2}$	$\frac{1}{2}$
1100	cyan	0	1	1
1101	lime	$\frac{1}{2}$	1	$\frac{1}{2}$
1110	sky	$\frac{1}{2}$	$\frac{1}{2}$	1
1111	white	1	1	1

Figure 3.   The fourteen target colors.

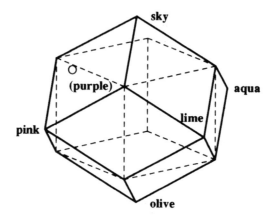

Figure 4. The rhombic dodecahedron.

square face into four equilateral right triangles. Next, extend the new vertices outward from the cube center so that all 14 vertices are equidistant from this center. (This changes the notion of color cube into color sphere, but this discrepancy will be resolved later.) By symmetry the two triangles joining at each cube edge lie in the same plane and the edge belonging to the original cube may be removed. A rhombus is left (a parallelogram with all four edges congruent). Repeating for each of 12 edges in the underlying cube thus yields the rhombic dodecahedron. This solid is well-known in lattice theory: it is the only "Archimedean dual" that can pack three-space, made clear by considering it the union of a white cube with six black pyramidal apexes that pack in a checkerboarding fashion. As with other Archimedean duals all faces are congruent and all dihedral angles equal—properties that make for fair dice. (Since six matching solids pack to fill space by the above, this dihedral is $\pi/3$ radians or 120 degrees.) The polyhedron appears in Fig. 4.

Dual Solids

Now consider the problem of finding the nearest vertex (target color) on this solid. For a test point lying along an edge of the solid there are merely two nearest vertices to be considered. The decision point for vertex choice occurs at the midpoint of that edge. This may be extended to find the region of space containing all test points nearest one vertex.

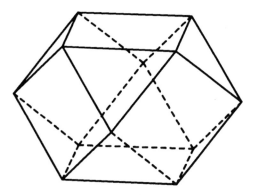

Figure 5.   The cuboctahedron.

By taking the midpoints of the three or four edges common to some vertex, a cutting plane may be defined in which all nearest points lie on one side. By replacing each of the 14 vertices with its related plane the solid becomes truncated. In this case, the process of truncation yields the dual solid (see Fig. 5).

As duality occurs in symmetric pairs, the original Archimedean solid—a *cuboctahedron*—is created. It is semiregular: not among Plato's canonical five because although the faces are all regular n-gons in symmetrical arrangement, the faces are not of identical type. This is another solid sharing the symmetry group of the dual octahedron-cube family. It can be formed from either of these parent solids by forming the convex hull of all edge midpoints. (That it may also be formed from the rhombic dodecahedron in this fashion attests to how "close" the latter comes to being among the select five. Its four-dimensional analog, a cell of 24 octahedra, is regular. In higher dimensions it vanishes together with the teapot and all other interesting regular solids, leaving merely hypertetrahedra, cubes, and their duals (Coexeter, 1948).) The cuboctahedron has six square and eight triangular faces, showing its lineage from both representative parents.

Proximity Testing

The properties of this solid form the crux of our algorithm. As with two-dimensional Voronai diagrams and their duals—common to problems concerning "nearest point to a set of given points"—the original question of nearest neighboring point to a test point has been dualized. The problem now is finding that face containing (or nearest to) a given point. Fortunately, this test can be made quickly by taking advantage of the quasi-regular nature of the regular cuboctahedron. An attribute of such solids is that select, closed, edge circuits not defining faces still lie in a common plane. This property is rare (the octahedron shares it, though not the cube) and makes for geodesic dome tents, which are easily assembled as each edge circuit becomes one long brace. In this case the faces are hexagons. They may be derived directly by slicing a cube along a plane perpendicular to one of its body diagonals, thereby exposing a face along an axis of three-fold rotational symmetry. As seen in Fig. 6a, this nicely reveals the color wheel of primaries and secondaries implicit in the color cube.

By taking all four body diagonals and matching hexagons, an "empty" cuboctahedron termed a "nolid" (Holden, 1971) appears as seen in Fig. 6b. The bounded indentations (occlusions in the shape of regular tetrahedra and half-octahedral pyramids) partition space into 14 distinct volumes. All points within a partition are associated with a matching nearest vertex on the rhombic dodecahedron. Thus, a test point's spatial partition may be identified by performing four inequality tests to locate the halfspaces in which the test point lies. Because the partitions may be extended outward to divide all of 3-space, the test remains valid for arbitrary points, making the algorithm well-defined for any input. This is

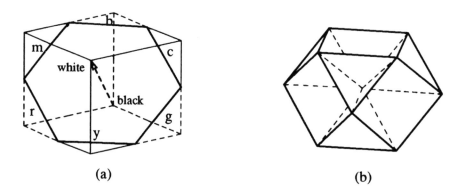

(a) (b)

Figure 6. Hexagonal construction.

Name	Faces	Vertices	Edges	Comments
Cube	6	8	12	"regular hexahedron"
Octahedron	8	6	12	dual of above
Cuboctahedron	14	12	24	connect others' mid-edges
Rhombic Dodecahedron	12	14	24	dual of above

Figure 7.   Select polyhedral solids.

important as certain triaxial color spaces, such as the *YIQ* basis used in commercial broadcasting (Limb *et al.*, 1977), can give rise to negative values of I and Q for strongly saturated colors. This extension accounts for the departure from a "color cube," alluded to when placing vertices at the cube faces' centers. For most data sets, the cuboctahedron nolid may be contained within a unit cube "case."

A summary of the solids encountered so far appears in Fig. 7. Notice that Euler's equation $F + V = E - 2$ is satisfied and that for duality F and V commute, leaving the right-hand term unchanged. Dual solids possess matching edge pairs, which are oriented to each other at right angles.

Related Methods

Spatial search methods, which divide volumes by means of planar half-space tests, have long been applied to rendering algorithms (Schumaker *et al.*, 1969), but universally employ conditional logic (in the form of a tree traversal) in the generation of test planes. The related geometric method of fixed, symmetric planes tested *en masse* rederives the "complete face" characterization of stellated polyhedra, wherein the intersection diagram between one arbitrary face plane and the entire remaining set is drawn. The canonical enumeration of solids thus generated is an open problem (the octahedron yields 1, the icosahedron 59) but graphics tools useful in their visualization exist (McKeown and Badler, 1980).

The hexagonal symmetry of the cube is explicit in other color spaces, such as HSV—Hue Saturation Value—(Smith, 1978), where it is recorded as the hue angle. Under this model, the six additional face colors are represented as desaturated primaries ($S = 1 \rightarrow S = 1/2$) and as secondaries of reduced value $(V = 1 \rightarrow V = 1/2)$, with other terms left unchanged. In particular, hue angles are still members of the original eight vertex set. Other hexagonally symmetric spaces include HSL (Foley and van Dam, 1982). A color space similar in treating the angular distribution of points about a gray axis is described in (Joblove and Greenberg, 1978). A general treatment of color spaces as topological solids containing axes of opposing colors (with related indexing methods) appears in Turkowski (1986).

Half-Space Testing

Because the half-space tests regard merely the sign and not the absolute perpendicular distance between point and plane, the normalized coefficients in the plane equation may be scaled arbitrarily. The goal is to remove irrational values or rational fractions, thus yielding arithmetically efficient tests. The plane equations that define the half-spaces are most easily derived by simple application of Pythagoras' theorem. The gray axis body diagonal shown in Figure 6a has endpoints at $[0, 0, 0]$ and $[1, 1, 1]$. Thus, for any test point (x, y, z) a boolean test may be derived, which reports the nearer endpoint using a distance inequality. For test points nearer the white point the following are true:

$$\sqrt{(x - 0)^2 + (y - 0)^2 + (z - 0)^2} > \sqrt{(x - 1)^2 + (y - 1)^2 + (z - 1)^2}$$

$$x^2 + y^2 + z^2 > (x - 1)^2 + (y - 1)^2 + (z - 1)^2$$

$$0 > -2x + 1 - 2y + 1 - 2z + 1$$

$$2(x + y + z) > 3$$

$$(x + y + z) > 1.5$$

This follows intuition, since x, y, and z contribute equally in symmetric fashion as the white point $[1, 1, 1]$ is approached from the origin, and the point of indecision is located at $[.5, .5, .5]$. For equations that test along the remaining three body diagonals, intuition is less helpful but the above approach remains useful in eliminating quadratic and radical terms.

The remaining diagonal endpoints are the cyclic coordinate permutations of the line $[(1, 0, 0); (0, 1, 1)]$, which yield three boolean tests of the form

$$\sqrt{(x-1)^2 + (y-0)^2 + (z-0)^2} > \sqrt{(x-0)^2 + (y-1)^2 + (z-1)^2}$$

$$(x-1)^2 + y^2 + z^2 > x^2 + (y-1)^2 + (z-1)^2$$

$$-2x + 1 > -2y + 1 - 2z + 1$$

$$-2x + 2y + 2z > 1$$

$$-x + y + z > 0.5$$

Algorithm Design

A four-bit code word may be formed directly from the signed tests by ORing successive code bits into a code word in a manner analogous to Sutherland's viewpoint clipping (Newman and Sproull, 1979). Bit signs and positions within the code word may be complemented and permuted arbitrarily, yielding $2^4 \cdot 4!$ or 384 distinct codings, corresponding to rotations and inversions of the solid. An important property of all codings is that any color's complement may be selected by complementing (or subtracting into 17) in that color's code word. Put another way, given a color C and its complement C', then Code $[C]$ + Code$[C']$ = 1111 and Red$[C]$ + Red$[C']$ = 1.0, and so on. To find a "canonical" representation of choice a boolean test polarity is chosen, which assigns black and white the codes 0000 and 1111, respectively. The two vacant code positions are of the permuted form 0001 and 1110 and relate to the fact that only seven (and not eight) distinct partitions appear in any hemisphere. Permutation of the dissimilar bit yields vacant code words at the consecutive mid-table locations 0111 and 1000, suggesting their potential use in recording two mid-level grayscale values. At this point the three primary colors occur within the first eight entries of the table. A final permutation allows them to appear in RGB order. The primaries are necessarily not consecutive because code words differing in only one bit position (as with successive even and odd integers) represent neighboring partitions, yet the primaries are nonadjacent. Thus, 14 of 16 possible code words are

V_r, V_g, V_b: **array** [0..15] **of real**;
$V_r \leftarrow$ [0.,.5 ,.5 , 1.,.0 , 0., 0.,.5 ,.5 , 1., 1., 1., 0.,.5 ,.5 ,1.];
$V_g \leftarrow$ [0.,.5 , 0., 0.,.5 , 1., 0.,.5 ,.5 , 1., 0.,.5 , 1., 1.,.5 ,1.];
$V_b \leftarrow$ [0., 0.,.5 , 0.,.5 , 0., 1.,.5 ,.5 , 0., 1.,.5 , 1.,.5 , 1.,1.];
map the floating triple $(R, G, B) \rightarrow (R', G', B')$ *thereby quantizing*
it; the return value is the vertex code / colormap index
integer function remap14(**real**: R, G, B, R', G', B')
    begin
    code: **integer** $\leftarrow$ 0;
    if $R + G + B > 1.5$ **then** code $\leftarrow$ code **bit-or** 8;
    if $-R + G + B > 0.5$ **then** code $\leftarrow$ code **bit-or** 4;
    if $R - G + B > 0.5$ **then** code $\leftarrow$ code **bit-or** 2;
    if $R + G - B > 0.5$ **then** code $\leftarrow$ code **bit-or** 1;
    $R' \leftarrow V_r$[code];
    $G' \leftarrow V_g$[code];
    $B' \leftarrow V_b$[code];
    return[code];
    end

Figure 8.   RGB onto RGB (four-bit).

employed. Absence (and potential treatment) of the remaining two table entries is discussed under the section "gray interior points." At this point a practical, standardized mapping of RGB onto a space of four-bit precision has been defined: the original goal. The software procedure that generates a code word and companion target vertex value appears in Fig. 8.

The function *remap14* is robust in that the vector $[.4\overline{9}, .4\overline{9}, .4\overline{9}]$ maps onto $[0, 0, 0]$ and the vector $[.5, .5, .5]$ maps onto $[1, 1, 1]$. In general, any point $[t, t, t]$ along the achromatic axis (as with gray-level input data for display on a color monitor) can generate only the black or white points as representative output. No multiplications take place in the routine, which makes for ready adaptation to scaled-integer values. For the common case of (unsigned) eight-bit color components, care must be taken because both the scaled value 1.5 and intermediate variable expressions may exceed the maximum unsigned byte value $2^8 - 1 = 255$.

The function *remap14* returns the code word (useful for the actual colormap value given to the frame buffer memory) and fills the true color in variables R', G', B', of use as when halftoning by error diffusion (Floyd and Steinberg, 1975). Because the decoding tables contain only three distinct values it is tempting to infer table elements implicitly through additional boolean logic. However, direct look-up is both faster and essential for use with color spaces not possessing six-fold symmetry about the achromatic axis (as with RGB and HSV). As an additional benefit, the use of a table allows the precomputation of 14 color descriptors in a chosen space of representation based on the RGB values listed in Fig. 3. An implementation accommodating RGB input pixels of arbitrary precision is part of the IM Raster Toolkit made available through the University of Waterloo (Paeth, 1986a, 1986b, 1987).

Three versus Four Bits

By way of comparison, the three-bit mapping case is seen to be of identical form with the above, except that a table look-up step is not needed to remap the code word into a representative set of values. This happens because in the three-bit case the half-space tests divide the three Cartesian axes allowing each bit in the code word to generate an associated axis value directly (Fig. 9).

This illustration makes it clear that the often programmed three-bit Cartesian case (most often conceptualized as a three-channel quantization operation) is of identical form to the four-bit polyhedral algorithm described—it is the minimal case common to both approaches. The major difference in the methods regards the orientation of the test planes. Whereas the three-bit version uses the cube's three planes of mirror

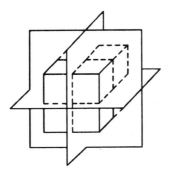

Figure 9.   Cube as Cartesian and polyhedral model.

symmetry, the four-bit case uses the cube's four axes of three-fold rotational symmetry.

Complexity Analysis

The three- and four-bit cases are computationally optimal in that the number of plane tests T for vertices V matches the information theoretic lower bound $T = \lceil \log_2 V \rceil$ exactly. They are optimal in an implementation sense because they are devoid of any conditional logic. That is, results of previous plane tests do not drive subsequent decisions. This complete decoupling implies that the half-space testing (program **if** statements) may be executed in parallel on hardware allowing concurrent computation. Each test contributes $0.25 \cdot \log_2 14$ bits of information, or 0.952, yielding an information content of 3.81 bits from the four boolean tests.

Gray Interior Points

As noted, the gray point is not represented in the choice of colors and cannot appear under this model. In fact, the point $[.5, .5, .5]$ is the common intersection of the test planes for both program routines. Because the target color vertices are created on the surface of a "color sphere" that circumscribes our polyhedron, there is no provision for allocating interior points. This is a major obstacle in generalizing this method. Explicit methods for interior testing are expensive. For instance, identifying the central gray subcube requires six inequality tests. Reduction to four by employing a bounding tetrahedron still doubles the total number of plane tests and complicates the code. Methods of extension to our color polyhedra approach will appear in a forthcoming paper (Paeth, in press).

Cartesian Quantization versus Polyhedra

For a 16-entry color table the lack of gray is not a major liability: a competitive $2 \times 3 \times 2$ Cartesian table (weighted in the green) cannot place any interior points, as at least one axis (the red and blue components) can represent only the extrema of their interval. Moreover, only 12 points are created.

On frame buffers providing additional precision the Cartesian approach becomes desirable. For instance, on a hypothetical five-bit device (32 colors) an excellent choice of table allocation is a $3 \times 3 \times 3$ Cartesian color "Rubik's" cube, which fills the table nearly to capacity (84%) and further places a target point (with surrounding cubical volume) at the central point (.5, .5, .5). (See Figure 2 in the Gem "Proper Treatment of Pixels as Integers" on page 254.) This approach requires as a worst-case six boolean tests for the six planes versus the theoretical lower bound of five. The operation may also proceed in parallel (three processes with each performing two consecutive plane tests) and the logic may be arranged conditionally so that a test point located above the higher (or beneath the lower) test plane need not be considered further. This reduces the total number of tests to three for a select cube corner (such as white) and lowers the average-case performance to 1.67 tests per axis, or to five overall. As with the three-bit case the target output color R', G', B' may be formed directly on a per-axis basis without resort to a code word. For efficiency reasons a 64-entry sparse table is still desirable to compute the LUT index defined as $I = 9R + 3G + B$, thereby forming a Cartesian product while avoiding integer multiplication.

It is not surprising that the eight vertices of the cube are present in all higher-order Cartesian models. What is surprising is that the 14 cubocta-hedron vertices can be derived from the $3 \times 3 \times 3$ Cartesian cube. This is possible because the latter's point lattice may be regarded as the union of a cube's vertices (8), face midpoints (6), edge midpoints (12) and central point (1), totaling 27. Here the cuboctahedron vertices are formed by the union of only the first two spatial symmetry groups.

Summary

An optimally efficient testing method for mapping RGB colors onto a reduced palette of four bits is described. Implementation is straightfor-ward and the predefined set of 14 target colors is highly symmetric. The exposition provides a good overview into descriptive solid geometry and the symmetries of cubic lattices.

See also A Fast HSL-to-RGB Transform (448); A Simple Method for Color Quantization: Octree Quantization (287)

See Appendix 2 for C Implementation (718)

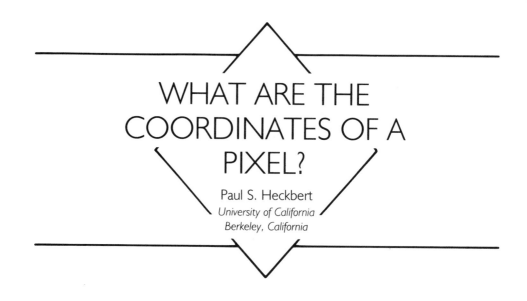

WHAT ARE THE COORDINATES OF A PIXEL?

Paul S. Heckbert
University of California
Berkeley, California

Did you ever get confused deciding whether pixels were centered at integer coordinates or centered halfway between the integers? We present here a consistent answer to this question.

When modeling, we use real numbers, but pixels have integer coordinates, so somewhere during rendering we must quantize the coordinates to integer values. How, exactly, do we perform this mapping? *Do we round or truncate?* Consistency is vital, but making the better choice is also important. This may seem like a petty question, but failure to address it can lead to misalignment, gaps or overlap between objects, or edge effects at the screen border. The question is especially important if we are anti-aliasing.

To clarify the problem, we distinguish between discrete images and continuous images, and also between discrete coordinates and continuous coordinates. A *discrete image* is an array of pixels, the sort of image with which we're familiar in computer graphics and image processing, and a *continuous image* is a function defined over a continuous domain, as in optics or the real world. In computer graphics we take a geometric description of a continuous image (for example, a list of polygons with floating point coordinates) and sample it at a discrete array of points to create a discrete image. The discrete image we render is an approximation of the continuous image. We call the coordinates in the discrete image *discrete coordinates* and the coordinates in the continuous image *continuous coordinates*. Discrete coordinates take on integer values at the sample points, which are the pixel centers. The mapping question is now reduced to a choice of phase (displacement) between continuous and discrete coordinates.

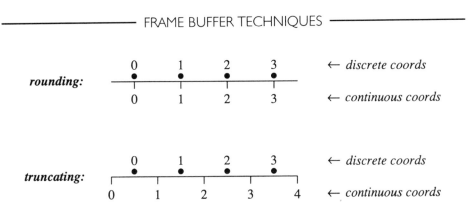

Figure 1. Rounding and truncating schemes for coordinate conversion.

If we round when converting floating point continuous coordinates to discrete coordinates, this is equivalent to aligning the continuous and discrete axes. Figure 1 shows the rounding mapping at top, for a hypothetical frame buffer four pixels on a side, with pixel centers marked by bullets. Rounding seems attractive at first, because continuous coordinates and discrete coordinates are equal. Unfortunately, the continuous range corresponding to our hypothetical frame buffer, using rounding, is the awkward range of $-.5$ to 3.5.

The better mapping choice is truncation, or more accurately, flooring, where continuous coordinates are converted to discrete coordinates by taking the floor function. In this scheme, there is a half-pixel phase shift between continuous coordinates and discrete coordinates as can be seen in Fig. 1, bottom. Continuous coordinates take on integer values halfway between pixels. The pixel with discrete coordinates (x, y) has its center at continuous coordinates $(x + 1/2, y + 1/2)$. Assuming as a first approximation that we reconstruct using a one-pixel-wide box filter, the continuous coordinate domain of pixel (x, y) is from x to $x + 1$ in x and from y to $y + 1$ in y. For our hypothetical frame buffer, the continuous coordinate range using truncation is 0 to 4—simpler numbers than with rounding. The simplicity of the coordinate range facilitates image scaling and other transformations.

In summary, both continuous and discrete coordinates have their place. Continuous coordinates are most appropriate when modeling, that is, when one is concerned with geometry, not with pixels. Discrete coordinates are most useful when working close to the pixel level, as in scan conversion or image processing. Note that discrete coordinates are not always integers: it is often useful to use floating point variables for discrete coordinates. When writing graphics software it is vital to be conscious of whether you are using continuous coordinates or discrete coordinates.

To convert from continuous to discrete or vice versa, where c is the continuous coordinate and d is the discrete coordinate,

$$d = floor\ (c)$$

$$c = d + \tfrac{1}{2}.$$

I developed the above dualist view of pixel coordinates while working on an image zoom algorithm at Xerox PARC in 1988. Thanks also to Alvy Ray Smith at Pixar for reinforcing my reverence for the pixel.

See also A Digital "Dissolve" Effect (221); Circles of Integral Radius on Integer Lattices (57); Precalculating Addresses for Fast Fills, Circles, and Lines (285)

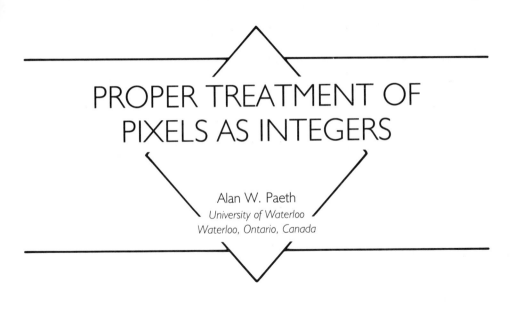

PROPER TREATMENT OF PIXELS AS INTEGERS

Alan W. Paeth
University of Waterloo
Waterloo, Ontario, Canada

Overview

Pixels are all-too-often viewed as collections of hardware bits, to be shifted, masked, and mapped. This three-part discussion illustrates shortcomings of this conceptual approach and suggests efficient alternatives, which give rise to more useful forms.

Proper Interpretation of Pixel Integers

The interpretation of the data bits present within any pixel is arbitrary. Most often, they are treated as unsigned integers used to specify intensity across a linear domain, such as *black → white*. A useful convention regards this integer as lying along the closed, unit interval [0..1]. Choice of this interval is consistent with the domains used in various color spaces, including XYZ and LUV space defined by the CIE (Commission International L'Eclairage) and the HSV space well-known in computer graphics (Smith, 1978). In the case of color pixels, three independent axes are represented along the interval [0.0..1.0].

Unfortunately, many software tools in existence implicitly adopt the interval [0..1). This commonly occurs within software that employs bit shifting as an efficient, reversible means to map between pixels with differing precisions. For instance, four-bit pixels on the range [0..15] may be mapped into eight-bit pixels on the range [0..255] by left shifting four bits, such that $1111 \rightarrow 11110000$. Right-shifting reconstructs the original

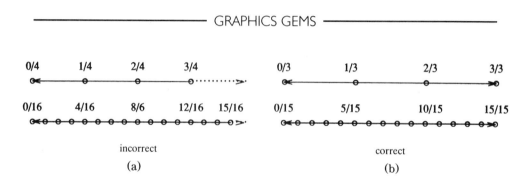

Figure 1. Pixel integers along the unit axis.

data without roundoff error—an important virtue. Moreover, under this scheme a pixel of select value (for example, 5/8 under a three-bit precision) may be represented exactly on any system of higher precision (the value 5/8 exists under three or more bits of precision). Here an n-bit pixel representation divides the unit axis into intervals of length 2^{-n}; converting between precisions m and n requires an (unsigned) multiplication of 2^{n-m}, which is conveniently represented as a left shift of $n - m$ bits. A major failing with this system is that white cannot be represented (see Fig. 1a). To take the common, worst case occurring with two-level bitmaps, mapping one-bit pixels onto eight bits yields the values 0.0 and 0.5, as the binary value .1 remains .100 when zeros are inserted from the right.

The proper approach substitutes the divisor $2^n - 1$ for the partitioning of the unit axis (see Fig. 1b). The adoption of this model yields a symmetric representation interval [0..1] that is closed under the operations complementation (with $\bar{x} = 1 - x$) and multiplication. This yields a number of benefits, notably the proper representation of the white point at 1.0. As an example, with $n = 8$, black and white in this system are 0/255 and 255/255, respectively, and *not* 0/256 and 255/256. Note that binary (one-bit) data under this scheme represent 0.0 and 1.0 exactly.

Adoption of this system means replacing bit shifts (multiplications by a value $2^{\pm m}$) by general multiplication and division. This is not a severe speed penalty. In practice, a scaling table can be constructed and a look-up operation used to find the appropriate mapped value. As with the previous method, mapping to a system of higher bit precision and back to the original system introduces no roundoff error.

Exact representation under the higher system is more difficult to achieve. When scaling up to a system of exactly twice the number of bits, it is guaranteed. Here the higher system $2^{2n} - 1$ can be factored as $(2^n - 1)(2^n + 1)$. The left-hand factor is the lower system, and the right-hand factor is simply an integral scale value. For instance, $n = 4$ bit data represents intensity values spaced by $1/15$. When scaling to $n = 8$ bit precision, $2^n + 1 = 17$, so scaling is by 17. Thus, $white_4$ (15) becomes $white_8$ (255) because $255 = 15 \times 17$. Similarly, the mapping between pixel indices of two- and four-bit precision (as appearing in Fig. 1b) merely requires multiplying or dividing by five.

In general, exact representation of all pixels under a lower system of m bits is possible in a higher n-bit system whenever n is a multiple of m. That is, $2^m - 1$ divides $2^n - 1$ *iff* m divides n, meaning that white in the lower system must divide white in the higher system. To illustrate this assertion rather than prove it rigorously, consider this: since 4 is a factor of 12, we assert that four-bit data has an exact representation in a twelve-bit system. Representing the factors $2^{12} - 1$ and $2^4 - 1$ in binary, 111111111111 can be divided by 1111 giving 000100010001, or 273. Thus, $4095 = 15 \times 273$, and the representation for white is still exact. More generally, multiplying any value in the four-bit system by 273 yields exact representation in the twelve-bit system.

Nonlinear Pixel Mappings

Nonlinear subdivision along an axis of representation is a worthwhile departure from the above first-order model. For instance, use of logarithmic encoding of pixels records intensities as "optical density"; this is a common practice in photometry. Here $P = \log_b I$ where P is the encoded pixel value, I is the intensity it represents, and $b = 0.1$ is the chosen base. It follows directly that the inverse map is $I = b^P$. The latter function may be made implicit in frame buffer look-up tables, allowing log-encoded pixel data to be stored internally and viewed directly. This approach has a number of benefits. First, because $\log(a) + \log(b) + \cdots + \log(n) = \log(a \times b \times \cdots \times n)$, summing images in encoded form yields the consecutive product of their constituent linear intensities, also in encoded form. Composition in this fashion models the physical superimpositioning of film transparencies, in which total transmitted light is computed by multiplying by the transparency of each successive media (Beer's Law). Second, the adjacent intensities represented by discretized pixels P and $P + 1$ differ by a constant ratio, because $b^{(P+1)}/b^{(P)} = b$ for any P. This means that quantization effects (visible steps in brightness) are not biased toward any part of the dynamic intensity range. The approach also has drawbacks. Input pixels of $I = 0$ (no light or full opacity) cannot be encoded under any base, as $\log 0 \rightarrow -\infty$. Also, summing two intensities I_1 and I_2 linearly must be computed by first returning to the linear domain and then re-encoding: $\log_b(I_1 + I_2) = \log_b(b^{\log_b I_1} + b^{\log_b I_2})$. In general, complex operations on the encoded domain will require these two recoding steps.

Useful alternatives exist, which resemble $\log x$ and which feature reduced quantization noise while lacking the latter's discontinuity at zero. Shifting and scaling the input domain gives the form $\log_b 1 + \mu x$ in which μ is an arbitrary scaling parameter. This function maps zero onto zero for any base; a unique choice of base fully constrains the function so $F: [0..1] \rightarrow [0..1]$, a valuable property. The correct choice is $F_\mu(x) = \log(1 + \mu x)/\log(1 + \mu)$, found by applying the identities $\log_{1+\mu}(1 + \mu) = 1$ and $\log_{1+\mu}(x) = \log_n(x)/\log_n(1 + \mu)$. Here the log is of arbitrary base; the denominator becomes a suitably scaled constant. The μ parameter may be tuned to set the slope at zero: $F_\mu'(0) = \mu/\ln(1 + \mu)$. In practice, $\mu = 255$ is a good choice and closely approximates the piecewise-linear $\mu-255$ law encoding used in digital telephony throughout North America. The latter maps voice data quantized at 12-bits precision onto eight bits for long distance transmission with increased channel capacity, and minimizes quantization effects otherwise present at low volumes.

A similar approach has been used successfully by the author for the accurate offset-press reproduction of digital color imagery to be included in ACM TOG journals (July, 1987). Here the original pixels of 12-bit linear precision showed marked step contouring at low levels when linearly coded at eight-bit precision, because pixel values differing by one unit in adjacent dark regions showed a distracting intensity step of roughly 6%. A custom display tool supporting both $\mu-255$ law input encoding plus CRT gamma correction reduced these effects to almost imperceptible levels and simultaneously fitted the high-precision linear data into a film recorder, which supported only eight-bit pixel channels. The equations used to encode pixels under $\mu-255$ law appear below; the fourth equation was used to ready data for the custom display tool described.

$$y = \frac{1}{8} \log_2(1 + 255x) \qquad\qquad M: [0.0..1.0] \rightarrow [0.0..1.0]$$

$$y = \frac{\text{sign}(x)}{8} \log_2(1 + 255|x|) \qquad M: [-1.0..1.0] \rightarrow [-1.0..1.0]$$

$$y = \frac{255}{8} \log_2(1 + x) \qquad\qquad M: [0..255] \rightarrow [0..255]$$

$$y = \frac{255}{8} \log_2\left(1 + \frac{17}{273}x\right) \qquad M: [0..4095] \rightarrow [0..255]$$

The fourth equation was inverted to create the correct look-up table (LUT) entries. This operation prefaces the customary inverse transformation used to linearize film/CRT response using the "gamma" model. The forward transformation of the latter was derived empirically from densitometry of film samples giving $I = V^{\gamma}$ with $\gamma_{system} = 2.8$, in which I is illuminated film intensity and V is CRT drive voltage (equivalent to LUT entries on systems with linear DAC, that is, Digital to Analog Converters). The film recorder provided $2^8 = 256$ LUT entries with values on the range $[0..1023]$ specifying linear drive voltage in 10-bit precision. Here is the pseudo-code used to fill the LUT:

```
lut: array [0..255] of integer;
for i ← 0 to 255 do
   γ: real ← 2.8; empirically derived
   t: real ← (1/255) × (2^(8i/255) − 1)
   lut[i] ← round (1023 × t^(1/γ))
endloop
```

253

Color Pixels and Cartesian Products

When a single pixel is used to represent a RGB color, most often three integer values are derived, which form the color primaries directly. The "quick and dirty" approach to uniform division of the color space (so that R, G, and B can be treated separately) very often slices up eight-bit pixels into three bits for red and green, and two bits for blue (the primary for which the eye is least sensitive).

This is an unnecessary oversimplification that leaves blue with only two mid-range intensities, which suggests itself when color is regarded as "bits" at the hardware level, not as "N discrete intensity steps." This approach is further suggested because the pixel channels for R, G, and B can be written individually through the proper setting of the write mask, but in practice, the color-mapped pixel is normally written as a single byte, not as three consecutive "inking" passes. One useful property of this power-of-two approach to color axis allocation is that a number of gray values are always present (that is, $R = G = B$) because the channel precisions are all multiples of each other.

A better approach is to form a color table containing a Cartesian product of intensities by using axis division that is not necessarily a power of two. For example, taking red $= [0..5]$, green $= [0..7]$, blue $= [0..4]$ (each suitably normalized to represent intensities on the range $[0.0..1.0]$) yields a color table of $6 \times 8 \times 5 = 240$ entries. Compared to the |RRRGGGBB| bit-allocation approach, the blue axis shows a 50% increase in mid-range specification.

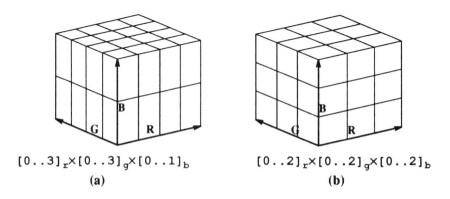

$$[0..3]_r \times [0..3]_g \times [0..1]_b$$
(a)

$$[0..2]_r \times [0..2]_g \times [0..2]_b$$
(b)

Figure 2. Cartesian color cubes.

General adoption of this method allows for more efficient use of the color map. For instance, consider the reduced scenario of 12 colors (as on a four-bit system in which four colors have been previously dedicated to the operating system). Here the bit plane scheme must allocate one bit to each of the three channels, totaling eight colors and leaving four unused. A better treatment would be to form the product $2 \times 3 \times 2$ with the axis of higher precision given to the green channel. Similarly, on a $2^5 = 32$ bit color system the allocation scheme |RRGGB| provides only on/off values in blue (see Fig. 2a). A better allocation is a $3 \times 3 \times 3$ volume, which additionally allows representation of mid-level gray (see Fig. 2b).

The latter approach is taken in the IM raster tool (Paeth, 1986a, 1986b, 1987), which provides *X*-window display of files containing color information at arbitrary bit precision. Here the creation of a systematic, uniform color space is essential in providing a shared color map common to all windows on the machine. As the hardware platform supports either four- or eight-bit color indices, conversion of input pixel precision onto the range [0.0..1.0] takes place as described in the first part of this Gem. At run-time, the low-level allocation routine is requested to build a product of evenly distributed factors whose product is no larger than $27/32 \approx 84.4\%$ of the hardware color table size. In practice, four- and eight-bit display architectures call the color allocator with values 13 or 216 respectively, yielding the factors $12 = (2\ 3\ 2)$ and $216 = (6\ 6\ 6)$ with channel allocation done in GRB order. Appearing in Fig. 3, the code has

split N into three (near) identical values R, G, and B
such that $N \geq R \times G \times B$ and $G \geq R \geq B$

Max ← Med ← Min ← 0;
while Min × Min × Min ≤ N **do** Min ← Min + 1;
Min ← Min − 1;
while Med × Med × Min ≤ N **do** Med ← Med + 1;
Med ← Med − 1;
Max ← n/(Min × Med);
G ← Max;
R ← Med;
B ← Min;

Figure 3.   Factoring into a Cartesian triple.

provision to alter the allocation order, which is occasionally useful when rendering predominantly sky-blue images.

The allocation $216 = (6\ 6\ 6)$ guarantees the existence of a gray axis along the body diagonal of the underlying color cube. The largest set possible on an eight-bit architecture is $6 \times 7 \times 6 = 252$. All factorings show significantly improved blue precision in comparison to the four possible blue values implicit under the common "three bits red and green, two for blue" scheme.

Extensions

The generalized use of Cartesian products may be combined with the nonlinear axis spacing described previously. This yields a nonlinear spacing of orthogonal planes, which define a color space in which points (color descriptors) lie in regions of varying density. This makes possible accurate color representation on frame buffers, which lack the pixel precision necessary for high-precision color (24-bit RGB), but which minimally provide color table indexing on a per-channel basis. Heckbert (1982) describes a means to create such custom color tables in which the density of color descriptors in the space increases in regions of commonly occurring colors within the input data.

Generally, nonlinear Cartesian products may be constructed *a priori*, which satisfy general constraints in the absence of any input data set. Two approaches are described by Paeth (1989a, 1989b); one allows the precise representation of a gray axis for color spaces of high nonlinearity as encountered on color hardcopy devices; the other is a symmetric space based on the theory of Chebyshev minimax approximation.

In their most general setting, "pixels as integers" serve as color table indices into a space that is both nonlinear and non-Cartesian: points may be distributed arbitrarily. A systematic, nonorthogonal approach to color descriptors and pixel indexing is described in the Gem "Mapping RGB Triples onto Four Bits" in this volume.

See Appendix 2 for C Implementation (**719**)

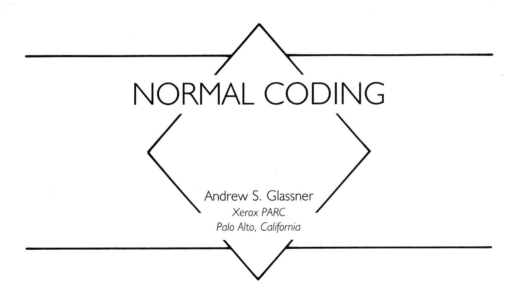

NORMAL CODING

Andrew S. Glassner
Xerox PARC
Palo Alto, California

A common technique for interactive lighting and surface design is to use an approach called *normal coding*. Using this technique, you can write a tool that gives the user interactive control over the lighting in a 3D scene, with options to add and delete lights, and to change the color and position of each light. The user may also interactively change some of the surface properties of the objects in the scene, such as specular and diffuse reflectivity.

The secret behind such an interactive system is that it is all done through the color map. Assume an eight-bit deep frame buffer, and an image rendered by a point-sampling Z-buffer (that is, there is exactly one nearest visible surface per pixel). When computing an image, typically we store the depth of the nearest visible surface in the Z-buffer, and the shaded color of that surface in the image buffer.

Suppose that we could turn any surface normal into an eight-bit number. Then instead of storing the color of the nearest object in the image buffer, we can store the eye-space surface normal of that object. When the final image is completed, each pixel in the image buffer contains the encoded eight-bit surface normal of the nearest visible object; we might rename the image buffer the *normal buffer*. The contents of the normal buffer will generally not look anything like a picture.

To make an image from the normal buffer, recall that there are only 256 different surface normals in the buffer—after all, each pixel is only eight bits deep. If the normal at some pixel has the bit pattern 00001001, it will be displayed on the screen with the color stored in color-map entry

9. To create an image, we need only compute the shading appropriate to each stored normal, and store that shade in the correct color-map entry. If a light is moved, we recompute the shading on each of the 256 normals, and write that new shading into the color map. The image is thus immediately updated to include the new lighting.

To make this scheme work, we need a way to encode and decode normals, or convert from normals to eight-bit entries and back again. This note suggests one way that works well.

Although this technique makes for a great interactive tool, it has some restrictions:

- You get only 256 unique normals in your image.

- You cannot distinguish between objects.

- You cannot use "local" light sources (that is, those with a position in space in addition to direction), since only the normal of the visible surface is stored at each point, not the spatial location of the surface.

- The image will show banding due to the quantization of normals.

- The interactive image will show aliasing artifacts, since there is only one sample per pixel.

Some of these problems can be overcome with some additional storage and processing; such remedies are discussed after we present the basic technique.

Some Encoding Methods

There are a couple of principles that we should keep in mind when building a normal encoding scheme. Typically we will not want to use all 256 entries in the color map. Often the image in the frame buffer will only occupy part of the screen; menus, controls, and a cursor may all be visible, and they must all have colors allocated. I suggest at a minimum that colors 0 and 255 be left untouched; typically these are used for black and white, to provide backgrounds, borders, text, and so forth. If a program decides to change these colors, that's fine, but the normal encoding process should leave them alone.

There are many ways to convert a normal into an eight-bit quantity. Perhaps the most obvious approaches are direct, 1-to-1 invertible mappings. Assume that all normals have unit length (that is, $x^2 + y^2 + z^2 = 1$). Most approaches save bits by encoding just the x and y components (we can easily recover the z component from x and y since $z = \sqrt{1 - x^2 - y^2}$; we choose the sign of z so that the normal points back to the viewer).

For example, consider the x component. We will use four bits to encode x, mapping -1.0 to 0, and $+1.0$ to 15. So x_e, the encoded value for x, is found by $x_e \leftarrow floor[(x + 1)*7.5]$. Similarly, $y_e \leftarrow floor[(y + 1)*7.5]$. We can combine these two four-bit values into a single eight-bit composite byte by storing x_e in the high four bits and y_e in the low four: $c \leftarrow (x_e*16) + y_e$. This sum represents c, the byte that encodes the normal.

To decode c back into components, first turn the high and low bits back into individual numbers: $x_e \leftarrow floor(c/16)$, $y_e \leftarrow c - (16*x_e)$. Now $x \leftarrow (x_e/7.5) - 1$ and $y \leftarrow (y_e/7.5) - 1$. As we saw above, $z \leftarrow \sqrt{1 - x^2 - y^2}$.

Another approach is to encode the x and y components of each normal in polar coordinates r and θ, four bits each ($r \leftarrow \sqrt{x^2 - y^2}$, $\theta \leftarrow arc\,tan(y/x)$). As before, we scale each of r and θ into numbers from 0 to 15 and store them in the low and high halves of the byte, as before.

Yet another encoding is to use a single value representing 1 of 256 positions along an equal-area spiral, which starts at the origin and winds outward. Each position along this spiral represents the head of a normal, which begins at the origin.

These approaches all require a special test to avoid the foreground and background colors. Some also have wasted entries. For example, consider the meaning of bit pattern $c = 11111110$ using the first encoding. Here, $x_e = 1111 = 15$, so $x = +1.0$, and $y_e = 1110 = 14$, so $y = 0.8666667$. Clearly there is no unit normal with these x and y components; in fact every bit pattern $1111xxxx$ is meaningless except for 11110000. So we've wasted 14 possible encodings (there are 16 possible sequences for $xxxx$ above; 1111 is reserved, and 0000 is okay, leaving 14 wasted).

Each bit pattern that we can't use gives us a smaller available range of normals to represent our image, making it look slightly worse.

A Better Encoding Method

The technique I use is to construct a pair of tables, one associating normals with indices, and the other associating indices with normals. To encode a normal, one looks it up in the table, and receives an index number giving the color-map entry for that normal. To decode, one looks up the index number in the other table, which provides a normal. This way the correspondence between normal bit patterns and geometric normals is not direct, and we get a greater range of possible normals. We can also use more sophisticated or expensive mappings, since they are computed only once and stored in the tables.

This approach is exactly analogous to the use of color maps in eight-bit frame buffers. One way (though not the best) to encode a color in eight bits is to use three bits for red, three bits for green, and two bits for blue (see "Pixels as Integers" in this volume). This would lock us into one particular color space, which directly associates a color with its bit pattern. A more general technique is to use a color map, which allows us to associate any color with any bit pattern; analagously, the technique mentioned here may be thought of as a *normal map*.

What might be the best such normal map or table? A first thought is to space normals equally on the surface of a hemisphere. But remember that we're viewing the image from a single, fixed location, and that the normals have already been transformed into eye space. We want most of the resolution near the normal pointing head-on toward us, and less to the sides, where we can see the changes less clearly. In other words, we want the perceived differences in the normals to be about equal.

One easy approach is to lay a grid over the unit circle, and use normals corresponding to grid centers within the circle. This is much like the first encoding technique described above (using four bits each for x and y), but we don't waste bit patterns that don't correspond to possible normals.

We wish to build two tables: *BtoNTable*[] converts a byte to a normal, and *NtoBTable*[] converts a normal to a byte. To build these tables, we place a grid of fixed size over the unit circle and scan the grid top–down, left–right, looking for cells whose center is within the circle. Suppose we

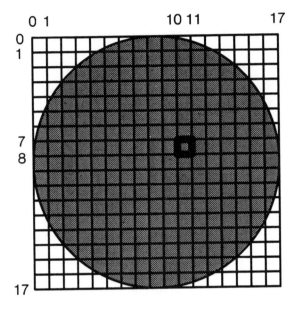

Figure 1. Using a 17-by-17 grid to encode normals. Cell $(10, 7)$ is highlighted.

have a grid 17 units on a side, and the cell under consideration is $(10, 7)$ (see Figs. 1 and 2). The (x, y) coordinates of this cell's normal are found by subtracting the cell's center at $(10.5, 7.5)$ from the circle's center at $(8.5, 8.5)$ and dividing by the radius, giving $((10.5 - 8.5)/8.5, (7.5 - 8.5)/8.5) = (0.2352941, - 0.1176471)$. Since in this case $x^2 + y^2 < 1$, this cell is within the unit circle. We can find $z = \sqrt{1.0 - (x^2 + y^2)}$, so the normal at this cell is $(0.2352941, - 0.1176471, 0.9647776)$.

Given that we now have a new normal to encode, how do we build the tables? Assume that table entries $[0 .. s]$ have been filled so far, so this is

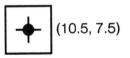 $(10.5, 7.5)$

Figure 2. Cell $(10, 7)$ is defined on the left and right by $x = 10$ and $x = 11$, and above and below by $y = 7$ and $y = 8$. Thus, the center is at $(10.5, 7.5)$.

the $s + 1st$ normal to be encoded. So now $BtoNTable[s + 1] \leftarrow$ $(0.2352941, -0.1176471, 0.9647776)$, which associates index $s + 1$ with this normal.

The other table, $NtoTable$, associates the color-map entry $s + 1$ with a quantized version of this normal. For this table, I use a 2D array corresponding to the quantized (x, y) coordinates that are equal to the cell index, so $NtoBTable[10][7] \leftarrow s + 1$.

On a 17-by-17 grid, 225 entries will be filled this way. Entries 0 and 255 are reserved for foreground and background colors (usually black and white, respectively). The others are available for use by the interactive tool. Table 1 provides the occupancy data for some other grid sizes.

Table 1. Cell Occupancy for Different Grid Sizes.

Size	Number of Cells Occupied	Density
12	112	0.7777778
13	137	0.8106509
14	156	0.7959183
15	177	0.7866667
16	208	0.8125
17*	225	0.7785467
18	256	0.7901235
19	293	0.8116344
20	316	0.79
21	349	0.7913832
22	384	0.7933884
23	421	0.7958412
24	448	0.7777778
25	489	0.7824
26	540	0.7988166
—		
35	973	0.7942857
36	1020	0.787037
37	1085	0.7925493
38	1124	0.7783933
—		
250	49080	0.78528
—		
1000	785456	0.78545

*Recommended for one-byte normal buffers.

262

It is interesting to note that an 18-by-18 grid has exactly 256 valid normals! We drop down one size to provide for the background, foreground, and auxiliary colors mentioned earlier. Note that with the method, a normal such as $(1.0, 0.0, 0.0)$ is never represented, since it lies on the boundary of the grid.

Improving the Method

There are a few things one can do to make life a little easier; we will address the five problems mentioned in the first section.

There's not much to be done about the limit of 256 normals if you have only an eight-bit image buffer. Of course, deeper buffers will provide more normals.

You can work with individual objects in several ways. One way is to allow the user to specify a material description, and apply that to all normals in the scene (so everything in the scene is made of that material). Some rendering programs can produce an object buffer, which contains an integer uniquely identifying the visible object at each pixel. You can set all pixels not equal to some object value to the background color, so only the selected object will change in appearance (the rest of the screen will be the background color). Of course, you'll have to store the original normal buffer so you can bring it back when another object is selected. When calculating a shade for a normal you may use a more complete shading equation, taking into account the object's color, diffuse and specular reflectance, and so on.

I don't have a good solution for handling local light sources; they require spatial information, which can vary on a pixel-by-pixel basis. There may be a more complex encoding scheme using more bits that handles these efficiently.

Banding is an artifact of this technique. Just as with color quantization, one can see bands of equal-normal regions of objects on the screen. This effect can be reduced by adding some low-level noise to each normal before quantization (this is similar to dithering). I have found that using random x and y perturbations in the range $-3/17$ to $+3/17$ gives good results.

If you provide interactive pointing on the screen (that is, in which the user may point to a spot and the light will be moved so it is head-on to that normal), you'll want to average a local region on the screen around the point being picked. This will compensate for both the quantization and the dithering. Another handy feature is to allow the user to point to where the highlight should appear, and then automatically calculate the position of the light to put the highlight at that spot.

I don't have any suggestions about the aliasing due to a single point per pixel. I don't think that's really much of a problem in an interactive tool, anyway—you're not making final images, just setting up parameters.

With some effort, the techniques in this note can be the heart of a useful, interactive lighting design program.

For other discussions of normal encoding and color-map techniques, see Heckbert (1984), and Sloan and Brown (1979).

See also Mapping RGB Triples onto Four Bits (233)

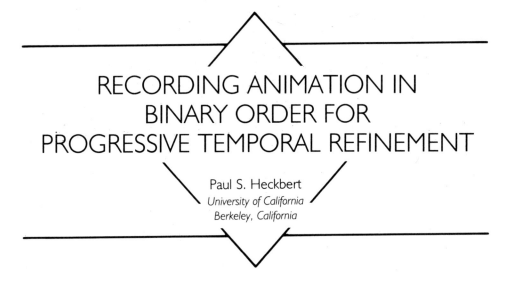

RECORDING ANIMATION IN BINARY ORDER FOR PROGRESSIVE TEMPORAL REFINEMENT

Paul S. Heckbert
University of California
Berkeley, California

Introduction

When recording hardware allows frames to be written multiple times, animation can be recorded in an order that provides progressive temporal refinement: halfway through the recording process, the animation is double-framed, one quarter of the way through recording, the animation is quadruple-framed, one eighth of the way through recording, the animation is octuple-framed, and so on. By recording frames in *binary order*, animation errors can be detected earlier than they would with sequential recording order. The technique is typically the same speed as sequential recording, and it is trivial to implement.

Double-Framed Order

A trick sometimes used in the animation production business is to record a double-framed animation in the process of recording a single-framed animation. This is done by first recording each of the even numbered pictures for two frames, yielding a double-framed animation, and then dropping in the odd numbered pictures for one frame each, yielding the finished, single-framed animation. For example, this *double-framed order* for an eight-frame animation is shown here:

i	0	1	2	3	4	5	6	7
start_frame	0	2	4	6	1	3	5	7
repeat_count	2	2	2	2	1	1	1	1

At each step i, picture number *start_frame* is recorded starting at frame *start_frame* and continuing for *repeat_count* consecutive frames. In this example, we'd have a double-framed animation after step 3 and a single-framed animation after step 7.

This trick requires that the recording hardware allow frames to be recorded multiple times. Most single-frame video recorders have this capability, but film recorders and write-once media do not. If frames are being rendered as they are recorded, then the trick also requires that the rendering process "have no history," that each frame can be rendered independent of the others. The benefit of the trick is that a rough draft of the animation is available halfway through the recording process for checking purposes.

Binary Order

This trick can be extended further to what we call *binary order*: on the way to generating a single-framed animation, we generate a double-framed animation at the halfway point, a quadruple-framed animation at the one-quarter point, an octuple-framed animation at the one-eighth point, and so on. Binary order is illustrated here for an eight-frame animation:

i	0	1	2	3	4	5	6	7
start_frame	0	4	2	6	1	5	3	7
repeat_count	8	4	2	2	1	1	1	1
i base 2	000	001	010	011	100	101	110	111
start_frame base 2	000	100	010	110	001	101	011	111

As shown in the table, step 0 records picture 0 over frames 0–7 (the entire duration of the animation), step 1 records picture 4 over frames 4–7, step 2 records picture 2 over frames 2–3, and so on. The sequence is obvious when i and *start_frame* are written in binary (last two rows of the table). Observe that *start_frame* is the bit-reversal of i, and that *repeat_count* is the largest power of two that divides *start_frame*. Incidentally, bit reversal crops up in many Fast Fourier Transform algorithms. The sequence is also related to breadth-first traversal of a binary tree.

Defining binary order in terms of bit reversal works only when the number of frames is a power of two, so we must generalize bit reversal to arbitrary sequence lengths. This can be done by noting that bit reversal of a sequence of length $n = 2^k$ consists of $k - 1$ stages of shuffles, where each shuffle brings all the even-numbered items to the front and all the odd-numbered items to the back (see Fig. 1, but note that these multi-stage shuffle diagrams are not FFT butterfly diagrams). The multiple-shuffle definition of binary order works for any sequence length. I call this generalization of bit reversal "turning a number inside-out." An algorithm is given here:

> *inside_out: turn a number "inside-out": a generalization of bit-reversal.*
>
> *For n = power of two, this is equivalent to bit-reversal.*
>
> *Turn the number a inside-out, yielding b. If $0 \le a < n$ then $0 \le b < n$. Also return $r = min(n - b,$ largest power of 2 dividing b)*

```
procedure inside_out(n, a: int; b, r: ref int);
note: b and r are returned via call-by-reference
k, m: int;
begin
     m ← n;
     r ← n;
     b ← 0;
     k ← 1;
     while k < n do
          if 2*a ≥ m then begin
            if b = 0 then r ← k;
            b ← b + k;
            a ← a - (m + 1)/2;
            m ← m/2;
          end;
          else m ← (m + 1)/2;
          k ← k*2;
          endloop;
       if r > n - b then r ← n - b;
     endproc;
```

We can now compute binary order for any sequence length. For example,

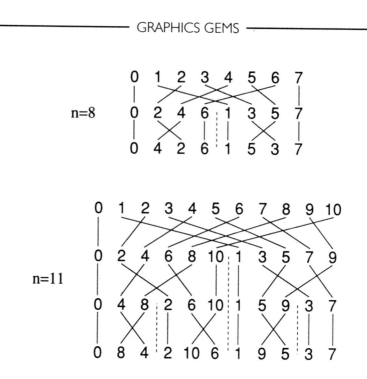

Figure 1. Bit reversal by multi-stage shuffle for sequences of length 8 and 11.

if *nframes* = 11:

i	0	1	2	3	4	5	6	7	8	9	10
start_frame	0	8	4	2	10	6	1	9	5	3	7
repeat_count	11	3	4	2	1	2	1	1	1	1	1

To record an *n*-frame animation in binary order, step a variable i from 0 to $n - 1$, and turn this number inside–out at each step:

```
for i ← 0 to nframes − 1 do
    inside_out(nframes, i, start_frame, repeat_count);
    here record picture number start_frame
        into frames start_frame through start_frame + repeat_count − 1
endloop;
```

Summary

By recording in binary order, the temporal resolution of animation can be progressively refined. If recording is terminated at any time, the animation is still presentable, since the entire duration has been recorded. The method uses one record operation for each frame, so it is as fast as simple, sequential order on most recorders. If frames are being rendered as they are recorded, binary recording order allows rough drafts of the animation to be previewed a fraction of the way through the rendering process, enabling early detection of errors. The ideas here obviously generalize to nontemporal and multidimensional sampling processes.

The technique described here was developed by the author at NYIT in 1981, and was used for video recording there. Others have employed similar techniques for progressive transmission of images, but few have addressed the treatment of data sizes that are not powers of two.

Some related references: Sloan and Tanimoto (1979), Knowlton (1980), and Bergman *et al.* (1986).

See Appendix 2 for C Implementation (**720**)

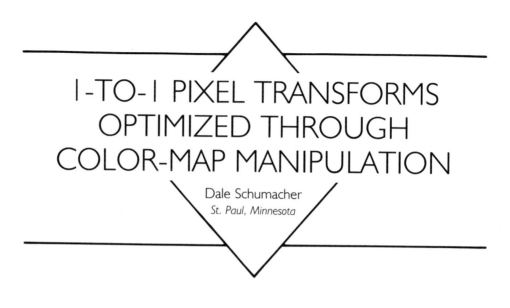

1-TO-1 PIXEL TRANSFORMS OPTIMIZED THROUGH COLOR-MAP MANIPULATION

Dale Schumacher
St. Paul, Minnesota

Many image manipulation suites include a number of tools that are analogous to common darkroom techniques. These tools can all be described as 1-to-1 pixel transforms, since the output pixel value is strictly a function of the input pixel value. When working with discrete pixel values, such as the integer range [0, 255], this kind of transform can often be implemented more efficiently by precomputing a look-up table of output values for every possible input value. As a further optimization, a color map can be used to implement this table look-up in hardware, and thus display the results of the transform at the next screen refresh.

Some examples of typical 1-to-1 transforms are photo-inversion, quantization (also known as posterization), gamma correction, and contrast adjustment. Photo-inversion simply replaces each pixel value with its grayscale opposite, like a photographic negative. Quantization divides the input range into a number of subranges and assigns the same value to each input value in each subrange. This creates a stair-step effect, which reduces the number of distinct output values that are used to represent the image. This kind of transform is often used to move images from a system that supports a large number of gray values, like 256, to a system that supports fewer gray values, like 16. Gamma correction is a nonlinear transform curve, which adjusts for the nonlinear response of image input or output devices to a linear range of inputs. This transform is analogous to overexposure and underexposure in photography. Finally, contrast enhancement is used to make light values lighter and dark values darker at the same time. Upper limits, above which all output will be white, and lower limits, below which all output will be black, define an input range between which output values are assigned in a linear ramp of gray values

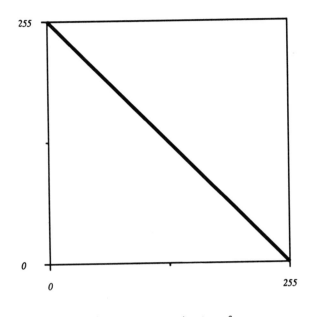

Figure 1. Photo-inversion transform.

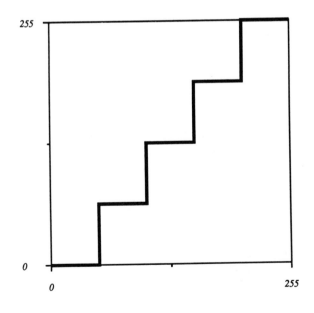

Figure 2. Quantization transform.

using the entire output range. This increases the total contrast of an image.

All of the transforms described above are 1-to-1 pixel transforms since the output pixel value depends only on the input pixel value. Techniques like convolution, which examines a neighborhood of input pixels, and dithering, which depends on the position in the image matrix as well as sometimes depending on the values of nearby pixels, are not 1-to-1 transforms. 1-to-1 transforms can be described as mathematical functions of the input pixel, and thus shown as a function graph. Figures 1, 2, 3, and 4 display input–output graphs of the transform functions described here. The input pixel values are along the horizontal axis and the output pixels values are along the vertical axis.

It is often convenient to work with image pixels as discrete grayscale values in an integer range such as $[0, 255]$ rather than idealized values in the continuous real number range $[0.0, 1.0]$. When implementing 1-to-1 transforms on a discrete input range, the number of possible input pixel values is usually much smaller than the number of pixels in the input image. Therefore, it is more efficient to precompute the output value corresponding to each possible input value, store these values in a look-up table, and use the look-up table to "compute" the output pixel value for each input pixel. This is particularly true as the transformation function gets more complex.

On a graphics system with a color map, the hardware can, in essence, provide a look-up table for you. The frame buffer holds index values into the color map and the color map stores the actual pixel value that corresponds to that index. To take advantage of this feature for implementing 1-to-1 pixel transforms, set aside a range of color map entries equal to the number of possible input pixel values. The index into the reserved color map range now corresponds to an input pixel value. The contents of each of those color map cells determines the actual output value of the pixel on the screen. Simply using that color map range as your precomputed look-up table causes the display hardware to do the look-up for each pixel for you as part of its normal operation. Changes to the color map appear on the screen almost immediately (at the next screen refresh). You never need to examine or change the pixel data actually in the frame buffer since it is always the input pixel value. The output pixel value is determined by the transform function look-up table that is loaded into the color map.

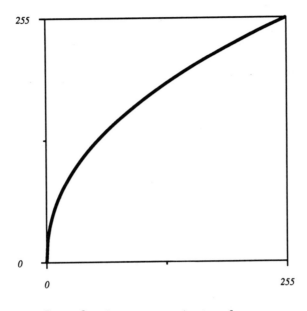

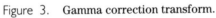

Figure 3. Gamma correction transform.

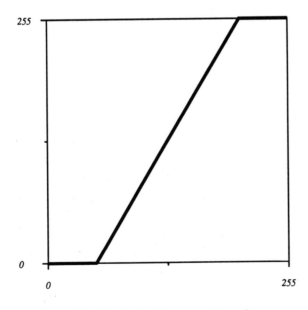

Figure 4. Contrast enhancement transform.

Using a color map to implement 1-to-1 pixel transforms allows real-time manipulation of transform parameters, like the upper and lower bounds of a contrast adjustment or the gamma value of a gamma-correction transform. Visual feedback showing the effect of the transform is immediate. This makes "tweaking" the transform parameters much more of an interactive try-it-and-see process. The results of even very complex transform functions can be shown quickly. When the desired resultant image is obtained, the images can be written to disk along with the color map in effect at the time, thus saving the transformed image.

See also Useful 1-to-1 Pixel Transforms (196)

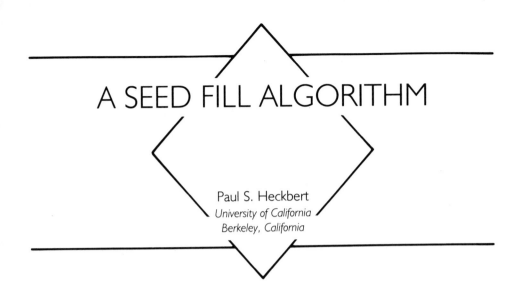

A SEED FILL ALGORITHM

Paul S. Heckbert
University of California
Berkeley, California

Provided here is pseudo code for seed fill. Given a seed point (x, y), it sets this pixel and all of its 4-connected neighbors with the same pixel value to a new pixel value. This is a useful operation in paint programs.

Unfortunately, many of the published algorithms for seed fill stress simplicity to the point of inefficiency. A near-optimal algorithm for seed fill is actually not much more complex than the simplest one, as demonstrated by the code here. Optimality can be measured by the number of times a pixel is read. One of the earliest published algorithms for seed fill reads each pixel twice (Smith, 1979). The algorithm here, which I developed in 1982, reads each pixel just a bit more than once on average, as does the similar algorithm described in Fishkin and Barsky (1985), which gives a good analysis of previous fill algorithms.

Our code stops filling with any change in pixel value, but other stopping rules, such as "stop at a specific pixel value" are often useful. The code could easily be generalized in this way.

> **fill:** *set the pixel at* (x, y) *and all of its 4-connected neighbors*
> *with the same pixel value to the new pixel value* nv.
> *A 4-connected neighbor is a pixel above, below, left, or right of a pixel.*

Pixel: **type** ← **int**;
Window: **type** ← **record** [xmin, ymin, xmax, ymax: **int**];   *inclusive window*

```
procedure fill(
        x, y: int;                                       seed point
        nv: int;                                         new pixel value
        win: Window;                                     screen window
        pixelread: function(x, y: int): Pixel;           procedure for reading pixels
        pixelwrite: procedure(x, y: int; pv: Pixel);     procedure for writing pixels
        );

start, x1, x2, dy: int;
ov: Pixel;                                  old pixel value

Segment: type ← record [y, xl, xr, dy: int];
        Filled horizontal segment of scanline y for xl ≤ x ≤ xr.
        Parent segment was on line y − dy. dy = 1 or −1

max: const int ← 10000;             max depth of stack
stack: array[0..max − 1] of Segment;  stack of filled segments
sp: int ← 0;                        stack pointer

 procedure push(y, xl, xr, dy: int);      push new segment on stack
begin
        if sp < max and y + dy ≥ win.ymin and y + dy ≤ win.ymax then begin
            stack[sp].y ← y;
            stack[sp].xl ← xl;
            stack[sp].xr ← xr;
            stack[sp].dy ← dy;
            sp ← sp + 1;
            end;
        endproc push;

procedure pop(y, xl, xr, dy: ref int);    pop segment off stack
begin
        sp ← sp − 1;
        dy ← stack[sp].dy;
        y ← stack[sp].y + dy;
        xl ← stack[sp].xl;
        xr ← stack[sp].xr;
        endproc pop;
```

begin *procedure fill*
    ov ← pixelread(x, y);   *read pixel value at seed point*
    if ov = nv **or** x < win.xmin **or** x > win.xmax **or** y < win.ymin **or** y > win.ymax **then**
      return;
    push(y, x, x, 1);   *needed in some cases*
    push(y + 1, x, x, −1);   *seed segment (popped 1st)*

    while sp > 0 **do**
      pop segment off stack and fill a neighboring scan line
      pop(y, x1, x2, dy);
      segment of scan line y − dy for x1 ≤ x ≤ x2 was previously filled,
      now explore adjacent pixels in scan line y
      x ← x1;
      while x ≥ win.xmin **and** pixelread(x, y) = ov **do**
          pixelwrite(x, y, nv);
          x ← x − 1;
          endloop;
      if x ≥ x1 **then goto** skip;
      start ← x + 1;
      if start < x1 **then** push(y, start, x1 − 1, −dy);   *leak on left?*
      x ← x1 + 1;
      loop do
          while x ≤ win.xmax **and** pixelread(x, y) = ov **do**
              pixelwrite(x, y, nv);
              x ← x + 1;
              endloop;
          push(y, start, x − 1, dy);
          if x > x2 + 1 **then** push(y, x2 + 1, x − 1, −dy); *leak on right?*
skip: x ← x + 1;
          while x ≤ x2 **and** pixelread(x, y) ≠ ov **do**
              x ← x + 1;
              endloop;
          start ← x;
          while x ≤ x2;
      endloop;
    endproc fill;

See also Filling a Region in a Frame Buffer (278)

See Appendix 2 for C Implementation (**721**)

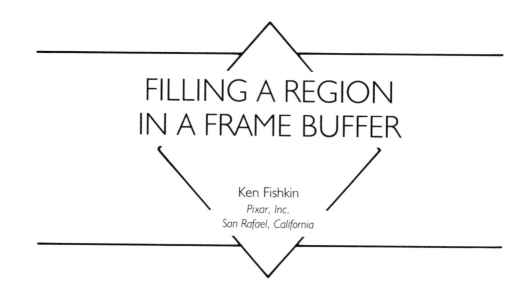

FILLING A REGION
IN A FRAME BUFFER

Ken Fishkin
Pixar, Inc.
San Rafael, California

Fill algorithms are a common graphics utility. They explore through a frame buffer from some seed point, finding all the pixels connected to that seed point that share some property (for example, all being the same color). Some function (for example, changing the color) is invoked exactly once on each pixel found.

This Gem doesn't worry about exactly what property you're looking for, or what function you want to invoke on each pixel: rather, it contains the "controller," which decides which pixels to look at and when. It assumes a boolean-valued function INSIDE(x, y), which returns *true* for any pixel that has the property you want, and a void-valued function SET(x, y), which changes the pixel as you wish. Furthermore, INSIDE(x, y) must return *false* if (x, y) has been SET(); commonly, a one-bit-per-pixel mask is used for this. The INSIDE and SET functions encapsulate the type of fill (interior fill, boundary fill, tint fill ...), while the controller sitting above it, contained in this gem, remains constant.

As terminology, the set of all pixels connected to the seed point that need to be filled comprise the *region*. A scanline of pixels, all of which are in the region, is termed a *span*. Figure 1a shows a sample "before" state of a frame buffer: pixels with a hollow circle inside them have the property we are interested in, and the pixel with a solid circle is the seed point. Figure 1b shows all SET() pixels with a solid circle, and outlines each span with a solid line.

Algorithms that do this exploration all work similarly: they start with a seed span, and then have a stack of unexplored spans, termed *shadows*, which they examine in classic graph-traversal fashion.

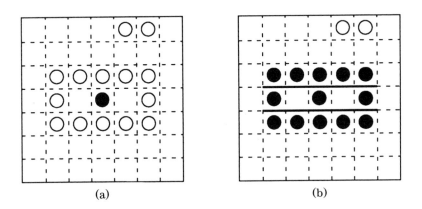

(a)   (b)

Figure 1. Filling a region.

When a shadow is pushed on the stack, it can have one of three possible relations to the span that is pushing it. It can overlap it at both edges (a "*W* turn"), it can overlap it at one edge (a "*U* turn"), or it can overlap it at neither edge (an "*S* turn") (see Fig. 2).

A detailed comparison of the most popular fill algorithms would take too long: the interested reader is referred to Fishkin and Barsky (1985). To make a long story short, they differ in how they handle S, U, and W turns, and in whether they need a bit-per-pixel.

The "canonical" fill algorithm, written by Smith (1982), works fine on S turns, but is nonoptimal on U and W turns. An extension to this, written by Levoy (1981), works fine on S and U turns, but is nonoptimal on W turns. Another, written by Shani (1980), works well on all three turns and doesn't require a bit-per-pixel, but has poor worst-case behavior. The gem you see here works fine on all three turns, and has the best average- and worst-case behavior of the four.

Figure 2. The three kinds of turns.

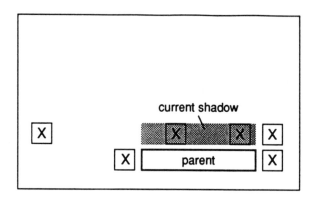

Figure 3.   About to process a shadow.

The algorithm works by maintaining a stack of shadows. A shadow is not an area that *has been* filled, but rather an area that *might be* filled: any sets of fillable pixels that intersect the shadow should be filled. In addition to the shadow, the stack remembers where the parent of the shadow (the "pusher" of this shadow) was; this lets it detect U, S, and W turns.

To process a particular shadow the algorithm marches across the shadow, finding all spans that the shadow touches. It calls SET() on each pixel in the span, and then pushes the new shadows cast by this new span. The pushing order is arranged in such a way that shadows that change direction, that is, shadows that are below an upward-moving span or above a downward-moving span are pushed last (and hence processed first). This is a heuristic based on the observation that turns are relatively rare and usually lead into relatively small areas; by processing them first, stack size is reduced.

To make this description more concrete, consider Figs. 3, 4, and 5. Figure 3 shows a frame buffer as we start to process a shadow. The parent of the shadow is shown, and the X-ed pixels are those pixels that are not inside the region.

In Figure 4, we have found the spans that contacted the current shadow. Then, in Figure 5, we push the new shadows on the stack cast by our two new spans (who become the parents of these new shadows). Child 2 does an S turn with respect to its parent, and hence pushes one shadow. Child 1 does a U turn with respect to its parent, and hence

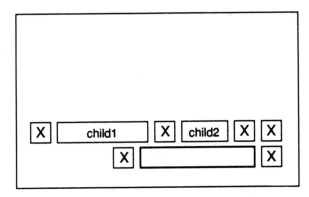

Figure 4.   Found the spans in the shadow.

pushes two shadows: one that continues in the current direction and one that reverses direction and explores the other lobe of the U. That shadow is pushed last (and processed first). Both shadows of child 1 are pushed before either shadow of child 2, as child 1 was discovered before child 2.

A good fill algorithm is one that reads as few pixels as possible. It can be shown that the algorithm in this Gem is optimal if the region has no holes. In other words, if the region is a solid, connected group of pixels, then the algorithm will read the necessary and sufficient set of pixels. In the worst case, a region full of holes (a grid), the algorithm will read 50%

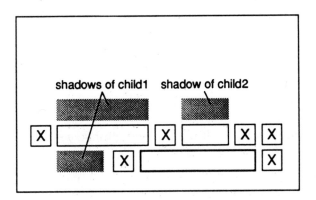

Figure 5.   The new shadows.

more pixels than it has to, as opposed to the 100% and 200% worst-case behaviors of earlier algorithms. One other feature is that the algorithm uses only increments, decrements, negations, assignments, and tests; this is handy for implementation on simple processors.

StackElement: **record** [
    myLx, myRx: **integer** *endpoints of this shadow*
    dadLx, dadRx: **integer** *and of my parent*
    myY: **integer**
    myDirection: TWO_VAL *records whether I'm above or below my parent:*
        can only have values of −1 or +1
];

assume a stack of StackElements,
and a Box-valued variable Limit, which indicates
the limits of the frame buffer window.

macro PUSH(left, right, dadl, dadr, y, dir)
    pushes a new shadow, going from left to right (inclusive) on line y,
    with a parent going from dadl to dadr (inclusive) on line y − dir

macro POP()
    pops the shadow on TOS into local variables
    lx, rx, y, direction, dadLx, and dadRx

macro STACK(dir, dadLx, dadRx, lx, rx, y)
    pushes one more shadow on the stack, given a newly discovered
    span and its parent: this is where S vs. U vs. W turns are handled
    pushrx ← rx + 1; pushlx ← lx − 1;
    PUSH(lx, rx, pushlx, pushrx, y + dir, dir);
    if rx > dadRx
        then PUSH(dadRx + 1, rx, pushlx, pushrx, y − dir, dir) *U turn to the right*
    if lx < dadLx
        then PUSH(lx, dadLx − 1, pushlx, pushrx, y − dir, dir) *U turn to the left*
    a W turn is just two U turns: both "if"s would evaluate true.

    main: fill a region with seed at (seedx, seedy)
Fill(seedx: **integer**, seedy: **integer**)
    find the span containing the seed point.

Suppose it goes from lx to rx, inclusive

PUSH(lx, rx, lx, rx, seedy + 1, 1);
PUSH(lx, rx, lx, rx, seedy − 1, −1);

while *stack is not empty* **do**
       POP();
       if y < Limit.top **or** y > Limit. bottom
           then loop;
       x ← lx + 1;
       if (wasIn ← INSIDE(lx, y))
       then begin
           SET(lx, y); lx ← lx − 1;
           while INSIDE(lx, y) **and** lx ≥ Limit.left **do**
                the left edge of the shadow contacts a span: walk over
                to its edge.
                SET(lx, y); lx ← lx − 1;
                endloop
       end

now enter the main loop: we are now looking at pixel x, and moving to the right. If wasIn is true, then I am currently inside a span of pixels whose left edge is at lx.

while (x ≤ Limit.right) **do**
    if wasIn
        then begin
        if INSIDE(x, y)
           then begin
               case 1: was inside, am still inside.
               SET(x, y)
               end
           else begin
               case 2: was inside, am no longer inside: just
               found the right edge of a span
               STACK(direction, dadLx, dadRx, lx, (x − 1), y);
               wasIn ← **false**
               end
        else begin
           if x > rx
               then exit;

```
if INSIDE(x, y)
    then begin
    SET(x, y);
    case 3: wasn't inside, am now: just found the
    start of a new run
    wasIn ← true;
    lx ← x;
    end
else begin
    case 4: wasn't inside, still isn't
    end
    x ← x + 1;
    end
    end
endloop
if wasIn
    then begin
    hit an edge of the frame buffer while inside a run
    STACK(direction, dadLx, dadRx, lx, (x − 1), y);
    end
endloop
return
```

See also A Seed Fill Algorithm (275)

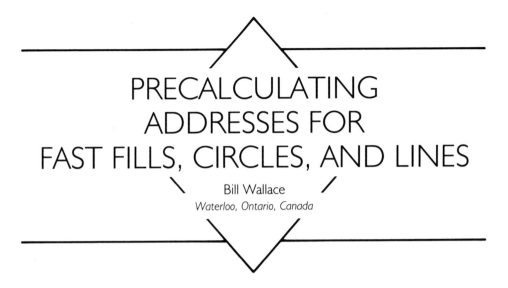

PRECALCULATING ADDRESSES FOR FAST FILLS, CIRCLES, AND LINES

Bill Wallace

Waterloo, Ontario, Canada

When adjacent pixels are accessed in an algorithm that needs to be fast, macro definitions (or inline functions) can be used, which precalculate one address and then use simple addition to find neighboring points. Assume *screen* is a pointer to a screen k bytes wide, eight bits deep (for ease of explanation, but this method can be used for arbitrary depth screens.) Then a fast fill algorithm can be written as follows:

```
macro Calculate Address(x, y) (y*k + x + screen address);
macro Move Left(address) (address + 1);
macro Move Right(address) (address − 1);
macro Move Up(address) (address − k);
macro Move Down (address) (address + k);

macro Plot(address, color) Put Byte (address, color);
macro Get Color(address) Get Byte (address);

fastfill( address, color, boundary color)
    begin
    if Get Color(address) ≠ boundary color
        then begin
        Plot(address, color);
        fastfill(Move Left(address), color, boundary color);
        fastfill(Move Right(address), color, boundary color);
        fastfill(Move Up(address), color, boundary color);
        fastfill(Move Down(address), color, boundary color);
        end;
    end;
```

This routine is called with something like

fastfill(Calculate Address(x, y), fill color, boundary color)

with the result being that everything in an area surrounded by the boundary color will be filled with the fill color.

This saves explicitly passing both x and y coordinates and saves two multiplies and four adds on each iteration of *fastfill*. Using this method with Bresenham's algorithm or with some line drawing algorithms saves one multiply and two adds per pixel. If the screen is 24 bits deep with separate base address, savings are increased correspondingly. One problem with this method is that there is no easy way to detect if the edge of the screen has been encountered. For the line drawing and circle algorithms, clipping can be performed before the line is drawn and for the fill algorithms it may or may not be a problem.

See also What Are the Coordinates of a Pixel? (246); Circles of Integral Radius on Integer Lattices (57); A Seed Fill Algorithm (275); Filling a Region in a Frame Buffer (278)

A SIMPLE METHOD FOR COLOR QUANTIZATION: OCTREE QUANTIZATION

Michael Gervautz, Werner Purgathofer
Technische Universität Wien
Wien, Austria

Introduction

A method for filling a color table is presented that produces pictures of similar quality as existing methods, but requires less memory and execution time. All colors of an image are inserted in an octree, and this octree is reduced from the leaves to the root in such a way that every pixel has a well-defined maximum error.

The human eye is able to distinguish about 200 intensity levels in each of the three primaries red, green, and blue. All in all, up to 10 million different colors can be distinguished. The RGB cube with 256 subdivisions on each of the red, green, and blue axes, as it is very often used, represents about 16.77 million colors and suffices for the eye. It enables display of color shaded scenes without visible color edges, and is therefore well-suited for computer graphics. Figure 1, on the back cover, shows a computer-generated image displayed with 16 million colors.

Color devices (mainly frame buffers) that allow for the projection of those 16 million colors at the same time are complicated and therefore expensive. On the other hand, even good dithering techniques produce relatively poor-quality pictures on cheap devices (Jarvis *et al.*, 1976). Therefore, devices with color tables are produced that allow the use of a small contingent K (for example, $K = 256$) of colors out of a larger palette (for example, 16 million colors).

When displaying images that contain more than K colors on such devices, the problem arises as to which K colors out of the possible colors will be selected and how the original colors are mapped onto the representatives to produce a satisfying picture. Such a selection is also needed for some other algorithms, such as the CCC-method for image encoding (Campbell *et al.*, 1986). The question is, how much expense can or will be invested in this job? This Gem presents a very simple but effective algorithm we called "octree quantization" to handle this task.

There are some existing solutions that have already been introduced. The simplest way to handle the problem is to divide the RGB cube into equal slices in each dimension and use the cross product of these (few) color levels of every primary for the color table. It is called "uniform quantization," and is depicted on the back cover in Fig. 2, which is the same image as Fig. 1, displayed with 64 colors. The "popularity algorithm" (Heckbert, 1982) chooses the K most frequently occurring colors for the color table, shown in Fig. 3 on the back cover. The "median cut algorithm" (Heckbert, 1982) tries to select K colors in such a way that each of these colors represents approximately the same number of pixels (see Fig. 4 on the back cover).

Principle of the Octree Quantization Method

The image is read sequentially. The first K different colors are used as initial entries to the color table. If another color is added, which means that the already processed part of the image has $K + 1$ different colors, some very near neighbors are merged into one and substituted by their mean. This step is repeated for every additional color, so that at any moment no more than K representatives are left. This property, of course, remains true after the image is completely processed.

The Octree

For this method a data structure has to be used that enables quick detection of colors that lie close together in the color space. An octree is well suited for this problem (Jakson and Tanimoto, 1980; Meagher, 1982). The RGB cube can easily be administered by an octree.

It suffices to use an octree of depth eight (two in the eighth is 256 levels in red, green, blue; eight in the eighth gives 16 million colors) to represent all possible colors. The red, green, and blue components (each between 0 and 255) are the coordinates within the octree.

Every exact color is represented by a leaf in depth eight. Intermediate nodes represent subcubes of the RGB space. The greater the depth of such a node, the smaller is the color subcube represented by it; therefore, the depth of a node is a measure for the maximum distance of its colors.

The Algorithm

The octree quantization is done in three phases:

- evaluation of the representatives
- filling the color table
- mapping the original colors onto the representatives.

These three steps are now described in detail using the color octree.

Evaluation of the Representatives

The octree is constructed only in those parts that are necessary for the image we want. At the beginning, the octree is empty. Every color that occurs in the image is now inserted by generating a leaf in depth eight; thereby, the color is represented exactly.

```
InsertTree (Tree : Octree, RGB : Color);
    inserts the color RGB into the subtree Tree

begin InsertTree
  if Tree = nil
    then NewAndInit (Tree);   produces and inits a new octree node.
  if Leaf                     we have reached the eighth level.
    then
      begin
        inc(Tree ^.ColorCount);      update the number of represented pixels
        AddColors (Tree ^.RGB, RGB);sum up the color values
      end
    else InsertTree (Next[Branch(RGB)], RGB);
  end;
```

In this way an incomplete octree is created, in which many branches are missing. Actually, this octree does not have to be filled with all the colors because every time the number of colors reaches $K + 1$, similar colors can be merged into one, so that there are never more than K colors left. We will call this action a reduction of the octree.

ReduceTree combines the successors of an intermediate node to one leaf node

GetReducible (*Tree*);	*finds a reducible node*
Sum ← (0, 0, 0);	
Children ← 0;	
for i:integer ← 0, 7 **do**	
if Next[i] < > nil	*there is an ith successor*
then	
begin	
Children ← Children + 1;	
AddColors (Sum, Tree ^.Next[i] ^.RGB)	
end;	
Tree ^.Leaf ← true;	*cut the tree at this level*
Tree ^.RGB ← Sum;	*the node represents the sum of all color values*
Size ← Size − Children + 1;	*of children*

Every time the number of leaves (that is, the number of representatives found up to the moment) exceeds K, the octree is reduced. The reduction begins at the bottom of the octree by always substituting some leaves by their predecessor.

Reducing the octree, the following criteria are relevant:

- From all reducible nodes, those that have the largest depths within the octree should be chosen first, for they represent colors that lie closest together.

- If there is more than one node in the largest depth, additional criteria could be used for an optimal selection. For example, reduce the node that represents the fewest pixels up to now. In this way the error sum will be kept small. Reduce the node that represents the most pixels up to now. In this case large areas will be uniformly filled in a slightly wrong color, and detailed shadings (like anti-aliasing) will remain.

To construct the color octree, the whole image has to be read once and all colors of the image have to be inserted into the octree.

Filling the Color Table

At the end, the K leaves of the octree contain the colors for the color table (the mean value of all represented colors = RGB/*ColorCount*). They can be written into the color table by recursively examining the octree. During this recursive tree traversal in every leaf node of the octree also its own color index is stored.

Mapping onto the Representatives

The mapping of the original colors onto their representatives can now be managed easily with the octree, too. Trying to find any original color in the reduced octree will end at a leaf in some depth. This node contains a color very similar to the one in search, and is therefore its representative. Since the index of the color table is stored there too, no further search has to be carried out.

If the original image used less than K colors, no reduction will have taken place, and the found color table entry will contain exactly the correct color. Otherwise, only the path to the leaf in depth eight was shortened by the reduction, so that the color will be displayed less exactly by the means of all the colors that had their paths over this node. Since the octree contains only K leaves, all original colors are mapped onto valid color table entries. For this, the image has to be read a second time.

> Quant (Tree : Octree, Original_Color : Color) : index;
>   *for the original color its representative*
>   *is searched for in the octree, and the index of*
>   *its color table entry is returned*
>
> **begin** *Quant*
>   **if** Leaf
>   **then** return Tree ^.ColorIndex   *stored color index in the tree*
>   **else** return Quant(Tree ^.Next[Branch (Original_Color)], Original_Color)
>   **end**;

The visual result using this octree quantization is of similar quality as the result using the median cut method (see Fig. 5 on the back cover).

Improvements

A significant portion of the execution time is spent with the search for an optimal reducible node every time a reduction of the octree has to take place. These nodes can be collected easily in an appropriate structure during the construction of the tree. They have to be sorted by depth to ensure quick access. An appropriate structure for this purpose has proved to be eight linear lists (one for every depth level) containing all reducible nodes. All nodes of one depth level are elements of the same list. The node with the largest depth can then be found quickly for reduction.

An intermediate node is inserted into its list of reducible nodes after its creation during *NewAndInit*.

At any given moment one level of the octree will be the depth in which the reductions take place. This depth is the level of the deepest intermediate nodes. At the beginning, this is level seven, and it moves toward the root during the octree construction. This "reduction level" states what the minimal distance between two representatives will already have to be. This minimal distance can never again decrease, even by adding more colors to the octree. Therefore, nothing beneath this reduction level + 1 will ever again be relevant, so that the insertion of colors can also stop at that depth. The depth of the octree is not constant, but decreases with lifetime.

Memory and Computational Expense

Let N be the number of pixels of the original image. If the image is run-length encoded, N can also be the number of runs of the image. The algorithm has to be modified slightly by using runs instead of pixels in the octree.

Let K be the number of representatives, that is, the size of the color table. Let D be the number of different colors in the original image.

In general the following equations hold:

$$N > D > K \quad \text{and} \quad N \gg K.$$

An upper bound for the memory used by the octree is $2.K - 1$ nodes, because there are K leaves and at the most (in the case of a bintree) $K - 1$ intermediate nodes. The algorithm needs very little memory! It is also independent of N and D, that is, of the image. Only the color table size is relevant.

Upper bounds for the number of steps for the insertions, for the generation of the color table, and for the quantization are

$$\text{Insertion:} N.MaxDepth.$$

N insertions take place, each of them not deeper than $MaxDepth$. $MaxDepth$ itself is a constant (≤ 8).

$$\text{Color table generation:} 2.K.$$

Table I. Comparison of the Quantization Techniques.

	Memory	Search for Representatives	Mapping	Picture Quality
Uniform Quant.	0	O(K)	O(N)	bad
Popularity algorithm	O(D)	O(N + D.1d K)	> O(N)	depends on data
Median Cut	O(D)	O(N + D.1d K)	O(N.1d K)	good
Octree Quant.	O(K)	O(N)	O(N)	good

To fill the color table the incomplete octree has to be examined once; for every node there is exactly one call to the procedure *InitColorTable*.

$$\text{Mapping:} N.MaxDepth$$

For every pixel the color index of its representative is found not deeper than in the maximum tree depth. Thus, the octree quantization algorithm is of $O(N)$, the larger part of the execution time is spent by I/O-operations.

Comparison with Other Methods

Table 1 gives a short comparison with the other mentioned methods.

Conclusion

A method was presented to find a color table selection for displaying an image on a screen. The picture quality of this "octree quantization" is as good as that for existing methods. The expense in terms of memory and execution time, however, lies significantly below the expense of those algorithms, especially in terms of the memory occupied, which is independent of the image complexity. The method is therefore well suited for microcomputers, too.

See also Mapping RGB Triples onto Four Bits (233)

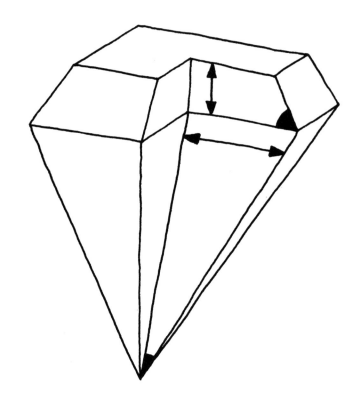

3D GEOMETRY

USEFUL 3D GEOMETRY

Andrew S. Glassner

Xerox PARC
Palo Alto, California

Record Sphere: [
    center: C,
    radius: r
    ]   (*see Fig. 1a*)
A sphere will be represented in upper case roman (A, B).

Record Plane: [
    normal: **N**,
    offset: d
    ]   (*see Fig. 1b*)
A Plane will be represented in upper case italic (J, K).

V3 Distance from Point to Plane

$d \leftarrow$ V3 Distance from Point (P) to Plane (J)   (*see Fig. 2*)
    $Q \leftarrow$ V3 Nearest Point on Plane (J) to Point (P)
    $d \leftarrow$ V3 Distance between Point (P) and Point (Q)

V3 Nearest Point on Plane to Point

$Q \leftarrow$ V3 Nearest Point on Plane (J) to Point (P)   (*see Fig. 3*)
    1. Q is on plane J, so $J_N \cdot Q + J_d = 0$.
    2. The vector Q − P is parallel to J_N, *so* $Q - P = kJ_N$ *for some k:*
    $Q = P - kJ_N$.
    3. Plug Q from 2 into 1: $J_N \cdot P - J_N \cdot kJ_N + J_d = 0$.
    4. Solve 3 for k: $k = \dfrac{J_d + J_N \cdot P}{J_N \cdot J_N}$.

    5. Plug k into 2 and find Q:

$$Q \leftarrow P - (\frac{J_d + J_N \cdot P}{J_N \cdot J_N})J_N.$$

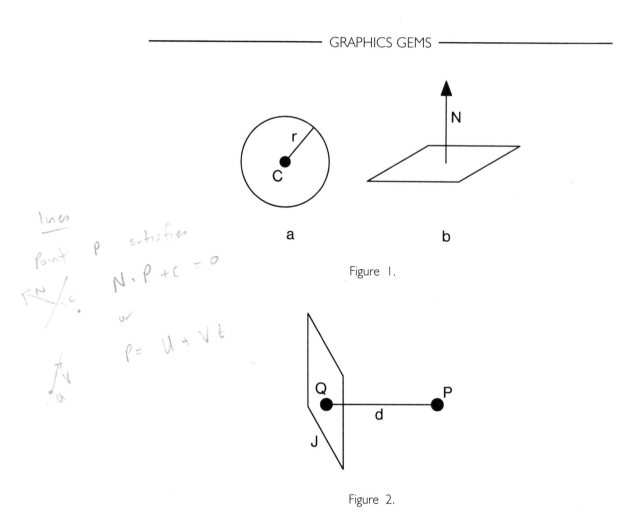

a

b

Figure 1.

(handwritten notes in margin)

lines

Point P satisfies

$N \cdot P + C = 0$

or

$P = U + Vt$

Figure 2.

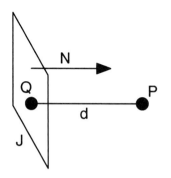

Figure 3.

V3 Point on Plane Nearest the Origin

$P \leftarrow$ V3 Point on Plane (J) Nearest the Origin

$\qquad P \leftarrow$ Nearest Point on Plane (J) to Point (0)

V3 Intersection of Line and Plane

$P \leftarrow$ V3 Intersection of Line (l) and Plane (J)

Plug in the expression for points on l into those on J.

$(l_U + l_V t) \cdot J_N + J_d = 0$

Now solve for t and plug back into the line equation.

$$t \leftarrow -\frac{J_d + (l_U \cdot J_N)}{l_V \cdot J_N}$$

l_V I think

$P \leftarrow l_U + l_V t$

line vector

starting pt of line

V3 Normalize

$\mathbf{A} \leftarrow$ V3 Normalize $(\mathbf{A})$

$$\mathbf{A} \leftarrow \frac{\mathbf{A}}{\text{V3 Length}(\mathbf{A})}$$

V3 Dot

$d \leftarrow$ V3 Dot$(\mathbf{A}, \mathbf{B})$

$\qquad d \leftarrow A_x B_x + A_y B_y + A_z B_z$

V3 Length

$d \leftarrow$ V3 Length $(\mathbf{A})$

$\qquad d \leftarrow \sqrt{\mathbf{A} \cdot \mathbf{A}}$

V3 Intersection of Sphere and Line

$P1, P2 \leftarrow$ V3 Intersection of Sphere (S) and Line (l)

$\qquad \mathbf{G} \leftarrow l_U - S_C$

$\qquad a \leftarrow l_V \cdot l_V$

$\qquad b \leftarrow 2(l_V \cdot \mathbf{G})$

$\qquad c \leftarrow (\mathbf{G} \cdot \mathbf{G}) - S_r^2$

$\qquad d \leftarrow b^2 - 4ac$

$\qquad$ **if** $d < 0$

$\qquad\qquad$ **then** "no intersection"

$\qquad\qquad$ **else**

$\qquad\qquad\qquad P1 \leftarrow (-b + \sqrt{d})/2a$

$\qquad\qquad\qquad P2 \leftarrow (-b - \sqrt{d})/2a$

299

V3 Point on Sphere Nearest Point

$Q \leftarrow$ V3 Point on Sphere (S) Nearest Point (P)
$\qquad Q \leftarrow S_C + S_r{}^*$V3 Normalize$(P - S_C)$

V3 Line through Two Points

$l \leftarrow$ V3 Line through Two Points (A, B)
$\qquad l_U \leftarrow A$
$\qquad l_V \leftarrow$ V3 Normalize$(B - A)$

V3 Distance from Point to Line

$d \leftarrow$ V3 Distance from Point (P) to Line (l)
$\qquad Q \leftarrow$ V3 Point on Line (l) Closest to Point (P)
$\qquad d \leftarrow$ V3 Distance from Point (P) to Point (Q)

V3 Point on Line Closest to Point

$Q \leftarrow$ V3 Point on Line (l) Closest to Point (P)
$\qquad$ *1. P lies on a plane with normal l_V: $P \cdot l_V + d = 0$.*
$\qquad$ *2. Find this plane and intersect it with the line:*
$\qquad J_N \leftarrow l_V$
$\qquad J_d \leftarrow -(P \cdot l_V)$
$\qquad Q \leftarrow$ V3 Intersection of Line (l) and Plane (J)

V3 Point on Line Nearest the Origin

$Q \leftarrow$ V3 Point on Line (l) Nearest the Origin
$\qquad Q \leftarrow$ V3 Point on Line (l) Closest to Point (0)

V3 Distance between Point and Point

$d \leftarrow$ V3 Distance between Point (P) and Point (Q)
$\qquad d \leftarrow$ V3 Length$(P - Q)$

V3 Parameter of Point on Line from Point to Point

$a \leftarrow$ V3 Parameter of Point (P) on Line from Point (Q) to Point (R)

$$a \leftarrow \frac{\text{V3 Distance from Point } (P) \text{ to Point } (Q)}{\text{V3 Distance from Point } (P) \text{ to Point } (Q + R)}$$

V3 Projection of Vector onto Plane

$\mathbf{V} \leftarrow$ V3 Projection of Vector $\mathbf{D}$ onto Plane J
$\qquad \mathbf{V} \leftarrow \mathbf{D} - (\mathbf{D} \cdot J_N)J_N$

See also Useful 2D Geometry (3)

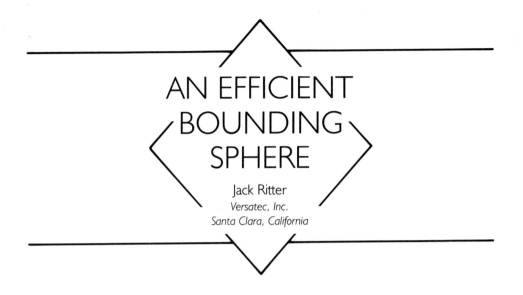

AN EFFICIENT BOUNDING SPHERE

Jack Ritter
Versatec, Inc.
Santa Clara, California

This gem is a method for finding a near-optimal bounding sphere for any set of N points in 3D space. It is Order (N), and extremely fast. The sphere calculated is about 5% bigger than the ideal minimum-radius sphere.

The algorithm is executed in two passes: the first pass finds two points that are close to maximally spaced. This pair describes the initial guess for the sphere. The second pass compares each point to the current sphere, and enlarges the sphere if the point is outside. The algorithm is as follows:

1. Make one (quick) pass through the N points. Find these six points:
   The point with minimum x, the point with maximum x,
   The point with minimum y, the point with maximum y,
   The point with minimum z, the point with maximum z.
This gives three pairs of points. Each pair has the maximum span for its dimension. Pick the pair with the maximum point-to-point separation (which could be *greater* than the maximum dimensional span). Calculate the initial sphere, using this pair of points as a diameter.

2. Make a second pass through the N points: for each point outside the current sphere, update the current sphere to the larger sphere passing through the point on one side, and the back side of the old sphere on the other side. Each new sphere will (barely) contain the old sphere, plus the new point, and usually some other outsiders as well. The number of updates needed will be a tiny fraction of N. In testing each point against the current sphere, the square of its distance from the current sphere's

center is compared to the square of the current sphere's radius, to avoid doing a *sqrt()* calculation.

The following pseudo code compares a point (x, y, z) with the current sphere [center = $(cenx, ceny, cenz)$, and radius = rad]. If (x, y, z) is outside the current sphere, $(cenx, ceny, cenz)$ and rad are updated to reflect the new sphere. The current square of the radius is maintained in *rad sq*:

> *given x, y, z, cenx, ceny, cenz, rad, and rad_sq*
>
> dx ← x − cenx;
> dy ← y − ceny;
> dz ← z − cenz;
> old_to_p_sq ← dx*dx + dy*dy + dz*dz;
> *do economical r**2 test before calc sqrt*
> **if** (old_to_p_sq > rad_sq)
>> **then**
>> *Point is outside current sphere. update.*
>> old_to_p ← $\sqrt{\text{old\_to\_p\_sq}}$;
>> rad ← (rad + old_to_p) /2.0;
>> *update square of radius for next compare*
>> rad_sq ← rad*rad;
>> old_to_new ← old_to_p − rad;
>> cenx ← (rad*cenx + old_to_new*x) /old_to_p;
>> ceny ← (rad*ceny + old_to_new*y) /old_to_p;
>> cenz ← (rad*cenz + old_to_new*z) /old_to_p;
>> **end**

The following two tests were run on a Sun 3/50 workstation (68020 with MC68881 floating point co-processor).

Case I

A spherical volume centered at the origin with a radius of 128, was randomly populated with 10,000 points. Five of these were forced to be at the edge of the sphere. This means that the optimal sphere should have a radius of 128. Results: center = $(3, 5, 4)$; radius = 133 (4% > ideal); processor time: 1.8 seconds.

Case 2

A cubic volume with a half-edge length of 128 was randomly populated with 10,000 points. Included were the eight corner points. This means that the ideal radius = $\sqrt{3} * 128 = 222$. Note: this is close to the worst case for this algorithm, because an orthogonally aligned box means that no corners will be found in the initial guessing phase. (A box rotated by any angle around any axis would allow corners to be found initially.) Results: center = $(5, 21, 2)$; radius = 237 (7% > ideal); processor time: 1.8 seconds.

A full C version of this algorithm can be found in the appendix.

See Appendix 2 for C Implementation (**723**)

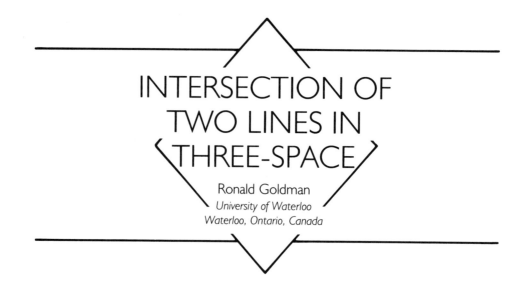

INTERSECTION OF TWO LINES IN THREE-SPACE

Ronald Goldman
University of Waterloo
Waterloo, Ontario, Canada

Let each line be defined by a point P_k and a unit direction vector $\mathbf{V}_k$, $k = 1, 2$. Then we can express each line parametrically by writing

$$L_1(t) = P_1 + \mathbf{V}_1 t \quad \text{and} \quad L_2(s) = P_2 + \mathbf{V}_2 s.$$

The intersection occurs when $L_1(t) = L_2(s)$ or equivalently when

$$P_1 + \mathbf{V}_1 t = P_2 + \mathbf{V}_2 s.$$

Subtracting P_1 from both sides and crossing with $\mathbf{V}_2$ yields

$$(\mathbf{V}_1 \times \mathbf{V}_2)t = (P_2 - P_1) \times \mathbf{V}_2.$$

Now dotting with $(\mathbf{V}_1 \times \mathbf{V}_2)$ and dividing by $|\mathbf{V}_1 \times \mathbf{V}_2|^2$ give us

$$t = \text{Det}\{(P_2 - P_1), \mathbf{V}_2, \mathbf{V}_1 \times \mathbf{V}_2\}/|\mathbf{V}_1 \times \mathbf{V}_2|^2.$$

Symmetrically, solving for s, we obtain

$$s = \text{Det}\{(P_2 - P_1), \mathbf{V}_1, \mathbf{V}_1 \times \mathbf{V}_2\}/|\mathbf{V}_1 \times \mathbf{V}_2|^2.$$

Two important observations follow:

- If the lines are parallel, the denominator $|\mathbf{V}_1 \times \mathbf{V}_2|^2 = 0$.
- If the lines are skew, s and t represent the parameters of the points of closest approach.

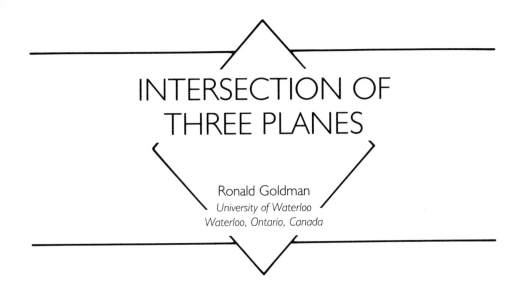

INTERSECTION OF THREE PLANES

Ronald Goldman
University of Waterloo
Waterloo, Ontario, Canada

Let each plane be defined by a point P_k and a unit normal vector $\mathbf{V}_k$, $k = 1, 2, 3$. Then the unique point of intersection can be written in closed form as

$$P_{\text{Int}} = \{(P_1 \cdot \mathbf{V}_1)(\mathbf{V}_2 \times \mathbf{V}_3) + (P_2 \cdot \mathbf{V}_2)(\mathbf{V}_3 \times \mathbf{V}_1)$$

$$+ (P_3 \cdot \mathbf{V}_3)(\mathbf{V}_1 \times \mathbf{V}_2)\}/\text{Det}(\mathbf{V}_1, \mathbf{V}_2, \mathbf{V}_3).$$

If two of the given planes are parallel there is no intersection. In this case the denominator $\text{Det}(\mathbf{V}_1, \mathbf{V}_2, \mathbf{V}_3)$ is zero.

MAPPING SUMMARY

Projecting a sphere onto the plane is not an easy problem. Cartographers, interested in making maps for navigation, have long known that one must make a variety of tradeoffs in such a projection. You may want to preserve distances, angles, headings, or areas, but you can't preserve them all at once.

Many styles of map projection have been developed for different goals: political boundaries, water navigation, land navigation, area calculation, and so on. The following two Gems discuss a variety of projections appropriate for computer graphics. They are useful for topics ranging from texture mapping to spherical function rendering.

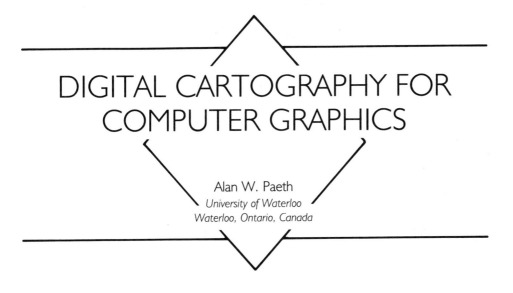

DIGITAL CARTOGRAPHY FOR COMPUTER GRAPHICS

Alan W. Paeth
University of Waterloo
Waterloo, Ontario, Canada

Overview

The mapping of a sphere onto a plane arises often in computer graphics. Direct applications include the automation of traditional map-making. Here the sphere represents a world globe and the plane represents the chart. Indirect applications include the creation of environment maps (Greene, 1986) or specialized applications such as the fireworks simulation that concludes this Gem. Most references on this topic lie at the subject's extreme points: on the specifics of practical cartography or on the mathematical theory of conformal mapping. This entry seeks the middle ground with emphasis on ease of computation. Cartographic terms (appearing in italics) and mathematical notation—particularly regarding spherical trigonometry—are employed preferentially.

Projection Properties

As the sphere cannot be *developed* onto a flat sheet (unlike a cylinder, cone, or plane of projection) distortions must necessarily be introduced in forming a chart, taking the form of local scale changes on both axes. A mathematical categorization of local scale changes reveals three principle and distinct projection classes: *conformal*, *equal-area*, and *equidistant*. Classes are exclusive with the first two of primary importance and of opposing nature. Conformality implies that small areas on the chart have true local scale. As a consequence all conformal projections preserve angles, but when used at global scales suffer severe distortion of shape. Common applications at both large and small scales include nautical charts and municipal maps, respectively. Equal-area maps allow the depiction of large land masses with reduced distortion of shape; exact area preservation makes them attractive for thematic census or statistical maps. Conversely, they suffer angular distortions of local scale. Equidistant projections maintain true scale along select curves; these and specialized projections seek a middle ground between the shape and angle distortions present in the first two classes. They are commonly employed for depicting areas of global extent in pleasing fashion. All proper maps can render a small, central portion of the globe with vanishingly small distortion as the earth's curvature then becomes negligible.

First Principles

Coordinates for a point P on a sphere of radius R centered about the origin O are most often given in terms of spherical coordinates (R, λ, ϕ). Here the z axis pierces the sphere at its north and south *poles*. Planes containing the origin O cut the sphere forming *great circles* of radius R —other planes of intersection form *small circles* of lesser radius. The xy plane perpendicular to the polar axis contains the *equator*, a great circle that bisects the sphere into a north and south *hemisphere*. Cartography universally employs λ to define *longitude* as the counterclockwise angular measure between the x axis and vector OP projected onto the xy plane. This is a *bearing* measure, which serves an identical function to the angle θ used in computer graphics to measure 2D rotation about the origin. Similarly, ϕ defines *latitude* or angular distance between OP and the z axis such that points on the equator have zero latitude and points at the north and south poles lie at $+\pi$ or $-\pi$ radians, respectively. This is an *azimuth* measurement specific to 3D spherical coordinates. The complementary *colatitude* (χ) measures the angle from the $+z$ axis: $\chi = \pi/2 - \phi$. Colatitude thus expresses great circle distance from this pole.

Spherical coordinate triples define a unique point in three-space; principle arguments are restricted to the range $-\pi \leq \lambda < \pi$ and $-\pi/2 \leq \phi \leq \pi/2$. For rendering using conventional graphics software these may be mapped into Cartesian 3D world coordinates by changing from spherical to rectangular form:

$$x = R \times \cos \lambda \times \cos \phi$$

$$y = R \times \sin \lambda \times \cos \phi$$

$$z = R \times \sin \phi.$$

Viewed at a finite distance the globe appears as under the *perspective* projection. The limiting case with view at infinity simplifies the foreshortening process, yielding the *orthographic* projection (Fig. 5a) in which exactly one hemisphere is depicted. Although not immediately conceptualized as map projections, both are members of the azimuthal family described later. The inverse mapping is

$$R = \sqrt{x^2 + y^2 + z^2}$$

$$\lambda = \tan^{-1} \frac{y}{x}$$

$$\phi = \tan^{-1} \frac{z}{\sqrt{x^2 + y^2}}.$$

In this form the *atan*2() function common in many subroutine libraries may be used to ensure proper four-quadrant operation.

Direct Charting of Databases

Geographic databases provide merely (ϕ, λ) latitude and longitude coordinate pairs, with R the derived distance from the earth's center to mean sea level by using a standardized *reference geoid*. For many purposes R may be set to the mean equatorial earth radius, a semimajor axis of length 6378.160 km. (True geodesy employs higher-order standard models to account for the oblate *figure* of the Earth; a polar flattening of $1/298.25$ yields an approximation for R with maximum elevation error less than 100 meters). For purposes of exposition only unit spheres are considered in what follows.

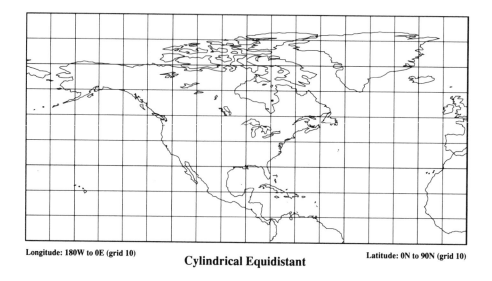

Cylindrical Equidistant   Latitude: 0N to 90N (grid 10)

Figure 1.   Equirectangular cylindrical projection.

Too often, a vector plot used to proof a cartographic data set uses the simple projection

$$x \leftarrow s \times \lambda$$
$$y \leftarrow s \times \phi,$$

which is implicit when executing commands of the form *plotxy* (λ, ϕ). Here s is a constant scale factor for both axes used to fit the data to the chart dimensions. The resulting *cylindrical equirectangular* map (see Fig. 1) represents the sphere at small scales and then only near the equator—many cartographers do not consider it a proper map. Fortunately, simple remedies exist

Cylindrical Maps

Maps of the cylindrical family allow a direct mapping of longitude lines, or *meridians*, onto equally spaced, vertical chart lines. Geometrically, this suggests projecting the globe onto an encasing vertical cylinder and then unwrapping to form a plane. Maps of this form are well-suited to computer graphics because the mapping function $M_2: (\phi, \lambda) \rightarrow (y, x)$

becomes one-dimensional $M_1: (\phi) \rightarrow (y)$ with λ scaled directly onto x, thereby simplifying the derivation of both forward and inverse projections. Cylindrical maps support clipping of λ in world coordinates when plotting on a surface of uniform width (a rectangular page or display). Mapping of screen (chart) coordinates back onto (ϕ, λ) is also straightforward, suggesting simplified direct selection and editing of the underlying cartographic data set.

On the globe the relative longitude scale shifts as a function of latitude. This effect accounts for the reduced distance between *meridians* (lines of constant longitude) measured along *parallels* of constant latitude. Because scales agree at the equator (where one degree is defined as sixty nautical miles) the scale ratio is $1:1$ and decreases to zero at either pole: $\cos(\phi)$ or $\sin(\chi)$ defines this ratio. Thus, a rectangular chart for a local region may use the adjusted scale

$$x \leftarrow s \times \lambda$$

$$y \leftarrow s \times \phi \times \sec \phi_{cen},$$

thereby providing an aspect ratio correct for a chosen parallel ϕ_{cen} and arbitrary chart scale s. This forms the *modified cylindrical equidistant projection*, which underlies many street and municipal maps. Note that a scaling of $\cos \phi$ along the x axis would also form a proper local aspect ratio (see *Sanson's Sinusoid*, below) but would alter the spacing of the parallels, which must be uniform for any cylindrical projection. By employing a secant multiplier, scale increases at high latitude: an arctic explorer looping the North Pole quickly traverses the chart's x extent; the y scale must accordingly be large. As this ratio is constant for the entire chart, trigonometric calculations need not appear in the innermost code loop performing the coordinate projection. Although computationally fast and more pleasing in appearance than direct coordinate plotting, the map is unsuited for large regions.

Mercator Projection

In the previous example, conformality was achieved along a chosen parallel by increasing the scale by $\sec \phi$ to offset the $\cos \phi$ change in aspect. By treating vertical scale change continually a map may be constructed as a montage of narrow strips having small ϕ (vertical) extent but with λ extent encircling the sphere. Away from the equator at $y = 0$, successive strips are joined together by offsetting them a distance $\sec \phi \, d\phi$ to accommodate the continuous change in scale. This graphically depicts the integral $y = \int \sec \phi \, d\phi$, which forms the basis of the *Mercator* projection. Solution of the integral and Taylor series expansion yields the inverse Gudermannian function and its arcfunction:

$$y = \mathrm{gd}^{-1}(\phi) = \log_e \tan\left(\frac{\phi}{2} + \frac{\pi}{4}\right)$$

$$= \phi + \frac{1}{6}\phi^3 + \frac{1}{24}\phi^5 + \frac{61}{5040}\phi^7 + O(\phi^9)$$

$$\phi = \mathrm{gd}(y) = 2\left(\tan^{-1}(e^y) - \frac{\pi}{4}\right)$$

$$= y + \frac{1}{6}y^3 - \frac{1}{24}y^5 + \frac{61}{5040}\phi^7 + O(y^9).$$

Because of conformality, true headings (the angle formed between a ground tack and a globe meridian) form true angles on conformal maps. Because the Mercator is additionally cylindrical, chart meridians are oriented in rectilinear fashion. Thus, lines of constant heading (called *loxodromes* or *rhumb lines*) may be plotted directly, explaining the projection's almost universal application in nautical charts. Despite these benefits, the map has the disadvantage of excessive distortion at high latitudes (see Fig. 2). Mercator was revolutionary in deriving a useful projection through analytic means. In particular, there is no simple geometrical model that depicts the projection's construction.

Sanson – Flamsteed Sinusoidal

This simple projection may be obtained by choosing the central meridian as the axis of constant spacing, or $y = s \times \phi$. Adjustment of the x axis yields a map that preserves area—a valuable property. Because the mapping function may once again be modeled as a one-dimensional

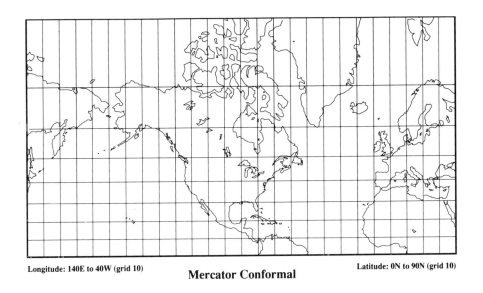

Longitude: 140E to 40W (grid 10)   **Latitude: 0N to 90N (grid 10)**

Mercator Conformal

Figure 2.   Mercator cylindrical projection.

function $M_1: (\lambda) \rightarrow (x)$ the useful properties of world-coordinate clipping (now on a vertical extent of constant height) and inverse mapping may again be claimed.

Consider a rectangular map of equally spaced parallels in which the central parallel represents the equator. At high latitudes the chart parallels represent small circles of reduced radius $\cos\phi$. The area of a strip bounded by two near parallels appears constant on the rectangular chart: the true globe area has decreased by an amount $\cos\phi$ because of reduction in the bounding parallels' circumferential length. Reducing the x scale of the chart by this factor maintains constant area between chart and globe. The resulting form resembles the modified cylindrical projection except that the sliding scale factor is now applied to the x axis:

$$x \leftarrow s \times \lambda \times \cos\phi$$

$$y \leftarrow s \times \phi.$$

This projection owes its name to the sinusoids that form the map edge and reference meridians (see Fig. 3) and can be derived as the limiting

313

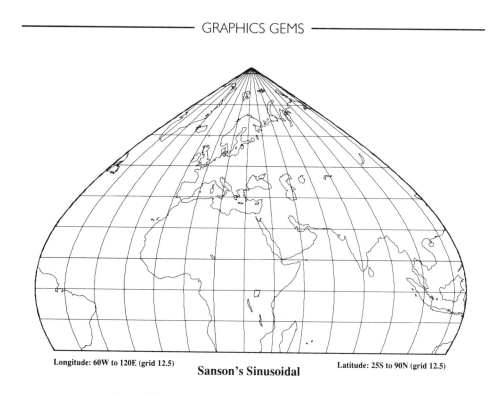

Longitude: 60W to 120E (grid 12.5)   **Sanson's Sinusoidal**   **Latitude: 25S to 90N (grid 12.5)**

Figure 3.   Sanson–Flamsteed equal-area projection.

case of *Bonne's* general projection of equispaced chart parallels. The sinusoidal projection is useful in replacing the polar discontinuity of cylindrical projections with a zero: the chart is bounded and depicts one hemisphere. Though attributed to Sanson, this chart was well-known to Mercator.

Azimuthal Projections

In this family a plane is placed tangent to the sphere and rays extended from a point of projection define a correspondence between points of intersection on the sphere and the chart. The projections are derived in polar form: spherical trigonometry provides a means of changing the underlying coordinate system, thus defining the point of tangency. With the North Pole serving as the point of tangency corresponding to the chart center, all great circles through this point (globe meridians) project as radials through the chart center. Polar bearing θ of chart radials is thus taken directly from the globe: $\theta = \lambda$. Distance away from the chart center ρ is defined using the angular measure for colatitude: $\rho = \chi = \pi/2 - \phi$. By applying the well-known polar to rectangular conversion formulae $x = r \cos \theta$, $y = r \sin \theta$, the entire family may be characterized by suitable choice of r as a function of ρ, which maps angular distance away from the globe's pole onto radial distance away from the chart center. This yields the program code:

polar azimuth projection of (ϕ, λ) onto (x, y)

$$\rho \leftarrow \frac{\pi}{2} - \phi \qquad \text{\textit{colatitude: N Pole is 0 degrees; Equator 90}}$$

$\theta \leftarrow \lambda$ *(more complex for oblique projections)*

$r \leftarrow f(\rho)$ *length of chart radial*

$x \leftarrow r \times \cos \theta$ *convert (r, θ) polar chart*

$y \leftarrow r \times \sin \theta$ *coordinates into rectangular (x, y)*

Reverse mapping from chart to spherical coordinates is accomplished by converting from rectangular to polar form and then applying the inverse function $\rho = f^{-1}(r)$. These function pairs are tabulated in Fig. 4, with short descriptions following. Note that for all functions $f(x) \approx f^{-1}(x) \approx x$ when $x \approx 0$; this may be verified through Taylor expansion. Sample azimuthal plots appear in Figs. 5a and 5b.

The *gnomonic* or *central* projection is neither conformal nor area preserving. By placing the ray origin at the sphere's center, all straight lines on the chart are *geodesics*—great circle paths of shortest distance—because any two projected rays define both the chart line and a plane that cuts the sphere through its center. Distortion grows to infinity along

Name	$r = f(\rho)$	$\rho = f(r)$
Gnomonic	$\tan \rho$	$\tan^{-1} r$
Stereographic	$2 \tan(\rho/2)$	$2 \tan^{-1} r/2$
Equidistant	ρ	r
Equal-Area	$2 \sin(\rho/2)$	$2 \sin^{-1} r/2$
Orthographic	$\sin \rho$	$\sin^{-1} r$

Figure 4.   Azimuthal projection parameters.

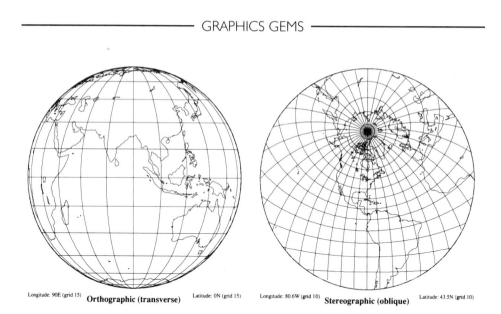

Longitude: 90E (grid 15) **Orthographic (transverse)** Latitude: 0N (grid 15)   Longitude: 80.6W (grid 10) **Stereographic (oblique)** Latitude: 43.5N (grid 10)

Figure 5. Azimuthal projections.

a hemisphere, requiring the omission or clipping of coordinates when $\rho \geq \pi/2$. R. Buckminster Fuller created a *dymaxion* gnomonic projection by centrally projecting the sphere onto an inscribing icosahedron, allowing great-circle routes to remain lines (albeit broken when crossing the edge between two non-conterminous faces) when developed as a sheet of 20 broken triangles.

The *stereographic* map places the point of projection at the tangent point's opposite pole or *antipode*. It is remarkable in being both conformal and circle preserving: circles of any radius (lines when the radius of curvature $\rightarrow \infty$) map freely between the chart and sphere. This feature may obviously be exploited in mixed proximity testing and clipping using both world and device coordinates. Because it renders an entire sphere onto a plane, it finds general scientific use in modeling spherically distributed point sets, as in crystallography. An example appears in Fig. 5b; note in particular that globe meridians (small circles) are nonconcentric circles on the chart.

The *azimuthal equidistant* projection equates r with colatitude (a rare case in which an angle measure appears directly and not as a trigonometric argument), thereby yielding a map that gives simultaneous bearing and radial distance for great-circle travel away from the chart

316

center. It finds application in the computation of heading and distance, as when aligning antennas for transoceanic broadcast—electromagnetic radiation follows geodesics.

The *azimuthal equal-area* projection employs a simple scale change to account for the area contributions of successive annuli away from the chart center as r changes incrementally. It resembles the *globular* projection derived for simplicity of construction that has been imprinted billions of times on journals of the National Geographic Society.

Spherical Coordinate Transformation

Azimuth projections have little value when projected merely at the North Pole. Spherical trigonometry may be employed to reorient the underlying polar coordinate system about a new tangent point (ϕ_0, λ_0). By applying coordinate transformations arbitrarily, the *aspect* of any projection may be changed from *normal* to *oblique*. As a special case, orientation at 90 degrees yields *transverse* projections (Figures 5a, 5b). The following equations reexpress the points (ϕ, λ) about the reference point (ϕ_0, λ_0) in terms of angular distance and radial bearing (ρ, θ) as required by the first two lines of the generic azimuthal pseudo-code. These formulae are also encountered when mapping from astronomical (ϕ, λ) pairs onto the celestial sphere in terms of horizon (compass) angle and elevation for an observer at a given location, or when computing great-circle distances and initial heading.

$$\rho = \cos^{-1}\left[\sin \phi \sin \phi_0 + \cos \phi \cos \phi_0 \cos(\lambda - \lambda_0)\right]$$

$$\theta = \sin^{-1}\left[\frac{\sin \phi - \sin \phi_0 \cos \rho}{\cos \phi_0 \sin \rho}\right],$$

in which θ's supplement $(\pi - \theta)$ or $(180° - \theta)$ is used when $(\lambda - \lambda_0) < 0$. This form maps latitude and longitude into counterclockwise bearing (longitude) and distance (colatitude). When employed to give conventional latitude or clockwise bearing, angular arguments α must be adjusted by use of angular complements: $\pi/2 - \alpha$; in many cases this is made implicit by reversing the roles of cos and sin. Subroutine implementation further requires $\cos^{-1}$ and $\sin^{-1}$ routines with full four-quadrant operation, that is, routines that return a properly signed angle.

General Projections

Azimuth maps may be generalized by moving the point of projection off the globe. This generality ultimately leads back to the *perspective* and *orthographic* projections. These and the cylindrical projections belong to the conics, the largest family of maps. Geometrically, a cone encircling a sphere possesses a central, symmetric point. Moving this apex onto the sphere flattens the cone into a tangential circle. Moving the apex to infinity creates a cylinder. The conic family includes pairs of both conformal and equal-area projections. The more accurate projections—the *Lambert Conformal Conic* and *Albers*— employ a *secant* cone, which cuts the globe at two *standard parallels*, thereby better fitting the sphere. The Lambert finds almost universal application in aeronautical sectionals, since it is conformal and represents great circle routes in nearly straight lines. H. C. Albers' projection is ideally suited to the depiction of continental land masses of large longitudinal extent and frequently appears in atlases of North America. (See also Albers Equal Area Conic Map Projection on page 321.)

Further generalization yields the polyconics, whose rendering was virtually intractable before the invention of the computer. The latter represent the broadest projection class in which $x = f(\phi, \lambda)$ and $y = g(\phi, \lambda)$. While excellent for problems of applied cartography, such forms are often both computationally intensive and lacking any closed-form inverses, leaving them unsuitable for direct application to problems arising in computer graphics. Instead, we return to a simple projection and related application.

Cylindrical Equal Area

This projection is obtained by wrapping a unit cylinder around a unit sphere and projecting parallels of latitude directly outward along planes normal to the polar axis. This geometrical derivation yields the pseudo-code

$$x \leftarrow s \times \lambda$$

$$y \leftarrow s \times \sin \phi.$$

As the cylinder is tangent along the equator, this thin region preserves area and angle. In regions of increasing latitude, the spherical shell located between parallels is a projected area, which is foreshortened by an amount $\cos \phi$ on the cylinder, thereby reducing the chart area along the y axis. However, this loss is perfectly offset by the increase in the chart's representation of each parallel's circumferential length, which grows by $\cos \phi$ as described for Sanson's sinusoidal projection.

As a consequence of this infinitesimal equation, a unit sphere and unit cylinder have identical surface area (known to the Greeks before Newton's calculus). As a quick check, the sphere's area is $4\pi r^2$ (or 4π steradians for a unit sphere). Similarly, the cylinder has unwrapped area $w \times h$ with $w = 2\pi r$ and $h = 2r$ giving $4\pi r^2$, in agreement. Being both cylindrical and computationally efficient, this projection—first attributed to Lambert—is another candidate to supplant the all-too-common direct $plotxy(\lambda, \phi)$ approach.

A Practical Application

Consider the rendering of an exploding fireworks shell, whose fragments show no underlying directional bias—the flame trails suggest a dandelion. How are the fragment vectors generated? Consider a stationary shell exploding at the origin (the type loathed by leather-clad pyrotechnicians)! Fragments have an equal likelihood in piercing an encompassing sphere—their flux density is equal per unit area. An equal-area projection (map) of the penetration will be a two-dimensional scatter plot with constant density. Turning the problem around, plotting random points of linear distribution along two independent axes of a 2D equal-area projection and then using the inverse projection forms a uniform spherical distribution.

The projection of choice is cylindrical (one axis of transformation is linear), suggesting the above cylindrical equal-area projection. Its inverse transformation is $\lambda = u$ and $\phi = \sin^{-1} v$ giving a chart running from $-\pi/2$ to $+\pi/2$ in u and from -1 to $+1$ in v. Here (ϕ, λ) are on the sphere and (u, v) are chart coordinates generated along their intervals using a conventional *random( )* routine with suitable offset and scaling. The inverse map forms corresponding (ϕ, λ) values. Finally, the (x, y, z) location of a particle is derived by conversion from spherical to rectangular coordinates:

$$x = R \cos \lambda \cos \phi = R \cos u \cos \sin^{-1} v$$

$$y = R \sin \lambda \cos \phi = R \sin u \cos \sin^{-1} v$$

$$z = R \sin \phi = R \sin \sin^{-1} v.$$

With $\sin^{-1} x = \cos^{-1}\sqrt{1 - x^2}$, the first two equations may be further simplified. $R = 1$ places the points in spherical distribution on a unit sphere about the origin. This yields the program code:

Distribute random points (x, y, z) uniformly on the unit sphere
with results also in (ϕ, λ) polar coordinates.
random() returns a random, uniform distribution on the range [0..1].

```
λ ← π × (2 × random() − 1)   [ − π..π]
z ← 2 × random() − 1          [ − 1..1]
s ← √1 − z²
x ← s × cos λ
y ← s × sin λ
φ ← atan2(z, s)               conventional four-quadrant tan⁻¹
```

The code distributes points linearly along the z axis because parallel cross-sections through a spherical shell generate annuli of equal edge area, as explained above. Axial bearing to x and y also form a linear distribution. The square root term scales the spatial distribution from cylindrical into spherical coordinates. With this tool in hand, one can immediately extend the fireworks model without further regarding the specifics of the underlying projection. Extensions might include fragments of randomized mass distribution with radial velocities in inverse proportion (thus conserving the center of mass), or parabolic fragment trajectories for particles of appreciable mass.

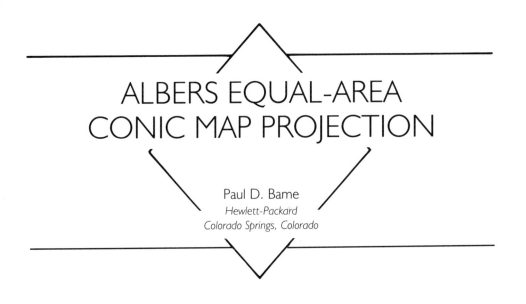

ALBERS EQUAL-AREA CONIC MAP PROJECTION

Paul D. Bame
Hewlett-Packard
Colorado Springs, Colorado

Map projections are used to show a portion of a sphere or ellipsoid, usually earth, in two dimensions in some reasonable way—they usually try to reduce a specific type of distortion. Different projection algorithms are suited to different types of maps. The Albers projection described here is a popular and suitable projection for North America—particularly the continental United States. Check with the U.S. Geological Survey Bulletin (Snyder, 1984) for details of other projection algorithms and their use.

The Albers projection is a particular way to project a sphere or ellipsoid onto a cone. The cone is then "unrolled," yielding the projected coordinates. Because the earth is an ellipsoid rather than a sphere, the calculations are pretty painful.

Imagine intersecting a cone with the earth so that the intersection is two circles of constant latitude (see Fig. 1). The latitudes of these circles of intersection are called *northlat* and *southlat* in the *albers_setup* routine and called "standard parallels" by USGS. Each point on the earth is projected onto the cone as if a normal from the surface of the cone at each point were intersected with the earth. At the standard parallels the normal is of zero length and the map projection has least distortion. Distortion increases with distance from these latitudes.

The standard parallels are usually chosen to be between the northern and southern limits of the map to be plotted so that the distortion is about equal everywhere. The standard parallels may span the equator but may not be equidistant from it. In addition to the standard parallels, a center

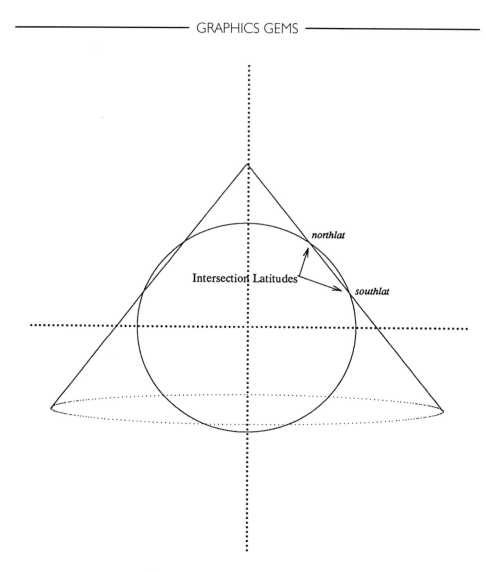

Figure 1.   Cone–ellipsoid intersection.

point (denoted by *originlon* and *originlat*) must be chosen for the projection in Fig. 2.

Projecting maps of the southern hemisphere is discussed in USGS. One simple method of projecting maps entirely in the southern hemisphere is to invert the sign of latitudes and projected Y values.

322

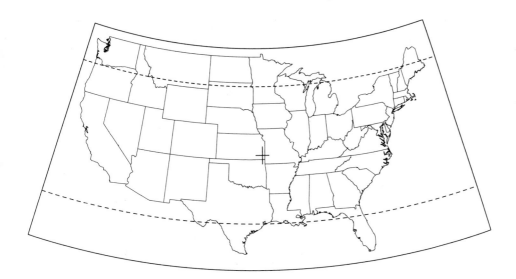

Figure 2. Continental United States projection. Dashed lines show standard parallels and a cross marks the center of the projection.

USGS Standard Parallels		
Region	North Parallel	South Parallel
Continental USA	45.5	29.5
North America	60.0	20.0
Alaska	65.0	55.0
Hawaii & Phillipines	18.0	8.0

Implementation

Implementing map projections is similar to implementing hash tables. One usually consults a reference, finds the appropriate algorithm, and translates the reference pseudo-code into the language of choice. Detailed understanding is often not required. Detailed description of the formulae presented here is not given. Those interested might derive the simpler spherical Albers projection and certainly should obtain USGS, from which most of the notation and math was taken.

Two functions are used repeatedly in the calculations. The first, denoted by $q \leftarrow F(lat)$, is given a latitude and produces q:

$$q \leftarrow (1 - e^2)\left[\frac{\sin(lat)}{1 - e^2 \sin^2(lat)} - \frac{1}{2e}\ln\left(\frac{1 - e\sin(lat)}{1 + e\sin(lat)}\right)\right],$$

where e is the eccentricity of the earth, which for the Clarke ellipsoid is 0.0822719. The following function, denoted by $m \leftarrow G(lat)$, produces m given a latitude:

$$m \leftarrow \cos\left(\frac{lat}{\sqrt{1 - e^2 \sin^2(lat)}}\right).$$

Both these functions have common and repeated terms and run-time may be saved by precomputing and reusing these terms. Also note that in the formulae to follow, m values are always squared before use, which suggests modifying $G(lat)$ to produce m^2 rather than m. For clarity, none of these enhancements are made here.

Several values are usually precomputed from the projection parameters to save compute time. These values are lon_0, the longitude at the center of the map; n, the "cone constant"; C and ρ_0—see USGS for specific definitions. The *albers_setup* routine calculates these values.

albers_setup(northlat, southlat, originlat, originlon)

begin

$lon_0 \leftarrow$ originlon

$q_1 \leftarrow F(southlat)$

$m_1 \leftarrow G(southlat)$

$q_2 \leftarrow F(northlat)$

$m_2 \leftarrow G(northlat)$

$q_0 \leftarrow F(originlat)$

$n \leftarrow \dfrac{m_1^2 - m_2^2}{q_2 - q_1}$

$C \leftarrow m_1^2 + nq_1$

$\rho_0 \leftarrow \sqrt{\dfrac{C - nq_0}{n}}$

end;

After this setup has been performed, the following routine is used to project each $[lon, lat]$ pair to a Cartesian $[x, y]$ pair:

albers_project(lon, lat, x, y)

begin

$\quad$ q $\leftarrow$ F(lat)

$\quad$ $\theta \leftarrow$ n(lon $-$ lon$_0$)

$\quad$ $\rho \leftarrow \sqrt{\dfrac{C - nq}{n}}$

$\quad$ *x and y are in terms of earth radii. Multiply each by earth's*
$\quad$ *radius in miles (kilometers) to convert to miles (kilometers)*

$\quad$ x $\leftarrow \rho \sin(\theta)$

$\quad$ y $\leftarrow \rho_0 - \rho \cos(\theta)$

$\quad$ **end;**

See Appendix 2 for C Implementation (**726**)

325

BOXES AND SPHERES SUMMARY

Many computer graphics applications involve rectangles and circles or boxes and spheres. The rectangle is common because it is the shape commonly assumed for a pixel; in 3D, the box corresponds to a popular voxel shape. The circle arises from the use of radially symmetric sampling and reconstruction filters, and the desire to render circles. Spheres are a popular shape for use as geometric primitives and bounding volumes.

Often one simply needs to know if a given rectangle and circle (or box and sphere) overlap. If the exact geometry of overlap is needed it may then be computed. A 2D algorithm for rectangles and circles was presented in the chapter on 2D Geometry. The following two Gems discuss the problem in 3D.

The first Gem provides an algorithm for scan-converting a sphere into an array of 3D voxels. This algorithm begins with the object, and the result is a list of boxes that are intersected. This technique may be adapted to other shapes, such as cylinders and cones. One would probably use it in an environment where a regular grid of voxels already existed, and membership was needed for each of a variety of primitives.

The second Gem is a more direct solution for a sphere and a given box. It is appropriate when the boxes are of different sizes, such as an adaptively subdivided space. It may also be applied to 3D ellipses, and generalized easily to higher dimensions.

See also Fast Circle–Rectangle Intersection Checking (51); Fast Ray–Box Intersection (395); A Simple Method for Box–Sphere Intersection Testing (335); Ray Tracing Gems

SPHERES-TO-VOXELS CONVERSION

Claudio Montani and Roberto Scopigno
Consiglio Nazionale delle Ricerche
Pisa, Italy

The use or prototyping of volumetric representation schemes based on three-dimensional cells—typical examples are the cubic frame buffer (Kaufman and Bakalash, 1988) or the octree (Meagher, 1982) schemes—often requires the availability of efficient routines for converting elementary solid objects into cells.

In this note we present a conversion algorithm from spheres to voxels. It accepts as input the definition of a sphere (in terms of its radius and center) and returns the set of voxels completely or partially contained into the space bounded by the surface of the sphere, that is, a 3D scan conversion of the sphere.

Based on the well-known Bresenham method for the discretization of a circle (Bresenham, 1977), our conversion algorithm can be easily extended to cylinders or cones, in which the main axis is parallel to either of the Cartesian axes.

The procedure *Circle* describes Bresenham's algorithm for the rasterization of the first (positive) quadrant of an origin-centered circle of radius R (R is an integer). Because of the symmetry of the circle, considering the first quadrant only is not restrictive, neither is referring to an origin-centered circle. The detailed analysis and explanation of this algorithm can be found in Rogers (1985). The pixels located by the algorithm for a circle of radius $R = 8$ are shown in Fig. 1.

```
Circle (R):
    begin
        x ← 0; y ← R;
        Δ ← 2(1 − R);
```

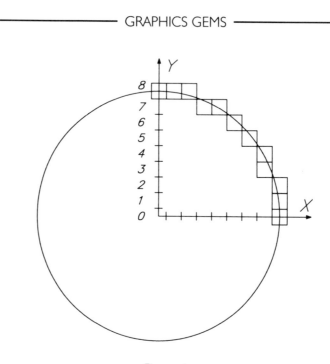

Figure 1.

```
limit ← 0;
Pixel (x, y);          Pixel(x, y) lights the pixel having (x, y) coordinate
while y ≥ limit do
      begin
          if Δ < 0
            then begin
                δ ← 2Δ + 2y − 1;
                if δ > 0
                    then begin
                        x ← x + 1; y ← y − 1;
                        Δ ← Δ + 2x − 2y + 2;
                        end;
                    else begin
                        x ← x + 1;
                        Δ ← Δ + 2x + 1;
                        end;
                end;
            else if Δ > 0
```

```
                   then begin
                        δ ← 2Δ − 2x − 1;
                        if δ > 0
                             then begin
                                  y ← y − 1;
                                  Δ ← Δ − 2y + 1;
                                  end;
                        else begin
                             x ← x + 1; y ← y − 1;
                             Δ ← Δ + 2x − 2y + 2;
                             end;
                        end;
                   else begin
                        x ← x + 1; y ← y − 1;
                        Δ ← Δ + 2x − 2y + 2;
                        end;
              Pixel(x, y);
         end;
    end loop;
end Circle;
```

The algorithm for the conversion from spheres to voxels applies Bresenham's method twice: first divide the sphere into horizontal slices, then discretize the slices. Though we will consider an origin-centered sphere, one can easily translate voxel coordinates with respect to the center.

The procedure *Sphere*(R) discretizes the first quadrant of the circle, with radius R, obtained by intersecting the origin-centered sphere with the plane $Z = 0$ (see Fig. 2). The abscissa of the rightmost pixel of each line $Y = y$ will represent the radius of the circle being discretized, which lies on the XZ plane of height y. Then, the procedure *Slice* is called before the y coordinate changes, that is, on the rightmost pixel of each line.

```
Sphere (R):
    begin
        x ← 0; y ← R;
        Δ ← 2(1 − R); limit ← 0;
        while y ≥ limit do
```

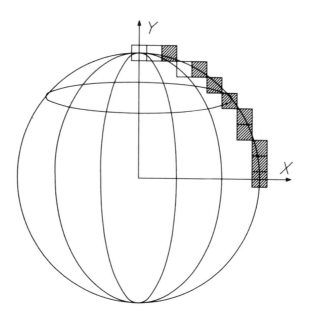

Figure 2.

```
begin
    if Δ < 0
        then begin
            δ ← 2Δ + 2y − 1;
            if δ > 0
                then begin
                    Slice(x, y);
                    x ← x + 1; y ← y − 1;
                    Δ ← Δ + 2x − 2y + 2;
                    end;
                else begin
                    x ← x + 1;
                    Δ ← Δ + 2x + 1;
                    end;
            end;
        else if Δ > 0
```

```
            then begin
                δ ← 2Δ − 2x − 1;
                if δ > 0
                        then begin
                                Slice(x, y);
                                y ← y − 1;
                                Δ ← Δ − 2y + 1;
                                end;
                        else begin
                                Slice(x, y);
                                x ← x + 1; y ← y − 1;
                                Δ ← Δ + 2x − 2y + 2;
                                end;
                end;
            else begin
                Slice(x, y);
                x ← x + 1; y ← y − 1;
                Δ ← Δ + 2x − 2y + 2;
                end;
            end;
        endloop;
    end Sphere;
```

The procedure $Slice(r, y)$ discretizes the first quadrant of the circle of radius r belonging to the plane $Y = y$. For each pixel determined by the procedure, the routine $Track(x, y, z)$ is called. In turn, the latter calls $Voxel(x, y, z)$ on the indices of the voxels belonging to the interval from $(x, y, -z)$ to (x, y, z). As is the case of the $Pixel$ routine used by the $Circle$ procedure, the $Voxel$ routine is implemention-dependent: the voxel coordinates could be stored, used to set an element in the cubic frame buffer, or used to build an octree.

```
    Slice(r, y):
        begin
            x ← 0; z ← r;
            Δ ← 2(1 − r); limit ← 0;
            Track(x, y, z);
            while z ≥ limit do
                    begin
                        if Δ < 0
```

```
then begin
        δ ← 2Δ + 2z − 1;
        if δ > 0
                then begin
                        x ← x + 1; z ← z − 1;
                        Δ ← Δ + 2x − 2z + 2;
                        Track(x, y, z);
                        Track( − x, y, z);
                        end;
                else begin
                        x ← x + 1; Δ ← Δ + 2x + 1;
                        Track(x, y, z);
                        Track( − x, y, z);
                        end;
        end;
else if Δ > 0
        then begin
                δ ← 2Δ − 2x − 1;
                if δ > 0
                        then begin
                                z ← z − 1;
                                Δ ← Δ − 2z + 1;
                                end;
                        else begin
                                x ← x + 1; z ← z − 1;
                                Δ ← Δ + 2x − 2z + 2;
                                Track(x, y, z);
                                Track( − x, y, z);
                                end;
                end;
        else begin
                x ← x + 1; z ← z − 1;
                Δ ← Δ + 2x − 2z + 2;
                Track(x, y, z);
                Track( − x, y, z);
                end;
        end;
    endloop;
end Slice;
```

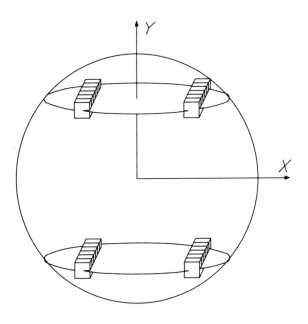

Figure 3.

Due to the symmetry of the sphere, if $x \neq 0$ the procedure *Slice* calls *Track* also on the point $(-x, y, z)$, while if $y \neq 0$ the procedure *Track* invokes *Voxel* also on the list of voxels in the interval from $(x, -y, -z)$ to $(x, -y, z)$.

It is worth noting that *Slice* does not call *Track* in case of vertical displacement; in fact, in this situation, the list of corresponding voxels has just been determined. In Fig. 3 the sets of voxels produced by the algorithm for the generic (x, y, z) point are depicted.

```
Track(x, y, z):
    begin
        for k: integer ← −z, k ← k + 1, k ≤ z do
            Voxel (x, y, k);
            endloop
        if y ≠ 0
            then
                for k: integer ← −z, k ← k + 1, k ≤ z do
                    Voxel(x, −y, k);
                    endloop;
    end Track;
```

While an $O(R^3)$ number of voxels is returned, the computational cost of the algorithm is proportional to R^2 (R being the radius of the sphere), with a small proportionality constant. This is true for two reasons: one is because the *Sphere* and *Slice* procedures only work on the positive quadrants of the circles to be discretized; the other is that the activation of *Sphere* with radius R causes the activation of *Slice* R times with parameter r (the radius of a slice) such that $1 < r \leq R$.

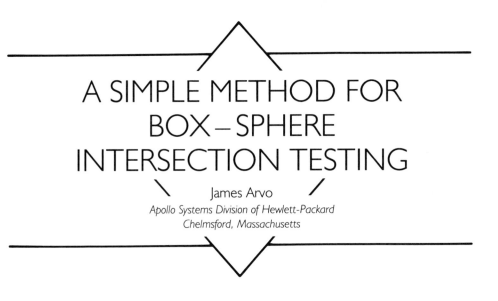

A SIMPLE METHOD FOR BOX–SPHERE INTERSECTION TESTING

James Arvo

Apollo Systems Division of Hewlett-Packard
Chelmsford, Massachusetts

Introduction

There are a number of computer graphics applications in which it is necessary to determine whether a sphere intersects an axis-aligned parallelepiped, or "box." In two dimensions this arises when rasterizing circles, which are two-dimensional spheres, into rectangular viewports, which are two-dimensional boxes. The intersection test is used to determine whether any portion of the circle is indeed visible before rasterizing. In three dimensions this operation may arise in spatial subdivision techniques that identify "voxels," or 3D boxes, pierced by the surfaces of various objects. If spheres are among the objects, or are used as bounding volumes for other objects, we need to test for 3D box–sphere intersection.

   This note describes a simple method for detecting intersections of n-dimensional boxes with n-dimensional spheres taken as either surfaces or solids. Applications for $n > 3$ are not addressed here, though the algorithm works in any dimension. For greatest generality all algorithms shown below take the dimension of the space, n, as an input parameter, though typical implementations would be optimized for either two or three dimensions.

Solid Objects

Suppose we wish to determine whether a solid n-dimensional box, B, intersects a solid n-dimensional sphere with center C and radius r. Here "solid" means that we include the interior as well as the boundary. Denote C by $(C_1, \ldots, C_n)$ and B by the closed intervals $[B_1^{min}, B_1^{max}]$, $\ldots, [B_n^{min}, B_n^{max}]$. We can perform this test by finding the point P on or in the box that is closest to the center of the sphere. If the distance between this point and C is no greater than r, then the box intersects the sphere. Thus, if the point $P \in R^n$ minimizes the distance function

$$\text{dist}(P) = \sqrt{(C_1 - P_1)^2 + \ldots + (C_n - P_n)^2}, \qquad (1)$$

subject to the constraints

$$B_i^{min} \leq P_i \leq B_i^{max} \quad \text{for } i = 1, \ldots, n, \qquad (2)$$

then the solids intersect if and only if $\text{dist}(P) \leq r$. As a simplification we will eliminate the square root by computing squared distances and comparing with r^2. It is a simple matter to find the P that minimizes the square of Eq. 1 because each term of the sum is nonnegative and can be minimized independently. If the ith coordinate of the sphere center satisfies the ith constraint, that is, if $B_i^{min} \leq C_i \leq B_i^{max}$, then setting $P_i = C_i$ reduces this term to zero. Otherwise, we set P_i equal to either B_i^{min} or B_i^{max} depending on which is closer. Summing the squares of the distances produces the minimum total squared distance. The algorithm in Fig. 1 uses this principle to determine whether a solid box intersects a solid sphere. The input parameters are the dimension n, box B, sphere

```
boolean function SolidBox_SolidSphere(n, B, C, r)
begin
    d_min ← 0;

    for i ← 1 . . . n do
        if C_i < B_i^min then d_min ← d_min + (C_i − B_i^min)²;
        else
            if C_i > B_i^max then d_min ← d_min + (C_i − B_i^max)²;
        endloop;

    if d_min ≤ r² then return [True]
    else return [False];

end;
```

Figure 1. An algorithm for intersecting a solid n-dimensional box with a solid n-dimensional sphere.

center C, and sphere radius r. The function value is returned as "True" if the objects intersect and "False" otherwise.

Hollow Objects

If we wish to make either or both of the objects hollow and test only their surfaces, we can do so by regarding total inclusion of one object inside the other as nonintersection. For instance, if we wish to test whether the surface of the sphere intersects the solid box, we can add a test for whether the box is entirely contained within the sphere and regard this as nonintersection. This is shown in the algorithm of Fig. 2, in which we've added the computation of the square distance from C to the farthest point of B. If this value, denoted d_{max}, is less than r^2, the entire box is inside the sphere and there is no intersection.

The approach is different if we wish to disregard the interior of the box. Here the constraints of Eq. 2 still hold but in order for the point P to be on the boundary of the box we require the additional constraint that $P_i = B_i^{min}$ or $P_i = B_i^{max}$ for some i. In the algorithm of Fig. 1 we see that this holds unless $C_i \in (B_i^{min}, B_i^{max})$ for all i. In this case we need to determine whether moving P to the nearest face of the box places it

```
boolean function SolidBox_HollowSphere(n, B, C, r)
begin
    d_max ← 0;
    d_min ← 0;

    for i ← 1...n do
        a ← (C_i − B_i^min)²;
        b ← (C_i − B_i^max)²;
        d_max ← d_max + max(a, b);
        if C_i ∉ [B_i^min, B_i^max] then d_min ← d_min + min(a,b);
        endloop;

    if r² ∈ [d_min, d_max] then return [True]
    else return [False];

end;
```

Figure 2. An algorithm for intersecting a solid n-dimensional box with a hollow n-dimensional sphere.

337

```
boolean function HollowBox_SolidSphere(n, B, C, r)
begin

    d_min ← 0;
    d_face ← infinity;

    for i ← 1...n do
        t ← min((C_i − B_i^min)^2, (C_i − B_i^max)^2);
        if C_i ∈ [B_i^min, B_i^max] then d_face ← min(d_face, t);
        else begin
            d_face = 0;
            d_min ← d_min + t;
        end
    endloop;
    if d_min + d_face ≤ r^2 then return [True]
    else return [False];

end;
```

Figure 3. An algorithm for intersecting a hollow n-dimensional box with a solid n-dimensional sphere.

outside the sphere. In Fig. 3 we have modified the algorithm to compute the smallest such adjustment, denoted d_{face}. We add this to the minimum distance between the box and C, and if the result remains less than r^2, the surface of the box intersects the solid sphere. The approaches in Fig. 2 and Fig. 3 can be combined to test for intersection between a hollow box and a hollow sphere.

Generalizing to Ellipsoids

We can easily generalize this idea to work with axis-aligned ellipsoids, that is, ellipsoids that result from scaling a sphere differently along the coordinate axes. We can specify such a ellipsoid in n-space by its center, $C \in R^n$, and a "radius" for each axis, $\alpha_1, \ldots, \alpha_n$. The point $P \in R^n$ is on or in such an ellipsoid if and only if

$$\left[\frac{C_1 - P_1}{\alpha_1} \right]^2 + \cdots + \left[\frac{C_n - P_n}{\alpha_n} \right]^2 \leq 1. \qquad (3)$$

boolean function SolidBox_SolidEllipsoid(n, B, C, α)
begin

$d_{min} \leftarrow 0;$

for $i \leftarrow 1 \ldots n$ **do**

if $C_i < B_i^{min}$ **then** $d_{min} \leftarrow d_{min} + \left[\dfrac{C_i - B_i^{min}}{\alpha_i}\right]^2;$

else

if $C_i > B_i^{max}$ **then** $d_{min} \leftarrow d_{min} + \left[\dfrac{C_i - B_i^{max}}{\alpha_i}\right]^2;$

endloop;

if $d_{min} \leq 1$ **then return** [True]
else return [False];

end;

Figure 4.   An algorithm for intersecting a solid n-dimensional box with a solid n-dimensional axis-aligned ellipsoid.

Modifying the algorithm in Fig. 1 to handle this type of ellipsoid results in the algorithm shown in Fig. 4. Here the scalar input parameter r has been changed to the array α. Modifications for either hollow boxes or hollow ellipsoids are analogous to those previously described.

See Appendix 2 for C Implementation (**730**)

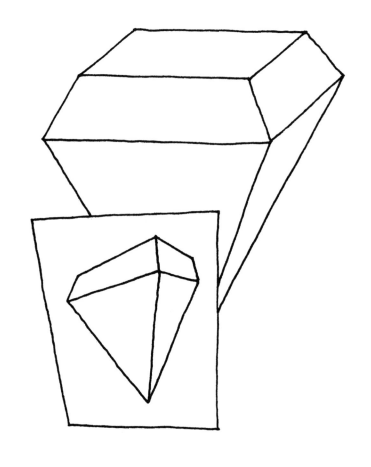

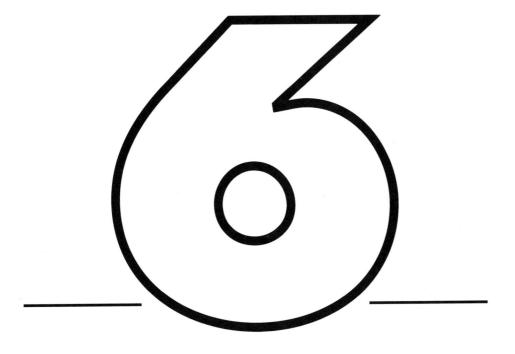

6

3D RENDERING

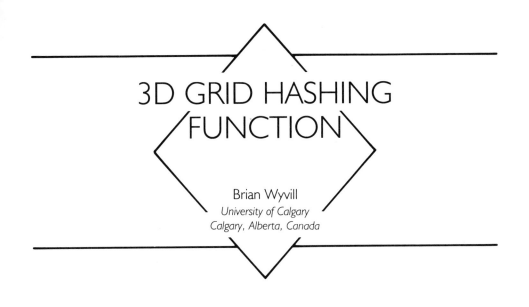

3D GRID HASHING FUNCTION

Brian Wyvill
University of Calgary
Calgary, Alberta, Canada

Voxel Subdivision

For various applications in computer graphics it is often necessary to sort objects into a 3D grid of cubes or *voxels* according to their position in space. One way of keeping track of which objects are stored in which voxels is simply to keep a 3D array of voxels in memory. Voxel grids don't have to be very large before this becomes impractical, since the size of the array goes up as the cube of the sides. Sometimes it is convenient to store the grid at a variety of resolutions; this is done using an octree. The tree divides into eight branches at every node. This corresponds to cutting the cube (node) along three orthogonal planes into eight sub-cubes. A node is subdivided if it is required to examine its contents in greater detail. If great depth is required, octrees can also use large amounts of memory. If many of the voxels are empty or the level of detail is known at the start, a table of pointers can be used to represent the grid. Each location in the table represents a group of neighboring voxels; a linked list allows access to the voxels in the group. Each voxel within the group points to a list of objects to be found in that particular voxel. The problem is how to make a good hash function that can be computed from the x, y, z location of the object to be stored. The function really acts as a sorting mechanism to distinguish groups of neighboring objects.

Computing the Hash Function

If the object position is characterized by the *origin*, an integer coordinate triple, (x, y, z), then the address in the hash table can be computed by combining the most significant few bits of each of x, y, and z. The table contains a relatively small number of entries, each one representing a group of voxels. Objects with the same hash address are in fact near neighbors, which are in the same group but not necessarily the same voxel.

To compute the address from the (x, y, z) triple it is necessary to know the length of the table and the number of voxels. For example, if the world is to be divided into a cube 256 voxels on a side then 256*256*256 (16,777,216) locations would be required to store the entire table. If the table was to be only 4096 locations in length, a table address could be

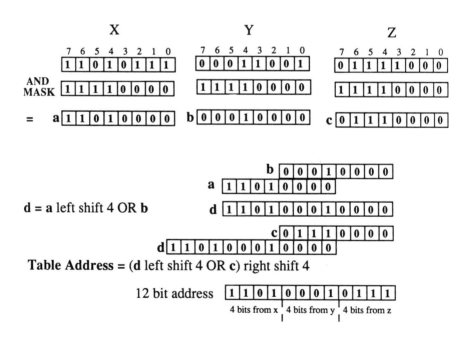

Figure 1. Finding a 12-bit address from x, y, z. In this example x, y, and z are shown as 1-byte values.

stored in four bits for each dimension. (addressed 0 to 4095). To ensure that an out-of-bounds index is not computed, x, y, and z must lie within a predefined range of positive values. For example, if range is set to 256 (8 bits) and the hash address is 12 bits then the top 4 bits of each of x, y, and z are used to compute this address. A bit mask is used to select the most significant four bits from the bottom eight bits of an x, y, z integer; in this example the mask is set to (11110000) (octal 360). (see Fig. 1). In the C example RANGE is set to 256, NBITS to 4.

Note that the following conditions must hold:

$$\log2(\text{RANGE}) \le \text{NBITS},$$

$$\text{MIXINT} \ge \text{RANGE}$$

$$0 \le x \le \text{RANGE} - 1$$

$$0 \le y \le \text{RANGE} - 1$$

$$0 \le z \le \text{RANGE} - 1$$

2 to the power NBITS*3 gives the length of the table.

See also Ray Tracing (383)

See Appendix 2 for C Implementation (**733**)

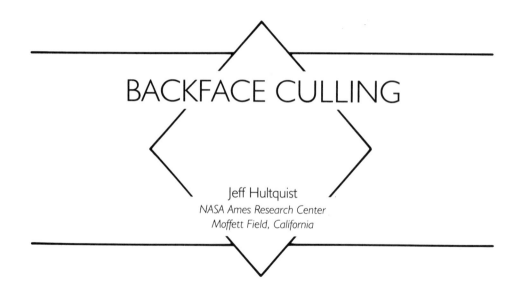

BACKFACE CULLING

Jeff Hultquist
NASA Ames Research Center
Moffett Field, California

Convex polygonal objects can be drawn rapidly by testing each face for visibility. We can construct the database for each shape so that the vertices around each face are listed in a counterclockwise order (such an object is called *oriented*).

Once all of the vertices of such an object are mapped into the two-dimensional screen coordinates, the visible faces will be "wrapped" in one direction, and the invisible faces will be wrapped in the other. We can test the wrapping direction of a face by taking adjacent vectors **BA** and **BC**, which lie along two edges of that face. The cross-product of these two edges is a vector that will point either into or out of the screen, depending on the wrapping direction.

To determine which edges of a convex oriented polygonal object are visible, we can test the visibility of each face. An edge shared by two visible faces is itself visible. An edge that aligns with only one visible face is on the silhouette of the object. All other edges are hidden from view.

This test can be used to determine which edges are visible on a convex, closed, and oriented object. First associate with each edge a "visibility count" initialized to zero, then examine each face of the object. Use the wrapping test described above to determine if the polygon is facing into or out of the screen. If it is facing out of the screen, then increment the visibility count for each of its edges. Once all of the faces have been processed, the visibility count for each edge will 0, 1, or 2. Edges with a

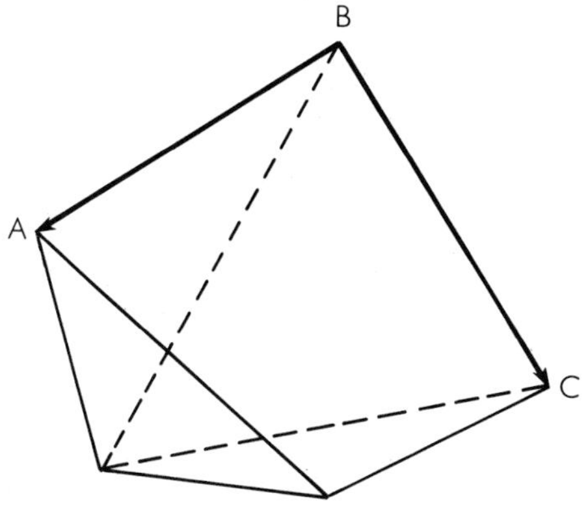

Figure 1.

count of 2 are fully visible, whereas a 1 indicates an edge that defines the silhouette of the object. Edges with a count of zero are fully obscured.

See also Scan Conversion Summary (75)

FAST DOT
PRODUCTS FOR
SHADING

Mark Lee

Amoco Production Company
Tulsa, Oklahoma

As images become more sophisticated, the illumination models used in generating the images are also generally more sophisticated. These illumination models become more and more expensive to compute. This article describes a method of reusing some of the computations to save on the total number of arithmetic operations necessary for evaluating the illumination model.

Several direction vectors are needed when using current illumination models. The following is a glossary of the vectors to be used in this article (see Fig. 1):

$\mathbf{L}$—the vector that points in the direction of the light source,

$\mathbf{V}$—the vector that points in the viewing direction,

$\mathbf{N}$—the normal to the reflecting or refracting surface,

$\mathbf{H}$—the normal to an imaginary surface that would reflect light perfectly from $\mathbf{L}$ to $\mathbf{V}$,

$\mathbf{H}'$—the normal to an imaginary surface that would refract light perfectly from $\mathbf{L}$ to $\mathbf{V}$,

$\mathbf{H_u}$—an unnormalized form of $\mathbf{H}$,

$\mathbf{H'_u}$—an unnormalized form of $\mathbf{H}'$.

The vectors $\mathbf{N}$, $\mathbf{L}$, $\mathbf{V}$, $\mathbf{H}$, and $\mathbf{H}'$ are assumed to have unit length. Also, all of these vectors are assumed to be oriented pointing away from the

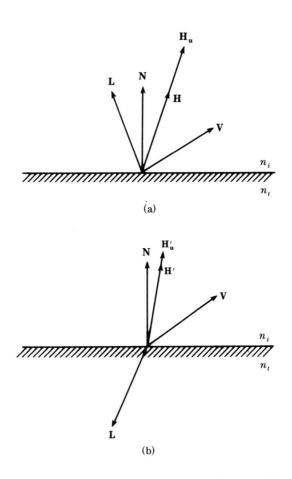

(a)

(b)

Figure 1. Geometry for the reflection and refraction of light.

surface. **H** is used whenever **L** and **V** lie on the same side of the surface $[(\mathbf{N} \cdot \mathbf{V})(\mathbf{N} \cdot \mathbf{L}) > 0]$ and **H′** is used whenever **L** and **V** lie on opposite sides of the surface $[(\mathbf{N} \cdot \mathbf{V})(\mathbf{N} \cdot \mathbf{L}) < 0]$.

Generally, the vectors **V**, **L**, and **N** are known at the time the illumination model is invoked. The vectors **H** and **H′** are usually generated within the illumination model to calculate the values $\mathbf{N} \cdot \mathbf{H}$, $\mathbf{N} \cdot \mathbf{H}'$, $\mathbf{V} \cdot \mathbf{H}$, and $\mathbf{V} \cdot \mathbf{H}'$ for use in computing the facet distribution function, D, the facet self-shadowing factor, G, and the Fresnel reflectance, F (Blinn, 1977; Cook and Torrance, 1982). Generally, however, by the time the terms D,

F, and G are to be evaluated, the terms $\mathbf{N} \cdot \mathbf{L}$ and $\mathbf{N} \cdot \mathbf{V}$ have been generated for use by other parts of the illumination model (diffuse reflectance, vector orientation and so forth). By utilizing the terms $\mathbf{N} \cdot \mathbf{L}$ and $\mathbf{N} \cdot \mathbf{V}$, the vectors $\mathbf{H}$ and $\mathbf{H}'$ need not be explicitly created. The remainder of this article will discuss calculating $\mathbf{N} \cdot \mathbf{H}$, $\mathbf{N} \cdot \mathbf{H}'$, $\mathbf{V} \cdot \mathbf{H}$, and $\mathbf{V} \cdot \mathbf{H}'$ given $\mathbf{L}$, $\mathbf{V}$, $\mathbf{N}$, $\mathbf{N} \cdot \mathbf{L}$, and $\mathbf{N} \cdot \mathbf{V}$.

Let's start by examining the case of the reflection of light (see Fig. 1a). Remember, $\mathbf{H}$ is the normal to an imaginary surface that would reflect light perfectly from $\mathbf{L}$ to $\mathbf{V}$. $\mathbf{H}$ is defined as

$$\mathbf{H} = \frac{\mathbf{L} + \mathbf{V}}{|\mathbf{L} + \mathbf{V}|},$$

(Cook, 1982; Glassner *et al.*, 1989; Hall, 1989). The terms $\mathbf{N} \cdot \mathbf{H}$ and $\mathbf{V} \cdot \mathbf{H}$ could be calculated by first forming the vector $\mathbf{H}$, and then calculating $\mathbf{N} \cdot \mathbf{H}$ and $\mathbf{V} \cdot \mathbf{H}$ directly. However, by using previously calculated information, namely $\mathbf{N} \cdot \mathbf{L}$ and $\mathbf{N} \cdot \mathbf{V}$, the number of arithmetic operations may be decreased.

Define $\mathbf{H}$ and $\mathbf{H_u}$ (the unnormalized form of $\mathbf{H}$) as follows:

$$\mathbf{H_u} = \mathbf{L} + \mathbf{V} \quad \text{and} \quad \mathbf{H} = \frac{\mathbf{H_u}}{|\mathbf{H_u}|}.$$

Remember, $|\mathbf{H_u}| = \sqrt{(\mathbf{H_u} \cdot \mathbf{H_u})}$, which means that

$$\mathbf{H_u} \cdot \mathbf{H_u} = (\mathbf{L} + \mathbf{V}) \cdot (\mathbf{L} + \mathbf{V})$$

$$= (\mathbf{L} \cdot \mathbf{L}) + 2(\mathbf{L} \cdot \mathbf{V}) + (\mathbf{V} \cdot \mathbf{V})$$

$$= 2(\mathbf{L} \cdot \mathbf{V}) + 2$$

$$\therefore |\mathbf{H_u}| = \sqrt{2(\mathbf{L} \cdot \mathbf{V}) + 2}.$$

Now the factors $\mathbf{N} \cdot \mathbf{H}$ and $\mathbf{V} \cdot \mathbf{H}$ can be rewritten as follows:

$$\mathbf{N} \cdot \mathbf{H} = \mathbf{N} \cdot \left(\frac{\mathbf{H_u}}{|\mathbf{H_u}|} \right)$$
$$= \frac{(\mathbf{N} \cdot \mathbf{H_u})}{|\mathbf{H_u}|}$$
$$= \frac{[\mathbf{N} \cdot (\mathbf{L} + \mathbf{V})]}{|\mathbf{H_u}|}$$
$$= \frac{[(\mathbf{N} \cdot \mathbf{L}) + (\mathbf{N} \cdot \mathbf{V})]}{|\mathbf{H_u}|}$$
$$= \frac{[(\mathbf{N} \cdot \mathbf{L}) + (\mathbf{N} \cdot \mathbf{V})]}{\sqrt{2(\mathbf{L} \cdot \mathbf{V}) + 2}}$$

$$\mathbf{V} \cdot \mathbf{H} = \mathbf{V} \cdot \left(\frac{\mathbf{H_u}}{|\mathbf{H_u}|} \right)$$
$$= \frac{(\mathbf{V} \cdot \mathbf{H_u})}{|\mathbf{H_u}|}$$
$$= \frac{[\mathbf{V} \cdot (\mathbf{L} + \mathbf{V})]}{|\mathbf{H_u}|}$$
$$= \frac{[(\mathbf{L} \cdot \mathbf{V}) + (\mathbf{V} \cdot \mathbf{V})]}{|\mathbf{H_u}|}$$
$$= \frac{[(\mathbf{L} \cdot \mathbf{V}) + 1]}{\sqrt{2(\mathbf{L} \cdot \mathbf{V}) + 2}}.$$

Now, compare the number of arithmetic operations needed by the two methods to calculate $\mathbf{N} \cdot \mathbf{H}$ and $\mathbf{V} \cdot \mathbf{H}$. First, define $\mathbf{V} = (v_x, v_y, v_z)$, $\mathbf{L} = (l_x, l_y, l_z)$, $\mathbf{N} = (n_x, n_y, n_z)$, and $\mathbf{H} = (h_x, h_y, h_z)$.

Direct algorithm, given, $\mathbf{L}$*,* $\mathbf{N}$*,* $\mathbf{V}$*,* $\mathbf{N} \cdot \mathbf{L}$*, and* $\mathbf{N} \cdot \mathbf{V}$
$h_x \leftarrow l_x + v_x$
$h_y \leftarrow l_y + v_y$
$h_z \leftarrow l_z + v_z$
$b \leftarrow \sqrt{(h_x * h_x) + (h_y * h_y) + (h_z * h_z)}$
$ndoth \leftarrow [(n_x * h_x) + (n_y * h_y) + (n_z * h_z)]/b$
$vdoth \leftarrow [(v_x * h_x) + (v_y * h_y) + (v_z * h_z)]/b$

New algorithm, given $\mathbf{L}$*,* $\mathbf{N}$*,* $\mathbf{V}$*,* $\mathbf{N} \cdot \mathbf{L}$*, and* $\mathbf{N} \cdot \mathbf{V}$
$a \leftarrow (l_x * v_x) + (l_y * v_y) + (l_z * v_z) + 1$
$b \leftarrow \sqrt{a + a}$
$ndoth \leftarrow [ndotl + ndotv]/b$
$vdoth \leftarrow a/b$

This implementation of the direct algorithm requires 9 additions/subtractions, 11 multiplications/divisions, and 1 square root, whereas the implementation of the new algorithm requires only 5 additions/subtractions, 5 multiplications/divisions, and 1 square root (for scalar-based machines). The difference comes from making more use of previously calculated information.

Now, let's examine the case of the refraction of light (see Fig. 1b). Let n_i be the index of refraction for the medium of incidence and n_t be the index of refraction for the medium of transmittance. From Hall (1989) and Glassner et $al.$ (1989), $\mathbf{H}'$ can be formulated as

$$\mathbf{H}' = \frac{-\left[\mathbf{L} + \left(\dfrac{\mathbf{V} + \mathbf{L}}{\dfrac{n_t}{n_i} - 1}\right)\right]}{\left|\mathbf{L} + \left(\dfrac{\mathbf{V} + \mathbf{L}}{\dfrac{n_t}{n_i} - 1}\right)\right|} = \frac{-\left(\dfrac{\dfrac{n_t}{n_i}\mathbf{L} + \mathbf{V}}{\dfrac{n_t}{n_i} - 1}\right)}{\left|\dfrac{\dfrac{n_t}{n_i}\mathbf{L} + \mathbf{V}}{\dfrac{n_t}{n_i} - 1}\right|} \quad \text{if } n_i < n_t,$$

and

$$\mathbf{H}' = \frac{\left[\mathbf{V} + \left(\dfrac{\mathbf{L} + \mathbf{V}}{\dfrac{n_i}{n_t} - 1}\right)\right]}{\left|\mathbf{V} + \left(\dfrac{\mathbf{L} + \mathbf{V}}{\dfrac{n_i}{n_t} - 1}\right)\right|} = \frac{\left(\dfrac{\dfrac{n_i}{n_t}\mathbf{V} + \mathbf{L}}{\dfrac{n_i}{n_t} - 1}\right)}{\left|\dfrac{\dfrac{n_i}{n_t}\mathbf{V} + \mathbf{L}}{\dfrac{n_i}{n_t} - 1}\right|} \quad \text{if } n_i > n_t.$$

Note, however, that

$$\frac{-\left(\dfrac{n_i}{n_t}\right)\left[-\dfrac{n_t}{n_i}\mathbf{L} - \mathbf{V}\right]}{-\left(\dfrac{n_i}{n_t}\right)\left[\dfrac{n_t}{n_i} - 1\right]} = \frac{\dfrac{n_i}{n_t}\mathbf{V} + \mathbf{L}}{\dfrac{n_i}{n_t} - 1},$$

which proves that all of these formulations of $\mathbf{H}'$ are really one and the same; therefore, we will choose

$$\mathbf{H}' = \cfrac{\left(\cfrac{\dfrac{n_i}{n_t}\mathbf{V} + \mathbf{L}}{\dfrac{n_i}{n_t} - 1}\right)}{\left|\cfrac{\dfrac{n_i}{n_t}\mathbf{V} + \mathbf{L}}{\dfrac{n_i}{n_t} - 1}\right|}$$

Unlike $\mathbf{H}$, $\mathbf{H}'$ does not exist for all configurations of $\mathbf{L}$ and $\mathbf{V}$. The first exception occurs when $n_i = n_t$. In this case, $\mathbf{H}'$ exists only when $\mathbf{L}$ and $\mathbf{V}$ are parallel to each other and point in opposite directions, in which case, $\mathbf{H}' = \mathbf{V}$; therefore, $\mathbf{N} \cdot \mathbf{H}' = \mathbf{N} \cdot \mathbf{V}$ and $\mathbf{V} \cdot \mathbf{H}' = 1$ when $\mathbf{H}'$ exists.

The second exception occurs when the law of refraction does not hold. Refraction is governed by Snell's law, which states that $n_i \sin \theta_i = n_t \sin \theta_t$ where θ_i is the angle of incidence and θ_t is the angle of transmittance. Since $-1 \le \sin \theta \le 1$ and $n_i, n_t > 1$, there exist $n_i, n_t, \theta_i, \theta_t$ such that Snell's law cannot be satisfied. Another constraint is that θ_i and θ_t must lie in the range $[0, \pi/2]$.

Suppose that $n_i < n_t$. Rearranging Snell's law gives $\sin \theta_i = (n_t/n_i)\sin \theta_t$. Obviously, the right-hand side of the equation can get larger than 1, whereas the left-hand side of the equation cannot. The point where $1 = (n_t/n_i)\sin \theta_t$ is called the critical angle, θ_c. Beyond this angle, total internal reflection occurs; therefore, the region of existence for $\mathbf{H}'$ is $0 \le \theta_t \le \theta_c$ for $n_i < n_t$.

Now, from Fig. 2, the angle between $\mathbf{V}$ and $\mathbf{L}$ is $(\pi/2 - \theta_i) + \pi/2 + \theta_t$. Using the facts that

$$\sin \theta_t = -\cos\left(\frac{\pi}{2} + \theta_t\right)$$

$$-\cos\left(\frac{\pi}{2} + \theta_t\right) \le -\cos\left(\frac{\pi}{2} + \theta_t + \left(\frac{\pi}{2} - \theta_i\right)\right)$$

$$-\mathbf{L} \cdot \mathbf{V} = -\cos\left(\frac{\pi}{2} + \theta_t + \left(\frac{\pi}{2} - \theta_i\right)\right),$$

353

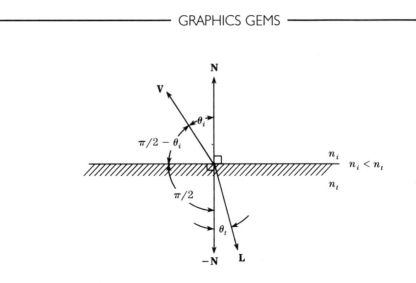

Figure 2.

we can derive the following:

$$\frac{n_i}{n_t} = \sin \theta_t$$

$$= -\cos\left(\frac{\pi}{2} + \theta_t\right)$$

$$\leq -\cos\left(\frac{\pi}{2} + \theta_t + \left(\frac{\pi}{2} - \theta_i\right)\right)$$

$$= -\mathbf{L} \cdot \mathbf{V}$$

$$\therefore \frac{n_i}{n_t} \leq -\mathbf{L} \cdot \mathbf{V}.$$

Also, $(n_i/n_t) < (n_t/n_i)$.

Suppose now that $n_t < n_i$. Rearranging Snell's law gives $(n_i/n_t)\sin \theta_i = \sin \theta_t$. The critical angle occurs at $(n_i/n_t)\sin \theta_i = 1$.

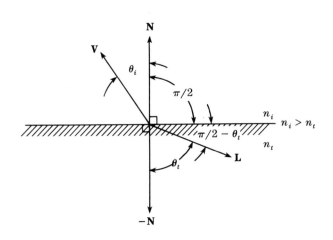

Figure 3.

From Fig. 3, the angle between $\mathbf{V}$ and $\mathbf{L}$ is $(\pi/2 - \theta_t) + \pi/2 + \theta_i$. Using the facts that

$$\sin \theta_i = -\cos\left(\frac{\pi}{2} + \theta_i\right)$$

$$-\cos\left(\frac{\pi}{2} + \theta_i\right) \leq -\cos\left(\frac{\pi}{2} + \theta_i + \left(\frac{\pi}{2} - \theta_t\right)\right)$$

$$-\mathbf{L} \cdot \mathbf{V} = -\cos\left(\frac{\pi}{2} + \theta_i + \left(\frac{\pi}{2} - \theta_t\right)\right),$$

we can derive the following:

$$\frac{n_t}{n_i} = \sin \theta_i$$

$$= -\cos\left(\frac{\pi}{2} + \theta_i\right)$$

$$\leq -\cos\left(\frac{\pi}{2} + \theta_i + \left(\frac{\pi}{2} - \theta_t\right)\right)$$

$$= -\mathbf{L} \cdot \mathbf{V}$$

$$\therefore \frac{n_t}{n_i} \leq -\mathbf{L} \cdot \mathbf{V}.$$

Also, $(n_t/n_i) < (n_i/n_t)$.

355

Combining the results for the cases $n_i < n_t$ and $n_t < n_i$, $\mathbf{H}'$ exists if $\min((n_i/n_t), (n_t/n_i)) \le -\mathbf{L} \cdot \mathbf{V}$.

The terms $\mathbf{N} \cdot \mathbf{H}'$ and $\mathbf{V} \cdot \mathbf{H}'$ could be calculated by first forming the vector $\mathbf{H}'$, and then calculating $\mathbf{N} \cdot \mathbf{H}'$ and $\mathbf{V} \cdot \mathbf{H}'$ directly. However, by reusing $\mathbf{N} \cdot \mathbf{L}$ and $\mathbf{N} \cdot \mathbf{V}$, the number of arithmetic operations may be decreased.

Define $\mathbf{H}'$ and $\mathbf{H}'_\mathbf{u}$ (the unnormalized form of $\mathbf{H}'$) as

$$\mathbf{H}'_\mathbf{u} = \frac{\dfrac{n_i}{n_t}\mathbf{V} + \mathbf{L}}{\dfrac{n_i}{n_t} - 1} \quad \text{and} \quad \mathbf{H}' = \frac{\mathbf{H}'_\mathbf{u}}{|\mathbf{H}'_\mathbf{u}|}.$$

$$\mathbf{H}'_\mathbf{u} \cdot \mathbf{H}'_\mathbf{u} = \left(\frac{\dfrac{n_i}{n_t}\mathbf{V} + \mathbf{L}}{\dfrac{n_i}{n_t} - 1} \right) \cdot \left(\frac{\dfrac{n_i}{n_t}\mathbf{V} + \mathbf{L}}{\dfrac{n_i}{n_t} - 1} \right)$$

$$= \left(\frac{1}{\dfrac{n_i}{n_t} - 1} \right)^2 \left[\left(\frac{n_i}{n_t}\right)^2 (\mathbf{V} \cdot \mathbf{V}) + 2\frac{n_i}{n_t}(\mathbf{L} \cdot \mathbf{V}) + (\mathbf{L} \cdot \mathbf{L}) \right]$$

$$= \left(\frac{1}{\dfrac{n_i}{n_t} - 1} \right)^2 \left[\left(\frac{n_i}{n_t}\right)^2 + 2\frac{n_i}{n_t}(\mathbf{L} \cdot \mathbf{V}) + 1 \right]$$

$$\therefore |\mathbf{H}'_\mathbf{u}| = \left| \frac{1}{\dfrac{n_i}{n_t} - 1} \right| \sqrt{ \left(\frac{n_i}{n_t}\right)^2 + 2\frac{n_i}{n_t}(\mathbf{L} \cdot \mathbf{V}) + 1 }$$

Take a look at the expression $(n_i/n_t)^2 + 2(n_i/n_t)(\mathbf{L} \cdot \mathbf{V}) + 1$. Since $(n_i/n_t)^2 + 1 > 0$, only $\mathbf{L} \cdot \mathbf{V}$ could be less than zero. The expression $2(n_i/n_t)(\mathbf{L} \cdot \mathbf{V})$ is smallest when $\mathbf{L} \cdot \mathbf{V} = -1$. Now, assuming $n_i \ne n_t$

and $\mathbf{L} \cdot \mathbf{V} = -1$,

$$\left(\frac{n_i}{n_t}\right)^2 + 2\frac{n_i}{n_t}(\mathbf{L} \cdot \mathbf{V}) + 1$$

$$= \left(\frac{n_i}{n_t}\right)^2 - 2\frac{n_i}{n_t} + 1$$

$$= \left(\frac{n_i}{n_t} - 1\right)^2 > 0.$$

Therefore, $(n_i/n_t)^2 + 2(n_i/n_t)(\mathbf{L} \cdot \mathbf{V}) + 1 > 0 \; \forall n_i \neq n_t$ and no check need be made for the square root of a negative number.

Now, the dot products $\mathbf{N} \cdot \mathbf{H}'$ and $\mathbf{V} \cdot \mathbf{H}'$ can be reformulated as

$$\mathbf{N} \cdot \mathbf{H}' = \mathbf{N} \cdot \left(\frac{\mathbf{H}'_\mathbf{u}}{|\mathbf{H}'_\mathbf{u}|}\right)$$

$$= \frac{(\mathbf{N} \cdot \mathbf{H}'_\mathbf{u})}{|\mathbf{H}'_\mathbf{u}|}$$

$$= \frac{1}{|\mathbf{H}'_\mathbf{u}|}\left[\mathbf{N} \cdot \left(\frac{\dfrac{n_i}{n_t}\mathbf{V} + \mathbf{L}}{\dfrac{n_i}{n_t} - 1}\right)\right]$$

$$= \frac{1}{|\mathbf{H}'_\mathbf{u}|\left(\dfrac{n_i}{n_t} - 1\right)}\left[\frac{n_i}{n_t}(\mathbf{N} \cdot \mathbf{V}) + (\mathbf{N} \cdot \mathbf{L})\right]$$

$$= \frac{1}{\left(\dfrac{n_i}{n_t} - 1\right)\left|\dfrac{1}{\dfrac{n_i}{n_t} - 1}\right|\sqrt{\left(\dfrac{n_i}{n_t}\right)^2 + 2\dfrac{n_i}{n_t}(\mathbf{L}\cdot\mathbf{V}) + 1}}$$

$$\times\left[\dfrac{n_i}{n_t}(\mathbf{N}\cdot\mathbf{V}) + (\mathbf{N}\cdot\mathbf{L})\right]$$

$$= \frac{1}{\text{sign}\left(\dfrac{n_i}{n_t} - 1\right)\sqrt{\left(\dfrac{n_i}{n_t}\right)^2 + 2\dfrac{n_i}{n_t}(\mathbf{L}\cdot\mathbf{V}) + 1}}$$

$$\times\left[\dfrac{n_i}{n_t}(\mathbf{N}\cdot\mathbf{V}) + (\mathbf{N}\cdot\mathbf{L})\right]$$

and

$$\mathbf{V}\cdot\mathbf{H}' = \mathbf{V}\cdot\left(\frac{\mathbf{H}'_\mathbf{u}}{|\mathbf{H}'_\mathbf{u}|}\right)$$

$$= \frac{(\mathbf{V}\cdot\mathbf{H}'_\mathbf{u})}{|\mathbf{H}'_\mathbf{u}|}$$

$$= \frac{1}{|\mathbf{H}'_\mathbf{u}|}\left[\mathbf{V}\cdot\left(\frac{\dfrac{n_i}{n_t}\mathbf{V} + \mathbf{L}}{\dfrac{n_i}{n_t} - 1}\right)\right]$$

$$= \frac{1}{|\mathbf{H}'_\mathbf{u}|\left(\dfrac{n_i}{n_t} - 1\right)}\left[\dfrac{n_i}{n_t}(\mathbf{V}\cdot\mathbf{V}) + (\mathbf{V}\cdot\mathbf{L})\right]$$

$$= \frac{1}{\left(\dfrac{n_i}{n_t} - 1\right)\left|\dfrac{1}{\dfrac{n_i}{n_t} - 1}\right|\sqrt{\left(\dfrac{n_i}{n_t}\right)^2 + 2\dfrac{n_i}{n_t}(\mathbf{L}\cdot\mathbf{V}) + 1}}$$

$$\times\left[\dfrac{n_i}{n_t}(\mathbf{V}\cdot\mathbf{V}) + (\mathbf{L}\cdot\mathbf{V})\right]$$

$$= \cfrac{1}{\text{sign}\left(\cfrac{n_i}{n_t} - 1\right)\sqrt{\left(\cfrac{n_i}{n_t}\right)^2 + 2\cfrac{n_i}{n_t}(\mathbf{L} \cdot \mathbf{V}) + 1}}$$

$$\times \left[\frac{n_i}{n_t} + (\mathbf{L} \cdot \mathbf{V})\right].$$

Once again, compare the number of arithmetic operations needed by the two methods to calculate $\mathbf{N} \cdot \mathbf{H}'$ and $\mathbf{V} \cdot \mathbf{H}'$. Define $\mathbf{H}' = (h'_x, h'_y, h'_z)$.

Direct algorithm, given $\mathbf{L}, \mathbf{N}, \mathbf{V}, \mathbf{N} \cdot \mathbf{L},$ *and* $\mathbf{N} \cdot \mathbf{V}$

```
ldotv ← [(l_x * v_x) + (l_y * v_y) + (l_z * v_z)]
if (n_i = n_t)
  then if (ldotv = −1)
    then begin
        H' ← V
        ndoth' ← ndotv
        vdoth' ← 1.0
      end
    else FLAG ← null
  else begin
      a ← n_i / n_t
      if (−ldotv ≥ min(a, n_t / n_i))
        then begin
            d ← a − 1
            h'_x ← [(a * v_x) + l_x] / d
            h'_y ← [(a * v_y) + l_y] / d
            h'_z ← [(a * v_z) + l_z] / d
            b ← √((h'_x * h'_x) + (h'_y * h'_y) + (h'_z * h'_z))
            ndoth' ← [(n_x * h'_x) + (n_y * h'_y) + (n_z * h'_z)] / b
            vdoth' ← [(v_x * h'_x) + (v_y * h'_y) + (v_z * h'_z)] / b
          end
        else FLAG = null
    end
```

New algorithm, given $\mathbf{L}, \mathbf{N}, \mathbf{V}, \mathbf{N} \cdot \mathbf{L},$ *and* $\mathbf{N} \cdot \mathbf{V}$

```
ldotv ← [(l_x * v_x) + (l_y * v_y) + (l_z * v_z)]
if (n_i = n_t)
```

then if (ldotv = −1)
    then begin
        ndoth′ ← ndotv
        vdoth′ ← 1.0
        end
    else FLAG ← **null**
else begin
    a ← n_i/n_t
    if (− ldotv ≥ min(a, n_t/n_i))
        then begin
            b ← [(a + ldotv + ldotv) ∗ a] + 1
            if (a > 1)
                then b ← $\sqrt{b}$
                else b ← $-\sqrt{b}$
            ndoth′ ← [(a ∗ ndotv) + ndotl]/b
            vdoth′ ← (a + ldotv)/b
        end
        else FLAG ← **null**
end

If *FLAG* = **null**, then **H′**, **N** · **H′**, and **V** · **H′** do not exist.

This implementation of the direct algorithm requires in the worst but most common case, 12 additions/subtractions, 22 multiplications/divisions, and 1 square root, whereas the implementation of the new algorithm requires only 7 additions/subtractions, 9 multiplications/divisions, and 1 square root. Once again, the difference comes from making more use of previously computed information.

See also Scan Conversion Summary (75)

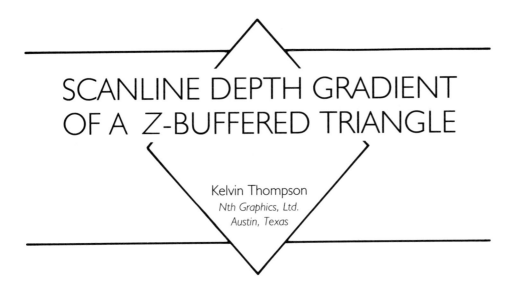

SCANLINE DEPTH GRADIENT OF A Z-BUFFERED TRIANGLE

Kelvin Thompson
Nth Graphics, Ltd.
Austin, Texas

Given a triangle with Z depth values at its vertices and basic geometry as shown in Fig. 1: if we render each scanline of the triangle in the direction shown, then for each increment in the X direction, the Z depth will change by

$$\frac{dz}{dx} = \frac{(z_2 - z_1)(y_3 - y_1) - (z_3 - z_1)(y_2 - y_1)}{(x_2 - x_1)(y_3 - y_1) - (x_3 - x_1)(y_2 - y_1)}.$$

That is, this is the Z slope of the triangle with respect to X. This slope can be used with a Bresenham's-like, DDA, or parallel-rendering algorithm (Swanson and Thayer, 1986; Niimi *et al.*, 1984).

The ratio above can also be used for Gouraud rendering. On systems with color look-up tables, you simply replace the Z values with color index values. On full-color systems you effectively need to have three parallel calculations—one for each color—in place of each Z calculation.

Proof

We calculate the X/Z slope by extending edge $P_1 P_2$ to point P_4, which is horizontal with point P_3 (see Fig. 2).

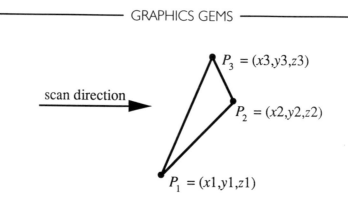

Figure 1.

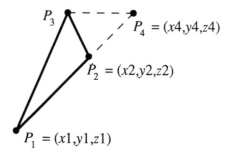

Figure 2.

By construction $y_4 = y_3$ and

$$\frac{x_4 - x_1}{y_4 - y_1} = \frac{x_2 - x_1}{y_2 - y_1}, \quad \text{and} \quad \frac{z_4 - z_1}{y_4 - y_1} = \frac{z_2 - z_1}{y_2 - y_1},$$

so

$$x_4 = \frac{x_2 - x_1}{y_2 - y_1}(y_3 - y_1) + x_1, \quad \text{and} \quad z_4 = \frac{z_2 - z_1}{y_2 - y_1}(y_3 - y_1) + z_1.$$

Hence the Z slope with respect to X is

$$\frac{z_4 - z_3}{x_4 - x_3} = \frac{\dfrac{z_2 - z_1}{y_2 - y_1}(y_3 - y_1) + z_1 - z_3}{\dfrac{x_2 - x_1}{y_2 - y_1}(y_3 - y_1) + x_1 - x_3}$$

$$= \frac{(z_2 - z_1)(y_3 - y_1) - (z_3 - z_1)(y_2 - y_1)}{(x_2 - x_1)(y_3 - y_1) - (x_3 - x_1)(y_2 - y_1)}.$$

See also Scan Conversion Summary (75)

SIMULATING FOG AND HAZE

Andrew S. Glassner

Xerox PARC
Palo Alto, California

One popular model for fog and haze is as a contrast-reducing medium. The fog is assigned an overall color, usually a light gray. The farther an object is from the viewer, the lower its contrast with respect to this fog color. We can approximate this contrast reduction on a point-by-point basis.

Suppose that the fog has RGB color $\mathbf{F}$, and point P on some object has color $\mathbf{K}$ (this is the color of P after all surface-dependent shading has been performed; that is, this is the color of the light radiated from P toward the viewer, measured at P). We can push the object color toward the fog color by interpolating the two: $\mathbf{K}' \leftarrow lerp(\alpha, \mathbf{K}, \mathbf{F})$. When $\alpha = 0$, the object is not at all colored by the fog; when $\alpha = 1$, the color has shifted to that of the fog.

The choice of α is governed by the properties of the fog. Assume that the fog is of constant density throughout the environment. Let d be the distance from the viewer at V to the point P being shaded, and σ be the density of fog per unit distance. Then the total fog between V and P is $\int_0^d \sigma\, dl = \sigma d$, so the proportion of fog we encounter along a sight line is linear with the distance to the point. A useful (though not very realistic) technique is to say that until distance d_{near} there should be no fog effect, and that after distance d_{far} nothing but fog should be visible. Then, since the fog density is constant, we can write α as a simple linear blend from d_{near} to d_{far}, so $\alpha = clamp(0, 1, (d - d_{near})/(d_{far} - d_{near}))$.

For example, suppose our colors are described in RGB, with object color $\mathbf{K} = (.1, .8, .3)$ and fog color $\mathbf{F} = (.6, .6, .6)$. If $d_{near} = 50$, d_{far}

364

= 550, and d = 100, then α = 0.1. Thus, the color we'd use for the point is $\mathbf{K}' \leftarrow \mathbf{K} + [0.1 \ (\mathbf{F} - \mathbf{K})] = (.1, .8, .3) + [.05, -.02, .03] = (.15, .78, .33)$. The approach here is equally applicable to more sophisticated color models than RGB.

In an environment where reflections and transmissions are visible, one may wish to apply contrast reduction to the transmitted and reflected light as well, simulating the dissipation of this light as it travels from one object to another. This is appropriate in both ray tracing and radiosity programs.

A popular technique in vector graphics is *depth cuing*, where the intensity of a stroke is diminished as a linear function of its distance from the viewer. This is a special case of the approach described here, using black as the fog color. Often in these systems d_{near} and d_{far} are set to the minimum and maximum depth component of all strokes in the scene.

Using a dark blue or black fog color is also appropriate for nighttime haze.

This note has presented a very simple model for fog and haze, appropriate for a quick hack or a special effect. More realistic and sophisticated models may be found in Blinn (1982), and Kajia and Von Herzen (1984).

See also Shadow Attenuation for Ray Tracing Transparent Objects (397)

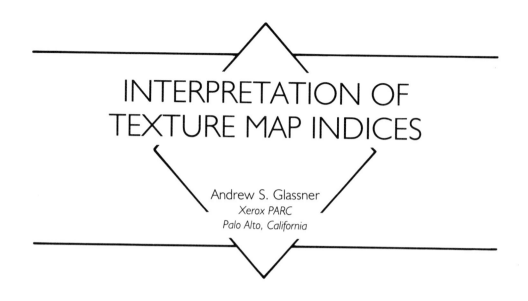

INTERPRETATION OF TEXTURE MAP INDICES

Andrew S. Glassner
Xerox PARC
Palo Alto, California

A typical rendering problem is to find the average value within some region of a texture map. Since this task can occur for every pixel (and in some Z-buffer systems, potentially many times per pixel), we would like to find this average as efficiently as possible. Several techniques have been proposed, such as the mip-map (Willams, 1983) for square regions, sum tables (Crow, 1984) for rectangular regions, refined sum tables for quadrilateral regions (Glassner, 1984), and the elliptically weighted average filter (Green and Heckbert, 1986) for elliptic regions.

In this note we restrict our attention to rectangular regions. Our problem is to find the average value within some axis-aligned rectangle of texture. Such a rectangle may be described by the points at opposite ends of one of its diagonals; in this note we choose these to be the points nearest and farthest from the origin of the texture coordinate system.

We define the texture to be available on the Cartesian product of the half-open intervals $[0, 1)$ in U and $[0, 1)$ in V. We diagram this in Fig. 1, using a solid line and a shaded pattern for available texture, and a dashed line for the boundary of the open intervals.

Figure 1.   The fundamental texture cell, from $[0, 0]$ to $(1, 1)$.

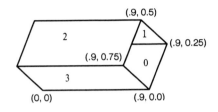

Figure 2. A textured cylinder.

Figure 3. The texture-space images of polygons 0, 1, and 2 in Figure 2.

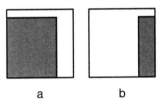

a   b

Figure 4. Two possible interpretations of polygon 3 in Figure 2. The texture is only specified by the rectangle corners $(0, 0)$ and $(.75, .9)$.

There are many ambiguities that can arise when one defines a texture rectangle with only two texture coordinates. For example, suppose we have an open, four-sided cylinder with $v = 0$ at the bottom and $v = .9$ at the top, and U running around the upper vertices from 0 to 0.75 in equal steps, as in Fig. 2.

Consider the three rectangles labeled 0, 1, and 2. Figure 3 shows the images of these rectangles in texture space.

Now consider rectangle 3 near the bottom of the image. It has texture coordinates with extremes $(0, 1)$ in V and $(0, .75)$ in U. The (u, v) extremes of this rectangle in texture space are then $(0, 0)$ and $(.75, .9)$.

367

Figure 4 shows two interpretations of mappings these points directly into texture space.

The first interpretation simply shows the region formed by those corners, but it's hardly a narrow slab like the other rectangles. We want the texture to wrap in little pieces around the cylinder, but the interpretation in Fig. 4a will cause the texture to fly all the way around, backwards, on the last piece. This looks very bad.

One common solution to this problem is to wrap texture space as a two-torus, and find the smallest rectangle on that surface. Thus, the right side of the texture is taped to the left side, and the top is taped to the bottom, as in many video games. Alternatively, we may wrap in only one direction, forming a cylinder. Then Fig. 4b is indeed the smallest rectangle on the cylinder, given our two points. Of course, we never actually construct the cylinder or torus; rather, the program checks the area of the possibilities. Of these rectangles the one with the smallest area is chosen.

A similar problem comes up when the texture coordinates are outside the unit square. Some applications might produce objects with texture coordinates of unknown extent; this can happen when a texture function is scaled up to replicate the texture on an object's surface. We would still like to render such objects sensibly. Before we can come up with an algorithm, though, we need to decide what it should mean to specify a texture coordinate such as $(1.3, 4.5)$.

There are many solutions to this problem. The texture could be treated as the fundamental cell for any of the symmetry groups with exclusively two- or four-fold symmetry. We could also devise complicated procedural answers. A really good analysis of this problem and the pros and cons of the different solutions makes for some interesting thinking. For simplicity in this article, we will just replicate the texture over the plane without transformation, as in Fig. 5.

You may prefer to reflect or rotate the texture as you repeat it.

The general idea is to determine if the desired texture spans one or more unit squares (we will call the texture-space unit square a *cell*). If the texture covers more than one cell we will find the contribution from each cell and add the contributions together. Each cell will be easy, since its coordinates will be within the unit square.

We begin with four texture coordinates as input: (u_1, v_2), (u_2, v_2), (u_3, v_3), and (u_4, v_4). From these we find the smallest axis-aligned box that encloses them all. Call the point on this enclosing box nearest the

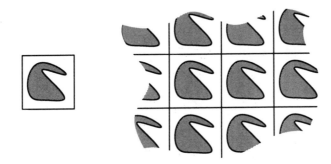

Figure 5. Replicating a single texture cell to create a larger texture.

origin S (for small), and the point farthest L (for large). We define two points, S' and L', and a translation vector $\mathbf{D}$, which we will use to build S and L:

1. $S' \leftarrow (min(u_i), min(v_i))$

2. $L' \leftarrow (max(u_i), max(v_i))$

3. $\mathbf{D} \leftarrow (frac(S'_u), frac(S'_v))$

4. $S \leftarrow S' - \mathbf{D}$

5. $L \leftarrow L' - \mathbf{D}$.

Steps 3 and 4 build S by translating S' into the unit square; L is then constructed in step 5 by translating L' by the same amount. So now $0 \leq S_u, S_v < 1$.

Next we will determine the sorts of cells that are overlapped by S and L. Figure 6 gives a decision tree for each of the nine different sorts of situations that can arise. A cell drawn with a solid circle in it means that there are one or more instances of that cell.

The tree in Fig. 6 contains rather more nodes than it must. For example, all four leaves in the lower left are of the same form: four corners plus one or more other pieces. If we're willing to redefine a solid circle to mean zero or more of these pieces, we can write a much smaller tree, as in Fig. 7.

369

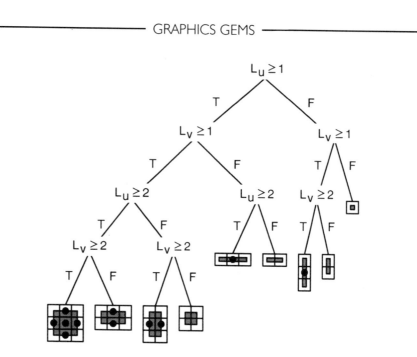

Figure 6.   A decision tree for determining how different types of cells should be used to create a replicated texture. Each solid dot indicates one or more instances of that type of cell.

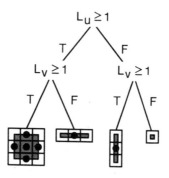

Figure 7.   A simplified form of Figure 6, where each dot represents zero or more instances of that type of cell.

This tree shows 16 different types of cells at the leaves. Our only remaining tasks are to find how many of the optional ones exist at each leaf with optional cells, and the geometry of each of these 16 different types of cells. Let us attack these problems in order.

Consider the rightmost leaf in Fig. 7—there are no optional cells, and the whole rectangle is in the unit texture square, so we're done.

Move left to the leaf with three cells stacked vertically. Consider that the bottom of the bottommost cell is $v = 0$, and the top of that cell is $v = 1$. If the V coordinate of point L is less than 2, then there are no intermediate cells, but otherwise there is one such cell for each additional integer increment of the top coordinate. Remember that we named the coordinate farthest from the origin L—in our left-handed system, this is the upper-right point. So the number of optional cells in the middle is $floor(L_v) - 1$.

Move left in the tree to the cell with the three horizontal cells. The same reasoning we just went through applies, but swap U and V. Thus, the number of center cells is $floor(L_u) - 1$.

Move now to the far-left leaf. There are four corner cells always there. Then we must consider the cells in the center of the top and bottom rows. This situation is analogous to the leaf immediately to the right, except now we must remember that there are $floor(L_u) - 1$ *pairs* of cells. The same argument holds for the center of the left and right columns; there are $floor(L_v) - 1$ pairs of these. The number of center cells is simply the product of the extensions of the two sides: $(floor(L_u) - 1)$ $(floor(L_v) - 1)$.

Now that we know how many of each kind of cell we need to find the sum, we need to be able to find the rectangle described by each cell. This is not too hard if we reason about one cell type at a time. If the cell contains the lower-left corner of the box, that point is point S. If it contains the upper-right corner, then the coordinates of that point in the unit square are $F = (frac(L_u), frac(L_v))$—remember that the optimal cells just discussed handle the integer parts of L. Although we have been careful about saying that the lines $u = 1$ and $v = 1$ are actually not part of our texture, most programs are happy to handle such values. I'm going to take advantage of this freedom now. In the following tables I often use the coordinates $u = 1$ or $v = 1$, rather than present the cell geometries as open intervals, which would then start to get messy (both logically and arithmetically). Figure 8 provides a summary of the 16 types of cells; their associated coordinates are given in Table 1.

371

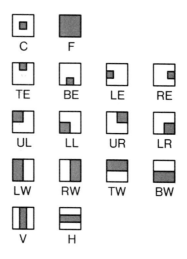

Figure 8.   The different types of cells and their names.

Table I.   Texture Sampling.

Cell Type	Occupied Region
C:	$(S_u, S_v), (L_u, L_v)$
F:	$(0, 0), (1, 1)$
TE:	$(S_u, S_v), (L_u, 1)$
BE:	$(S_u, 0), (L_u, L_v)$
LE:	$(0, S_v), (L_u, L_v)$
RE:	$(S_u, S_v), (1, L_v)$
UL:	$(0, S_v), (L_u, 1)$
LR:	$(S_u, 0), (1, L_v)$
LL:	$(0, 0), (L_u, L_v)$
UR:	$(S_u, S_v), (1, 1)$
LW:	$(0, 0), (L_u, 1)$
BW:	$(0, 0), (1, L_v)$
RW:	$(S_u, 0), (1, 1)$
TW:	$(0, S_v), (1, 1)$
V:	$(S_u, 0), L_u, 1)$
H:	$(0, S_v), (1, L_v)$

These are all the tools necessary to write a program that can integrate any axis-aligned rectangle.

We can express the algorithm formed by the decision tree above in pseudo-code:

map (S, L) { S and L are two input points in the 2d UV system. $S_u \le L_u, S_v \le L_v.$

This returns the sum of all samples in that rectangle; divide by the area of the rectangle for the average value.

We use the function GetSum(type, S, L) which takes a cell type and the two original input points and returns the sum of all samples in that types of cell in that rectangle.

```
vc ← floor(L_v) − 1      The number of vertical cells in tall strips
hc ← floor(L_u) − 1      The number of horizontal cells in wide strips
if L_u ≥ 1 then
        if L_v ≥ 1 then
                sum ← GetSum(UR, S, L) + GetSum(UL, S, L) +
                        GetSum(LR, S, L) + GetSum(LL, S, L)
                if vc > 0 then sum ← sum +
                        [vc * (GetSum(LW, S, L) + GetSum(RW, S, L))]
                if hc > 0 then sum ← sum +
                        [hc * (GetSum(TW, S, L) + GetSum(BW, S, L))]
                if hc * vc > 0 then sum ← sum + [(hc * vc) * GetSum(F, S, L)]
        else
                sum ← GetSum(LE, S, L) + GetSum(RE, S, L)
                if hc > 0 then sum ← sum + [hc * GetSum(H, S, L)]
else
        if L_v ≥ 1 then
                sum ← GetSum(TE, S, L) + GetSum(BE, S, L)
                if vc > 0 then sum ← sum + [vc * GetSum(V, S, L)]
        else
                sum ← GetSum(C, S, L)
        return[sum]
}
```

GetSum(type, S, L) {

We assume a routine GetSumTableRectangle which will take two points A *and* B, $A_u \leq B_u$, $A_v \leq B_v$, *and returns the average value in the rectangle formed by* A *and* B.

TexturePoint A, B;

select type **from**

C: **begin**	$A \leftarrow (S_u, S_v)$;	$B \leftarrow (L_u, L_v)$; **end;**
F: **begin**	$A \leftarrow (0, 0)$;	$B \leftarrow (1, 1)$; **end;**
TE: **begin**	$A \leftarrow (S_u, S_v)$;	$B \leftarrow (L_u, 1)$; **end;**n
BE: **begin**	$A \leftarrow (S_u, 0)$;	$B \leftarrow (L_u, L_v)$; **end;**
LE: **begin**	$A \leftarrow (0, S_v)$;	$B \leftarrow (L_u, L_v)$; **end;**
RE: **begin**	$A \leftarrow (S_u, S_v)$;	$B \leftarrow (1, L_v)$; **end;**
UL: **begin**	$A \leftarrow (0, S_v)$;	$B \leftarrow (L_u, 1)$; **end;**
LR: **begin**	$A \leftarrow (S_u, 0)$;	$B \leftarrow (1, L_v)$; **end;**
LL: **begin**	$A \leftarrow (0, 0)$;	$B \leftarrow (L_u, L_v)$; **end;**
UR: **begin**	$A \leftarrow (S_u, S_v)$;	$B \leftarrow (1, 1)$; **end;**
LW: **begin**	$A \leftarrow (0, 0)$;	$B \leftarrow (L_u, 1)$; **end;**
BW: **begin**	$A \leftarrow (0, 0)$;	$B \leftarrow (1, L_v)$; **end;**
RW: **begin**	$A \leftarrow (S_u, 0)$;	$B \leftarrow (1, 1)$; **end;**
TW: **begin**	$A \leftarrow (0, S_v)$;	$B \leftarrow (1, 1)$; **end;**
V: **begin**	$A \leftarrow (S_u, 0)$;	$B \leftarrow (L_u, 1)$; **end;**
H: **begin**	$A \leftarrow (0, S_v)$;	$B \leftarrow (1, L_v)$; **end;**

endselect;

return [GetSumRect(A, B)];

};

As I mentioned at the start, you may want to reflect or rotate the texture as you tile the plane. You'll need to keep track of the right transformation at each cell. It's then a simple matter to either reflect or rotate the indices to the correct form.

The bookkeeping necessary to make sure this all comes out straight over repeated cells is not trivial, but it's not particularly hard—just messy. Figure 9 shows the eight transformations with their geometric and algebraic meanings.

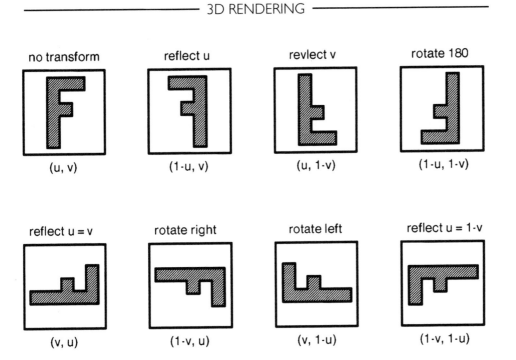

no transform
(u, v)

reflect u
(1-u, v)

revlect v
(u, 1-v)

rotate 180
(1-u, 1-v)

reflect u = v
(v, u)

rotate right
(1-v, u)

rotate left
(v, 1-u)

reflect u = 1-v
(1-v, 1-u)

Figure 9. There are eight ways to rigidly transform a square cell. Each has a simple interpretation in terms of transformed texture coordinates.

See also Multidimensional Sum Tables (376)

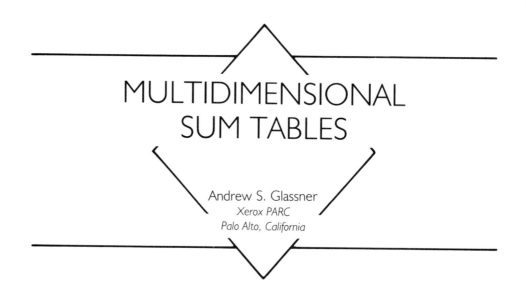

MULTIDIMENSIONAL SUM TABLES

Andrew S. Glassner
Xerox PARC
Palo Alto, California

Sum tables were introduced to computer graphics by Crow (1984) as a technique for rapidly integrating rectangular areas of texture. They are popular for two-dimensional texture mapping, where they are used to find the average texture value in some rectangular region. You can find them discussed in the statistics literature as joint cumulative probability distribution functions on n variables (Ross, 1976).

One may generalize the sum table method to an arbitrary number of dimensions, in order to find the average value within a rectangular box of any number of sides. I needed the average value in 3D boxes when building an interactive slicing program. The user moved a slicing plane through a 3D volume of intensity values, and I constantly updated a display with the grayscale "slice" of the volume represented by the current position of the plane. There wasn't enough time to render this image at full resolution and still stay interactive, so I rendered the image at low resolution (originally 32 by 32 samples, where each sample was a big box on the screen). I wanted each of these samples to represent the average density in the 3D box spanned by four points on the 3D sample grid; a 3D sum table was just the right technique to find these averages quickly.

Let's briefly review the two-dimensional sum table. Given a sampled input $I(x, y)$, a sum table $S(x, y)$ is built from the samples of I so that $S(x, y) = \sum_{j=0}^{x}\sum_{k=0}^{y} I(j, k)$. Thus, each point on the sum table is the sum of all intensities in the box formed by that point and the origin.

To find the average value in some rectangle with corners UR (upper-right), UL (upper-left), LR (lower-right), and LL (lower-left), we first find the sum of all values in that box, and then divide by the area of the box.

The beauty of sum tables is that you can quickly find the total value in that region by computing

$$\text{Sum of samples in box} = S(\text{UR}) - S(\text{UL}) - S(\text{LR}) + S(\text{LL}). \quad (1)$$

So then the average value may be found by

$$\text{Average} = (\text{Sum of samples in box})/(\text{Area of box}). \quad (2)$$

Why does Eq. 1 work? Figure 1 suggests a pictorial explanation. The box we want can be found by finding the sum at UR, and by then removing the extraneous area to the left and below of LL by removing the sums at UL and LR. But we have implicitly removed the area that is both to the left and below of LL two times, so we explicitly add it back in once, so it is only subtracted from the total once.

Equation 1 can also help us build the sum table in the first place. The brute-force way to build a sum table is to loop through all the pixels below and to the left of each sample you want to compute. A smarter way to go is to pretend you wanted to find the sum in the box formed by the sample at (x, y) and its neighbors immediately left, below, and below-left:

$$S(x, y) - S(x - 1, y) - S(x, y - 1) + S(x - 1, y - 1) = I(x, y).$$

$$(3)$$

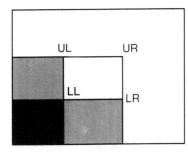

Figure 1. The sum of all values in a rectangle may be found by combining the sum table value at the four corners.

We don't have to divide the sum because the area of this box is exactly 1. We can just rewrite this for $S(x, y)$:

$$S(x, y) = I(x, y) + S(x - 1, y) + S(x, y - 1) - S(x - 1, y - 1).$$

(4)

This shows that we can use the previously filled-in entries in the sum table and the image itself to help build new entries.

A common technique for generalizing something is to see what happens when you go one dimension higher, and then see if you can find the arbitrary case by induction. Let's try this and move from 2D to a 3D sum table.

Figure 2 shows a three-dimensional sum table and a box we would like to sample (for clarity in the figure we have suppressed the space beyond point P). Suppose that the point P is at (x, y, z), and the opposite diagonal Q is at $(x - \Delta x, y - \Delta y, z - \Delta z)$. In Figure 3a we have shown the eight octants of the original 3D image as defined by the planes of the box we're investigating. Figure 3b labels each of the eight octants created

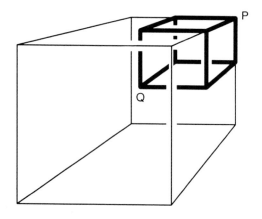

Figure 2.   In 3D, the near corner Q and far corner P define the diagonal of a box of 3D texture.

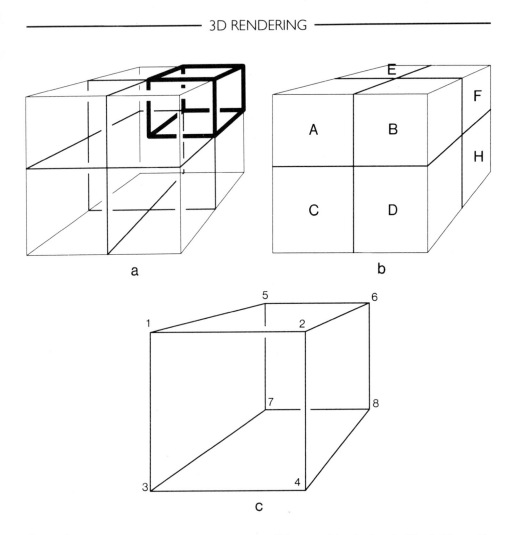

Figure 3. Figure 3a shows the eight octants in 3D created by the box in Fig. 2. Figure 3b provides labels for these octants. Figure 3c labels the eight vertices of the sampled box.

by the planes of this box; note that the box we wish to sample is labeled F. Figure 3c labels the vertices of the box.

We would like to find the sum of all samples in box F. Suppose that we have built a sum table in three dimensions. To clarify how the table is built, we will say that Σn is the sum of all samples in box n. Then we can write each Si (the value of the sum table at vertex i) as a sum of these octant sums:

$$S1 = \Sigma C + \Sigma A$$
$$S2 = \Sigma C + \Sigma A + \Sigma B + \Sigma D$$
$$S3 = \Sigma C$$
$$S4 = \Sigma C + \Sigma D$$
$$S5 = \Sigma C + \Sigma A + \Sigma E + \Sigma G$$
$$S6 = \Sigma C + \Sigma B + \Sigma A + \Sigma D + \Sigma E + \Sigma F + \Sigma G$$
$$S7 = \Sigma C + \Sigma G$$
$$S8 = \Sigma C + \Sigma D + \Sigma G + \Sigma H.$$

Now that we have a 3D sum table, we need to know how to combine the values at the vertices of the box to find ΣF, the sum of the values in octant F. The correct combination is given by

$$\Sigma F = S1 - S2 - S3 + S4 - S5 + S6 + S7 - S8. \tag{5}$$

If we divide ΣF by its volume we get the average value in that box.

We can now state our generalization of sum table methods, which says that you can find the total value inside any box by finding the sum table values at each vertex and then combining those sum table values. But the correct coefficients are important; we would like to find a simple way to determine which sum table values need to be added and which need to be subtracted—Eq. 5 was simply produced out of thin air.

Look back at Fig. 1, where we wanted the value at the upper-right corner of the box. We started by adding the sum table value at that point, and then subtracted off the values at each of the two vertices of the box that were one step away from our sample point, and then added back the vertex of the box that was two steps away.

Now look at Figs. 2 and 3 and Eq. 5, and observe that we did exactly the same thing for the 3D box. $S6$ itself was added, vertices that were one step away from $S6$ were subtracted, vertices two steps away were added, and vertex $S3$ (the only vertex three steps away) was subtracted.

What's going on? Intuitively, each time we take a step we're cleaving away a half-space of sums. When we take two steps we're restoring some of the space that was removed more than once. When we step again, we compensate for too many subtractions by adding some spaces back in, and so on.

In d dimensions, you can easily enumerate all the points in a d-dimensional box by generating all the binary numbers from 0 to 2^{d-1}. Each bit position corresponds to an axis. You can interpret a zero bit as telling you to stay put, and a one bit as instructing you to move along the corresponding axis. You then look up the sum table value S at the point you've constructed. If you moved along an even number of axes then you add S into your running sum; if you moved along an odd number of axes then you subtract it.

In the following pseudo-code, we find the average value in some box in a d-dimensional space. P is the location of the box corner farthest from the origin, represented by an array of d numbers. The box we want to sample has side lengths given by the entries in an array *sideLength[]*—see Fig. 4 for an illustration of this setup. We assume that there's a function *SumTable[]*, which will take as input a point and return the value of the sum table at that n-dimensional point.

```
Find-sum-at(P, sideLength[], d) {
  sum ← 0
  for i ← 0, 2^(d-1) do
   Q ← P
   for j ← 0, d do        check each axis for movement
     mask ← 2^j
     if i bit-and mask then {   move along this axis?
           count ← count + 1;
           Q_j ← Q_j − sideLength[j];
           };
     endloop;
   if count mod 2 = 0
     then sum ← sum + SumTable[Q];
     else sum ← sum − SumTable[Q];
  endloop;
  return(sum);
  };
```

There are all kinds of nice symmetry patterns to be found in the points generated, their coefficients, and the volumes they sample.

See also Interpretation of Texture Map Indices (366)

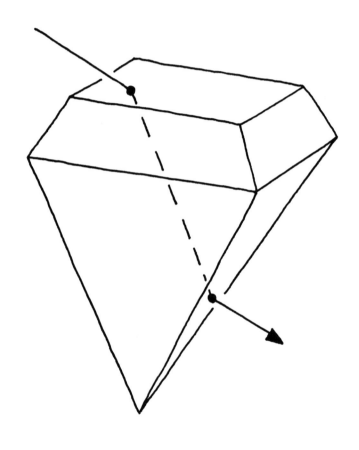

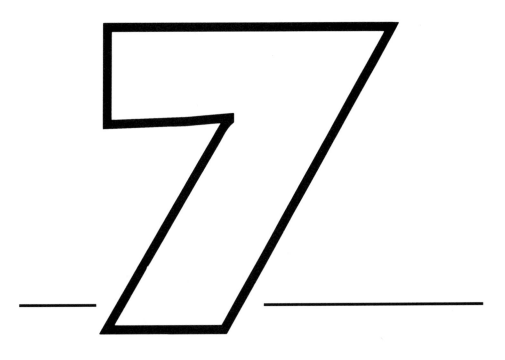

RAY TRACING

A SIMPLE RAY REJECTION TEST

Jack Ritter
Versatec, Inc.
Santa Clara, California

Here is a simple method for fast ray tracing that can trivially reject eye rays that don't intersect with objects in the scene.

For each object: Compute its axis-aligned 3D bounding box. Project the box's eight corners onto the screen and find the 2D bounding box that surrounds them. This box should be in screen space. (Tighter bounding polyhedra could be used as well.)

To test a ray against an object, check if the pixel through which the ray passes is in the object's 2D box. If not, reject it.

This is much faster than doing a 3D distance check of the ray against the object's bounding volume.

The benefit would be most pronounced in scenes that don't involve a lot of reflection and refraction, since these phenomena generate rays that don't originate from the eye. However, the early development stage of any ray tracer will benefit from this technique, since frequent initial bugs necessitate many renderings, and any speed-up will save time, particularly if only opaque objects are considered at first.

This 2D box scheme can be used to calculate automatically the field-of-view (fov) angle of the synthetic camera construct used in most 3D systems. The user must define the camera's location, the "look-at" point, and the "up" point, but the lens's angle can be automatically computed so as to encompass the whole scene. Here, fov is actually the half-angle from the center of the scene to the screen's edge, in radians.

Assume the center of the screen is at $(0, 0)$. The method is as follows: pick an initial fov known to encompass the scene. A fov of 60 degrees (meaning the edge-to-edge angle is 120 degrees) should suffice for all but the most severely distorted scenes. Calculate the camera based on this. Make a dry run through the scene, without rendering.

For each object in the scene, just calculate the 2D bounding box, as described above. Find the edge of the box farthest away from the screen's center, and call this distance *max_edge*.

Pick the maximum *max_edge*, for the whole scene. Call it *max_max_edge*. Calculate the distance from the eye to the screen's center. Call it *eye_to_screen*. The new fov will be

$$\text{fov} = \arctan(max\_max\_width / eye\_to\_screen).$$

Now you can run through the data again and render, using fov; all objects will be in the picture, with a little border to spare. Note, *eye_to_screen* must be in the same units as *max_max_width*. The conversion is dependent on the particular camera model being implemented. The screen's aspect ratio is not a factor.

A more refined variation of the ideas presented here was published in Bronsvoort *et al.* (1984).

See also Efficient Generation of Sampling Jitter Using Look-up Tables (64); Fast Line–Edge Intersections on a Uniform Grid (29); Transforming Axis-Aligned Bounding Boxes (548)

RAY – OBJECT INTERSECTION SUMMARY

The intersection of a ray and an object is perhaps the most critical step when ray tracing. Because it is at the heart of the inner loop of any ray tracing algorithm, a ray/object intersection algorithm should be as efficient as possible. There are many strategic and tactical methods available for optimizing various ray/object intersections; the following Gems present a few of those techniques.

See also Efficient Generation of Sampling Jitter Using Look-up Tables (64); Fast Line–Edge Intersections on a Uniform Grid (29); Transforming Axis-Aligned Bounding Boxes (548)

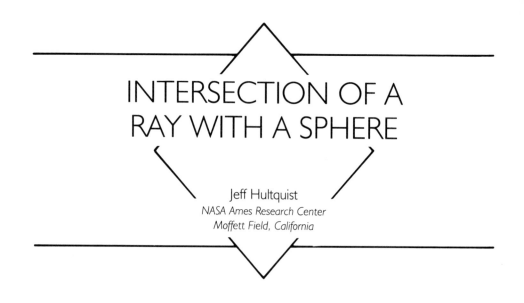

INTERSECTION OF A RAY WITH A SPHERE

Jeff Hultquist
NASA Ames Research Center
Moffett Field, California

Intersecting a ray with a sphere is one of the simplest of problems. When viewed in the plane defined by the ray and the center of the sphere, the geometry of the problem looks like that presented in Fig. 1.

We need to find the point P at which the ray first intersects the sphere. We observe that

$$v^2 + b^2 = c^2$$

$$d^2 + b^2 = r^2$$

$$d = \sqrt{r^2 - (c^2 - v^2)}$$

If we let **V** be the unit vector in the direction of the ray, then the point of intersection can be found like so . . .

```
v = EO · V;
disc = r² − ((EO · EO) − v²)
if(disc < 0)
    then no intersection
    else begin
        d = √disc;
        P = E + (v − d)V;
    end;
```

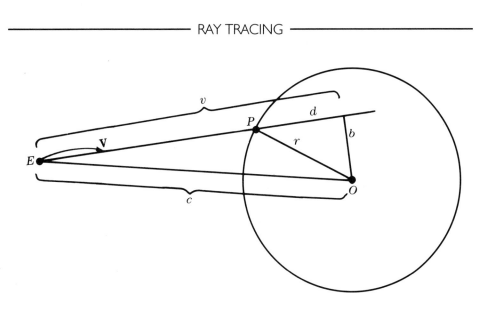

Figure 1.

See also Efficient Generation of Sampling Jitter Using Look-up Tables (64); Fast Line–Edge Intersections on a Uniform Grid (29); Transforming Axis-Aligned Bounding Boxes (548)

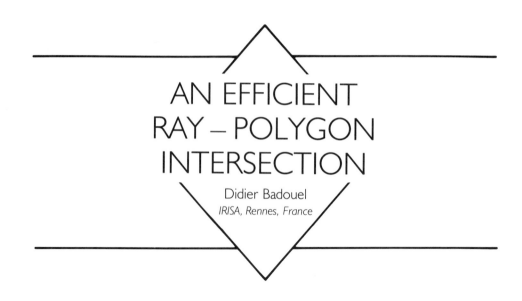

AN EFFICIENT RAY – POLYGON INTERSECTION

Didier Badouel

IRISA, Rennes, France

Using a ray tracing method with polygonal databases, we must define a fast algorithm to compute ray–polygon intersection. The following algorithm is quite similar to but faster than the barycentric approach described in Snyder and Barr (1987).

The goal of the algorithm is first to determine if a ray goes through the polygon, and then to determine the coordinates of the intersection point and parameters, to localize this point with respect to the polygon's vertices. These parameters are used to compute the interpolated normal at this point, and can be used also to compute the entry of a texture map.

First Step: Intersecting the Embedding Plane

This step is common with the other intersection algorithms but can be presented again. A polygon is described by its vertices V_i ($i \in \{0, \dots, n-1\}$, $n \geq 3$). Let x_i, y_i, and z_i the coordinates of the vertex V_i. The normal of the plane containing the polygon, $\mathbf{N}$, is computed with the cross product:

$$\vec{\mathbf{N}} = \overrightarrow{V_0V_1} \times \overrightarrow{V_0V_2}.$$

For each point P of the plane, the quantity $P \cdot \mathbf{N}$ is constant. This constant value is computed by the dot product $d = -V_0 \cdot \mathbf{N}$. The implicit representation of the plane,

$$\mathbf{N} \cdot P + d = 0, \tag{1}$$

is computed once, and then stored in the polygon description.

Let the parametric representation of the ray be

$$r(t) = O + \mathbf{D}t. \tag{2}$$

The evaluation of the parameter t corresponding to the intersection point can be obtained using the equations (1) and (2):

$$t = -\frac{d + \mathbf{N} \cdot O}{\mathbf{N} \cdot \mathbf{D}}. \tag{3}$$

This calculation requires 12 floating operations and three tests:

- If polygon and ray are parallel ($\mathbf{N} \cdot \mathbf{D} = 0$), the intersection is rejected.

- If the intersection is behind the origin of the ray ($t \leq 0$), the intersection is rejected.

- If a closer intersection has been already found for the ray ($t > t_{ray}$), the intersection is rejected.

Second Step: Intersecting the Polygon

A parametric resolution is now presented. This solution is based on triangles. If a polygon has n vertices ($n > 3$), it will be viewed as a set of $n - 2$ triangles. For this reason, the resolution is restricted to convex polygons. The point P (see Fig. 1) is given by

$$\overrightarrow{V_0 P} = \alpha \overrightarrow{V_0 V_1} + \beta \overrightarrow{V_0 V_2}. \tag{4}$$

The point P will be inside the triangle ($\triangle\, V_0\, V_1\, V_2$) if

$$\alpha \geq 0, \beta \geq 0, \text{ and } \alpha + \beta \leq 1.$$

Equation (4) has three components:

$$\begin{cases} x_P - x_0 = \alpha(x_1 - x_0) + \beta(x_2 - x_0) \\ y_P - y_0 = \alpha(y_1 - y_0) + \beta(y_2 - y_0) \\ z_P - z_0 = \alpha(z_1 - z_0) + \beta(z_2 - z_0). \end{cases} \tag{5}$$

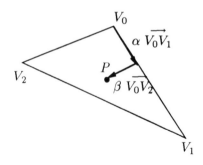

Figure 1. Parametric representation of the point P.

A solution exists and is unique. To reduce this system, we wish to project the polygon onto one of the primary planes, either xy, xz, or yz. If the polygon is perpendicular to one of these planes, its projection onto that plane will be a single line. To avoid this problem, and to make sure that the projection is as large as possible, we find the dominant axis of the normal vector and use the plane perpendicular to that axis. As in Snyder and Barr (1987), we compute the value i_0,

$$i_0 = \begin{cases} 0 & \text{if } |\mathbf{N}_x| = \max(|\mathbf{N}_x|, |\mathbf{N}_y|, |\mathbf{N}_z|) \\ 1 & \text{if } |\mathbf{N}_y| = \max(|\mathbf{N}_x|, |\mathbf{N}_y|, |\mathbf{N}_z|) \\ 2 & \text{if } |\mathbf{N}_z| = \max(|\mathbf{N}_x|, |\mathbf{N}_y|, |\mathbf{N}_z|). \end{cases}$$

Consider i_1 and i_2 (i_1 and $i_2 \in \{0, 1, 2\}$), the indices different from i_0. They represent the primary plane used to project the polygon. Let (u, v) be the two-dimensional coordinates of a vector in this plane; the coordinates of $\overrightarrow{V_0P}$, $\overrightarrow{V_0V_1}$, and $\overrightarrow{V_0V_2}$, projected onto that plane, are

$$u_0 = P_{i_1} - V_{0_{i_1}} \qquad u_1 = V_{1_{i_1}} - V_{0_{i_1}} \qquad u_2 = V_{2_{i_1}} - V_{0_{i_1}}$$

$$v_0 = P_{i_2} - V_{0_{i_2}} \qquad v_1 = V_{1_{i_2}} - V_{0_{i_2}} \qquad v_2 = V_{2_{i_2}} - V_{0_{i_2}}$$

Equations 5 then reduce to

$$\begin{cases} u_0 = \alpha.u_1 + \beta.u_2 \\ v_0 = \alpha.v_1 + \beta.v_2 \end{cases}.$$

The solutions are

$$\alpha = \frac{\det\begin{pmatrix} u_0 & u_2 \\ v_0 & v_2 \end{pmatrix}}{\det\begin{pmatrix} u_1 & u_2 \\ v_1 & v_2 \end{pmatrix}} \quad \text{and} \quad \beta = \frac{\det\begin{pmatrix} u_1 & u_0 \\ v_1 & v_0 \end{pmatrix}}{\det\begin{pmatrix} u_1 & u_2 \\ v_1 & v_2 \end{pmatrix}}.$$

The interpolated normal from the point P may be computed by

$$\mathbf{N}_P = (1 - (\alpha + \beta))\mathbf{N}_0 + \alpha\mathbf{N}_1 + \beta\mathbf{N}_2.$$

Pseudo-Code for a Ray – Triangle Intersection

O: **point**;   *Origin of the ray*
D: **vector**;   *Direction of the ray*
P: **point**;   *Intersection point*
V: **array**[0..2] **of point**;   *Polygon vertices*

```
P ← O + Dt;
i₁ and i₂ are in the polygon description.
```

$u_0 \leftarrow P[i_1] - V[0][i_1];$
$v_0 \leftarrow P[i_2] - V[0][i_2];$
$u_1 \leftarrow V[1][i_1] - V[0][i_1];$
$u_2 \leftarrow V[2][i_1] - V[0][i_1];$
$v_1 \leftarrow V[1][i_2] - V[0][i_2];$
$v_2 \leftarrow V[2][i_2] - V[0][i_2];$
if $u_1 = 0$
      then $\beta \leftarrow u_0/u_2;$
         if $0 \le \beta \le 1$
               then $\alpha \leftarrow (v_0 - \beta * v_2)/v_1;$
      else $\beta \leftarrow (v_0 * u_1 - u_0 * v_1)/(v_2 * u_1 - u_2 * v_1);$
         if $0 \le \beta \le 1$
               then $\alpha \leftarrow (u_0 - \beta * u_2)/u_1;$
The values α and β are the interpolation parameters.
return ($\alpha \ge 0$ **and** $\beta \ge 0$ **and** $(\alpha + \beta) \le 1$)

See also Efficient Generation of Sampling Jitter Using Look-up Tables (64); Fast Line–Edge Intersections on a Uniform Grid (29); Transforming Axis-Aligned Bounding Boxes (548)

See Appendix 2 for C Implementation (**735**)

393

FAST RAY – POLYGON INTERSECTION

Andrew Woo
SAS Institute Inc.
Don Mills, Ontario, Canada

In many rendering programs, the polygon tends to be the main primitive available to model complex surfaces. In addition, many surfaces that are expressed in some complex form (such as quadric, parametric, and implicit surfaces) are often broken down to polygons during the rendering stage for the simple reason that most systems can easily and efficiently render polygons. Thus, special attention should be paid to ray–polygon intersections.

In ray tracing, ray–polygon intersection involves two processes: intersection against the plane on which the polygon lies, and a check if the intersection point on the plane is inside the polygon. If each polygon has associated with it a bounding box (parallel to the axes), we can use this bounding box to speed up ray–polygon intersection: after the intersection with the plane, if the point intersected lies outside the bounding box, then the inside–outside check can again be avoided. This check basically acts as an approximate inside–outside test and requires only an additional six comparisons at worst.

This quick check can be used as a secondary culler for your favorite intersection culler in ray tracing, especially when the candidate set of objects to be intersected is large. I have tested this method against a uniform voxel traversal algorithm with the ray bounding box check (which requires bounding boxes for the objects, anyway), and it pays off handsomely.

> *See also* Efficient Generation of Sampling Jitter Using Look-up Tables (64); Fast Line–Edge Intersections on a Uniform Grid (29); Transforming Axis-Aligned Bounding Boxes (548)

FAST RAY – BOX INTERSECTION

Andrew Woo
SAS Institute, Inc.
Don Mills, Ontario, Canada

A fast intersection scheme with the bounding box is proposed. It assumes that parallel planes form the box, where each set is parallel to one axis. This approach is very similar to the bounding box evaluation discussed by Haines (1989), except that it cuts down on the number of floating point operations and returns the intersection point with the box, which is required under some circumstances—for instance, in voxel traversal—to identify the first voxel that the ray pierces.

Assume we are working in 3D. We first search for three candidate planes that the ray can possibly intersect, that is, we cull away back facing planes forming the box. From these three candidate planes, the maximum of the hit distances with the candidate planes must be the closest plane the ray hits (with the condition that the hit is inside the box; otherwise there is no hit).

As an example, in 2D, let $x1$, $x2$, $y1$, $y2$ be the boundaries of the box (see Fig. 1). In this case, with the ray origin in the lower-right corner, the candidate planes are $x2$ and $y1$. tx and ty hit distances are then calculated from the ray origin to $x2$ and $y1$, respectively. Since $tx > ty$, $x2$ is the closest plane hit by the ray.

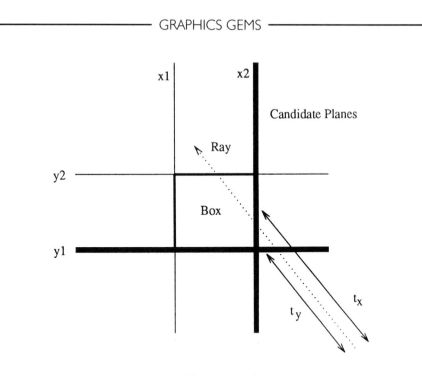

Figure 1.

See also Efficient Generation of Sampling Jitter Using Look-up Tables (64); Fast Line–Edge Intersections on a Uniform Grid (29); Transforming Axis-Aligned Bounding Boxes (548)

See Appendix 2 for C Implementation (**736**)

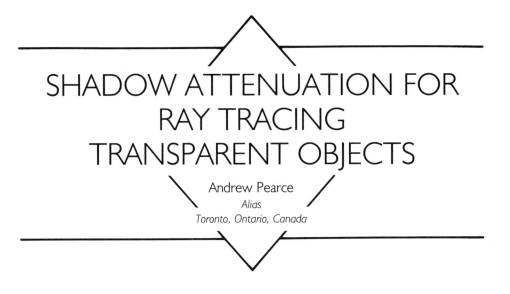

SHADOW ATTENUATION FOR RAY TRACING TRANSPARENT OBJECTS

Andrew Pearce
Alias
Toronto, Ontario, Canada

This trick attempts to avoid constant intensity shadows from transparent objects when ray tracing. It's loosely based on Sweeney's (1984) trick for ambient light.

In reality, light transmitted through a transparent object produces caustics in the object's shadow. Unfortunately, traditional ray tracing does not take this effect into account. Recently researchers have attacked this problem in several ways; by backwards ray tracing (Arvo, 1986), which involves tracing rays from a point light source, through the transparent object, and recording the resulting illumination as it falls on the occluded surface; by pencil tracing (Shinya *et al.*, 1987), where bundles of rays are traced from a point light source, through an optical system—the transparent object—to create illuminance polygons on the occluded surfaces; and by grid pencil tracing (Shinya *et al.*, 1989), which is similar to pencil tracing except the illuminance polygons are scan converted into an illuminance map to avoid aliasing problems, and the light source may be an area source.

All of these techniques produce very impressive images, but they require a lot of effort to implement. An alternative, which ignores caustics, is to attenuate the light based on the distance a shadow ray travels through a transparent object and on the object's optical depth (the object's transparency). Unfortunately, this approach may require a power and/or an exponential function; it does not allow for the light to appear focused in one particular region; it requires remembering all of the shadow intersections, since they may be found in no specific order, and a sense of optical medium must be determined for the shadow ray.

A trick I prefer is to attenuate the intensity of the light source based on the cosine of the incident angle of the shadow ray with the transparent object at each intersection along the shadow ray. The amount of attenuation is controlled by a scale value, which has a range from 0.0 to 1.0. The rationale for this trick is that shadows from glasses of water or crystal balls tend to focus light more toward the center of the shadow where the angle between the light rays and the surface normal is small. This is not always true; the focus can be totally outside of the shadow altogether, usually seen from objects with a high index of refraction. This trick is good enough to fool the eye on objects with small indices of refraction, such as glass ashtrays, plastic marbles, or bottles of beer.

The new transparency term multiplier (t_m) is calculated

$$t_m = \text{MAX}\Big[0, 1 + (\vec{S} \cdot \vec{N})t_s\Big],$$

where

$\vec{S}$ is the normalized shadow ray direction vector

$\vec{N}$ is the surface normal vector (*facing the eye*)

t_s is the scale factor for the effect (0.0 to 1.0).

The actual transparency value (k_t) for the object is assumed to lie in the range 0.0 to 1.0. The final transparency value for the object (k_t') is computed

$$k_t' = k_t t_m.$$

If $t_s = 0.0$, the shadow will be of constant intensity (equivalent to the transparency of the object) regardless of the angle of incidence. If $t_s = 1.0$, the shadowing will be complete when the angle between $\vec{N}$ and $\vec{S}$ is 90 degrees; the shadowing will be equivalent to the transparency of the object when the angle between $\vec{N}$ and $\vec{S}$ is 180 degrees.

The term t_m is computed for every transparent surface intersected by the shadow ray and factored into k_t', which is initialized to 1.0 for the shadow ray. Of course all of this work is wasted if the shadow ray strikes an opaque surface, which is why Haines' idea of testing opaque objects for shadowing before checking transparent objects should be used in conjunction with this technique.

Setting $t_s = 0.6$ works well in most cases. This trick can be used in conjunction with integrating transparency over the distance traveled through the object, resulting in a detailed shadow.

See also Simulating Fog and Haze (364); Efficient Generation of Sampling Jitter Using Look-up Tables (64); Fast Line–Edge Intersections on a Uniform Grid (29); Transforming Axis-Aligned Bounding Boxes (548)

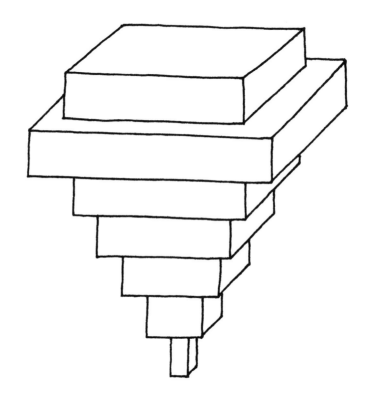

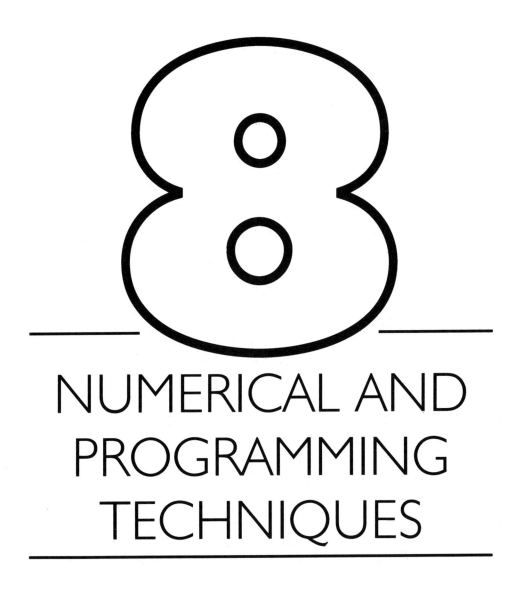

NUMERICAL AND PROGRAMMING TECHNIQUES

ROOT FINDING SUMMARY

Finding the roots of an equation is a common task in computer graphics. In 3D, the operation is very common in ray tracing, when object/ray intersections are computed using the implicit form for an object; the intersections of the object and ray are then represented by the zeros of the equation formed by plugging the explicit form of the ray into the explicit form of the object. In 2D, some applications of root-finding include the determination of bounding boxes and accurate tracing of curves.

The following Gems discuss numerical root finding. Linear and quadratic equations are trivial, and the solutions well-known. Cubic and quartic equations may also be solved analytically, but it takes some care to make sure the solution is stable; the first Gem addresses that question.

The second and third Gems are more general numerical solutions, which are designed to find the zeros of a function efficiently and robustly.

See also Ray Tracing (383); Distance Measures Summary (423)

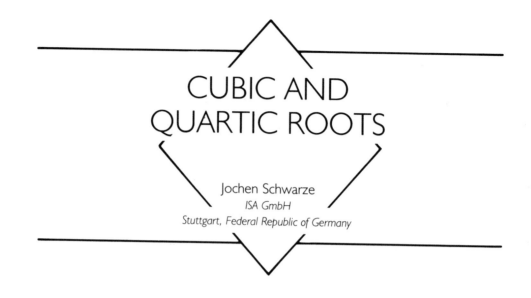

CUBIC AND QUARTIC ROOTS

Jochen Schwarze
ISA GmbH
Stuttgart, Federal Republic of Germany

The ray–object intersection used in ray tracing requires the solution of cubic and quartic equations as soon as more complex objects like splines and tori are to be supported. Iterative algorithms are often slow and numerically unstable. Start values and the number of noncomplex roots are hard to determine.

An approach to finding cubic and quartic roots analytically is presented in the following. Sample code in C shows a possible implementation with intermediate variables and case decisions for time efficiency. It uses double precision arithmetic; no complex numbers and operations are required.

Solution of the Cubic

A cubic equation of the form

$$c_3 x^3 + c_2 x^2 + c_1 x + c_0 = 0$$

is first divided by c_3, giving the normal form

$$x^3 + Ax^2 + Bx + C = 0.$$

Substitution of

$$x = y - \frac{A}{3}$$

eliminates the quadratic term, yielding

$$y^3 + 3py + 2q = 0.$$

Using Cardano's Formula (G. Cardano, 1501–1576), the determinant is

$$D = q^2 + p^3$$

$$u,v = \sqrt[3]{-q \pm \sqrt{D}} \,,$$

and the roots are

$$y_1 = u + v$$

$$y_{2,3} = -\frac{u+v}{2} \pm \frac{\sqrt{3}}{2}(u-v)i.$$

Three cases can be distinguished:

$D > 0$:   one real (y_1), two conjugated complex values (y_2, y_3)

$D = 0$:   two real values, $y_2 = y_3$

$D < 0$:   three different real values.

In the case of $D < 0$ (the so-called *casus irreducibilis*), trigonometric substitution helps to find all three solutions without the need for complex arithmetics:

$$\cos \varphi = -\frac{q}{\sqrt{-p^3}}$$

$$y_1 = 2\sqrt{-p}\,\cos\frac{\varphi}{3}$$

$$y_{2,3} = -2\sqrt{-p}\,\cos\frac{\varphi \pm \pi}{3}.$$

Resubstitution yields the correct values for x.

405

Solution of the Quartic

A quartic equation,

$$c_4 x^4 + c_3 x^3 + c_2 x^2 + c_1 x + c_0 = 0,$$

is divided by c_4:

$$x^4 + Ax^3 + Bx^2 + Cx + D = 0,$$

and substitution of

$$x = y - \frac{A}{4}$$

eliminates the cubic term

$$y^4 + py^2 + qy + r = 0.$$

The resolvent cubic is then

$$z^3 - \frac{p}{2}z^2 - rz + \frac{rp}{2} - \frac{q^2}{8} = 0.$$

With z being one root of the above equation, the roots of the quartic can be obtained by solving the two quadratic equations

$$y^2 \pm y\sqrt{2z - p} + z \mp \sqrt{z^2 - r} = 0.$$

Resubstitution yields the correct values for x.

Implementation

The three functions *SolveQuadric( )*, *SolveCubic( )*, and *SolveQuartic( )* take both an array of coefficients and an array of solutions as parameters. They return the number of noncomplex solutions and put the roots into the second array. Double and triple solutions are detected in the code but are returned only once.

Incorrect results produced by floating point precision errors have the most serious effects with small numbers around zero. A function *IsZero( )* is required for such values to be recognized. The extent of the appropriate epsilon surrounding *EQN_EPS* should be set accordingly.

Intermediate variables are used to avoid redundant floating point operations. More optimization could be done by checking for division by one, and other special cases. The *IsZero( )* function could be inline coded if supported by the compiler.

The presented solution for cubic and quartic roots allows easy implementation and adaption. It is sufficiently fast and accurate to meet the requirements of graphics applications.

See Appendix 2 for C Implementation (738)

A BÉZIER CURVE – BASED ROOT-FINDER

Philip J. Schneider
University of Geneva
Geneva, Switzerland

Introduction

Mathematics, especially geometry and linear algebra, is fundamental to computer graphics. One important class of problems that arises frequently is that of finding the root or roots of functions—for example, finding the intersection of a ray with a torus or the intersection of two curves. More often than not, the polynomials one must solve are of high enough degree that no closed-form solution exists. This Gem describes an algorithm for finding all the roots of such higher-order equations. This algorithm was developed in the context of an interactive two-dimensional curve-drawing system (Schneider, 1988), and was originally used to solve the problem described in "Solving the Nearest-Point-on-Curve Problem" in this volume. Variants on this root-finding algorithm have apparently been discovered independently by a number of researchers, but it appears to be relatively unknown.

The root-finding algorithm presented here is a variant of the bisection method. By exploiting certain characteristics of Bézier curves, we are able to find all the roots of equations with no closed form. A common approach to problems such as these is to use Newton–Raphson iteration, a method that begins with an initial "guess" at a solution, and iteratively converges on the root. Unfortunately, texts describing Newton iteration usually begin their explanation with a phrase such as, "Assume you have an initial guess u . . . ." The method described here, on the other hand, needs no such initial guess, and works recursively to find the root or roots. The basic method can be stated quite briefly:

1. Convert the equation to Bernstein–Bézier form.

2. Find the roots of the equation by finding the intersection(s) of the resulting Bézier curve with the horizontal 0-axis.

Conversion to Bernstein – Bézier form

Functional curves have the general form $y = f(x)$, where f is some polynomial. This can be recast as a parametric polynomial:

$$Graph(t) = (x(t), y(t))$$

$$= (X, Y).$$

The question is now: what is the Bézier control polygon for *Graph*? That is, we seek control points $V_i = (x_i, y_i)$ in the plane that satisfy

$$(X, Y) = \sum_{i=0}^{n} V_i B_i^n(t).$$

The x and y components are independent, so the above vector-valued equation is really two scalar equations:

$$X = \sum_{i=0}^{n} x_i B_i^n(t)$$

$$Y = \sum_{i=0}^{n} y_i B_i^n(t).$$

By the linear precision property of Bézier curves (Boehm *et al.*, 1984; Farin, 1988), we know that we can rewrite the function as

$$Graph(t) = \sum_{i=0}^{n} \left(\frac{i}{n}, y_i \right) B_i^n(t).$$

That is, the control points of the Bernstein–Bézier form of *Graph* are spaced evenly in the interval [0, 1] (the x direction, if you will).

So, it remains to determine the coefficients of Y, which will correspond to the y component of the control points of the Bernstein–Bézier form of *Graph*. This is relatively straightforward. What follows is a description of a method due to Lane (1989) for converting from the power basis to Bézier basis. Given

$$P(t) = \sum_{i=0}^{n} A_i t^i, \qquad t \in [0, 1],$$

we want $\{Y_i\}_0^n$ such that

$$P(t) = \sum_{i=0}^{n} \binom{n}{i} t^i (1 - t)^{n-i}.$$

A simple algorithm for the conversion is:

```
for j: integer ← 1, j + 1, while j ≤ n do
    begin
                    1
        c ←  ───────────;
              (n + 1 − j)
        d ← 1;
        e ← c;
        for i: integer ← n, i − 1, while i ≥ j do
            begin
                Yᵢ ← dYᵢ + eYᵢ₋₁;
                d ← d − c;
                e ← e + c;
            end;
        endloop;
    end;
endloop;
```

Then, $\{Y_i\}_0^n$ are the desired coefficients, and the final form of the equation is:

$$Graph(t) = \sum_{i=0}^{n} \left(\frac{i}{n}, Y_i \right) B_i^n(t).$$

The attentive reader may object that the range of the polynomial above is fixed at $[0, 1]$. For polynomials that do not naturally fall into this form, one may apply the Cauchy criterion (Collins and Loos, 1976) to find the root bounding interval, and then map this onto the $[0, 1]$ interval.

Finding the Roots

An example of a fifth-degree curve for which we must find the roots is shown in Fig. 1. The roots of the polynomial are exactly those values of t where the Bernstein–Bézier curve crosses the horizontal axis (the t-axis). In general, the values of coefficients of arbitrary polynomials given in power basis form provide no intuition regarding the shape of the functional curve, and are of little direct help in finding roots. However, the values of coefficients (that is, control points) of Bézier curves are very intuitively related to the shape of the curve. We can exploit several characteristics of Bézier curves in order to help us find the roots. These

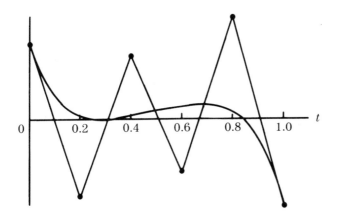

Figure 1.   A fifth-degree polynomial in Bézier form.

characteristics are as follows:

1. The convex hull property—the curve itself will always lie within the convex hull of the control points.

2. The variation-diminishing property—the curve is an approximation to the control polygon that is "smoother" than the control polygon. More specifically, any straight line will intersect the curve at most as many times as the straight line intersects the control polygon.

3. Repeated subdivision of the curve yields control points that converge on the curve itself in the limit.

These observations lead to a simple recursive algorithm, which appears in Fig. 2. The algorithm starts by counting the number of sign changes in the list of Bézier control points (the coefficients)—this corresponds to the number of times the control polygon crosses the t-axis. By Descartes' Law of Signs, and the variation-diminishing property of Bézier curves, we know that the number of roots in an interval will be less than or equal to the number of such crossings. If there are no sign changes, the Bézier

```
FindRoots (V)
        V: array[0..n] of point; Control points of Bezier representation
begin
    if (control polygon does not cross t-axis)
      then return NoRoots;
    else if ((control polygon crosses t-axis once) and
            (control polygon is flat enough or recursion limit reached))
            then return (t-intercept of chord from V[0] to V[n] as the root)
    else begin
            subdivide the Bezier curve V at midpoint, using deCasteljau's algorithm;
            FindRoots(left half);
            FindRoots(right half);
            return (all solutions thereby generated);
            end;
        end;
    end.
```

Figure 2. The root-finding algorithm.

curve cannot cross the t-axis, and there are no roots, so we just return. If there is one sign change, we check if the Bézier control polygon is flat enough or if we have reached the recursion depth limit. By "flat enough," we mean that the control polygon is close enough to a straight line so that we can approximate the root in that region by taking the intersection of a chord from the first to last control points with the t-axis as the root—this exploits the convex hull and variation-diminishing properties.

When there is more than one sign, there may be more than one root in the interval. In this case, we subdivide the current control polygon in the center of the current interval using deCasteljau's algorithm—this gives us two new Bézier curves, each of which represent exactly half the current curve. We then call *FindRoots* recursively on each new subcurve. The roots found at the "bottom" of each recursive call are gathered together, and make up the set of roots for the original equation.

Whether we subdivide at any particular recursive depth due to the control polygon not being flat enough or because there is more than one t-axis crossing, subdivision creates smaller and smaller subcurves. Because each subcurve resulting from an application of deCasteljau's algorithm is shorter than the curve from which it came from, and because the new control points converge toward the curve, the algorithm can be viewed as "homing in" on the point at which the curve itself crosses the t-axis.

As stated earlier, we can stop the recursion when the control polygon of the current polynomial is flat enough; that is, when the control polygon is close enough to a line segment (and crosses the t-axis just once), the root can be approximated by the point of intersection of the t-axis and a line segment drawn from the first to the last control points. Our problem now is to determine how flat is flat enough for a specified acceptable error. For a control polygon crossing just once, (see Fig. 3 for an example), we can define a bounding box whose top and bottom are parallel to the line connecting the first and last control points, and whose ends are perpendicular to the top and bottom. Then, the error of the solution is then bounded by half the distance between the points at which the bounding box intercepts the t-axis (or one or both endpoints of the interval $[0, 1]$, if the intersection point(s) lie outside this interval). When the error of the solution is within the desired precision of the root approximation, we compute the intersection of the line from the first to last with the t-axis, and return. Because we are doing binary subdivision

413

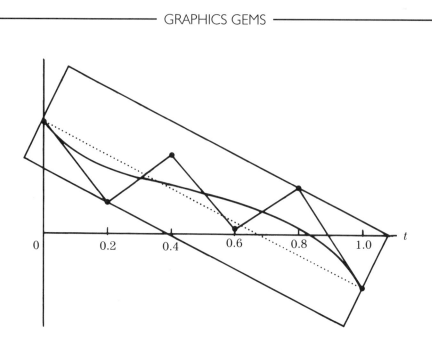

Figure 3. Bounding box for a fifth-degree polynomial.

of the fifth-degree polynomial, and because the t-values are bounded between 0 and 1, we can easily compute the relationship between the depth of the recursive subdivision and the desired error. At the top level (before any subdivision), the interval is [0, 1] and the expected error is 0.5. Each binary subdivision therefore cuts the expected error in half, so we merely stop the recursion when we have reached a depth corresponding to the base 2 logarithm of the desired error bound. For example, if our desired precision is $\frac{1}{128}$, or $\frac{1}{2^7}$, we set our depth limit to 7 (assuming the "top level" is considered to have depth 1).

A variation on this algorithm can be used to provide an initial bound and guess for using Newton–Raphson iteration. Note that our algorithm here finds an interval in which a root exists (when there is one t-axis crossing). An initial guess might be to use the midpoint of such an interval or the intersection method described earlier. This may be an essential modification if one wishes to find roots of very high-degree functions, because excessive repeated subdivision of high-degree Bézier curves tends to accumulate floating-point errors, which can lead to imprecise roots.

A C implementation of this algorithm appears in the appendix, in the file *point_on_curve.c*. The routine of interest is *FindRoots*; the arguments to this routine are the control points of the Bézier curve, the degree of the curve, an array of real numbers in which to store the root(s) it finds, and the current recursive depth. The routine returns the number of roots found. In that sample implementation, the degree of the root-finder is fixed at 5 for simplicity.

See Appendix 2 for C Implementation (**787**)

USING STURM SEQUENCES TO BRACKET REAL ROOTS OF POLYNOMIAL EQUATIONS

D. G. Hook, P. R. McAree
The University of Melbourne
Parkville, Melbourne, Australia

Introduction

The polynomial

$$y = a_n x^n + a_{n-1} x^{n-1} + \cdots + a_1 x + a_0 \equiv f(x)$$

with real coefficients $a_0, a_1, \ldots, a_n$ is a continuous graph on the (x, y)-plane whose real roots correspond to the values of x where $f(x)$ touches or crosses the axis $y = 0$. Recall that a polynomial of degree n has n roots, and that these may be real or complex and they need not be distinct. In his treatise *Mém. présentes par divers savants*, Charles Sturm, (1835) detailed a method for finding the exact number of real roots of $f(x) = 0$ in the interval $a < x < b$. The approach provides a convenient and computationally efficient technique for bracketing roots of $f(x) = 0$. Once a root is bracketed, root polishing techniques, such as bisection, false position, Brent's method, and Newton–Raphson, can be used to obtain accurate estimates.

The Theorem of Sturm

Sturm's Theorem: There exists a set of real polynomials $f_1(x)$, $f_2(x), \ldots, f_m(x)$ whose degrees are in descending order, such that if $b > a$, the number of distinct real roots of $f(x) = 0$ in the interval $x = a$ to $x = b$ is given by the difference $N = s(a) - s(b)$, where $s(a)$ and $s(b)$ are the number of sign changes in the sequence $f, f_1, f_2, \ldots, f_m$ at $x = a$ and $x = b$ respectively.

Thus, to determine the number of distinct real roots of $f(x) = 0$ in the interval (a, b), it suffices to establish the difference in the number of sign changes in the Sturm sequence of $f(x)$ between limits $x = a$ and $x = b$. The real roots of $f(x) = 0$ obviously fall in the interval $(-\infty, +\infty)$. Applying the Sturm theorem to this interval gives the total number of such roots, while applying the Sturm theorem to the intervals $(-\infty, 0)$ and $(0, +\infty)$ yields, respectively, the number of negative and the number of positive real roots of $f(x) = 0$.

Of the variety of methods for constructing the Sturm sequence of the polynomial $f(x)$, we give the most widely used (see, for example, Turnbull, 1957 or Wilkinson, 1988). Set $f_1(x) = f(x)$ and $f_2(x) = f'(x)$. Then set $f_3(x)$ equal to the remainder, with its sign reversed, of the division $f_1(x)/f_2(x)$. Subsequent terms in the sequence are found using the same process of polynomial division. In general if the members f_{k-1} and f_k have been found, f_{k+1} will be the remainder after dividing f_{k-1} by f_k and reversing its sign. This process of polynomial division is continued until the remainder term becomes a constant.

Every polynomial $f(x)$ with real coefficients has a Sturm sequence that will yield the total number of distinct real roots of $f(x)$. If $f(x)$ has repeated roots each member of the sequence $f_1, f_2, \ldots, f_m$ will share a greatest common multiplier $G = (x - \alpha)^p(x - \beta)^q \ldots$, where powers $p, q, \ldots$ are integers. The members of the Sturm sequence can be written $f_1 = G\phi_1, f_2 = G\phi_2, \ldots, f_m = G\phi_m$, where

$$\phi = (x - \alpha)(x - \beta) \ldots (x - \lambda).$$

The repeated roots $\alpha, \beta, \ldots$ can be found by other methods (for example, synthetic division) after all of the distinct roots have been found.

Example

The polynomial

$$f(x) = x^3 + 3x^2 - 1$$

has the following Sturm sequence:

$$f_1 = x^3 + 3x^2 - 1, \; f_2 = 3x^2 + 6x, \; f_3 = 2x + 1, \; f_4 = 9/4.$$

The table below shows the signs for each member of the Sturm sequence at different values of x. From it we see that the polynomial $f(x)$ has three real roots α, β, γ, which satisfy the following inequalities:

$$-3 < \alpha < -2, \qquad -1 < \beta < 0, \qquad 0 < \gamma < 1.$$

	$f_1(x)$	$f_2(x)$	$f_3(x)$	$f_4(x)$	sign changes
$x = -\infty$	$-$	$+$	$-$	$+$	3
$x = -3$	$-$	$+$	$-$	$+$	3
$x = -2$	$+$	0	$-$	$+$	2
$x = -1$	$+$	$-$	$-$	$+$	2
$x = 0$	$-$	0	$+$	$+$	1
$x = +1$	$+$	$+$	$+$	$+$	0
$x = +\infty$	$+$	$+$	$+$	$+$	0

Constructing the Sturm Sequence

Algorithm A (Driving Algorithm)

Given a polynomial

$$f(x) = a[n]x^n + a[n-1]x^{n-1} + \cdots + a[1]x + a[0],$$

create the Sturm sequence $f_1, f_2, \ldots f_m$.

A1　Set f_1 equal to $f(x)$, and set f_2 equal to $f'(x)$.

A2　For $k = 0, 1, \ldots, \text{order}(f_2)$, set $f_2[k] = f_2[k]/\text{abs}(f_2[\text{order}(f_2)])$

A3　Set $k = 3$. While $\text{order}(f_k) \neq 0$, do algorithm B (*which takes parameters f_{k-2}, f_{k-1}, and sets f_k*), do step A4, set $k = k + 1$. Set $f_k[0] = -f_k[0]$. Stop.

A4 (*reverse the signs of the coefficients of the polynomial and normalize against the leading coefficient.*) For $j = 0, 1, \ldots,$ order(f_k), set $f_k[j] = -f_k[j]/\text{abs}(f_k[\text{order}(f_k)])$.

Algorithm B (Pseudo-division of polynomials to give remainder)

Given polynomials

$$u(x) = u[m]x^m + u[m - 1]x^{m-1} + \cdots + u[1]x + u[0],$$
$$v(x) = v[n]x^n + v[n - 1]x^{n-1} + \cdots + v[1]x + v[0],$$

where $v[n] = \pm 1.0$ and $m > n > 0$, this algorithm finds polynomial $r(x)$, which is the remainder of the polynomial division $u(x)/v(x)$.

B1   Copy $u(x)$ into $r(x)$.

B2   If $v[\text{Order}(v)] < 0.0$, do steps B3, B4; otherwise do steps B5, B6. Stop.

B3 $k = \text{Order}(u) - \text{Order}(v) - 1$. While $k \geq 0$ do $r[k] = -r[k]$, $k = k - 2$.   Do step B4 for $k = \text{Order}(u) - \text{Order}(v)$, Order (u) $- \text{Order}(v) - 1, \ldots, 0$

B4 $j = \text{Order}(v) + k - 1, \text{Order}(v) + k - 2, \ldots, k, r[j] = -r[j] - r[\text{Order}(v) + k]v[j - k]$.

B5   Do step B6, for $k = \text{Order}(u) - \text{Order}(v), \text{Order}(u) - \text{Order}(v)$ $- 1, \ldots, 0$

B6 $j = \text{Order}(v) + k - 1, \text{Order}(v) + k - 2, \ldots, k, r[j] = r[j] - r[\text{Order}(v) + k]v[j - k]$.

Counting the Sign Changes
Algorithm C

Given the Sturm sequence $f_1, f_2, \ldots, f_m$, count the number of sign changes for the sequence at a given x. S is the number of sign changes.

C1 Set $S = 0$. Do steps C2, C3 for $k = 2, 3, \ldots, m$. Stop.

C2 If $x = +\infty$

$$a = f_{k-1}[\text{order}(f_{k-1})], \ b = f_k[\text{order}(f_k)].$$

If $x = -\infty$

if order (f_{k-1}) is odd, $a = -f_{k-1}[\text{order}(f_{k-1})]$,
otherwise $a = f_{k-1}[\text{order}(f_{k-1})]$.

if order(f_k) is odd, $b = -f_k[\text{order}(f_k)]$,
otherwise $b = f_k[\text{order}(f_k)]$.

if $x = 0.0$

$$a = f_{k-1}[0], \ b = f_k[0]$$

otherwise

$$a = f_{k-1}(x), \ b = f_k(x).$$

C3 If $a \cdot b < 0.0$ or $a = 0.0$, $S = S + 1$.

Some operations in this algorithm can be avoided if we make use of the following characteristics of Sturm sequences (Turnbull, 1957; Wilkinson, 1988):

1. Contiguous members of the sequence cannot evaluate to zero at the same value of x.

2. If $f_k = 0$, the signs of f_{k-1} and f_{k+1} are equal in magnitude but opposite in sign.

Consequently, there are circumstances when the polynomial f_{k+1} does not need to be evaluated once the value of f_{k-1} is known.

Method of Bisection

The Sturm method can be used to isolate any real root of $f(x) = 0$—say the kth in order of decreasing values—using the method of bisection.

Suppose we have an interval (a, b) such that

$$b > a; s(a) - s(\infty) \geq k; s(b) - s(\infty) < k.$$

By the Sturm theorem, the interval (a, b) must contain the kth root, λ_k of $f(x) = 0$. Repeated bisection of the interval (a, b) will isolate λ_k to an interval (a_p, b_p), of width $(b - a)/s^p$ after p steps, and provided $s(a_p) - s(b_p) = 1$, λ_k will be the only distinct real root of $f(x)$ in this interval. Algorithm D below, is based on the analysis by Wilkinson (1988).

Algorithm D (Bisection Method)

Given a Sturm sequence for the polynomial $f(x)$ and an interval (a, b) known to contain the kth root of $f(x) = 0$, this algorithm isolates an interval that contains only the kth root.

D1 Determine $s(a)$, $s(b)$. Do steps D2, D3 until $s(a) - s(b) = 1$. Stop.

D2 set $c = (a + b)/2$ and determine $s(c)$.

D3 if $s(c) - s(\infty) \geq k$ set $a = c$, otherwise set $b = c$.

The time taken by algorithm D is independent of the separation of the roots of $f(x) = 0$ and is exceptionally stable even when the roots are pathologically close. Algorithm D could be used to find λ_k to any desired accuracy; once an interval containing the root has been isolated, however, faster convergence is possible using the known information about $f(x)$ at each step. Bracketing methods, such as classical bisection, false position, and Brent's method, are more stable than open methods, such as Newton–Raphson and the secant method. Note that classical bisection relies on $f(x)$ changing sign across any interval containing an odd number of real roots. It should not be confused with algorithm D.

Conclusions

We have used algorithms A, B, C, and D in a ray tracer that renders algebraic surfaces of arbitrary order. The points where each ray intersects the surface correspond to the real roots of a polynomial whose order is the same as the surface. These polynomials are frequently ill-conditioned. In this application we used the modified false position algorithm to polish the roots. It converges in almost quadratic time, is extremely stable, and is generally faster than adaptive methods (such as Brent's method) when the polynomial is unpredictable. In similar situations we recommend it.

Sturm's method can also be used to find the complex roots of a polynomial. The approach is detailed in Pinkert (1976).

See Appendix 2 for C Implementation (**743**)

DISTANCE MEASURES SUMMARY

Calculating distance is an important and common operation in computer graphics. Often an exact answer is not important. For example, suppose you are writing a 2D drawing program, and you are contemplating writing the code to do selection: the user clicks the mouse, and the nearest object is selected. Since the operation is interactive, you do not need an exact solution for the distance to each nearby object; taking the minimum of estimated distances is probably good enough. If the wrong object is occasionally selected, the user may move closer to the one desired and click again.

A 3D application for an approximate distance metric could be tracing the path of a moving, charged particle through a volume filled with static charged particles. Only those static charges closer than some threshold (determined by their charge) will influence the moving particle; an approximate distance is enough to determine if a charge is "close enough" to influence the moving particle. More common applications in 3D include an extension of the 2D example to a 3D drawing program; determining "near" implicit functions for testing in a ray tracing system; and finding candidates for collision detection in a dynamics system.

The following Gems present distance approximations in 2D and 3D. Note that you can generalize a 2D distance metric $d = f(d1, d2)$ to 3D by writing $d3 = f(d1, f(d2, d3))$, and then expanding the result for $d3$. This process may be iterated to higher dimensions if needed.

See also Root Finding Summary (403)

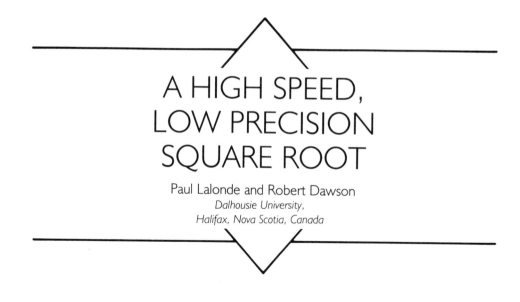

A HIGH SPEED, LOW PRECISION SQUARE ROOT

Paul Lalonde and Robert Dawson
Dalhousie University,
Halifax, Nova Scotia, Canada

Traditional methods for evaluating square roots using iterative methods are often too slow for use either in interactive systems or when large numbers of square roots must be evaluated. Often, particularly in computer graphics, the precision required is much less than that computed. For instance, the *sqrt*() function in most C library implementations returns a double precision result, even when passed a single precision operand.

When only a few digits of accuracy are required a faster approach can be used. The technique is to use the most significant bits of the mantissa as an index into a table of square roots. By using this looked-up value and halving the exponent, a low-precision square root function can be built that runs much faster than iterative methods.

A review of floating point formats is in order. A floating point number in binary is of the form $2^{\pm ee\ldots e} * \pm mm\ldots m$, where m and e represent bits. All floating point numbers can be expressed in normalized form, in which a number takes the form $eeeeeeee \pm 1.mmmmmmm$. Since any floating point number can be normalized, most systems assume normalization and store only the fractional part. For illustrative purposes we will consider a floating point type with an eight-bit exponent, one-bit sign, and seven-bit mantissa, stored in the form $[2\char94]e_7 e_6 e_5 e_4 e_3 e_2 e_1 e_0[*] \pm [1.]m_6 m_5 m_4 m_3 m_2 m_1 m_0$.

$$\sqrt{2^m \cdot n} = 2^{\frac{m}{2}} \sqrt{n} \qquad (1)$$

Equation 1 shows that the operation of taking a square root of a floating point number reduces to halving the exponent and finding the

```
e ← exponent(V)

i ← mantissa(V)

if (e bit-and 1)              the exponent is odd
        set the high bit of i

e ← e/2                divide e by two — recall equation 1
                       (This division must preserve sign)

j ← T[i]

U ← 2^e*1.j
```

Figure 1.

square root of the mantissa. As an odd exponent cannot be divided by 2, we break the number into an even exponent $e_7 e_6 e_5 e_4 e_3 e_2 e_1 0$, and a *quaternary mantissa*, $e_0 m_6 m_5 m_4 m_3 m_2 m_1 m_0$, in the range [1..4). The sign bit of the mantissa is ignored, but may be used to flag an error if negative. This stores all the values of [1..4) with no loss of information from the original floating point representation.

A look-up table is created during the application's initialization, which stores the square roots of the values $2 {^\wedge} e_0 * 1.m_6 m_5 m_4 m_3 m_2 m_1 m_0$.

```
build_table(precision: integer, table: array [0..2^precision+1] of integer)
        i, j: integer;
        f, sf: real;
begin
        for i: integer ← 0, 2^precision − 1
            f ← 1.i
            table[i] ← mantissa(√f);
            f ← 2*1.i
            table[i + 2^precision] ← mantissa(√f);
            endloop;
end
```

Figure 2.

425

Once the table, T, is built, the algorithm to find a square root, U, of a given floating point number V is as follows. Let p be the required precision in bits, and i be an integer $p + 1$ bits wide. Pseudo-code to build the table is given in Fig. 2. Pseudo-code for extracting the square root is shown in Fig. 1. Sample code illustrating this process is shown in the appendix. This code is in no way optimal. An assembler implementation of a similar algorithm executed almost five times faster than the C implementation. Note that we are halving the exponent as a signed variable; a simple shift right will not preserve the sign bit.

This whole process, once the table is generated, can be performed with one bitwise *and*, two bitwise *or*s, one bitwise *test* and five shift operations. Clearly this is faster than any iterative square root process. The main disadvantages are the time required to build the table of square roots, which adds to the application's start-up time, and the memory required to store the table. For n bits of precision, 2^{n+1} words of memory are required. For example, a seven-bit table requires 256 bytes.

Similar techniques can be used for other periodic and logarithmically periodic functions.

See Appendix 2 for C Implementation (**756**)

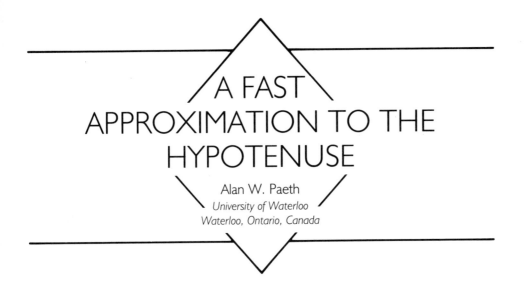

A FAST APPROXIMATION TO THE HYPOTENUSE

Alan W. Paeth
University of Waterloo
Waterloo, Ontario, Canada

Overview

A fast approximation to the hypotenuse (Pythagorean distance) $h = (x^2 + y^2)^{1/2}$ and its related approximation error is derived. The method is useful in providing accept/reject distance tests in 2D graphics. These are commonly used in providing "gravity fields" or other proximity tests for circle or ellipse selection (see concluding code).

Derivation

When forming a boolean proximity test for a known distance d, the inequality may be rewritten in the form $d^2 \geq x^2 + y^2$ thereby removing the square root. A useful approximation for h should do likewise and ideally dispense with multiplication as well. To derive such a form, consider (without loss of generality) the case $x > y > 0$. Next, normalize the test:

$$h = x\sqrt{\frac{x^2}{x^2} + \frac{y^2}{x^2}} = x\sqrt{1 + \left[\frac{y}{x}\right]^2} = x + \frac{1}{2}\left[\frac{x}{y}\right]^2 - \frac{1}{8}\left[\frac{x}{y}\right]^4 + O\left(\left[\frac{x}{y}\right]^6\right).$$

The last form is the direct Taylor expansion. Retaining terms through the quadratic gives $h' = x \cdot (1 + \frac{1}{2}(y/x)^2)$ with cubic accuracy. This form is commonly employed in libraries offering a high-precision *hypot* as the conventional form is prone to severe loss of accuracy: for $|y| < |x|$ it holds that $y^2 \ll x^2$ and the sum within the radicand discards much of y's original precision.

Factoring the expansion as $h' = x + 1/2 \cdot y \cdot (y/x)$ and then further approximating by considering $(y/x) \approx 1$ (when it in fact lies on the range $[0..1]$) yields the valuable approximation $h' = x + \frac{1}{2}y$. The error is not as great as may be expected because the oversize constant approximation to (y/x) is in part offset by the Taylor series truncation, since the first omitted term is negative. By discarding the original assumption that $x > y > 0$, this may be rewritten as

$$h \le h' = \max(|x|, |y|) + 1/2 \cdot \min(|x|, |y|).$$

For many languages, minimum and maximum operations involve costly conditional logic. Operation count may be reduced by noting that $\max(a, b) + \min(a, b) = a + b$ for all a and b yielding the well-known form

$$h \le h' = |x| + |y| - 1/2 \cdot \min(|x|, |y|).$$

Note that the code is symmetric about the axis $x = y = 1$ within the first quadrant. Absolute value operations on the input arguments allow for four-quadrant operation, yielding isometric distance lines of eight-fold symmetry (see Fig. 1) in close relation with the circular Euclidean norm.

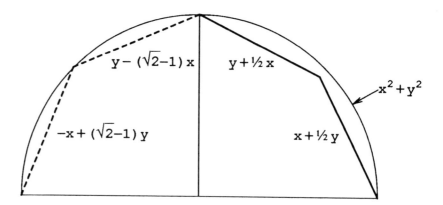

Figure 1. Equations of (approximate) unit distance.

```
integer function idist(integer: x1, y1, x2, y2)
begin
    min: integer;
    if (x2 ← x2 − x1) < 0 then x2 ← −x2;
    if (y2 ← y2 − y1) < 0 then y2 ← −y2;
    if x2 > y2 then min ← y2 else min ← x2;
    return [x2 + y2 − rshift(min, 1)];
end
```

Figure 2.   Approximate vector length.

For greatest speed the $1/2 \cdot |y|$ scaling operation may be replaced by a single bit shift right. As this operation is on nonnegative quantities, concerns regarding rounding direction and arithmetic versus logical shifting vanish. The code is of general use when presented as the distance between two points, as in Fig. 2 above. Calls of the form $idist(x1, y1, 0, 0)$ provide vector length by measuring point-origin distance with little added expense.

Error Analysis

Consider the locus of points at unit distance from the origin $(\cos\theta, \sin\theta)$ within the first octant $(\cos\theta > \sin\theta)$. The deviation between this ideal arc and the approximated distance is then $\mathrm{dev}(\theta) = \cos\theta + \frac{1}{2}\sin\theta - 1$. Differentiation locates the points of minimum and maximum deviation at $2\sin\theta = \cos\theta$. The minimum lies at $\theta = 0$ where the functions $h(0, 1) = h'(0, 1) = 1$ are in perfect agreement. The maximum (found by dividing both terms by $\cos\theta$) lies at $\theta \approx 26.5°$ at the point $(\cos\tan^{-1}(1/2), \sin\tan^{-1}(1/2))$. Substitution into the approximate hypotenuse equation for h' yields the vector length $(5/4)\cos\tan^{-1}(1/2) = (5/2)\sin\tan^{-1}(1/2) = \frac{1}{2}\sqrt{5} \approx 1.118$. Thus, vector estimates are too large by a worst-case value of no more than 12%, but are never small. Note that this is a relative error as calculations were in reference to an exact unit vector. Scaling h' by an overall value of 94% splits the difference in error but discards the valuable property $h'(x, y) \geq h(x, y)$ for all x and y. When coded in integer precision, the quantized relative error may be smaller

```
integer function PntOnCirc(integer: x_p, y_p, x_c, y_c, r)
        begin
returns true IF a test point (x_p, y_p) is to within a
pixel of the circle of center (x_c, y_c) and radius r;
see also C source comments
        d: integer ← idist(x_p, y_b, x_c, y_c);
        if r > d then return[0];                far-in
        if 9 × r < 8 × (d − 1) then return[0];  far-out
full test: r < hypot(xp − xc, yp − yc) < r + 1
        x_p ← x_p − x_c;
        y_p ← y_p − Y_c;
        d ← x_p² + y_p²;
        if d < r² then return[0];               near-in
        r ← r + 1
        if d > r² then return[0];               near-out
        return[1];                              WITHIN
        end
```

Figure 3.   Point-on-circle test.

than its theoretic bound because of the loss of one bit of precision inherent in the halving operation. While maintaining the containment property, this effect must nonetheless be accounted for in carefully crafted program code (See C-language source comments).

If slightly greater accuracy is desired at the cost of one multiplication, the $1/2 \cdot$ min term may be scaled downwards to provide a tighter fit (Fig. 1, left). The optimal scale factor occurs when this value is $0.414 + \approx \sqrt{2} - 1 = \tan(\pi/8)$. Note that this brings both methods into agreement at $h(1, 1) = h'(1, 1) = \sqrt{2}$ so that the approximation is now exact at eight principle compass points. This change moves the angle for worst-case deviation from $26.5° +$ to the symmetric portion of the octant at $\pi/8$ radians (22.5°). The worst-case error is then reduced to $\cos(\pi/8) + \tan(\pi/8) \sin(\pi/8) = \sec(\pi/8) \approx 1.0824$. This change maintains the valuable property $h'(x, y) \geq h(x, y)$ with equality holding *iff* $|x| = |y|$ or $x = 0$ or $y = 0$. For many applications the multiplication is not worth the marginal gain in accuracy.

Given the bounded nature of the estimate, a bracketing interval test may be made in which points either too near and too far from a reference length are discarded. A range check of this nature is used as a circle pick mechanism within the "Lemming" portable graphics editor (Paeth, 1988). Here the approximation is used to discard unlikely selection candidates quickly without resorting to multiplication unless necessary, while yielding no concessions to accuracy (see Fig. 3).

Note that all arguments are integers and that no intermediate floating point calculations appear. As the final squaring operations double the number of bits in integers x_p, y_p, and r, 16-bit architectures will require integer variables of 32-bit precision to accommodate arguments with values outside of the byte range (± 127).

See also A Fast 2D Point-on-Line Test (49); Trigonometric Functions at Select Points (18)

See Appendix 2 for C Implementation (758)

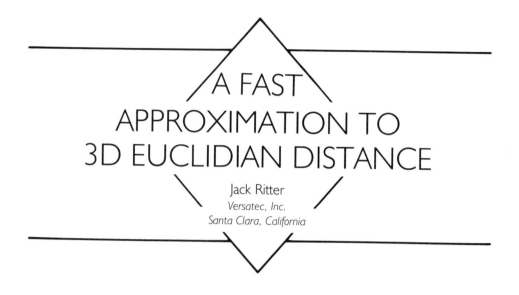

A FAST APPROXIMATION TO 3D EUCLIDIAN DISTANCE

Jack Ritter
Versatec, Inc.
Santa Clara, California

This Gem is a fast approximation to 3D Euclidian distance $(\sqrt{dx * dx + dy * dy + dz * dz})$. It could be used in ray tracing for quickly calculating ray versus bounding volume distances, or object to object distances in general.

It takes advantage of the fact that the sum of the lengths of the three components of a 3D vector is a rough approximation of the vector's length. This way of measuring distance is also called "Manhattan distance."

If the vector has only one nonzero component, the Manhattan distance is exactly correct. This is the best case. The worst case is where all three components are equal in length (d): then the Manhattan distance will be $d + d + d = 3 * d$, where the true Euclidian distance is $\sqrt{3} * d$. The worst case is off by a factor of $3 / \sqrt{3} \approx 1.7$. The algorithm below compromises between these extreme conditions, giving a maximum error much less than 1.7. The algorithm is as follows:

1. Find these three values: ABS(dx), ABS(dy), ABS(dz).

2. Sort them (3 compares, 0–3 swaps).

3. Approximate distance = max + (1/4)med + (1/4)min.

This approximation is accurate within ±13%.
  Two successively more refined step 3 formulae are

$$\text{max} + (5/16)\text{med} + (1/4)\text{min (has } \pm 9\% \text{ error)}$$
$$\text{max} + (11/32)\text{med} + (1/4)\text{min (has } \pm 8\% \text{ error)}.$$

In all cases, the coefficients are fractions whose denominators are powers of 2. This avoids division. The numerators can be calculated by shifting and adding, avoiding multiplication. This allows very simple fixed point arithmetic, which is faster than the 3D Euclidian calculation, even with a floating point coprocessor.

If the vector components are floating point values, they may need to be scaled before being converted to integers. If the maximum length vector we would expect is 100 or more, for example, then no scaling need be done; a span of 100 is enough resolution, given that we are only accurate to ±8% to begin with. If the span is, say, 1.0, then we need to scale up.

More generally, this algorithm is an alternative to finding the square root of the sum of three squares, which need not mean distance, or anything spatial at all.

Here is pseudo-code for the 13% version, where scaling is needed. A scale of 1024 is used, which can be accomplished by shifting by 10. This means that the code contains no multiplies, divides, or square roots, and is all in fixed point.

```
approx_length_13(dx, dy, dz) :real
    dx, dy, dz: real;
    begin
        maxc, medc, minc: integer;
        Convert the reals to scaled integers.
        maxc ← abs ( 1shift(dx, 10) );
        medc ← abs ( 1shift(dy, 10) );
        minc ← abs ( 1shift(dz, 10) );
        Sort. Need only find max.
        if maxc < medc
                then swap(maxc, medc);
        if maxc < minc
                then swap(maxc, minc);
        Compute 1/4 of med & min in 1 step.
        medc ← medc + minc;
        maxc ← maxc + rshift(medc, 2);
        return ( (real) rshift(maxc, 10) );
        end
```

433

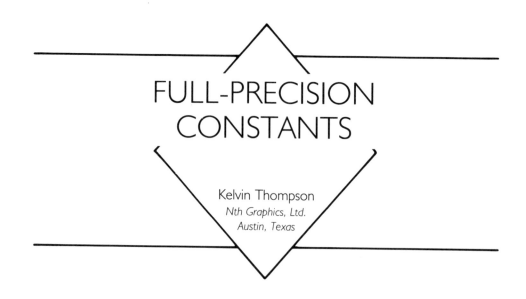

FULL-PRECISION CONSTANTS

Kelvin Thompson
Nth Graphics, Ltd.
Austin, Texas

Most extended-precision floating point formats store the equivalent of 14–16 decimal digits of precision (see "Converting between Bits and Digits" in this volume); many of us have trouble remembering this many digits in some important constants. Here are some constants whose precision should satisfy any floating point format.

$$\pi \approx 3.14159265358979323846264338327950288419716939937511$$

$$\sqrt{2} \approx 1.41421356237309504880168872420969807856967187537691$$

$$\sqrt{3} \approx 1.73205080756887729352744634150587236694280525381041$$

$$\log_e 2 \approx 0.69314718055994530941723212145817656807550013436025511$$

Another way to get full precision in a constant is simply to use a math library routine to initialize a global variable, then use that variable as a constant. A pseudo-code example follows:

pi: **real** ← 3*acos(0.5).

(Unfortunately, some math libraries aren't accurate to full precision.)

CONVERTING BETWEEN BITS AND DIGITS

Kelvin Thompson
The University of Texas at Austin

Problem statement

Find out how many binary bits correspond to a given number of decimal digits ... or vice versa.

Solution

If b is the number of bits and d the number of digits, satisfy the relation

$$2^b = 10^d.$$

Solving for each variable in terms of the other, we get

$$b = d \cdot \log_2 10 \approx d \cdot 3.3219280948873623478703$$

$$d = b \cdot \log_{10} 2 \approx b \cdot 0.30102999566398119521 3739.$$

Example

The IEEE single-precision floating point format has 23 bits of precision; this is equivalent to about 6.9 decimal digits of precision.

435

STORAGE-FREE SWAPPING

Brian Wyvill
University of Calgary
Calgary, Alberta, Canada

I first noticed this little Gem in some C code written by my brother, Geoff Wyvill. It is often the case that the values of two variables have to be swapped. The usual way that this is done is to declare a temporary variable to store the value of one of the two items to be swapped, then overwrite the variable with the value of the other. The idea of this Gem is to use three exclusive *or* operations to avoid declaring a temporary variable. The following pseudo-code does this:

    a ← a xor b;
    b ← b xor a;
    a ← a xor b;

This is best illustrated by example:

	Value of a	Value of b
	5	6
a ← a xor b (101 xor 110 = 011)	3	6
b ← b xor a (110 xor 011 = 101)	3	5
a ← a xor b (011 xor 101 = 110)	6	5

This method will work regardless of the data type of the variables to be swapped since it is good for any bit pattern. In C a macro can be defined whose arguments can be of any type:

#**define** SWAP(a, b) {a↑ = b; b↑ = a; a↑ = b;}

Using a macro not only saves storage, but also avoids the overheads of a function call.

See also Median Finding on a 3×3 Grid (171)

GENERATING
RANDOM INTEGERS

Andrew S. Glassner
Xerox PARC
Palo Alto, California

Suppose you want to generate a random integer n from the range $[l, h]$. You would like to have equal probability of getting any integer in the set $\{l, l + 1, l + 2, \ldots, h - 1, h\}$. The typical way to do this is to start with a random-number generator that returns a floating point number in the range $[0, 1]$; call this real number u.

To convert u to the range $[l, h]$ you might be tempted to simply scale u into the new range by using the expression $n \leftarrow round[l + (h - l)u]$. This would be a bad idea. To see why, consider the fragment of the real number line shown in Fig. 1, where $l = 3$ and $h = 5$. Then $[l + (h - l)u]$ will be in the closed interval $[3, 5]$. When you take the integer part of this, you're likely to get only 3 or 4; you will get 5 only when $u = 1.0$, which should be a rare event. What you really want in this example is to scale u into the open interval $(2.5, 5.5)$, as shown in Fig. 2. Then when you round to the nearest integer you'll be equally likely to get 3, 4, or 5. To simulate this open interval, offset the ends of the original range by an amount Δ slightly smaller than 0.5; perhaps 0.4999.

So to compute a random integer n in the range $[l, h]$ from a random real u in the range $[0, 1]$, choose a number Δ slightly smaller than 0.5,

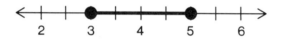

Figure 1. The closed interval $[3, 5]$. Rounding points in this interval will virtually never return 5.

438

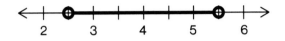

Figure 2.   The open interval $(2.5, 5.5)$. Rounding points in this interval you are equally likely to get 3, 4, or 5.

create two new temporary variables $l' \leftarrow l - \Delta$ and $h' \leftarrow h + \Delta$, and use the formula $n \leftarrow round[l' + (h' - l')u]$.

See also A Digital "Dissolve" Effect (221)

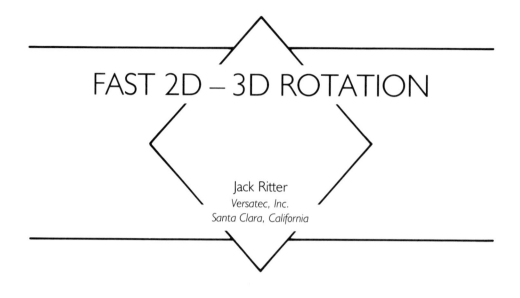

FAST 2D – 3D ROTATION

Jack Ritter
Versatec, Inc.
Santa Clara, California

This Gem shows a way to rotate a point around the origin quickly and accurately. The rotation can be in 2D or 3D. In general, rotated coordinates (X', Y') are derived from (X, Y) by

$$X' \leftarrow X*\cos(\theta) - Y*\sin(\theta)$$

$$Y' \leftarrow X*\sin(\theta) + Y*\cos(\theta). \qquad (1)$$

The problem is that computing $sin(\ )$ and $cos(\ )$ is very costly. The method described here makes use of a precomputed table of sine values, scaled such that 16-bit fixed point multiplies can be used. No floating point calculations or trig functions are used.

The table is defined for the first quadrant, to save storage. Rotations in the other three quadrants can be transformed into first quadrant rotations by reflection and/or transposition.

You generate the table with any desired resolution. Let's say you want to be able to rotate a point in increments of degrees. This means that the table will have 91 entries (the number of gradations + 1). The table is pregenerated via the following technique:

```
for i = 0, +1, i ≤ 90
    table[i] ← 16384*sin(i*DtoR)
endloop
```

The last entry in the table, table[90], will hold the maximum value: 16384. This means that the table can be held in 16-bit words.

From Eq. 1, we see that to compute X' and Y', we need to compute four terms: $X*\cos$, $Y*\sin$, $X*\sin$, and $Y*\cos$. Each of these four is of the form "coordinate*$\sin(\theta)$" or "coordinate*$\cos(\theta)$." Thus, we need only to know how to calculate these two forms.

The algorithm is as follows:

> *To calculate the form "coordinate $*$ $\sin(\theta)$":*
> index ← $\lfloor \theta \rfloor$
> value ← Rshift(coordinate $*$ table[index], 14)
> *To calculate the form "coordinate $*$ $\cos(\theta)$":*
> index ← $\lfloor \theta \rfloor$
> value ← Rshift(coordinate $*$ table[90 − index], 14)

In each case, the multiply by the table value occurs before the right shift of 14, which corrects for the scaling. The multiply creates an intermediate 32-bit value. The final value is 16 bits. The table, as well as the input coordinate values, must be 16-bit words, so that integer multiplies are generated.

The $\cos(\theta)$ form differs from the $\sin(\theta)$ form only in that the indexing is from the *end* of the table. This is why there must be 91 entries.

If you successively accumulate θ, as in a tumbling object, you must wrap around from 0 to 360, or from 360 to 0, depending on whether θ is being incremented or decremented. Wrap-around is clumsy in the 90 gradation case. If the table holds 128 gradations, for example, instead of 90, wrap around is trivial:

> $\theta \leftarrow \theta + \Delta\theta$ *increment, possibly causing wrap.*
> $\theta \leftarrow \theta$ bit-**and** 511   *correct for wrap.*

$\Delta\theta$ can be positive or negative.

The table has only 16 bits of accuracy. Successive rotations may eventually cause an object to deform. For higher accuracy, use 32-bit values. On the 68020, for example, you would do a "quad word" multiply (any 32-bit processor has some way to hold an intermediate 64-bit product).

See also Rotation Tools (465); Rotation Matrix Methods Summary (455); Bit Patterns for Encoding Angles (442)

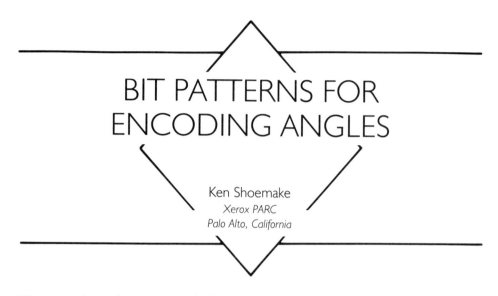

BIT PATTERNS FOR ENCODING ANGLES

Ken Shoemake
Xerox PARC
Palo Alto, California

The question often arises of what units to use for angles, and most folks only consider two choices: radians and degrees. There is another choice, however, which is often used for computer music.

You can use a fixed-point fraction of 2π, or 360 degrees—it's the same either way. The implicit binary point is just above the high-order bit. This notation melds perfectly with two's complement integer arithmetic. The high-order bit can be viewed as either a sign bit or a fraction bit; plus and minus 180 degrees are indistinguishable, both being represented by (0).100000. As you increment an angle, it naturally wraps around at 360 degrees. All your bits are meaningful; each angle has a unique bit pattern.

The two high bits tell you which quadrant you're in, and make it cheap to use a quarter wave look-up table for sines and cosines.

Instead of deciding between degrees and radians, you use a natural unit that varies between 0 and 1, and one that makes sense.

Here are some examples to give you the idea.

Binary Fixed Point	Degrees	Radians
0.000000000	0	0
0.010000000	90	$\pi/2$
0.100000000	-180 or $+180$	$-\pi$ or $+\pi$
0.111000000	-45 or $+315$	$-\pi/4$ or $+7\pi/4$

See also Rotation Tools (465); Rotation Matrix Methods Summary (455); Fast 2D–3D Rotation (440)

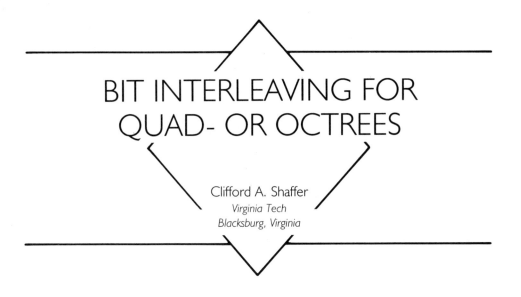

BIT INTERLEAVING FOR QUAD- OR OCTREES

Clifford A. Shaffer
Virginia Tech
Blacksburg, Virginia

The linear quad- or octree is an alternative to the traditional tree structure based on explicit pointers to nodes. The linear representation can reduce the total storage requirements for a quadtree. It stores only the leaves from the original tree structure, in the order that those nodes would be visited during a traversal of the tree. The internal nodes and pointers of the explicit tree are replaced by position descriptors describing the path from the root of the tree to the leaf node. Alternatively, the linear representation can be viewed as storing square blocks from the image in a sorted list. The sort key is obtained by bit interleaving the coordinates of the upper-left corner of each such block.

Below is pseudo-code for bit interleaving 2D coordinates (a similar process can be used for three dimensions). The result is a 32-bit address code, whose lower four bits tell the size of the block represented by that address. You could also view the address as a series of two-bit codes, with each code telling which way to branch in a quadtree to reach the node. In that case, the lower four bits tell the number of branches to take. Thus, a 32-bit code can store addresses for quadtrees with 15 levels (counting the root), equivalent to a 2D image with $2^{14} \times 2^{14}$ pixels. In 3D, a 32-bit code word can represent an address in a 2^9 pixel cube; higher resolution would require a longer code word.

Since the bit interleaving function is heavily used in a linear quad- or octree system, its efficiency is crucial. The code presented here makes use of look-up tables. The general approach to creating the interleaved value is to break the 32-bit work into 4 bytes, and use look-up tables to calculate directly the value of each byte from the corresponding four bits of the two input coordinates. Following the interleaving code are functions to extract the x, y, and depth values from an interleaved address. Note that *MAX_DEPTH* defines how big the interleaved value can be, that is, how may levels the tree may have. Any particular tree has an actual value (*max_depth*) that corresponds to the resolution of that tree's image. The alternative is to interpret all x and y values in terms of the maximum possible resolution ($2^{MAX-DEPTH}$). *MAX_DEPTH* also has the effect of limiting the size of the x and y coordinate values—in our case, only the lower 14 bits are used.

macro MAX_DEPTH 14; *Maximum possible depth*
byteval *is the look-up table for coordinate interleaving. Given a four-bit portion of the* (x, y)*coordinates, return the bit interleaving. Notice that this table looks like the order in which the pixels of a* 16×16 *Pixel image would be visited.*

```
byteval: array [0..15][0..15] of integer ← [
  [  0,   1,   4,   5,  16,  17,  20,  21,  64,  65,  68,  69,  80,  81,  84,  85],
  [  2,   3,   6,   7,  18,  19,  22,  23,  66,  67,  70,  71,  82,  83,  86,  87],
  [  8,   9,  12,  13,  24,  25,  28,  29,  72,  73,  76,  77,  88,  89,  92,  93],
  [ 10,  11,  14,  15,  26,  27,  30,  31,  74,  75,  78,  79,  90,  91,  94,  95],
  [ 32,  33,  36,  37,  48,  49,  52,  53,  96,  97, 100, 101, 112, 113, 116, 117],
  [ 34,  35,  38,  39,  50,  51,  54,  55,  98,  99, 102, 103, 114, 115, 118, 119],
  [ 40,  41,  44,  45,  56,  57,  60,  61, 104, 105, 108, 109, 120, 121, 124, 125],
  [ 42,  43,  46,  47,  58,  59,  62,  63, 106, 107, 110, 111, 122, 123, 126, 127],
  [128, 129, 132, 133, 144, 145, 148, 149, 192, 193, 196, 197, 208, 209, 212, 213],
  [130, 131, 134, 135, 146, 147, 150, 151, 194, 195, 198, 199, 210, 211, 214, 215],
  [136, 137, 140, 141, 152, 153, 156, 157, 200, 201, 204, 205, 216, 217, 220, 221],
  [138, 139, 142, 143, 154, 155, 158, 159, 202, 203, 206, 207, 218, 219, 222, 223],
  [160, 161, 164, 165, 176, 177, 180, 181, 224, 225, 228, 229, 240, 241, 244, 245],
  [162, 163, 166, 167, 178, 179, 182, 183, 226, 227, 230, 231, 242, 243, 246, 247],
  [168, 169, 172, 173, 184, 185, 188, 189, 232, 233, 236, 237, 248, 249, 252, 253],
  [170, 171, 174, 175, 186, 187, 190, 191, 234, 235, 238, 239, 250, 251, 254, 255]];
```

bytemask *is the mask for byte interleaving—mask out the nonsignificant bit positions. This is determined by the depth of the node. For example, a node of depth 0 is at the root. Thus, there are no branches and no bits are significant. The bottom four bits (the depth) are always retained. Values are described in hexidecimal notation.*

bytemask: **array** [0..MAX_DEPTH] **of integer** ← [0xf,
  0xc000000f, 0xf000000f, 0xfc00000f, 0xff00000f,
  0xffc0000f, 0xfff0000f, 0xfffc000f, 0xffff000f,
  0xffffc00f, 0xfffff00f, 0xfffffc0f, 0xffffff0f,
  0xfffffcf, 0xffffffff];

integer interleave(x, y, depth, max_depth)
Return the interleaved code for a quadtree node at depth depth whose upper left hand corner has coordinates (x, y) in a tree with maximum depth max_depth.
begin
  addr: **integer**; *Assumes 32-bit integers.*
  Scale x, y values to be consistent with maximum coord size and depth of tree.
  x ← lshift(x, MAX_DEPTH−max_depth);
  y ← lshift(y, MAX_DEPTH−max_depth);

Calculate the bit interleaving of the x, y values that have now been appropriately shifted, and place this interleave in the address portion of addr. *Note that the binary representations of* x *and* y *are being processed from right to left.*
  addr ← depth;
  addr ← addr **bit-or** lshift(byteval[y **bit-and** 03][x **bit-and** 03], 4);
  addr ← baddr **bit-or**
          lshift(byteval[rshift(y, 2) **bit-and** 0xf][rshift(x, 2) **bit-and** 0xf], 8);
  addr ← addr **bit-or**
          lshift(byteval[rshift(y, 6) **bit-and** 0xf][rshift(x, 6) **bit-and** 0xf], 16);
  addr ← addr **bit-or**
          lshift(byteval[rshift(y, 10) **bit-and** 0xf][rshift(x, 10) **bit-and** 0xf], 24);
  addr ← addr **bit-and** bytemask[depth];
  return (addr);
end;

The next two arrays are used in calculating the (x, y) coordinate of the upper left-hand corner of a node from its bit interleaved address. Given an eight-bit number, the arrays return the effect of removing every other bit (the y bits precede the x bits).

xval: **array** [0..255] **of integer** ← [

```
[ 0,   1,   0,   1,   2,   3,   2,   3,   0,   1,   0,   1,   2,   3,   2,   3],
[ 4,   5,   4,   5,   6,   7,   6,   7,   4,   5,   4,   5,   6,   7,   6,   7],
[ 0,   1,   0,   1,   2,   3,   2,   3,   0,   1,   0,   1,   2,   3,   2,   3],
[ 4,   5,   4,   5,   6,   7,   6,   7,   4,   5,   4,   5,   6,   7,   6,   7],
[ 8,   9,   8,   9,  10,  11,  10,  11,   8,   9,   8,   9,  10,  11,  10,  11],
[12,  13,  12,  13,  14,  15,  14,  15,  12,  13,  12,  13,  14,  15,  14,  15],
[ 8,   9,   8,   9,  10,  11,  10,  11,   8,   9,   8,   9,  10,  11,  10,  11],
[12,  13,  12,  13,  14,  15,  14,  15,  12,  13,  12,  13,  14,  15,  14,  15],
[ 0,   1,   0,   1,   2,   3,   2,   3,   0,   1,   0,   1,   2,   3,   2,   3],
[ 4,   5,   4,   5,   6,   7,   6,   7,   4,   5,   4,   5,   6,   7,   6,   7],
[ 0,   1,   0,   1,   2,   3,   2,   3,   0,   1,   0,   1,   2,   3,   2,   3],
[ 4,   5,   4,   5,   6,   7,   6,   7,   4,   5,   4,   5,   6,   7,   6,   7],
[ 8,   9,   8,   9,  10,  11,  10,  11,   8,   9,   8,   9,  10,  11,  10,  11],
[12,  13,  12,  13,  14,  15,  14,  15,  12,  13,  12,  13,  14,  15,  14,  15],
[ 8,   9,   8,   9,  10,  11,  10,  11,   8,   9,   8,   9,  10,  11,  10,  11],
[12,  13,  12,  13,  14,  15,  14,  15,  12,  13,  12,  13,  14,  15,  14,  15]]
```

yval: **array** [0..255] **of integer** ← [

```
[ 0,   0,   1,   1,   0,   0,   1,   1,   2,   2,   3,   3,   2,   2,   3,   3],
[ 0,   0,   1,   1,   0,   0,   1,   1,   2,   2,   3,   3,   2,   2,   3,   3],
[ 4,   4,   5,   5,   4,   4,   5,   5,   6,   6,   7,   7,   6,   6,   7,   7],
[ 4,   4,   5,   5,   4,   4,   5,   5,   6,   6,   7,   7,   6,   6,   7,   7],
[ 0,   0,   1,   1,   0,   0,   1,   1,   2,   2,   3,   3,   2,   2,   3,   3],
[ 0,   0,   1,   1,   0,   0,   1,   1,   2,   2,   3,   3,   2,   2,   3,   3],
[ 4,   4,   5,   5,   4,   4,   5,   5,   6,   6,   7,   7,   6,   6,   7,   7],
[ 4,   4,   5,   5,   4,   4,   5,   5,   6,   6,   7,   7,   6,   6,   7,   7],
[ 8,   8,   9,   9,   8,   8,   9,   9,  10,  10,  11,  11,  10,  10,  11,  11],
[ 8,   8,   9,   9,   8,   8,   9,   9,  10,  10,  11,  11,  10,  10,  11,  11],
[12,  12,  13,  13,  12,  12,  13,  13,  14,  14,  15,  15,  14,  14,  15,  15],
[12,  12,  13,  13,  12,  12,  13,  13,  14,  14,  15,  15,  14,  14,  15,  15],
[ 8,   8,   9,   9,   8,   8,   9,   9,  10,  10,  11,  11,  10,  10,  11,  11],
[ 8,   8,   9,   9,   8,   8,   9,   9,  10,  10,  11,  11,  10,  10,  11,  11],
[12,  12,  13,  13,  12,  12,  13,  13,  14,  14,  15,  15,  14,  14,  15,  15],
[12,  12,  13,  13,  12,  12,  13,  13,  14,  14,  15,  15,  14,  14,  15,  15]]
```

integer getx(addr, max_depth)
Return the x coordinate of the upper left-hand corner of addr *for a tree with maximum depth* max_depth.

begin
  x: **integer;**
  x ← xval[rshift(addr, 4) **bit-and** 0xf]; *do bottom two bits.*
  x ← x **bit-or** lshift(xval[rshift(addr, 8) **bit-and** 0xff]], 2); *next four bits.*
  x ← x **bit-or** lshift(xval[rshift(addr, 16) **bit-and** 0xff]], 6); *next four bits.*
  x ← x **bit-or** lshift(xval[rshift(addr, 24) **bit-and** 0xff]], 10); *top four bits.*
  x ← rshift(x, MAX_DEPTH − max_depth); *scale to tree depth.*

  return *(x);*
  end;

integer getx(addr, max_depth)
Return the y coordinate of the upper left hand corner of addr *for a tree with maximum depth* max_depth.

begin
  y: **integer;**
  y ← yval[rshift(addr, 4) **bit-and** 0xf]; *do bottom two bits.*
  y ← y **bit-or** lshift(yval[rshift(addr, 8) **bit-and** 0xff]], 2); *next four bits.*
  y ← y **bit-or** lshift(yval[rshift(addr, 16) **bit-and** 0xff]], 6); *next four bits.*
  y ← y **bit-or** lshift(yval[rshift(addr, 24) **bit-and** 0xff]], 10); *top four bits.*
  y ← rshift(y, MAX_DEPTH − max_depth); *scale to tree depth.*

  return (y);
  end;

integer getdepth(addr)
  Return the depth of the node. Simply return the bottom four bits.
begin
  return (addr **bit-and** 0xf);
  end;

See Appendix 2 for C Implementation (**759**)

A FAST HSL-TO-RGB TRANSFORM

Ken Fishkin
Pixar, Inc.
San Rafael, California

Three common color spaces used in computer graphics are RGB, HSV, and HSL color space. RGB color space is by far the most common, and is practically the lingua franca of computer graphics color spaces: its axes (R, G, and B) refer to the amount of red, green, and blue light that a pixel emits. The other two are *perceptual* color spaces, whose axes represent more perceptual qualities: the hue, the saturation, and the value or lightness.

The use of HSV and HSL color spaces for computer graphics arose at almost the same time. HSV was first proposed by Smith (1978), and HSL by the Core committee (Graphics Standards Planning Committee, 1979). The HSV-to-RGB and RGB-to-HSV transformations are simple and fast. While the RGB-to-HSL transformation is also simple and fast, the HSL-to-RGB transformation is about twice as slow, and now nearly as simple, as the HSV-to-RGB transformation.

This Gem fills in the "missing link," supplying an improved HSL-to-RGB transformation that is nearly the same as the HSV-to-RGB transformation. It does this by "massaging" the HSV-to-RGB transformation into an HSL-to-RGB transformation.

Hue (H) is defined the same in the two systems. Value (V) and lightness (L) are defined as

$$V \equiv \text{MAX}(R, G, B), \quad \text{and} \quad L \equiv (\text{MIN} + \text{MAX})/2.$$

Saturation is defined differently: "HSV Saturation" S_v is defined as

$$S_v \equiv \frac{V - \text{MIN}}{V},$$

while "HSL Saturation" S_L is defined as

$$S_L \equiv \frac{\text{MAX} - \text{MIN}}{\text{MAX} + \text{MIN}} \text{ if } L \le 1/2,$$

$$\equiv \frac{\text{MAX} - \text{MIN}}{2 - \text{MAX} - \text{MIN}} \text{ if } L > 1/2.$$

This Gem just computes V and S_ν from L and S_L, and then does standard HSV to RGB, with a little strength reduction and common subexpression elimination thrown in.

A pseudo-code description of the algorithm follows:

> *given H, S_L, L on* [0 $\cdots$ 1], *compute R, G, B on* [0 $\cdots$ 1]
>
> **if** $L \le \dfrac{1}{2}$
> > **then** $\nu \leftarrow L\,(1.0 + S_L)$;
> > **else** $\nu \leftarrow L + S_L - L \cdot S_L$;
>
> **if** $\nu = 0$
> > **then** $R \leftarrow G \leftarrow B \leftarrow 0.0$;
> > **else begin**
> > > min $\leftarrow 2L - \nu$;
> > > $S_\nu \leftarrow (\nu - \text{min})/\nu$;
> > > $H \leftarrow 6H$; *map onto* [0 $\cdots$ 6)
> > > sextant: **int** $\leftarrow$ floor(H);
> > > fract: **real** $\leftarrow H -$ sextant;
> > > vsf: **real** $\leftarrow \nu \cdot S_\nu \cdot$ fract;
> > > mid1; **real** $\leftarrow$ min + vsf;
> > > mid2: **real** $\leftarrow \nu -$ vsf;
> > > $[R, G, B] = $ **select** sextant **from**
> > > > 0: [ν, mid1, min];
> > > > 1: [mid2, ν, min];
> > > > 2: [min, ν, min1];
> > > > 3: [min, mid2, ν];
> > > > 4: [mid1, min, ν];
> > > > 5: [ν, min, mid2];
> > > > **endcase;**
> > **end**

See also Mapping RGB Triples onto Four Bits (233)
See Appendix 2 for C Implementation (**763**)

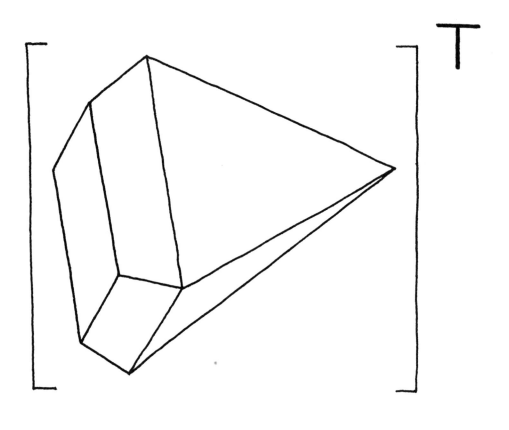

T

9

MATRIX
TECHNIQUES

MATRIX IDENTITIES

Kelvin Thompson
The University of Texas at Austin

Below are some matrix identities that are useful for a number of purposes: constructing and decomposing transforms; optimizing matrix multiplication routines (see "Fast Matrix Multiplication" in this volume); and understanding the subtleties of matrix concatenation.

$$
\begin{bmatrix} a & b & c & 0 \\ d & e & f & 0 \\ g & h & i & 0 \\ 0 & 0 & 0 & 1 \end{bmatrix}
\begin{bmatrix} 1 & 0 & 0 & 0 \\ 0 & 1 & 0 & 0 \\ 0 & 0 & 1 & 0 \\ x & y & z & 1 \end{bmatrix}
=
\begin{bmatrix} a & b & c & 0 \\ d & e & f & 0 \\ g & h & i & 0 \\ x & y & z & 1 \end{bmatrix}
$$

$$
\begin{bmatrix} 1 & 0 & 0 & 0 \\ 0 & 1 & 0 & 0 \\ 0 & 0 & 1 & 0 \\ x_1 & y_1 & z_1 & 1 \end{bmatrix}
\begin{bmatrix} 1 & 0 & 0 & 0 \\ 0 & 1 & 0 & 0 \\ 0 & 0 & 1 & 0 \\ x_2 & y_2 & z_2 & 1 \end{bmatrix}
=
\begin{bmatrix} 1 & 0 & 0 & 0 \\ 0 & 1 & 0 & 0 \\ 0 & 0 & 1 & 0 \\ x_1 & y_1 & z_1 & 1 \end{bmatrix}
$$

$$
+
\begin{bmatrix} 1 & 0 & 0 & 0 \\ 0 & 1 & 0 & 0 \\ 0 & 0 & 1 & 0 \\ x_2 & y_2 & z_2 & 1 \end{bmatrix}
$$

453

$$
\begin{bmatrix} a & b & c & 0 \\ d & e & f & 0 \\ g & h & i & 0 \\ 0 & 0 & 0 & 1 \end{bmatrix}
\begin{bmatrix} x & 0 & 0 & 0 \\ 0 & y & 0 & 0 \\ 0 & 0 & z & 0 \\ 0 & 0 & 0 & 1 \end{bmatrix}
=
\begin{bmatrix} ax & by & cz & 0 \\ dx & ey & fz & 0 \\ gx & hy & iz & 0 \\ 0 & 0 & 0 & 1 \end{bmatrix}
$$

$$
\begin{bmatrix} x & 0 & 0 & 0 \\ 0 & y & 0 & 0 \\ 0 & 0 & z & 0 \\ 0 & 0 & 0 & 1 \end{bmatrix}
\begin{bmatrix} a & b & c & 0 \\ d & e & f & 0 \\ g & h & i & 0 \\ 0 & 0 & 0 & 1 \end{bmatrix}
=
\begin{bmatrix} ax & bx & cx & 0 \\ dy & ey & fy & 0 \\ gz & hz & iz & 0 \\ 0 & 0 & 0 & 1 \end{bmatrix}
$$

The identities below simply say that (1) the product of two *linear* matrices is a linear matrix, and (2) the product of two *affine* matrices is an affine matrix.

$$
\begin{bmatrix} ? & ? & ? & 0 \\ ? & ? & ? & 0 \\ ? & ? & ? & 0 \\ 0 & 0 & 0 & 1 \end{bmatrix}
\begin{bmatrix} ? & ? & ? & 0 \\ ? & ? & ? & 0 \\ ? & ? & ? & 0 \\ 0 & 0 & 0 & 1 \end{bmatrix}
=
\begin{bmatrix} ? & ? & ? & 0 \\ ? & ? & ? & 0 \\ ? & ? & ? & 0 \\ 0 & 0 & 0 & 1 \end{bmatrix}
\tag{1}
$$

$$
\begin{bmatrix} ? & ? & ? & 0 \\ ? & ? & ? & 0 \\ ? & ? & ? & 0 \\ ? & ? & ? & 1 \end{bmatrix}
\begin{bmatrix} ? & ? & ? & 0 \\ ? & ? & ? & 0 \\ ? & ? & ? & 0 \\ ? & ? & ? & 1 \end{bmatrix}
=
\begin{bmatrix} ? & ? & ? & 0 \\ ? & ? & ? & 0 \\ ? & ? & ? & 0 \\ ? & ? & ? & 1 \end{bmatrix}
\tag{2}
$$

See also Transformation Identities (485)

454

ROTATION MATRIX METHODS SUMMARY

Matrix techniques form the heart of geometric transformations used in computer graphics. A good grounding in linear algebra can help a programmer navigate through the various types of projections and transformations in common use. Typically a user should be shielded from the mathematics of matrix manipulations, which are just a convenient mechanism for accomplishing certain goals. A good command of matrix techniques can help a programmer write systems that insulate the user from the underlying representation.

The following Gems present a variety of matrix techniques that help in various rotation tasks. Matrix methods for 3D rotation are considered difficult or abstruse by many programmers, but this does not have to be. The following Gems provide some basic tools and fundamentals that can help you master the application of matrices in computer graphics.

See also Rotation Tools (465); Bit Patterns for Encoding Angles (442); Fast 2D–3D Rotation (440)

TRANSFORMING AXES

Kelvin Thompson
The University of Texas at Austin

Problem Statement

Sometimes an interactive 3D application needs to know roughly which way a set of transformed coordinate axes are pointing on the screen. For example, the application may want to know if the x-axis of a given modeling space is pointing into or out of the screen after the axis undergoes a sequence of modeling and viewing transforms; this could help the application understand the orientation of an object on the screen. Even if the application knows only the net transform for the object, it can still calculate the approximate orientation of the object's axes quite efficiently.

Solution

Given an arbitrary 4×4 matrix $\mathbf{A} = [a_{ij}]$ that transforms 3D points in an "input" space to 3D points in an "output" screen space in the usual manner,

$$\begin{bmatrix} x_{\text{in}} & y_{\text{in}} & z_{\text{in}} & 1 \end{bmatrix} \begin{bmatrix} a_{11} & a_{12} & a_{13} & a_{14} \\ a_{21} & a_{22} & a_{23} & a_{24} \\ a_{31} & a_{32} & a_{33} & a_{34} \\ a_{41} & a_{42} & a_{43} & a_{44} \end{bmatrix} = \begin{bmatrix} \alpha & \beta & \gamma & \omega \end{bmatrix} \quad (1)$$

$$x_{\text{out}} = \frac{\alpha}{\omega}, \qquad y_{\text{out}} = \frac{\beta}{\omega}, \qquad z_{\text{out}} = \frac{\gamma}{\omega}. \quad (2)$$

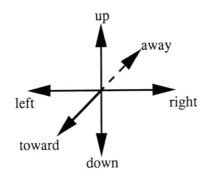

Figure 1. General directions.

Figure 1 shows six "general directions" in screen space ("toward" and "away" are directly in and out of the screen). To determine the general direction of an "input" axis after it is transformed to the screen space, we check the sign of the appropriate ratio in Tables 1 or 2. Generally we use Table 1; however, if a_{i4} is zero for some entry in Table 1 ($i \neq 4$, since a_{44} should never be zero), then we use the corresponding entry in Table 2.

If the "output" space is the usual left-handed eye space, with the eye looking toward positive z, sign conventions are as follows: if a given quotient is negative, the transformed axis is pointing in the upper direction indicated at the top of the column; if the quotient is positive, the axis points toward the lower direction. (For example, if a quotient in the middle column is negative, then the corresponding axis is pointing down.)

Table 1. General Direction Ratios.

	Toward/Away	Down/Up	Left/Right
x-axis	$\dfrac{a_{13}a_{44} - a_{43}a_{14}}{a_{14}a_{44}}$	$\dfrac{a_{12}a_{44} - a_{42}a_{14}}{a_{14}a_{44}}$	$\dfrac{a_{11}a_{44} - a_{41}a_{14}}{a_{14}a_{44}}$
y-axis	$\dfrac{a_{23}a_{44} - a_{43}a_{24}}{a_{24}a_{44}}$	$\dfrac{a_{22}a_{44} - a_{42}a_{24}}{a_{24}a_{44}}$	$\dfrac{a_{21}a_{44} - a_{41}a_{24}}{a_{24}a_{44}}$
z-axis	$\dfrac{a_{33}a_{44} - a_{43}a_{34}}{a_{34}a_{44}}$	$\dfrac{a_{32}a_{44} - a_{42}a_{34}}{a_{34}a_{44}}$	$\dfrac{a_{31}a_{44} - a_{41}a_{34}}{a_{34}a_{44}}$

Table 2.   Zero-Case Direction Ratios.

	Toward/Away	Down/Up	Left/Right
x-axis	a_{13}/a_{44}	a_{12}/a_{44}	a_{11}/a_{44}
y-axis	a_{23}/a_{44}	a_{22}/a_{44}	a_{21}/a_{44}
z-axis	a_{33}/a_{44}	a_{32}/a_{44}	a_{31}/a_{44}

On the other hand, if the "output" space is a right-handed eye space, with the eye looking toward negative z, the positions of the "toward" and "away" labels need to be swapped (or the sign tests in the first column reversed).

We don't have to do any floating-point division to determine the signs of the ratios. The sign of each quotient can be determined by the XOR of the sign bits of the dividend and divisor.

Proof

Let us take the case of whether the x-axis points toward or away from the viewer. All vectors along the x-axis take the form $[x\,0\,0\,1]$, and we will want to look at the z coordinate of the transformed vector. Doing the arithmetic from Eqs. (1) and (2), we see that the transformed z coordinate will be

$$\frac{xa_{13} + a_{43}}{xa_{14} + a_{44}}.$$

Similarly, the transformed origin $[0\,0\,0\,1]$ has a z coordinate of a_{43}/a_{44}. If we subtract the transformed origin from the transformed x vector, we get

$$\frac{xa_{13} + a_{43}}{xa_{14} + a_{44}} - \frac{a_{43}}{a_{44}}. \tag{3}$$

If we now let x approach positive infinity, and apply L'Hospital's rule

where appropriate, this becomes

$$\frac{a_{13}}{a_{14}} - \frac{a_{43}}{a_{44}} = \frac{a_{13}a_{44} - a_{43}a_{14}}{a_{14}a_{44}},$$

which is exactly the upper-left entry in Table 1. If this ratio is negative, the transformed x-axis points in the negative z direction; if it is positive, it points toward positive z.

Next, if a_{14} is zero, we simply use $x = 1$ in Eq. 3 and get a_{13}/a_{44}, which agrees with Table 2. Derivations of other entries in the table are similar.

FAST MATRIX MULTIPLICATION

Kelvin Thompson
The University of Texas at Austin

Problem Statement

Speed up routines that multiply matrices, perhaps at the expense of code size and readability.

Solutions

First, remove unnecessary floating point operations. If you are multiplying matrices that you know contain 1's or 0's in certain positions, remove multiplication and addition by the appropriate terms. It may be useful to write special routines for multiplying affine and linear matrices—see "Matrix Identities" in this volume.

Second, unwind loops. Routines like *V3MatMul* in the Vector C Library are compact, but they waste unnecessary time updating loop variables and performing array look-ups. Such programs run faster when written as a strict sequence of operations with constant-valued indices into arrays. For example, pseudo-code to multiply two general 4 × 4 matrices would contain a sequence of sixteen assignments similar to

$$\text{m\_out}[0][0] \leftarrow \text{m1}[0][0] * \text{m2}[0][0] +$$

$$\text{m1}[0][1] * \text{m2}[1][0] +$$

$$\text{m1}[0][2] * \text{m2}[2][0] +$$

$$\text{m1}[0][3] * \text{m2}[3][0].$$

(It may not be necessary to unwind loops if you know your compiler is smart enough to unwind or vectorize loops for you.)

Finally, when programming in C, use register pointers (see "How to Use C Register Variables to Point to 2D Arrays" in this volume); many C compilers won't use registers unless you explicitly tell them to do so.

$$\left[\triangleright \right]^{\mathsf{T}}$$

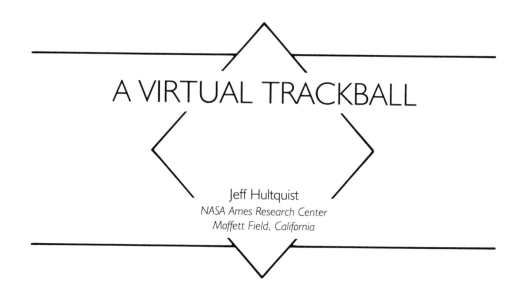

A VIRTUAL TRACKBALL

Jeff Hultquist
NASA Ames Research Center
Moffett Field, California

This simple code is the heart of a virtual manipulator that mimics a trackball. Using the mouse, a user can select any point on the trackball and rotate the entire scene about the center of rotation. The variables *oldMouse* and *newMouse* hold the successive positions of the cursor in object coordinates. The trackball is centered at point C and has radius r (see Fig. 1).

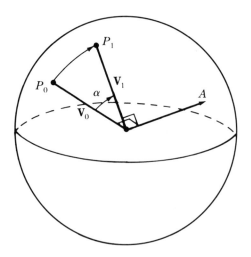

Figure 1.

```
ray0 ← [[oldMouse.x, oldMouse.y, 0], [0,0,1]];
ray1 ← [[newMouse.x, newMouse.y, 0], [0,0,1]];
P₀ ← intersectSphere(ray0, C, r);
P₁ ← intersectSphere(ray1, C, r);
```
$\mathbf{V}_0 \leftarrow (P_0 - C) / |(P_0 - C)|;$
$\mathbf{V}_1 \leftarrow (P_1 - C) / |(P_1 - C)|;$
$\mathbf{A} \leftarrow \mathbf{V}_0 \times \mathbf{V}_1;$
$\alpha \leftarrow \arcsin(|\mathbf{A}|)$
if $(\mathbf{V}_0 \cdot \mathbf{V}_1 < 0)$
   then $\alpha \leftarrow \alpha + \pi / 2;$
rotateAboutAxis$(\mathbf{A}, \alpha);$

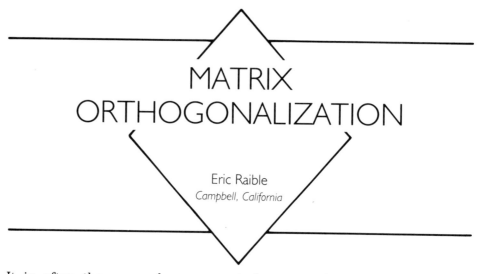

MATRIX ORTHOGONALIZATION

Eric Raible
Campbell, California

It is often the case when successively composing rotations that the resulting matrix becomes nonorthogonal. This leads to skewing and scaling effects. Although there are several common algorithms to re-orthogonalize matrices (for example, Gram Schmidt), I prefer the following.

We reorthogonalize the matrix R by computing an approximation to a correction matrix $C = (R^TR)^{-1/2}$, which, if premultiplied by R, would give an orthogonal matrix. (To see that RC is indeed orthogonal, it suffices to show that $(RC)^T = (RC)^{-1}$, since the inverse of an orthogonal matrix is also its transpose. This is easily done.)

It is difficult to find C directly, so we instead find an approximation to C by computing the matrix analog to Taylor Series expansion of $(1 + x)^{-1/2}$ about $x = 0$.

Since R is close to orthogonal, R^TR will be close to the identity matrix, and $X = R^TR - I$ will be close to the zero matrix. Thus, we can compute C by doing the Taylor expansion of $C = (R^TR)^{-1/2} = [I + (R^TR - I)]^{-1/2} = [I + X]^{-1/2}$ about $X = 0I$, to give us

$$C = I - (1/2)X + (3/8)X^2 - (5/16)X^3 + O(X^4).$$

There are two ways of increasing the accuracy of this approximation. The first is to increase the number of terms (the next ones are $35/128$, $-63/256$, $231/1024$, and $-429/2048$). The second is to repeat this procedure (and using only the first two or three terms). Exactly which approach to take depends on how the loop that evaluates C is coded, and how far the original matrix is from orthogonal. A little experimentation should determine the best approach for your application.

See Appendix 2 for C Implementation (**765**)

464

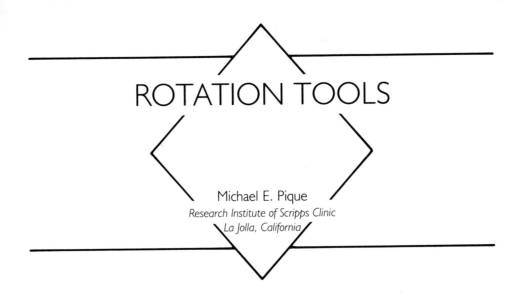

ROTATION TOOLS

Michael E. Pique
Research Institute of Scripps Clinic
La Jolla, California

Here are some facts and techniques you'll want to have at hand when working with rotations. This section uses the following conventions: row vectors go on the left and are post-multiplied by matrices on the right; points are row vectors.

True for any 3×3 rotation matrix R:

- R is normalized: the squares of the elements in any row or column sum to unity, or $+1$.

- R is orthogonal: the dot product (sum of the products of corresponding elements) of any pair of rows is zero, likewise the dot product of any pair of columns.

- The rows of R represent the coordinates in the original space of unit vectors along the coordinate axes of the rotated space.

- The columns of R represent the coordinates in the rotated space of unit vectors along the coordinate axes of the original space.

- The determinant of R is $+1$. (Reflection matrices have determinants of -1.)

Converting between Matrix and Axis-Amount Representations

The only rotation matrix generating formula you'll ever need: the matrix that rotates about an arbitrary axis through the origin is

$$R = rotation\_about\_axis\_by\_angle(\mathbf{axis}, \theta)$$

$$= \begin{bmatrix} tx^2 + c & txy + sz & txz - sy \\ txy - sz & ty^2 + c & tyz + sx \\ txz + sy & tyz - sx & tz^2 + c \end{bmatrix},$$

where x, y, and z are the components of a unit-vector (use $V3\,Normalize$ function) along the axis, θ is the angular amount of rotation, and $s = \sin\theta$, $c = \cos\theta$, $t = 1 - \cos\theta$. See Rogers and Adams (1976), or any classical mechanics text for the derivation. See Barry *et al.* (1971) for hints on doing this using only integer arithmetic.

When the rotation angle is small, approximate $\sin\theta$ by θ (in radians, don't forget) and $\cos\theta$ by 1:

$$R = \begin{bmatrix} 1 & z\theta & -y\theta \\ z\theta & 1 & x\theta \\ y\theta & -x\theta & 1 \end{bmatrix}.$$

One way of interpreting this approximation is as the product of successive rotations about the three coordinate axes, with angles small enough that the order in which the rotations are applied makes no significant difference. The vector sum of these three increments implicitly defines an axis and magnitude of rotation.

To find the axis and angle of a rotation, given the matrix, find θ from

$$\cos\theta = (R[0][0] + R[1][1] + R[2][2] - 1)/2;$$

then providing $\sin \theta \neq 0$,

$$axis.x = \frac{R[1][2] - R[2][1]}{2 \sin \theta}$$

$$axis.y = \frac{R[2][0] - R[0][2]}{2 \sin \theta}$$

$$axis.z = \frac{R[0][1] - R[1][0]}{2 \sin \theta}.$$

See Pars (1965). There is a unique solution except that a negative rotation amount about a reversed axis yields the same matrix, as of course do multiples of 360° added to the amount. The axis is undefined when the angular amount is zero or a multiple of 360°.

Nesting

The effect of multiple rotations is cumulative, and dependent on their order of application. After a rotation, A, is applied to an object the object is considered rotated by A from its original (unspecified) orientation. If the object is subjected to a second rotation B whose direction (axis) turns with rotation A, then rotation B is *nested* within rotation A. The object's final position and orientation then depends on both rotations. The instantaneous relation between any two spaces can always be completely described by a single translation combined with a single rotation. The translation part is the amount by which the origin of B is moved from the origin of A: the coordinates of B's origin in space A, represented here by the vector $_bT_a$, in which the subscript letters indicate the names of the spaces. The rotation part of the relation is $_bR_a$, the rotation of space B with respect to space A.

Nesting space G within space F by rotation $_gR_f$ means calculating the relationship $_gR_a$ between space G and a reference space A, sometimes called *composition* or *concatenation*. We always define the relation in the *parent* space's coordinate system.

To nest space G inside space F, describe the orientation of F with respect to some reference space A by the 3×3 matrix $_fR_a$ and the orientation of G with respect to F by $_gR_f$. Describe the origin point of F in space A by the 1×3 row translation vector $_fT_a$ and the origin point (pivot point) of G in F by $_gT_f$. Then the orientation of G with respect to A is $_gR_a = (_gR_f)(_fR_a)$, a matrix times a matrix, and the origin of G with respect to A is $_gT_a = (_fT_a) + (_gT_f)(_fR_a)$, a vector plus a vector.

Letting $R1$, $R2$, and $R3$ be any transformations and the symbol '$\bigcirc$' represent the nesting operation, nesting is associative: $(R1 \bigcirc R2) \bigcirc R3 = R1 \bigcirc (R2 \bigcirc R3)$. When calculating multilevel nesting, this permits evaluating intermediate results in the order that allows the most reuse of relations common to several nesting chains. Note that the innermost space is on the left of the list and the outermost on the right, when following the post-multiplication convention. Mnemonic: the innermost space is closest to the point being transformed, the vector that will go at the left of the concatenated matrices.

Transformation Inverses

Given the rotation and translation relationship of space C with respect to space B, $_cR_b$ and $_cT_b$, we can write the inverse relationship, that of B with respect to C, as: $_bR_c = (_cR_b)^{-1} = (_cR_b)^T$ and $_bT_c = (_cT_b)^{-1} = -(_cT_b)(_bR_c)$. It is convenient that the inverse of the rotation component is just its transpose.

To handle inverses mixed with nesting, $(R1 \bigcirc R2)^{-1} = R2^{-1} \bigcirc R1^{-1}$; and in general $(R1 \bigcirc R2 \bigcirc \cdots Rn)^{-1} = Rn^{-1} \bigcirc \cdots R2^{-1} \bigcirc R1^{-1}$.

Iteration: Applying and Accumulating Changes to a Matrix

A change matrix specifies the direction and amount of a change to a transformation matrix: $M \leftarrow MC$. When applied repeatedly, numerical error accumulates and the matrix must be reconditioned every dozen or so updates. Tountas and Katz (1971) renormalize the matrix at the end of each cycle or by renormalizing the rows and columns in alternate cycles. Since the rows and columns are almost unit vectors, they approximate the normalization factor $1/\sqrt{x^2 + y^2 + z^2}$ by the faster $1/(0.5 + 0.5(x^2 + y^2 + z^2))$.

When the user's hand moves a control device, the image of the object controlled by the device should move in the same direction. To achieve such kinesthetic correspondence, one must compensate for the effects of nesting. For example, a simple y mouse-motion or z-axis dial rotation would become translations and rotations about arbitrary 3D directions after the viewing direction compensation. See Britton *et al.* (1978) and Pique (1986) for details and worked examples.

In brief, store the device increment (mouse movement, dial change, ...) into a 3D vector *motion* and rotate it backwards by the current viewing matrix before applying it to the object's old modelling matrix to yield the new modelling matrix:

modelling_translation ← (motion)(viewing_rotation^T) + modelling_translation

modelling_rotation ← renormalize_matrix((modelling_rotation) rotation_about_axis_
  by_angle((motion)(viewing_rotation^T),|motion|))

Note |motion| is the V3Length function. This is the scalar amount of the motion: the translation distance or the rotation angle.

MATRIX INVERSION

Richard Carling
Independent Graphics Consultant
Bedford, Massachusetts

This Gem demonstrates how to calculate the inverse and adjoint of a 4-by-4 matrix.

Computation of the inverse of a matrix $M(M^{-1})$ is an important step in many image synthesis algorithms. Typically the projection of objects from world space to image space is accomplished with a transformation matrix. The inverse of this projection may be represented by the inverse of the transformation matrix.

The inverse matrix is used freely in computer graphics papers and published algorithms, but routines for its calculation are usually left to the reader. There are several methods for calculating the inverse of a matrix; the one presented here is one of the easiest to follow, though it is not the fastest. If the inverse of a matrix larger than 4-by-4 is needed or if speed is critical, other methods of calculating the inverse may be more suitable.

A common use of the inverse matrix is in texture mapping applications, where screen coordinates need to be mapped back onto the surface of an object in world space. The inverse is also useful in ray tracing, when one wishes to intersect a parametrically defined object. Rather than actually transform the object from it's parametric space into world space, the ray is inverse-transformed into the object's canonical space, where the intersection is typically easier and faster. One example of this technique is described in Blinn (1989).

The inverse is also useful for transforming from one device space to another. For example, the shadow map technique of Williams (1978) requires transforming a point in screen space to a 3D coordinate system defined by the light source. In this algorithm, a depth buffer is constructed by rendering the scene from the point of view of the light source. To determine if a particular point is in shadow, one finds its line of sight in the coordinate system of the light source, and looks up (from the depth buffer) the nearest surface visible from the light in that direction. If the point in question is farther from the light than the stored object, it is blocked by that object and is in shadow. This calculation requires taking a screen space coordinate and transforming it first into world space, and then into the space of the light source for look-up in the depth buffer.

The adjoint matrix ($M*$) is similar to the inverse, except for a scaling factor. In particular, $M* = (1/\det(M))M^{-1}$ (each element $\mathrm{ad}_{ij} = \mathrm{inv}_{ij}/\det$), where det is the determinant of the original matrix. If the matrix is singular, then $\det = 0$, so there is no inverse matrix. However, computing the adjoint does not require the determinant. The two main advantages of the adjoint are that it always exists, and that it is easier and faster to calculate than the inverse.

The distinction between the adjoint and the inverse may be demonstrated by observing the transformation of a vector. Suppose one calculates a vector V' by transforming an input V by a matrix M: $V' = VM$. We can post-multiply V' by M^{-1} to recover V: $V'' = V'M^{-1} = V$. Suppose instead we use the adjoint, then $V'' = V'M* = VMM* = VM(1/\det(M))M^{-1} = (1/\det(M))V$. Thus, using the adjoint rather than the inverse gets us back to the original input vector, but it has been scaled by $1/\det(M)$. A common use for the adjoint is for transforming surface normals, which typically must be rescaled to unit length after transformation, anyway, so there is no penalty for this scaling created by use of the adjoint.

See Appendix 2 for C Implementation (**766**)

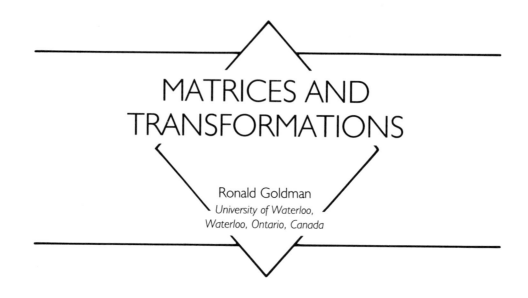

MATRICES AND TRANSFORMATIONS

Ronald Goldman
University of Waterloo,
Waterloo, Ontario, Canada

People often struggle to find the 4×4 matrices for affine or projective transformations that are not relative to the origin or the coordinate axes, but rather relative to some arbitrary points or lines. Often they proceed by transforming the problem to the origin and coordinate axes, finding the transformation matrix relative to this canonical position, and then transforming back to an arbitrary location. All this extra work is unnecessary. Here we describe the 4×4 matrices for the following transformations:

- Translation

- Rotation

- Mirror Image

- Scaling
  —Uniform
  —Nonuniform

- Projections
  —Orthogonal
  —Parallel
  —Perspective

Each of these transformations in any arbitrary position can be defined in terms of three basic matrices: the tensor product, the cross product, and the identity matrix. We include the definitions of these basic building blocks along with the affine and projective transformation matrices.

Notation

a. Identity

$$I = \begin{vmatrix} 1 & 0 & 0 \\ 0 & 1 & 0 \\ 0 & 0 & 1 \end{vmatrix}$$

b. Tensor Product

$$v \otimes w = \begin{vmatrix} v_1 w_1 & v_1 w_2 & v_1 w_3 \\ v_2 w_1 & v_2 w_2 & v_2 w_3 \\ v_3 w_1 & v_3 w_2 & v_3 w_3 \end{vmatrix} = \begin{pmatrix} v_1 \\ v_2 \\ v_3 \end{pmatrix} * \begin{pmatrix} w_1 & w_2 & w_3 \end{pmatrix}$$

c. Cross Product

$$w \mathrm{x}\_ = \begin{vmatrix} 0 & w_3 & -w_2 \\ -w_3 & 0 & w_1 \\ w_2 & -w_1 & 0 \end{vmatrix}$$

Observations

a. $u * I = u$

b. $u * (v \otimes w) = (u \cdot v) w$

c. $u * (w \mathrm{x}\_) = w \mathrm{x} u$

Translation

$$w = \text{translation vector}$$

$$T(w) = \begin{vmatrix} I & 0 \\ w & 1 \end{vmatrix}$$

Rotation

$$L = \text{Axis line}$$
$$w = \text{Unit vector parallel to } L$$
$$Q = \text{Point on } L$$
$$\Theta = \text{Angle of rotation}$$
$$R(w, \Theta) = (\cos \Theta)\mathrm{I} + (1 - \cos \Theta)w \otimes w + (\sin \Theta)w\mathrm{x}\_$$

$$R(w, \Theta, Q) = \begin{vmatrix} R(w, \Theta) & 0 \\ Q - Q^*R(w, \Theta) & 1 \end{vmatrix}$$

Mirror Image

$$S = \text{Mirror plane}$$
$$n = \text{Unit vector perpendicular to } S$$
$$Q = \text{Point on } S$$

$$M(n, Q) = \begin{vmatrix} \mathrm{I} - 2(n \otimes n) & 0 \\ 2(Q \cdot n)n & 1 \end{vmatrix}$$

Scaling

$$Q = \text{Scaling origin}$$
$$c = \text{Scaling factor}$$
$$w = \text{Unit vector parallel to scaling direction}$$

a.   Uniform scaling

$$S(Q, c) = \begin{vmatrix} c\mathrm{I} & 0 \\ (1 - c)Q & 1 \end{vmatrix}$$

b. Nonuniform scaling

$$S(Q, c, w) = \begin{vmatrix} I - (1 - c)(w \otimes w) & 0 \\ (1 - c)(Q \cdot w)w & 1 \end{vmatrix}$$

Projection

S = Image plane

n = Unit vector perpendicular to S

Q = Point on S

w = Unit vector parallel to projection direction

R = Perspective point

a. Orthogonal projection

$$Oproj(n, Q) = \begin{vmatrix} I - n \otimes n & 0 \\ (Q \cdot n)n & 1 \end{vmatrix}$$

b. Parallel projection

$$Pproj(n, Q, w) = \begin{vmatrix} I - (n \otimes w)/(w \cdot n) & 0 \\ [Q \cdot n)/(w \cdot n)]w & 1 \end{vmatrix}$$

c. Perspective projection

$$Persp(n, Q, R) = \begin{vmatrix} [(R - Q) \cdot n]I - n \otimes R & -^t n \\ (Q \cdot n)R & R \cdot n \end{vmatrix}$$

EFFICIENT POST-CONCATENATION OF TRANSFORMATION MATRICES

Joseph M. Cychosz
Purdue University
W. Lafayette, Indiana

Introduction

Presented in this paper are the computations required for efficient, direct, post-concatenation of standard 4×4 transformation matrices. The use of post-concatenated transformation matrices has a wide variety of applications, notably in computer graphics. This paper compares the costs of computing the resulting transformation through direct post-concatenation, versus using a standard 4×4 matrix multiply.

Post-concatenation of transformation matrices is used extensively in computer graphics, as well as other applications that require the hierarchical transformation of points, lines, and surfaces in three-space. A detailed explanation of the use of concatenated transformation matrices can be found in several sources, including Foley and Van Dam (1982) and Gasson (1983). Two examples of their use are the viewing of hierarchically constructed models, and the computation of end effector position and orientation of robotic arms. Shown in Fig. 1 is an example of a 3D transformation resulting from the concatenation of several individual transformation matrices that translate the vertical bar to the origin, rotate it 90° counterclockwise, and then translate it back.

Typical implementations of the post-concatenation computation first construct the transformation matrix, then form the product of the transformation matrix with the current transformation matrix, and finally copy the resulting matrix onto the current transformation matrix, thereby yielding a new current transformation matrix. Figure 2 depicts the coded

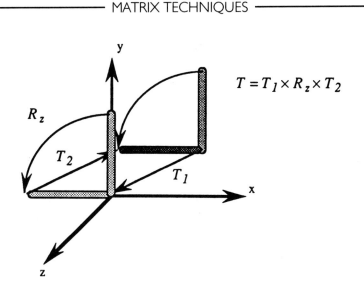

$$T = T_1 \times R_z \times T_2$$

Figure 1. Example use of concatenated transformation matrices.

implementation of a rotation about the x-axis using this approach. This type of implementation not only requires a full matrix multiply but also extra computation in forming the transformation and in copying the resulting matrix. A more efficient method would perform the post-concatenation directly on the current transformation matrix.

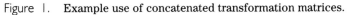

```
function    rotx    (M, a)
M: matrix4;          Current transformation matrix
a: real;             Angle of rotation about the x axis
begin
        T: matrix4 ← I;          ident (T)
        T[1][1] = T[2][2] = cos (a);
        T[1][2] = sin (a);
        T[2][1] = −T[1][2];
        R: matrix4 ← M × T;     mmult (R, M, T)
        M ← R;                  mcopy (M, R)
        end
```

Figure 2. Typical implementation of a transformation operation.

Direct Post-Concatenation

Presented in this section are the computations required for direct post-concatenation of standard transformations onto the current transformation matrix. By relying on the sparseness of the transformation matrix (that is, the number of zero and one elements in the matrix), direct post-concatenation can be performed efficiently by computing only the elements of the current transformation matrix that actually change. In the following examples the transformation matrix is shown on the right, while the appropriate pseudo-code fragment for post-concatenating the matrix to the current transformation is shown on the left. The current transformation matrix, represented by M in the code fragments, is not shown. It is assumed to be a general 4×4 matrix (that is, **matrix4**).

x-axis rotation:

```
c: real ← cos (a);  s: real ← sin (a);
for i: integer ← 0, i ← i + 1 while i < 4 do
    t: real ← M[i][1];
    M[i][1] ← tc − M[i][2] s;
    M[i][2] ← ts + M[i][2] c;
endloop;
```

$$R_x(a) = \begin{vmatrix} 1 & 0 & 0 & 0 \\ 0 & cos(a) & sin(a) & 0 \\ 0 & -sin(a) & cos(a) & 0 \\ 0 & 0 & 0 & 1 \end{vmatrix}$$

y-axis rotation:

```
c: real ← cos (a);  s: real ← sin (a);
for i: integer ← 0, i ← i + 1 while i < 4 do
    t: real ← M[i][0];
    M[i][0] ← tc + M[i][2] s;
    M[i][2] ← M[i][2] c − ts;
endloop;
```

$$R_y(a) = \begin{vmatrix} cos(a) & 0 & -sin(a) & 0 \\ 0 & 1 & 0 & 0 \\ sin(a) & 0 & cos(a) & 0 \\ 0 & 0 & 0 & 1 \end{vmatrix}$$

z-axis rotation:

```
c: real ← cos (a);  s: real ← sin (a);
for i: integer ← 0, i ← i + 1 while i < 4 do
    t: real ← M[i][0];
    M[i][0] ← tc + M[i][1] s;
    M[i][1] ← ts − M[i][1] c;
endloop;
```

$$R_z(a) = \begin{vmatrix} cos(a) & sin(a) & 0 & 0 \\ -sin(a) & cos(a) & 0 & 0 \\ 0 & 0 & 1 & 0 \\ 0 & 0 & 0 & 1 \end{vmatrix}$$

scaling:

for i: **integer** ← 0, i ← i + 1 **while** i < 4 **do**
    M[i][0] ← M[i][0] s_x;
    M[i][1] ← M[i][1] s_y;
    M[i][2] ← M[i][2] s_z;
endloop;

$$S_{xyz}(s_x, s_y, s_z) = \begin{vmatrix} s_x & 0 & 0 & 0 \\ 0 & s_y & 0 & 0 \\ 0 & 0 & s_z & 0 \\ 0 & 0 & 0 & 1 \end{vmatrix}$$

translation:

for i: **integer** ← 0, i ← i + 1 **while** i < 4 **do**
    M[i][0] ← M[i][0] + M[i][3] t_x;
    M[i][1] ← M[i][1] + M[i][3] t_y;
    M[i][2] ← M[i][2] + M[i][3] t_z;
endloop;

$$T_{xyz}(t_x, t_y, t_z) = \begin{vmatrix} 1 & 0 & 0 & 0 \\ 0 & 1 & 0 & 0 \\ 0 & 0 & 1 & 0 \\ t_x & t_y & t_z & 1 \end{vmatrix}$$

perspective:
    (*along z-axis, image plane at origin, eye at z = d*)

f: **real** ← $-1/d$;
for i: **integer** ← 0, i ← i + 1 **while** i < 4 **do**
    M[i][3] ← M[i][3] + M[i][2] f;
    M[i][2] ← 0;
endloop;

$$P_z(d) = \begin{vmatrix} 1 & 0 & 0 & 0 \\ 0 & 1 & 0 & 0 \\ 0 & 0 & 0 & -1/d \\ 0 & 0 & 0 & 1 \end{vmatrix}$$

Table I. Operational Cost Comparison.

Transformation	Adds	Multiplies
Standard		
4 × 4 matrix multiply	48	64
Direct Concatenation		
rotation	8	12
scaling	0	12
transformation	12	12
perspective	4	4

479

Table 2. Computational Comparison for Various CPUs.

Machine	Rotation			Scaling			Translation			Perspective			Comments
	std	Direct	Speedup	std	Direct	Speedup	std	Direct	Speedup	std	Direct	Speedup	
Ardent Titan	3.192	.627	5.1	2.818	.279	10.1	2.806	.351	8.0	2.815	.158	17.8	16 Mhz MIPS R2000
Convex C-220	2.433	.300	8.1	2.300	.133	17.3	2.333	.150	15.6	2.300	.100	23.0	
Gould NP1	4.467	.400	11.2	4.167	.233	17.8	4.283	.333	12.9	3.833	.200	19.2	Arithmetic Accelerator
SGI 4D/20G	1.830	.350	5.2	1.650	.160	10.3	1.650	.150	11.0	1.630	.110	14.8	12.5 Mhz MIPS 2000A
Sun 4/280	2.550	.650	3.9	2.200	.217	10.1	2.167	.267	8.1	2.200	.183	12.0	16 Mhz SPARC, FPU1, 32kb cache

Computational Cost Comparison

The direct methods require considerably less computation than a standard 4×4 matrix multiply. Table 1 compares the operational costs of direct post-concatenation with that of standard matrix multiplication. Table 2 compares the computational costs for each of the transformations for a variety of computers. Each type of transformation has three columns for each of the CPUs. The first column shows the CPU time in seconds required using a standard 4×4 matrix multiply to perform the concatenation; the second column shows the CPU time for direct concatenation; and the third shows the speedup of the direct approach over the standard approach. The CPU time reported represents the time required to perform 10,000 concatenation operations.

See Appendix 2 for C Implementation (**770**)

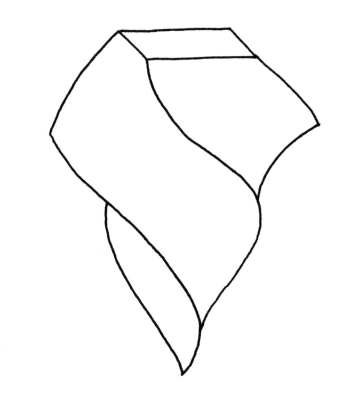

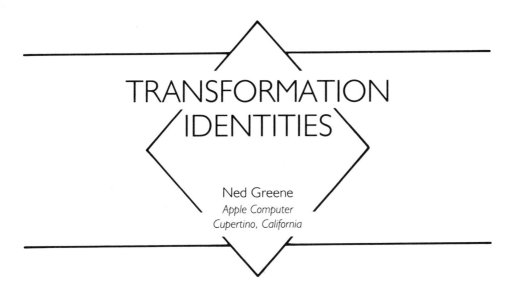

TRANSFORMATION IDENTITIES

Ned Greene
Apple Computer
Cupertino, California

Introduction

3D graphics systems usually perform coordinate transformations with 4×4 matrices created by concatenating primitive geometric transformations such as rotation and translation. Algebraic manipulation of transformation expressions is crucial to a variety of problems that arise in modeling and motion specification. Often it is necessary, for example, to reorder transformations or to find equivalent parameter sets for different representations of the same transformation. Some problems of this type are simple and intuitive, but often this is not the case, since solution may involve algebraic manipulation of 3×3 or 4×4 matrices having coefficients that are trigonometric expressions. This collection of identities is intended to make working with transformation expressions easier and more intuitive.

Notation

Primitive geometric transformations are specified as follows:

$T_{u, v, w}(A, B, C)$ translate A in u, B in v, C in w
(subscripts u, v, w encompass the six possible combinations of x, y, and z)

$R_u(D)$ rotate by angle D about axis u

$S_{u,v,w}(E, F, G)$ scale u axis by E, v axis by F, w axis by G (subscripts u, v, w encompass the six possible combinations of x, y, and z)

$K_{u,v}(J)$ skew u axis relative to v axis by angle J, $-\pi/2 < J < \pi/2$

$P(\theta, N, F)$ perspective transformation where θ is the vertical view angle ($0 < \theta < \pi$), N is the z coordinate of the near clipping plane, and F is the z coordinate of the far clipping plane.

In keeping with the usual conventions in computer graphics, the xyz coordinate frame is right-handed, direction of rotations is established by the right-hand rule, and points are represented by row matrices. Thus, mapping a point from a local to a global coordinate system is done as follows:

$$[x_G \, y_G \, z_G \, w_G] = [x_L \, y_L \, z_L \, 1] |M|,$$

where M is a concatenation of transformation matrices. 4×4 matrix expressions for the above primitive transformations are given in the appendix.

Transformation Identities

Throughout this paper u, v, w are arbitrary distinct coordinate axes. For identities that depend on the handedness of the coordinate frame, two versions are given with the right-hand version labelled (#R) and the left-hand version labelled (#L). Since we are assuming that the xyz axes are a right-handed coordinate frame, u, v, w is a right-handed coordinate frame for ($u = x$, $v = y$, $w = z$), ($u = y$, $v = z$, $w = x$), and ($u = z$, $v = x$, $w = y$). The three other combinations of axes, ($u = z$, $v = y$, $w = x$), ($u = y$, $v = x$, $w = z$), and ($u = x$, $v = z$, $w = y$) are left-handed coordinate frames.

Reversing the order of translation and scaling is simple and intuitive:

$$T_{u,v,w}(A, B, C)S_{u,v,w}(D, E, F) = S_{u,v,w}(D, E, F)T_{u,v,w}(AD, BE, CF)$$

$$(1)$$

$$S_{u,v,w}(A, B, C)T_{u,v,w}(D, E, F)$$

$$= T_{u,v,w}(D/A, E/B, F/C)S_{u,v,w}(A, B, C),$$

$$A \neq 0, B \neq 0, C \neq 0. \quad (2)$$

The following rules for exchanging the order of translation and rotation are related to formulas for rotating a 2D point:

$$T_{u,v,w}(A, B, C)R_u(D)$$

$$= R_u(D)T_{u,v,w}(A, B\cos(D) - C\sin(D), C\cos(D) + B\sin(D))$$

$$(3R)$$

$$T_{u,v,w}(A, B, C)R_u(D)$$

$$= R_u(D)T_{u,v,w}(A, B\cos(D) + C\sin(D), C\cos(D) - B\sin(D))$$

$$(3L)$$

$$R_u(A)T_{u,v,w}(B, C, D)$$

$$= T_{u,v,w}(B, C\cos(A) + D\sin(A), D\cos(A) - C\sin(A))R_u(A)$$

$$(4R)$$

$$R_u(A)T_{u,v,w}(B, C, D)$$

$$= T_{u,v,w}(B, C\cos(A) - D\sin(A), D\cos(A) + C\sin(A))R_u(A).$$

$$(4L)$$

The order of translation and skewing can be easily reversed:

$$T_{u,v,w}(A,B,C)K_{u,v}(D)$$

$$= K_{u,v}(D)T_{u,v,w}(A + B\tan(D), B, C), \; -\pi/2 < D < \pi/2 \quad (5)$$

$$K_{u,v}(A)T_{u,v,w}(B,C,D)$$

$$= T_{u,v,w}(B - C\tan(A), C, D)K_{u,v}(A), \; -\pi/2 < A < \pi/2. \quad (6)$$

Rotation and isotropic scaling commute:

$$R_u(A)S_{x,y,z}(B,B,B) = S_{x,y,z}(B,B,B)R_u(A). \quad (7)$$

This identity shows that even when angles are normalized to a standard interval (say, $-\pi$ to π), there are always at least two parameter sets of rotation angles that generate the same rotation:

$$R_u(A)R_v(B)R_w(C) = R_u(\pi + A)R_v(\pi - B)R_w(\pi + C). \quad (8)$$

Special cases involving rotation of π or $\pi/2$ (see also Rule 20).

$$R_u(\pi) = S_{u,v,w}(1, -1, -1) \quad (9)$$

$$R_u(\pi)R_v(\pi) = R_w(\pi) \quad (10)$$

$$R_u(A)R_v(\pi) = R_v(\pi)R_u(-A) \quad (11)$$

$$R_u(\pi/2)R_v(A) = R_w(-A)R_u(\pi/2) \quad (12R)$$

$$R_u(\pi/2)R_v(A) = R_w(A)R_u(\pi/2) \quad (12L)$$

$$R_u(-\pi/2)R_v(A) = R_w(A)R_u(-\pi/2) \quad (13R)$$

$$R_u(-\pi/2)R_v(A) = R_w(-A)R_u(-\pi/2) \quad (13L)$$

A rotation can be expressed as three skews:

$$R_u(A) = K_{v,w}(-A/2)K_{w,v}(\mathrm{atan}(\sin(A)))K_{v,w}(-A/2), \quad -\frac{\pi}{2} < A < \frac{\pi}{2}$$

(14R)

$$R_u(A) = K_{v,w}(A/2)K_{w,v}(-\mathrm{atan}(\sin(A)))K_{v,w}(A/2), \quad -\frac{\pi}{2} < A < \frac{\pi}{2}$$

(14L)

A paper on image rotation by Paeth (1986) is based on this identity, which was independently discovered by Heckbert (Greene, 1983).

A rotation can also be expressed as a combination of skews and scales:

$$R_u(A) = S_{u,v,w}(1, 1/\cos(A), \cos(A))K_{w,v}(B)K_{v,w}(-A)$$

$$= S_{u,v,w}(1, \cos(A), 1/\cos(A))K_{v,w}(-B))K_{w,v}(A),$$

$$-\frac{\pi}{2} < A < \frac{\pi}{2}$$

$$B = \mathrm{atan}(\sin(A)\cos(a))$$

(15R)

$$R_u(A) = S_{u,v,w}(1, 1/\cos(A), \cos(A))K_{v,v}(-B)K_{v,w}(A)$$

$$= S_{u,v,w}(1, \cos(A), 1/\cos(A))K_{w,v}(B))K_{w,v}(-A),$$

$$-\frac{\pi}{2} < A < \frac{\pi}{2}$$

$$B = \mathrm{atan}(\sin(A)\cos(A))$$

(15L)

Skewing and isotropic scaling commute:

$$S_{x,y,z}(A, A, A)K_{u,v}(B) = K_{u,v}(B)S_{x,y,z}(A, A, A).$$

(16)

The order of skewing and anisotropic scaling can be reversed:

$$S_{u,v,w}(A, B, C)K_{u,v}(D) = K_{u,v}(E)S_{u,v,w}(A, B, C),$$

$$A \neq 0, \ -\pi/2 < D < \pi/2$$

$$E = \mathrm{atan}(B\tan(D)/A).$$

(17)

489

A special case for which skewing and anisotropic scaling commute follows:

$$S_{u,v,w}(A,1,1)K_{v,w}(B) = K_{v,w}(B)S_{u,v,w}(A,1,1) \qquad (18).$$

The following identity shows that anisotropic scaling following rotation introduces skew:

$$R_u(A)S_{u,v,w}(B,C,D)$$

$$= K_{w,v}(H)K_{v,w}(G)S_{u,v,w}(B,E,F)R_u(A), \qquad A \neq 0, \quad -\frac{\pi}{2} < A < \frac{\pi}{2}$$

$$Q = (C-D)/(\tan(A) + \cot(A))$$

$$F = C + (D-C)/(1 + \tan^2(A))$$

$$E = \big(Q(D-C)\sin(A)\cos(A)$$

$$+F\big(D\sin^2(A) + C\cos^2(A)\big)\big)/F$$

$$G = -\text{atan}((C-D)/(E(\tan(A) + \cot(A))))$$

$$H = -\text{atan}((C-E)\cos(A)/(Q\cos(A) + F\sin(A))). \qquad (19R)$$

For a left-handed coordinate frame, the signs of G and H are reversed.
Two special cases follow, for which rotation and anisotropic scaling commute:

$$S_{u,v,w}(A,B,C)R_u(\pi) = R_u(\pi)S_{u,v,w}(A,B,C) \qquad (20)$$

$$S_{u,v,w}(A,1,1)R_u(B) = R_u(B)S_{u,v,w}(A,1,1). \qquad (21)$$

A skew can be expressed as two rotations and a scale:

$$K_{u,v}(A) = R_w(B)S_{u,v,w}(C,D,1)R_w(E), \quad -\pi/2 < A < \pi/2$$

$$C = \left(\tan(A) \pm \sqrt{4 + \tan^2(A)}\right)\Big/2$$

$$D = 1/C$$

$$B = -\text{atan}(C)$$

$$E = B + \pi/2 \tag{22R}$$

For a left-handed coordinate frame, the sign of A is reversed.
Identities for exchanging the order of skews follow:

$$K_{u,v}(A)K_{u,w}(B)$$

$$= K_{u,w}(B)K_{u,v}(A), -\pi/2 < A < \pi/2, -\pi/2 < B < \pi/2 \tag{23}$$

$$K_{u,v}(A)K_{u,v}(B)$$

$$= K_{u,v}(B)K_{u,v}(A) = K_{u,v}(\text{atan}(\tan(A) + \tan(B))),$$

$$-\frac{\pi}{2} < A < \frac{\pi}{2}, -\frac{\pi}{2} < B < \frac{\pi}{2}. \tag{24}$$

Expressions involving perspective follow:

$$P(A,B,C) = P(D,B,C)S_{x,y,z}(E,E,1) = S_{x,y,z}(E,E,1)P(D,B,C)$$

$$E = \tan(D/2)\big/\tan(A/2), \quad 0 < A < \pi, \quad 0 < D < \pi, \quad 0 < B < C. \tag{25}$$

The previous identity shows that changing camera angle is equivalent to a 2D zoom.

$$DP(A,B,C) = S_{x,y,z}(D,D,D)P(A,BD,CD), \quad D > 0. \tag{26}$$

Matrix expressions on the two sides of the equation differ by scale factor D, so from the standpoint of transforming homogeneous coordinates, $P(A,B,C)$ is equivalent to $S_{x,y,z}(D,D,D)P(A,BD,CD)$.

Appendix

Identities are based on the following matrix representations of primitive transformations. We assume a right-handed coordinate frame, rotation according to the right-hand rule, that points are represented as row matrices, and that points rotate in a fixed coordinate frame.

$$
\text{translation } T_{x,y,z}(A,B,C)
\begin{bmatrix}
1 & 0 & 0 & 0 \\
0 & 1 & 0 & 0 \\
0 & 0 & 1 & 0 \\
A & B & C & 1
\end{bmatrix}
\qquad
\text{scaling } S_{x,y,z}(A,B,C)
\begin{bmatrix}
A & 0 & 0 & 0 \\
0 & B & 0 & 0 \\
0 & 0 & C & 0 \\
0 & 0 & 0 & 1
\end{bmatrix}
$$

$$
x \text{ rotation } R_x(A)
\begin{bmatrix}
1 & 0 & 0 & 0 \\
0 & \cos A & \sin A & 0 \\
0 & -\sin A & \cos A & 0 \\
0 & 0 & 0 & 1
\end{bmatrix}
\qquad
y \text{ rotation } R_y(A)
\begin{bmatrix}
\cos A & 0 & -\sin A & 0 \\
0 & 1 & 0 & 0 \\
\sin A & 0 & \cos A & 0 \\
0 & 0 & 0 & 1
\end{bmatrix}
$$

$$
z \text{ rotation } R_z(A)
\begin{bmatrix}
\cos A & \sin A & 0 & 0 \\
-\sin A & \cos A & 0 & 0 \\
0 & 0 & 1 & 0 \\
0 & 0 & 0 & 1
\end{bmatrix}
$$

$$
\text{skew } x \text{ with respect to } y \; K_{x,y}(A)
\begin{bmatrix}
1 & 0 & 0 & 0 \\
\tan A & 1 & 0 & 0 \\
0 & 0 & 1 & 0 \\
0 & 0 & 0 & 1
\end{bmatrix}
\qquad
\text{skew } y \text{ with respect to } x \; K_{y,x}(A)
\begin{bmatrix}
1 & \tan A & 0 & 0 \\
0 & 1 & 0 & 0 \\
0 & 0 & 1 & 0 \\
0 & 0 & 0 & 1
\end{bmatrix}
$$

$$
\text{skew } x \text{ with respect to } z \; K_{x,z}(A)
\begin{bmatrix}
1 & 0 & 0 & 0 \\
0 & 1 & 0 & 0 \\
\tan A & 0 & 1 & 0 \\
0 & 0 & 0 & 1
\end{bmatrix}
\qquad
\text{skew } z \text{ with respect to } x \; K_{z,x}(A)
\begin{bmatrix}
1 & 0 & \tan A & 0 \\
0 & 1 & 0 & 0 \\
0 & 0 & 1 & 0 \\
0 & 0 & 0 & 1
\end{bmatrix}
$$

$$
\text{skew } y \text{ with respect to } z \; K_{y,z}(A)
\begin{bmatrix}
1 & 0 & 0 & 0 \\
0 & 1 & 0 & 0 \\
0 & \tan A & 1 & 0 \\
0 & 0 & 0 & 1
\end{bmatrix}
\qquad
\text{skew } z \text{ with respect to } y \; K_{z,y}(A)
\begin{bmatrix}
1 & 0 & 0 & 0 \\
0 & 1 & \tan A & 0 \\
0 & 0 & 1 & 0 \\
0 & 0 & 0 & 1
\end{bmatrix}
$$

$$
\text{perspective } P(A,B,C)
\begin{bmatrix}
a & 0 & 0 & 0 \\
0 & a & 0 & 0 \\
0 & 0 & b & 1 \\
0 & 0 & c & 0
\end{bmatrix}
$$

where

$$a = 1/\tan(A/2)$$

$$b = (C + B)/(C - B)$$

$$c = 2BC/(B - C).$$

The perspective matrix transforms the viewing volume—the region of the viewing pyramid between the clipping planes—to a cube extending from -1 to 1 on each axis.

Acknowledgements

Most of the research for this paper was done at the New York Institute of Technology in 1983. I would like to thank former colleagues Paul Heckbert and Pat Hanrahan for their help at that time. In addition, Paul Heckbert contributed identities (14) and (22) and reviewed this manuscript.

See also Matrix Identities (453)

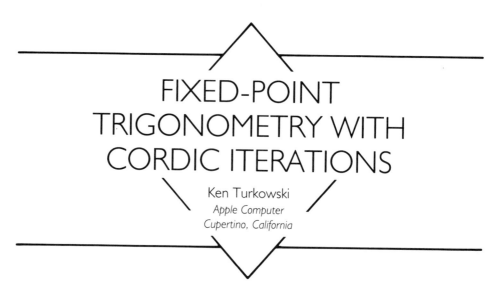

FIXED-POINT TRIGONOMETRY WITH CORDIC ITERATIONS

Ken Turkowski
Apple Computer
Cupertino, California

Introduction to the CORDIC Technique

CORDIC is an acronym that stands for COordinate Rotation DIgital Computer, and was coined by Volder (1959). Its concepts have been further developed to include calculation of the Discrete Fourier Transform (Despain, 1974), exponential, logarithm, forward and inverse circular and hyperbolic functions, ratios and square roots (Chen, 1972; Walther, 1971), and has been applied to the anti-aliasing of lines and polygons (Turkowski, 1982).

It is an iterative fixed-point technique that achieves approximately one more bit of accuracy with each iteration. In spite of merely linear convergence, the inner loop is very simple, with arithmetic that consists only of shifts and adds, so it is competitive with (and even outperforms) floating-point techniques with quadratic convergence, for the accuracy typically required for two-dimensional raster graphics.

CORDIC Vector Rotation

To rotate a vector $[x \quad y]$ through an angle θ, we perform the linear transformation

$$[x' \quad y'] = [x \quad y] \begin{bmatrix} \cos\theta & \sin\theta \\ -\sin\theta & \cos\theta \end{bmatrix}. \tag{1}$$

If this transformation is accomplished by a sequence of rotations θ_i such that

$$\theta = \sum_i \theta_i,\qquad(2)$$

we then have

$$[x'\ \ y'] = [x\ \ y]\prod_i \begin{bmatrix} \cos\theta_i & \sin\theta_i \\ -\sin\theta_i & \cos\theta_i \end{bmatrix},\qquad(3)$$

where the product is performed on the right with increasing i. We next factor out a $\cos\theta_i$ from the matrix:

$$[x'\ \ y'] = [x\ \ y]\left\{\prod_i \cos\theta_i \begin{bmatrix} 1 & \tan\theta_i \\ -\tan\theta_i & 1 \end{bmatrix}\right\}$$

$$= \left\{\prod_j \cos\theta_j\right\}[x\ \ y]\prod_i \begin{bmatrix} 1 & \tan\theta_i \\ -\tan\theta_i & 1 \end{bmatrix}.\qquad(4)$$

Then we constrain the θ_i's such that

$$\tan\theta_i \pm_i 2^{-i},\qquad(5)$$

where the sign is chosen for each i so that Eq. 2 is fulfilled to the desired accuracy. We arrive at

$$[x'\ \ y'] = \left\{\prod_j \cos(\tan^{-1} 2^{-j})\right\}[x\ \ y]\left\{\prod_i \begin{bmatrix} 1 & \pm_i 2^{-i} \\ \mp_i 2^{-i} & 1 \end{bmatrix}\right\}$$

$$= \left\{\prod_j \frac{1}{\sqrt{1+2^{-2j}}}\right\}[x\ \ y]\prod_i \begin{bmatrix} 1 & \pm_i 2^{-i} \\ \mp_i 2^{-i} & 1 \end{bmatrix}.\qquad(6)$$

495

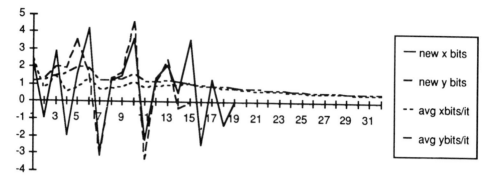

Figure 1.

Eq. 6 is even simpler than it looks. The factor in braces is a constant for a fixed number of iterations, so it may be precomputed. The matrix multiplications are nothing more than shifts and adds (or subtracts).

The convergence of this product is guaranteed in an interval greater than $-90° \le \theta \le 90°$ when i starts out at 0, although it converges faster when i begins at -1 (that is, the first shift is upward, the rest downward). Typical convergence is illustrated in Fig. 1 using approximately 16 bit registers. Note that no new bits of accuracy are added after about 16 iterations, but until that point, approximately one bit of accuracy is added per iteration.

The scale factor converges two bits per iteration and is accurate to 16 bits after 9 iterations, so the limit value could be safely used for all practical numbers of iterations, and has the value 0.2715717684432241 when i starts at -1, and the value 0.6072529350088813 when i starts at 0.

The recommended algorithm is then

$$[x' \quad y'] = 0.27157177[x \quad y] \prod_{i=-1}^{N-2} \begin{bmatrix} 1 & \pm_i 2^{-i} \\ \mp_i 2^{-i} & 1 \end{bmatrix}, \qquad (7)$$

or in words, start with the largest subangle and either add it or subtract it in such a way as to bring the desired angle closer to zero, and perform the

496

matrix multiplication corresponding to that subrotation with shifts and adds (or subtracts). Continue on in the manner for the specified number of iterations. Multiply the result by the constant scale factor.

Note that two extra bits are needed at the high end due to the scale factor. It is difficult to assess the error due to finite word length, but 32-bit registers work well in practice. Expect to have about 2–3 LSB's of noise, even if 32 iterations are performed.

If the original vector was $[r \quad 0]$, rotation by θ performs a polar-to-rectangular conversion. If r is 1, it generates sines and cosines. Rectangular-to-polar conversion can be accomplished by determining the sense of the rotation by the sign of y at each step.

See also Trig Summary (12); Rotation Matrix Methods Summary (455); Bit Patterns for Encoding Angles (442); Fast 2D–3D Rotation (440); Using Quaternions for Coding 3D Transformations (498)

See Appendix 2 for C Implementation (**773**)

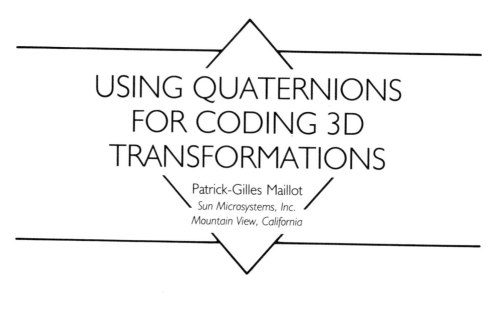

USING QUATERNIONS FOR CODING 3D TRANSFORMATIONS

Patrick-Gilles Maillot
Sun Microsystems, Inc.
Mountain View, California

Introduction

This paper presents some fundamentals of a mathematical element called a *quaternion*. A theoretical study emphasizes the characteristic properties of these elements and the analogy that can be made between the geometrical interpretation of 3D transformations and the subgroup of *unit* quaternions.

We also give a practical application of quaternions for the coding of 3D transformations and some basic algorithms for orthogonal coordinate systems displacements.

Quaternions were introduced in 1843 by Sir William R. Hamilton. They are useful primarily in the coding of natural movements in a 3D space, as it has been realized in the *PATK3D* software (Maillot, 1983), or to perform movements along parametric curves (Shoemake, 1985). Quaternions may also be used when coding transformations in Constructive Solid Geometry (CSG) trees as used in MCAD systems or applications, as well as when coding the hierarchical transformation trees of visualization software, such as proposed by the PHIGS (PHIGS, 1987) standard.

This paper describes a way to code and evaluate 3D transformations using a different method than coding 4×4 matrices. The initial researches on the material presented here have been conducted at the University Claude Bernard, Lyon I, France. In 1983, the graphic group was working on formalization of scene composition and natural movements coding in space. Some mathematical demonstrations presented here are due to E. Tosan (Tosan, 1982), who is a mathematician researcher of the computing sciences group.

A mathematical definition of the quaternion division ring, **Q**, is proposed to demonstrate some of the particularities and properties of the quaternions, as well as the definition of the operations that can be applied to them.

The analogy that can be made between this algebraic element and the geometry of 3D transformations will be described. This is constructed over a subgroup of quaternions having a particular property.

Some examples of code are proposed that show two basic transformations involving only some simple algebraic computations.

Definition of the Quaternions

A quaternion is a mathematical element noted

$$q = c + xi + yj + zk,$$

with c, x, y, z: real numbers, and i, j, K: imaginary numbers. It is also written in condensed notation:

$$q = c + u,$$

with $u = xi + yj + zk$ called the *pure* part of the quaternion, and c the *real* part of the quaternion.

Let us supply **Q**, the set of quaternions, with two operations: addition,

$$q + q' = (c + c') + (x + x')i + (y + y')j + (z + z')k$$

and multiplication, defined on the base $\{1, i, j, k\}$:

$$i^2 = j^2 = k^2 = -1$$

$$ij = k, \ ji = -k; \ jk = i, \ kj = -i; \ ki = j, \ ik = -j.$$

If we develop the multiplication, we obtain:

$$qq' = (c + xi + yj + zk)(c' + x'i + y'j + z'k)$$

$$= (cc' - xx' - yy' - zz') + (yz' - y'z + cx' + c'x)i$$

$$+ (zx' - z'x + cy' + c'y)j + (xy' - x'y + cz' + c'z)k.$$

Or, if we use the condensed notation,

$$qq' = (c + u)(c' + u')$$

$$= (cc' - u \cdot u') + (u \times u' + \langle cu' \rangle + \langle c'u \rangle),$$

with

$$u \cdot u' = xx' + yy' + zz': \text{inner product.}$$

$$\langle cu \rangle = cxi + cyj + czk$$

$$u \times u' = (yz' - zy', zx' - xz', xy' - yz'): \text{cross product.}$$

Notes

- If we write $u = s\mathbf{N}$ and $u' = s'\mathbf{N}$, with s and s' being real numbers, and $\mathbf{N} = (N_x, N_y, N_z)$ a unit vector of $\mathbf{R}^3$, so that $|\mathbf{N}|^2 = 1$, we find the product of complex numbers, with $\mathbf{N}$ instead of the imaginary number i.

Then

$$qq' = (c + s\mathbf{N})(c' + s'\mathbf{N})$$

$$= (cc' - ss'\mathbf{N} \cdot \mathbf{N}) + (\mathbf{N} \times \mathbf{N} + \langle cs'\mathbf{N} \rangle + \langle c'sN \rangle)$$

$$= (cc' - s's) + \langle (cs' + c's)\mathbf{N} \rangle.$$

- If we write $q = q' = \mathbf{N}$, or $c = c' = 0$ and $s = s' = 1$, we finally find

$$\mathbf{N}^2 = -ss'\mathbf{N} \cdot \mathbf{N} = -1.$$

Properties of the Quaternions

The addition of quaternions has an *identity* element,

$$0 = 0 + 0i + 0j + 0k,$$

and an *inverse* element,

$$-q = -c - xi - yj - zk.$$

The multiplication of quaternions has an *identity* element,

$$1 = 1 + 0i + 0j + 0k.$$

The quaternions have some *conjugate* elements,

$$q = c + u; \quad \bar{q} = c - u.$$

It is possible to define a magnitude for q by applying the *hermitian* inner product of q into $\bar{q}$:

$$q\bar{q} = (c^2 + u \cdot u) + (u \times u - \langle cu \rangle + \langle cu \rangle)$$

$$= c^2 + x^2 + y^2 + z^2$$

$$= \bar{q}q = |q|^2, \text{ magnitude of } q.$$

The quaternions have some *inverse* elements:

$$q^{-1} = \frac{1}{|q|^2}\bar{q}.$$

The multiplication is *not commutative*. If it was commutative, we would have had

$$qq' = q'q.$$

Then,

$$(c + u)(c' + u') = (c' + u')(c + u)$$

$$\Rightarrow u \times u' = u' \times u \Rightarrow u \times u' = 0.$$

The multiplication is *distributive over* the addition:

$$q(v + w) = qv + qw \qquad (v + w)q = vq + wq.$$

In conclusion, we may write that

- **Q** is closed under quaternion addition.

- **Q** is closed under quaternion multiplication.

- $(\mathbf{Q}, +, \cdot)$ is a division ring.

Properties of the Set of Unit Quaternions

This paragraph focuses on the subset quaternions of unit magnitude. These are the particular quaternions that are of interest in this application.

Let us consider the quaternions so that $|q| = 1$, or $c^2 + u \cdot u = 1$, and $c^2 + s^2 = 1$, (if $u = s\mathbf{N}$); then we can write any *unit* quaternion as $q = \cos(\theta) + \sin(\theta)\mathbf{N}$.

Then, for this particular set of quaternions,

- The multiplication of the conjugate of two quaternions is the conjugate of the multiplication of the quaternions.

$$\overline{qq'} = (cc' - u \cdot u') - (u \times u' + \langle cu' \rangle + \langle c'u \rangle)$$

$$\overline{q'}\,\overline{q} = (c' - u')(c - u)$$

$$= (cc' - u' \cdot u) + ((-u') \times (-u) - \langle cu' \rangle - \langle c'u \rangle)$$

$$= (cc' - u \cdot u') - (u \times u' + \langle cu' \rangle + \langle c'u \rangle)$$

$$= \overline{qq'}$$

- The magnitude of the multiplication of two quaternions is the multiplication of the magnitudes of the quaternions.

$$|qq'|^2 = (qq')(\overline{qq'})$$

$$= qq'\overline{q}'\overline{q} = q|q'|^2\overline{q}$$

$$= |q|^2|q'|^2$$

- If two quaternions have a magnitude of 1, then the product of these two quaternions will also have a magnitude of 1.

$$|q| = |q'| = 1 \Rightarrow |qq'| = 1$$

$$(\cos(\theta) + \sin(\theta)\mathbf{N})(\cos(\phi) + \sin(\phi)\mathbf{N}) = \cos(\theta + \phi) + \sin(\theta + \phi)\mathbf{N}$$

- The conjugate of a unit quaternion is its inverse.

$$|q| = 1 \Rightarrow q^{-1} = \overline{q}$$

The set of unit quaternions is a multiplicative subgroup of the non-null quaternions.

Rotations in a 3D Space

Rotations can be expressed using a geometrical formulation. Figure 1 graphically presents the rotation of a vector around a given axis.

Let $P' = Rot_{(a, \mathbf{N})}(P)$ be the transformation of point P by the rotation of angle θ around the axis $\mathbf{N}$. We can write:

$$\mathbf{H} = \overrightarrow{OH}$$

$$\mathbf{P'} = \overrightarrow{OP'} = \overrightarrow{OH} + \overrightarrow{HP'} = \mathbf{H} + \mathbf{U'}$$

$$\mathbf{P} = \overrightarrow{OP} = \overrightarrow{OH} + \overrightarrow{HP} = \mathbf{H} + \mathbf{U},$$

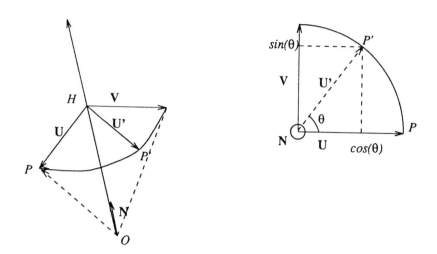

Figure 1. Geometrical representation of a rotation.

and then,

$$\mathbf{U} = \mathbf{P} - \mathbf{H}.$$

In the plane formed by (PHP'), we can set

$$\mathbf{U}' = \cos(\theta)\mathbf{U} + \sin(\theta)\mathbf{V},$$

with $\mathbf{U} \perp \mathbf{V}$, $\mathbf{V} \perp \mathbf{N}$, and $|\mathbf{V}| = |\mathbf{U}|$, that is to say, $\mathbf{V} = \mathbf{N} \times \mathbf{U} = \mathbf{N} \times (\mathbf{P} - \mathbf{H}) = \mathbf{N} \times \mathbf{P}$. On the ($O, \mathbf{N}$) axis, $\overrightarrow{OH}$ is the projection of $\overrightarrow{OP}$ on $\mathbf{N}$, and then $\overrightarrow{OH} = \mathbf{H} = \mathbf{N} (\mathbf{N} \cdot \mathbf{P})$, which gives the formulas

$$\overrightarrow{OP'} = \mathbf{H} + \mathbf{U}' = \mathbf{N}(\mathbf{N} \cdot \mathbf{P}) + (\cos(\theta)\mathbf{U} + \sin(\theta)\mathbf{V})$$

$$= \mathbf{N}(\mathbf{N} \cdot \mathbf{P}) + \cos(\theta)(\mathbf{P} - \mathbf{N}(\mathbf{N} \cdot \mathbf{P})) + \sin(\theta)\mathbf{N} \times \mathbf{P}$$

$$= \cos(\theta)\mathbf{P} + (1 - \cos(\theta))\mathbf{N}(\mathbf{N} \cdot \mathbf{P}) + \sin(\theta)\mathbf{N} \times \mathbf{P}.$$

This can be written in a matrix formulation:

$$Rot_{(\theta, \mathbf{N})} = \cos(\theta)\mathbf{I}_3 + (1 - \cos(\theta))\mathbf{N}^T\mathbf{N} + \sin(\theta)\mathbf{A_N},$$

with

$$\mathbf{N} = [N_1, N_2, N_3], \mathbf{I}_3 = \begin{bmatrix} 1 & 0 & 0 \\ 0 & 1 & 0 \\ 0 & 0 & 1 \end{bmatrix}, \mathbf{A_N} = \begin{bmatrix} 0 & N_3 & -N_2 \\ -N_3 & 0 & N_1 \\ N_2 & -N_1 & 0 \end{bmatrix}$$

The geometry formulation presented above can be expressed in an algebraic formulation:

Let $p = (0, v) = xi + yj + zk$ be a *pure* quaternion.

Let $q = (c, u)$ be a *unit* quaternion.

We can define

$$R_q(p) = qp\bar{q}$$

$$= (c, u)p(c, -u)$$

$$= (c, u)(0, v)(c, -u)$$

$$= (c, u)(v \cdot u, -v \times u + \langle cv \rangle)$$

$$= (c(v \cdot u) - u \cdot (-v \times u) - c(u \cdot v), u \times (-v \times u)$$

$$+ \langle c(u \times v) \rangle + \langle c(-v \times u + \langle cv \rangle) \rangle + (v \cdot u)u)$$

$$= (0, -u \times (u \times v) + \langle 2c(u \times v) \rangle + \langle c^2 v \rangle + (v \cdot u)u)$$

$$= (0, (u \cdot v)u - \langle (u \cdot u)v \rangle + \langle 2c(u \times v) \rangle$$

$$+ \langle c^2 v \rangle + \langle (v \cdot u)u \rangle)$$

$$= (0, \langle (c^2 - u \cdot u)v \rangle + \langle 2(v \cdot u)u \rangle + \langle 2c(u \times v) \rangle).$$

And because q is a unit quaternion, that is, $q = (c, u) = (c, s\mathbf{N})$ with $c = \cos(\theta)$ and $s = \sin(\theta)$,

$$R_q(p) = \left(0, \langle (c^2 - s^2)v \rangle + \langle 2s^2(\mathbf{N} \cdot v)\mathbf{N} \rangle + \langle 2sc(\mathbf{N} \times v) \rangle \right)$$

$$= \left(0, \langle \cos(2\theta)v \rangle + \langle (1 - \cos(2\theta))(\mathbf{N} \cdot v)\mathbf{N} \rangle \right.$$

$$\left. + \langle \sin(2\theta)(\mathbf{N} \times v) \rangle \right)$$

R_q can be interpreted as the rotation of angle 2θ around the axis $\mathbf{N} = N_1 i + N_2 j + N_3 k$. As a reciprocity, $Rot_{(\theta, \mathbf{N})}$ is represented by the quaternion

$$q = \cos(\theta/2) + \sin(\theta/2)\mathbf{N}$$

$$\mathbf{N} = N_1 i + N_2 j + N_3 k.$$

Notes

$$R_{qq'} = R_q \circ R_{q'}$$

$$R_{qq'}(p) = (qq')p(\overline{qq'})$$

$$= q(q'p\overline{q})\overline{q}'$$

$$= R_q(R_{q'}(p))$$

$$R_{qq'} = R_q \circ R_{q'}.$$

If we state that $-\pi \le \theta \le \pi$, then $-\pi/2 \le \theta/2 \le \pi/2$, and then

$$-q = -\cos(\theta/2) - \sin(\theta/2)\mathbf{N} = \cos(-\theta/2) + \sin(-\theta/2)(-\mathbf{N})$$

$$R_{-q} = Rot_{(-\theta, -\mathbf{N})} = Rot_{(\theta, \mathbf{N})}.$$

The algebraic formulation can be directly used in computing the displacement of orthonormal (orthogonal and normalized) coordinate systems.

If we make an analogy between the points $P = [x, y, z]$ of a nonhomogeneous space with the pure quaternions $p = xi + yj + zk$, it is possible to represent the displacements $Tr_{(\mathbf{U})} \circ Rot_{(\theta, \mathbf{N})}$ of the space with the following functions:

$$p \rightarrow p' = M_{(u, r)}(p) = u + rp\bar{r},$$

with p, p', u being pure quaternions, and r a unit quaternion.

We can write

$$Tr_{(\mathbf{U})} = M_{(u, 1)}: p' = p + u$$

$$Rot_{(\theta, \mathbf{N})} = M_{(0, r)} = M_{(0, \cos(\theta/2) + \sin(\theta/2)\mathbf{N})}$$

$$Id = M_{(0, 1)}: Identity \; transform.$$

We can also define the property

$$M_{(u, r)} \circ M_{(u', r')}(p) = u + r(u' + r'p\bar{r}')\bar{r}$$

$$M_{(u, r)} \circ M_{(u', r')}(p) = (u + ru'\bar{r}) + (rr')p(\overline{rr'})$$

$$M_{(u, r)} \circ M_{(u', r')}(p) = M_{(u + ru'\bar{r}, rr')}.$$

We have defined a multiplication $*$ over the elements (u, r):

$$(u, r) * (u', r') = (u + ru'\bar{r}, rr')$$

$$M_{(u, r)} * M_{(u', r')} = M_{(u, r)} \circ M_{(u', r')}.$$

We can now evaluate displacements in a 3D space using only algebraic elements (u, r).

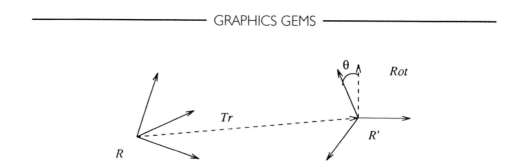

Figure 2.   Movement from one orthonormal base to another.

By setting the initial coordinate system to Id, we can represent the movements of orthonormal bases (see Fig. 2).

$$R' = R \circ Tr_{(\mathbf{V})} \circ Rot_{(\theta, \mathbf{N})}$$

$$(u', r') = (u, r) * (v, \cos(\theta/2) + \sin(\theta/2)\mathbf{N})$$

We can also represent series of displacements as explained in Fig. 3.

$$(u, r) = (u_0, r_0) * (v_1, s_1) * (v_2, s_2) * \ldots * (v_n, s_n),$$

where $(v_i, s_i) = (v_i, \cos(\theta_i/2) + \sin(\theta_i/2)\mathbf{N})$ represents the transformation $Tr_{(\mathbf{V})} \circ Rot_{(\theta, \mathbf{N})}$.

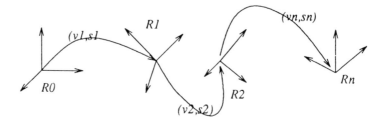

Figure 3.   Series of movements from one orthonormal base to another.

Notes

Let R_0 and R_1 be two given orthonormal bases. The transformation from R_0 to R_1 has an algebraic representation:

$$(u_1, r_1) = (u_0, r_0) * (v, s)$$

$$(v, s) = (u_0, r_0)^{-1} * (u_1, r_1)$$

$$(v, s) = (-\bar{r}_0 u_0 r_0, \bar{r}_0) * (u_1, r_1)$$

$$(v, s) = (-\bar{r}_0 (u_1 - u_0) r_0, \bar{r}_0 r_1).$$

Algorithmic Implementation

The use of quaternions is a good way of coding 3D transformations. It requires less space than a 4×4 matrix (only 7 elements instead of 16) and the functions that are necessary for the implementation of a pre-/post-translation or a pre-/post-rotation are short and simple to code.

The pseudo-code examples that follow have been implemented in the *PATK3D* software, and have already been presented in a FORTRAN-like code (Maillot, 1986). A C language version is given in the appendix section. In the *PATK3D* package, the observer's position is initially $[1, 0, 0]$, looking at the point $[0, 0, 0]$. There are three primitives that control the position and visualization direction of the observer.

- The first one sets the observer at a given position, $[x, y, z]$, and initializes the visualization direction to be in the X decreasing, that is, *looking in the X decreasing direction*.

- Another primitive can be used to set the visualization direction while not changing the observer position. It only needs a point in 3D, which is equivalent to saying: *look at the point* $[x, y, z]$.

- The last primitive is more general and gives to the *PATK3D* user the capability of moving in the 3D space using a displacement descriptor.

This descriptor is coded as a string where the user specifies a series of movements such as: *forward 10, turn right 20 degrees, pitch 30 degrees*, and so on.

Once all the observer's movements are described by the user, a 4×4 matrix is calculated using the observer's resulting quaternion. This matrix is accumulated with the other matrices of the visualization pipeline to produce the final matrix used in the single model-coordinate-to-device-coordinate transformation.

The functions presented here deal only with the kernel part of the observer's position and visualization direction primitives. We define the following structures:

P: **point** $\leftarrow [-1.0, 0.0, 0.0]$ is used to keep trace of the observer's position. It actually codes the orthonormal world coordinate base in respect to the observer.

Q: **array** $[0..3]$ **of real** $\leftarrow [1.0, 0.0, 0.0, 0.0]$ is the quaternion itself. The first element, $Q[0]$, keeps the real part of the quaternion, while the three other elements represent the components of the pure part of the quaternion.

M: **matrix4** is the matrix that will be calculated from P and Q. **M** will be coded like this:

$$\mathbf{M} = \begin{bmatrix} 1 & tx & ty & tz \\ 0 & m_{1,1} & m_{1,2} & m_{1,3} \\ 0 & m_{2,1} & m_{2,2} & m_{2,3} \\ 0 & m_{3,1} & m_{3,2} & m_{3,3} \end{bmatrix}.$$

The *set_obs_position* primitive sets new values for the observer's eye's position in the space.

name: set_obs_position(*position*: **point**)

begin

Set the values of the eye's position.
The position here represents the position of the orthonormal base
in respect to the observer.
$P \leftarrow -position$;
Set the visualization to be in the decreasing x-axis.
$Q \leftarrow [1.0, 0.0, 0.0, 0.0]$;
end;

P and Q (Fig. 4) have the following values:

$$P: [-2.0, 0.0, 0.0],$$

$$Q: [1.0, 0.0, 0.0, 0.0].$$

The *translate_quaternion* function computes translation movements for a given quaternion. i is the axis of the translation, while x is the parameter that characterizes the translation for the quaternion. w should be set to -1 if the observer moves in respect to the scene, or to 1 if the scene moves in respect to the observer.

```
name: translate_quaternion(x: real, i, w: integer)
begin
        j, k: integer;
        A, B, D, E, F: real;

        Does the observer move in respect to the scene?
        if w < 0 then P[i − 1] ← P[i − 1] − x;
        else begin

                The scene moves in respect to the observer.
                Compute the successor axis of i [1, 2, 3];
                and then the successor axis of j [1, 2,3];
                j ← i + 1;
                if j > 3 then j ← 1;
                k ← j + 1;
                if k > 3 then k ← 1;
                A ← Q[j]; B ← Q[k]; F ← Q[0]; E ← Q[i];
                P[i − 1] ← P[i − 1] + x*(E*E + F*F − A*A − B*B);
                D ← x + x;
                P[j − 1] ← P[j − 1] + D*(E*A + F*B);
                P[k − 1] ← P[k − 1] + D*(E*B + F*A);
                end;
        end;
```

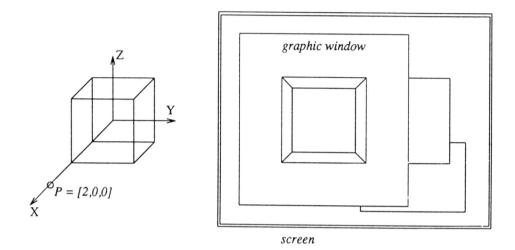

Figure 4.   A simple graphic scene, and the user's screen.

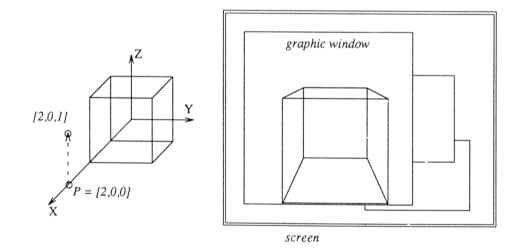

Figure 5.   The result of a translation of vector [0, 0, 1].

P and Q (Fig. 5) get the following values:

$$P: [-2.0, 0.0, -1.0],$$

$$Q: [1.0, 0.0, 0.0, 0.0].$$

The *rotate_quaternion* function computes rotation based movements for a given quaternion. i is the axis number of the rotation, while x and y are the parameters that characterize the rotation for the quaternion. w follows the same rule as for *translate_quaternion*. x and y are typically the cosine and sine of the half-rotation angle.

```
name: rotate_quaternion(x, y: real, i, w: integer)
begin
      j, k: integer;
      E, F, R1: real;
      Compute the successor axis of i [1, 2, 3,] and j [1, 2, 3];
      j ← i + 1;
      if j > 3 then j ← 1;
      k ← j + 1;
      if k > 3 then k ← 1;
      E ← Q[i];
      Q[i] ← E*x + w*y*Q[0];
      Q[0] ← Q[0]*x − w*y*E;
      E ← Q[j];
      Q[j] ← E*x + y*Q[k];
      Q[k] ← Q[k]*x − y*E;
      if w < 0 then begin
            Compute a new position if the observer moves in respect to the scene.
            j ← j − 1; k ← k − 1;
            R1 ← x*x − y*y;
            F ← 2.*x*y;
            E ← P[j];
            P[j] ← E*R1 + F*P[k];
            P[k] ← P[k]*R1 − F*E;
            end;
      end;
```

P and Q (Fig. 6) get the following values:

$$P: [-2.24, 0.0, 0.0],$$

$$Q: [0.97, 0.0, 0.23, 0.0].$$

The *evaluate_matrix* primitive (re)computes the matrix corresponding to the observer's position and visualization direction given by P and Q. The method presented here is the direct application of the mathematical formulae. Faster ways to evaluate the matrix can be found.

```
name: evaluate_matrix( )
begin
      e, f: real;
      r: array [0..3] of real;
      i, j, k: integer;
      We will need some square values!
      for i: integer ← 0, i < 4 do
        r[i] ← Q[i]*Q[i];
        i ← i + 1;
        endloop;
      Compute each element of the matrix.
      j is the successor of i (in 1, 2, 3), where k is the successor of j.
      for i: integer ← 1, i < 4 dO
        j ← i + 1;
        if j > 3 then j ← 1;
        k ← j + 1;
        if k > 3 then k ← 1;
        e ← 2.*Q[i]*Q[j];
        f ← 2.*Q[k]*Q[0];
        M[j][i] ← e − f;
        M[i][j] ← e + f;
        M[i][i] ← r[i] + r[0] − r[j] − r[k];
        M[0][i] ← P[i − 1];
        M[i][0] ← 0.0;
        endloop;
      M[0][0] ← 1.0;
      end;
```

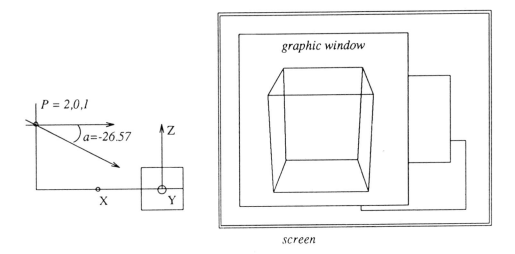

Figure 6. The result of a rotation of angle -26.57 degrees around the y-axis to look at the point $[0, 0, 0]$.

As an example, the matrix resulting from P and Q values of Fig. 6 is given below.

$$\mathbf{M} = \begin{bmatrix} 1.0 & -2.24 & 0.0 & 0.0 \\ 0.0 & 0.89 & 0.0 & 0.45 \\ 0.0 & 0.0 & 1.0 & 0.0 \\ 0.0 & -0.45 & 0.0 & 0.89 \end{bmatrix}$$

See also Rotation Matrix Methods Summary (455); Bit Patterns for Encoding Angles (442); Fast 2D–3D Rotation (440); Fixed-Point Trigonometry with CORDIC Iterations (494)

See Appendix 2 for C Implementation (**775**)

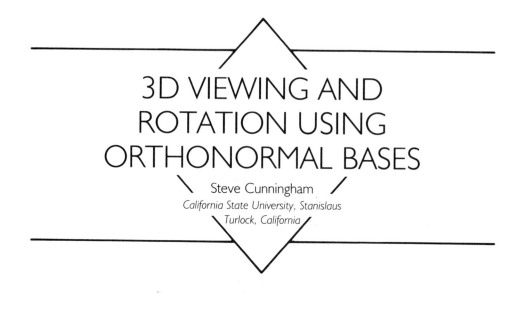

3D VIEWING AND ROTATION USING ORTHONORMAL BASES

Steve Cunningham
California State University, Stanislaus
Turlock, California

This note discusses the general viewing transformation and rotations about a general line. It contrasts the common textbook approach to this problem with an approach based on orthonormal bases from linear algebra and shows that a straightforward piece of mathematics can improve the implementations of viewing and rotation transformations in actual work.

The common approach to viewing and general rotation operations treats these as a translation followed by a sequence of rotations about the coordinate axes in model space, and seems to go back to Newman and Sproull (1979). The viewing transformation requires three of these rotations, whereas the general rotation requires four. The entries in these rotation matrices are trigonometric functions of angles which are not readily seen, though the actual computations rarely use the trig functions; the entries are computed from the components of vectors derived from the translated eye vector as the rotations proceed. See Newman and Sproull for more details; this same approach has been used in Hearn and Baker (1986) and other books. Some books, such as Foley and Van Dam (1982) discuss a (U, V, N) viewplane coordinate system such as we build below, but still use rotations to build the actual viewing transformation.

The approach we suggest was developed independently but is not original to this note. It appears in Berger (1986), where it seems a bit obscure, as well as in Salmon and Slater (1987), where it is developed more formally, but is not widely known. No graphics texts seem to use this approach to general rotations in 3-space. The approach is straightforward: after the usual translation of the view reference point to the origin, use the eye point and up point in the viewing information to compute an orthonormal basis (U, V, N) for 3-space for which the eye vector is one component (the z-axis analogue) and the up vector is projected onto another (the y-axis analogue). Then the viewing transformation is simply a change of basis and its matrix is directly written from the orthonormal (U, V, N) basis. The general rotation is much the same, with the up vector taken randomly, and the desired rotation applied after the initial viewing transformation; the inverse of the viewing transformation is then applied.

The advantages of the orthonormal basis approach are twofold: there is a logical basis for the approach, which comes naturally from linear algebra, and the computation involves fewer steps. I have found that students can apply these ideas in their own code more quickly and accurately than they can using the traditional approach.

The New Approach

Consider a standard setup for 3D viewing (there are variations, but this uses standard information common to them all):

- A view reference point VRP

- An eye point EP

- An "up point" UP

From these we compute two vectors:

- An eye vector EV as the vector from VRP to EP

- An up vector UV as the vector from VRP to UP,

and we have the situation shown in Fig. 1.

The new process starts in the same way as the standard process: by defining a translation to move the view reference point to the origin. This

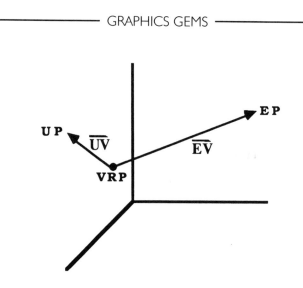

Figure I.   A standard viewing environment.

has the standard matrix form

$$T_0 = \begin{bmatrix} 1 & 0 & 0 & 0 \\ 0 & 1 & 0 & 0 \\ 0 & 0 & 1 & 0 \\ -xv & -yv & -zv & 0 \end{bmatrix}$$

Next compute the orthonormal basis for the space as seen by the viewer, as follows:

1. Normalize EV and call the result N.

2. Normalize UV and continue to call the result UV.

3. Compute V_1 orthogonal to N by setting $V_1 = UV - (N \cdot UV)N$, (as shown in Fig. 2).

4. Normalize V_1 and call the result V.

5. Compute the cross product $U = V \times N$.

This creates a new coordinate system within the original model space that represents the coordinates of the desired viewing space. This coordinate system is shown in Fig. 3.

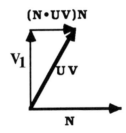

Figure 2. Orthogonalizing UV and N.

Then the change of basis from (X, Y, Z)-space to (U, V, N)-space (assuming that matrices multiply on the right of their operands) has U as its first row, V as its second row, and N as its third row. The inverse of this matrix is the transformation from (U, V, N)-space to (X, Y, Z)-space and provides the construction of the rotation part of the matrix M of the viewing transformation. Since U, V, and N are orthonormal, this inverse is the transpose of the matrix above; the first three rows of M have U as the first column, V as the second column, N as the third column, and the rest are zero. Finally, the viewing transformation is $T_0 M$. It is easier to compute than the standard transformation and is as efficient to apply (if all three rotations are computed and multiplied together) or more efficient

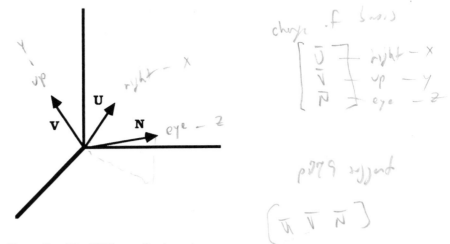

Figure 3. The UVN coordinate system.

519

(if the rotations are applied separately). The actual matrix of this transformation is the output of the *BuildViewTransform* function below.

Rotations about a General Line

The usual approach to a rotation by an angle α about a general line is to move the line so it goes through the origin (a translation), rotate the line into the XZ-plane, rotate the resulting line to align with the z-axis, perform the desired rotation by α now, reverse the two earlier rotations, and then reverse the translation. This requires five rotations and two translations, and suffers from the same difficulties as the viewing transformation: the angles are not easy to see and the computations are obscure.

The approach above to the viewing transformation extends easily to these rotations. The line is assumed to be given by a point $P = (xp, yp, zp)$ and a direction vector $D = \langle A, B, C \rangle$. Then the plane perpendicular to the line at the given point has equation

$$A(x - xp) + B(y - yp) + C(z - zp) = 0.$$

Let T be the translation that moves P to the origin. Pick any point $Q = (x, y, z)$ in the plane and let $UP = (x - xp, y - yp, z - zp)$, as shown in Fig. 4. Let N be the result when D is normalized, and let V be

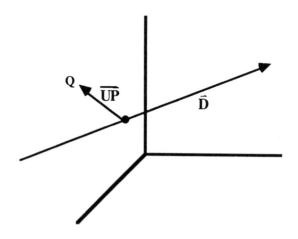

Figure 4.   The setup for general rotations.

the result when UP is normalized. Then compute U as in the viewing transformation to complete the (U, V, N) triple, and build the change-of-basis matrix M with U, V, and N as the first, second, and third columns, respectively.

Now let R be the matrix of the rotation by α about the z-axis, and let N and S be the (trivially computed) inverses of M and T, respectively. Then the matrix of the rotation by Q about the line is $TMRNS$, which requires fewer matrices and less computation than the traditional method of rotation about the coordinate axes. There is another benefit for students and for floating-point speed: it uses no trigonometric functions except those in the matrix R.

Pseudo-code for Constructing the Viewing Transformation

The following pseudo-code produces the matrix for the viewing transformation with the three standard view specification points as input. It is expanded into actual C code in an appendix. No pseudo-code is given for the general rotation, since the matrices M and N of the previous section are easily computed by the pseudo-code above (and the code in the appendix) if the last translation step is omitted.

```
BuildViewTransform(VRP, EP, UP, T)
   Input: points VRP, EP, UP as in the text
   Output: transformation matrix T
   Compute vector N ← EP − VRP and normalize N
   Compute vector V ← VP − VRP
   Make vector V orthogonal to N and normalize V
   Compute vector U ← V × N (cross product)
   Write the vectors U, V, and N as the first three rows of the
      first, second, and third columns of T, respectively,
   Compute the fourth row of T to include the translation of
      VRP to the origin
```

See Appendix 2 for C Implementation (778)

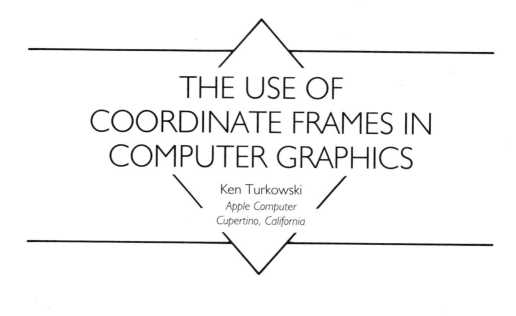

THE USE OF COORDINATE FRAMES IN COMPUTER GRAPHICS

Ken Turkowski
Apple Computer
Cupertino, California

Introduction

Coordinates have no meaning without reference to their corresponding basis vectors (and origin). When we express one set of basis vectors (and origin) with respect to another, we establish a new *coordinate frame* in terms of the old. This coordinate frame can also be used to transform the coordinates in one frame to those of another.

We will see that coordinate frames are easy to construct and can simplify the construction of coordinate transformations without the explicit use of trigonometry.

Vectors and Points

We will need to distinguish between 3D vectors and 3D points. A vector has a magnitude and a direction, but does not have a location, whereas a point has only a location, and no magnitude or direction. A vector cannot be moved, but it can be scaled and rotated. A point cannot be scaled or rotated, although it can be moved; a group of points can, however, be rotated or moved relative to each other. A linear transformation is appropriate for vectors, whereas an affine transformation is appropriate for points. There is a unique origin in a vector space, but an origin is arbitrary in an affine (point) space. These properties are summarized in the table below:

Attribute	Vector	Point
represents	magnitude and direction	location
origin	unique	arbitrary
transformation	linear	affine
	scale	move
	rotate	

When points and vectors are represented by three components, they can be distinguished only by context. We may sometimes represent them by four coordinates (x, y, z, w), in what is called *homogeneous coordinates*. We interpret a 4-vector as a point in 3D by its projection onto the hyperplane $w = 1$, that is, $(x/w, y/w, z/w)$. The indeterminate form at $w = 0$ is resolved by taking the limit as w approaches 0 from above: the point approaches infinity in a particular direction; hence the *vector* interpretation.

By convention, we will represent points as homogeneous 4-vectors with $w = 1$ whenever possible. For example, we represent the point 1 unit along the x-axis as

$$\begin{bmatrix} 1 & 0 & 0 & 1 \end{bmatrix},$$

whereas the x-axis (a vector) itself is represented as

$$\begin{bmatrix} 1 & 0 & 0 & 0 \end{bmatrix}.$$

In nonhomogeneous coordinates, they are both represented as

$$\begin{bmatrix} 1 & 0 & 0 \end{bmatrix},$$

so only context can distinguish them.

Coordinate Frames

We shall usually represent a coordinate frame for three-dimensional points with a 4×3 matrix:

$$
\mathbf{F} = \begin{bmatrix} \mathbf{X} \\ \mathbf{Y} \\ \mathbf{Z} \\ O \end{bmatrix} = \left[\begin{array}{ccc} X_x & X_y & X_z \\ \hline Y_x & Y_y & Y_z \\ \hline Z_x & Z_y & Z_z \\ \hline O_x & O_y & O_z \end{array} \right]. \tag{1}
$$

This establishes a local reference frame within a more global frame by representing the local origin and the x-, y-, and z-axes in terms of the global coordinates in the rows of the matrix. In particular,

$$
O = \begin{bmatrix} O_x & O_y & O_z \end{bmatrix}, \tag{2}
$$

is a point that represents the origin of the local coordinate frame, represented in the coordinates of the global reference frame.

The local x-axis,

$$
\mathbf{X} = \begin{bmatrix} X_x & X_y & X_z \end{bmatrix}, \tag{3}
$$

is a vector (not a point), with both magnitude and direction.

Similar sorts of interpretations are appropriate for the y- and z-axes. There is no requirement that the vectors $\mathbf{X}$, $\mathbf{Y}$, and $\mathbf{Z}$ be mutually orthogonal, although they should be linearly independent.

The matrix representation of this coordinate frame is more than just a convenient representation; it is in fact related to the more familiar 4×4 graphics transformation matrix (Newman and Sproull, 1979):

$$
\mathbf{F}_4 = \left[\begin{array}{c|c} \mathbf{F} & \begin{matrix} 0 \\ 0 \\ 0 \end{matrix} \\ \hline & 1 \end{array} \right] = \left[\begin{array}{c|c} \mathbf{X} & 0 \\ \hline \mathbf{Y} & 0 \\ \hline \mathbf{Z} & 0 \\ \hline O & 1 \end{array} \right] = \left[\begin{array}{ccc|c} X_x & X_y & X_z & 0 \\ \hline Y_x & Y_y & Y_z & 0 \\ \hline Z_x & Z_y & Z_z & 0 \\ \hline O_x & O_y & O_z & 1 \end{array} \right], \tag{4}
$$

where the 0's and 1 in the right column underscore the interpretation of $\mathbf{X}$, $\mathbf{Y}$, and $\mathbf{Z}$ as vectors, and O as a point.

A 4-vector with $w = 0$, will not be affected by the translation portion (bottom row) of a 4×4 matrix transformation, whereas the 4-vector with $w \neq 0$ will.

We illustrate the effect of a coordinate transformation on the homogeneous representation of the x-axis (a vector) with a 4×4 matrix multiplication:

$$\begin{bmatrix} 1 & 0 & 0 & 0 \end{bmatrix} \begin{bmatrix} X_x & X_y & X_z & 0 \\ Y_x & Y_y & Y_z & 0 \\ Z_x & Z_y & Z_z & 0 \\ O_x & O_y & O_z & 1 \end{bmatrix} = \begin{bmatrix} X_x & X_y & X_z & 0 \end{bmatrix}. \quad (5)$$

With the fourth component zero, we see that a vector transforms into a vector, and not just any vector: the x-axis transforms into the vector $\begin{bmatrix} X_x & X_y & X_z & 0 \end{bmatrix}$, the top row of the transformation matrix. It is easy to see that the y- and z-axes transform into the second and third rows of the matrix, respectively.

The transformation of the origin (a point) yields

$$\begin{bmatrix} 0 & 0 & 0 & 1 \end{bmatrix} \begin{bmatrix} X_x & X_y & X_z & 0 \\ Y_x & Y_y & Y_z & 0 \\ Z_x & Z_y & Z_z & 0 \\ O_x & O_y & O_z & 1 \end{bmatrix} = \begin{bmatrix} O_x & O_y & O_z & 1 \end{bmatrix}, \quad (6)$$

the bottom row of the matrix. This is consistent with the definition we gave it earlier.

Since the transformation of an arbitrary vector

$$\begin{bmatrix} V_x & V_y & V_z & 0 \end{bmatrix} \begin{bmatrix} X_x & X_y & X_z & 0 \\ Y_x & Y_y & Y_z & 0 \\ Z_x & Z_y & Z_z & 0 \\ O_x & O_y & O_z & 1 \end{bmatrix}$$

$$= \begin{bmatrix} V_x X_x + V_y Y_x + V_z Z_x & V_x X_y + V_y Y_y + V_z Z_y \\ & V_x X_z + V_y Y_z + V_z Z_z & 0 \end{bmatrix} \quad (7)$$

doesn't depend at all on the last row (translation), we will generally omit it, as well as the last column, to obtain the familiar 3×3 linear transformation matrix for 3D vectors:

$$\begin{bmatrix} V_x & V_y & V_z \end{bmatrix} \begin{bmatrix} X_x & X_y & X_z \\ Y_x & Y_y & Y_z \\ Z_x & Z_y & Z_z \end{bmatrix}$$

$$= \begin{bmatrix} V_x X_x + V_y Y_x + V_z Z_x & V_x X_y + V_y Y_y + V_z Z_y & V_x X_z + V_y Y_z + V_z Z_z \end{bmatrix}$$

$$(8)$$

We will use this as the intrinsic coordinate frame for 3D vectors, whereas the 4×3 matrix (see Eq. 1) will be used as the intrinsic coordinate frame for 3D points, where we extend the operations of linear algebra to affine algebra as follows:

$$\begin{bmatrix} P_x & P_y & P_z \end{bmatrix} \begin{bmatrix} X_x & X_y & X_z \\ Y_x & Y_y & Y_z \\ Z_x & Z_y & Z_z \\ O_x & O_y & O_z \end{bmatrix}$$

$$= \begin{bmatrix} P_x X_x + P_y Y_x + P_z Z_x + O_x & P_x X_y + P_y Y_y + P_z Z_y + O_y \end{bmatrix}$$

$$P_x X_z + P_y Y_z + P_z Z_z + O_z \big]. \quad (9)$$

This definition is consistent with the treatment of 3D points as homogeneous 4-vectors, as in Eq. 6.

We now show some examples of how the use of coordinate frames can simplify tremendously problems in computer graphics.

Examples: Using Coordinate Frames to Solve Problems

Example 1: Find the simple plane rotation that aligns the x-axis to the y-axis.

If the x-axis $[1, 0]$ rotates into the y-axis $[0, 1]$, the y-axis rotates into the negative x-axis $[-1, 0]$. Therefore, the desired transformation is

$$\mathbf{R}_{90} = \begin{bmatrix} \mathbf{X} \\ \mathbf{Y} \end{bmatrix} = \begin{bmatrix} X_x & X_y \\ \hline Y_x & Y_y \end{bmatrix} = \begin{bmatrix} 0 & 1 \\ \hline -1 & 0 \end{bmatrix}. \tag{10}$$

Example 2: Find the simple plane rotation that aligns the x-axis to the direction $[1, 1]$.

From the previous example, we know that the new y-axis must be aligned with $[1 \quad 1]\mathbf{R}_{90} = [-1 \quad 1]$, so that the desired matrix is

$$\mathbf{R}_{45} = \begin{bmatrix} \mathbf{X} \\ \mathbf{Y} \end{bmatrix} = \frac{1}{\sqrt{2}} \begin{bmatrix} 1 & 1 \\ \hline -1 & 1 \end{bmatrix}.$$

The normalization factor comes about because the Euclidean norm of each of the two rows is $\sqrt{2}$. Without this, the transformation would enlarge vectors as well as rotate them.

Example 3: Find the simple plane rotation that rotates an arbitrary normalized vector $\mathbf{V}$ into another normalized vector $\mathbf{W}$.

We approach this by first rotating $\mathbf{V}$ to align it to the x-axis, then rotating it to align it to $\mathbf{W}$. In order to determine the first rotation, it is easier to specify the rotation from the x-axis to $\mathbf{V}$, and then invert it.

Rotating the x-axis to $\mathbf{V}$ is accomplished by the matrix

$$\mathbf{R}_{\mathbf{V}} = \begin{bmatrix} \mathbf{V} \\ \mathbf{V}\mathbf{R}_{90} \end{bmatrix} = \begin{bmatrix} V_x & V_y \\ \hline -V_y & V_x \end{bmatrix}.$$

Since this is an orthogonal matrix (all pure rotations are orthogonal), its

527

inverse is equal to its transpose:

$$
\mathbf{R}_{\mathbf{V}}^{-1} = \begin{bmatrix} \mathbf{V} \\ \mathbf{VR}_{90} \end{bmatrix}^{\mathrm{T}} = \begin{bmatrix} V_x & -V_y \\ V_y & V_x \end{bmatrix}.
$$

The rotation from the x-axis to $\mathbf{W}$ is found similarly:

$$
\mathbf{R}_{\mathbf{W}} = \begin{bmatrix} \mathbf{W} \\ \mathbf{WR}_{90} \end{bmatrix} = \begin{bmatrix} W_x & W_y \\ -W_y & W_x \end{bmatrix}.
$$

Therefore, the desired transformation is the concatenation

$$
\mathbf{R}_{\mathbf{V}\to\mathbf{W}} = \mathbf{R}_{\mathbf{V}}^{-1}\mathbf{R}_{\mathbf{W}} = \begin{bmatrix} \mathbf{V} \\ \mathbf{VR}_{90} \end{bmatrix}^{\mathrm{T}} \begin{bmatrix} \mathbf{W} \\ \mathbf{WR}_{90} \end{bmatrix} = \begin{bmatrix} V_x & -V_y \\ V_y & V_x \end{bmatrix} \begin{bmatrix} V_x & V_y \\ -W_y & W_x \end{bmatrix}
$$

$$
= \begin{bmatrix} V_xW_x + V_yW_y & V_xW_y - V_yW_x \\ -(V_xW_y - V_yW_x) & V_xW_x + V_yW_y \end{bmatrix} \tag{11}
$$

Example 4: Find the skewing transformation suitable for italicizing letters by $\frac{1}{4}$ unit in x for every unit in y.

We basically just want to remap the y-axis to $[\frac{1}{4} \quad 1]$ while the x-axis remains the same:

$$
\mathbf{K} = \begin{bmatrix} 1 & 0 \\ \frac{1}{4} & 1 \end{bmatrix}.
$$

Example 5: Find the rotation that takes the vector $(1/\sqrt{3})[1 \quad 1 \quad 1]$ onto the x-axis, through the plane that contains them both.

The axis of rotation can be obtained as

$$
\mathbf{N} = \frac{\mathbf{V} \times \mathbf{X}}{|\mathbf{V} \times \mathbf{X}|} = \frac{[1 \quad 1 \quad 1] \times [1 \quad 0 \quad 0]}{|[1 \quad 1 \quad 1] \times [1 \quad 0 \quad 0]|} = \frac{1}{\sqrt{2}}[0 \quad 1 \quad -1],
$$

where $\mathbf{X}$ is the x-axis. An orthogonal third vector can be obtained by crossing this with the given vector:

$$
\mathbf{M} = \frac{\mathbf{N} \times \mathbf{V}}{|\mathbf{N} \times \mathbf{V}|} = \frac{[0 \quad 1 \quad -1] \times [1 \quad 1 \quad 1]}{|[0 \quad 1 \quad -1] \times [1 \quad 1 \quad 1]|} = \frac{1}{\sqrt{6}}[2 \quad -1 \quad -1].
$$

These three vectors then make up an orthonormal coordinate frame:

$$
\mathbf{Q} = \begin{bmatrix} \mathbf{V} \\ \mathbf{M} \\ \mathbf{N} \end{bmatrix} = \left[\begin{array}{c|c|c} \dfrac{1}{\sqrt{3}} & \dfrac{1}{\sqrt{3}} & \dfrac{1}{\sqrt{3}} \\ \hline \dfrac{2}{\sqrt{6}} & -\dfrac{1}{\sqrt{6}} & -\dfrac{1}{\sqrt{6}} \\ \hline 0 & \dfrac{1}{\sqrt{2}} & -\dfrac{1}{\sqrt{2}} \end{array} \right].
$$

This transformation takes the x-axis onto the vector $(1/\sqrt{3}\,)[1 \quad 1 \quad 1]$, and takes the z-axis onto the axis of rotation. In order to simplify the rotation, we would like to have the inverse of this, namely, to transform the axis of rotation onto the z-axis. Since $\mathbf{Q}$ is an orthogonal matrix, its inverse is simply the transpose:

$$
\mathbf{Q}^{-1} = \mathbf{Q}^{\mathrm{T}} = \begin{bmatrix} \dfrac{1}{\sqrt{3}} & \dfrac{2}{\sqrt{6}} & 0 \\ \dfrac{1}{\sqrt{3}} & -\dfrac{1}{\sqrt{6}} & \dfrac{1}{\sqrt{2}} \\ \dfrac{1}{\sqrt{3}} & -\dfrac{1}{\sqrt{6}} & -\dfrac{1}{\sqrt{2}} \end{bmatrix}.
$$

It can be verified that the vector $(1/\sqrt{3}\,)[1 \quad 1 \quad 1]$ maps onto the x-axis, that the axis of rotation, $(1/\sqrt{2}\,)[0 \quad 1 \quad -1]$, maps onto the z-axis, and that the x-axis maps onto

$$
\mathbf{X'} = \begin{bmatrix} \dfrac{1}{\sqrt{3}} & \dfrac{2}{\sqrt{6}} & 0 \end{bmatrix}.
$$

A simple rotation about the z-axis in this frame would have the y-axis map into

$$
\mathbf{Y'} = \mathbf{X'R}_{z90} = \begin{bmatrix} -\dfrac{2}{\sqrt{6}} & \dfrac{1}{\sqrt{3}} & 0 \end{bmatrix},
$$

where

$$
\mathbf{R}_{z90} = \begin{bmatrix} 0 & 1 & 0 \\ -1 & 0 & 0 \\ 0 & 0 & 1 \end{bmatrix} \tag{12}
$$

is the 3D analog of Eq. 10, and rotates the x-axis onto the y-axis around the z-axis. Putting this together into a transformation, we have

$$\mathbf{R} = \begin{bmatrix} \dfrac{1}{\sqrt{3}} & \dfrac{2}{\sqrt{6}} & 0 \\[2ex] -\dfrac{2}{\sqrt{6}} & \dfrac{1}{\sqrt{3}} & 0 \\[2ex] 0 & 0 & 1 \end{bmatrix}.$$

We then need to go back to our original frame by using $\mathbf{Q}$; the composite transformation is

$$\mathbf{T} = \mathbf{Q}^{\mathsf{T}}\mathbf{R}\mathbf{Q} = \begin{bmatrix} \dfrac{1}{\sqrt{3}} & \dfrac{2}{\sqrt{6}} & 0 \\[2ex] \dfrac{1}{\sqrt{3}} & -\dfrac{1}{\sqrt{6}} & \dfrac{1}{\sqrt{2}} \\[2ex] \dfrac{1}{\sqrt{3}} & -\dfrac{1}{\sqrt{6}} & -\dfrac{1}{\sqrt{2}} \end{bmatrix} \begin{bmatrix} \dfrac{1}{\sqrt{3}} & \dfrac{2}{\sqrt{6}} & 0 \\[2ex] -\dfrac{2}{\sqrt{6}} & \dfrac{1}{\sqrt{3}} & 0 \\[2ex] 0 & 0 & 1 \end{bmatrix}$$

$$\times \begin{bmatrix} \dfrac{1}{\sqrt{3}} & \dfrac{1}{\sqrt{3}} & \dfrac{1}{\sqrt{3}} \\[2ex] \dfrac{2}{\sqrt{6}} & -\dfrac{1}{\sqrt{6}} & -\dfrac{1}{\sqrt{6}} \\[2ex] 0 & \dfrac{1}{\sqrt{2}} & -\dfrac{1}{\sqrt{2}} \end{bmatrix}$$

$$= \begin{bmatrix} \dfrac{1}{\sqrt{3}} & -\dfrac{1}{\sqrt{3}} & -\dfrac{1}{\sqrt{3}} \\[2ex] \dfrac{1}{\sqrt{3}} & \dfrac{1}{2\sqrt{3}} + \dfrac{1}{2} & \dfrac{1}{2\sqrt{3}} - \dfrac{1}{2} \\[2ex] \dfrac{1}{\sqrt{3}} & \dfrac{1}{2\sqrt{3}} - \dfrac{1}{2} & \dfrac{1}{2\sqrt{3}} + \dfrac{1}{2} \end{bmatrix},$$

a somewhat formidable expression. No trigonometry per se has been used for this derivation—only cross products, vector normalization, and matrix multiplication. We generalize this in the next example.

Example 6: Find the rotation that takes an arbitrary normalized vector **V** to another normalized vector **W**, through the plane that contains them both.

Generalizing our experience with Example 3 and Example 5, we have the matrix that transforms **V** onto the x-axis, and the axis of the plane of rotation onto the z-axis:

$$\mathbf{Q}^{\mathrm{T}} = \begin{bmatrix} \mathbf{V} \\ \mathbf{M} \\ \mathbf{N} \end{bmatrix}^{\mathrm{T}}, \tag{13}$$

where

$$\mathbf{N} = \frac{\mathbf{V} \times \mathbf{W}}{|\mathbf{V} \times \mathbf{W}|} \tag{14}$$

is the axis of rotation, and

$$\mathbf{M} = \frac{\mathbf{N} \times \mathbf{V}}{|\mathbf{N} \times \mathbf{V}|} \tag{15}$$

is the third vector that completes a dextral orthogonal basis. The image of **W** in $\mathbf{Q}^{\mathrm{T}}$ is:

$$\mathbf{W}' = \mathbf{W}\mathbf{Q}^{\mathrm{T}}. \tag{16}$$

The transformation that rotates the x-axis (that is, the image of **V**) onto **W**' (the image of **W**) is

$$\mathbf{R} = \begin{bmatrix} \mathbf{W}' \\ \mathbf{W}'\mathbf{R}_{z90} \\ \mathbf{Z} \end{bmatrix}, \tag{17}$$

where

$$\mathbf{Z} = \begin{bmatrix} 0 & 0 & 1 \end{bmatrix}$$

is the z-axis. The desired transformation is then

$$\mathbf{R}_{\mathbf{v} \to \mathbf{w}} = \mathbf{Q}^{\mathrm{T}} \mathbf{R} \mathbf{Q}. \tag{18}$$

Example 7: For a general transformation on a set of points, suppose that we would like to scale the x-axis by 2, the y-axis by 3, the z-axis by 4, and we want to reorient the object described in terms of those points so that the new x-axis points in the direction $(1/\sqrt{3})[1 \quad 1 \quad 1]$, the y-axis points in the direction $[1 \quad 0 \quad 0]$, and the z-axis points in the direction $(1/\sqrt{2})[0 \quad 1 \quad -1]$, and further, that the whole object be shifted in position by $[10 \quad 20 \quad -27]$.

Just copying these specifications into a 4×3 matrix, we get

$$\mathbf{T} = \begin{bmatrix} \dfrac{2}{\sqrt{3}} & \dfrac{2}{\sqrt{3}} & \dfrac{2}{\sqrt{3}} \\ 3 & 0 & 0 \\ 0 & \dfrac{4}{\sqrt{2}} & -\dfrac{4}{\sqrt{2}} \\ 10 & 20 & -27 \end{bmatrix}.$$

Note that this transformation is more complex than others that we have encountered before, and would be virtually impossible to describe in terms of elementary rotation, scaling, skewing, and translation operations, yet it was extremely simple to describe and implement in terms of a coordinate frame.

532

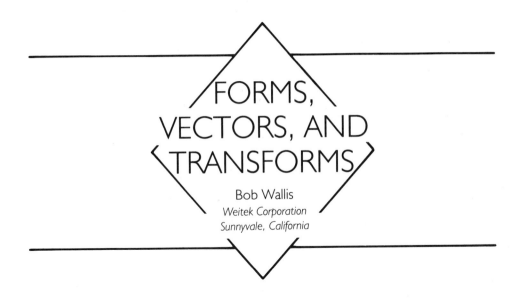

FORMS, VECTORS, AND TRANSFORMS

Bob Wallis
Weitek Corporation
Sunnyvale, California

Introduction

The modern concept of a tensor as a linear machine that contracts forms with vectors to produce scalars is an excellent mental model for dealing with certain types of graphics problems. It helps to eliminate much of the confusion that exists in dealing with questions such as how surface normals, Bézier control points, and so on, are affected by geometrical transformations.

Many graphics programmers tend to get confused when attempting to perform operations such as the rendering of bicubic patches, lighting calculations, and so forth, in different coordinate systems. The following is a tutorial that describes a way of thinking about mathematical quantities, such as polynomial coefficients and surface normals, which the author has found useful in problems involving coordinate system transformations. The key point is that *all arrays of numbers are not necessarily vectors*.

The Modern View of a Tensor

Older books on tensors seem obsessed with their transformation properties, classifying them as covariant and contravariant. The modern concept (Misner *et al.*, 1973) is that a tensor is sort of a dot product machine that accepts as inputs two different types of mathematical quantities, vectors and forms. It contracts these via an inner product to produce a scalar quantity, which should be invariant to coordinate system changes. While the full-blown generality of modern differential geometry is definitely overkill for dealing with simple graphics problems, the concept of separating forms and vectors is very helpful in avoiding mathematical blunders when dealing with coordinate system transformations. For example, in evaluating the homogeneous line equation

$$p = \alpha x + \beta y + \gamma = \langle \alpha\beta\gamma \rangle [x\, y\, 1] \qquad point\ on\ line\ if\ p = 0$$

$$\langle \alpha\beta\gamma \rangle = \omega_j;\ j = 1,2,3 \qquad 1\text{-}form\ of\ plane\ equation\ coefficients$$

$$[x\, y\, 1] = v_j;\ j = 1, 2, 3 \qquad\qquad vector, \qquad (1)$$

It is important to recognize that the surface normal, or array of plane equation coefficients (Greek letters) is a different sort of mathematical object than the $[x\, y\, 1]$ (Roman letters) vector. When we change coordinate systems, the vital thing to remember is that the scalar output of the tensor, p in Eq. 1, should remain invariant. Different disciplines have different notations for segregating forms and vectors. Quantum mechanics uses the bra-ket notation; some tensor books use subscripts and superscripts. Most graphics programmers use column vectors and row vectors, but in the nomenclature of this paper, what is normally called a column vector really isn't a vector at all, but a 1-form. For most practical problems in graphics, it is sufficient to use conventional subscript notation. However, one must be very careful about which index is summed over which. For example, expressing Eq. 1 in index notation we have

$$p = \sum \omega_j v_j = \sum \omega_i I_{ij} v_j = \sum \left(\omega_i T_{ij}^{-1} \right) \left(T_{jk} v_k \right)$$

$$p = \sum \omega'_j v'_j \qquad invariant\ in\ primed\ coords$$

$$v'_j = \sum T_{jk} v_k \qquad how\ to\ transform\ vector$$

$$\omega'_j = \sum \omega_i T_{ij}^{-1} \qquad how\ to\ transform\ 1\text{-}form.$$

In the above, I is the identity transform (Kroneker's delta), and there is an implied summation over any repeated index. In most literature on tensors, the summation sign is also implied. The advantage of writing everything down with index notation (instead of row and column vectors, for instance) is that it extends easily to higher-dimensional problems, minimizes the likelihood of blunders such as an inappropriate matrix transpose, and can be translated directly to nested *for* loops when coding up the result.

Triangular Interpolants

As a further example of the difference between 1-forms and vectors, consider the problem of linear interpolation within a triangle. This typically comes up in tiling surfaces that have been tesellated into triangles. Here, it becomes necessary to interpolate z-depth and/or intensity at each pixel within the triangle. If the interpolator is viewed as a contraction between a group of three forms and a dual group of three vectors, it is possible to write down the correct answer by inspection.

Figure 1 illustrates one way of viewing 1-forms. Consider the density of a 1-form at a particular point x, y to be the scalar you get when you

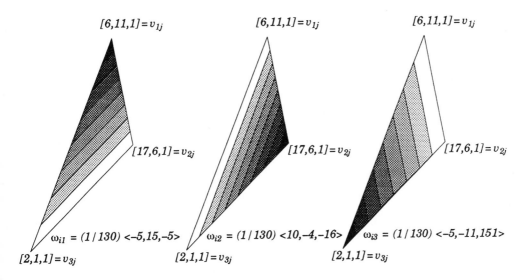

Figure 1.

535

contract it with $[x, y, 1]$. These are indicated in the figure as waves of increasing density (darkness), which sweep across the triangle whose vertices (in this example) are at $[6, 11]$, $[17, 6]$, $[2, 1]$. The 1-forms are the duals of the basis vectors for the triangle, and as such, the ith 1-form starts with a density of 0, and hits a density of exactly 1 when it rolls over the ith vertex of the triangle. It is 0 at the other two vertices. This is really just a fancy way of saying that the vertices of the triangle and its associated 1-forms are inverses of one another. That is, invert the matrix whose rows are the triangle's vertices, and you get a matrix whose columns are the dual 1-forms.

$$v_{ij} = \begin{bmatrix} 6 & 11 & 1 \\ 17 & 6 & 1 \\ 2 & 1 & 1 \end{bmatrix} \qquad \omega_{ij} = (1/130)\begin{bmatrix} -5 & 10 & -5 \\ 15 & -4 & -11 \\ -5 & -16 & 151 \end{bmatrix}$$

$$I_{ik} = \sum \omega_{ij} v_{jk} \qquad \textit{Orthogonality}$$

$$\omega_{ij} = v_{ij}^{-1} \qquad \textit{Inverse of } 3 \times 3 \textit{ matrix}$$

These 3 forms (which always sum to $\langle 0, 0, 1 \rangle$) are precisely the blending functions required for our interpolator. All one has to do is weight the ith form by the value we would like to have at the ith vertex of the triangle, and add the blending functions together:

$$z_i \qquad\qquad \textit{desired value at } i\textit{th vertex}$$

$$\Omega_i = \sum \omega_{ij} z_j \qquad \textit{form to interpolate } [x, y, 1].$$

The problem could have been reduced to two dimensions by locating the coordinate system origin at one of the triangle's vertices, but the geometrical interpretation given here would be the same in either case. The above interpolator is sometimes seen under the name of *barycentric coordinates*.

The determinant of the v matrix tells us the handedness and area of the triangle. If a 3D triangle is viewed nearly edge-on, the 2D projection becomes a sliver, and the determinant approaches 0. This would seem to cause numerical range problems for the interpolator, but if it is implemented with integer math, and its output is ignored for points outside the triangle, 2's complement overflows and underflows don't matter. However, if the determinant does reach 0, the problem has to be recast as interpolating along a line.

As a further example, consider the problem of subdividing parametric polynomial curves:

$$\mu_j = \begin{bmatrix} 1 & u & u^2 & u^3 \dots \end{bmatrix} \qquad parameter\ of\ curve,\ u = [0, 1]$$

$$M_{ij} = \qquad blending\ functions\ of\ curve$$

$$Z_{ij} = \qquad jth\ component\ of\ ith\ control\ point$$

$$p_j = \begin{bmatrix} x & y & z \end{bmatrix} \qquad output\ point$$

$$p_m = \sum \mu_i M_{ij} Z_{jm} = \sum (\mu_i T_{ij})(T_{jk}^{-1} M_{kl} Z_{lm}) = \sum \mu_i' M_{ij} Z_{jm}'$$

$$Z_{im}' = \sum (M_{ij}^{-1} T_{jk}^{-1} M_{kl}) Z_{lm} = \sum S_{il} Z_{lm}$$

For the specific case of a cubic Bézier subdivided in two, the upper half is a reparametrization of the u parameter such that

$$u' = 2u - 1 \qquad maps\ [0.5, 1] \to [0, 1]$$

The T, M, S matrices are:

$$T_{ij} = \begin{bmatrix} 1 & -1 & 1 & -1 \\ 0 & 2 & -4 & 6 \\ 0 & 0 & 4 & -12 \\ 0 & 0 & 0 & 8 \end{bmatrix} \qquad M_{ij} = \begin{bmatrix} 1 & 0 & 0 & 0 \\ -3 & 3 & 0 & 0 \\ 3 & -6 & 3 & 0 \\ -1 & 3 & -3 & 1 \end{bmatrix}$$

$$S_{ij} = (1/8) \begin{bmatrix} 1 & 3 & 3 & 1 \\ 0 & 2 & 4 & 2 \\ 0 & 0 & 4 & 4 \\ 0 & 0 & 0 & 8 \end{bmatrix}$$

537

Although this well-known result can be derived by more elegant means, the brute-force matrix approach is just as easy for any type or degree of curve, and for any linear subdivision. All the algebraic work is in the matrix inverse.

It should be emphasized that unless the M blending functions of the curve add to unity (as was the case for the triangular interpolant), the control points don't have any geometrical vector significance, since they lose invariance with the origin of the coordinate system. See Goldman (1985) for an excellent discussion of these types of issues.

Cramer's Rule and Adjoint Matrices

A very useful tool in dealing with problems such as those discussed here is a utility for inverting matrices using exact integer arithmetic. The approaches described here can then be applied directly without any tedious algebra, and used to provide insight toward a more closed-form solution (if needed).

Since computational efficiency is of no concern, the much-maligned Cramer's Rule is ideally suited for this. If done in integer arithmetic, it is free of roundoff error, is easy to code, and will always produce an adjoint, even if the matrix is singular. A sample collection of routines set up to solve the Bézier subdivision example is provided in the appendix.

See Appendix 2 for C Implementation (780)

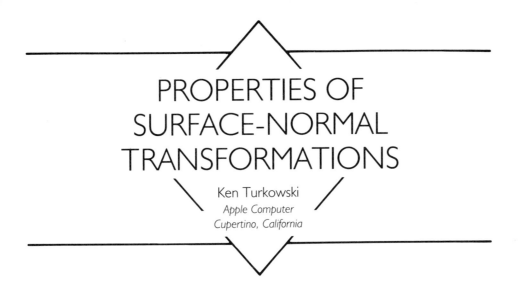

PROPERTIES OF SURFACE-NORMAL TRANSFORMATIONS

Ken Turkowski
Apple Computer
Cupertino, California

Why Is a Normal Vector Not Just a Difference between Two Points?

In Fig. 1a, we illustrate a rectangle and its normals, $\mathbf{N}_i$, that have been modeled as straight line segments. Figure 1b shows an affine transformation of the rectangle and its normals, where the endpoints of the straight line segments representing the normals have been transformed in the same way as other points that make up the rectangle. Note that these so-called normal vectors are no longer perpendicular to the surface. This occurs because we applied an *anisotropic* transformation, that is, one that is not equal in all directions.

Is this the type of behavior that we expect from normal vectors? I think not. This leads us to believe that normals behave differently under transformations than the surfaces to which they correspond. The transformations are related, though, by the requirement that the surfaces and their normals remain orthogonal. We use this property to derive the normal transformation matrix from the point transformation matrix.

Transformation of Normal Vectors under Affine Modeling Transformations

Given a planar surface, a tangent vector can be expressed as the difference between two points on the surface

$$\mathbf{T}_1 = P_1 - P_0. \tag{1}$$

539

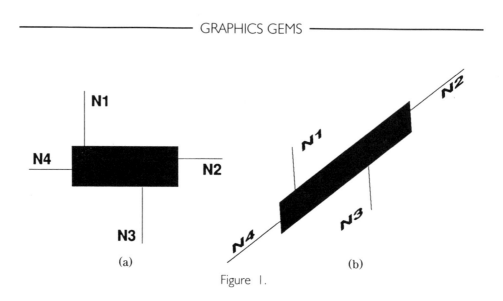

Figure 1.

The normal to the surface can be calculated from

$$\mathbf{N} = \mathbf{T}_1 \times \mathbf{T}_2, \tag{2}$$

for any two noncolinear tangent vectors $\mathbf{T}_1$ and $\mathbf{T}_2$.

If a surface is not planar, the tangents and normal can still be defined systematically. For a parametric surface (that is, x, y, and z as a function of u and v), we have

$$\mathbf{T}_u = \frac{\partial(x, y, z)}{\partial u}, \qquad \mathbf{T}_v = \frac{\partial(x, y, z)}{\partial v}, \qquad \mathbf{N} = \mathbf{T}_u \times \mathbf{T}_v, \tag{3}$$

while for an implicit surface described by $f(x, y, z) = 0$, we have

$$\mathbf{N} = \nabla f(x, y, z), \tag{4}$$

with a tangent represented by any nonzero vector such that

$$\mathbf{T} \cdot \mathbf{N} = 0. \tag{5}$$

Regardless of the type of surface, we know that the normal is orthogonal to the tangent by construction, so that

$$\mathbf{T} \cdot \mathbf{N} = \mathbf{T}\mathbf{N}^{\mathrm{T}} = 0. \tag{6}$$

When a surface is transformed by the affine modeling matrix $\mathbf{M}$,

$$\tilde{\mathbf{p}}' = \tilde{\mathbf{p}}\mathbf{M}, \tag{7}$$

where

$$\mathbf{M} = \begin{bmatrix} \mathbf{M}_{00} & \mathbf{M}_{01} & \mathbf{M}_{02} & 0 \\ \mathbf{M}_{10} & \mathbf{M}_{11} & \mathbf{M}_{12} & 0 \\ \mathbf{M}_{20} & \mathbf{M}_{21} & \mathbf{M}_{22} & 0 \\ \mathbf{M}_{30} & \mathbf{M}_{31} & \mathbf{M}_{32} & 1 \end{bmatrix}, \tag{8}$$

and $\tilde{\mathbf{p}}$ is a representative of a set of points (in homogeneous coordinates) that define the surface, then the tangent vector is transformed by the matrix $\mathbf{M}_T$:

$$\mathbf{T}' = \mathbf{T}\mathbf{M}_T, \tag{9}$$

where

$$\mathbf{M}_T = \begin{bmatrix} \mathbf{M}_{00} & \mathbf{M}_{01} & \mathbf{M}_{02} \\ \mathbf{M}_{10} & \mathbf{M}_{11} & \mathbf{M}_{12} \\ \mathbf{M}_{20} & \mathbf{M}_{21} & \mathbf{M}_{22} \end{bmatrix} \tag{10}$$

is the submatrix of $\mathbf{M}$ that excludes translations, as can be verified by applying Eq. 1, Eq. 8, and Eq. 7.

In order to have the relation between tangent and normal vectors hold, we apply Eq. 6:

$$\mathbf{T} \cdot \mathbf{N} = \mathbf{T}\mathbf{M}_T\mathbf{M}_T^{-1}\mathbf{N}^T = (\mathbf{T}\mathbf{M}_T) \cdot \left(\mathbf{N}\mathbf{M}_T^{-1T}\right) = \mathbf{T}' \cdot \mathbf{N}' = 0, \tag{11}$$

or

$$\mathbf{N}' = \mathbf{N}\mathbf{M}_N = \mathbf{N}\mathbf{M}_T^{-1T}, \tag{12}$$

which implies that the normal vector is transformed by the *transpose of the inverse* of the tangent's transformation matrix. This is a well-known theorem of tensor algebra, where $\mathbf{T}$ is called a covariant tensor of rank 1, and $\mathbf{N}$ is a contravariant tensor of rank 1.

Certain types of modeling transformations give rise to simple representations of the normal transformation matrix. Translations do not affect the normal or tangent transformations, so these two are the identity transformation. Below, we give examples of other special transformations.

Isotropic Transformations

Often, a modeling transformation consists of uniform (isotropic) scaling. This type of transformation has the following representative tangent matrix:

$$\mathbf{M}_T = \begin{bmatrix} s & 0 & 0 \\ 0 & s & 0 \\ 0 & 0 & s \end{bmatrix}, \tag{13}$$

where s is a nonzero scalar. The inverse transpose of this matrix (suitable for transforming normals) is

$$\mathbf{M}_N = \mathbf{M}_T^{-1T} = \begin{bmatrix} \dfrac{1}{s} & 0 & 0 \\ 0 & \dfrac{1}{s} & 0 \\ 0 & 0 & \dfrac{1}{s} \end{bmatrix} = \frac{1}{s^2}\mathbf{M}_T, \tag{14}$$

a scalar multiple of the tangent transformation matrix.

Orthogonal Transformations

In the case where $\mathbf{M}_T$ is an orthogonal matrix (that is, the modeling matrix $\mathbf{M}$ is composed only of rotations and translations), its inverse is simply the transpose; since the transpose of the transpose of a matrix is the original matrix itself, normals are transformed by the same matrix as the tangents, and hence,

$$\mathbf{M}_N = \mathbf{M}_T. \tag{15}$$

Composition of Transformations

If a modeling transformation is composed of a concatenation of simpler transformations, the composite normal transformation is just the concatenation of the corresponding simpler normal transformations. That is, if

$$\mathbf{M}_T = \mathbf{M}_{T1}\mathbf{M}_{T2}\ldots\mathbf{M}_{Tk}, \tag{16}$$

then

$$\mathbf{M}_N = \mathbf{M}_{N1}\mathbf{M}_{N2}\ldots\mathbf{M}_{Nk}. \tag{17}$$

This can be verified by substitution of Eqs. 16, 17, and 12 into Eq. 11.

Transformations of Metric Properties

In Euclidean space, the L_2 norm of a vector is given by

$$|\mathbf{V}|_2 = \sqrt{\mathbf{V} \cdot \mathbf{V}} = \sqrt{\mathbf{V}\mathbf{V}^T}. \tag{18}$$

Under the transformation

$$\mathbf{V} = \mathbf{W}\mathbf{A}, \tag{19}$$

we have

$$|\mathbf{W}|_2 = \sqrt{(\mathbf{W}\mathbf{A})(\mathbf{W}\mathbf{A})^T} = \sqrt{\mathbf{W}\mathbf{A}\mathbf{A}^T\mathbf{W}^T} = \sqrt{\mathbf{W}\mathbf{G}\mathbf{W}^T}, \tag{20}$$

where the matrix

$$\mathbf{G} = \mathbf{A}\mathbf{A}^T \tag{21}$$

is known as the *first fundamental matrix* (Faux and Pratt, 1979) or *metric tensor*, and represents the fact that the space is in general non-Euclidean, that is, the length of a vector in this space is not simply the square root of the sum of the squares of the components of the vector. Such a space is called a Riemannian space, and comes about because the modeling matrix **A** is not in general isotropic (scaling is not equal in all dimensions).

In a Euclidean space, $\mathbf{G} = \mathbf{1}$ (the identity matrix), and the norm becomes the familiar Euclidean one.

Applications to Computer Graphics: Back-Face Culling

Performance in a computer graphics display system can be improved if polygons facing away from the view point are removed before scan-conversion. This is facilitated with an operation involving the plane equation of the polygon in question:

$$N_x x + N_y y + N_z z - d = \mathbf{N} \cdot P - d = 0, \tag{22}$$

where

$$\mathbf{N} = \begin{bmatrix} N_x & N_y & N_z \end{bmatrix} \tag{23}$$

is the outward-facing normal to the polygon,

$$P = \begin{bmatrix} x & y & z \end{bmatrix} \tag{24}$$

is any point on the plane of the polygon, and d is the closest distance of the plane to the origin, measured in the direction of the normal—positive if the normal points toward the origin from the plane, and negative if it points away.

Back-facing polygons can be identified by

$$\mathbf{N} \cdot E - d < 0, \tag{25}$$

where E is the view point. This can also be represented as

$$\tilde{\mathbf{N}} \cdot \tilde{\mathbf{E}} < 0, \tag{26}$$

where

$$\tilde{\mathbf{N}} = \begin{bmatrix} N_x & N_y & N_z & -d \end{bmatrix} \quad \text{and} \quad \tilde{\mathbf{E}} = \begin{bmatrix} E_x & E_y & E_z & 1 \end{bmatrix} \tag{27}$$

represent the plane and view point in homogeneous coordinates.

Suppose now that the polygon is defined in a coordinate system different than the "world" coordinate system. This is commonly called modeling space, and usually has an affine transformation $\mathbf{M}$ relating it to world space as in Eq. 7 by

$$\tilde{\mathbf{P}}_w = \tilde{\mathbf{P}}_m \mathbf{M}. \tag{28}$$

If the plane equation is given in modeling space, we can transform the view point into modeling space and do the back-face culling there:

$$\tilde{\mathbf{N}} \cdot \tilde{\mathbf{E}} \mathbf{M}^{-1} < 0. \tag{29}$$

We can alternatively do the culling in world space by noting that

$$\tilde{\mathbf{N}} \cdot \tilde{\mathbf{E}} \mathbf{M}^{-1} = \tilde{\mathbf{N}} (\tilde{\mathbf{E}} \mathbf{M}^{-1})^{\mathrm{T}} = \tilde{\mathbf{N}} \mathbf{M}^{-1\mathrm{T}} \tilde{\mathbf{E}}^{\mathrm{T}} = (\tilde{\mathbf{N}} \mathbf{M}^{-1\mathrm{T}}) \cdot \tilde{\mathbf{E}}, \tag{30}$$

so we can transform the plane from modeling to world space with the inverse transpose of the full modeling matrix.

Either way, we need to invert the modeling matrix, whether we do the back-face culling in modeling or world space.

Applications to Computer Graphics: Shading

When computing shading in a simple three-dimensional graphics system, it is sometimes advantageous to transform a *directional* light vector $\mathbf{I}$ from the world space into the modeling space. Central to the Lambert shading computation, for example, is the calculation of the dot product:

$$d = \frac{\mathbf{N}_w \mathbf{I}_w^{\mathrm{T}}}{|\mathbf{N}_w||\mathbf{I}_w|}. \tag{31}$$

In a typical scan-conversion system, the light vector is normalized once when the light is placed in the scene, and doesn't need to be normalized again. The surface normal, however, is usually interpolated from the polygon's vertex normals, so it needs to be renormalized at every pixel in the polygon. (This is true if the normals are linearly interpolated in a Cartesian space. If the normals are interpolated on the surface of a sphere, using spherical coordinates or quaternions, no renormalization is required.)

Applying the normal transformation rule (Eq. 12), we get the equivalent relation in modeling space:

$$d = \frac{\mathbf{N}_w \mathbf{I}_w^{\mathrm{T}}}{|\mathbf{N}_w||\mathbf{I}_w|} = \frac{\mathbf{N}_m \mathbf{M}_{\mathrm{N}} \mathbf{I}_w^{\mathrm{T}}}{|\mathbf{N}_m \mathbf{M}_{\mathrm{N}}||\mathbf{I}_w|} = \frac{\mathbf{N}_m \cdot \left(\mathbf{I}_w \mathbf{M}_{\mathrm{N}}^{\mathrm{T}}\right)}{|\mathbf{N}_m \mathbf{M}_{\mathrm{N}}||\mathbf{I}_w|}, \tag{32}$$

which implies that we need to transform only one vector (the light vector) instead of all of the polygon's vertex normals. But wait! There's a pesky transformation in the denonominator as well. Looking back to Eq. 20, we find that

$$|\mathbf{N}_m \mathbf{M}_{\mathrm{N}}| = \sqrt{\mathbf{N}_m \mathbf{M}_{\mathrm{N}} \mathbf{M}_{\mathrm{N}}^{\mathrm{T}} \mathbf{N}_m^{\mathrm{T}}} = \sqrt{\mathbf{N}_m \mathbf{G} \mathbf{N}_m^{\mathrm{T}}}, \tag{33}$$

where $\mathbf{G}$ is the first fundamental matrix of the Riemannian modeling space.

Normalizing the surface normal at each pixel costs:

Modeling space:	one 3×3 matrix–vector multiplications and one 3-vector dot product
World space:	one 3-vector dot product

Since one matrix-vector multiplication is composed of three dot products, it costs three extra dot products per pixel to do the shading calculations in modeling space. Thus, it seems like it is always advantageous to do the shading calculations in world space.

There is another reason not to compute shading in model space: the components of the vector as normalized by Eq. 33 do not necessarily have a magnitude less than or equal to one. This is an important consideration if the shading calculations are to be done in fixed-point because the magnitudes need to be bounded. For a given unit of energy (power consumption multiplied by time), fixed-point computations are always faster than floating-point, so high-performance graphics systems especially need to perform shading in world space.

If one can be assured, however, that all scaling will be isotropic, it is possible to save a few matrix-vector multiplications per polygon by subsuming the scale factor in Eq. 14 into the transformed light vector, thereby guaranteeing a Euclidean norm and bounded vector magnitudes. However, the increased flexibility afforded by nonrestricted modeling matrices far outweighs any performance improvement afforded by shading in modeling space.

Conclusions

Normals are transformed by the inverse transpose of the modeling transformation.

Anisotropic transformations make metric computations (distance, length, norm) more complex: three extra 3-vector dot products.

It is slightly more advantageous to perform back-face culling in modeling space. The extra cost in world space is one multiplication and one 4×4 matrix transpose.

It costs three extra 3-vector dot products per pixel to perform shading computations in modeling rather than world space if anisotropic scaling is allowed. It costs $(n - 1)$ extra 3×3 matrix-vector multiplications per polygon in world space.

Unless the interface to the graphics library prevents anisotropic scaling (none currently do), the shading software should accommodate it. This is accomplished most efficiently and robustly in world space.

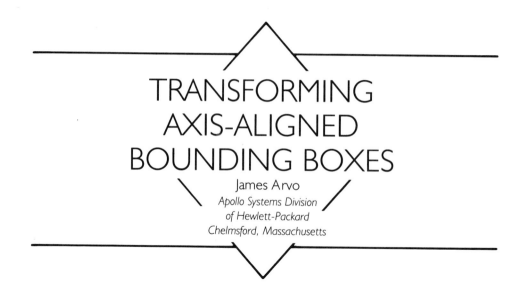

TRANSFORMING AXIS-ALIGNED BOUNDING BOXES

James Arvo
Apollo Systems Division
of Hewlett-Packard
Chelmsford, Massachusetts

A very common type of three-dimensional bounding volume is the axis-aligned box, a parallelepiped with each face perpendicular to one coordinate axis. The appeal of this shape is its simplicity. It is ubiquitous in ray tracing because it is among the simplest objects to test for ray intersection. It is also widely used to accelerate the rendering of display lists by facilitating quick visibility tests for collections of drawing primitives.

In both contexts it is frequently necessary to construct a bounding box of an object to which an affine transformation has been applied, typically by means of a 3×3 modeling matrix, M, followed by a translation, T. A simple and frequently acceptable means of constructing such a box is to transform the bounding box of the original object and enclose the resulting arbitrary parallelepiped by an axis-aligned box. This is equivalent to transforming the eight vertices of the original box and finding the extrema of the resulting coordinates. Since each point transformation requires nine multiplies and nine adds, this would entail 144 arithmetic operations and a minimum of 21 compares. This naive approach is wasteful because it ignores the information embodied in the cube's symmetry. We will show how to take advantage of this information.

We address two common methods of encoding a bounding box, B. The first is the use of three intervals, $[B_x^{min}, B_x^{max}]$, $[B_y^{min}, B_y^{max}]$, $[B_z^{min}, B_z^{max}]$. Aside from ordering, this is equivalent to storing two opposing vertices. The second method is to store the box center, $(B_x^{cent}, B_y^{cent}, B_z^{cent})$, and the box *half-diagonal*, $(B_x^{diag}, B_y^{diag}, B_z^{diag})$, which is the positive vector from the center of the box to the vertex with the three largest components. Both of these representations are amenable to very efficient transformation.

The algorithm shown in Fig. 1 transforms box A, encoded as intervals, into another axis-aligned box, B, of the same form. The algorithm is based on the following observation. To compute a component of the transformed box, say, the maximum along the ith axis, we need only consider which of the eight vertices produces the maximal product with the ith row of the matrix. There are two possibilities for each component of the potential vertex: the minimum or the maximum of the interval for that axis. By forming both products for each component and summing the largest terms, we arrive at the maximal value. The minimal value is found by summing the smaller terms. The translation component of the matrix does not influence these choices and is simply added in.

The algorithm shown in Fig. 2 transforms box A, now encoded as a center and half-diagonal vector, into another axis-aligned box, B, of the same form. In this form the new center, B^{cent}, is obtained by simply applying the affine transformation to A^{cent}. The ith component of the new half-diagonal, B_i^{diag}, is obtained by selecting the signed half-

procedure Transform_Interval_Box(M, T, A, B)
begin
    for i = 1...3 **do**

        Start with a degenerate interval at T_i to account for translation.

        $B_i^{min} \leftarrow T_i$;
        $B_i^{max} \leftarrow T_i$;

        Add in extreme values obtained by computing the products of the mins and maxes with the elements of the i'th row of M

        for j = 1...3 **do**
            $a \leftarrow M_{i,j} * A_j^{min}$;
            $b \leftarrow M_{i,j} * A_j^{max}$;
            $B_i^{min} \leftarrow B_i^{min} + \min(a, b)$;
            $B_i^{max} \leftarrow B_i^{max} + \max(a, b)$;
            endloop;
        endloop;
    end;

Figure 1. An algorithm for transforming an axis-aligned bounding box, A, stored as three intervals into another box, B, of the same form.

procedure Transform_CenterDiag_Box(M, T, A, B)
begin
    for i = 1...3 **do**

        Initialize the output variables by zeroing the new half-diagonal and setting the new center equal to the translation T.

$$B_i^{cent} \leftarrow T_i;$$
$$B_i^{diag} \leftarrow 0;$$

        Compute the i'th coordinate of the center by adding $M_{i,\,*} \cdot A^{cent}$, and the i'th coordinate of the half-diagonal by adding $|M_{i,\,*}| \cdot A^{diag}$.

        for j = 1...3 **do**
$$B_i^{cent} \leftarrow B_i^{cent} + M_{i,\,j} * A_j^{cent};$$
$$B_i^{diag} \leftarrow B_i^{diag} + |M_{i,\,j}| * A_j^{diag};$$
        endloop;
    endloop;
end;

Figure 2. An algorithm for transforming an axis-aligned bounding box, A, stored as a center and a half-diagonal into another box, B, of the same form.

diagonal of A, which results in the maximal product with the ith row of M. Here "signed" means allowing each component to be either positive or negative independently. This generates all eight half-diagonals of box A, pointing from A^{cent} to each vertex. We achieve the maximum product with the row of M by making each of its three terms positive, negating the negative elements of M. Because A^{cent} is a positive vector, this is equivalent to taking the absolute value of each element of M, as shown in Fig. 2.

The cost of both of these algorithms is only 36 arithmetic operations and 9 compares. Note that in the first algorithm both $min(a, b)$ and $max(a, b)$ can be computed with one compare, and in the second algorithm each absolute value is counted as one compare.

See Appendix 2 for C Implementation (785)

CONSTRUCTING SHAPES SUMMARY

There are many approaches to constructing geometric shapes. One may begin with a small set of geometric primitives, such as polygons and quadric surfaces, and combine them using some or all of the constructive solid geometry operators. One may create a shape using free-form deformation of a simpler initial shape. Other techniques for creating 3D objects abound in the literature and commercial products.

The Gems in this section provide some techniques useful for some of these approaches. Rather than algorithms for shape construction, these Gems provide some of the essential pieces used by such algorithms to create shapes from contours, determine surface normals, or orient reference frames. These methods may then be coupled with other procedures to form powerful shape synthesis tools.

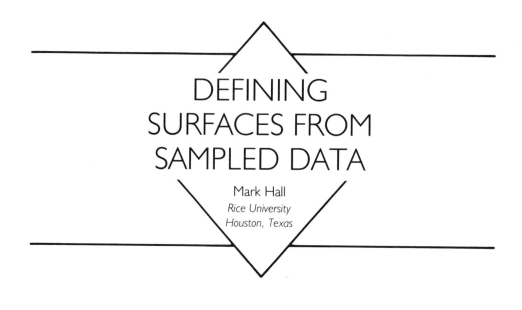

DEFINING SURFACES FROM SAMPLED DATA

Mark Hall
Rice University
Houston, Texas

The Problem

This article will describe how to create surface descriptions from regularly spaced data values on a three-dimensional grid.

Many disciplines deal with a scalar data field whose values are known on a regular three-dimensional grid as depicted in Fig. 1. Examples are seismic data, electron microscopy data, NMR and CT scan data, and barometric pressure. It is often useful to look at surfaces defined as a collection of points with a given value. The surface is called a *level set*. For example, CT scan data records material densities. Bone has a different density than the softer tissues around it. Finding the boundary between bone and soft tissue results in a surface representation of the bone. Another example of a familiar level set is a single line of barometric pressure on a weather map.

Assumptions

The original data is considered to be samples of a continuous field function over space. Having a continuous function is important because it allows inferences about the surface location. If the data values are floating point numbers, the chance that a data value will be exactly equal to the desired level is negligible. If two samples of a continuous function bracket the level set value (one is more and one is less), there must be a member of the level set on any path between the two sample points.

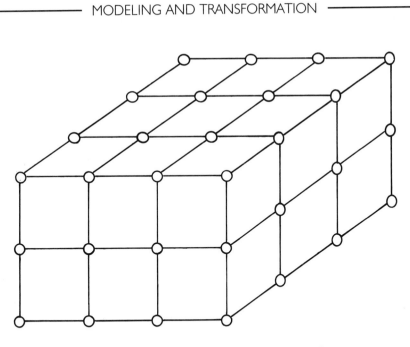

Figure 1.   Function values known at corner nodes.

A second assumption about the data values is that the distance between samples is small enough to avoid aliasing. In simple terms the samples must be spaced closely enough to detect the smallest feature in which you are interested. This is the three-dimensional equivalent of the Nyquist sampling theorem for one-dimensional signals. If the samples are too far apart, accurate reconstruction of the surfaces generally will not be possible.

Methods

Three examples of surface-finding techniques are found in Wyvill *et al.* (1986), Lorenson and Cline (1987), and Bloomenthal (1988). This article will describe similarities in the techniques.

The basic idea is to look at a "cube" for which we know the function value at each corner. We compare the corner values to the desired surface value, the level. For any cube with at least one corner value above

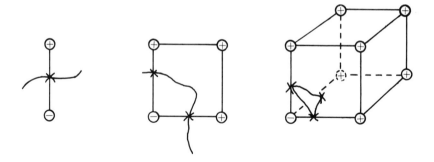

Figure 2.   Adjacent nodes define contours in one, two, and three dimensions.

and one corner value below the level, we know that the surface exists inside the cube.

Consider scaling the corner values by subtracting the desired level from each sampled value. Then the desired level set is composed of points with value zero. For a given cube edge, if the endpoints are of opposite sign, the surface must pass through the edge. The exact location of the surface vertex is determined by assuming that the field values along an edge linearly interpolate the corner values. For a cube face, if the surface intersects edges on the face, the surface must intersect the face as well. The cube face intersections can be combined to form a representation of the surface inside the cube, as shown in Fig. 2. All three methods perform a variation of these steps to define polygonal representations of a surface within each cube.

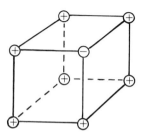

Figure 3.   An example.

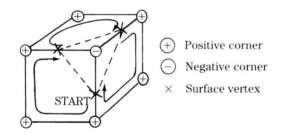

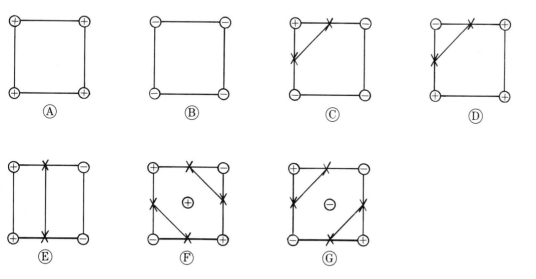

Figure 4. Bloomenthal's solution of the example.

As an example, the cube in Fig. 3 has seven positive vertices and a single negative vertex. Bloomenthal's (1988) method would be given one of the surface vertices as a starting point, as in Fig. 4. From that point, the algorithm proceeds toward the positive corner, and then clockwise on the face to the "right," as defined by the travel direction. When another surface vertex is encountered, a polygon edge is added and the process repeats until all surface vertices have been found.

Bloomenthal's method differs from the other two in that it is an algorithmic approach while the others are table-driven. It has the addi-

Figure 5. Wyvill's seven cases (from Wyvill *et al.*, 1986).

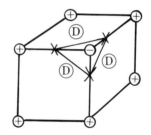

Figure 6.   Wyvill solution of the example.

tional benefit of allowing adaptive refinement of the cubic mesh around regions of high surface curvature. That is, more sample points can be used around certain areas of the surface. For cases where additional field values can be generated, this allows a better surface fit.

Wyvill *et al.*'s method (1986) is based on considering the corner values of each face. There are only seven possible face configurations, as shown in Fig. 5. Note that the difference between case *F* and case *G* is the value at the center of the face. An average of the corner values is usually sufficient for the center value. Under Wyvill's method, each visible face of the cube would be an example of case *D*, as shown in Fig. 6. The three edges create the corners of a triangle in the cube.

Lorenson and Cline's method (1987) looks at the signs of all the corners in a cube. They number the cube vertices and edges as in Fig. 7.

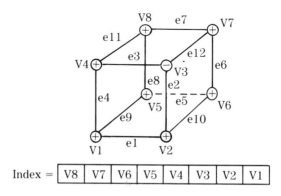

Index =	V8	V7	V6	V5	V4	V3	V2	V1

Figure 7.   Lorenson and Cline's (1987) edge and vertex numbering.

The vertex signs create an index into a look-up table. The table describes the triangles formed by each pattern of vertex signs. Our example would be described by the index 11111011 binary, or 251 decimal. Entry 251 would describe a single triangle formed by vertices on edges 2, 3, and 12.

There is a problem with the last method. It is possible for adjoining cubes to have an inconsistent interpretation of their shared face (Dürst, 1988). An example is the difference between cases F and G in Wyvill's notation. A hole in the surface can result from these different interpretations. In practice, this problem seldom arises.

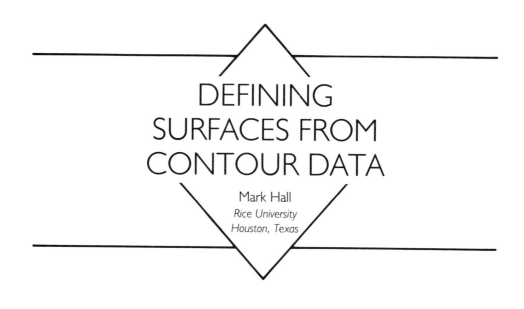

DEFINING SURFACES FROM CONTOUR DATA

Mark Hall
Rice University
Houston, Texas

Problem Statement

Given a set of two-dimensional contours of an object, create a set of polygons in three dimensions describing the object.

The problem with finding polyhedra from a selection of two-dimensional contours is that there is in general no way to join contours together correctly. When the individual contours are defined, all the connectivity information is limited to the contour plane. There is no information about the relationship between adjacent contours. At best, heuristic rules can be used to recreate the connectivity between successive contour layers. But there is no way to use the contours to recreate the correct connections in all cases.

Examples of Difficulties

The hardest problem in reconstructing a surface from planar contours concerns how to deal with *branching*. Finding polygons to connect a single contour to several closed contours on the next level is difficult. In more general terms, the contours or their enclosed regions on successive levels may not have the same topology.

Figure 1 demonstrates the branching problem. One level contains a single contour. The next contour level contains three distinct contours. It is not obvious how to joint the two contour levels with polygons. Figure 2 depicts another problem. One contour level contains a single closed

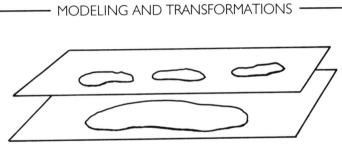

Figure 1.

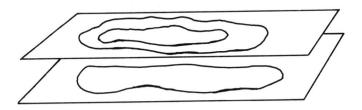

Figure 2.

curve. The adjacent contour contains several, one enclosing the other. Figure 3 shows another difficulty that can arise. One contour level contains a closed curve. The next contour level contains a single contour line. There is no obvious method of defining a surface between the two contour levels.

Methods

There are several methods that work for some situations. A relatively simple configuration occurs when each contour level contains a single

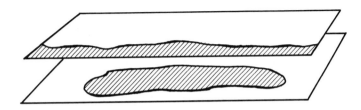

Figure 3.

top view   side view

Figure 4. Simple case—a single closed contour on each level.

closed curve. The algorithms of Fuchs *et al.* (1977) or Ganapathy and Dennehy (1982) work well for this simple case. They seek positions on the adjacent contours that are near each other to define corners of polygons spanning the contour levels, as shown in Fig. 4.

In more complicated cases, the method of Anjyo *et al.* (1987) often works, but not always. It tries to transform each pair of adjacent contour levels into a number of the simple situations solved above. The algorithm assumes that each level defines a number of closed areas called regions. For a pair of levels, the upper and lower regions are tested against each other to determine how the regions overlap. Each region has associated with it a value, which is the number of regions from the other level overlapping the region. Call this number the *count* of a region. A region with count zero is a local minimum or maximum, so the surface is defined as the enclosed region. A pair of regions that overlap only each other define the simple situation of Fig. 4. Regions that have count greater than one are involved in branching, as depicted in Fig. 5. The region L overlaps two regions $U1$ and $U2$ in the next contour level. The algorithm seeks to divide region L into regions $L1$ and $L2$ as in Fig. 6. Each pair $(L1, U1)$ and $(L2, U2)$ can then be handled easily. The crux of the problem is how to find a good place to split L. The article is vague about how to go about the splitting process.

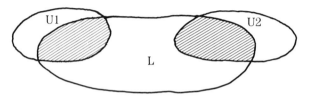

Figure 5. An example of branching.

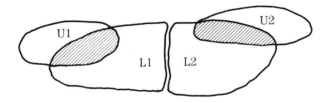

Figure 6. Branching converted to several simple cases.

For data in the form of a scalar quantity known over a three-dimensional grid, the methods developed to find polygonal approximations to implicit surfaces work well.

See also Defining Surfaces from Sampled Data (552)

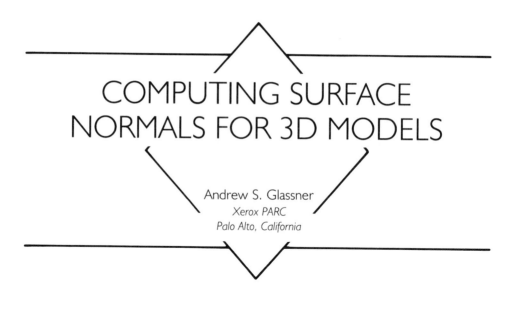

COMPUTING SURFACE NORMALS FOR 3D MODELS

Andrew S. Glassner
Xerox PARC
Palo Alto, California

Introduction

In this note we focus on polygonal approximations to smooth surfaces. Such surfaces may be made to appear smooth rather than faceted, using smooth-shading techniques such as those proposed by Gouraud (1971b) and Phong (1973). These techniques require a surface normal to be defined at each vertex in the model. This note discusses some methods for generating such normals.

Swept Contours

We begin with an important special class of shape: swept contours. Examples of these shapes are prisms and surfaces of revolution. Such shapes are defined by a planar curve (or contour), which is then translated along a path or rotated about an axis, as shown in Fig. 1. If our input consists only of the contour, how might we find a surface normal for points on the swept-out surface?

Reducing the dimension of a problem is often a good way to simplify its analysis. An easy way to eliminate one dimension for this problem is to generate normals for just the 2D contour curve, and then transform those normals with the curve as the contour is swept (see "Properties of

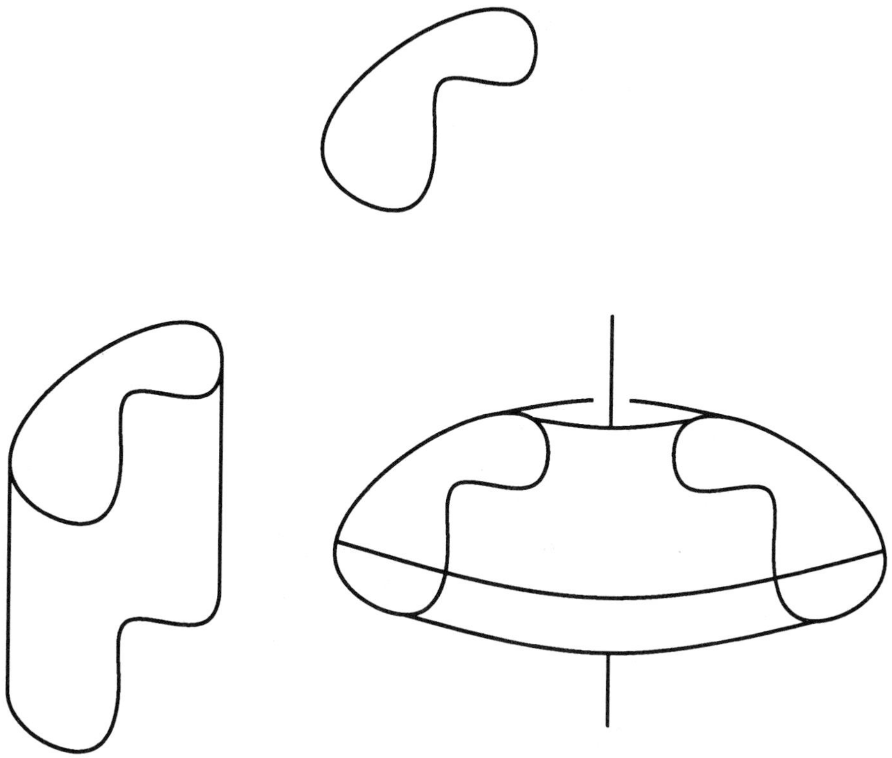

Figure 1. A contour, and the results of translation along a straight line and rotation about an axis.

Surface-Normal Transformations'' in this volume). We now need only find planar normals to the planar contour.

Figure 2 shows a contour and a distinguished point P for which we wish to find a normal; we discuss three approaches. Technique A finds the normals of the two segments adjacent to P, and averages those (Fig. 2a). Technique B finds the line joining the two vertices adjacent to P, and uses the normal of that line as the normal at P (Fig. 2b). Both of these approaches are implicitly using the Mean Value Theorem, which guarantees that somewhere between two points on a continuous curve, the curve obtains a slope parallel to the line through those points. We can take a more direct, constructive approach to this result. Recall that the derivative of a curve at a point may be computed as the limit of the slope of a line that passes on either side of that point; that is,

$$\frac{\mathrm{d}f}{\mathrm{d}x}(x_0) \approx \frac{f(x_0 + \epsilon) - f(x_0 - \epsilon)}{(x_0 + \epsilon) - (x_0 - \epsilon)}.$$

Let us directly compute $x_0 + \epsilon$ and $x_0 - \epsilon$ as those points that are some small distance ϵ away from P along the lines joining P; these are on the circle of radius ϵ centered at P. Then the slope of that line may be used as the average slope at P, as shown in Fig. 2c. The choice of ϵ may be made somewhat arbitrarily; about $1/2$ the distance along the shorter of the two edges has worked well for me. Note that this is a distance along the *nonzero* edges radiating from P; the next defined point after P may be P itself (this can happen when one wishes to define a double point for an interpolated curve).

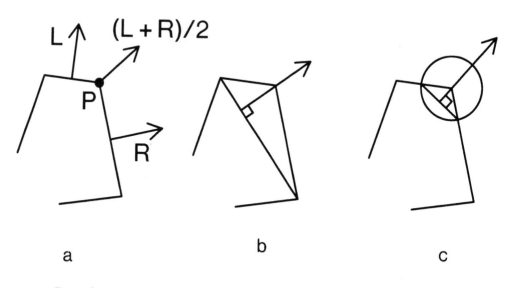

Figure 2. Different methods for computing the vertex normal on a contour.

3D Polyhedra

The more general problem of computing normals at vertices of arbitrary 3D polyhedra may also be approached in several ways. By far the most common approach is that suggested by Gouraud (1971), which simply averages the normal of each polygon that shares that vertex (see Fig. 3).

We may adapt the latter two techniques of the previous section, but there is a problem. In 2D, we found two points that together determined a unique line; this is because only two edges could leave a vertex in a profile curve. In 3D, we need exactly three points to determine a plane. If a vertex has three edges radiating from it, we may find the vertex on the far end of each edge, pass a plane through these points, and use the plane normal as the vertex normal (see Fig. 4a). The problem with this approach is that many vertices will have more or less than three edges. If a vertex has only two edges, the two neighboring vertices do not determine a unique plane; if a vertex has more than three edges, there typically will be no single plane that will pass through all the neighbor vertices. One

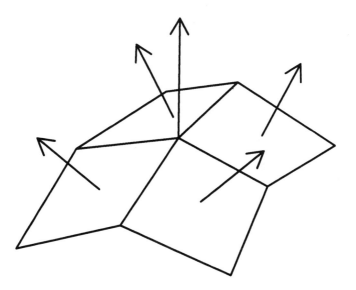

Figure 3.   Computing a vertex normal by averaging neighbor polygon normals.

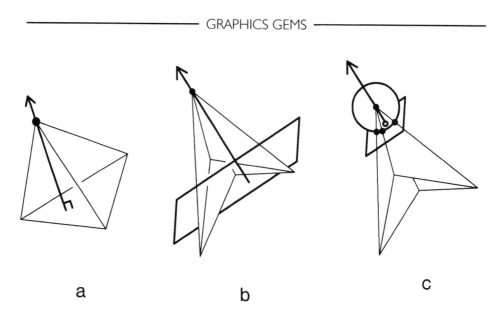

a   b   c

Figure 4. Different methods for computing the vertex normal on a polyhedron.

approach in this latter case is to find the least-squares solution to the points, resulting in the plane that most nearly interpolates the points (Fig. 4b). Techniques for finding this plane are well-known; see Lawson and Hanson (1974).

This approximate solution may also be applied to a more local approximation of the derivative, found by traveling only some distance along each edge sharing P (Fig. 4c).

In practice, the simple averaging of the normals of adjacent polygons works quite well, as long as the polygons interpolate the surface "reasonably." (It is interesting to consider just what that word means in this context.) If the polygons are a poor approximation to the surface, then I think that flattened silhouettes and badly approximated intersections with other surfaces will usually be more objectionable symptoms than poor shading. These latter effects may be alleviated with the technique of Max (1989).

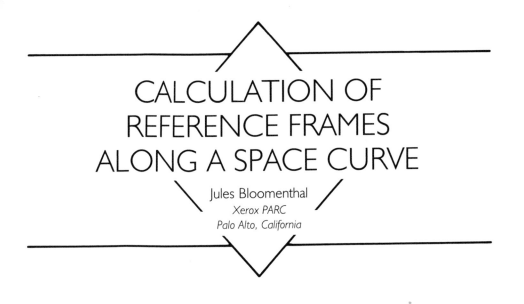

CALCULATION OF REFERENCE FRAMES ALONG A SPACE CURVE

Jules Bloomenthal
Xerox PARC
Palo Alto, California

Three-dimensional space curves can represent the path of an object or the boundary of a surface patch. They can also participate in various free-form geometric constructions. For example, the *generalized cylinder* (a cylinder with arbitrary cross-sections along a central, space curve axis) is used in computer graphics to good effect. Establishing reference frames for the cross-sections of a generalized cylinder, or for any other geometric use, is the subject of this Gem.

We restrict the central axis to the familiar three-dimensional cubic curve, which we represent by its polynomial coefficients, the three-dimensional vectors $\mathbf{A}$, $\mathbf{B}$, $\mathbf{C}$, and $\mathbf{D}$. A point P on the curve is computed according to its parametric position, t:

$$P = \mathbf{A}t^3 + \mathbf{B}t^2 + \mathbf{C}t + \mathbf{D}.$$

When constructing a polygonal generalized cylinder, each cross-section must be aligned properly with its neighbors so that the structure does not twist. This alignment is usually provided by a *reference frame*, a point and three orthogonal vectors that define position and orientation along the central axis of the cylinder (see Fig. 1).

One of the more intuitive reference frames is due to Frenet (see Fig. 2); the frame consists of a unit length tangent, $\mathbf{T}$, to the central axis; a principal normal, $\mathbf{N}$; and a binormal, $\mathbf{B}$. $\mathbf{T}$ is computed simply as the unit length velocity vector, $\mathbf{V}$; $\mathbf{V}$ is the derivative of the curve

$$\mathbf{V} = 3\mathbf{A}t^2 + 2\mathbf{B}t + \mathbf{C}.$$

567

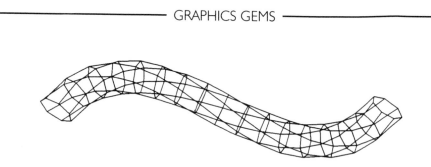

Figure 1. Polygons resulting from twisting reference frames.

The principal normal is often defined to be in the direction of curvature, $\mathbf{K} = \mathbf{V} \times \mathbf{Q} \times \mathbf{V}/|\mathbf{V}|^4$. $\mathbf{Q}$ is the acceleration of the curve, that is, the derivative of velocity, $6\mathbf{A}t + 2\mathbf{B}$. Thus,

$$\mathbf{T} = \mathbf{V}/|\mathbf{V}|, \mathbf{N} = \mathbf{K}/|\mathbf{K}|, \text{ and } \mathbf{B} = \mathbf{T} \times \mathbf{N}.$$

The Frenet frame is convenient because it can be analytically computed at arbitrary points along the curve. Unfortunately, it is undefined wherever the curvature is degenerate, such as at points of inflection or along straight sections of curve. Worse, the curvature vector can suddenly reverse direction on either side of an inflection point, inflicting a violent twist in a progression of Frenet frames.

This problem was discussed by Shani and Ballard (1984), who proposed an iterative solution to minimize torsion, that is, rotation around the tangent to a curve. This technique was used to compute reference frames for the tree branches in J. Bloomenthal (1985).

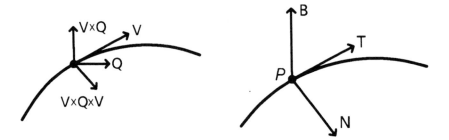

Figure 2. Curvature (left) and a Frenet frame (right).

Papers by Klok (1986) and M. Bloomenthal (1988) discuss rotation minimizing frames in some detail. They both observe that a rotation minimizing frame does not necessarily produce the intuitively desired result; in the case of a helical curve, for example, the Frenet frame appears more desirable.

The idea behind rotation minimizing frames is to define an initial reference frame at the beginning of the curve and then propagate the frame along the curve using small, local rotations. This method is immune to degeneracies in the curvature vector; it does not, unfortunately, permit analytical computation of a reference frame.

The first frame usually can be computed using curvature, as illustrated in Fig. 2. If the curvature is degenerate, then $\mathbf{N}$ can be any unit length vector perpendicular to $\mathbf{T}$. Given the initial frame, subsequent frames are generated, *in order*, by computing P and $\mathbf{T}$ at the new location on the curve. The old reference frame is then rotated such that the old $\mathbf{T}$ aligns itself with the new $\mathbf{T}$. The rotation creates a new $\mathbf{N}$ and $\mathbf{B}$, which, with the new P and $\mathbf{T}$, define a new reference frame. The axis of rotation is given by $\mathbf{T0} \times \mathbf{T1}$ and $\alpha = \cos^{-1}((\mathbf{T0} \cdot \mathbf{T1})/(|\mathbf{T0}||\mathbf{T1}|))$. In Fig. 3, $\{P0, \mathbf{T0}, \mathbf{N0}, \mathbf{B0}\}$ becomes $\{P1, \mathbf{T1}, \mathbf{N1}, \mathbf{B1}\}$.

As the curve becomes relatively straight, the difference between $\mathbf{T0}$ and $\mathbf{T1}$ becomes small. If $\mathbf{T0} = \mathbf{T1}$, their cross-product is undefined and no axis is available to perform the rotation: this is not a problem, because the amount of rotation is zero.

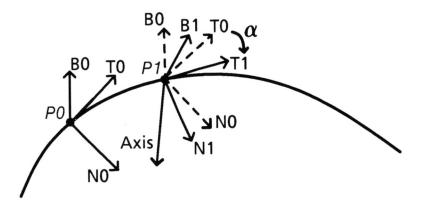

Figure 3.   Computing a reference frame from the previous frame.

Although the tangent is needed to compute the reference frame, only the point P, normal $\mathbf{N}$, and binormal $\mathbf{B}$ are needed to transform the cross-section into the plane defined by $\mathbf{N}$ and $\mathbf{B}$.

If (C_x, C_y) is on the cross-section (Fig. 4), $(P_x + C_x \mathbf{N_x} + C_y \mathbf{B_x}, P_y + C_x \mathbf{N_y} + C_y \mathbf{B_y}, P_z + C_x \mathbf{N_z} + C_y \mathbf{B_z})$ is a three-dimensional point properly positioned on the surface of the generalized cylinder. This is conveniently expressed in matrix form:

$$P_{surface} = \begin{bmatrix} C_x, C_y, 1 \end{bmatrix} [\mathbf{M}], \quad \text{where } \mathbf{M} = \begin{bmatrix} \mathbf{N_x} & \mathbf{N_y} & \mathbf{N_z} \\ \mathbf{B_x} & \mathbf{B_y} & \mathbf{B_z} \\ P_x & P_y & P_z \end{bmatrix}.$$

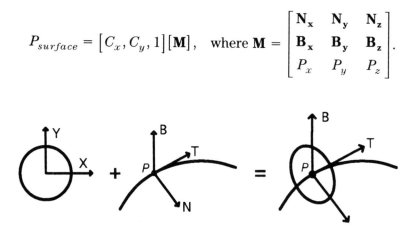

Figure 4.   Positioning and orienting a cross-section.

Note that the results depend on the distance between successive reference frames. Reference frames a small distance apart will, naturally, follow the path of the curve more closely. With large distances it is possible to miss turns of the curve; such an error is then propagated along the curve. Implementors may find it advantageous to create several intermediate reference frames in order to establish one at a desired location. Also, a cross-section at the beginning of a closed curve will not necessarily align with the cross-section at the end of the curve.

Figure 5 was created with the technique described here; note that the cross-sections change as they progress along the curve. Also, there are more cross-sections where the curvature is relatively high. The number of cross-sections can also depend on the change in cross-sections (whether radius or shape).

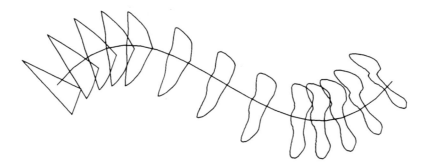

Figure 5.   A generalized cylinder with changing cross-sections.

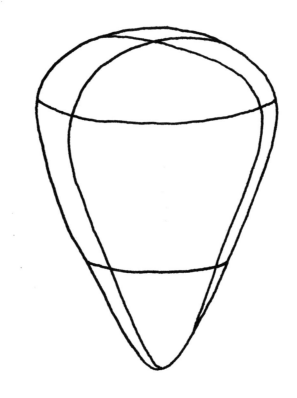

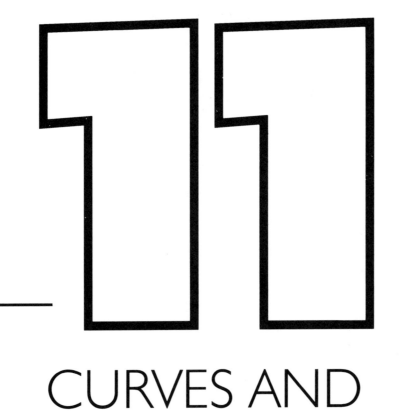

CURVES AND
SURFACES

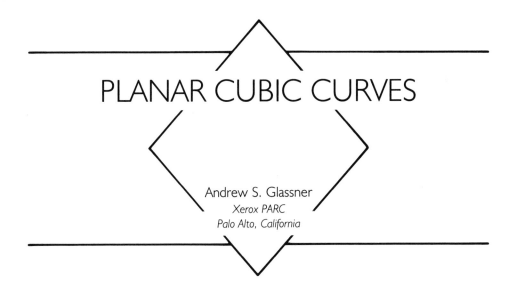

PLANAR CUBIC CURVES

Andrew S. Glassner
Xerox PARC
Palo Alto, California

I find that planar cubic curves pop up all over the place in computer graphics. They're useful for all sorts of interpolation and blending in modeling and animation. For example, a good slow-in/slow-out curve for motion control may be built from a cubic. Simple cubics are also useful tools for interactive drawing programs, and they can be used as filters to modulate some scalar parameter.

Let's focus just on 1D curves. Suppose that we write our cubic as $y = f(x)$. To define a cubic you need to provide four parameters—these can then be turned into the four coefficients of f so $f(x)$ can be evaluated at any x. The way I specify such a cubic is to provide the (x, y) coordinates and the slope of the curve at the start and the end of an interval. Suppose the interval goes from x_L (low) to x_H (high). The input consists of the points (x_L, y_L) and (x_H, y_H) and the associated slopes m_L and m_H at those points (see Fig. 1):

$$f(x_L) = y_L \qquad f(x_H) = y_H$$

$$f'(x_L) = m_L \qquad f'(x_H) = m_H,$$

where f' is the derivative of f. Calculation of the coefficients is much easier if we map the input interval $[x_L, x_H]$ to the interval $[0, 1]$. Since this will change the scaling of the axes relative to each other, we need to adjust the values of the slopes as well. We will define a new function g,

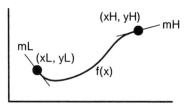

Figure 1. Specifying a cubic curve with two points and corresponding slopes.

which will mimic f over the unit interval (see Fig. 2):

$$g(0) = y_L = y_0 \qquad\qquad g(1) = y_H = y_1$$

$$g'(0) = m_L \frac{\Delta x}{\Delta y} = m_0 \qquad g'(1) = m_H \frac{\Delta x}{\Delta y} = m_1,$$

where $\Delta x = x_H - x_L$ and $\Delta y = y_H - y_L$. (We have renamed the y and m values with the subscripts 0 and 1 to emphasize that they are the values for g, not f.) Our function g and its derivative g' look like this:

$$g(x) = ax^3 + bx^2 + cx + d$$

$$g'(x) = 3ax^2 + 2bx + c$$

Examination shows that $g(0) = d$, and since by definition $g(0) = y_0$, we have $d = y_0$. Similar reasoning holds for $g'(0) = c = m_0$. We can find

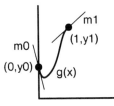

Figure 2. Remapping the curve into the unit interval [0, 1] requires scaling the slopes.

a and *b* by simultaneously solving $g(1)$ and $g'(1)$. The resulting coefficients are summarized below:

$$a = m_0 + m_1 + 2(y_0 - y_1)$$

$$b = 3(y_1 - y_0) - m_1 - 2m_0$$

$$c = m_0$$

$$d = m_1.$$

An important special case is when $y_0 = 0$ and $y_1 = 1$; this arises when one is interpolating between two values smoothly. The above coefficients then simplify to

$$a = m_0 + m_1 - 2$$

$$b = 3 - m_1 - 2m_0$$

$$c = m_0$$

$$d = y_0.$$

An even more special case is when $m_0 = m_1 = 0$. This is useful when you want first-order continuity between a series of interpolated values that are held constant between transitions (see Fig. 3). To blend from value v_0 to v_1, let α go from 0 to 1, and calculate $v_\alpha = lerp(f(\alpha), v_0, v_1)$.

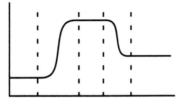

Figure 3.   Interpolating between constant segments uses endpoint derivatives of 0.

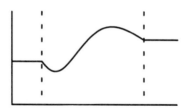

Figure 4. Clamping the input range to (x_L, x_H) is equivalent to holding the endpoint values constant outside the interval, so the curve doesn't fly off to extreme values.

The coefficients for the process are given by

$$a = -2$$

$$b = 3$$

$$c = d = 0.$$

Incidentally, another good way to do this sort of interpolation is to use a piece of the cosine curve. (Again using the interval $[0, 1]$, you could use $g(x) = 1 - ([\cos(\pi x) + 1]/2)$.)

To evaluate $f(x)$, we remap the input to the unit interval and find the value of g:

$$f(x) = g\left(\frac{x - x_L}{x_H - x_L}\right).$$

This indirect approach is much easier than solving for the cubic directly on the input range. If you evaluate f outside the interval $[x_L, x_H]$, you may find that it quickly shoots off into huge positive or negative numbers. Typically one clamps the input domain in this case (see Fig. 4):

$$f(x) = g\left(clamp\left(x_L, x_H, \frac{x - x_L}{x_H - x_L}\right)\right).$$

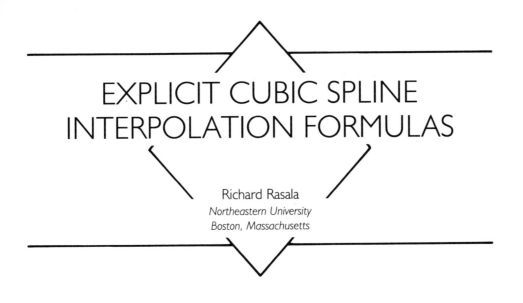

EXPLICIT CUBIC SPLINE INTERPOLATION FORMULAS

Richard Rasala
Northeastern University
Boston, Massachusetts

Introduction

This article will show how to compute the uniform cubic spline that passes through a sequence of points: $P_0, P_1, \ldots, P_i, P_{i+1}, \ldots$. For each i, we will construct additional Bézier control points Q_i and R_i such that the cubic Bézier curve defined by the four control points P_i, Q_i, R_i, P_{i+1} is the spline segment between P_i and P_{i+1}. For background information on splines and on the Bézier representation of a cubic polynomial, see Bartels *et al.* (1987) or Farin (1988).

The spline smoothness conditions (based on agreement of first and second derivatives) yield two sets of equations:

$$P_i - R_{i-1} = Q_i - P_i \tag{1}$$

$$P_i - 2R_{i-1} + Q_{i-1} = R_i - 2Q_i + P_i. \tag{2}$$

The first equations suggest that we introduce as fundamental quantities the difference vectors or "tangents":

$$\mathbf{D}_i = P_i - R_{i-1} = Q_i - P_i \tag{3}$$

Then, using simple algebra, we can eliminate the Q's and R's from Eqs. 1 and 2 to obtain a set of equations that relate the $\mathbf{D}$'s directly to the P's:

$$\mathbf{D}_{i+1} + 4\mathbf{D}_i + \mathbf{D}_{i-1} = P_{i+1} - P_{i-1} \tag{4}$$

579

The heart of the computation becomes finding expressions for the $\mathbf{D}$'s given the P's. We must break up the discussion into two separate cases: closed loops and open curves.

Closed Loops

The key to finding expressions in the closed loop case is to exploit the symmetries in the equations. We assume that there are n points $P_0 \ldots P_{n-1}$ in the loop and that the spline curve wraps around from P_{n-1} to P_0. We extend the notation so that for $0 \leq i < n$: $P_{i-n} = P_{i+n} = P_i$ and $\mathbf{D}_{i-n} = \mathbf{D}_{i+n} = \mathbf{D}_i$. The equations (4) are valid for $0 \leq i < n$. Thus, there are n equations for the n unknowns $\mathbf{D}_i$. These equations are invariant under "rotational" permutation of the indices. Thus, with proper notation, the expression for $\mathbf{D}_i$ in terms of the P_j's must involve coefficients that are independent of i. In addition, "reflection" of the indices about i will reverse the direction of each vector $\mathbf{D}_i$ while interchanging symmetric points P_j. Thus, in the expression for $\mathbf{D}_i$, the coefficients of points P_j symmetric relative to i must have opposite signs.

To exploit these remarks on symmetry, we need one additional notation. If n is odd, let $n = 2m + 1$, and, if n is even, let $n = 2m + 2$. Then, we can compute each $\mathbf{D}_i$ by an expression of the following form:

$$\mathbf{D}_i = \sum_{k=1}^{m} a_k(P_{i+k} - P_{i-k}).$$

It remains to explain how to compute the coefficients a_k. The rule depends on whether n is odd or even. If n is odd,

$$a_k = -f_{m-k}/f_m$$

where

$$f_0 = 1, \quad f_1 = -3, \quad \text{and} \quad f_j = -4f_{j-1} - f_{j-2} \quad \text{for} \quad j \geq 2.$$

If n is even,

$$a_k = -g_{m-k}/g_m$$

Table 1. The Quantities f_j and g_j.

j	0	1	2	3	4	5	6	7
f_j	1	-3	11	-41	153	-571	2131	-7953
g_j	1	-4	15	-56	209	-780	2911	-10864

Table 2. Interpolation Coefficients for Closed Loops of n Points with n Odd.

n	m	a_1	a_2	a_3	a_4	a_5	a_6	a_7
3	1	0.3333						
5	2	0.2727	-0.0909					
7	3	0.2683	-0.0732	0.0244				
9	4	0.2680	-0.0719	0.0196	-0.0065			
11	5	0.2680	-0.0718	0.0193	-0.0053	0.0018		
13	6	0.2679	-0.0718	0.0192	-0.0052	0.0014	-0.0005	
15	7	0.2679	-0.0718	0.0192	-0.0052	0.0014	-0.0004	0.0001

Table 3. Interpolation Coefficients for Closed Loops of n Points with n Even.

n	m	a_1	a_2	a_3	a_4	a_5	a_6	a_7
4	1	0.2500						
6	2	0.2677	-0.0667					
8	3	0.2679	-0.0714	0.0179				
10	4	0.2679	-0.0718	0.0191	-0.0048			
12	5	0.2679	-0.0718	0.0192	-0.0051	0.0013		
14	6	0.2679	-0.0718	0.0192	-0.0052	0.0014	-0.0003	
16	7	0.2679	-0.0718	0.0192	-0.0052	0.0014	-0.0004	0.0001

where

$$g_0 = 1, \quad g_1 = -4, \quad \text{and} \quad g_j = -4g_{j-1} - g_{j-2} \quad \text{for} \quad j \geq 2.$$

The values of the sequences f_j and g_j for small j are given in Table 1. The numerical values of the corresponding coefficients a_k are given in Tables 2 and 3. These tables can be stored in a spline computation routine and used for the special cases $3 \leq n \leq 14$. By $n = 15$, the coefficients a_k for $1 \leq k \leq 7$ have converged within four-decimal accuracy to constant values that are independent of the parity of n. In addition, the coefficient a_7 is already so small that higher coefficients can be ignored in computation of splines for graphics displays. Thus, for $n \geq 15$, $\mathbf{D}_i$ can be computed by a *fixed formula*, which uses only the seven difference vectors $(P_{i+k} - P_{i-k})$ corresponding to $1 \leq k \leq 7$.

Open Curves

The key to finding expressions in the open curve case is to reduce the computation to the closed loop case. We will define a degenerate closed loop that folds back upon itself in such a way that certain tangents in the closed loop are equal to the desired tangents in the original open curve. For convenience of notation, we assume that there are $n + 1$ points $P_0 \ldots P_n$ in the open curve. The endpoints P_0 and P_n are special and there are only $n - 1$ constraint equations corresponding to $\mathbf{D}_i$ with $0 < i < n$. Thus, the initial and final tangent vectors $\mathbf{D}_0$ and $\mathbf{D}_n$ are undetermined and may be freely chosen. In practice, these tangent vectors are often taken to be zero but we need not assume this.

It turns out that the vectors $\mathbf{D}_i$ for $0 < i < n$ can be expressed simply in terms of the points P_i for $0 < i < n$ and the points $Q_0 = P_0 + \mathbf{D}_0$ and $R_{n-1} = P_n - \mathbf{D}_n$. To capture this we introduce the following notation:

$$T_0 = P_0 + \mathbf{D}_0 \qquad T_n = P_n - \mathbf{D}_n \qquad T_i = P_i \quad \text{for} \quad 0 < i < n.$$

We extend the points $T_0 \ldots T_n$ to a degenerate closed loop of $2n$ points by "reflecting back" from T_n using the definition

$$T_{2n-i} = T_i \quad \text{for} \quad 0 < i < n.$$

By comparison of the equations for the original open curve and the new degenerate closed loop, it is easy to see that $\mathbf{D}_i$ is also the tangent at T_i in the degenerate closed loop. Thus, the formula of the preceding section

Table 4.   Interpolation Coefficients for Open Curves of $n + 1$ Points.

n	m	a_1	a_2	a_3	a_4	a_5	a_6	a_7
2	1	0.2500						
3	2	0.2677	-0.0667					
4	3	0.2679	-0.0714	0.0179				
5	4	0.2679	-0.0718	0.0191	-0.0048			
6	5	0.2679	-0.0718	0.0192	-0.0051	0.0013		
7	6	0.2679	-0.0718	0.0192	-0.0052	0.0014	-0.0003	
8	7	0.2679	-0.0718	0.0192	-0.0052	0.0014	-0.0004	0.0001

may be used. To do this, set

$$T_{-i} = T_i \quad \text{for} \quad 0 < i < n,$$

and set $m = n - 1$. Then, we can compute each $\mathbf{D}_i$ by an expression of the following form:

$$D_i = \sum_{k=1}^{m} a_k(T_{i+k} - T_{i-k}).$$

In this formula, $2m = 2n - 2$ points appear even though there are only $n + 1$ distinct T's. Thus, most points occur in this formula twice, once as original points and once as reflected points. The coefficients a_k are already familiar from the even-order closed loop case and may be tabulated as shown in Table 4. Of course, Table 4 is identical to Table 3 except for the first column. Thus, in practice, one should probably store the coefficient tables indexed by m rather than by n.

Remarks

The formulas in this article are related to formulas of Schoenberg (1973). There, Schoenberg treats only the open curve case and uses a B-spline basis rather than Bézier cubics. His formulas are more complex than ours because Bézier cubics appear to be a better choice of basis and because no advantage is taken of reducing the open curve case to the closed loop case.

The coefficients a_k in the expression for $\mathbf{D}_i$ decrease by roughly a factor of four as k increases. This decrease is so rapid that for practical purposes $\mathbf{D}_i$ is influenced by at most seven pairs of points on either side of P_i. This estimate is in fact somewhat pessimistic. If all points P_i lie within a square of size 1024, then each $\mathbf{D}_i$ is influenced by at most five pairs of points on either side of P_i. Thus, interpolating splines exhibit "semilocal" control... a change in one P_j affects only a relatively small number of nearby $\mathbf{D}_i$.

The formulas for $\mathbf{D}_i$ are quite easy to program. In addition, if one P_j is later changed, it is trivial to incrementally update each affected $\mathbf{D}_i$.

FAST SPLINE DRAWING

Julian Gomez
MacroMind, Inc.
San Francisco, California

Splines are often expressed as the matrix product

$$[\mathbf{T}] \quad [\mathbf{C}] \quad [\mathbf{G}], \tag{1}$$

where $[\mathbf{T}] = [t^3 \quad t^2 \quad t \quad 1]$, $[\mathbf{C}]$ is the coefficient matrix for the spline basis, and $[\mathbf{G}]$ is the geometry matrix of control points. For cubic splines, both $[\mathbf{C}]$ and $[\mathbf{G}]$ are 4×4 matrices. A common method of generating the spline involves first evaluating t over the range $[0, 1]$ in equal increments to generate an array of vectors; that is, the ith entry of the array would be the product $[t_i^3 \quad t_i^2 \quad t_i \quad 1] [\mathbf{C}] [\mathbf{G}]$. Generally, $t_i = i \cdot \Delta t$. The second step is handing the array to the graphics software to be drawn as a vector list through the current transformation matrix $[\mathbf{M}]$.

A faster method involves extending Eq. 1 to include $[\mathbf{M}]$ in the product

$$[\mathbf{T}] \quad [\mathbf{C}] \quad [\mathbf{G}] \quad [\mathbf{M}]. \tag{2}$$

To draw the spline it is then necessary simply to calculate $[\mathbf{T}]$ for t_i and draw that vector. In pseudo-code this would look like the following:

```
Push( );
PreMultiply(G);
PreMultiply(C);
for i ← 0; i ≤ nChords; i ← i + 1
    T[0] ← 1;
    T[1] ← t;
    T[2] ← T[1] * t;
```

585

```
        T[3] ← T[2] * t;
        if i = 0 then MoveTo(T); else DrawTo(T);
        t ← t + Δt;
        endloop;
    Pop( );
```

This technique combines the spline drawing operation with the geometrical transformation, at the cost of two matrix multiplies, for which the hardware is presumably optimized, anyway. Since all operations are done at the same time it eliminates the time, space, and code required to generate this temporary array.

See also Line Drawing Summary (98)

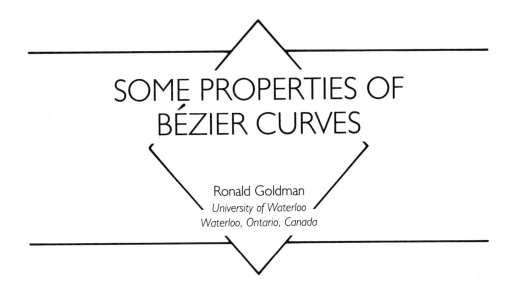

SOME PROPERTIES OF BÉZIER CURVES

Ronald Goldman
University of Waterloo
Waterloo, Ontario, Canada

Most of the properties of Bézier curves can be derived from the de Casteljau evaluation algorithm (see Fig. 1). Here we show how quickly to differentiate Bézier curves and how easily to convert between the Bézier and monomial form.

Notation

Let $B(t)$ be the Bézier curve with control points $P_0, \ldots, P_n$. Then by definition

$$B(t) = \sum_k \binom{n}{k} t^k (1 - t)^{n-k} P_k.$$

Let $M(t)$ be the monomial curve with coefficients $C_0, \ldots, C_n$. Then we define

$$M(t) = \sum_k \binom{n}{k} C_k t^k.$$

Notice that to the standard monomial form, we have added the binomial coefficient $\binom{n}{k}$. This will make all our algorithms simpler later on. To convert from this version of the monomial form to the standard monomial form is very easy; simply multiply C_k by $\binom{n}{k}$.

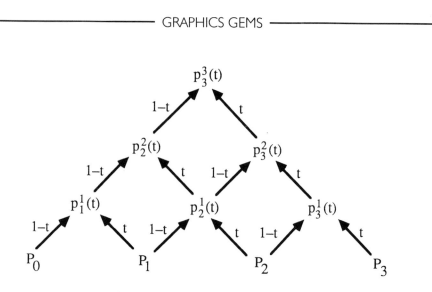

Figure 1. De Casteljau algorithm.

Remarks

We shall illustrate all of our algorithms in figures for cubic curves, but these algorithms work quite generally for polynomials of arbitrary degree n.

Much the same algorithms (evaluation, differentiation, and conversion) will work for B-spline curves if we replace the de Casteljau algorithm for Bézier curves by the de Boor algorithm for B-spline curves.

Bézier Curves

1. The de Casteljau Evaluation Algorithm for Bézier Curves (Fig. 1). Let

$$p_k^0(t) = P_k \qquad k = 0, \ldots, n$$

$$p_k^r(t) = (1 - t)p_{k-1}^{r-1}(t) + tp_k^{r-1}(t) \qquad k = r, \ldots, n.$$

Then the Bézier curve with control points $P_0, \ldots, P_n$ is given by

$$B(t) = p_n^n(t).$$

We illustrate this algorithm for cubic Bézier curves in Fig. 1. Here the control points are placed at the base of a triangular array and the recursion is illustrated by labeling the arrows with the coefficients $(1 - t)$ and t. The final result, that is, a point on the curve at parameter value t, emerges at the apex of the triangle.

2. Differentiation of Bézier Curves (Fig. 2).
   Let

$$p_k^0(t) = P_k \qquad k = 0, \ldots, n$$

$$p_k^r(t) = -p_{k-1}^{r-1}(t) + p_k^{r-1}(t) \qquad r = 1, \ldots, m$$

$$p_k^r(t) = (1 - t)p_{k-1}^{r-1}(t) + tp_k^{r-1}(t) \qquad r = m + 1, \ldots, n$$

Then

$$B^{(m)}(t) = \{n!/(n - m)!\} p_n^n(t).$$

Here the point is that to differentiate a Bézier curve, all we need to do is

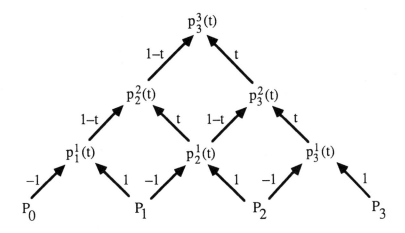

Figure 2. Differentiation algorithm.

589

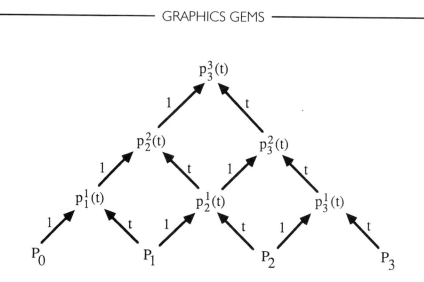

Figure 3.   Monomial evaluation algorithm.

to differentiate the de Casteljau algorithm. But to differentiate the de Casteljau algorithm m times, we need only differentiate the coefficients t and $(1 - t)$ in m levels of the algorithm and multiply the final result by $n!/(n - m)!$; we need not differentiate the terms $p_k^r(t)$ at all! In fact, though we chose to differentiate the first m levels of the algorithm, we could actually differentiate any m levels and still get the correct answer. We illustrate this differentiation algorithm by finding the first derivative of a cubic Bézier curve in Fig. 2. (Remember that the result at the apex of the triangle must be multiplied by $n = 3$.) Notice that all we did is differentiate the labels on the first levels of the de Casteljau algorithm of Fig. 1.

Curves in Monomial Form

3. Evaluation Algorithm for Curves in Monomial Form (Fig. 3). Let

$$p_k^0(t) = P_k \qquad k = 0, \dots, n$$

$$p_k^r(t) = p_{k-1}^{r-1}(t) + t p_k^{r-1}(t) \qquad k = r, \dots, n.$$

Then the monomial curve with coefficients $P_0, \ldots, P_n$ is given by

$$M(t) = p_n^n(t).$$

Notice that this algorithm is just the de Casteljau algorithm for Bézier curves with the coefficient $(1 - t)$ replaced by 1. This algorithm works because the monomials $\binom{n}{k}t^k$ are the same as the Bernstein basis functions $\binom{n}{k}t^k(1 - t)^{n-k}$, except that $(1 - t)$ is replaced by 1. This evaluation algorithm is much less efficient than evaluation by Horner's method. We illustrate it here only because our conversion algorithms are based on this evaluation technique.

4. Differentiation Algorithm for Curves in Monomial Form.
Let

$$p_k^0(t) = P_k \qquad k = 0, \ldots, n$$

$$p_k^r(t) = p_k^{r-1}(t) \qquad r = 1, \ldots, m$$

$$p_k^r(t) = p_{k-1}^{r-1}(t) + t p_k^{r-1}(t) \qquad r = m + 1, \ldots, n.$$

Then

$$M^{(m)}(t) = \{n!/(n - m)!\} p_n^n(t).$$

This differentiation algorithm mimics the differentiation algorithm for Bézier curves. That is, only the coefficients 1 and t are differentiated. This technique works because

$$t^n = t t^{n-1} \quad \text{and} \quad (t^n)' = n t^{n-1}.$$

That is, to differentiate t^n, we differentiate t and multiply the result by n.

Conversion between Bézier and Monomial Form

5. Conversion from Monomial to Bézier Form (Fig. 4).
Let the monomial coefficients be $P_0, \ldots, P_n$, and let

$$p_k^0(t) = P_k \qquad k = 0, \ldots, n$$

$$p_k^r(t) = p_{k-1}^{r-1}(t) + p_k^{r-1}(t) \qquad k = r, \ldots, n.$$

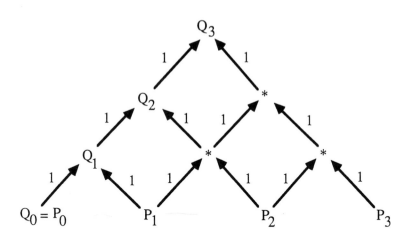

Figure 4. Conversion from monomial to Bézier form.

Then the Bézier control points $Q_0, \ldots, Q_n$ are given by

$$Q_k = p_k^k(t).$$

Notice that this algorithm is just the evaluation algorithm for monomial form with 1 substituted for t. Also the diagram is just Pascal's triangle in reverse (Fig. 4).

6. Conversion from Bézier to Monomial Form (Fig. 5).
Let the Bézier control points be $Q_0, \ldots, Q_n$, and let

$$p_k^0(t) = P_k \qquad k = 0, \ldots, n$$

$$p_k^r(t) = -p_{k-1}^{r-1}(t) + p_k^{r-1}(t) \qquad k = r, \ldots, n.$$

Then the monomial coefficients $P_0, \ldots, P_n$ are given by

$$P_k = p_k^k(t).$$

Notice that this algorithm is just the differentiation algorithm for Bézier curves where we have differentiated every level of the recursion. Also the diagram is just forward differencing (Fig. 5).

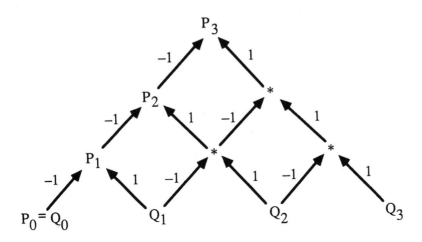

Figure 5. Conversion from Bézier to monomial form.

Observation

We can also convert from Bézier to monomial form by dividing a Bézier curve by either t^n or $(1 - t)^n$. That is, if we let $u = t/(1 - t)$, then

$$B(t)/(1 - t)^n = \sum_k \binom{n}{k} t^k (1 - t)^{n-k} P_k/(1 - t)^n = \sum_k \binom{n}{k} u^k P_k.$$

Thus, we can evaluate $B(t)/(1 - t)^n$ by applying Horner's method to $\sum_k \binom{n}{k} u^k P_k$, and we can then retrieve $B(t)$ by multiplying the result by $(1 - t)^n$. This procedure is faster than converting directly to monomial form using the algorithm described above. Again this method illustrates the close connection between the Bézier and monomial form. This technique can be used to derive properties of the Bernstein polynomials and Bézier curves. For example, that the Bernstein polynomials $\binom{n}{k} t^k (1 - t)^{n-k}$, $k = 0, \ldots, n$, form a basis and satisfy Descartes' Law of Signs follows easily from the corresponding facts about the monomial basis $\binom{n}{k} u^k$, $k = 0, \ldots, n$, by applying this conversion procedure.

See also A Bézier Curve–Based Root-Finder (408)

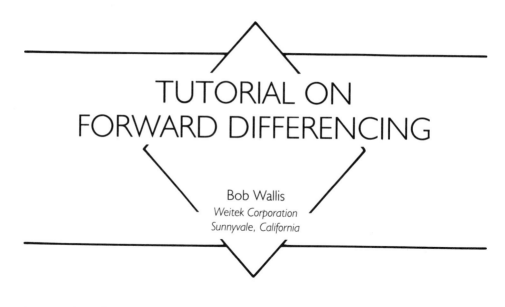

TUTORIAL ON FORWARD DIFFERENCING

Bob Wallis

Weitek Corporation
Sunnyvale, California

Introduction

A collection of mathematical tools and tricks for reasoning about forward differencing algorithms is presented.

Forward differencing provides a very fast technique for evaluating polynomials at uniformly spaced intervals. Although recursive subdivision has many advantages, it is less efficient when implemented on RISC processors because of all the load/store traffic involved in the stack operations. The basic tools for deriving forward differencing DDAs come from the field of numerical analysis. They are Newton's forward formula, Stirling's numbers, and a technique known as subtabulation.

Del Operator and the DDA

If we evaluate the cubic polynomial

$$y_k = 5 + 4k + 3k^2 + 2k^3 = \sum \alpha_i k^i \qquad (1)$$

at $k = 0, 1, 2..$ and tabulate the *forward differences*:

$$\Delta^1 y_k = y_{k+1} - y_k \qquad \text{\textit{first forward difference}}$$

$$\Delta^2 y_k = \Delta^1 y_{k+1} - \Delta^1 y_k \qquad \text{\textit{second forward difference}}$$

$$\Delta^3 y_k = \Delta^2 y_{k+1} - \Delta^2 y_k, \qquad \text{\textit{third forward difference}}$$

we obtain the table:

k	y	Δ^1	Δ^2	Δ^3
0	5	9	18	12
1	14	27	30	12
2	41	57	42	12
3	98	99	54	12
4	197	153	66	
5	350	219		
6	569			

The DDA algorithm exploits this pattern by running the above construction *backwards* to reconstruct the polynomial from its forward differences. For example, the code fragment below will reproduce the y column of the above table exactly.

```
y₀ ← 5
Δ¹y₀ ← 9
Δ²y₀ ← 18
Δ³y₀ ← 12
k ← 0
until finished do
    y_{k+1} ← y_k + Δ¹y_k
    Δ¹y_{k+1} ← Δ¹y_k + Δ²y_k
    Δ²y_{k+1} ← Δ²y_k + Δ³y₀
    k ← k + 1
endloop
```

Newton's Formula and Factorial Polynomials

There is an easy way to convert between the polynomial coefficients of Eq. (1) $(5, 4, 3, 2)$ and the associated DDA coefficients $(5, 9, 18, 12)$. It involves converting ordinary polynomials to *factorial polynomials*,

595

which are defined as follows:

$$k^{(1)} = k$$

$$k^{(2)} = k(k - 1)$$

$$k^{(3)} = k(k - 1)(k - 2)$$

$$k^{(n)} = k(k - 1)\ldots(k - n + 1)$$

Polynomials in this form permit discrete analogs of Taylor's formula, derivatives, and so on. For example, the *del* operator applied to a factorial power behaves exactly like a continuous derivative:

$$\Delta k^{(n)} = nk^{(n-1)}.$$

The counterpart of Taylor's formula is Newton's formula:

$$y_k = \sum_{j=0}^{N} \left(k^{(j)}/j!\right) \Delta^j y_0. \tag{2}$$

For example, converting the polynomial in Eq. 1 to this form yields

$$y_k = 5 + 9k + 18k(k - 1)/2 + 12k(k - 1)(k - 2)/6.$$

The mathematics of finite differences is full of elegant recurrences, and surprising inversion formulas. Since these are well-described elsewhere (Scheid, 1968; Ralston, 1965; Graham *et al.*, 1989), this tutorial will use a different approach. This is basically the brute-force matrix inverse method presented in "Forms, Vectors, and Transformations" in this volume.

We can convert from ordinary powers to k to factorial polynomials of k using Stirling's numbers of the first kind. The first six of these expressed as matrix transforms are

$$
\begin{bmatrix} 1 & k^1 & k^2 & k^3 & k^4 & k^5 \end{bmatrix}
\begin{bmatrix}
1 & 0 & 0 & 0 & 0 & 0 \\
0 & 1 & -1 & 2 & -6 & 24 \\
0 & 0 & 1 & -3 & 11 & -50 \\
0 & 0 & 0 & 1 & -6 & 35 \\
0 & 0 & 0 & 0 & 1 & -10 \\
0 & 0 & 0 & 0 & 0 & 1
\end{bmatrix}
$$

$$
= \sum k^i S_{ij} = \begin{bmatrix} 1 & k^{(1)} & k^{(2)} & k^{(3)} & k^{(4)} & k^{(5)} \end{bmatrix}.
$$

The inverse relationship uses Stirling's numbers of the second kind:

$$
\begin{bmatrix} 1 & k^{(1)} & k^{(2)} & k^{(3)} & k^{(4)} & k^{(5)} \end{bmatrix}
\begin{bmatrix}
1 & 0 & 0 & 0 & 0 & 0 \\
0 & 1 & 1 & 1 & 1 & 1 \\
0 & 0 & 1 & 3 & 7 & 15 \\
0 & 0 & 0 & 1 & 6 & 25 \\
0 & 0 & 0 & 0 & 1 & 10 \\
0 & 0 & 0 & 0 & 0 & 1
\end{bmatrix}
$$

$$
= \sum k^{(i)} S_{ij}^{-1} = \begin{bmatrix} 1 & k^1 & k^2 & k^3 & k^4 & k^5 \end{bmatrix}.
$$

If we use this to convert from a polynomial in power series format, such as Eq. (1), to one in the form of Newton's formula (Eq. (2)), we can just read off the DDA coefficients we want. Introducing a diagonal factorial matrix F, whose ii entry is $i!$, we can derive the desired result by starting with a power series, and introducing matched pairs of transforms that keep the relationship invariant. However, one must be very careful which indices are summed over rows, and which are summed over columns:

$$
y_k = \sum \alpha_m k^m = \sum k^m I_{mn} \alpha_n = \sum k^m \left(S_{mn} F_{no}^{-1} \right) \left(F_{op} S_{pq}^{-1} \alpha_q \right)
$$

$$
y_k = \sum (k^{(i)}/i!)(C_{ij}\alpha_j).
$$

Comparing this to Ralston (1965), we have

$$\Delta^i y_0 = \sum C_{ij}\alpha_j = \sum \left(F_{ij}S_{jk}^{-1}\right)\alpha_k.$$

The resulting C matrix, up to $N = 5$, is

$$\begin{bmatrix} 1 & 0 & 0 & 0 & 0 & 0 \\ 0 & 1 & 1 & 1 & 1 & 1 \\ 0 & 0 & 2 & 6 & 14 & 30 \\ 0 & 0 & 0 & 6 & 36 & 150 \\ 0 & 0 & 0 & 0 & 24 & 240 \\ 0 & 0 & 0 & 0 & 0 & 120 \end{bmatrix} \begin{bmatrix} 1 \\ \alpha^1 \\ \alpha^2 \\ \alpha^3 \\ \alpha^4 \\ \alpha^5 \end{bmatrix} = \begin{bmatrix} 1 \\ \Delta^1 y_0 \\ \Delta^2 y_0 \\ \Delta^3 y_0 \\ \Delta^4 y_0 \\ \Delta^5 y_0 \end{bmatrix}.$$

Using this, we can easily convert the $(5, 4, 3, 2)$ 1-form (see "Forms, Vectors, and Transformations" in this volume) of power series coefficients in Eq. 1 to the $(5, 9, 18, 12)$ 1-form of DDA coefficients. The same method can be used to derive conversions between any pair of formats that are related by linear weights of their coefficients.

In the case of Bézier format, the *del* operator becomes involved in a rather amazing fashion. It turns out that if we convert a curve from Bézier format to power series format, the coefficients end up being related to the forward differences of the control points (vectors in bold type):

$$\boldsymbol{Z}_j = \qquad\qquad\qquad\qquad j\text{th } control\ point$$

$$\boldsymbol{f}(t) = \sum_{j=0}^{N} \binom{N}{j} t^j (1 - t)^{N-j} \boldsymbol{Z}_j \qquad Bézier\ form$$

$$= \sum_{j=0}^{N} t^j \binom{N}{j} \Delta^j \boldsymbol{Z}_0 \qquad\qquad power\ series\ form$$

so it is an easy manner to convert Bézier to power series, and then apply the C matrix.

598

Determining the Step Size

If we have a polynomial in a *continuous* variable $t = [0, 1]$, then to use the DDA method, we have to decide how many samples we want in the interval. If this is N, our discrete variable becomes

$$h = 1/N \qquad N \text{ steps from } 0 \to 1$$

$$k = t/h = Nt. \qquad continuous \to discrete$$

An example of the effect of decreasing step sizes on the rendering of an outline font is shown in Fig. 1.

A simple geometrical argument can be used to derive a relationship between step size and error. It is based on the assumption that the curve can be treated as if it were *locally circular* (see Fig. 2).

A reasonable strategy for selecting h is to pick a value such that the maximum error in pixel space between the exact curve and its piecewise linear approximation is less than some tolerance:

$$R^2 = (ds/2)^2 + (R - e)^2. \qquad Pythagorean\ theorem$$

Ignoring e^2, this reduces to

$$e = ds^2/(8R). \qquad error\ from\ finite\ step\ size \qquad (3)$$

Figure 1.

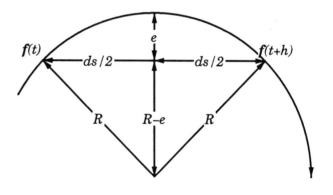

Figure 2.

Denoting vector quantities in bold type,

$$\boldsymbol{v} = d\boldsymbol{f}/dt \qquad \textit{first derivative = velocity of curve}$$

$$ds/dt = |\boldsymbol{v}| \qquad \textit{change in arc length with respect to } t \qquad (4)$$

$$\boldsymbol{a} = d\boldsymbol{v}/dt \qquad \textit{second derivative = acceleration of curve}$$

$$1/R = |\boldsymbol{v}|^3/|\boldsymbol{v} \times \boldsymbol{a}| \qquad \textit{from differential geometry} \qquad (5)$$

$$dt = h \qquad \textit{time step same as step size} \qquad (6)$$

$$e = h^2|\boldsymbol{v} \times \boldsymbol{a}|/(8|\boldsymbol{v}|) \qquad \textit{combining } (3),(4),(5),(6) \qquad (7)$$

Equation 7 gives us a fairly tight error bound as long as the "locally circular" assumption holds. However, when curves have cusps the velocity goes to zero, and Eq. 5 becomes meaningless. A more conservative bound that works with cusps can be derived as

$$|\boldsymbol{v} \times \boldsymbol{a}| \le |\boldsymbol{v}|\,|\boldsymbol{a}| \qquad (8)$$

$$e = h^2|\boldsymbol{a}|/8. \qquad \textit{combining } (7),(8) \qquad (9)$$

Equation 9 turns out to be a standard result from numerical analysis (Scheid, 1986; Ralston, 1965). Applying this to the case of a cubic Bézier curve is easy:

$$Z_j = \qquad\qquad\qquad\qquad j\text{th } control\ point$$

$$a(t) = 6\big[(1 - t)\,\Delta^2 Z_0 + t\,\Delta^2 Z_1\big] \qquad acceleration$$

Since the magnitude of a is a linear function of t, the max must occur at either $t = 0$ or $t = 1$.

$$e = (3/4)h^2\,max\big(|\Delta^2 Z_0|, |\Delta^2 Z_1|\big) \qquad for\ a\ cubic\ Bézier \qquad (10)$$

Subdividing Forward Differences

Prior to the publication of Lien *et al.* (1987), it was not widely recognized that you could change the step size without completely recalculating the forward differences, thus giving DDA algorithms some of the advantages of recursive subdivision. The technique has actually been known for a long time in the field of numerical analysis (Scheid, 1986; Ralston, 1965), but was disguised under the name of *subtabulation*.

In Lien *et al.*, the step size is halved until the pixel space increment is less than a pixel. This section will describe a slightly different approach, in which the step size is reduced until the error of Eq. 9 is less than some tolerance, yielding a piecewise linear approximation to the curve. The advantage of combining the step estimator with the calculation of the DDA coefficients is that the same quantities are involved in both computations.

The subdivision formulae may be derived using the same matrix technique as used in section 4:

$$y_k = \sum (k^{(j)}/j!)\,\Delta^j y_0 = \sum k^l S_{lm} F_{mn}^{-1}\,\Delta^n y_0.$$

If we want to transform the step size, this is the same as transforming the k parameter:

$$k'^j = \sum k^i T_{ij}.$$

Some simple manipulations give us a transformation matrix that converts DDA coefficients from one step size to another:

$$\Delta_t^i = \sum C_{ij} \Delta^j = \sum \left(F_{mn} S_{no}^{-1} T_{op} S_{pq} F_{qr}^{-1} \right) \Delta^r.$$

For the case of a cubic, and a halving of h, the relevant matrices are

$$S_{ij} = \begin{bmatrix} 1 & 0 & 0 & 0 \\ 0 & 1 & -1 & 2 \\ 0 & 0 & 1 & -3 \\ 0 & 0 & 0 & 1 \end{bmatrix} \qquad F_{ij} = \begin{bmatrix} 1 & 0 & 0 & 0 \\ 0 & 1 & 0 & 0 \\ 0 & 0 & 2 & 0 \\ 0 & 0 & 0 & 6 \end{bmatrix}$$

$$T_{ij} = \begin{bmatrix} 1 & 0 & 0 & 0 \\ 0 & 2 & 0 & 0 \\ 0 & 0 & 4 & 0 \\ 0 & 0 & 0 & 8 \end{bmatrix} \qquad C_{ij} = (1/16) \begin{bmatrix} 16 & 0 & 0 & 0 \\ 0 & 8 & -2 & 1 \\ 0 & 0 & 4 & -2 \\ 0 & 0 & 0 & 2 \end{bmatrix}.$$

For a quintic polynomial, the result is

$$C_{ij}(1/256) \begin{bmatrix} 256 & 0 & 0 & 0 & 0 & 0 \\ 0 & 128 & -32 & 16 & -10 & 7 \\ 0 & 0 & 64 & -32 & 20 & -14 \\ 0 & 0 & 0 & 32 & -24 & 18 \\ 0 & 0 & 0 & 0 & 16 & -16 \\ 0 & 0 & 0 & 0 & 0 & 8 \end{bmatrix}.$$

For the cubic case, the final result is very simple, and can be expressed in terms of *del* operators as

$$\Delta_{1/2}^3 = \Delta^3/8$$

$$\Delta_{1/2}^2 = \Delta^2/4 - \Delta_{1/2}^3$$

$$\Delta_{1/2}^1 = \left(\Delta^1 - \Delta_{1/2}^2 \right)/2. \tag{11}$$

It should be pointed out that there exist much more elegant ways to derive the above relationships. They involve the calculus of the *del* operator, and result in very nice closed form solutions. See Scheid (1968) and Ralston (1965). The advantage of the matrix approach is that it puts all the algebra into the matrix inverse routine, and provides a uniform tool to attack a wide variety of problems.

Implementation for Bézier Cubics

Once the forward differences of the Bézier control points have been calculated, the conversion from Bézier format to DDA format, for $h = 1$, is easy:

$$\Delta^1 f_0 = 3\left(\Delta^1 Z_0 + \Delta^2 Z_0\right) + \Delta^3 Z_0 \qquad \textit{first DDA forward diff.}$$

$$\Delta^2 f_0 = 6\left(\Delta^2 Z_0 + \Delta^3 Z_0\right) \qquad \textit{second DDA forward diff.}$$

$$\Delta^3 f_0 = 6\,\Delta^3 Z_0. \qquad \textit{third DDA forward diff.}$$

Equation 10 may then be used to calculate the error for this (unity) step size. The recursion of Eq. 11 can then be applied repeatedly, each time reducing the error by a factor of $(1/4)$. When this is below the error tolerance (or we hit a min step size), we can drop directly to the inner DDA loop.

A major concern with any DDA scheme is the control of accumulated roundoff error (Chang *et al.*, 1989). The binary subdivision of Eq. 11 is very attractive in this regard because all the divides are by powers of two, so the resultant coefficients can be represented without error (given a binary fraction with enough bits to the right of the decimal point).

If coded in assembler on a 32-bit CPU with lots of registers, the most straightforward technique is to use 64-bit double precision adds for the DDA, putting the binary decimal point between the most and least significant words. This results in a very fast inner loop, capable of producing up to 1024 points per curve, with no roundoff.

Another alternative is to use three linked Bresenham-type DDAs, maintaining separate fractional parts. This has the advantage that it will work for nonbinary subdivisions, but results in a much bigger inner loop.

For a small number of steps, roundoff is less of a concern, and a single precision DDA is usually sufficient.

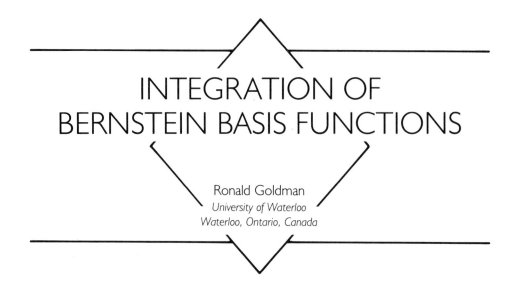

INTEGRATION OF
BERNSTEIN BASIS FUNCTIONS

Ronald Goldman
University of Waterloo
Waterloo, Ontario, Canada

We can use the de Casteljau algorithm to integrate the Bernstein basis functions

$$B_k^n(t) = \binom{n}{k} t^k (1 - t)^{n-k}.$$

If we read the de Casteljau algorithm from the apex down, the functions at the nodes are the Bernstein basis functions, where the degree n functions reside in order on the nth level of the diagram. We illustrate this principle in Fig. 1 for $n = 3$.

This diagram is just a consequence of the well-known recurrence

$$B_k^n(t) = (1 - t)B_k^{n-1}(t) + tB_{k-1}^{n-1}(t).$$

In fact Fig. 1 is simply an illustration of this recurrence.

Now suppose that we wish to integrate some basis function $B_k^n(t)$. The procedure is simply to extend the diagram down one more level from $B_k^n(t)$ to where $B_k^{n+1}(t)$ and $B_{k+1}^{n+1}(t)$ would ordinarily reside. Then through the two new nodes draw lines parallel to the two new opposing edges and clip the diagram below these edges. Summing the leaf nodes either to the upper left or the upper right and dividing by $(n + 1)$ yields the desired integral.

We illustrate this algorithm in Figs. 2 and 3 for the basis function $B_1^3(t)$. Referring to Fig. 3, we have

$$\int B_1^3(t)\,\mathrm{dt} = \{\alpha_0^3(t) + \alpha_1^4(t)\}/4,$$

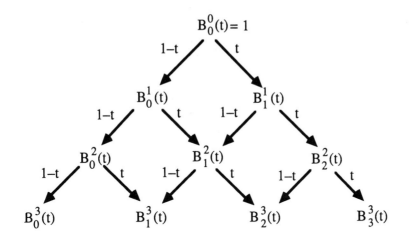

Figure 1. Bernstein basis functions.

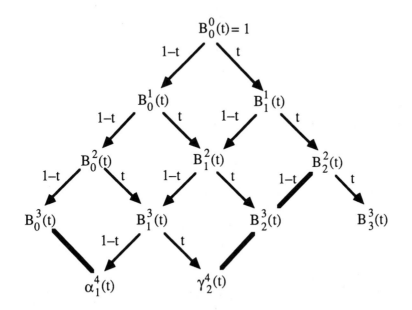

Figure 2. Integration, step 1: Extend the diagram and draw the clipping lines.

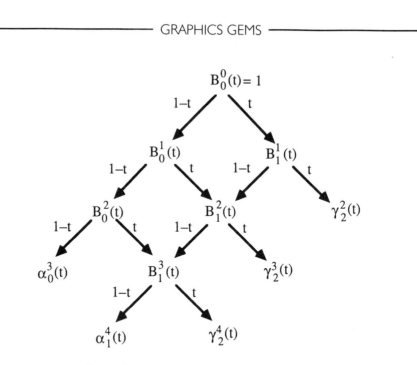

Figure 3.   Integration, step 2: Clip the diagram.

and

$$\int B_1^3(t)\,\mathrm{dt} = \{\gamma_2^2(t) + \gamma_2^3(t) + \gamma_2^4(t)\}/4.$$

Notice, therefore, that

$$\{\alpha_0^3(t) + \alpha_1^4(t)\} - \{\gamma_2^2(t) + \gamma_2^3(t) + \gamma_2^4(t)\} = \text{constant}.$$

Much the same technique works for integrating the B-splines.

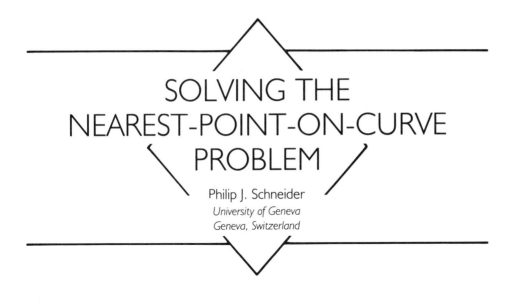

SOLVING THE NEAREST-POINT-ON-CURVE PROBLEM

Philip J. Schneider
University of Geneva
Geneva, Switzerland

Introduction

Consider the following scenario: you have an interactive curve-drawing system that maintains a piecewise Bézier representation of the curves appearing on the screen. The user can manipulate the curves by selecting control points and moving them about, by adding or deleting curves, and so on. However, the user has no direct "handle" onto the curve itself—he or she cannot select points on the curve directly. The ability to manipulate curves freely would allow the user to select points on the curve at which to further subdivide the curve, interactively trace along the curve with a mouse, find the point on a curve closest to some other point on the screen (for example, a vertex of a triangle), find the distance from such a point to the curve, and so on. Unfortunately, the "space" to which the user has access is the world of Cartesian coordinates (window coordinates, or some real two-dimensional space mapped onto the screen), while the "space" of the Bézier curve is that of the parametric domain of the curve. This Gem presents an algorithm for solving this problem.

This algorithm was developed in the context of an interactive two-dimensional curve-drawing system (Schneider, 1988), which maintained a piecewise cubic Bézier representation of free-form curves; these were generated by fitting the parametric curves to digitized points input (that is, "sketched in") by the user. (See "An Algorithm For Automatically Fitting Digitized Curves" in this volume.)

Problem Statement

The basic problem can be stated in this manner: given a parametric curve Q and a point P, both in the plane, find the point on the curve closest to P (that is, find the parameter value t such that the distance from P to $Q(t)$ is a minimum). Our approach begins with the geometric observation that the line segment (whose length we wish to minimize) from P to $Q(t)$ is perpendicular to the tangent of the curve at $Q(t)$, as shown in Fig. 1. The equation we wish to solve for t is

$$[Q(t) - P] \cdot Q'(t) = 0. \tag{1}$$

In our particular case, curve Q is a cubic Bernstein–Bézier polynomial,

$$Q(t) = \sum_{i=0}^{n} V_i B_i^n(t), \qquad t \in [0, 1],$$

where the V_i are the control points. The Bernstein polynomials of degree n are defined by

$$B_i^n(t) = \binom{n}{i} t^i (1 - t)^{n-i}, \qquad i = 0, \ldots, n,$$

where $\binom{n}{i}$ is the binomial coefficient $n!/(n-i)!i!$. The tangent curve Q'

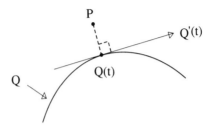

Figure 1.   Distance from an arbitrary point to a parametric curve.

for the above curve Q can also be represented in Bernstein–Bézier form:

$$Q'(t) = n \sum_{i=0}^{n-1} (V_{i+1} - V_i) B_i^{n-1}(t).$$

Conversion of Bézier Form

We are dealing with cubics, so polynomial Q is of degree three, and Q' is of degree two. $Q - P$ is also of degree three, so the polynomial described by Eq. 1 is (in general) of degree five. Thus, we can restate our problem as one of finding the roots of this fifth-degree polynomial. There is no closed-form solution for solving this problem, so we must turn to some other technique to find the roots (see "A Bézier Curve–Based Root-Finder" in this volume). The basic technique is first to convert the equation to Bernstein–Bézier form, and then to use a recursive algorithm to find the roots. The remainder of this Gem describes the conversion of this fifth-degree equation to Bernstein–Bézier form, to which one can then apply the previously mentioned root-finder.

We can rewrite Eq. 1 as a single polynomial of degree five. Let

$$Q_1(t) = Q(t) - P \tag{2}$$

$$Q_2(t) = Q'(t). \tag{3}$$

Then, Eq. (1) can be written

$$Q_1(t) \cdot Q_2(t) = 0. \tag{4}$$

Expanding Eq. (2),

$$Q_1(t) = Q(t) - P$$

$$= \sum_{i=0}^{n} V_i B_i^n(t) - P$$

$$= \sum_{i=0}^{n} c_i B_i^n(t),$$

where $c_i = V_i - P$.

Expanding Eq. (3),

$$Q_2(t) = n \sum_{i=0}^{n-1} (V_{i+1} - V_i) B_i^{n-1}$$

$$= \sum_{i=0}^{n-1} d_i B_i^{n-1},$$

where $d_i = n(V_{i+1} - V_i)$. Then, Eq. (4) can be written as

$$0 = \sum_{i=0}^{n} c_i B_i^n(t) \cdot \sum_{j=0}^{n-1} d_j B_j^{n-1}(t)$$

$$= \sum_{i=0}^{n} \sum_{j=0}^{n-1} c_i \cdot d_j B_i^n(t) B_j^{n-1}(t)$$

$$= \sum_{i=0}^{n} \sum_{j=0}^{n-1} c_i \cdot d_j \binom{n}{i}(1-t)^{n-i}t^i \binom{n-1}{j}(1-t)^{n-1-j}t^j$$

$$= \sum_{i=0}^{n} \sum_{j=0}^{n-1} c_i \cdot d_j \binom{n}{i}\binom{n-1}{j}(1-t)^{(2n-1)-(i+j)}t^{i+j}$$

$$= \sum_{i=0}^{n} \sum_{j=0}^{n-1} c_i \cdot d_j \frac{\binom{n}{i}\binom{n-i}{j}}{\binom{2n-1}{i+j}} B_{i+j}^{2n-1}(t)$$

$$= \sum_{i=0}^{n} \sum_{j=0}^{n-1} c_i \cdot d_j z_{i,j} B_{i+j}^{2n-1}(t)$$

$$= \sum_{i=0}^{n} \sum_{j=0}^{n-1} w_{i,j} B_{i+j}^{2n-1}(t),$$

where $z_{i,j} = \binom{n}{i}\binom{n-i}{j} / \binom{2n-1}{i+j}$, and $w_{i,j} = c_i \cdot d_j z_{i,j}$.

Note that the $w_{i,j}$ are not two-dimensional coordinates—they are real numbers, and thus represent only one component of the Bézier control points for this function (the y component, if you will). The other component, x, for each control point $w_{i,j}$ is $i + j/n + (n - 1)$; this is explained further in "A Bézier Curve–Based Root-Finder." At this point, we have the equation in the desired Bernstein–Bézier form, and can apply the method found in the Gem mentioned earlier.

C code implementing the conversion described here, and the root-finding algorithm associated with it, may be found in the appendix in the file "*point_on_curve.c*." For simplicity, this sample implementation is for cubic curves only—generalization should be relatively straightforward. The example case specifies a single cubic Bézier curve and an arbitrary point, and computes the point on the curve nearest that arbitrary point. The routine *ConvertToBezierForm* creates the fifth-degree Bézier equation, which is passed to the routine *FindRoots*. *FindRoots* will then return from zero to three roots, which we evaluate to find the points on the curve. By comparing the distances from those points on the curve to the arbitrary point, and also considering the endpoints of the curve, we can find our desired result—the point on the curve closest to the arbitrary point, and also its parameter value.

See also A Fast 2D Point-on-Line Test (49)

See Appendix 2 for C Implementation (787)

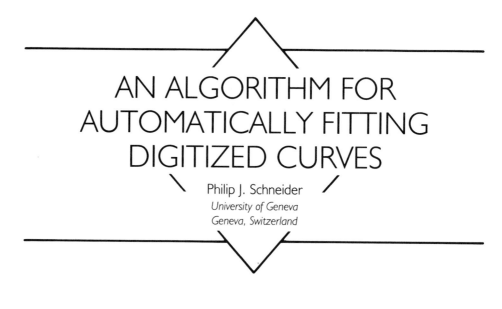

AN ALGORITHM FOR AUTOMATICALLY FITTING DIGITIZED CURVES

Philip J. Schneider
University of Geneva
Geneva, Switzerland

Introduction

A new curve-fitting method is introduced. This adaptive algorithm automatically (that is, with no user intervention) fits a piecewise cubic Bézier curve to a digitized curve; this has a variety of uses, from drawing programs to creating outline fonts from bitmap fonts. Of particular interest is the fact that it fits geometrically continuous (G^1) curves, rather than parametrically continuous (C^1) curves, as do most previous approaches.

Curve fitting has been the subject of a fair amount of attention, even before computer graphics came along. The term *spline* comes from drafting jargon: to draw a smooth curve passing through a set of points, the draftsman would place a weight (also a term that has survived into CAGD methods) on each point, and then place a flexible wooden strip (the spline) onto the weights. The spline had slots running lengthwise, which fitted onto the top of the weights, allowing the spline to assume a "natural" and smooth shape. Pavlidis (1983) notes that theories of mechanical elasticity can be used to show that such spline curves exhibit C^2 continuity, and are equivalent to piecewise cubic polynomial curves. Because of this, piecewise polynomial curves are referred to as *splines*, and such curves have been used to mathematically interpolate discrete data sets. Readers interested in interpolation should consult any numerical analysis text, such as Conte and deBoor (1972), or Bartels *et al.* (1987).

This article discusses a method for approximation of digitized curves with piecewise cubic Bézier segments. Such an algorithm is useful in interactive drawing systems, converting bitmapped or otherwise digitized figures (such as fonts) to a parametric curve representation, and the like.

Many techniques have been brought to bear on the problem of this type of curve-fitting: splines (Reinsch, 1967; Grossman, 1970); purely geometric methods (Flegal cited in Reeves, 1981); B-splines (Yamaguchi, 1978; Wu *et al.*, 1977; Giloi, 1978; Lozover and Preiss, 1981; Yang *et al.*, 1986; Dierckx, 1982; Vercken *et al.*, 1987; Ichida *et al.*, 1977; Chong, 1980); hermite polynomials (Plass and Stone, 1983); hyperbolic splines in tension (Kozak, 1986; Schweikert, 1966; Cline, 1974); cubic splines in tension (Cline, 1974; Dube, 1987; Schweikert, 1966); conic sections (Bookstein, 1979); conic splines (Pavlidis, 1983); conic arcs and straight-line segments (Albano, 1974); and circular arcs and straight-line segments (Piegl, 1986). A more detailed description of these solutions may be found in Schneider (1988) and Reeves (1981).

However, each of these approaches has some shortcoming—some of the earlier methods apply only to scalar functions, many require a great deal of intervention by the user, some produce representations that are inappropriate for free-form curves (for example, circular arcs and straight-line segments), and all of the parametric polynomial methods but Plass and Stone's (1983) produce curves that are parametrically continuous, but they note of their method that "...it sometimes does not converge at all."

Bézier Curves

The curve representation that is used in this algorithm in approximating the digitized curve is the Bézier curve. Accordingly, we briefly review the basics: the curves known as Bézier curves were developed (independently) in 1959 by P. de Casteljau and in 1962 by P. Bézier. Numerous references exist; see Boehm *et al.*, (1984) and Davis (1975). A Bézier curve of degree n is defined in terms of Bernstein polynomials:

$$Q(t) = \sum_{i=0}^{n} V_i B_i^n(t), \qquad t \in [0, 1],$$

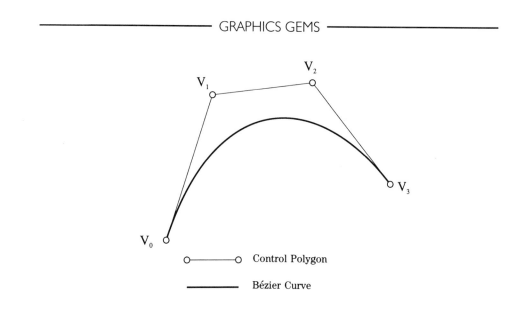

Figure 1. A single cubic Bézier segment.

where the V_i are the control points, and the $B_i^n(t)$ are the Bernstein polynomials of degree n.

$$B_i^n(t) = \binom{n}{i} t^i (1 - t)^{n-i}, \qquad i = 0, \ldots, n,$$

where $\binom{n}{i}$ is the binomial coefficient $n!/(n - i)!i!$. See Fig. 1 for an example of a cubic Bézier curve. Bézier curves generally are evaluated using a recursive algorithm due to de Casteljau. The algorithm is based on the *recursion* property of Bernstein polynomials:

$$B_i^n(t) = (1 - t)B_{i-1}^{n-1} + tB_{i-1}^{n-1}(t).$$

The kth derivative of a Bézier curve is given by

$$\frac{d^k}{dt^k}Q(t) = \frac{n!}{(n - k)!} \sum_{i=0}^{n-k} \Delta^k V_i B_i^{n-k}(t),$$

where $\Delta^1 V_i = \Delta V_i = V_{i+1} - V_i$, and where $\Delta^k V_i = \Delta^k V_{i+1} - \Delta^{k-1} V_i$,

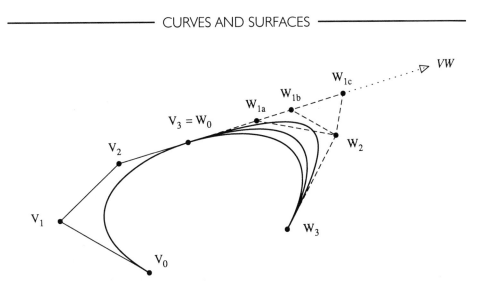

Figure 2. G^1 continuity condition for cubic Bézier curves.

(Watkins, 1987; Boehm *et al.*, 1984). Thus, for $t = 0$ (the left endpoint),

$$\frac{d^k}{dt^k}Q(0) = \frac{n!}{(n-k)!}\Delta^k V_0.$$

For $k = 1$,

$$\frac{dQ}{dt} = Q'(t) = n \sum_{i=0}^{n-1} (V_{i+1} - V_i)B_i^{n-1}(t),$$

which makes more obvious the fact that the tangent vector direction (at the left of the segment) is determined by the line segment from V_0 to V_1. A similar condition holds for the right end.

The implication of this fact is that to enforce continuity at the joints, the second-to-last control point of one segment must be collinear with the last control point (which is also the first control point of the adjoining segment) and the second control point of the adjoining segment. See Fig. 2 for an example; the second control point of the right-hand segment (the one with control points W_i) must be located along the half-line labeled VW.

Any sort of complete treatment of continuity conditions is well beyond the scope of this article—interested readers may wish to consult DeRose (1985). Briefly, we note that if the distance between the control point on the left side of the joint and the shared control point is equal to the distance between the shared control point and its neighbor on the right, the tangent vectors will be equal in magnitude and direction. This condition is known as *parametric continuity*, denoted C^1. However, for many applications, this is too restrictive—notice that for the joint to appear smooth, all that is required is that only the tangent *directions* be equivalent, a condition known as *geometric continuity*, denoted G^1. Getting back to the figure, this implies that the shared control point and its two neighbors need only be colinear—the respective distances do not affect the appearance of smoothness at the joint. The curve-fitting algorithm exploits this extra degree of freedom—we employ a least-squares fitting method, which sets these distances so that the error (that is, distance) between the digitized points of the fitted curve is minimized. This has several advantages: first, we can fit the curve with fewer segments; second, parametrically continuous curves correspond to the family of curves drawn by the motion of a particle that moves at a continuous velocity. This is a too much of a restriction for bitmapped fonts, for example; for hand-drawn curves, the restriction is patently wrong.

Fitting the Curve

Following Plass and Stone (1983), a parametric curve $Q(t)$ can be thought of as the projection of a curve in X, Y, t space onto the X–Y plane. Then, we can think of the problem as finding the curve in X, Y, t space whose projection best approximates the digitized curve in the X–Y lane. "Best" is defined in terms of minimization of the sum of squared distances from the digitized curve to the parametric curve.

We state without proof that the curves defined by the projections of the 3-space curve on the X–t and Y–t planes are single-valued (scalar) curves. Thus, if one could devise some scheme relating the X and Y coordinates of each point, one could apply a conventional least-squares function-fitting technique, with the addition constraints of tangent vector direction considered, in X and Y simultaneously. As we are working with

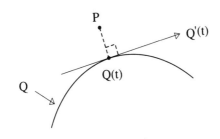

Figure 3. The distance from P to $Q(t)$.

parametric representations, the "scheme" relating the X and Y coordinates is the parametric value t associated with each point. As none are provided, we must look for a way to estimate accurately a value of t for each digitized point. A traditional approach to this problem is to use *chord-length parameterization*.

Once each point has an associated t-value, we can fit a cubic Bézier segment to the set of points (a process described later), and compute the error by comparing the distances between each digitized point p_k and the point with parametric value t_k on the generated curve.

The square distance between a given point P and a point $Q(t)$ on a parametric curve Q is

$$dist = \| P - Q(t) \|. \tag{1}$$

Refer to Fig. 3 for a diagram of this. The general problem can be stated in this manner: given a set of points in the plane, find a curve that fits those points to within some given tolerance. In our case, the curve with which we wish to approximate the points is a cubic Bernstein–Bézier curve, and our fitting criterion is to minimize the sum of the squared distances from the points to their corresponding points on the curve. Formally, we wish to minimize a function S, where S is defined by

$$S = \sum_{i=1}^{n} \left[d_i - Q(u_i) \right]^2 \tag{2}$$

$$= \sum_{i=1}^{n} \left[d_i - Q(u_i) \right] \cdot \left[d_i - Q(u_i) \right], \tag{3}$$

where d_i are the (x, y) coordinates of the given points, and u_i is the parameter value associated with d_i.

In the next set of equations, the following definitions hold:

- V_0 and V_3, the first and last control points, are given—they are set to be equal to the first and last digitized points in the region we are trying to fit.

- $\hat{t}_1$ and $\hat{t}_2$ are the unit tangent vectors at V_0 and V_3, respectively.

- $V_1 = \alpha_1 \hat{t}_1 + V_0$, and $V_2 = \alpha_2 \hat{t}_2 + V_3$; that is, the two inner control points are each some distance α from their the nearest end control point, in the tangent vector direction.

Recall that as we are enforcing G^1 continuity, V_1 and V_2 can be placed anywhere along the half-lines defined by $\hat{t}_1$ and $\hat{t}_2$, respectively. Our problem can be defined as finding α_1 and α_2 to minimize S. That is, we wish to solve these two equations for α_1 and α_2, thereby determining the remaining two control points (that is, V_1 and V_2) of the cubic Bézier segment:

$$\frac{\partial S}{\partial \alpha_1} = 0 \tag{4}$$

$$\frac{\partial S}{\partial \alpha_2} = 0. \tag{5}$$

Expanding Eq. (4),

$$\frac{\partial S}{\partial \alpha_1} = \sum_{i=1}^{n} 2[d_i - Q(u_i)] \cdot \frac{\partial Q(u_i)}{\partial \alpha_1}.$$

Expanding the second term, we get

$$\frac{\partial Q(u_i)}{\partial \alpha_1} = \frac{\partial}{\partial \alpha_1} \left(V_0 B_0^3(u_i) + (\alpha_1 \hat{t}_1 + V_0) B_1^3(u_i) \right.$$

$$+ (\alpha_2 \hat{t}_2 + V_3) B_2^3(u_i) + V_3 B_3^3(u_i) \big)$$

$$= \hat{t}_1 B_1^3(u_i).$$

Thus,

$$\frac{\partial S}{\partial \alpha_1} = \sum_{i=1}^{n} 2[d_i - Q(u_i)] \cdot \hat{t}_1 B_1^3(u_i) = 0.$$

Rearranging, we get

$$\sum_{i=1}^{n} B_1^3(u_i)Q(u_i) \cdot \hat{t}_1 = \sum_{i=1}^{n} \hat{t}_1 B_1^3(u_i) \cdot d_i.$$

For convenience, define

$$A_{i,1} = \hat{t}_1 B_1^3(u_i).$$

Then,

$$\sum_{i=1}^{n} Q(u_i) \cdot A_{i,1} = \sum_{i=1}^{n} d_i \cdot A_{i,1}. \tag{6}$$

Expanding $Q(u_i)$,

$$\sum_{i=1}^{n} Q(u_i) \cdot A_{i,1}$$

$$= \sum_{i=1}^{n} A_{i,1} \cdot \left(V_0 B_0^3(u_i) + \alpha_1 A_{i,1} + V_0 B_1^3(u_i) \right.$$

$$\left. + \alpha_2 A_{i,2} + V_3 B_2^3(u_i) + V_3 B_3^3(u_i) \right)$$

$$= \sum_{i=1}^{n} A_{i,1} \cdot V_0 B_0^3(u_i) + \alpha_1 \sum_{i=1}^{n} A_{i,1}^2 + \sum_{i=1}^{n} A_{i,1} \cdot V_0 B_1^3(u_i)$$

$$+ \alpha_2 \sum_{i=1}^{n} A_{i,1} \cdot A_{i,2} + \sum_{i=1}^{n} A_{i,1} \cdot V_3 B_2^3(u_i) + \sum_{i=1}^{n} A_{i,1} \cdot V_3 B_3^3(u_i)$$

Equation (6) becomes

$$\left(\sum_{i=1}^{n} A_{i,1}^2 \right) \alpha_1 + \left(\sum_{i=1}^{n} A_{i,1} \cdot A_{i,2} \right) \alpha_2$$

$$= \sum_{i=1}^{n} \left(d_i - \left(V_0 B_0^3(u_i) + V_0 B_1^3(u_i) + V_3 B_2^3(u_i) + V_3 B_3^3(u_i) \right) \right) \cdot A_{i,1}$$

Similarly, for $\partial S / \partial \alpha_2$,

$$\left(\sum_{i=1}^{n} A_{i,1} \cdot A_{i,2} \right) \alpha_1 + \left(\sum_{i=1}^{n} A_{i,2}^2 \right) \alpha_2$$

$$= \sum_{i=1}^{n} \left(d_i - \left(V_0 B_0^3(u_i) + V_0 B_1^3(u_i) + V_3 B_2^3(u_i) + V_3 B_3^3(u_i) \right) \right) \cdot A_{i,2}$$

If we represent the previous two equations by

$$c_{1,1} \alpha_1 + c_{1,2} \alpha_2 = X_1$$

$$c_{2,1} \alpha_1 + c_{2,2} \alpha_2 = X_2,$$

we need only solve

$$\begin{pmatrix} c_{1,1} & c_{1,2} \\ c_{2,1} & c_{2,2} \end{pmatrix} \begin{pmatrix} \alpha_1 \\ \alpha_2 \end{pmatrix} = \begin{pmatrix} X_1 \\ X_2 \end{pmatrix}$$

for α_1 and α_2. If we let

$$\mathscr{C} = \begin{pmatrix} c_{1,1} & c_{1,2} \\ c_{2,1} & c_{2,2} \end{pmatrix} = \begin{pmatrix} C_1 & C_2 \end{pmatrix}$$

$$\mathscr{X} = \begin{pmatrix} X_1 \\ X_2 \end{pmatrix},$$

Then, using Cramer's Rule, the solution to

$$\begin{pmatrix} \alpha_1 \\ \alpha_2 \end{pmatrix} = \mathscr{C}^{-1} \mathscr{X}$$

is

$$\alpha_1 = \frac{\det(\mathscr{X} \ C_2)}{\det(C_1 \ C_2)}$$

$$\alpha_1 = \frac{\det(C_1 \ \mathscr{X})}{\det(C_1 \ C_2)}$$

Our algorithm that attempts to fit a single cubic Bézier segment to a set of points appears in Fig. 4. We begin by computing approximate tangents at the endpoints of the digitized curve. This can be accomplished by fitting a least-squares line to the points in the neighborhood of the endpoints, or by averaging vectors from the endpoints to the next n points, and so on. Next, we assign an initial parameter value u_i to each point d_i, using chord-length parameterization. At this point, we use the technique described to fit a cubic Bézier segment to the points—the first and last control points are positioned at the first and last digitized points in the region we are working on, and the inner two control points are placed a distance α_1 and α_2 away from the first and last control points, in the direction of the unit tangent vectors previously computed. We then compute the error between the Bézier curve and the digitized points, noting the point that is the farthest distance from the curve. If the fit is acceptable, we draw or otherwise output the curve. If the fit is not acceptable, we could break the digitized points into two subsets at the point of greatest error, compute the unit tangent vector at the point of splitting, and recursively try to fit Bézier curves to these two new subcurves. Consider, though, that our initial chord-length parameterization is only a very rough approximation; if we had a better parameterization of the points, we might have been able to fit the curve without further recursive processing. Fortunately, there is a technique available to us. Referring back to Eq. 1, our t is that chord-length-generated approximate parameter. We can use Newton–Raphson iteration to get a better t—in general, the formula is

$$ t \leftarrow t - \frac{f(t)}{f'(t)}. \tag{7} $$

Referring back to Fig. 3, we wish to solve

$$ [Q(t) - P] \cdot Q'(t) = 0 \tag{8} $$

for t. In our case, then, we reduce the t for each point by

$$ \frac{Q_1 t \cdot Q_2 t}{[Q_1(t) \cdot Q_2(t)]'}. \tag{9} $$

```
FitCurve(d, ε)
        d     : array[ ] of point; Array of digitized points
        ε     : double;            User-specified error
begin
        Compute t̂₁ and t̂₂, the unit tangent
                vectors at the ends of the digitized points;
        FitCubic(d, t̂₁, t̂₂, ε);
end

FitCubic(d, t̂₁, t̂₂, ε)
        d     : array[ ] of point; Array of digitized points
        t̂₁, t̂₂ : vector;           Endpoint tangents
        ε     : double;            User-specified error
begin
        Compute chord-length parameterization of digitized points:
        Fit a single cubic Bezier curve to digitized points:
        Compute the maximum distance from points
        to curve:
        if error < ε
          then begin
                DrawBezierCurve:
                return;
                end;
        if error < ψ
          then begin
                for i: integer ← 0. i ← 1. while i < maxIterations do
                  begin
                        Reparameterize the points:
                        Fit a single cubic Bezier curve to digitized points:
                        Compute the maximum distance from points to
                         curve:
                        if error < ε
                          then begin
                                DrawBezierCurve:
                                return;
                                end
                  end
              endloop
          else begin
                Compute unit tangent at point of maximum error:
                Call FitCubic on the "left" side:
                Call FitCubic on the "right" side:
             end
          end
      end
```

Figure 4.

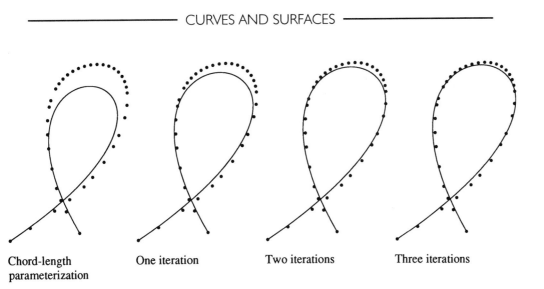

| Chord-length parameterization | One iteration | Two iterations | Three iterations |

Figure 5. Use of the iterative process to improve the fitting of the cubic.

This technique was first used by Grossman (1970) and later by Plass and Stone (1983) in their algorithms. This iteration can greatly improve the fit of the curve to the points: see Fig. 5, for an example of the process.

Newton–Raphson iteration is fairly inexpensive and tends to converge rather quickly. Thus, one might want to attempt this improvement every time. However, if the initial fit is very poor, it may be best not even to attempt the improvement. So, we compare the error to some value ψ, which we set to some small multiple or power of the user-specified error ϵ. This value ψ is implementation-dependent, but is easy to determine empirically. Additionally, since the incremental improvement decreases quickly with each successive iteration, we set a limit on the number of attempts we make (the author found that a value of four or five is appropriate). Finally, we note that while this Newton–Raphson iteration is cheap, the associated fitting attempts are not. The astute reader may notice, then, that we have placed more emphasis on minimizing the number of segments generated than on execution speed. Even so, the algorithm is generally more than fast enough for interactive use, even with a very large number of points to fit. In addition, it is very stable—the author has not seen a case when the algorithm failed to converge quickly on a satisfactory and correct fit.

One final note: the least-squares mathematics fails when there are only two points in the digitized subcurve to be fitted. In this case, we adopt a

623

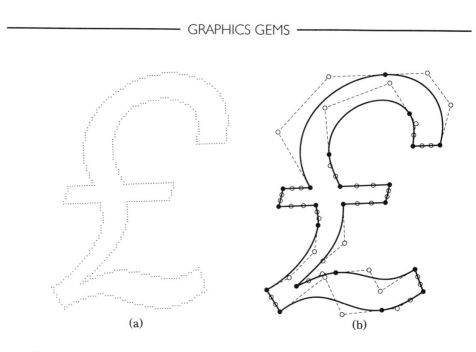

(a)   (b)

Figure 6.   A digitized glyph, showing the original samples and the fitted curves.

method from Schmitt *et al.*, (1986), and plane the inner two control points at a distance from the outer two control points equal to one-third of the distance between the two points, along the unit tangents at each endpoint.

Examples of the fitting algorithm being applied to a digitized font and to a hand-sketched curve appear in Figs. 6 and 7. The large dots indicate the cubic Bézier control points—the filled dots are the first and last control points in each curve (which are shared with the curve's neighbors), and the hollow dots are the "inner" control points.

Implementation Notes

Several points should be made with respect to implementation. First, the implementor may want to preprocess the digitized data prior to calling the fitting routine. Such preprocessing might include: removing coinci-

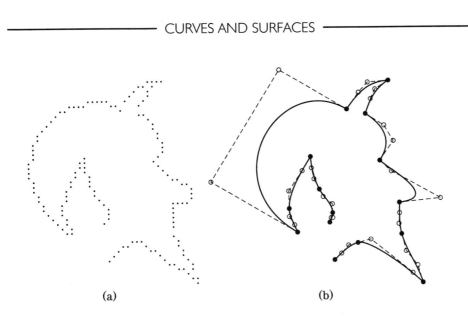

(a)   (b)

Figure 7.   A hand-sketched curve, showing the original samples and the fitted curves.

dent and/or nearly coincident data points, filtering the points with a little convolution (makes tangent computation more reliable), and locating corners. By "corners" we mean regions in the digitized curve where there should be a discontinuity; such points can be located by looking at the angle created by a point and its neighbors. These corners divide the original curve into a number of distinct subcurves, each of which can be fitted independently. Second, negative α values occasionally are generated when the points are very irregularly spaced. In this case, one can either split the points and try to fit each subcurve, or employ the heuristic mentioned earlier.

A sample C implementation of the algorithm is included in the appendix, in the file *fit_cubic.c*. Inputs to the routine *FitCurve* are the array of digitized points, their number, and the desired (squared) error value. When Bézier curves are generated, the routine *DrawBezierCurve* is called to output the curve; this routine must be supplied by the implementor, and simply consists of drawing or otherwise outputting the curve defined by the control points with which it is called.

Conclusion

We have presented an adaptive, automatic algorithm for fitting piecewise cubic Bézier curves to digitized curves. This algorithm elegantly parallels adaptive subdivision for curve evaluation, and shares with that technique that characteristic that regions of lower curvature are more coarsely refined than those of higher curvature. Advantages over previous approaches are complete automaticity, geometric continuity, stability, and extreme ease of implementation.

See Appendix 2 for C Implementation (**797**)

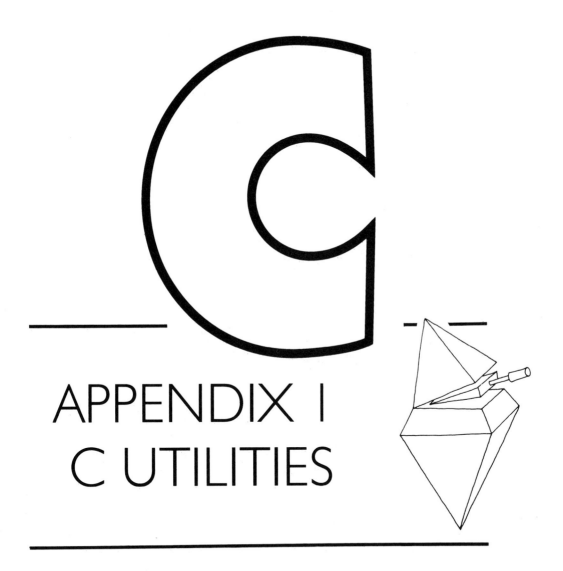

APPENDIX I
C UTILITIES

GRAPHICS GEMS
C HEADER FILE

Andrew Glassner

```c
/* GraphicsGems.h */

/*********************/
/* 2d geometry types */
/*********************/

typedef struct Point2Struct {    /* 2d point */
    double x, y;
    } Point2;
typedef Point2 Vector2;

typedef struct IntPoint2Struct { /* 2d integer point */
    int x, y;
    } IntPoint2;

typedef struct Matrix3Struct {    /* 3-by-3 matrix */
    double element[3][3];
    } Matrix3;

typedef struct Box2dStruct {      /* 2d box */
    Point2 min, max;
    } Box2;


/*********************/
/* 3d geometry types */
/*********************/

typedef struct Point3Struct {    /* 3d point */
    double x, y, z;
    } Point3;
typedef Point3 Vector3;

typedef struct IntPoint3Struct { /* 3d integer point */
    int x, y, z;
    } IntPoint3;
```

```c
typedef struct Matrix4Struct {       /* 4-by-4 matrix */
    double element[4][4];
    } Matrix4;

typedef struct Box3dStruct {         /* 3d box */
    Point3 min, max;
    } Box3;



/***********************/
/* one-argument macros */
/***********************/

/* absolute value of a */
#define ABS(a)          (((a)<0) ? -(a) : (a))

/* round a to nearest integer towards 0 */
#define FLOOR(a)        ((a)>0 ? (int)(a) : -(int)(-a))

/* round a to nearest integer away from 0 */
#define CEILING(a) \
((a)==(int)(a) ? (a) : (a)>0 ? 1+(int)(a) : -(1+(int)(-a)))

/* round a to nearest int */
#define ROUND(a)        ((a)>0 ? (int)(a+0.5) : -(int)(0.5-a))

/* take sign of a, either -1, 0, or 1 */
#define ZSGN(a)         (((a)<0) ? -1 : (a)>0 ? 1 : 0)

/* take binary sign of a, either -1, or 1 if >= 0 */
#define SGN(a)          (((a)<0) ? -1 : 0)

/* shout if something that should be true isn't */
#define ASSERT(x) \
if (!(x)) fprintf(stderr," Assert failed: x\n");

/* square a */
#define SQR(a)          ((a)*(a))
```

630

```c
/***********************/
/* two-argument macros */
/***********************/

/* find minimum of a and b */
#define MIN(a,b)        (((a)<(b))?(a):(b))

/* find maximum of a and b */
#define MAX(a,b)        (((a)>(b))?(a):(b))

/* swap a and b (see Gem by Wyvill) */
#define SWAP(a,b)       { a^=b; b^=a; a^=b; }

/* linear interpolation from l (when a=0) to h (when a=1)*/
/* (equal to (a*h)+((1-a)*l) */
#define LERP(a,l,h)     ((l)+(((h)-(l))*(a)))

/* clamp the input to the specified range */
#define CLAMP(v,l,h)  ((v)<(l) ? (l) : (v) > (h) ? (h) : v)


/***************************/
/* memory allocation macros */
/***************************/

/* create a new instance of a structure (see Gem by Hultquist) */
#define NEWSTRUCT(x)  (struct x *)(malloc((unsigned)sizeof(struct x)))

/* create a new instance of a type */
#define NEWTYPE(x)    (x *)(malloc((unsigned)sizeof(x)))
```

```c
/********************/
/* useful constants */
/********************/

#define PI              3.141592 /* the venerable pi */
#define PITIMES2        6.283185 /* 2 * pi */
#define PIOVER2         1.570796 /* pi / 2 */
#define E               2.718282 /* the venerable e */
#define SQRT2           1.414214 /* sqrt(2) */
#define SQRT3           1.732051 /* sqrt(3) */
#define GOLDEN          1.618034 /* the golden ratio */
#define DTOR            0.017453 /* convert degrees to radians */
#define RTOD            57.29578 /* convert radians to degrees */


/************/
/* booleans */
/************/

#define TRUE            1
#define FALSE           0
#define ON              1
#define OFF             0
typedef int boolean;                    /* boolean data type */
typedef boolean flag;                   /* flag data type */
```

632

2D AND 3D
VECTOR C LIBRARY

Andrew Glassner

```c
#include "GraphicsGems.h"

/******************/
/*   2d Library   */
/******************/

/* returns squared length of input vector */
double V2SquaredLength(a)
Vector2 *a;
{    return((a->x * a->x)+(a->y * a->y));
    };

/* returns length of input vector */
double V2Length(a)
Vector2 *a;
{
    return(sqrt(V2SquaredLength(a)));
    };

/* negates the input vector and returns it */
Vector2 *V2Negate(v)
Vector2 *v;
{
    v->x = -v->x;   v->y = -v->y;
    return(v);
    };

/* normalizes the input vector and returns it */
Vector2 *V2Normalize(v)
Vector2 *v;
{
double len = V2Length(v);
    if (len != 0.0) { v->x /= len;   v->y /= len; };
    return(v);
    };
```

```c
/* scales the input vector to the new length and returns it */
Vector2 *V2Scale(v, newlen)
Vector2 *v;
double newlen;
{
double len = V2Length(v);
    if (len != 0.0) { v->x *= newlen/len;    v->y *= newlen/len; };
    return(v);
    };

/* return vector sum c = a+b */
Vector2 *V2Add(a, b, c)
Vector2 *a, *b, *c;
{
    c->x = a->x+b->x;   c->y = a->y+b->y;
    return(c);
    };

/* return vector difference c = a-b */
Vector2 *V2Sub(a, b, c)
Vector2 *a, *b, *c;
{
    c->x = a->x-b->x;   c->y = a->y-b->y;
    return(c);
    };

/* return the dot product of vectors a and b */
double V2Dot(a, b)
Vector2 *a, *b;
{
    return((a->x*b->x)+(a->y*b->y));
    };

/* linearly interpolate between vectors by an amount alpha */
/* and return the resulting vector. */
/* When alpha=0, result=lo.  When alpha=1, result=hi. */
Vector2 *V2Lerp(lo, hi, alpha, result)
Vector2 *lo, *hi, *result;
double alpha;
{
    result->x = LERP(alpha, lo->x, hi->x);
    result->y = LERP(alpha, lo->y, hi->y);
    return(result);
    };
```

```
/* make a linear combination of two vectors and return the result.
*/
/* result = (a * ascl) + (b * bscl) */
Vector2 *V2Combine (a, b, result, ascl, bscl)
Vector2 *a, *b, *result;
double ascl, bscl;
{
    result->x = (ascl * a->x) + (bscl * b->x);
    result->y = (ascl * a->y) + (bscl * b->y);
    return(result);
    };

/* multiply two vectors together component-wise */
Vector2 *V2Mul (a, b, result)
Vector2 *a, *b, *result;
{
    result->x = a->x * b->x;
    result->y = a->y * b->y;
    return(result);
    };

/* return the distance between two points */
double V2DistanceBetween2Points(a, b)
Point2 *a, *b;
{
double dx = a->x - b->x;
double dy = a->y - b->y;
    return(sqrt((dx*dx)+(dy*dy)));
    };

/* return the vector perpendicular to the input vector a */
Vector2 *V2MakePerpendicular(a, ap)
Vector2 *a, *ap;
{
    ap->x = -a->y;
    ap->y = a->x;
    return(ap);
    };

/* create, initialize, and return a new vector */
Vector2 *V2New(x, y)
double x, y;
{
Vector2 *v = NEWTYPE(Vector2);
    v->x = x;   v->y = y;
    return(v);
    };
```

```
/* create, initialize, and return a duplicate vector */
Vector2 *V2Duplicate(a)
Vector2 *a;
{
Vector2 *v = NEWTYPE(Vector2);
    v->x = a->x;   v->y = a->y;
    return(v);
    };


/* multiply a point by a matrix and return the transformed point */
Point2 *V2MulPointByMatrix(p, m)
Point2 *p;
Matrix3 *m;
{
double w;
    p->x = (p->x * m->element[0][0]) +
            (p->y * m->element[1][0]) + m->element[2][0];
    p->y = (p->x * m->element[0][1]) +
            (p->y * m->element[1][1]) + m->element[2][1];
    w    = (p->x * m->element[0][2]) +
            (p->y * m->element[1][2]) + m->element[2][2];
    if (w != 0.0) { p->x /= w;   p->y /= w; }
    return(p);
    };


/* multiply together matrices c = ab */
/* note that c must not point to either of the input matrices */
Matrix3 *V2MatMul(a, b, c)
Matrix3 *a, *b, *c;
{
int i, j, k;
    for (i=0; i<3; i++) {
        for (j=0; j<3; j++) {
            c->element[i][j] = 0;
        for (k=0; k<3; k++) c->element[i][j] +=
                a->element[i][k] * b->element[k][j];
            };
        };
    return(c);
    };
```

```
/*****************/
/*   3d Library   */
/*****************/

/* returns squared length of input vector */
double V3SquaredLength(a)
Vector3 *a;
{
    return((a->x * a->x)+(a->y * a->y)+(a->z * a->z));
    };

/* returns length of input vector */
double V3Length(a)
Vector3 *a;
{
    return(sqrt(V3SquaredLength(a)));
    };

/* negates the input vector and returns it */
Vector3 *V3Negate(v)
Vector3 *v;
{
    v->x = -v->x;   v->y = -v->y;   v->z = -v->z;
    return(v);
    };

/* normalizes the input vector and returns it */
Vector3 *V3Normalize(v)
Vector3 *v;
{
double len = V3Length(v);
    if (len != 0.0) { v->x /= len;   v->y /= len; v->z /= len; };
    return(v);
    };

/* scales the input vector to the new length and returns it */
Vector3 *V3Scale(v, newlen)
Vector3 *v;
double newlen;
{
double len = V3Length(v);
    if (len != 0.0) {
    v->x *= newlen/len;   v->y *= newlen/len;   v->z *= newlen/len;
    };
    return(v);
    };
```

```
/* return vector sum c = a+b */
Vector3 *V3Add(a, b, c)
Vector3 *a, *b, *c;
{
    c->x = a->x+b->x;   c->y = a->y+b->y;   c->z = a->z+b->z;
    return(c);
    };

/* return vector difference c = a-b */
Vector3 *V3Sub(a, b, c)
Vector3 *a, *b, *c;
{
    c->x = a->x-b->x;   c->y = a->y-b->y;   c->z = a->z-b->z;
    return(c);
    };

/* return the dot product of vectors a and b */
double V3Dot(a, b)
Vector3 *a, *b;
{
    return((a->x*b->x)+(a->y*b->y)+(a->z*b->z));
    };

/* linearly interpolate between vectors by an amount alpha */
/* and return the resulting vector. */
/* When alpha=0, result=lo.  When alpha=1, result=hi. */
Vector3 *V3Lerp(lo, hi, alpha, result)
Vector3 *lo, *hi, *result;
double alpha;
{
    result->x = LERP(alpha, lo->x, hi->x);
    result->y = LERP(alpha, lo->y, hi->y);
    result->z = LERP(alpha, lo->z, hi->z);
    return(result);
    };

/* make a linear combination of two vectors and return the result. */
/* result = (a * ascl) + (b * bscl) */
Vector3 *V3Combine (a, b, result, ascl, bscl)
Vector3 *a, *b, *result;
double ascl, bscl;
{
    result->x = (ascl * a->x) + (bscl * b->x);
    result->y = (ascl * a->y) + (bscl * b->y);
    result->y = (ascl * a->z) + (bscl * b->z);
    return(result);
    };
```

```c
/* multiply two vectors together component-wise and return the result */
Vector3 *V3Mul (a, b, result)
Vector3 *a, *b, *result;
{
    result->x = a->x * b->x;
    result->y = a->y * b->y;
    result->z = a->z * b->z;
    return(result);
    };

/* return the distance between two points */
double V3DistanceBetween2Points(a, b)
Point3 *a, *b;
{
double dx = a->x - b->x;
double dy = a->y - b->y;
double dz = a->z - b->z;
    return(sqrt((dx*dx)+(dy*dy)+(dz*dz)));
    };

/* return the cross product c = a cross b */
Vector3 *V3Cross(a, b, c)
Vector3 *a, *b, *c;
{
    c->x = (a->y*b->z) - (a->z*b->y);
    c->y = (a->z*b->x) - (a->x*b->z);
    c->z = (a->x*b->y) - (a->y*b->x);
    return(c);
    };

/* create, initialize, and return a new vector */
Vector3 *V3New(x, y, z)
double x, y, z;
{
Vector3 *v = NEWTYPE(Vector3);
    v->x = x;   v->y = y;   v->z = z;
    return(v);
    };

/* create, initialize, and return a duplicate vector */
Vector3 *V3Duplicate(a)
Vector3 *a;
{
Vector3 *v = NEWTYPE(Vector3);
    v->x = a->x;   v->y = a->y;   v->z = a->z;
    return(v);
    };
```

```
/* multiply a point by a matrix and return the transformed point */
Point3 *V3MulPointByMatrix(p, m)
Point3 *p;
Matrix4 *m;
{
double w;
    p->x = (p->x * m->element[0][0]) + (p->y * m->element[1][0]) +
        (p->z * m->element[2][0]) + m->element[3][0];
    p->y = (p->x * m->element[0][1]) + (p->y * m->element[1][1]) +
        (p->z * m->element[2][1]) + m->element[3][1];
    p->z = (p->x * m->element[0][2]) + (p->y * m->element[1][2]) +
        (p->z * m->element[2][2]) + m->element[3][2];
    w =      (p->x * m->element[0][3]) + (p->y * m->element[1][3]) +
        (p->z * m->element[2][3]) + m->element[3][3];
    if (w != 0.0) { p->x /= w;  p->y /= w;  p->z /= w; }
    return(p);
    };


/* multiply together matrices c = ab */
/* note that c must not point to either of the input matrices */
Matrix4 *V3MatMul(a, b, c)
Matrix4 *a, *b, *c;
{
int i, j, k;
    for (i=0; i<4; i++) {
        for (j=0; j<4; j++) {
            c->element[i][j] = 0;
            for (k=0; k<4; k++) c->element[i][j] +=
                a->element[i][k] * b->element[k][j];
            };
        };
    return(c);
    };


/* binary bcd by Silver and Terzian.  See Knuth */
/* both inputs must be >= 0 */
gcd(u, v)
int u, v;
{
int k, t, f;
    if ((u<0) || (v<0)) return(1); /* error if u<0 or v<0 */
    k = 0;  f = 1;
    while ((0 == (u%2)) && (0 == (v%2))) {
        k++;  u>>=1;  v>>=1,   f*=2;
        };
    if (u&01) { t = -v;  goto B4; } else { t = u; }
    B3: if (t > 0) { t >>= 1; } else { t = -((-t) >> 1); };
    B4: if (0 == (t%2)) goto B3;
```

```
    if (t > 0) u = t; else v = -t;
    if (0 != (t = u - v)) goto B3;
    return(u*f);
    };


/***********************/
/*   Useful Routines   */
/***********************/


/* return roots of ax^2+bx+c */
/* stable algebra derived from Numerical Recipes by Press et al.*/
int quadraticRoots(a, b, c, roots)
double a, b, c, *roots;
{
double d, q;
int count = 0;
    d = (b*b)-(4*a*c);
    if (d < 0.0) { *roots = *(roots+1) = 0.0;  return(0); };
    q = -0.5 * (b + (SGN(b)*sqrt(d)));
    if (a != 0.0)  { *roots++ = q/a; count++; }
    if (q != 0.0) { *roots++ = c/q; count++; }
    return(count);
    };



/* generic 1d regula-falsi step.  f is function to evaluate */
/* interval known to contain root is given in left, right */
/* returns new estimate */
double RegulaFalsi(f, left, right)
double (*f)(), left, right;
{
double d = (*f)(right) - (*f)(left);
    if (d != 0.0) return (right - (*f)(right)*(right-left)/d);
    return((left+right)/2.0);
    };


/* generic 1d Newton-Raphson step. f is function, df is derivative */
/* x is current best guess for root location. Returns new estimate */
double NewtonRaphson(f, df, x)
double (*f)(), (*df)(), x;
{
double d = (*df)(x);
    if (d != 0.0) return (x-((*f)(x)/d));
    return(x-1.0);
    };
```

```
/* hybrid 1d Newton-Raphson/Regula Falsi root finder. */
/* input function f and its derivative df, an interval */
/* left, right known to contain the root, and an error tolerance */
/* Based on Blinn */
double findroot(left, right, tolerance, f, df)
double left, right, tolerance;
double (*f)(), (*df)();
{
double newx = left;
    while (ABS((*f)(newx)) > tolerance) {
        newx = NewtonRaphson(f, df, newx);
        if (newx < left || newx > right)
            newx = RegulaFalsi(f, left, right);
        if ((*f)(newx) * (*f)(left) <= 0.0) right = newx;
            else left = newx;
        };
    return(newx);
    };
```

MEMORY ALLOCATION IN C

Jeff Hultquist

```c
/* To improve the readability of C sources, we can replace lines like */
/* ptr = (OBJ *) malloc(sizeof(OBJ)) with the shorter ptr = NEW(OBJ) */
/* using a macro   */

#define NEW(baz)   (baz *) malloc(sizeof(baz))


/* We might also want to replace malloc with our own routine, which */
/* tests for a successful result. */

char *my_malloc(unsigned bytes)
{
    char *tmp = malloc(bytes);
    if (! tmp) {
        handle_error_condition();
    }
    return(tmp);
}
```

TWO USEFUL C MACROS

Eric Raible

```
/*
Although Ansi C (and hence prototypes) are becoming more
widespread, there is still a need for backward compatability
with traditional (K + R) C. To accomodate this need, programmers
will often repeat the declarations for global procedures
within an #ifdef - one copy with prototype information, the
other without. The following approach allows for only one
declaration per procedure instead of two.
*/

#ifdef _STDC_
#define Proto(arglist) arglist
#else
#define Proto(arglist) ()
#endif
extern double tan Proto(double));
extern int strcmp Proto((char *, char *));

/* Note that the double parentheses are needed to      */
/* allow the passing of a variable number of arguments in this */
/* C-preprocessor macro. */

/* In any C program that has a large number of globals, a robust *
/* way of keeping the definitions and the declarations consistent
/* is to use the following approach. The file globals.h looks like

#ifdef DEFINE_GLOBALS
#define GLOBAL
#define INIT(x) = x
#else
#define GLOBAL extern
#define INIT(x)
#endif

GLOBAL char *prompt_string INIT("prompt> ");
GLOBAL int   lines_read     INIT (0);
GLOBAL int   line_buf[100];
GLOBAL float epsilon        INIT (.0001);

/* Then exactly one source file #defines DEFINE_GLOBALS */
/* before #including globals.h. This will allocate space for and *
/* initialize all of the globals. Every other file simply #include
/* globals.h. */
```

HOW TO BUILD CIRCULAR STRUCTURES IN C

Kelvin Thompson

```
/*
When programming in C, it is sometimes necessary to make different
structs point to one another in a circular fashion. For example,
make a component of struct type A point to struct type B, and
vice versa.  The most obvious way of doing this involves references
to undefined structs, and will confuse many compilers. A solution to
this problem is to typedef the interlocking structs to aliases, then
use the aliases to describe the references. For example,
*/

/* attach aliases to struct types */
typedef struct aa aa_type;
typedef struct bb bb_type;

/* use aliases in struct definition */
struct aa {bb_type *bb_pointer; };
struct bb {aa_type *aa_pointer; };

/* Structs aa and bb can also contain other components. */
```

HOW TO USE C REGISTER VARIABLES TO POINT TO 2D ARRAYS

Kelvin Thompson

```
/*
When programming in C, it is efficient to use a register variable
to point to a 2D array of values, for exmaple a 4 x 4 array of
doubles. The more obvious ways of expressing this idea will confuse
many compilers. One solution is to put the matrix in a struct as
the Vector C Library does.
*/

typedef struct {double element[4][4];  } Matrix4;

void func1 (matrix_pointer)
register Matrix4 *matrix_pointer;
{
    matrix_pointer->element[row][col] = expression;
}

/* Another solution to this problem is to use direct pointer typing. *

void func2 (matrix_pointer)
register double (*matrix_pointer) [4][4];
{
    (*matrix_pointer) [row][col] = expression;
}

/* Both methods are somewhat awkward. Sometimes it is helpful to */
/* define a macro to access a matrix via a register. */

#define M1(ptr,row,col)    ((ptr)->element [row][col])
#define M2(ptr,row,col)    ((*(ptr)) [row][col])

/* See Fast Matrix Multiplication in this volume for hints on */
/* speeding up matrix multiplication. */
```

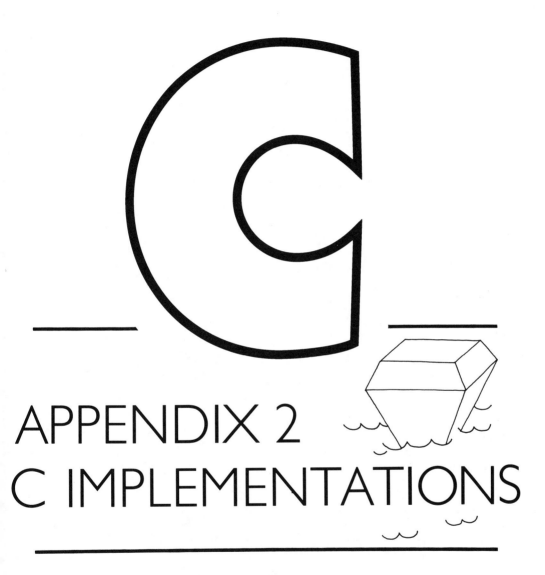

APPENDIX 2
C IMPLEMENTATIONS

GENERATING RANDOM POINTS IN TRIANGLES

(page 24)

Greg Turk

```
/*****************************************************************
Compute relative areas of sub-triangles that form a convex polygon.
There are vcount-2 sub-triangles, each defined by the first point
in the polygon and two other adjacent points.

This procedure should be called once before using
square_to_polygon().

Entry:
  vertices - list of the vertices of a convex polygon
  vcount   - number of vertices of polygon
Exit:
  areas - relative areas of sub-triangles of polygon
*****************************************************************/

triangle_areas (vertices, vcount, areas)
    Point3 vertices[];
    int vcount;
    float areas[];
{
    int i;
    float area_sum = 0;
    Vector3 v1,v2,v3;

  /* compute relative areas of the sub-triangles of polygon */

    for (i = 0; i < vcount - 2; i++) {
        V3Sub(&vertices[i+1], &vertices[0], &v1);
        V3Sub(&vertices[i+2], &vertices[0], &v2);
        V3Cross(&v1, &v2, &v3);
        areas[i] = LengthVector3(&v3);
        area_sum += areas[i];
    }

  /* normalize areas so that the sum of all sub-triangles is one */

    for (i = 0; i < vcount - 2; i++)
        areas[i] /= area_sum;
}
```

```
/****************************************************************/
Map a point from the square [0,1] x [0,1] into a convex polygon.
Uniform random points in the square will generate uniform random
points in the polygon.

The procedure triangle_areas() must be called once to compute
'areas', and then this procedure can be called repeatedly.

Entry:
   vertices - list of the vertices of a convex polygon
   vcount   - number of vertices of polygon
   areas    - relative areas of sub-triangles of polygon
   s,t      - position in the square [0,1] x [0,1]
Exit:
  p - position in polygon
****************************************************************/

square_to_polygon (vertices, vcount, areas, s, t, p)
    Point3 vertices[];
    int vcount;
    float areas[];
    float s,t;
    Point3 *p;
{
    int i;
    float area_sum = 0;
    float a,b,c;

  /* use 's' to pick one sub-triangle, weighted by relative */
  /* area of triangles */

    for (i = 0; i < vcount - 2; i++) {
        area_sum += areas[i];
        if (area_sum >= s)
            break;
    }

  /* map 's' into the interval [0,1] */

    s = (s - area_sum + areas[i]) / areas[i];

  /* map (s,t) to a point in that sub-triangle */

    t = sqrt(t);

    a = 1 - t;
    b = (1 - s) * t;
    c = s * t;

    p->x = a * vertices[0].x + b * vertices[i+1].x + c * vertices[i+2].x;
    p->y = a * vertices[0].y + b * vertices[i+1].y + c * vertices[i+2].y;
    p->z = a * vertices[0].z + b * vertices[i+1].z + c * vertices[i+2].z;
}
```

FAST LINE–EDGE
INTERSECTIONS ON
A UNIFORM GRID

(page 29)

Andrew Shapira

```
#define OCTANT(f1, f2, f3, f4, f5, i1, s1, r1, r2) \
    for (f1, f2, f3, nr = 0; f4; f5) { \
        if (nr < const) { \
            if (i1) \
                r1(&C); \
            else \
                vertex(&C); \
        } \
        else { \
            s1; \
            if (nr -= const) { \
                r2(&C); \
                r1(&C); \
            } \
            else \
                vertex(&C); \
        } \
    }

find_intersections(Pptr, Qptr)
IntPoint2    *Pptr, *Qptr;        /* P and Q as described in gem text */
{
    IntPoint2    P, Q;            /* P and Q, dereferenced for speed */
    IntPoint2    C;               /* current grid point */
    int          nr;             /* remainder */
    int          deltax, deltay; /* Q.x - P.x, Q.y - P.y */
    int          const;          /* loop-invariant constant */

    P.x = Pptr->x;
    P.y = Pptr->y;
    Q.x = Qptr->x;
    Q.y = Qptr->y;
    deltax = Q.x - P.x;
    deltay = Q.y - P.y;
```

```
    /* for reference purposes, let theta be the angle from P to Q */

    if ((deltax >= 0) && (deltay >= 0) && (deltay < deltax))
                                      /* 0 <= theta < 45 */
        OCTANT(C.x = P.x + 1, C.y = P.y, const = deltax - deltay,
                C.x < Q.x, C.x++, nr += deltay, C.y++, up, left)
    else if ((deltax > 0) && (deltay >= 0) && (deltay >= deltax))
                                      /* 45 <= theta < 90 */
        OCTANT(C.y = P.y + 1, C.x = P.x, const = deltay - deltax,
                C.y < Q.y, C.y++, nr += deltax, C.x++, right, down)
    else if ((deltax <= 0) && (deltay >= 0) && (deltay > -deltax))
                                      /* 90 <= theta < 135 */
        OCTANT(C.y = P.y + 1, C.x = P.x, const = deltay + deltax,
                C.y < Q.y, C.y++, nr -= deltax, C.x--, left, down)
    else if ((deltax <= 0) && (deltay > 0) && (deltay <= -deltax))
                                      /* 135 <= theta < 180 */
        OCTANT(C.x = P.x - 1, C.y = P.y, const = -deltax - deltay,
                C.x > Q.x, C.x--, nr += deltay, C.y++, up, right)
    else if ((deltax <= 0) && (deltay <= 0) && (deltay > deltax))
                                      /* 180 <= theta < 225 */
        OCTANT(C.x = P.x - 1, C.y = P.y, const = -deltax + deltay,
                C.x > Q.x, C.x--, nr -= deltay, C.y--, down, right)
    else if ((deltax < 0) && (deltay <= 0) && (deltay <= deltax))
                                      /* 225 <= theta < 270 */
        OCTANT(C.y = P.y - 1, C.x = P.x, const = -deltay + deltax,
                C.y > Q.y, C.y--, nr -= deltax, C.x--, left, up)
    else if ((deltax >= 0) && (deltay <= 0) && (-deltay > deltax))
                                      /* 270 <= theta < 315 */
        OCTANT(C.y = P.y - 1, C.x = P.x, const = -deltay - deltax,
                C.y > Q.y, C.y--, nr += deltax, C.x++, right, up)
    else if ((deltax >= 0) && (deltay < 0) && (-deltay <= deltax))
                                      /* 315 <= theta < 360 */
        OCTANT(C.x = P.x + 1, C.y = P.y, const = deltax + deltay,
                C.x < Q.x, C.x++, nr -= deltay, C.y--, down, left)
    else {}                           /* P = Q */
}

vertex(I)
IntPoint2    *I;
{
    /* Note: replace printf with code to process vertex, if desired */
    (void) printf("vertex at %d %d\n", I->x, I->y);
}

left(I)
IntPoint2    *I;
{
```

```c
    /* Note: replace printf with code to process leftward */
    /* intersection, if desired */
    (void) printf("left from %d %d\n", I->x, I->y);
}

up(I)
IntPoint2    *I;
{
    /* Note: replace printf with code to process upward */
    /* intersection, if desired */
    (void) printf("up from %d %d\n", I->x, I->y);
}

right(I)
IntPoint2    *I;
{
    /* Note: replace printf with code to process rightward */
    /* intersection, if desired */
    (void) printf("right from %d %d\n", I->x, I->y);
}

down(I)
IntPoint2    *I;
{
    /* Note: replace printf with code to process downward */
    /* intersection, if desired */
    (void) printf("down from %d %d\n", I->x, I->y);
}
```

A FAST 2D
POINT-ON-LINE TEST

(page 49)

Alan Paeth

```c
int PntOnLine(px,py,qx,qy,tx,ty)
   int px, py, qx, qy, tx, ty;
   {
/*
 * given a line through P:(px,py) Q:(qx,qy) and T:(tx,ty)
 * return 0 if T is not on the line through      <--P--Q-->
 *        1 if T is on the open ray ending at P: <--P
 *        2 if T is on the closed interior along:   P--Q
 *        3 if T is on the open ray beginning at Q:    Q-->
 *
 * Example: consider the line P = (3,2), Q = (17,7). A plot
 * of the test points T(x,y) (with 0 mapped onto '.') yields:
 *
 *     8 | . . . . . . . . . . . . . . . . . 3 3
 *   Y 7 | . . . . . . . . . . . . . 2 2 Q 3 3      Q = 2
 *     6 | . . . . . . . . . . . 2 2 2 2 . . . .
 *   a 5 | . . . . . . . . . 2 2 2 2 2 . . . . .
 *   x 4 | . . . . . . 2 2 2 2 2 . . . . . . . .
 *   i 3 | . . . 2 2 2 2 2 . . . . . . . . . . .
 *   s 2 | 1 1 P 2 2 . . . . . . . . . . . . .    P = 2
 *     1 | 1 1 . . . . . . . . . . . . . . . . .
 *     +-------------------------------------------
 *      1 2 3 4 5 X-axis 10          15          19
 *
 * Point-Line distance is normalized with the Infinity Norm
 * avoiding square-root code and tightening the test vs the
 * Manhattan Norm. All math is done on the field of integers.
 * The latter replaces the initial ">= MAX(...)" test with
 * "> (ABS(qx-px) + ABS(qy-py))" loosening both inequality
 * and norm, yielding a broader target line for selection.
 * The tightest test is employed here for best discrimination
 * in merging collinear (to grid coordinates) vertex chains
 * into a larger, spanning vectors within the Lemming editor.
 */
```

```c
if ( ABS((qy-py)*(tx-px)-(ty-py)*(qx-px)) >=
    (MAX(ABS(qx-px), ABS(qy-py)))) return(0);
if (((qx<px)&&(px<tx)) || ((qy<py)&&(py<ty))) return(1);
if (((tx<px)&&(px<qx)) || ((ty<py)&&(py<qy))) return(1);
if (((px<qx)&&(qx<tx)) || ((py<qy)&&(qy<ty))) return(3);
if (((tx<qx)&&(qx<px)) || ((ty<qy)&&(qy<py))) return(3);
return(2);
}
```

FAST CIRCLE–RECTANGLE
INTERSECTION CHECKING
(page 51)

Clifford A. Shaffer

```
#include "gems.h"

boolean Check_Intersect(R, C, Rad)

/* Return TRUE iff rectangle R intersects circle with centerpoint C and
    radius Rad. */
 Box2 *R;
 Point2 *C;
 double Rad;
{
 double Rad2;

 Rad2 = Rad * Rad;
 /* Translate coordinates, placing C at the origin. */
 R->max.x -= C->x;   R->max.y -= C->y;
 R->min.x -= C->x;   R->min.y -= C->y;

 if (R->max.x < 0)                /* R to left of circle center */
     if (R->max.y < 0)            /* R in lower left corner */
         return ((R->max.x * R->max.x + R->max.y * R->max.y) < Rad2);
     else if (R->min.y > 0)       /* R in upper left corner */
         return ((R->max.x * R->max.x + R->min.y * R->min.y) < Rad2);
     else                         /* R due West of circle */
         return(ABS(R->max.x) < Rad);
 else if (R->min.x > 0)           /* R to right of circle center */
     if (R->max.y < 0)            /* R in lower right corner */
         return ((R->min.x * R->min.x) < Rad2);
 else if (R->min.y > 0)           /* R in upper right corner */
     return ((R->min.x * R->min.x + R->min.y + R->min.y) < Rad2);
 else                             /* R due East of circle */
     return (R->min.x < Rad);
 else                             /* R on circle vertical centerline */
     if (R->max.y < 0)            /* R due South of circle */
     return (ABS(R->max.y) < Rad);
 else if (R->min.y > 0)           /* R due North of circle */
     return (R->min.y < Rad);
 else                             /* R contains circle centerpoint */
     return(TRUE);
}
```

NICE NUMBERS FOR
GRAPH LABELS

(page 61)

Paul Heckbert

```c
/*
 * label.c: demonstrate nice graph labeling
 *
 * Paul Heckbert   2 Dec 88
 */

#include <stdio.h>
#include <math.h>
#include "gem.h"

double nicenum();

/* expt(a,n)=a^n for integer n */

#ifdef POW_NOT_TRUSTWORTHY
/* if roundoff errors in pow cause problems, use this: */

double expt(a,  n)
double  a;
register  int  n;
{
    double x;

    x = 1.;
    if (n>0) for (; n>0; n--) x *= a;
    else for (; n<0; n++) x /= a;
    return x;
}

#else
#define expt(a, n)  pow(a, (double)(n))
#endif
```

```c
#define NTICK 5             /* desired number of tick marks */

main(ac, av)
int ac;
char **av;
{
    double min, max;

    if (ac!=3) {
        fprintf(stderr, "Usage: label <min> <max>\n");
        exit(1);
    }
    min = atof(av[1]);
    max = atof(av[2]);
    loose_label(min, max);
}

/*
 * loose_label: demonstrate loose labeling of data range from min to
 *              max.    (tight method is similar)
 */

loose_label(min, max)
double min, max;
{
    char str[6], temp[20];
    int nfrac;
    double d;                    /* tick mark spacing */
    double graphmin, graphmax;        /* graph range min and max
    double range, x;

    /* we expect min!=max */
    range = nicenum(max-min, 0);
    d = nicenum(range/(NTICK-1), 1);
    graphmin = floor(min/d)*d;
    graphmax = ceil(max/d)*d;
    nfrac = MAX(-floor(log10(d)), 0);
                                /* # of fractional digits to show */
    sprintf(str, "%%.%df", nfrac);  /* simplest axis labels */

    printf("graphmin=%g graphmax=%g increment=%g\n",
                graphmin, graphmax, d);
    for (x=graphmin; x<graphmax+.5*d; x+=d) {
        sprintf(temp, str, x);
        printf("(%s)\n", temp);
    }
}
```

```
/*
 * nicenum: find a "nice" number approximately equal to x.
 * Round the number  if round=1, take ceiling if round=0
 */

static double nicenum(x, round)
double x;
int round;
{
    int exp;                        /* exponent of x */
    double f;                       /* fractional part of x */
    double nf;                      /* nice, rounded fraction */

    exp = floor(log10(x));
    f = x/expt(10., exp);           /* between 1 and 10 */
    if (round)
        if (f<1.5) nf = 1.;
        else if (f<3.) nf = 2.;
        else if (f<7.) nf = 5.;
        else nf = 10.;
    else
        if (f<=1.) nf = 1.;
        else if (f<=2.) nf = 2.;
        else if (f<=5.) nf = 5.;
        else nf = 10.;
    return nf*expt(10., exp);
}
```

EFFICIENT GENERATION OF SAMPLING JITTER USING LOOK-UP TABLES

(page 64)

Joseph M. Cychosz

```
/*         Jitter.c - Sampling jitter generation routines.
/*
/*    Description:
/*         Jitter.c contains the routines for generation of sampling
/*         jitter using look-up tables.
/*
/*    Contents:
/*         Jitter1   Generate random jitter function 1.
/*         Jitter2   Generate random jitter function 2.
/*         JitterInit    Initialize look-up tables.
/*


#define            NRAN       1024      /* Random number table length */

static  double     URANX[NRAN],         /* Random number tables          */
                   URANY[NRAN];
static  int        IRAND[NRAN];         /* Shuffle table  */
static  int        MASK = NRAN-1;       /* Mask for jitter mod function */
extern  double     xranf();             /* Random number generator pro- */
                                        /* ducing uniform numbers 0 to 1 */


/*         Jitter1 - Generate random jitter.         */

void       Jitter1  (x,y,s,xj,yj)
           int x, y;                    /* Pixel location  */
           int s;                       /* Sample number for the pixel */
           double  *xj, *yj;            /* Jitter (x,y)    */
{
           *xj = URANX[ (x + (y<<2) + IRAND[(x+s)&MASK]) & MASK ];
           *yj = URANY[ (y + (x<<2) + IRAND[(y+s)&MASK]) & MASK ];
}
```

```
/*       Jitter2 - Generate random jitter.       */

void     Jitter2 (x,y,s,xj,yj)
         int x, y;                   /* Pixel location */
         int s;                      /* Sample number for the pixel */
         double *xj, *yj;            /* Jitter (x,y)   */
{
         *xj = URANX[ ((x | (y<<2)) + IRAND[(x+s)&MASK]) & MASK ];
         *yj = URANY[ ((y | (x<<2)) + IRAND[(y+s)&MASK]) & MASK ];
}


/*       JitterInit - Initialize look-up tables.       */

void     JitterInit   ()
{
         int i;

         for ( i = 0 ; i < NRAN ; i++ ) URANX[i] = xranf();
         for ( i = 0 ; i < NRAN ; i++ ) URANY[i] = xranf();
         for ( i = 0 ; i < NRAN ; i++ ) IRAND[i] = (int) (NRAN *
                xranf());
}
```

FAST ANTI-ALIASING POLYGON SCAN CONVERSION

(page 76)

Jack Morrison

```
/*
 * Anti-aliased polygon scan conversion by Jack Morrison
 *
 * This code renders a polygon, computing subpixel coverage at
 * 8 times Y and 16 times X display resolution for anti-aliasing.
 * One optimization left out for clarity is the use of incremental
 * interpolations. X coordinate interpolation in particular can be
 * with integers. See Dan Field's article in ACM Transactions on
 * Graphics, January 1985 for a fast incremental interpolator.
 */
#include "gems.h"

#define SYBYRES   8         /* subpixel Y resolution per scanline */
#define SUBXRES  16         /* subpixel X resolution per pixel */
#define MAX_AREA (SUBYRES*SUBXRES)
#define MODRES (y)   ((y) &7)      /*subpixel Y modulo */
#define MAX_X    0x7FFF   /* subpixel X beyond right edge */

typedef struct SurfaceStruct {  /* object shading surface info */
    int red, green, blue;         /* color components */
    } Surface;
/*
 * In  real life, SurfaceStruct will contain many more parameters as
 * required by the shading and rendering programs, such as diffuse
 * and specular factors, texture information, transparency, etc.
 */

typedef struct VertexStruct  {    /* polygon vertex */
    Vector3  model, world,        /* geometric information */
            normal, image;
    int y;                        /* subpixel display coordinate */
    } Vertex;

Vertex *Vleft, *VnextLeft;        /* current left edge */
Vertex *Vright, *VnextRight;      /* current right edge */

struct  SubPixel {                /* subpixel extents for scanline */
    int xLeft, xRight;
    } sp[SUBYRES];

int xLmin, xLmax;                 /* subpixel x extremes for scanline */
int XRmax, xRmin;                 /* (for optimization shortcut) */

/* Compute sub-pixel x coordinate for vertex */
extern int screenX(/* Vertex *v */);

/* Interpolate vertex information */
extern void vLerp(/* double alpha, Vertex *Va, *Vb, *Vout */);
```

```
/* Render polygon for one pixel, given coverage area */
/*   and bitmask */
extern void renderPixel(/* int x, y, Vertex *V,
                           int area, unsigned mask[],
                           Surface *object */);

/*
 * Render  shaded  polygon
 */
drawPolygon(polygon, numVertex, object)
     Vertex    polygon[];        /*clockwise clipped vertex list */
     int numVertex;              /*number of vertices in polygon */

     Surface *object;            /* shading parms for this object */
{
     Vertex *endPoly;            /* end of polygon vertex list */
     Vertex VscanLeft, VscanRight;   /* interpolated vertices */
                                     /* at scanline */
     double aLeft, aRight;            /* interpolation ratios */
     struct SubPixel *sp_ptr;        /* current subpixel info */
     int xLeft, xNextLeft;           /* subpixel coordinates for */
     int  xRight, xNextRight;        /* active polygon edges */
     int  i,y;

/* find vertex with minimum y (display coordinate) */
Vleft = polygon;
for  (i=1; i<numVertex; i++)
     if  (polygon[i].y < Vleft ->y)
          Vleft = &polygon[i];
endPoly = &polygon[numVertex-1];

/* initialize scanning edges */
Vright = VnextRight = VnextLeft = Vleft;

/* prepare bottom of initial scanline - no coverage by polygon */
for (i=0; i<SUBYRES; i++)
     sp[i].xLeft = sp[i].xRight = -1;
xLmin = xRmin = MAX_X;
xLmax = xRmax = -1;

/* scan convert for each subpixel from bottom to top */
for (y+Vleft->y; ; y++)     {

     while (y == VnextLeft->y) {    /* reached next left vertex */
          VnextLeft = (Vleft+VnextLeft) + 1;  /* advance */
          if (VnextLeft > endPoly)            /* (wraparound) */
               VnextLeft = polygon;
          if (VnextLeft == Vright)   /* all y's same?  */
               return;               /* (null polygon) */
          xLeft = screenX(Vleft);
          xNextLeft = screenX(VnextLeft);
     }

     while (y == VnextRight->y) { /*reached next right vertex */
          VnextRight = (Vright=VnextRight) -1;
          if (VnextRight < polygon)            /* (wraparound) */
               VnextRight = endPoly;
```

```
                xRight = screenX(Vright);
                xNextRight = screenX(VnextRight);
        }

        if (y>VnextLeft->y || y>VnextRight->y)  {
                    /* done, mark uncovered part of last scanline */
            for (; MODRES(y); y++)
                sp[MODRES(y)].xLeft = sp[MODRES(y)].xRight = -1;
            renderScanline(Vleft, Vright, y/SUBYRES, object);
            return;
        }

/*
 * Interpolate sub-pixel x endpoints at this y,
 * and update extremes for pixel coherence optimization
 */

        sp_ptr = &sp[MODRES(y)];
        aLeft = (double)(y - Vleft->y) / (VnextLeft->y - Vleft->y);
        sp_ptr->xLeft = LERP(aLeft, xLeft, xNextLeft);
        if (sp_ptr->xLeft < xLmin)
            xLmin = sp_ptr->xLeft;
        if (sp_ptr->xLeft > xLmax)
            xLmax = sp_ptr->xLeft;

        aRight = (double)(y - Vright->y) / (VnextRight->y
                        - Vright->y);
        sp_ptr->xRight = LERP(aRight, xRight, xNextRight);
        if (sp_ptr->xRight < xRmin)
            xRmin = sp_ptr->xRight;
        if (sp_ptr->xRight > xRmax)
            xRmax = sp_ptr->xRight;

        if (MODRES(y) == SUBYRES-1)   {    /* end of scanline */
                /* interpolate edges to this scanline */
            vLerp(aLeft, Vleft, VnextLeft, &VscanLeft);
            vLerp(aRight, Vright, VnextRight, &VscanRight);
            renderScanline(&VscanLeft, &VscanRight, y/SUBYRES,
                object);
            xLmin = xRmin = MAX_X;           /* reset extremes */
            xLmax = xRmax = -1;
        }
    }
}

/*
 * Render one scanline of polygon
 */

renderScanline(Vl, Vr, y, object)
    Vertex *Vl, *Vr;  /* polygon vertices interpolated */
                      /* at scanline */
    int y;            /* scanline coordinate */
    Surface *object;  /* shading parms for this object */
{
    Vertex Vpixel;      /*object info interpolated at one pixel */
    unsigned mask[SUBYRES];  /*pixel coverage bitmask */
    int x;              /* leftmost subpixel of current pixel */
```

```
        for (x=SUBXRES*FLOOR(xLmin/SUBXRES); x<=xRmax; x+=SUBXRES) {
            vLerp((double)(x-xLmin)/(xRmax-xLmin), Vl, Vr, &Vpixel);
            computePixelMask(x, mask);
            renderPixel(x/SUBXRES, y, &Vpixel,
                        /*computePixel*/Coverage(x), mask, object);
        }
    }

/*
 * Compute number of subpixels covered by polygon at current pixel
 */
/*computePixel*/Coverage(x)
        int x;              /* left subpixel of pixel */
    {
        int   area              /* total covered area */
        int partialArea;        /* covered area for current subpixel y */
        int xr = x+SUBXRES-1; /*right subpixel of pixel */
        int y;

        /* shortcut for common case of fully covered pixel */
        if (x>xLmax && x<xRmin)
            return MAX_AREA;

        for (area=y=0; y<SUBYRES; y++) {
            partialArea = MIN(sp[y].xRight, xr)
                - MAX(sp[y].xLeft, x) + 1;
            if (partialArea>0)
                area += partialArea;
        }
        return area;
    }

/* Compute bitmask indicating which subpixels are covered by
 * polygon at current pixel. (Not all hidden-surface methods
 * need this mask. )
 */
computePixelMask(x, mask)
        int x;              /* left subpixel of pixel */
        unsigned mask[];        /* output bitmask */
    {
        static unsigned leftMaskTable[] =
            { 0xFFFF, 0x7FFF, 0x3FFF, 0x1FFF, 0x0FFF, 0x07FF, 0x03FF,
              0x01FF, 0x00FF, 0x007F, 0x003F, 0x001F, 0x000F,
              0x0007, 0x0003, 0x0001  };
        static unsigned rightMaskTable[] =
            { 0x8000, 0xC000, 0xE000, 0xF000, 0xF800, 0xFC00,
                0xFE00, 0xFF00, 0xFF80, 0xFFC0, 0xFFE0, 0xFFF0,
                0xFFF8, 0xFFFC, 0xFFFE, 0xFFFF  };
        unsigned leftMask, rightMask;           /* partial masks */
        int xr = x+SUBXRES-1;               /* right subpixel of pixel */
        int y;

    /* shortcut for common case of fully covered pixel */
        if (x>xLmax && x<xRmin)   {
            for (y=0; y<SUBYRES; y++)
                mask[y] = 0xFFFF;
        } else   {
```

```
        for (y=0; y<SUBYRES; y++) {
            if (sp[y].xLeft < x)   /* completely left of pixel*/
                leftMask = 0xFFFF;
            else if (sp[y].xLeft > xr)  /* completely right */
                leftMask = 0;
            else
                leftMask = leftMaskTable[sp[y].xLeft -x];

            if (sp[y].xRight > xr)      /* completely */
                                       /* right of pixel*/
                rightMask = 0xFFFF;
            else if (sp[y].xRight < x)     /*completely left */
                rightMask = O;
            else
                rightMask = rightMaskTable[sp[y].xRight -x];
            mask[y] = leftMask & rightMask;
        }
    }
}
```

GENERIC CONVEX
POLYGON SCAN
CONVERSION AND CLIPPING

(page 84)

Paul Heckbert

```c
/* poly.h: definitions for polygon package */

#ifndef POLY_HDR
#define POLY_HDR

#define POLY_NMAX 8   /* max #sides to a polygon; change if needed */

typedef struct {              /* A POLYGON VERTEX */
    double sx, sy, sz, sw;    /* screen space position  */
                             /* (sometimes homo.) */
    double x, y, z;          /* world space position */
    double u, v, q;          /* texture position */
                             /* (sometimes homogeneous) */
    double r, g, b;          /* (red,green,blue) color */
    double nx, ny, nz;       /* world space normal vector */
} Poly_vert;
/* update poly.c if you change this structure */

typedef struct {              /* A POLYGON */
    int n;                   /* number of sides */
    int mask;                /* interpolation mask for vertex elems */
    Poly_vert vert[POLY_NMAX]; /* vertices */
} Poly;
/*
 * mask is an interpolation mask whose kth bit indicates whether the kth
 * double in a Poly_vert is relevant.
 * For example, if the valid attributes are sx, sy, and sz, then set
 *   mask = POLY_MASK(sx) | POLY_MASK(sy) | POLY_MASK(sz);
 */

typedef struct {              /* A BOX (TYPICALLY IN SCREEN SPACE) */
    double x0, x1;           /* left and right */
    double y0, y1;           /* top and bottom */
    double z0, z1;           /* near and far */
} Poly_box;
```

```
typedef struct {              /* WINDOW: A DISCRETE 2-D RECTANGLE */
    int x0, y0;               /* xmin and ymin */
    int x1, y1;               /* xmax and ymax (inclusive) */
} Window;

#define POLY_MASK(elem) (1 << (&poly_dummy->elem - \
                            (double *)poly_dummy))

#define POLY_CLIP_OUT 0           /* polygon entirely outside box */
#define POLY_CLIP_PARTIAL 1       /* polygon partially inside */
#define POLY_CLIP_IN 2            /* polygon entirely inside box */

extern Poly_vert *poly_dummy;  /* used superficially by */
                               /* POLY_MASK macro */

void    poly_print(/* str, p */);
void    poly_vert_label(/* str, mask */);
void    poly_vert_print(/* str, v, mask */);
int     poly_clip_to_box(/* p1, box */);
void    poly_clip_to_halfspace(/* p, q, index, sign, k, name */);
void    poly_scan(/* p, win, pixelproc */);

#endif


/*
 * poly.c: simple utilities for polygon data structures
 */

#include "poly.h"

Poly_vert *poly_dummy;       /* used superficially by POLY_MASK macro */

/*
 * poly_print: print Poly p to stdout, prefixed by the label str */

void poly_print(str, p)
char *str;
Poly *p;
{
    int i;

    printf("%s: %d sides\n", str, p->n);
    poly_vert_label("        ", p->mask);
    for (i=0; i<p->n; i++) {
        printf("    v[%d] ", i);
        poly_vert_print("", &p->vert[i], p->mask);
    }
}
```

```c
void poly_vert_label(str, mask)
char *str;
int mask;
{
    printf("%s", str);
    if (mask&POLY_MASK(sx))    printf("   sx   ");
    if (mask&POLY_MASK(sy))    printf("   sy   ");
    if (mask&POLY_MASK(sz))    printf("   sz   ");
    if (mask&POLY_MASK(sw))    printf("   sw   ");
    if (mask&POLY_MASK(x))     printf("   x    ");
    if (mask&POLY_MASK(y))     printf("   y    ");
    if (mask&POLY_MASK(z))     printf("   z    ");
    if (mask&POLY_MASK(u))     printf("   u    ");
    if (mask&POLY_MASK(v))     printf("   v    ");
    if (mask&POLY_MASK(q))     printf("   q    ");
    if (mask&POLY_MASK(r))     printf("   r    ");
    if (mask&POLY_MASK(g))     printf("   g    ");
    if (mask&POLY_MASK(b))     printf("   b    ");
    if (mask&POLY_MASK(nx))    printf("   nx   ");
    if (mask&POLY_MASK(ny))    printf("   ny   ");
    if (mask&POLY_MASK(nz))    printf("   nz   ");
    printf("\n");
}

void poly_vert_print(str, v, mask)
char *str;
Poly_vert *v;
int mask;
{
    printf("%s", str);
    if (mask&POLY_MASK(sx)) printf(" %6.1f", v->sx);
    if (mask&POLY_MASK(sy)) printf(" %6.1f", v->sy);
    if (mask&POLY_MASK(sz)) printf(" %6.2f", v->sz);
    if (mask&POLY_MASK(sw)) printf(" %6.2f", v->sw);
    if (mask&POLY_MASK(x))  printf(" %6.2f", v->x);
    if (mask&POLY_MASK(y))  printf(" %6.2f", v->y);
    if (mask&POLY_MASK(z))  printf(" %6.2f", v->z);
    if (mask&POLY_MASK(u))  printf(" %6.2f", v->u);
    if (mask&POLY_MASK(v))  printf(" %6.2f", v->v);
    if (mask&POLY_MASK(q))  printf(" %6.2f", v->q);
    if (mask&POLY_MASK(r))  printf(" %6.4f", v->r);
    if (mask&POLY_MASK(g))  printf(" %6.4f", v->g);
    if (mask&POLY_MASK(b))  printf(" %6.4f", v->b);
    if (mask&POLY_MASK(nx)) printf(" %6.3f", v->nx);
    if (mask&POLY_MASK(ny)) printf(" %6.3f", v->ny);
    if (mask&POLY_MASK(nz)) printf(" %6.3f", v->nz);
    printf("\n");
}
```

```
/*
 * poly_scan.c: point-sampled scan conversion of convex polygons
 *
 * Paul Heckbert   1985, Dec 1989
 */

#include <stdio.h>
#include <math.h>
#include "poly.h"

/*
 * poly_scan: Scan convert a polygon, calling pixelproc at
 * each pixel with an interpolated Poly_vert structure.
 *    Polygon can be clockwise or ccw.
 * Polygon is clipped in 2-D to win, the screen space window.
 *
 * Scan conversion is done on the basis of Poly_vert fields sx and sy.
 * These two must always be interpolated, and only they have
 * special meaning to this code; any other fields are
 * blindly interpolated regardless of their semantics.
 *
 * The pixelproc subroutine takes the arguments:
 *
 *   pixelproc(x, y, point)
 *   int x, y;
 *   Poly_vert *point;
 *
 * All the fields of point indicated by p->mask will be
 * valid inside pixelproc except sx and sy.
 * If they were computed, they would have values
 * sx=x+.5 and sy=y+.5, since sampling is done at pixel centers.
 */

void poly_scan(p, win, pixelproc)
register Poly *p;            /* polygon */
Window *win;             /* 2-D screen space clipping window */
void (*pixelproc)();          /* procedure called at each pixel */
{
    register int i, li, ri, y, ly, ry, top, rem, mask;
    double ymin;
    Poly_vert l, r, dl, dr;

    if (p->n>POLY_NMAX) {
        fprintf(stderr, "poly_scan: too many vertices: %d\n", p->n);
        return;
    }
```

```
    ymin = HUGE;
    for (i=0; i<p->n; i++)        /* find top vertex (y points down) */
        if (p->vert[i].sy < ymin) {
            ymin = p->vert[i].sy;
            top = i;
        }

    li = ri = top;                /* left and right vertex indices */
    rem = p->n;                   /* number of vertices remaining */
    y = ceil(ymin-.5);               /* current scan line */
    ly = ry = y-1;                /* lower end of left & right edges */
    mask = p->mask & ~POLY_MASK(sy); /* stop interpolating screen y */

    while (rem>0) { /* scan in y, activating new edges on left & */
                    /* right as scan line passes over new vertices */

        while (ly<=y && rem>0) {  /* advance left edge? */
            rem--;
            i = li-1;                 /* step ccw down left side */
            if (i<0) i = p->n-1;
            incrementalize_y(&p->vert[li], &p->vert[i], &l,
                        &dl, y, mask);
            ly = floor(p->vert[i].sy+.5);
            li = i;
        }
        while (ry<=y && rem>0) {  /* advance right edge? */
            rem--;
            i = ri+1;                 /* step cw down right edge */
            if (i>=p->n) i = 0;
            incrementalize_y(&p->vert[ri], &p->vert[i], &r,
                        &dr, y, mask);
            ry = floor(p->vert[i].sy+.5);
            ri = i;
        }

        while (y<ly && y<ry)
                    /* do scanlines till end of l or r edge */
            if (y>=win->y0 && y<=win->y1)
              if (l.sx<=r.sx) scanline(y, &l, &r, win, pixelproc, mask);
              else            scanline(y, &r, &l, win, pixelproc, mask);
            y++;
            increment(&l, &dl, mask);
            increment(&r, &dr, mask);
        }
    }
}
```

```
/* scanline: output scanline by sampling polygon at Y=y+.5 */

static scanline(y, l, r, win, pixelproc, mask)
int y, mask;
Poly_vert *l, *r;
Window *win;
void (*pixelproc)();
{
    int x, lx, rx;
    Poly_vert p, dp;

    mask &= ~POLY_MASK(sx);             /* stop interpolating screen x */
    lx = ceil(l->sx-.5);
    if (lx<win->x0) lx = win->x0;
    rx = floor(r->sx-.5);
    if (rx>win->x1) rx = win->x1;
    if (lx>rx) return;
    incrementalize_x(l, r, &p, &dp, lx, mask);
    for (x=lx; x<=rx; x++) {             /* scan in x, generating pixels */
        (*pixelproc)(x, y, &p);
        increment(&p, &dp, mask);
    }
}

/*
 * incrementalize_y: put intersection of line Y=y+.5 with edge
 * between points p1 and p2 in p, put change with respect to y in dp
 */

static incrementalize_y(p1, p2, p, dp, y, mask)
register double *p1, *p2, *p, *dp;
register int mask;
int y;
{
    double dy, frac;

    dy = ((Poly_vert *)p2)->sy - ((Poly_vert *)p1)->sy;
    if (dy==0.) dy = 1.;
    frac = y+.5 - ((Poly_vert *)p1)->sy;

    for (; mask!=0; mask>>=1, p1++, p2++, p++, dp++)
        if (mask&1) {
            *dp = (*p2-*p1)/dy;
            *p = *p1+*dp*frac;
        }
}
```

```
/*
 * incrementalize_x: put intersection of line X=x+.5 with
 * edge between points p1 and p2 in p,
 *  put change with respect to x in dp
 */

static incrementalize_x(p1, p2, p, dp, x, mask)
register double *p1, *p2, *p, *dp;
register int mask;
int x;
{
    double dx, frac;

    dx = ((Poly_vert *)p2)->sx - ((Poly_vert *)p1)->sx;
    if (dx==0.) dx = 1.;
    frac = x+.5 - ((Poly_vert *)p1)->sx;

    for (; mask!=0; mask>>=1, p1++, p2++, p++, dp++)
        if (mask&1) {
            *dp = (*p2-*p1)/dx;
            *p = *p1+*dp*frac;
        }
}

static increment(p, dp, mask)
register double *p, *dp;
register int mask;
{
    for (; mask!=0; mask>>=1, p++, dp++)
        if (mask&1)
            *p += *dp;
}


/*
 * poly_clip.c: homogeneous 3-D convex polygon clipper
 *
 * Paul Heckbert   1985, Dec 1989
 */

#include "poly.h"

#define SWAP(a, b, temp)  {temp = a; a = b; b = temp;}
#define COORD(vert, i)   ((double *)(vert))[i]

#define CLIP_AND_SWAP(elem, sign, k, p, q, r) { \
    poly_clip_to_halfspace(p, q, &v->elem-(double *)v, sign, sign*k); \
    if (q->n==0) {p1->n = 0; return POLY_CLIP_OUT;} \
    SWAP(p, q, r); \
}
```

```
/*
 * poly_clip_to_box: Clip the convex polygon p1 to the screen space box
 * using the homogeneous screen coordinates (sx, sy, sz, sw) of each
 * vertex, testing if v->sx/v->sw > box->x0 and v->sx/v->sw < box->x1,
 * and similar tests for y and z, for each vertex v of the polygon.
 * If polygon is entirely inside box, then POLY_CLIP_IN is returned.
 * If polygon is entirely outside box, then POLY_CLIP_OUT is returned.
 * Otherwise, if the polygon is cut by the box, p1 is modified and
 * POLY_CLIP_PARTIAL is returned.
 */

int poly_clip_to_box(p1, box)
register Poly *p1;
register Poly_box *box;
{
    int x0out = 0, x1out = 0, y0out = 0, y1out = 0, z0out = 0,
        z1out = 0;
    register int i;
    register Poly_vert *v;
    Poly p2, *p, *q, *r;

    /* count vertices "outside" with respect to each */
    /* of the six planes */
    for (v=p1->vert, i=p1->n; i>0; i--, v++) {
        if (v->sx < box->x0*v->sw) x0out++;    /* out on left */
        if (v->sx > box->x1*v->sw) x1out++;    /* out on right */
        if (v->sy < box->y0*v->sw) y0out++;    /* out on top */
        if (v->sy > box->y1*v->sw) y1out++;    /* out on bottom */
        if (v->sz < box->z0*v->sw) z0out++;    /* out on near */
        if (v->sz > box->z1*v->sw) z1out++;    /* out on far */
    }

    /* check if all vertices inside */
    if (x0out+x1out+y0out+y1out+z0out+z1out == 0) return POLY_CLIP_IN;

    /* check if all vertices are "outside" any of the six planes */
    if (x0out==p1->n || x1out==p1->n || y0out==p1->n ||
        y1out==p1->n || z0out==p1->n || z1out==p1->n) {
        p1->n = 0;
        return POLY_CLIP_OUT;
    }
```

```
    /*
     * now clip against each of the planes that might cut the polygon,
     * at each step toggling between polygons p1 and p2
     */
    p = p1;
    q = &p2;
    if (x0out) CLIP_AND_SWAP(sx, -1., box->x0, p, q, r);
    if (x1out) CLIP_AND_SWAP(sx,  1., box->x1, p, q, r);
    if (y0out) CLIP_AND_SWAP(sy, -1., box->y0, p, q, r);
    if (y1out) CLIP_AND_SWAP(sy,  1., box->y1, p, q, r);
    if (z0out) CLIP_AND_SWAP(sz, -1., box->z0, p, q, r);
    if (z1out) CLIP_AND_SWAP(sz,  1., box->z1, p, q, r);

    /* if result ended up in p2 then copy it to p1 */
    if (p==&p2)
        bcopy(&p2, p1, sizeof(Poly)-
            (POLY_NMAX-p2.n)*sizeof(Poly_vert));
    return POLY_CLIP_PARTIAL;
}

/*
 * poly_clip_to_halfspace: clip convex polygon p against a plane,
 * copying the portion satisfying sign*s[index] < k*sw into q,
 * where s is a Poly_vert* cast as a double*.
 * index is an index into the array of doubles at each vertex, such that
 * s[index] is sx, sy, or sz (screen space x, y, or z).
 * Thus, to clip against xmin, use
 *   poly_clip_to_halfspace(p, q, XINDEX, -1., -xmin);
 * and to clip against xmax, use
 *   poly_clip_to_halfspace(p, q, XINDEX,  1.,  xmax);
 */

void poly_clip_to_halfspace(p, q, index, sign, k)
Poly *p, *q;
register int index;
double sign, k;
{
    register int m;
    register double *up, *vp, *wp;
    register Poly_vert *v;
    int i;
    Poly_vert *u;
    double t, tu, tv;

    q->n = 0;
    q->mask = p->mask;
```

```
        /* start with u=vert[n-1], v=vert[0] */
        u = &p->vert[p->n-1];
        tu = sign*COORD(u, index) - u->sw*k;
        for (v= &p->vert[0], i=p->n; i>0; i--, u=v, tu=tv, v++) {
        /* on old polygon (p), u is previous vertex, v is current vertex */
        /* tv is negative if vertex v is in */
            tv = sign*COORD(v, index) - v->sw*k;
            if (tu<=0. ^ tv<=0.) {
                /* edge crosses plane; add intersection point to q */
                t = tu/(tu-tv);
                vp = (double *)v;
                wp = (double *)&q->vert[q->n];
                for (m=p->mask; m!=0; m>>=1, up++, vp++, wp++)
                    if (m&1) *wp = *up+t*(*vp-*up);
                q->n++;
            }
            if (tv<=0.)        /* vertex v is in, copy it to q */
                q->vert[q->n++] = *v;
        }
    }


/*
 * scantest.c: use poly_scan() for Gouraud shading and z-buffer demo.
 * Given the screen space X, Y, and Z of N-gon on command line,
 * print out all pixels during scan conversion.
 * This code could easily be modified to actually read and write pixels
 *
 * Paul Heckbert   Dec 1989
 */

#include <stdio.h>
#include <math.h>
#include "poly.h"

#define XMAX 1280     /* hypothetical image width */
#define YMAX 1024     /* hypothetical image height */

#define FRANDOM()  ((rand()&32767)/32767.)
        /* random number between 0 and 1 */

void pixelproc();
```

```
main(ac, av)
int ac;
char **av;
{
    int i;
    Poly p;
    static Window win = {0, 0, XMAX-1, YMAX-1};
            /* screen clipping window */

    if (ac<2 || ac != 2+3*(p.n = atoi(av[1]))) {
        fprintf(stderr,
            "Usage: scantest N X1 Y1 Z1 X2 Y2 Z2 ... XN YN ZN\n");
        exit(1);
    }
    for (i=0; i<p.n; i++) {
        p.vert[i].sx = atof(av[2+3*i]);   /* set screen space x,y,z */
        p.vert[i].sy = atof(av[3+3*i]);
        p.vert[i].sz = atof(av[4+3*i]);
        p.vert[i].r = FRANDOM();   /* random vertex colors, for kicks */
        p.vert[i].g = FRANDOM();
        p.vert[i].b = FRANDOM();
    }
    /* interpolate sx, sy, sz, r, g, and b in poly_scan */
    p.mask = POLY_MASK(sx) | POLY_MASK(sy) | POLY_MASK(sz) |
        POLY_MASK(r) | POLY_MASK(g) | POLY_MASK(b);

    poly_print("scan converting the polygon", &p);

    poly_scan(&p, &win, pixelproc); /* scan convert! */
}

static void pixelproc(x, y, point)
            /* called at each pixel by poly_scan */
int x, y;
Poly_vert *point;
{
    printf("pixel (%d,%d) screenz=%g rgb=(%g,%g,%g)\n",
        x, y, point->sz, point->r, point->g, point->b);

    /*
     * in real graphics program you could read and write pixels, e.g.:
     *
     *   if (point->sz < zbuffer_read(x, y)) {
     *       image_write_rgb(x, y, point->r, point->g, point->b);
     *       zbuffer_write(x, y, point->sz);
     *   }
     */
}
```

```
/*
 * fancytest.c: subroutine illustrating the use of poly_clip and
poly_scan
 * for Phong-shading and texture mapping.
 * Note: lines enclosed in angle brackets "<", ">" should be
 * replaced with the code described.
 * Makes calls to hypothetical packages "shade", "image", "texture",
 * "zbuffer".
 * Paul Heckbert   Dec 1989
 */

#include <stdio.h>
#include <math.h>
#include "poly.h"

#define XMAX 1280      /* hypothetical image width */
#define YMAX 1024      /* hypothetical image height */
#define LIGHT_INTEN 255        /* light source intensity */

void pixelproc();

fancytest()
{
    int i;
    double WS[4][4]; /* world space to screen space transform */
    Poly p;         /* a polygon */
    Poly_vert *v;

    static Poly_box box = {0, XMAX-1, 0, YMAX-1, -32678, 32767};
    /* 3-D screen clipping box */

    static Window win = {0, 0, XMAX-1, YMAX-1};
    /* 2-D screen clipping window */

    <initialize world space position (x,y,z), normal (nx,ny,nz), and
    texture position (u,v) at each vertex of p; set p.n>
    <set WS to world-to-screen transform>

    /* transform vertices from world space to homogeneous */
    /*    screen space */
    for (i=0; i<p.n; i++) {
        v = &p.vert[i];
        mx4_transform(v->x, v->y, v->z, 1.,
            WS, &v->sx, &v->sy, &v->sz, &v->sw);
    }
```

```
    /* interpolate sx, sy, sz, sw, nx, ny, nz, u, v in poly_clip */
    p.mask = POLY_MASK(sx) | POLY_MASK(sy) | POLY_MASK(sz) |
        POLY_MASK(sw) | POLY_MASK(nx) | POLY_MASK(ny) | POLY_MASK(nz) |
        POLY_MASK(u) | POLY_MASK(v);

    poly_print("before clipping", &p);
    if (poly_clip_to_box(&p, &box) == POLY_CLIP_OUT) /* clip polygon */
        return;                           /* quit if off-screen */

    /* do homogeneous division of screen position, texture position */
    for (i=0; i<p.n; i++) {
        v = &p.vert[i];
        v->sx /= v->sw;
        v->sy /= v->sw;
        v->sz /= v->sw;
        v->u /= v->sw;
        v->v /= v->sw;
        v->q = 1./v->sw;
    }
    /*
     * previously we ignored q (assumed q=1),
     *   henceforth ignore sw (assume sw=1)
     * Interpolate sx, sy, sz, nx, ny, nz, u, v, q in poly_scan
     */
    p.mask &= ~POLY_MASK(sw);
    p.mask |= POLY_MASK(q);

    poly_print("scan converting the polygon", &p);
    poly_scan(&p, &win, pixelproc); /* scan convert! */
}

static void pixelproc(x, y, pt)
    /* called at each pixel by poly_scan */
int x, y;
Poly_vert *pt;
{
    int sz, u, v, inten;
    double len, nor[3], diff, spec;
```

```
          sz = pt->sz;
          if (sz < zbuffer_read(x, y)) {
                len = sqrt(pt->nx*pt->nx + pt->ny*pt->ny + pt->nz*pt->nz);
                nor[0] = pt->nx/len;          /* unitize the normal vector */
                nor[1] = pt->ny/len;
                nor[2] = pt->nz/len;
                shade(nor, &diff, &spec);
                                /* compute specular and diffuse coeffs*/
                u = pt->u/pt->q;          /* do homogeneous div. of texture pos */
                v = pt->v/pt->q;
                inten = texture_read(u, v)*diff + LIGHT_INTEN*spec;
                image_write(x, y, inten);
                zbuffer_write(x, y, sz);
          }
}

/* mx4_transform: transform 4-vector p by matrix m */
/*    yielding q: q = p*m */

mx4_transform(px, py, pz, pw, m, qxp, qyp, qzp, qwp)
double px, py, pz, pw, m[4][4], *qxp, *qyp, *qzp, *qwp;
{
     *qxp = px*m[0][0] + py*m[1][0] + pz*m[2][0] + pw*m[3][0];
     *qyp = px*m[0][1] + py*m[1][1] + pz*m[2][1] + pw*m[3][1];
     *qzp = px*m[0][2] + py*m[1][2] + pz*m[2][2] + pw*m[3][2];
     *qwp = px*m[0][3] + py*m[1][3] + pz*m[2][3] + pw*m[3][3];
}
```

680

CONCAVE POLYGON SCAN CONVERSION

(page 87)

Paul Heckbert

```
/*
 * concave: scan convert nvert-sided concave non-simple polygon
 * with vertices at (point[i].x, point[i].y) for i in
 * [0..nvert-1] within the window win by
 * calling spanproc for each visible span of pixels.
 * Polygon can be clockwise or counterclockwise.
 * Algorithm does uniform point sampling at pixel centers.
 * Inside-outside test done by Jordan's rule: a point is
 * considered inside if an emanating ray intersects the polygon
 * an odd number of times.
 * drawproc should fill in pixels from xl to xr inclusive on scanline y,
 * e.g:
 *   drawproc(y, xl, xr)
 *   int y, xl, xr;
 *   {
 *       int x;
 *       for (x=xl; x<=xr; x++)
 *           pixel_write(x, y, pixelvalue);
 *   }
 *
 *   Paul Heckbert 30 June 81, 18 Dec 89
 */

#include <stdio.h>
#include <math.h>
#include <gem.h>            /* header file for gems */

#define ALLOC(ptr, type, n) \
        ASSERT(ptr = (type *)malloc((n)*sizeof(type)))

typedef  struct {          /* window: a discrete 2-D rectangle */
    int x0, y0;            /* xmin and ymin */
    int x1, y1;            /* xmax and ymax (inclusive) */
} Window;
```

```
typedef  struct  {            /* a polygon edge */
    double x;
        /* x coordinate of edge's intersection with current scanline *
    double dx;    /* change in x with respect to y */
    int i;    /* edge number: edge i goes from pt[i] to pt[i+1] */
} Edge;

static int n;                 /* number of vertices */
static Point2 *pt;            /* vertices */

static int nact;              /* number of active edges */
static Edge *active;  /* active edge list:edges crossing scanline y */

int compare_ind(), compare_active();

concave(nvert, point, win, spanproc)
int nvert;                    /* number of vertices */
Point2 *point;                /* vertices of polygon */
Window *win;                  /* screen clipping window */
void (*spanproc)();           /* called for each span of pixels */
{
    int k, y0, y1, y, i, j, xl, xr;
    int *ind;       /* list of vertex indices, sorted by pt[ind[j]].y */

    n = nvert;
    pt = point;
    if (n<=0) return;
    ALLOC(ind, int, n);
    ALLOC(active, Edge, n);

    /* create y-sorted array of indices ind[k] into vertex list */
    for (k=0; k<n; k++)
        ind[k] = k;
    qsort(ind, n, sizeof ind[0], compare_ind);
                                /* sort ind by pt[ind[k]].y */

    nact = 0;                        /* start with empty active list */
    k = 0;                        /* ind[k] is next vertex to process */
    y0 = MAX(win->y0, ceil(pt[ind[0]].y-.5));
                                            /* ymin of polygon */
    y1 = MIN(win->y1, floor(pt[ind[n-1]].y-.5));
                                            /* ymax of polygon */

    for (y=y0; y<=y1; y++) {  /* step through scanlines */
```

```
/* scanline y is at y+.5 in continuous coordinates */
/* Check vertices between previous scanline */
/* and current one, if any */

for (; k<n && pt[ind[k]].y<=y+.5; k++) {
    /* to simplify, if pt.y=y+.5, pretend it's above */
    /* invariant: y-.5 < pt[i].y <= y+.5 */
    i = ind[k];
  /*
    * insert or delete edges before and after
    * vertex i  (i-1 to i, and i to i+1) from active
    * list if they cross scanline y
    */
    j = i>0 ? i-1 : n-1;   /* vertex previous to i */
    if (pt[j].y <= y-.5)
    /* old edge, remove from active list */
        delete(j);
    else if (pt[j].y > y+.5)
    /* new edge, add to active list */
        insert(j, y);
    j = i<n-1 ? i+1 : 0;   /* vertex next after i */
    if (pt[j].y <= y-.5)
    /* old edge, remove from active list */
        delete(i);
    else if (pt[j].y > y+.5)
    /* new edge, add to active list */
        insert(i, y);
}

/* sort active edge list by active[j].x */
qsort(active, nact, sizeof active[0], compare_active);

/* draw horizontal segments for scanline y */
for (j=0; j<nact; j+=2) { /* draw horizontal segments */
/* span 'tween j & j+1 is inside, span tween */
/* j+1 & j+2 is outside */
    xl = ceil(active[j].x-.5);   /* left end of span */
    if (xl<win->x0) xl = win->x0;
    xr = floor(active[j+1].x-.5);
                                     /* right end of span */
    if (xr>win->x1) xr = win->x1;
    if (xl<=xr)
            (*spanproc)(y, xl, xr);
                                     /* draw pixels in span */
    active[j].x += active[j].dx;
                            /* increment edge coords */
    active[j+1].x += active[j+1].dx;
}
}
}
```

```
static delete(i)        /* remove edge i from active list */
int i;
{
    int j;

    for (j=0; j<nact && active[j].i!=i; j++);
    if (j>=nact) return;
        /* edge not in active list; happens at win->y0*/
    nact--;
    bcopy(&active[j+1], &active[j], (nact-j)*sizeof active[0]);
}

static insert(i, y)        /* append edge i to end of active list */
int i, y;
{
    int j;
    double dx;
    Point2 *p, *q;

    j = i<n-1 ? i+1 : 0;
    if (pt[i].y < pt[j].y) {p = &pt[i]; q = &pt[j];}
    else                   {p = &pt[j]; q = &pt[i];}
    /* initialize x position at intersection of edge with scanline y *
    active[nact].dx = dx = (q->x-p->x)/(q->y-p->y);
    active[nact].x = dx*(y+.5-p->y)+p->x;
    active[nact].i = i;
    nact++;
}

/* comparison routines for qsort */
compare_ind(u, v) int *u, *v; {return pt[*u].y <= pt[*v].y ? -1 : 1;}
compare_active(u, v) Edge *u, *v; {return u->x <= v->x ? -1 : 1;}
```

684

DIGITAL LINE DRAWING

(page 99)

Paul Heckbert

```c
/*
 * digline: draw digital line from (x1,y1) to (x2,y2),
 * calling a user-supplied procedure at each pixel.
 * Does no clipping.  Uses Bresenham's algorithm.
 * Paul Heckbert  3 Sep 85
 */

#include <gem.h>
digline(x1, y1, x2, y2, dotproc)
int x1, y1, x2, y2;
void (*dotproc)();
{
    int d, x, y, ax, ay, sx, sy, dx, dy;

    dx = x2-x1;   ax = ABS(dx)<<1;   sx = SGN(dx);
    dy = y2-y1;   ay = ABS(dy)<<1;   sy = SGN(dy);

    x = x1;
    y = y1;
    if (ax>ay) {          /* x dominant */
        d = ay-(ax>>1);
        for (;;) {
            (*dotproc)(x, y);
            if (x==x2) return;
            if (d>=0) {
                y += sy;
                d -= ax;
            }
            x += sx;
            d += ay;
        }
    }
    else {                  /* y dominant */
        d = ax-(ay>>1);
        for (;;) {
            (*dotproc)(x, y);
            if (y==y2) return;
            if (d>=0) {
                x += sx;
                d -= ay;
            }
            y += sy;
            d += ax;
        }
    }
}
```

SYMMETRIC DOUBLE STEP
LINE ALGORITHM

(page 101)

Brian Wyvill

```c
#define swap(a,b)                {a^=b; b^=a; a^=b;}
#define absolute(i,j,k)          ( (i-j)*(k = ( (i-j)<0 ? -1 : 1)))
int
symwuline(a1, b1, a2, b2) int a1, b1, a2, b2;
{
    int         dx, dy, incr1, incr2, D, x, y, xend, c, pixels_left;
    int         x1, y1;
    int         sign_x, sign_y, step, reverse, i;

    dx = absolute(a2, a1, sign_x);
    dy = absolute(b2, b1, sign_y);
    /* decide increment sign by the slope sign */
    if (sign_x == sign_y)
        step = 1;
    else
        step = -1;

    if (dy > dx) {          /* chooses axis of greatest movement (make
                             * dx) */
        swap(a1, b1);
        swap(a2, b2);
        swap(dx, dy);
        reverse = 1;
    } else
        reverse = 0;
    /* note error check for dx==0 should be included here */
    if (a1 > a2) {          /* start from the smaller coordinate */
        x = a2;
        y = b2;
        x1 = a1;
        y1 = b1;
    } else {
        x = a1;
        y = b1;
        x1 = a2;
        y1 = b2;
    }
}
```

```c
/* Note dx=n implies 0 - n or (dx+1) pixels to be set */
/* Go round loop dx/4 times then plot last 0,1,2 or 3 pixels */
/* In fact (dx-1)/4 as 2 pixels are already plottted */
xend = (dx - 1) / 4;
pixels_left = (dx - 1) % 4;       /* number of pixels left over at the
                                   * end */
plot(x, y, reverse);
plot(x1, y1, reverse);            /* plot first two points */
incr2 = 4 * dy - 2 * dx;
if (incr2 < 0) { /* slope less than 1/2 */
    c = 2 * dy;
    incr1 = 2 * c;
    D = incr1 - dx;

    for (i = 0; i < xend; i++) {        /* plotting loop */
        ++x;
        --x1;
        if (D < 0) {
                            /* pattern 1 forwards */
            plot(x, y, reverse);
            plot(++x, y, reverse);
                            /* pattern 1 backwards */
            plot(x1, y1, reverse);
            plot(--x1, y1, reverse);
            D += incr1;
        } else {
            if (D < c) {
                /* pattern 2 forwards */
                plot(x, y, reverse);
                plot(++x, y += step, reverse);
                /* pattern 2 backwards */
                plot(x1, y1, reverse);
                plot(--x1, y1 -= step, reverse);
            } else {
                /* pattern 3 forwards */
                plot(x, y += step, reverse);
                plot(++x, y, reverse);
                /* pattern 3 backwards */
                plot(x1, y1 -= step, reverse);
                plot(--x1, y1, reverse);
            }
            D + = incr2;
        }
    }           /* end for */
```

[handwritten annotations in margins] always smaller · always large · plot is odd. If reverse = 0, plot (x, y) plots @ x, y · if reverse = 1, x is y, and y is x. Nonetheless, on calling plot true x, true y get illuminated ⇒ just a cute way to keep from unrolling loop too much.

```
          /* plot last pattern */
        if (pixels_left) {
            if (D < 0) {
                plot(++x, y, reverse);   /* pattern 1 */
                if (pixels_left > 1)
                    plot(++x, y, reverse);
                if (pixels_left > 2)
                    plot(--x1, y1, reverse);
            } else {
                if (D < c) {
                    plot(++x, y, reverse);    /* pattern 2  */
                    if (pixels_left > 1)
                        plot(++x, y += step, reverse);
                    if (pixels_left > 2)
                        plot(--x1, y1, reverse);
                } else {
                  /* pattern 3 */
                    plot(++x, y += step, reverse);
                    if (pixels_left > 1)
                        plot(++x, y, reverse);
                    if (pixels_left > 2)
                        plot(--x1, y1 -= step, reverse);
                }
            }
        }          /* end if pixels_left */
    }
    /* end slope < 1/2 */
    else {               /* slope greater than 1/2 */
        c = 2 * (dy - dx);
        incr1 = 2 * c;
        D = incr1 + dx;
        for (i = 0; i < xend; i++) {
            ++x;
            --x1;
            if (D > 0) {
              /* pattern 4 forwards */
                plot(x, y += step, reverse);
                plot(++x, y += step, reverse);
              /* pattern 4 backwards */
                plot(x1, y1 -= step, reverse);
                plot(--x1, y1 -= step, reverse);
                D += incr1;
            } else {
                if (D < c) {
                  /* pattern 2 forwards */
                    plot(x, y, reverse);
                    plot(++x, y += step, reverse);
```

```
                    /* pattern 2 backwards */
                        plot(x1, y1, reverse);
                        plot(--x1, y1 -= step, reverse);
                    } else {
                      /* pattern 3 forwards */
                        plot(x, y += step, reverse);
                        plot(++x, y, reverse);
                      /* pattern 3 backwards */
                        plot(x1, y1 -= step, reverse);
                        plot(--x1, y1, reverse);
                    }
                    D += incr2;
                }
            }           /* end for */
        /* plot last pattern */
        if (pixels_left) {
            if (D > 0) {
                plot(++x, y += step, reverse);        /* pattern 4 */
                if (pixels_left > 1)
                    plot(++x, y += step, reverse);
                if (pixels_left > 2)
                    plot(--x1, y1 -= step, reverse);
            } else {
                if (D < c) {
                    plot(++x, y, reverse);     /* pattern 2  */
                    if (pixels_left > 1)
                         plot(++x, y += step, reverse);
                    if (pixels_left > 2)
                         plot(--x1, y1, reverse);
                } else {
                  /* pattern 3 */
                    plot(++x, y += step, reverse);
                    if (pixels_left > 1)
                         plot(++x, y, reverse);
                    if (pixels_left > 2) {
                        if (D > c) /* step 3 */
                            plot(--x1, y1 -= step, reverse);
                        else /* step 2 */
                           plot(--x1, y1, reverse);
                        }
                }
            }
        }
    }
}
/* non-zero flag indicates the pixels needing swap back. */
plot(x, y, flag) int x, y, flag;
{
    if (flag)
        setpixel(y, x);
    else
        setpixel(x, y);
}
```

689

RENDERING
ANTI-ALIASED LINES

(page 105)

Kelvin Thompson

```
/* HARDWARE ASSUMPTIONS:
/*     * 32-bit, signed ints
/*     * 8-bit pixels, with initialized color table
/*     * pixels are memory mapped in a rectangular fashion */

/* FIXED-POINT DATA TYPE */
typedef  int FX;
# define FX_FRACBITS 16   /* bits of fraction in FX format */
# define FX_0         0   /* zero in fixed-point format */


/* ASSUMED MACROS:
/*    SWAPVARS(v1,v2) -- swaps the contents of two variables
/*    PIXADDR(x,y) -- returns address of pixel at (x,y)
/*    COVERAGE(FXdist) -- lookup macro for pixel coverage
/*        given perpendicular distance; takes a fixed-point
/*        integer and returns an integer in the range [0,255]
/*    SQRTFUNC(FXval) -- lookup macro for sqrt(1/(1+FXval^2))
/*        accepts and returns fixed-point numbers
/*    FIXMUL(FX1,FX2) -- multiplies two fixed-point numbers
/*        and returns the product as a fixed-point number   */

/* BLENDING FUNCTION:
/*   'cover' is coverage -- in the range [0,255]
/*   'back' is background color -- in the range [0,255] */
#define BLEND(cover,back)  ((((255-(cover))*(back))>>8)+(cover))

/* LINE DIRECTION bits and tables */
#define DIR_STEEP  1  /* set when abs(dy) > abs(dx) */
#define DIR_NEGY   2  /* set whey dy < 0 */
```

```
/* pixel increment values
/*    -- assume PIXINC(dx,dy) is a macro such that:
/*    PIXADDR(x0,y0) + PIXINC(dx,dy) = PIXADDR(x0+dx,y0+dy)  */
static int adj_pixinc[4] =
        { PIXINC(1,0), PIXINC(0,1), PIXINC(1,0), PIXINC(0,-1) };
static int diag_pixinc[4] =
        { PIXINC(1,1), PIXINC(1,1), PIXINC(1,-1), PIXINC(1,-1) };
static int orth_pixinc[4] =
        { PIXINC(0,1), PIXINC(1,0), PIXINC(0,-1), PIXINC(1,0) };

/* Global 'Pmax' is initialized elsewhere.  It is the
   "maximum perpendicular distance" -- the sum of half the
   line width and the effective pixel radius -- in fixed format */
FX Pmax;


/**************    FUNCTION ANTI_LINE    **************/

void Anti_Line ( X1, Y1, X2, Y2 )
int X1, Y1, X2, Y2;
{
int       Bvar,     /* decision variable for Bresenham's */
          Bainc,    /* adjacent-increment for 'Bvar' */
          Bdinc;    /* diagonal-increment for 'Bvar' */
FX        Pmid,     /* perp distance at Bresenham's pixel */
          Pnow,     /* perp distance at current pixel (ortho loop) */
          Painc,    /* adjacent-increment for 'Pmid' */
          Pdinc,    /* diagonal-increment for 'Pmid' */
          Poinc;    /* orthogonal-increment for 'Pnow'--also equals 'k' */
char      *mid_addr,  /* pixel address for Bresenham's pixel */
          *now_addr;  /* pixel address for current pixel */
int       addr_ainc,  /* adjacent pixel address offset */
          addr_dinc,  /* diagonal pixel address offset */
          addr_oinc;  /* orthogonal pixel address offset */
int dx,dy,dir;        /* direction and deltas */
FX slope;             /* slope of line */
int temp;

/* rearrange ordering to force left-to-right */
if  ( X1 > X2 )
    { SWAPVARS(X1,X2);   SWAPVARS(Y1,Y2); }

/* init deltas */
dx = X2 - X1;  /* guaranteed non-negative */
dy = Y2 - Y1;
```

```
/* calculate direction (slope category) */
dir = 0;
if ( dy < 0 )    { dir |= DIR_NEGY;  dy = -dy; }
if ( dy > dx )   { dir |= DIR_STEEP; SWAPVARS(dx,dy); }

/* init address stuff */
mid_addr = PIXADDR(X1,Y1);
addr_ainc = adj_pixinc[dir];
addr_dinc = diag_pixinc[dir];
addr_oinc = orth_pixinc[dir];

/* perpendicular measures */
slope =  (dy << FX_FRACBITS) / dx;
Poinc = SQRTFUNC( slope );
Painc = FIXMUL( slope, Poinc );
Pdinc = Painc - Poinc;
Pmid = FX_0;

/* init Bresenham's */
Bainc = dy << 1;
Bdinc = (dy-dx) << 1;
Bvar = Bainc - dx;

do
    {
    /* do middle pixel */
    *mid_addr = BLEND( COVERAGE(abs(Pmid)), *mid_addr );

    /* go up orthogonally */
    for (
        Pnow = Poinc-Pmid,   now_addr = mid_addr+addr_oinc;
        Pnow < Pmax;
        Pnow += Poinc,       now_addr += addr_oinc
        )
      *now_addr = BLEND( COVERAGE(Pnow), *now_addr );

    /* go down orthogonally */
    for (
        Pnow = Poinc+Pmid,   now_addr = mid_addr-addr_oinc;
        Pnow < Pmax;
        Pnow += Poinc,       now_addr -= addr_oinc
        )
      *now_addr = BLEND( COVERAGE(Pnow), *now_addr );
```

```c
/* update Bresenham's */
if ( Bvar < 0 )
    {
    Bvar += Bainc;
    mid_addr = (char *) ((int)mid_addr + addr_ainc);
    Pmid += Painc;
    }
else
    {
    Bvar += Bdinc;
    mid_addr = (char *) ((int)mid_addr + addr_dinc);
    Pmid += Pdinc;
    }

--dx;
} while ( dx >= 0 );
}
```

TWO-DIMENSIONAL CLIPPING: A VECTOR-BASED APPROACH

(page 121)

Hans Spoelder and Fons Ullings

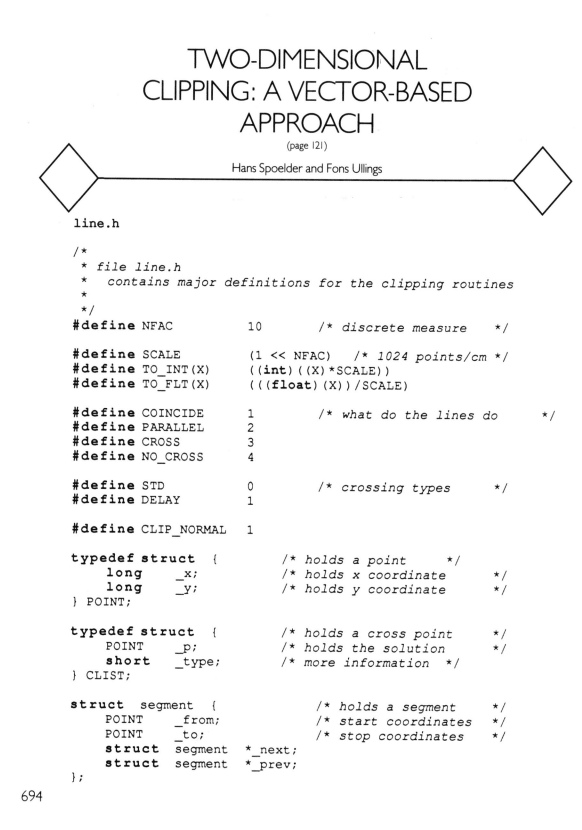

line.h

```
/*
 * file line.h
 *   contains major definitions for the clipping routines
 *
 */
#define NFAC            10          /* discrete measure    */

#define SCALE           (1 << NFAC)   /* 1024 points/cm */
#define TO_INT(X)       ((int)((X)*SCALE))
#define TO_FLT(X)       (((float)(X))/SCALE)

#define COINCIDE        1           /* what do the lines do    */
#define PARALLEL        2
#define CROSS           3
#define NO_CROSS        4

#define STD             0           /* crossing types      */
#define DELAY           1

#define CLIP_NORMAL     1

typedef struct  {           /* holds a point      */
    long    _x;             /* holds x coordinate      */
    long    _y;             /* holds y coordinate      */
} POINT;

typedef struct  {           /* holds a cross point     */
    POINT   _p;             /* holds the solution      */
    short   _type;          /* more information  */
} CLIST;

struct  segment  {                  /* holds a segment     */
    POINT   _from;                  /* start coordinates   */
    POINT   _to;                    /* stop coordinates    */
    struct  segment *_next;
    struct  segment *_prev;
};
```

694

```c
#define SEGMENT          struct  segment

struct  contour {               /* holds a contour       */
    short    _no;               /* contour counter       */
    short    _status;           /* holds information     */
    short    _cnt;              /* number of elements    */
    SEGMENT  *_s;               /* the segments          */
    struct   contour *_next;    /* linked list           */
    long     _minx;             /* coordinates of box    */
    long     _miny;
    long     _maxx;
    long     _maxy;
};

#define CONTOUR          struct  contour

#define ACTIVE           01          /* polygon attributes */
#define NORMAL           02

#define SET_ON(p)        ((p)->_status |=  ACTIVE)
#define SET_NORMAL(p)        ((p)->_status |= NORMAL)

#define SET_OFF(p)       ((p)->_status &= ~ACTIVE)
#define SET_INVERSE(p)       ((p)->_status &= ~NORMAL)

#define IS_ON(p) ((p)->_status & ACTIVE)
#define IS_NORMAL(p)  ((p)->_status & NORMAL)

extern  CONTOUR   *CL;

CONTOUR  *get_contour_ptr();

extern  short    C_COUNT;

box.h

/*
 * file box.h
 *   a short include file is better then no include file
 */
typedef struct {            /* guess what this is              */
    long     _lowx;
    long     _lowy;
    long     _highx;
    long     _highy;
} BOX;
```

bio1.c

```c
/*
 * file  bio.c
 *   contains the basic operations
 *
 */
#include    <stdio.h>
#include    "line.h"

/*
 * def_contour
 *
 *   Purpose:
 *   add a contour to the list
 *   NOTE: coordinates must already be converted into longs!
 *
 *   x     x coordinates of the end points of segments
 *   y     y coordinates of the end points of segments
 *   n     number of coordinate pairs
 *   no    contour number (id), does no have to be unique!
 *   type      type of clip operation desired CLIP_NORMAL means
 *        clip everything inside the contour
 */
def_contour(x, y, n, no, type)
long     x[], y[];
int n, no, type;
{
    short     i;
    long      dx1, dx2, dy1, dy2;
    long      minx, miny, maxx, maxy;
    CONTOUR   *cp;
    SEGMENT   *sp, *spp;

    if((cp = CL) == (CONTOUR *)NULL) {
        cp = CL = NEWTYPE(CONTOUR);
    }
    else {
        while(cp->_next != (CONTOUR *)NULL)
            cp = cp->_next;
        i = cp->_no;
        cp = cp->_next = NEWTYPE(CONTOUR);
    }
```

```
cp->_next = (CONTOUR *)NULL;
cp->_no = no;
SET_ON(cp);
if(type == CLIP_NORMAL)
    SET_INVERSE(cp);
else
    SET_NORMAL(cp);
minx = miny = 1000000;
maxx = maxy = -1;
for(i=0; i<n; i++) {
    if(i == 0) {
        cp->_s = sp = NEWTYPE(SEGMENT);
        sp->_from._x = x[0];
        sp->_from._y = y[0];
        sp->_to._x   = x[1];
        sp->_to._y   = y[1];
    }
    else {
    /*
     * if necessary stretch the contour
     * and skip the point
     */
        dx1 = sp->_to._x - sp->_from._x;
        dy1 = sp->_to._y - sp->_from._y;
        dx2 = x[(i == n-1) ? 0 : i+1] - sp->_to._x;
        dy2 = y[(i == n-1) ? 0 : i+1] - sp->_to._y;
        if(dy2*dx1 == dy1*dx2) {
            sp->_to._x = x[(i == n-1) ? 0 : i+1];
            sp->_to._y = y[(i == n-1) ? 0 : i+1];
        }
        else {
            spp = sp;
            sp = sp->_next = NEWTYPE(SEGMENT);
            sp->_prev = spp;
            sp->_from._x = x[i];
            sp->_from._y = y[i];
            sp->_to._x = x[(i == n-1) ? 0 : i+1];
            sp->_to._y = y[(i == n-1) ? 0 : i+1];
        }
    }
```

```
/*
 * calculate the enclosing box
 */
        if(x[i] < minx)
            minx = x[i];
        if(x[i] > maxx)
            maxx = x[i];
        if(y[i] < miny)
            miny = y[i];
        if(y[i] > maxy)
            maxy = y[i];

    }
    cp->_minx = minx;
    cp->_maxx = maxx;
    cp->_miny = miny;
    cp->_maxy = maxy;
    sp->_next = cp->_s;
    cp->_s->_prev = sp;
    cp->_next = (CONTOUR *)NULL;
}

/*
 * get_contour_ptr
 *
 *   PURPOSE
 *   get the pointer to a contour given its id
 *   with multiple id's first fit algorithm is
 *   used. Returns NULL in case of error.
 *
 *   no    id of contour
 */
CONTOUR  *get_contour_ptr(no)
int no;
{
    CONTOUR  *cp;

    if((cp = CL) == (CONTOUR *)NULL)
        return((CONTOUR *)NULL);
    else {
        while(cp != (CONTOUR *)NULL) {
            if(cp->_no == no)
                return(cp);
            else
                cp = cp->_next;
        }
        return((CONTOUR *)NULL);
    }
}
```

```
/*
 * del_contour
 *
 *   PURPOSE
 *   delete contour(s) from the list with id
 *   no
 */
del_contour(no)
int no;
{
    CONTOUR  *cp, *cpp;
    CONTOUR  *qp = (CONTOUR *)NULL;
    SEGMENT  *sp, *spp;

    if((cp = CL) == (CONTOUR *)NULL)
        return;
    while(cp != (CONTOUR *)NULL) {
        if(cp->_no == no) {
            sp = cp->_s;
            do {
                spp = sp->_next;
                free(sp);
                sp = spp;
            } while(sp != cp->_s);
            cpp = cp->_next;
            free(cp);
            if(qp)
                qp->_next = cpp;
            else
                CL = cpp;
            cp = cpp;
        }
        else {
            qp = cp;
            cp = cp->_next;
        }
    }
}
```

cross1.c

```c
/*
 * file cross.c:
 *   calculate the intersections
 */
#include      <math.h>
#include      "line.h"
#include      "box.h"
/*
 * cross_calc:
 *
 *   PURPOSE
 *   calculate the intersections between the polygon
 *   stored in poly and the linesegment stored in l
 *   and put the intersections into psol.
 *
 *   poly     pointer to the structure containing the polygon
 *   l    pointer to the structure containing the linesegment
 *   psol     pointer to the pointer where intersections are stored
 *   nsol     current number of intersections stored
 *   nsmax    maximum storage in psol for intersections
 *        if nsol exceeds nsmax additional storage is allocated
 *
 */
cross_calc(poly, l, psol, nsol, nsmax)
CONTOUR   *poly;
SEGMENT   *l;
CLIST     **psol;
short     *nsol, nsmax;
{
     SEGMENT   *p;
     CLIST     *sol;
     double    s;
     long      x, y, a, b, c;
     int psort(), type;

     sol = *psol;
     p = poly->_s;
     do {
/*
 * calculate the a, b and c coefficients and determine the
 * type of intersection
 */
```

700

```c
        a = (p->_to._y - p->_from._y)*(l->_to._x - l->_from._x) -
            (p->_to._x - p->_from._x)*(l->_to._y - l->_from._y);
        b = (p->_from._x - l->_from._x)*(l->_to._y - l->_from._y) -
            (p->_from._y - l->_from._y)*(l->_to._x - l->_from._x);
        c = (p->_from._x - l->_from._x)*(p->_to._y - p->_from._y) -
            (p->_from._y - l->_from._y)*(p->_to._x - p->_from._x);
    if(a == 0)
        type = (b == 0) ? COINCIDE : PARALLEL;
    else {
        if(a > 0) {
            if((b >= 0 && b <= a) &&
               (c >= 0 && c <= a))
                type = CROSS;
            else
                type = NO_CROSS;
        }
        else {
            if((b <= 0 && b >= a) &&
               (c <= 0 && c >= a))
                type = CROSS;
            else
                type = NO_CROSS;
        }
    }
/*
 * process the interscetion found
 */
        switch(type) {
            case NO_CROSS: case PARALLEL:
                break;

            case CROSS:
                if(b == a || c == a || c == 0)
                    break;
                if(b == 0 &&
                   p_where(&(p->_prev->_from), &(p->_to), l) >= 0)
                    break;
                s = (double)b/(double)a;
                if(l->_from._x == l->_to._x)
                    x = l->_from._x;
                else
                    x = p->_from._x +
                        (int)((p->_to._x - p->_from._x)*s);
                if(l->_from._y == l->_to._y)
                    y = l->_from._y;
                else
                    y = p->_from._y +
                        (int)((p->_to._y - p->_from._y)*s);
```

```
        if(*nsol == nsmax) {
            nsmax *= 2;
            *psol = sol = (CLIST *) realloc(sol,
                nsmax*sizeof(CLIST));
        }
        sol[*nsol]._p._x = x;
        sol[*nsol]._p._y = y;
        sol[*nsol]._type = STD;
        *nsol += 1;
        break;

    case COINCIDE:
        if(p_where(&(p->_prev->_from),
            &(p->_next->_to), 1) > 0)
            break;
        if(l->_from._x != l->_to._x) {
            if((max(l->_from._x, l->_to._x) <
                min(p->_from._x, p->_to._x)  ) ||
               (min(l->_from._x, l->_to._x) >
                max(p->_from._x, p->_to._x))    )
                break;
            if(min(l->_from._x, l->_to._x) <
               min(p->_from._x, p->_to._x) ) {
                if(*nsol == nsmax) {
                    nsmax *= 2;
                    *psol = sol = (CLIST *) realloc(sol,
                        nsmax*sizeof(CLIST));
                }
                sol[*nsol]._p._x = p->_from._x;
                sol[*nsol]._p._y = p->_from._y;
                sol[*nsol]._type = DELAY;
                *nsol += 1;
            }
            if(max(l->_from._x, l->_to._x) >
               max(p->_from._x, p->_to._x) ) {
                if(*nsol == nsmax) {
                    nsmax *= 2;
                    *psol = sol = (CLIST *) realloc(sol,
                        nsmax*sizeof(CLIST));
                }
                sol[*nsol]._p._x = p->_to._x;
                sol[*nsol]._p._y = p->_to._y;
                sol[*nsol]._type = DELAY;
                *nsol += 1;
            }
        }
        else {
```

702

```c
            if((max(l->_from._y, l->_to._y) <
                min(p->_from._y, p->_to._y)  ) ||
               (min(l->_from._y, l->_to._y) >
                max(p->_from._y, p->_to._y)) )
                break;
            if(min(l->_from._y, l->_to._y) <
               min(p->_from._y, p->_to._y) ) {
                if(*nsol == nsmax) {
                    nsmax *= 2;
                    *psol = sol = (CLIST *) realloc(sol,
                        nsmax*sizeof(CLIST));
                }
                sol[*nsol]._p._x = p->_from._x;
                sol[*nsol]._p._y = p->_from._y;
                sol[*nsol]._type = DELAY;
                *nsol += 1;
            }
            if(max(l->_from._y, l->_to._y) >
               max(p->_from._y, p->_to._y) ) {
                if(*nsol == nsmax) {
                    nsmax *= 2;
                    *psol = sol = (CLIST *) realloc(sol,
                        nsmax*sizeof(CLIST));
                }
                sol[*nsol]._p._x = p->_to._x;
                sol[*nsol]._p._y = p->_to._y;
                sol[*nsol]._type = DELAY;
                *nsol += 1;
            }
        }
        break;
    }
    p = p->_next;
} while(p != poly->_s);
qsort(sol, *nsol, sizeof(CLIST), psort);
}
```

```
/*
 * p_where
 *
 *   PURPOSE
 *   determine position of point p1 and p2 relative to
 *   linesegment l.
 *   Return value
 *   < 0  p1 and p2 lie at different sides of l
 *   = 0  one of both points lie on l
 *   > 0  p1 and p2 lie at same side of l
 *
 *   p1    pointer to coordinates of point
 *   p2    pointer to coordinates of point
 *   l     pointer to linesegment
 *
 */
p_where(p1, p2, l)
POINT      *p1, *p2;
SEGMENT    *l;
{
    long      dx, dy, dx1, dx2, dy1, dy2, p_1, p_2;

    dx  = l->_to._x - l->_from._x;
    dy  = l->_to._y - l->_from._y;
    dx1 = p1->_x - l->_from._x;
    dy1 = p1->_y - l->_from._y;
    dx2 = p2->_x - l->_to._x;
    dy2 = p2->_y - l->_to._y;
    p_1 = (dx*dy1 - dy*dx1);
    p_2 = (dx*dy2 - dy*dx2);
    if(p_1 == 0 || p_2 == 0)
        return(0);
    else {
        if((p_1 > 0 && p_2 < 0) || (p_1 < 0 && p_2 > 0))
            return(-1);
        else
            return(1);
    }
}
```

```
/*
 * p_inside
 *
 *    PURPOSE
 *    determine if the point stored in pt lies inside
 *    the polygon stored in p
 *    Return value:
 *    FALSE       pt lies outside p
 *    TRUE        pt lies inside  p
 *
 *    p    pointer to the polygon
 *    pt   pointer to the point
 */
boolean   p_inside(p, pt)
CONTOUR   *p;
POINT     *pt;
{
    SEGMENT   l, *sp;
    CLIST     *sol;
    short     nsol = 0, nsmax = 2, reduce = 0, i;
    boolean   on_contour(), odd;

    l._from._x = p->_minx-2;
    l._from._y = pt->_y;
    l._to._x   = pt->_x;
    l._to._y   = pt->_y;
    sol = (CLIST *) calloc(2, sizeof(CLIST));
    cross_calc(p, &l, &sol, &nsol, nsmax);
    for(i=0; i<nsol-1; i++)
        if(sol[i]._type == DELAY && sol[i+1]._type == DELAY)
            reduce++;
    free(sol);
    odd = (nsol - reduce) & 0x01;
    return(odd ? !on_contour(p, pt) : FALSE);
}

/*
 * function used for sorting
 */
psort(p1, p2)
CLIST     *p1, *p2;
{
    if(p1->_p._x != p2->_p._x)
        return(p1->_p._x - p2->_p._x);
    else
        return(p1->_p._y - p2->_p._y);
}
```

```
/*
 * on_contour
 *
 * PURPOSE
 * determine if the point pt lies on the
 * contour p.
 * Return value
 * TRUE       point lies on contour
 * FALSE      point lies not on contour
 *
 * p    pointer to the polygon structure
 * pt   pointer to the point
 */
boolean   on_contour(p, pt)
CONTOUR   *p;
POINT     *pt;
{
    SEGMENT   *sp;
    long      dx1, dy1, dx2, dy2;

    sp = p->_s;
    do {
        if((pt->_x >= min(sp->_from._x, sp->_to._x)) &&
           (pt->_x <= max(sp->_from._x, sp->_to._x))     ) {
               dx1 = pt->_x - sp->_from._x;
               dx2 = sp->_to._x - pt->_x;
               dy1 = pt->_y - sp->_from._y;
               dy2 = sp->_to._y - pt->_y;
               if(dy1*dx2 == dy2*dx1)
                       return(TRUE);
        }
        sp = sp->_next;
    } while(sp != p->_s);
    return(FALSE);
}

clip1.c

/*
 * file clip.c
 *   contains the actual clipping routines
 */
#include    <stdio.h>
#include    "line.h"
```

```
/*
 * vis_vector
 *
 *   PURPOSE
 *   actual user interface. Draws a clipped line
 *   NOTE: coordinates are given in converted LONGS!
 *
 *   xf, yf    from coordinates of vector to be drawn
 *   xt, yt    to coordinates of vector to be drawn
 */
vis_vector(xf, yf, xt, yt)
long      xf, yf, xt, yt;
{
     SEGMENT   l;

     if(xf == xt && yf == yt)
          return;
     l._from._x = xf;
     l._from._y = yf;
     l._to._x   = xt;
     l._to._y   = yt;
/*
 * start at top of list
 */
     clip(CL, &l);
}


/*
 * clip
 *
 *   PURPOSE
 *
 *   p    pointer to polygon
 *   l    pointer to line segment
 */
clip(p, l)
CONTOUR   *p;
SEGMENT   *l;
{
     SEGMENT   *sp, ss;
     CLIST     *sol;
     POINT     pt;
     boolean   up, delay, inside, p_inside(), disjunct();
     int i;
     short     nsol, nsmax = 2;
```

```
/*
 * list exhausted do what you like
 * we want to plot
 */
    if(p == (CONTOUR *)NULL) {
        move((l->_from._x), (l->_from._y));
        cont((l->_to._x), (l->_to._y));
        return;
    }
/*
 * polygon is switched off
 * take next one
 */
    if(!IS_ON(p)) {
        clip(p->_next, l);
        return;
    }
/*
 * comparison on basis of the
 * enclosing rectangle
 */
    if(disjunct(p, l)) {
        if(!IS_NORMAL(p)) {
            clip(p->_next, l);
        }
        return;
    }
/*
 * calculate possible intersections
 */
    sol = (CLIST *) calloc(2, sizeof(CLIST));
    sol[0]._p._x = l->_from._x;
    sol[0]._p._y = l->_from._y;
    sol[0]._type = STD;
    sol[1]._p._x = l->_to._x;
    sol[1]._p._y = l->_to._y;
    sol[1]._type = STD;
    nsol = 2;
    cross_calc(p, l, &sol, &nsol, nsmax);
    pt._x = sol[0]._p._x;
    pt._y = sol[0]._p._y;
```

```
/*
 * determine status of first point
 */
    inside = p_inside(p, &pt);
    if((!inside && IS_NORMAL(p)) || (inside && !IS_NORMAL(p)))
        up = TRUE;
    else
        up = FALSE;
    delay = FALSE;
/*
 * process list of intersections
 */
    for(i=1; i<nsol; i++) {
        if(!up) {
            ss._from._x = sol[i-1]._p._x;
            ss._from._y = sol[i-1]._p._y;
            ss._to._x = sol[i]._p._x;
            ss._to._y = sol[i]._p._y;
            clip(p->_next, &ss);
        }
        if(!delay) {
            if(sol[i]._type != DELAY)
                up = (up) ? FALSE : TRUE
            else
                delay = TRUE;
        }
        else {
            up = (up) ? FALSE : TRUE;
            delay = FALSE;
        }
    }
    free(sol);
}

/*
 * disjunct
 *
 * PURPOSE
 * determine if the box enclosing the polygon
 * stored in p and the box enclosing the line
 * segment stored in l are disjunct.
 * Return TRUE if disjunct else FALSE
 *
 * p    points to the polygon structure
 * l    points to the linesegment structure
 *
 */
boolean   disjunct(p, l)
CONTOUR   *p;
SEGMENT   *l;
```

```c
{
    if((max(l->_from._x, l->_to._x) < p->_minx) ||
        (min(l->_from._x, l->_to._x) > p->_maxx) ||
            (max(l->_from._y, l->_to._y) < p->_miny) ||
        (min(l->_from._y, l->_to._y) > p->_maxy)    )
        return(TRUE);
    else
        return(FALSE);
}

#define DEBUG
#ifdef DEBUG
move(x, y)
long    x, y;
{
    printf("(%d,%d) ->", x, y);
}

cont(x, y)
long    x, y;
{
    printf("(%d,%d)\n", x, y);
}

#endif
```

MEDIAN FINDING ON
A 3×3 GRID

(page 171)

Alan Paeth

```
#define s2(a,b)  {register int t; if ((t=b-a)<0) {a+=t; b-=t;}}
#define mn3(a,b,c)  s2(a,b); s2(a,c);
#define mx3(a,b,c)  s2(b,c); s2(a,c);
#define mnmx3(a,b,c)  mx3(a,b,c); s2(a,b);
#define mnmx4(a,b,c,d)  s2(a,b); s2(c,d); s2(a,c); s2(b,d);
#define mnmx5(a,b,c,d,e)  s2(a,b); s2(c,d); mn3(a,c,e); mx3(b,d,e);
#define mnmx6(a,b,c,d,e,f)  s2(a,d); s2(b,e); s2(c,f);\
                            mn3(a,b,c); mx3(d,e,f);
med3x3(b1, b2, b3)
    int *b1, *b2, *b3;
/*
 * Find median on a 3x3 input box of integers.
 * b1, b2, b3 are pointers to the left-hand edge of three
 * parallel scan-lines to form a 3x3 spatial median.
 * Rewriting b2 and b3 as b1 yields code which forms median
 * on input presented as a linear array of nine elements.
 */
    {
    register int r1, r2, r3, r4, r5, r6;
    r1 = *b1++; r2 = *b1++; r3 = *b1++;
    r4 = *b2++; r5 = *b2++; r6 = *b2++;
    mnmx6(r1, r2, r3, r4, r5, r6);
    r1 = *b3++;
    mnmx5(r1, r2, r3, r4, r5);
    r1 = *b3++;
    mnmx4(r1, r2, r3, r4);
    r1 = *b3++;
    mnmx3(r1, r2, r3);
    return(r2);
    }


/* t2(i,j) transposes elements in A[] such that A[i] <= A[j] */

#define t2(i, j)  s2(A[i-1], A[j-1])
```

```
int median25(A)
    int A[25];
    {
/*
 * median25(A) partitions the array A[0..24] such that element
 * A[12] is the median and subarrays A[0..11] and A[13..24]
 * are partitions containing elements of smaller and larger
 * value (rank), respectively.
 *
 * The exchange table lists element indices on the range 1..25,
 * this accounts for the "-1" offsets in the macro t2 and in
 * the final return value used to adjust subscripts to C-code
 * conventions (array indices begin at zero).
 */
    t2( 1, 2); t2( 4, 5); t2( 3, 5); t2( 3, 4); t2( 7, 8);
    t2( 6, 8); t2( 6, 7); t2(10,11); t2( 9,11); t2( 9,10);
    t2(13,14); t2(12,14); t2(12,13); t2(16,17); t2(15,17);
    t2(15,16); t2(19,20); t2(18,20); t2(18,19); t2(22,23);
    t2(21,23); t2(21,22); t2(24,25); t2( 3, 6); t2( 4, 7);
    t2( 1, 7); t2( 1, 4); t2( 5, 8); t2( 2, 8); t2( 2, 5);
    t2(12,15); t2( 9,15); t2( 9,12); t2(13,16); t2(10,16);
    t2(10,13); t2(14,17); t2(11,17); t2(11,14); t2(21,24);
    t2(18,24); t2(18,21); t2(22,25); t2(19,25); t2(19,22);
    t2(20,23); t2( 9,18); t2(10,19); t2( 1,19); t2( 1,10);
    t2(11,20); t2( 2,20); t2( 2,11); t2(12,21); t2( 3,21);
    t2( 3,12); t2(13,22); t2( 4,22); t2( 4,13); t2(14,23);
    t2( 5,23); t2( 5,14); t2(15,24); t2( 6,24); t2( 6,15);
    t2(16,25); t2( 7,25); t2( 7,16); t2( 8,17); t2( 8,20);
    t2(14,22); t2(16,24); t2( 8,14); t2( 8,16); t2( 2,10);
    t2( 4,12); t2( 6,18); t2(12,18); t2(10,18); t2( 5,11);
    t2( 7,13); t2( 8,15); t2( 5, 7); t2( 5, 8); t2(13,15);
    t2(11,15); t2( 7, 8); t2(11,13); t2( 7,11); t2( 7,18);
    t2(13,18); t2( 8,18); t2( 8,11); t2(13,19); t2( 8,13);
    t2(11,19); t2(13,21); t2(11,21); t2(11,13);
    return(A[13-1]);
    }
```

ORDERED DITHERING

(page 176)

Stephen Hawley

```c
/* Program to generate dithering matrices.
 * written by Jim Blandy, Oberlin College, jimb@occs.oberlin.edu
 * Gifted to, documented and revised by Stephen Hawley,
 * sdh@flash.bellcore.com
 *
 * Generates a dithering matrix from the command line arguments.
 * The first argument, size, determines the dimensions of the
 * matrix: 2^size by 2^size
 * The optional range argument is the range of values to be
 * dithered over. By default, it is (2^size)^2, or simply the
 * total number of elements in the matrix.
 * The final output is suitable for inclusion in a C program.
 * A typical dithering function is something like this:
 * extern int dm[], size;
 *
 * int
 * dither(x,y, level)
 * register int x,y, level;
 * {
 *    return(level > dm[(x % size) + size * (y % size)]);
 * }
 */

main(argc, argv)
int argc;
char **argv:
{
    register int size, range;

    if (argc >= 2) size = atoi(argv[1]);
    else size = 2;

    if (argc == 3) range = atoi(argv[2]);
    else range = (1 << size) * (1 << size);

    printdither (size, range);
}
```

```c
printdither (size, range)
register int size, range;
{
    register int l = (1 << size), i;
    /*
     * print a dithering matrix.
     * l is the length on a side.
     */
    range = range / (l * l);
    puts ("int dm[] = {");
    for (i=0; i < l*l; i++) {
        if (i % l == 0) /* tab in 4 spaces per row */
            printf ("    ");
        /* print the dither value for this location
         * scaled to the given range
         */
        printf ("%4d", range * dithervalue(i / l, i % l, size));

        /* commas after all but the last */
        if (i + 1 < l * l)
            putchar (',');
        /* newline at the end of the row */
        if ((i + 1) % l == 0)
            putchar ('\n');
    }
    puts ("\n}; ");
}
dithervalue (x, y, size)
register int x, y, size;
{
    register int d;
    /*
     * calculate the dither value at a particular
     * (x, y) over the size of the matrix.
     */
    d=0;
    while (size-->0) {
        /* Think of d as the density. At every iteration,
         * d is shifted left one and a new bit is put in the
         * low bit based on x and y. If x is odd and y is even,
         * or x is even and y is odd, a bit is put in. This
         * generates the checkerboard seen in dithering.
         * This quantity is shifted left again and the low bit of
         * y is added in.
         * This whole thing interleaves a checkerboard bit pattern
         * and y's bits, which is the value you want.
         */
        d = (d <<1 | (x&1 ^ y&1))<<1 | y&1;
        x >>= 1;
        y >>= 1;
    }
    return (d);
}
```

A DIGITAL "DISSOLVE"
EFFECT

(page 221)

Mike Morton

```c
int reg;                /* current sequence element */
reg = 1;                /* start in any non-zero state */
if (reg & 1)            /* is the bottom bit set? */
    reg = (reg >>1) ^ MASK;   /* yes: toss out 1 bit; */
                              /* XOR in mask */
else reg = reg >>1;     /* no: toss out 0 bit */


dissolve1 (height, width)   /* first version of the dissolve
                               /* algorithm */
    int height, width;      /* number of rows, columns */
{
    int pixels, lastnum;    /* number of pixels; */
                            /* last pixel's number */
    int regwidth;           /* "width" of sequence generator */
    register long mask;     /* mask to XOR with to*/
                            /* create sequence */
    register unsigned long element;
                            /* one element of random sequence */
    register int row, column;
                            /* row and column numbers for a pixel */

    /* Find smallest register which produces enough pixel numbers */
    pixels = height * width; /* compute number of pixels */
                             /* to dissolve */
    lastnum = pixels-1;     /* find last element (they go 0..lastnum) */
    regwidth = bitwidth (lastnum); /* how wide must the */
                                   /* register be? */
    mask = randmasks [regwidth];   /* which mask is for that width? */

    /* Now cycle through all sequence elements. */

    element = 1;     /* 1st element (could be any nonzero) */
```

```c
    do {
        row = element / width; /* how many rows down is this pixel? */
        column = element % width;   /* and how many columns across? */
        if (row < height) /* is this seq element in the array? */
            copy (row, column);  /* yes: copy the (r,c)'th pixel */

        /* Compute the next sequence element */
        if (element & 1)        /* is the low bit set? */
            element = (element >>1)^mask; /* yes: shift value, */
                                        /* XOR in mask */
        else element = (element >>1); /* no: just shift the value */
    } while (element != 1);         /* loop until we return   */
                                    /* to original element */
    copy (0, 0);                    /* kludge: the loop doesn't produce (0,0) */
}                                   /* end of dissolve1() */



int bitwidth (N)  /* find "bit-width" needed to represent N */
    unsigned int N;       /* number to compute the width of */
{
    int width = 0;   /* initially, no bits needed to represent N */
    while (N != 0) {    /* loop 'til N has been whittled down to 0 */
        N >>= 1;      /* shift N right 1 bit (NB: N is unsigned) */
        width++;      /* and remember how wide N is */
    }             /* end of loop shrinking N down to nothing *
    return (width);    /* return bit positions counted */

}                       /* end of bitwidth() */



dissolve2 (height, width)   /* fast version of the dissolve algorithm */
    int height, width;    /* number of rows, columns */
{
    int rwidth, cwidth;   /* bit width for rows, for columns */
    int regwidth;         /* "width" of sequence generator */
    register long mask;   /* mask to XOR with to create sequence */
    register int rowshift;   /* shift distance to get row */
                            /* from element */
    register int colmask; /* mask to extract column from element */
    register unsigned long element; /* one element of random */
                                /* sequence */
    register int row, column;   /* row and column for one pixel */
```

```
        /* Find the mask to produce all rows and columns. */

    rwidth = bitwidth (height); /* how many bits needed for height? */
    cwidth = bitwidth (width);  /* how many bits needed for width? */
    regwidth = rwidth + cwidth; /* how wide must the register be? */
    mask = randmasks [regwidth]; /* which mask is for that width? */

/* Find values to extract row and col numbers from each element. */
    rowshift = cwidth; /* find dist to shift to get top bits (row) */
    colmask = (1<<cwidth)-1;    /* find mask to extract  */
                                /* bottom bits (col) */

        /* Now cycle through all sequence elements. */

    element = 1;  /* 1st element (could be any nonzero) */
    do {
        row = element >> rowshift; /* find row number for this pixel */
        column = element & colmask; /* and how many columns across? */
        if ((row < height)      /* does element fall in the array? */
            && (column < width))    /* ...must check row AND column */
        copy (row, column);     /* in bounds: copy the (r,c)'th pixel */

        /* Compute the next sequence element */
        if (element & 1)        /* is the low bit set? */
        element = (element >>1)^mask; /* yes: shift value, /*
                                /* XOR in mask */
        else element = (element >>1); /* no: just shift the value */
    } while (element != 1);     /* loop until we return to */
                                /*  original element */

    copy (0, 0);        /* kludge: element never comes up zero */
}                       /* end of dissolve2() */
```

MAPPING RGB TRIPLES
ONTO FOUR BITS

(page 233)

Alan Paeth

```
remap8(R, G, B, R2, G2, B2)
    float R, G, B, *R2, *G2, *B2;
    {
/*
 * remap8 maps floating (R,G,B) triples onto quantized
 * (R2,B2,B2) triples and returns the code (vertex)
 * value/color table entry for the quantization. The
 * points (eight) are the vertices of the cube.
 */
    int code;
    *R2 = *G2 = *B2 = 0.0;
    code = 0;
    if (R >= 0.5) { *R2 = 1.0; code |= 1; }
    if (G >= 0.5) { *G2 = 1.0; code |= 2; }
    if (B >= 0.5) { *B2 = 1.0; code |= 4; }
    return(code);
    }

/*
 * remap14 maps floating (R,G,B) triples onto quantized
 * (R2,B2,B2) triples and returns the code (vertex)
 * value/color table entry for the quantization. The
 * points (fourteen) are the vertices of the cuboctahedron.
 */

float rval[] = { 0.,.5 ,.5 , 1.,.0 , 0., 0.,.5,
                 .5 , 1., 1., 1., 0.,.5 ,.5 , 1.};
float gval[] = { 0.,.5 , 0., 0.,.5 , 1., 0.,.5,
                 .5 , 1., 0.,.5 , 1., 1.,.5 , 1.};
float bval[] = { 0., 0.,.5 , 0.,.5 , 0., 1.,.5,
                 .5 , 0., 1.,.5 , 1.,.5 , 1., 1.};

int remap14(R, G, B,  R2, G2, B2)
    float R, G, B, *R2, *G2, *B2;
    {
    int code = 0;
    if ( R + G + B > 1.5) code |= 8;
    if (-R + G + B > 0.5) code |= 4;
    if ( R - G + B > 0.5) code |= 2;
    if ( R + G - B > 0.5) code |= 1;
    *R2 = rval[code];
    *G2 = gval[code];
    *B2 = bval[code];
    return(code);
    }
```

PROPER TREATMENT OF
PIXELS AS INTEGERS

(page 249)

Alan Paeth

```c
#define Min      code[2]
#define Med      code[1]
#define Max      code[0]
#define NCODE    3

/*
 * A call to getplanes of the form:
 * getplanes(&red, &green, &blue, 256, "grb");
 *
 * fills the first three integer pointers with (near) identical
 * values which maximize red*green*blue <= 256. The final parameter
 * string defines tie-break order, here green>=red>=blue (the usual
 * default). The present code procedure calls "err(string, arg)"
 * given bad parameters; it is a simple task to rewrite the code as
 * a function which returns a success/failure code(s), as needed.
 *
 * In the example given above the code fills in the values
 * red = 6, green = 7, blue = 6.
 */

getplanes(r, g, b, n, bias)
    int *r, *g, *b;
    char *bias;
    {
    int i, code[NCODE];
    if(strlen(bias) != NCODE )
        err("bias string \"%s\" wrong length",bias);
    Min = Med = Max = 0;
    *r = *g = *b = 0;
    while(Min*Min*Min <= n) Min++;
    Min--;
    while(Med*Med*Min <= n) Med++;
    Med--;
    Max = n/(Min*Med);
    for( i = 0; i < NCODE; i++ )
        {
        switch(bias[i])
            {
            case 'r': case 'R': *r = code[i]; break;
            case 'g': case 'G': *g = code[i]; break;
            case 'b': case 'B': *b = code[i]; break;
            default: err("bad bias character: \'%c\'",bias[i]); break;
            }
        }
    if (!(*r && *g && *b)) err("bias string \"%s\" deficient", bias);
    }
```

RECORDING ANIMATION IN BINARY ORDER FOR PROGRESSIVE TEMPORAL REFINEMENT

(page 265)

Paul Heckbert

```c
/*
 * binrec.c: demonstrate binary recording order
 * Paul Heckbert   Jan 90
 */

#include <stdio.h>
main(ac, av)
int ac;
char **av;
{
    int nframes, i, start_frame, repeat_count;
    if (ac!=2) {
        fprintf(stderr, "Usage: binrec <nframes>\n");
        exit(1);
    }
    nframes = atoi(av[1]);

    printf("step startframe repeatcount\n");
    for (i=0; i<nframes; i++) {
        inside_out(nframes, i, &start_frame, &repeat_count);
        printf(" %2d      %2d           %2d\n", i, start_frame,
            repeat_count);
    }
}

/*
 * inside_out: turn a number "inside-out": a generalization of bit-
 * reversal.
 * For n = power of two, this is equivalent to bit-reversal.
 *
 * Turn the number a inside-out, yielding b.  If 0<=a<n then 0<=b<n.
 * Also return r = min(n-b, largest power of 2 dividing b)
 */
inside_out(n, a, b, r)
int n, a, *b, *r;
{
    int k, m;
    *r = m = n;
    for (*b=0, k=1; k<n; k<<=1)
        if (a<<1>=m) {
            if (*b==0) *r = k;
            *b += k;
            a -= m+1>>1;
            m >>= 1;
        }
        else m = m+1>>1;
    if (*r>n-*b) *r = n-*b;
}
```

A SEED FILL ALGORITHM

(page 275)

Paul Heckbert

```
/*
 * fill.c : simple seed fill program
 * Calls pixelread() to read pixels, pixelwrite() to write pixels.
 *
 * Paul Heckbert  13 Sept 1982, 28 Jan 1987
 */

typedef struct  {         /* window: a discrete 2-D rectangle */
    int x0, y0;           /* xmin and ymin */
    int x1, y1;           /* xmax and ymax (inclusive) */
} Window;

typedef int Pixel;        /* 1-channel frame buffer assumed */

Pixel pixelread();

typedef struct {short y, xl, xr, dy;} Segment;
/*
 * Filled horizontal segment of scanline y for xl$<=$x$<=$xr.
 * Parent segment was on line y-dy.  dy=1 or -1
 */

#define MAX 10000         /* max depth of stack */

#define PUSH(Y, XL, XR, DY)    /* push new segment on stack */ \
    if (sp<stack+MAX && Y+(DY)>=win->y0 && Y+(DY)<=win->y1) \
    {sp->y = Y; sp->xl = XL; sp->xr = XR; sp->dy = DY; sp++;}

#define POP(Y, XL, XR, DY)     /* pop segment off stack */ \
    {sp--; Y = sp->y+(DY = sp->dy); XL = sp->xl; XR = sp->xr;}
```

```
/*
 * fill: set the pixel at (x,y) and all of its 4-connected neighbors
 * with the same pixel value to the new pixel value nv.
 * A 4-connected neighbor is a pixel above, below, left, or right of
 * a pixel.
 */

fill(x, y, win, nv)
int x, y;      /* seed point */
Window *win;   /* screen window */
Pixel nv;      /* new pixel value */
{
    int l, x1, x2, dy;
    Pixel ov;       /* old pixel value */
    Segment stack[MAX], *sp = stack;        /* stack of filled segments */

    ov = pixelread(x, y);        /* read pv at seed point */
    if (ov==nv || x<win->x0 || x>win->x1 || y<win->y0 || y>win->y1)
        return;
    PUSH(y, x, x, 1);            /* needed in some cases */
    PUSH(y+1, x, x, -1);         /* seed segment (popped 1st) */

    while (sp>stack) {
        /* pop segment off stack and fill a neighboring scan line */
        POP(y, x1, x2, dy);
        /*
         * segment of scan line y-dy for x1<=x<=x2 was
         * previously filled,
         * now explore adjacent pixels in scan line y
         */
        for (x=x1; x>=win->x0 && pixelread(x, y)==ov; x--)
            pixelwrite(x, y, nv);
        if (x>=x1) goto skip;
        l = x+1;
        if (l<x1) PUSH(y, l, x1-1, -dy);        /* leak on left? */
        x = x1+1;
        do {
            for (; x<=win->x1 && pixelread(x, y)==ov; x++)
                pixelwrite(x, y, nv);
            PUSH(y, l, x-1, dy);
            if (x>x2+1) PUSH(y, x2+1, x-1, -dy); /* leak on right? */
skip:       for (x++; x<=x2 && pixelread(x, y)!=ov; x++);
            l = x;
        } while (x<=x2);
    }
}
```

AN EFFICIENT BOUNDING SPHERE

(page 301)

Jack Ritter

```c
/* Routine to calculate tight bounding sphere over    */
/* a set of points in 3D */
/* This contains the routine find_bounding_sphere(), */
/* the struct definition, and the globals used for parameters. */
/* The abs() of all coordinates must be < BIGNUMBER */
/* Code written by Jack Ritter and Lyle Rains. */

#include <stdio.h>
#include <math.h>

#define BIGNUMBER 100000000.0                /* hundred million */
struct Point3Struct {double x,y,z;};  /* The only struct used. */

/* GLOBALS. These are used as input and output parameters. */

struct Point3Struct caller_p,cen;
double rad;
int NUM_POINTS;

/* Call with no parameters. Caller must set NUM_POINTS */
/* before calling. */
/* Caller must supply the routine GET_iTH_POINT(i), which loads his */
/* ith point into the global struct caller_p. (0 <= i < NUM_POINTS). */
/* The calling order of the points is irrelevant. */
/* The final bounding sphere will be put into the globals */
/* cen and rad. */


find_bounding_sphere()
{
register int i;
register double dx,dy,dz;
register double rad_sq,xspan,yspan,zspan,maxspan;
double old_to_p,old_to_p_sq,old_to_new;
struct Point3Struct xmin,xmax,ymin,ymax,zmin,zmax,dia1,dia2;
```

```
/* FIRST PASS: find 6 minima/maxima points */
xmin.x=ymin.y=zmin.z= BIGNUMBER; /* initialize for min/max compare */
xmax.x=ymax.y=zmax.z= -BIGNUMBER;
for (i=0;i<NUM_POINTS;i++)
    {
    GET_iTH_POINT(i); /* load global struct caller_p with */
                      /* his ith point. */
    if (caller_p.x<xmin.x)
        xmin = caller_p; /* New xminimum point */
    if (caller_p.x>xmax.x)
        xmax = caller_p;
    if (caller_p.y<ymin.y)
        ymin = caller_p;
    if (caller_p.y>ymax.y)
        ymax = caller_p;
    if (caller_p.z<zmin.z)
        zmin = caller_p;
    if (caller_p.z>zmax.z)
        zmax = caller_p;
    }
/* Set xspan = distance between the 2 points xmin & xmax (squared) */
dx = xmax.x - xmin.x;
dy = xmax.y - xmin.y;
dz = xmax.z - xmin.z;
xspan = dx*dx + dy*dy + dz*dz;

/* Same for y & z spans */
dx = ymax.x - ymin.x;
dy = ymax.y - ymin.y;
dz = ymax.z - ymin.z;
yspan = dx*dx + dy*dy + dz*dz;

dx = zmax.x - zmin.x;
dy = zmax.y - zmin.y;
dz = zmax.z - zmin.z;
zspan = dx*dx + dy*dy + dz*dz;

/* Set points dia1 & dia2 to the maximally seperated pair */
dia1 = xmin; dia2 = xmax; /* assume xspan biggest */
maxspan = xspan;
if (yspan>maxspan)
    {
    maxspan = yspan;
    dia1 = ymin; dia2 = ymax;
    }
if (zspan>maxspan)
    {
    dia1 = zmin; dia2 = zmax;
    }
```

724

```
/* dia1,dia2 is a diameter of initial sphere */
/* calc initial center */
cen.x = (dia1.x+dia2.x)/2.0;
cen.y = (dia1.y+dia2.y)/2.0;
cen.z = (dia1.z+dia2.z)/2.0;
/* calculate initial radius**2 and radius */
dx = dia2.x-cen.x;  /* x componant of radius vector */
dy = dia2.y-cen.y;  /* y componant of radius vector */
dz = dia2.z-cen.z;  /* z componant of radius vector */
rad_sq = dx*dx + dy*dy + dz*dz;
rad = sqrt(rad_sq);

/* SECOND PASS: increment current sphere */

for (i=0;i<NUM_POINTS;i++)
    {
    GET_iTH_POINT(i); /* load global struct caller_p  */
                      /* with his ith point. */
    dx = caller_p.x-cen.x;
    dy = caller_p.y-cen.y;
    dz = caller_p.z-cen.z;
    old_to_p_sq = dx*dx + dy*dy + dz*dz;
    if (old_to_p_sq > rad_sq)          /* do r**2 test first */
        {    /* this point is outside of current sphere */
        old_to_p = sqrt(old_to_p_sq);
        /* calc radius of new sphere */
        rad = (rad + old_to_p) / 2.0;
        rad_sq = rad*rad;       /* for next r**2 compare */
        old_to_new = old_to_p - rad;
        /* calc center of new sphere */
        cen.x = (rad*cen.x + old_to_new*caller_p.x) / old_to_p;
        cen.y = (rad*cen.y + old_to_new*caller_p.y) / old_to_p;
        cen.z = (rad*cen.z + old_to_new*caller_p.z) / old_to_p;
        /* Suppress if desired */
        printf("\n New sphere: cen,rad = %f %f %f    %f",
            cen.x,cen.y,cen.z,  rad);
        }
    }
}                 /* end of find_bounding_sphere()   */
```

ALBERS EQUAL-AREA
CONIC MAP PROJECTION

(page 321)

Paul Bame

```
/*
 * Albers Conic Equal-Area Projection
 * Formulae taken from "Map Projections Used by the U.S.
 * Geological Survey" Bulletin #1532
 *
 * Equation reference numbers and some variable names taken
 * from the reference.
 * To use, call albers setup() once and then albers_project()
 * for each coordinate pair of interest.
 */

#include <stdio.h>
#include <math.h>

/*
 * This is the Clarke 1866 Earth spheroid data which is often
 * used by the USGS - there are other spheroids however - see the
 * book.
 */

/*
 * Earth radii in different units */
#define CONST_EradiusKM (6378.2064)              /* Kilometers */
#define CONST_EradiusMI (CONST_EradiusKM/1.609)       /* Miles */
#define CONST_Ec        (0.082271854)         /* Eccentricity */
#define CONST_Ecsq      (0.006768658)    /* Eccentricity squared */
```

```
/*
 * To keep things simple, assume Earth radius is 1.0. Projected
 * coordinates (X and Y obtained from albers project ()) are
 *  dimensionless and may be multiplied by any desired radius
 *  to convert to desired units (usually Kilometers or Miles).
 */
#define CONST_Eradius 1.0

/* Pre-computed variables */
static double middlelon;               /* longitude at center of map */
static double bigC, cone_const, r0);      /* See the reference */

static
calc_q_msq(lat, qp, msqp)
double lat;
double *qp;
double *msqp;
/*
 * Given latitude, calculate 'q' [eq 3-12]
 * if msqp is != NULL, m^2   [eq. 12-15].
 */
{
    double s, c, es;

    s = sin(lat);
    es = s * CONST_Ec;

    *qp = (1.0 - CONST_Ecsq) * ((s / (1 - es * es))-
        (1 / (2 * CONST_Ec)) * log((1 - es) / (1 + es)));

    if (msqp != NULL)
    {
        c = cos(lat);
        *msqp = c * c/ (1 - es * es);
    }
}
```

```
albers_setup(southlat, northlat, originlon, originlat)
double southlat, northlat;
double originlon;
double originlat;
/*
 * Pre-compute a bunch of variables which are used by the
 * albers_project()
 *
 * southlat   Southern latitude for Albers projection
 * northlat   Northern latitute for Albers projection
 * originlon  Longitude for origin of projected map
 * originlat  Latitude for origin of projected map -
 *                      often (northlat + southlat) / 2
 */
{
    double q1, q2, q0;
    double m1sq, m2sq;

    middlelon = originlon;

    cal_q_msq(southlat, &q1, &m1sq);
    cal_q_msq(northlat, &q2, &m2sq);
    cal_q_msq(originlat, &q0, NULL);

    cone_const = (m1sq - m2sq) / (q2 - q1);
    bigC = m1sq + con_const * q1;
    r0 = CONST_Eradius * sqrt(bigC - cone_const *q0) / cone_const
}

/*****************************************************************/

albers_project(lon, lat, xp, yp)
double lon, lat;
double *xp, *yp;
/*
 * Project lon/lat (in radians) according to albers_setup and
 * return the results via xp, yp. Units of *xp and *yp are same
 * as the units used by CONST_Eradius.
 */
{
    double q, r, theta;
    calc_q_msq(lat, &q, NULL);
    theta = cone_const * (lon -middlelon);
    r = CONST_Eradius * sqrt(bigC - cone_const * q) / cone_const;
    *xp = r * sin(theta);
    *yp = r0 - r * cos(theta);
```

```
#ifdef TESTPROGRAM

/*
 * Test value from the USGS book. Because of roundoff, the
 * actual values are printed for visual inspection rather
 * than guessing what constitutes "close enough".
 */
/* Convert a degress, minutes pair to radians */
#define DEG_MIN2RAD(degrees, minutes) \
    ((double) ((degrees + minutes / 60.0) * M_PI / 180.0))

#define Nlat DEG_MIN2RAD(29, 30)    /* 29 degrees, 30' North Lat */
#define Slat DEG_MIN2RAD(45, 30)
#define Originlat DEG_MIN2RAD(23, 0)
#define Originlon DEG_MIN2RAD(-96, 0) /* West longitude is negative */

#define Testlat DEG_MIN2RAD(35, 0)
#define Testlon DEG_MIN2RAD(-75, 0)

#define TestX 1885.4727
#define TestY 1535.9250

main()
{
    int i;
    double x, y;

/* Setup is also from USGS book test set */
    albers_setup(Slat, Nlat, Originlon, Originlat);

    albers_project(Testlon, Testlat, &x, &y);
    printf("%.41f, %.41f =?= %.41f, %.41f/n",
        x * CONST_EradiusKM, y * CONST_EradiusKM,
        TestX, TestY);
}
#endif        /* TESTPROGRAM */
```

A SIMPLE METHOD
FOR BOX–SPHERE
INTERSECTION TESTING

(page 335)

Jim Arvo

```
/*
 *   This routine tests for intersection between an n-dimensional
 *   axis-aligned box and an n-dimensional sphere.  The mode argument
 *   indicates whether the objects are to be regarded as surfaces or
 *   solids.  The values are:
 *
 *      mode
 *
 *       0    Hollow Box, Hollow Sphere
 *       1    Hollow Box, Solid  Sphere
 *       2    Solid  Box, Hollow Sphere
 *       3    Solid  Box, Solid  Sphere
 *
 */
int Box_Sphere_Intersect( n, Bmin, Bmax, C, r, mode )
int     n;        /* The dimension of the space.            */
float   Bmin[];   /* The minium of the box for each axis.   */
float   Bmax[];   /* The maximum of the box for each axis.  */
float   C[];      /* The sphere center in n-space.          */
float   r;        /* The radius of the sphere.              */
int     mode;     /* Selects hollow or solid.               */
    {
    float   a, b;
    float   dmin, dmax;
    float   r2 = SQR( r );
    int     i, face;
```

```
switch( mode )
    {
    case 0: /* Hollow Box - Hollow Sphere */
        dmin = 0;
        dmax = 0;
        face = FALSE;
        for( i = 0; i < n; i++ ) {
            a = SQR( C[i] - Bmin[i] );
            b = SQR( C[i] - Bmax[i] );
            dmax += MAX( a, b );
            if( C[i] < Bmin[i] ) {
                face = TRUE;
                dmin += a;
                }
            else if( C[i] > Bmax[i] ) {
                face = TRUE;
                dmin += b;
                }
            else if( MIN( a, b ) <= r2 ) face = TRUE;
            }
        if(face && ( dmin <= r2 ) && ( r2 <= dmax)) return(TRUE);
        break;

    case 1: /* Hollow Box - Solid Sphere */
        dmin = 0;
        face = FALSE;
        for( i = 0; i < n; i++ ) {
            if( C[i] < Bmin[i] ) {
                face = TRUE;
                dmin += SQR( C[i] - Bmin[i] );
                }
            else if( C[i] > Bmax[i] ) {
                face = TRUE;
                dmin += SQR( C[i] - Bmax[i] );
                }
            else if( C[i] - Bmin[i] <= r ) face = TRUE;
            else if( Bmax[i] - C[i] <= r ) face = TRUE;
            }
        if( face && ( dmin <= r2 ) ) return( TRUE );
        break;
```

```
case 2: /* Solid Box - Hollow Sphere */
    dmax = 0;
    dmin = 0;
    for( i = 0; i < n; i++ ) {
        a = SQR( C[i] - Bmin[i] );
        b = SQR( C[i] - Bmax[i] );
        dmax += MAX( a, b );
        if( C[i] < Bmin[i] ) dmin += a; else
        if( C[i] > Bmax[i] ) dmin += b;
        }
    if( dmin <= r2 && r2 <= dmax ) return( TRUE );
    break;

case 3: /* Solid Box - Solid Sphere */
    dmin = 0;
    for( i = 0; i < n; i++ ) {
        if( C[i] < Bmin[i] ) dmin += SQR(C[i] - Bmin[i] ); else
        if( C[i] > Bmax[i] ) dmin += SQR( C[i] - Bmax[i] );
        }
    if( dmin <= r2 ) return( TRUE );
    break;

} /* end switch */

return( FALSE );
}
```

3D GRID HASHING FUNCTION

(page 343)

Brian Wyvill

```c
/* Test Program for 3D hash function.
In C the hash function can be defined in a macro which
avoids a function call
and the bit operations are defined in the language.
*/


#include <stdio.h>
#include <math.h>


#define RANGE      256
#define NBITS      4
#define RBITS      4
#define MASK       0360
#define HASH(a,b,c)  ((((a&MASK)<<NBITS|b&MASK)<<NBITS|c&MASK)>>RBITS)
#define HSIZE       1<<NBITS*3
#define ABS(x)  (int)(x<0 ? -x : x)
#define TRUE 1
#define FALSE 0


typedef  struct {
  double  x,y,z;
} Triple, *RefTriple;


typedef struct {    /* linked list of objects to be stored */
  Triple origin;
  struct Object *link;
} Object, *RefObject;


typedef struct {  /* linked list of voxels (object pointers) */
  RefObject objectList;
  struct Voxel *link;
} Voxel, *RefVoxel;


RefVoxel table[HSIZE];   /* Table of pointers to Voxels */
```

```
checkrange(z) double z;
{
  if (z < 0 || z >= RANGE) fprintf(stderr,"%f out of range\n",z),
      exit();
}

double getcoord()
{
  char buf[80];
  double z;
  scanf("%s",buf);
  z = atof(buf);
  checkrange(z);
  return z;
}

main()
{
  Triple a;
  while (TRUE) {
    printf("Enter object position x y z ===> ");
    a.x = getcoord();
    a.y = getcoord();
    a.z = getcoord();
    printf("\ncoord: %d %d %d Hashes to
%d\n",ABS(a.x),ABS(a.y),ABS(a.z),
        HASH(ABS(a.x), ABS(a.y), ABS(a.z) ));
  };
}
```

734

AN EFFICIENT RAY–POLYGON
INTERSECTION

(page 390)

Didier Badouel

```c
/* the value of t is computed.
 * i1 and i2 come from the polygon description.
 * V is the vertex table for the polygon and N the
 * associated normal vectors.
 */
P[0] = ray.O[0] + ray.D[0]*t;
P[1] = ray.O[1] + ray.D[1]*t;
P[2] = ray.O[2] + ray.D[2]*t;
u0 = P[i1] - V[0][i1]; v0 = P[i2] - V[0][i2];
inter = FALSE; i = 2;
do {
    /* The polygon is viewed as (n-2) triangles. */
    u1 = V[i-1][i1] - V[0][i1]; v1 = V[i-1][i2] - V[0][i2];
    u2 = V[i  ][i1] - V[0][i1]; v2 = V[i  ][i2] - V[0][i2];

    if (u1 == 0)      {
        beta = u0/u2;
        if ((beta >= 0.)&&(beta <= 1.)) {
            alpha = (v0 - beta*v2)/v1;
            inter = ((alpha >= 0.)&&(alpha+beta) <= 1.));
        }
    } else {
        beta = (v0*u1 - u0*v1)/(v2*u1 - u2*v1);
        if ((beta >= 0.)&&(beta <= 1.)) {
            alpha = (u0 - beta*u2)/u1;
            inter = ((alpha >= 0)&&((alpha+beta) <= 1.));
        }
    }
} while ((!inter)&&(++i < poly.n));

if (inter) {
    /* Storing the intersection point. */
    ray.P[0] = P[0]; ray.P[1] = P[1]; ray.P[2] = P[2];
    /* the normal vector can be interpolated now or later. */
    if (poly.interpolate) {
        gamma = 1 - (alpha+beta);
        ray.normal[0] = gamma * N[0][0] + alpha * N[i-1][0] +
         beta * N[i][0];
        ray.normal[1] = gamma * N[0][1] + alpha * N[i-1][1] +
          beta * N[i][1];
        ray.normal[2] = gamma * N[0][2] + alpha * N[i-1][2] +
          beta * N[i][2];
    }
}
return (inter);
```

735

FAST RAY–BOX
INTERSECTION

(page 395)

Andrew Woo

```
#define  NUMDIM   3
#define  RIGHT    0
#define  LEFT     1
#define  MIDDLE   2

char HitBoundingBox(minB,maxB, origin, dir,coord)
double minB[NUMDIM], maxB[NUMDIM];            /*box */
double origin[NUMDIM], dir[NUMDIM];              /*ray */
double coord[NUMDIM];                         /* hit point */
{
      char inside = TRUE;
      char quadrant[NUMDIM];
      register int i;
      int whichPlane;
      double maxT[NUMDIM];
      double candidatePlane[NUMDIM];

      /* Find candidate planes; this loop can be avoided if
      rays cast all from the eye(assume perpsective view) */
      for (i=0; i<NUMDIM; i++)
            if(origin[i] < minB[i]) {
                  quadrant[i] = LEFT;
                  candidatePlane[i] = minB[i];
                  inside = FALSE;
            }else if (origin[i] > maxB[i]) {
                  quadrant[i] = RIGHT;
                  candidatePlane[i] = maxB[i];
                  inside = FALSE;
            }else        {
                  quadrant[i] = MIDDLE;
            }

      /* Ray origin inside bounding box */
      if(inside) {
            coord = origin;
            return (TRUE);
      }
```

```
/* Calculate T distances to candidate planes */
for (i = 0; i < NUMDIM; i++)
    if (quadrant[i] != MIDDLE && dir[i] !=0.)
        maxT[i] = (candidatePlane[i]-origin[i]) / dir[i];
    else
        maxT[i] = -1.;

/* Get largest of the maxT's for final choice of intersection */
whichPlane = 0;
for (i = 1; i < NUMDIM; i++)
    if (maxT[whichPlane] < maxT[i])
        whichPlane = i;

/* Check final candidate actually inside box */
if (maxT[whichPlane] < 0.) return (FALSE);
for (i = 0; i < NUMDIM; i++)
    if (whichPlane != i) {
        coord[i] = origin[i] + maxT[whichPlane] *dir[i];
        if ((quadrant[i] == RIGHT && coord[i] < minB[i]) ||
            (quadrant[i] == LEFT && coord[i] > maxB[i]))
            return (FALSE);      /* outside box */
    }else {
        coord[i] = candidatePlane[i];
    }
return (TRUE);                          /* ray hits box */
```

CUBIC AND QUARTIC ROOTS

(page 404)

Jochen Schwarze

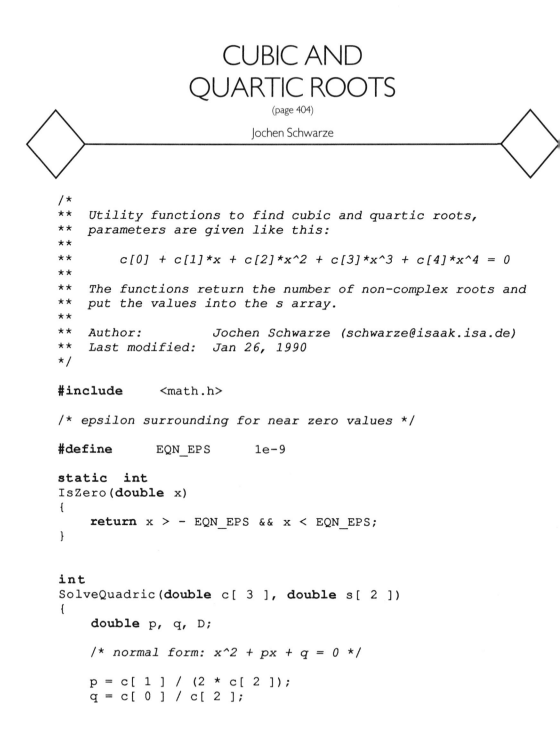

```
/*
**   Utility functions to find cubic and quartic roots,
**   parameters are given like this:
**
**       c[0] + c[1]*x + c[2]*x^2 + c[3]*x^3 + c[4]*x^4 = 0
**
**   The functions return the number of non-complex roots and
**   put the values into the s array.
**
**   Author:        Jochen Schwarze (schwarze@isaak.isa.de)
**   Last modified: Jan 26, 1990
*/

#include     <math.h>

/* epsilon surrounding for near zero values */

#define     EQN_EPS     1e-9

static  int
IsZero(double x)
{
    return x > - EQN_EPS && x < EQN_EPS;
}


int
SolveQuadric(double c[ 3 ], double s[ 2 ])
{
    double p, q, D;

    /* normal form: x^2 + px + q = 0 */

    p = c[ 1 ] / (2 * c[ 2 ]);
    q = c[ 0 ] / c[ 2 ];
```

```
D = p * p - q;

if    (IsZero(D))
{
      s[ 0 ] = - p;
      return 1;
}
else if (D < 0)
{
      return 0;
}
else if (D > 0)
{
      double sqrt_D = sqrt(D);

      s[ 0 ] =   sqrt_D - p;
      s[ 1 ] = - sqrt_D - p;
      return 2;
}
}


int
SolveCubic(double c[ 4 ], double s[ 3 ])
{
    int       i, num;
    double    sub;
    double    A, B, C;
    double    sq_A, p, q;
    double    cb_p, D;

    /* normal form: x^3 + Ax^2 + Bx + C = 0 */

    A = c[ 2 ] / c[ 3 ];
    B = c[ 1 ] / c[ 3 ];
    C = c[ 0 ] / c[ 3 ];

    /*  substitute x = y - A/3 to eliminate quadric term:
     x^3 +px + q = 0 */

    sq_A = A * A;
    p = 1.0/3 * (- 1.0/3 * sq_A + B);
    q = 1.0/2 * (2.0/27 * A * sq_A - 1.0/3 * A * B + C);
```

```
/* use Cardano's formula */

cb_p = p * p * p;
D = q * q + cb_p;

if    (IsZero(D))
{
    if (IsZero(q))        /* one triple solution */
    {
        s[ 0 ] = 0;
        num = 1;
    }
    else                  /* one single and one double solution */
    {
        double u = cbrt(-q);
        s[ 0 ] = 2 * u;
        s[ 1 ] = - u;
        num = 2;
    }
}
else if (D < 0) /* Casus irreducibilis: three real solutions */
{
    double phi = 1.0/3 * acos(-q / sqrt(-cb_p));
    double t = 2 * sqrt(-p);

    s[ 0 ] =   t * cos(phi);
    s[ 1 ] = - t * cos(phi + M_PI / 3);
    s[ 2 ] = - t * cos(phi - M_PI / 3);
    num = 3;
}
else                      /* one real solution */
{
    double sqrt_D = sqrt(D);
    double u = cbrt(sqrt_D - q);
    double v = - cbrt(sqrt_D + q);

    s[ 0 ] = u + v;
    num = 1;
}

/* resubstitute */

sub = 1.0/3 * A;

for (i = 0; i < num; ++i)
    s[ i ] -= sub;

return num;
}
```

```
int
SolveQuartic(double c[ 5 ], double s[ 4 ])
{
    double   coeffs[ 4 ];
    double   z, u, v, sub;
    double   A, B, C, D;
    double   sq_A, p, q, r;
    int      i, num;

    /* normal form: x^4 + Ax^3 + Bx^2 + Cx + D = 0 */

    A = c[ 3 ] / c[ 4 ];
    B = c[ 2 ] / c[ 4 ];
    C = c[ 1 ] / c[ 4 ];
    D = c[ 0 ] / c[ 4 ];

    /*  substitute x = y - A/4 to eliminate cubic term:
    x^4 + px^2 + qx + r = 0 */

    sq_A = A * A;
    p = - 3.0/8 * sq_A + B;
    q = 1.0/8 * sq_A * A - 1.0/2 * A * B + C;
    r = - 3.0/256*sq_A*sq_A + 1.0/16*sq_A*B - 1.0/4*A*C + D;

    if (IsZero(r))
    {
        /* no absolute term: y(y^3 + py + q) = 0 */

        coeffs[ 0 ] = q;
        coeffs[ 1 ] = p;
        coeffs[ 2 ] = 0;
        coeffs[ 3 ] = 1;

        num = SolveCubic(coeffs, s);

        s[ num++ ] = 0;
    }
    else
    {
        /* solve the resolvent cubic ... */

        coeffs[ 0 ] = 1.0/2 * r * p - 1.0/8 * q * q;
        coeffs[ 1 ] = - r;
        coeffs[ 2 ] = - 1.0/2 * p;
        coeffs[ 3 ] = 1;

        (void) SolveCubic(coeffs, s);
```

```
    /* ... and take the one real solution ... */

    z = s[ 0 ];

    /* ... to build two quadric equations */

    u = z * z - r;
    v = 2 * z - p;

    if   (IsZero(u))
        u = 0;
    else if (u > 0)
        u = sqrt(u);
    else
        return 0;

    if (IsZero(v))
        v = 0;
    else if (v > 0)
        v = sqrt(v);
    else
        return 0;

    coeffs[ 0 ] = z - u;
    coeffs[ 1 ] = v;
    coeffs[ 2 ] = 1;

    num = SolveQuadric(coeffs, s);

    coeffs[ 0 ]= z + u;
    coeffs[ 1 ] = - v;
    coeffs[ 2 ] = 1;

    num += SolveQuadric(coeffs, s + num);
}

    /* resubstitute */

sub = 1.0/4 * A;

for (i = 0; i < num; ++i)
    s[ i ] -= sub;

return num;
}
```

USING STURM SEQUENCES TO BRACKET REAL ROOTS OF POLYNOMIAL EQUATIONS

(page 416)

D.G. Hook and P.R. McAree

```
#
# Makefile
#
#    command file for make to compile the solver.

solve: main.o sturm.o util.o
    cc -o solve main.o sturm.o util.o -lm
```

```c
/*
 * solve.h
 *
 *    some useful constants and types.
 */
#define     MAX_ORDER        12
/* maximum order for a polynomial */

#define     RELERROR         1.0e-14
/* smallest relative error we want */

#define     MAXPOW           32
/* max power of 10 we wish to search to */

#define     MAXIT            800
/* max number of iterations */

/* a coefficient smaller than SMALL_ENOUGH is considered to
   be zero (0.0). */

#define     SMALL_ENOUGH     1.0e-12
```

```
/*
 * structure type for representing a polynomial
 */
typedef      struct  p {
                 int      ord;
                 double  coef[MAX_ORDER];
} poly;

extern   int      modrf();
extern   int      numroots();
extern   int      numchanges();
extern   int      buildsturm();

extern   double  evalpoly();



/*
 * util.c
 *
 *   some utlity functions for root polishing and evaluating
 * polynomials.
 */
#include  <math.h>
#include  <stdio.h>
#include  "solve.h"

/*
 * evalpoly
 *
 *   evaluate polynomial defined in coef returning its value.
 */
double
evalpoly (ord, coef, x)
    int      ord;
    double  *coef, x;
{
    double  *fp, f;

    fp = &coef[ord];
    f = *fp;

    for (fp--; fp >= coef; fp--)
    f = x * f + *fp;

    return(f);
}
```

```
/*
 * modrf
 *
 *    uses the modified regula-falsi method to evaluate the root
 * in interval [a,b] of the polynomial described in coef. The
 * root is returned is returned in *val. The routine returns zero
 * if it can't converge.
 */
int
modrf(ord, coef, a, b, val)
      int     ord;
      double  *coef;
      double  a, b, *val;
{
      int     its;
      double  fa, fb, x, lx, fx, lfx;
      double  *fp, *scoef, *ecoef;

      scoef = coef;
      ecoef = &coef[ord];

      fb = fa = *ecoef;
      for (fp = ecoef - 1; fp >= scoef; fp--) {
          fa = a * fa + *fp;
          fb = b * fb + *fp;
      }

      /*
       * if there is no sign difference the method won't work
       */
      if (fa * fb > 0.0)
          return(0);

      if (fabs(fa) < RELERROR) {
          *val = a;
          return(1);
      }

      if (fabs(fb) < RELERROR) {
          *val = b;
          return(1);
      }

      lfx = fa;
      lx = a;
```

```c
    for (its = 0; its < MAXIT; its++) {

        x = (fb * a - fa * b) / (fb - fa);

        fx = *ecoef;
        for (fp = ecoef - 1; fp >= scoef; fp--)
                fx = x * fx + *fp;

        if (fabs(x) > RELERROR) {
                if (fabs(fx / x) < RELERROR) {
                    *val = x;
                    return(1);
                }
        } else if (fabs(fx) < RELERROR) {
                *val = x;
                return(1);
        }

        if ((fa * fx) < 0) {
                b = x;
                fb = fx;
                if ((lfx * fx) > 0)
                    fa /= 2;
        } else {
                a = x;
                fa = fx;
                if ((lfx * fx) > 0)
                    fb /= 2;
        }

        lx = x;
        lfx = fx;
    }

    fprintf(stderr, "modrf overflow %f %f %f\n", a, b, fx);

    return(0);
}
```

746

```c
/*
 * main.c
 *
 *   a sample driver program.
 */
#include <stdio.h>
#include <math.h>
#include "solve.h"

/*
 * a driver program for a root solver.
 */
main()
{
    poly      sseq[MAX_ORDER];
    double    min, max, roots[MAX_ORDER];
    int       i, j, order, nroots, nchanges, np, atmin, atmax;

    /*
     * get the details...
     */

    printf("Please enter order of polynomial: ");
    scanf("%d", &order);

    printf("\n");

    for (i = order; i >= 0; i--) {
            printf("Please enter coefficient number %d: ", i);
            scanf("%lf", &sseq[0].coef[i]);
    }

    printf("\n");

    /*
     * build the Sturm sequence
     */
    np = buildsturm(order, sseq);

    printf("Sturm sequence for:\n");

    for (i = order; i >= 0; i--)
            printf("%lf ", sseq[0].coef[i]);

    printf("\n\n");

    for (i = 0; i <= np; i++) {
            for (j = sseq[i].ord; j >= 0; j--)
                printf("%lf ", sseq[i].coef[j]);
            printf("\n");
    }

    printf("\n");
```

747

```
/*
 * get the number of real roots
 */
nroots = numroots(np, sseq, &atmin, &atmax);

if (nroots == 0) {
        printf("solve: no real roots\n");
        exit(0);
}

/*
 * calculate the bracket that the roots live in
 */
min = -1.0;
nchanges = numchanges(np, sseq, min);
for (i = 0; nchanges != atmin && i != MAXPOW; i++) {
        min *= 10.0;
        nchanges = numchanges(np, sseq, min);
}

if (nchanges != atmin) {
        printf("solve: unable to bracket all negetive roots\n");
        atmin = nchanges;
}

max = 1.0;
nchanges = numchanges(np, sseq, max);
for (i = 0; nchanges != atmax && i != MAXPOW; i++) {
        max *= 10.0;
        nchanges = numchanges(np, sseq, max);
}

if (nchanges != atmax) {
        printf("solve: unable to bracket all positive roots\n");
        atmax = nchanges;
}

nroots = atmin - atmax;

/*
 * perform the bisection.
 */
sbisect(np, sseq, min, max, atmin, atmax, roots);
```

```
       /*
        * write out the roots...
        */
       if (nroots == 1) {
               printf("\n1 distinct real root at x = %f\n", roots[0]);
       } else {
               printf("\n%d distinct real roots for x: ", nroots);

               for (i = 0; i != nroots; i++)
                   printf("%f ", roots[i]);
               printf("\n");
       }
}


/*
 * sturm.c
 *
 * the functions to build and evaluate the Sturm sequence
 */
#include <math.h>
#include <stdio.h>
#include "solve.h"

/*
 * modp
 *
 * calculates the modulus of u(x) / v(x) leaving it in r, it
 * returns 0 if r(x) is a constant.
 * note: this function assumes the leading coefficient of v
 * is 1 or -1
 */
static int
modp(u, v, r)
       poly      *u, *v, *r;
{
       int       k, j;
       double    *nr, *end, *uc;

       nr = r->coef;
       end = &u->coef[u->ord];

       uc = u->coef;
       while (uc <= end)
               *nr++ = *uc++;

       if (v->coef[v->ord] < 0.0) {
```

```
                for (k = u->ord - v->ord - 1; k >= 0; k -= 2)
                    r->coef[k] = -r->coef[k];

                for (k = u->ord - v->ord; k >= 0; k--)
                    for (j = v->ord + k - 1; j >= k; j--)
                        r->coef[j] = -r->coef[j] - r->coef[v->ord + k]
                        * v->coef[j - k];
        } else {
                for (k = u->ord - v->ord; k >= 0; k--)
                    for (j = v->ord + k - 1; j >= k; j--)
                        r->coef[j] -= r->coef[v->ord + k] * v->coef[j - k];
        }

        k = v->ord - 1;
        while (k >= 0 && fabs(r->coef[k]) < SMALL_ENOUGH) {
            r->coef[k] = 0.0;
            k--;
        }

        r->ord = (k < 0) ? 0 : k;

        return(r->ord);
}


/*
 * buildsturm
 *
 *   build up a sturm sequence for a polynomial in smat, returning
 * the number of polynomials in the sequence
 */
int
buildsturm(ord, sseq)
        int     ord;
        poly    *sseq;
{
        int     i;
        double  f, *fp, *fc;
        poly    *sp;

        sseq[0].ord = ord;
        sseq[1].ord = ord - 1;
```

```
        /*
         * calculate the derivative and normalise the leading
         * coefficient.
         */
        f = fabs(sseq[0].coef[ord] * ord);
        fp = sseq[1].coef;
        fc = sseq[0].coef + 1;
        for (i = 1; i <= ord; i++)
                *fp++ = *fc++ * i / f;


        /*
         * construct the rest of the Sturm sequence
         */
        for (sp = sseq + 2; modp(sp - 2, sp - 1, sp); sp++) {

            /*
             * reverse the sign and normalise
             */
            f = -fabs(sp->coef[sp->ord]);
            for (fp = &sp->coef[sp->ord]; fp >= sp->coef; fp--)
                    *fp /= f;
        }

        sp->coef[0] = -sp->coef[0];       /* reverse the sign */

        return(sp - sseq);
}

/*
 * numroots
 *
 *     return the number of distinct real roots of the polynomial
 * described in sseq.
 */
int
numroots(np, sseq, atneg, atpos)
        int        np;
        poly       *sseq;
        int        *atneg, *atpos;
{
        int        atposinf, atneginf;
        poly       *s;
        double     f, lf;

        atposinf = atneginf = 0;
```

```
    /*
     * changes at positve infinity
     */
    lf = sseq[0].coef[sseq[0].ord];

    for (s = sseq + 1; s <= sseq + np; s++) {
            f = s->coef[s->ord];
            if (lf == 0.0 || lf * f < 0)
                    atposinf++;
        lf = f;
    }

    /*
     * changes at negative infinity
     */
    if (sseq[0].ord & 1)
            lf = -sseq[0].coef[sseq[0].ord];
    else
            lf = sseq[0].coef[sseq[0].ord];

    for (s = sseq + 1; s <= sseq + np; s++) {
            if (s->ord & 1)
                f = -s->coef[s->ord];
            else
                f = s->coef[s->ord];
            if (lf == 0.0 || lf * f < 0)
                atneginf++;
            lf = f;
    }

    *atneg = atneginf;
    *atpos = atposinf;

    return(atneginf - atposinf);
}

/*
 * numchanges
 *
 * return the number of sign changes in the Sturm sequence in
 * sseq at the value a.
 */
int
numchanges(np, sseq, a)
    int     np;
    poly    *sseq;
    double  a;
```

```c
{
    int     changes;
    double  f, lf;
    poly    *s;

    changes = 0;

    lf = evalpoly(sseq[0].ord, sseq[0].coef, a);

    for (s = sseq + 1; s <= sseq + np; s++) {
            f = evalpoly(s->ord, s->coef, a);
            if (lf == 0.0 || lf * f < 0)
                changes++;
            lf = f;
    }

    return(changes);
}

/*
 * sbisect
 *
 *   uses a bisection based on the sturm sequence for the polynomial
 * described in sseq to isolate intervals in which roots occur,
 * the roots are returned in the roots array in order of magnitude.
 */
sbisect(np, sseq, min, max, atmin, atmax, roots)
    int     np;
    poly    *sseq;
    double  min, max;
    int     atmin, atmax;
    double  *roots;
{
    double  mid;
    int     n1, n2, its, atmid, nroot;

    if ((nroot = atmin - atmax) == 1) {

            /*
             * first try a less expensive technique.
             */
            if (modrf(sseq->ord, sseq->coef, min, max, &roots[0]))
                return;
```

```
            /*
             * if we get here we have to evaluate the root the hard
             * way by using the Sturm sequence.
             */
            for (its = 0; its < MAXIT; its++) {
                    mid = (min + max) / 2;

                    atmid = numchanges(np, sseq, mid);

                    if (fabs(mid) > RELERROR) {
                        if (fabs((max - min) / mid) < RELERROR) {
                            roots[0] = mid;
                            return;
                        }
                    } else if (fabs(max - min) < RELERROR) {
                        roots[0] = mid;
                        return;
                    }

                    if ((atmin - atmid) == 0)
                        min = mid;
                    else
                        max = mid;
            }

        if (its == MAXIT) {
                fprintf(stderr, "sbisect: overflow min %f max %f\
                    diff %e nroot %d n1 %d n2 %d\n",
                    min, max, max - min, nroot, n1, n2);
            roots[0] = mid;
        }

        return;
}

/*
 * more than one root in the interval, we have to bisect...
 */
for (its = 0; its < MAXIT; its++) {

        mid = (min + max) / 2;

        atmid = numchanges(np, sseq, mid);

        n1 = atmin - atmid;
        n2 = atmid - atmax;
```

```
        if (n1 != 0 && n2 != 0) {
                sbisect(np, sseq, min, mid, atmin, atmid, roots);
                sbisect(np, sseq, mid, max, atmid, atmax, &roots[n1]);
                break;
        }

        if (n1 == 0)
                min = mid;
        else
                max = mid;
}


if (its == MAXIT) {
        fprintf(stderr, "sbisect: roots too close together\n");
        fprintf(stderr, "sbisect: overflow min %f max %f diff %e\
                nroot %d n1 %d n2 %d\n",
                min, max, max - min, nroot, n1, n2);
        for (n1 = atmax; n1 < atmin; n1++)
        roots[n1 - atmax] = mid;
}
}
```

A HIGH-SPEED, LOW PRECISION SQUARE ROOT

(page 424)

Paul Lalonde and Robert Dawson

```
/* SPARC implementation of a fast square root by table
 * lookup.
 * SPARC floating point format is as follows:
 *
 * BIT 31      30  23  22   0
 *     sign    exponent mantissa
 */

#include <math.h>
static short sqrttab[0x100]; /* declare table of square roots */
void build_table()
{
    unsigned short i;
    float f;
    unsigned int *fi=&f;        /* to access the bits of a float in */
                                /* C quickly we must misuse pointers */
    for(i=0; i<= 0x7f; i++)
    {
        *fi = 0;

        /* Build a float with the bit pattern i as mantissa
         * and an exponent of 0, stored as 127
         */

        *fi = (i << 16) | (127 << 23);
        f = sqrt(f);

        /* Take the square root then strip the first 7 bits of
         * the mantissa into the table
         */

        sqrttab[i] = (*fi & 0x7fffff) >> 16;

        /* Repeat the process, this time with an exponent of
         * 1, stored as 128
         */
```

```
            *fi = 0;
            *fi = (i << 16) | (128 << 23);
            f = sqrt(f);
            sqrttab{i+0x80] = (*fi & 0x7fffff) >> 16;
      }
}

/*
 * fsqrt - fast square root by table lookup
 */

float fsqrt(float n)
{
      unsigned int *num = &n;   /* to access the bits of a float in C
                                 * we must misuse pointers */

      short e;                         /* the exponent */
      if (n == 0) return (0);   /* check for square root of 0 */
      e = (*num >> 23) - 127;   /* get the exponent - on a SPARC the */
                                /* exponent is stored with 127 added */
      *num & = 0x7fffff:        /* leave only the mantissa */
      if (e & 0x01) *num | = 0x800000;
                                /* the exponent is odd so we have to */
                                /* look it up in the second half of  */
                                /* the lookup table, so we set the   */
                                /* high bit                          */
      e >>= 1:                  /* divide the exponent by two */
                                /* note that in C the shift */
                                /* operators are sign preserving */
                                /* for signed operands */
      /* Do the table lookup, based on the quaternary mantissa,
       * then reconstruct the result back into a float
       */
      *num = ((sqrttab[*num >> 16]) << 16) | ((e + 127) << 23);
      return (n);
}
```

A FAST APPROXIMATION TO THE HYPOTENUSE

(page 427)

Alan Paeth

```c
int idist(x1, y1, x2, y2)
    int x1, y1, x2, y2;
        {
/*
 * gives approximate distance from (x1,y1) to (x2,y2)
 * with only overestimations, and then never by more
 * than (9/8) + one bit uncertainty.
 */
    if ((x2 -= x1) < 0) x2 = -x2;
    if ((y2 -= y1) < 0) y2 = -y2;
    return (x2 + y2 - (((x2>y2) ? y2 : x2) >> 1) );
    }

int PntOnCirc(xp, yp, xc, yc, r)
    int xp, yp, xc, yc, r;
        {
/* returns true IFF a test point (xp, yp) is to within a
 * pixel of the circle of center (xc, yc) and radius r.
 * "d" is an approximate length to circle's center, with
 * 1.0*r < dist < 1.12*r < (9/8)*r used for coarse testing.
 * The 9/8 ratio suggests the code: (x)<<3 and ((x)<<3)-(x).
 * Variables xp, yp, r and d should be of 32-bit precision.
 *
 * Note: (9/8) forms a very tight, proper inner bound but
 * must be slackened by one pixel for the outside test (#2)
 * to account for the -1/2 pixel absolute error introduced
 * when "idist" halves an odd integer; else rough clipping
 * will trim occasional points on the circle's perimeter.
 */
    int d = idist(xp, yp, xc, yc);
    if (   r >      d)  return(0);      /* far-in  */
    if (9*r < 8*(d-1))  return(0);      /* far-out */
/* full test: r < hypot(xp-xc,yp-yc) < r+1 */
    xp -= xc;
    yp -= yc;
    d = xp*xp + yp*yp;
    if (d < r*r) return(0);             /* near-in */
    r += 1;
    if (d > r*r) return(0);             /* near-out */
    return(1);                          /* WITHIN */
    }
```

BIT INTERLEAVING FOR QUAD- OR OCTREES

(page 443)

Clifford A. Shaffer

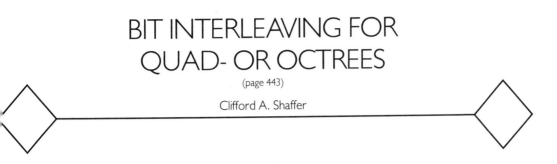

```c
#define B_MAX_DEPTH 14    /* maximum depth allowed */

/* byteval is the lookup table for coordinate interleaving.  Given a
   4 bit portion of the (x, y) coordinates, return the bit interleaving.
   Notice that this table looks like the order in which the pixels of
   a 16 X 16 pixel image would be visited. */
int byteval[16][16] =
     {  0,   1,   4,   5,  16,  17,  20,  21,  64,  65,  68,  69,  80,  81,  84,  85,
        2,   3,   6,   7,  18,  19,  22,  23,  66,  67,  70,  71,  82,  83,  86,  87,
        8,   9,  12,  13,  24,  25,  28,  29,  72,  73,  76,  77,  88,  89,  92,  93,
       10,  11,  14,  15,  26,  27,  30,  31,  74,  75,  78,  79,  90,  91,  94,  95,
       32,  33,  36,  37,  48,  49,  52,  53,  96,  97, 100, 101, 112, 113, 116, 117,
       34,  35,  38,  39,  50,  51,  54,  55,  98,  99, 102, 103, 114, 115, 118, 119,
       40,  41,  44,  45,  56,  57,  60,  61, 104, 105, 108, 109, 120, 121, 124, 125,
       42,  43,  46,  47,  58,  59,  62,  63, 106, 107, 110, 111, 122, 123, 126, 127,
      128, 129, 132, 133, 144, 145, 148, 149, 192, 193, 196, 197, 208, 209, 212, 213,
      130, 131, 134, 135, 146, 147, 150, 151, 194, 195, 198, 199, 210, 211, 214, 215,
      136, 137, 140, 141, 152, 153, 156, 157, 200, 201, 204, 205, 216, 217, 220, 221,
      138, 139, 142, 143, 154, 155, 158, 159, 202, 203, 206, 207, 218, 219, 222, 223,
      160, 161, 164, 165, 176, 177, 180, 181, 224, 225, 228, 229, 240, 241, 244, 245,
      162, 163, 166, 167, 178, 179, 182, 183, 226, 227, 230, 231, 242, 243, 246, 247,
      168, 169, 172, 173, 184, 185, 188, 189, 232, 233, 236, 237, 248, 249, 252, 253,
      170, 171, 174, 175, 186, 187, 190, 191, 234, 235, 238, 239, 250, 251, 254, 255};

/* bytemask is the mask for byte interleaving - masks out the
   non-significant bit positions.  This is determined by the
   depth of the node. For example, a node of depth 0 is at the root.
   Thus, there are no branchs and no bits are significant.
   The bottom 4 bits (the depth) are always retained.
   Values are in octal notation. */
int bytemask[B_MAX_DEPTH + 1] = {017,
       030000000017,036000000017,037400000017,037700000017,
       037760000017,037774000017,037777000017,037777600017,
       037777740017,037777770017,037777776017,037777777417,
       037777777717,037777777777};
```

```
long *interleave(addr, x, y, depth, max_depth)
/* Return the interleaved code for a quadtree node at depth depth
whose upper left hand corner has coordinates (x, y) in a tree with
maximum depth max_depth.  This function receives and returns a
pointer to addr, which is either a long interger or (more typically)
an array of long integers whose first integer contains the
interleaved code. */
 long *addr;
 int max_depth, depth;
 int x, y;
{

/* Scale x, y values to be consistent with maximum coord size */
/* and depth of tree */
 x <<= (B_MAX_DEPTH - max_depth);
 y <<= (B_MAX_DEPTH - max_depth);

/* calculate the bit interleaving of the x, y values that have now
    been appropriately shifted, and place this interleave in the address
    portion of addr.  Note that the binary representations of x and y are
    being processed from right to left */

 *addr = depth;
 *addr |= byteval[y & 03][x & 03] << 4;
 *addr |= byteval[(y >> 2) & 017][(x >> 2) & 017] << 8;
 *addr |= byteval[(y >> 6) & 017][(x >> 6) & 017] << 16;
 *addr |= byteval[(y >> 10) & 017][(x >> 10) & 017] << 24;
 *addr &= bytemask[depth];

/* if there were unused portions of the x and y addresses then  */
/* the address was too large for the depth values given.  */
/*  Return address built */
 return (addr);
}
```

```c
/* The next two arrays are used in calculating the (x, y) coordinates
   of the upper left-hand corner of a node from its bit interleaved
   address.  Given an 8 bit number, the arrays return the effect of
   removing every other bit (the y bits preceed the x bits). */

int xval[256] = { 0, 1, 0, 1, 2, 3, 2, 3, 0, 1, 0, 1, 2, 3, 2, 3,
                  4, 5, 4, 5, 6, 7, 6, 7, 4, 5, 4, 5, 6, 7, 6, 7,
                  0, 1, 0, 1, 2, 3, 2, 3, 0, 1, 0, 1, 2, 3, 2, 3,
                  4, 5, 4, 5, 6, 7, 6, 7, 4, 5, 4, 5, 6, 7, 6, 7,
                  8, 9, 8, 9,10,11,10,11, 8, 9, 8, 9,10,11,10,11,
                 12,13,12,13,14,15,14,15,12,13,12,13,14,15,14,15,
                  8, 9, 8, 9,10,11,10,11, 8, 9, 8, 9,10,11,10,11,
                 12,13,12,13,14,15,14,15,12,13,12,13,14,15,14,15,
                  0, 1, 0, 1, 2, 3, 2, 3, 0, 1, 0, 1, 2, 3, 2, 3,
                  4, 5, 4, 5, 6, 7, 6, 7, 4, 5, 4, 5, 6, 7, 6, 7,
                  0, 1, 0, 1, 2, 3, 2, 3, 0, 1, 0, 1, 2, 3, 2, 3,
                  4, 5, 4, 5, 6, 7, 6, 7, 4, 5, 4, 5, 6, 7, 6, 7,
                  8, 9, 8, 9,10,11,10,11, 8, 9, 8, 9,10,11,10,11,
                 12,13,12,13,14,15,14,15,12,13,12,13,14,15,14,15,
                  8, 9, 8, 9,10,11,10,11, 8, 9, 8, 9,10,11,10,11,
                 12,13,12,13,14,15,14,15,12,13,12,13,14,15,14,15};

int yval[256] = { 0, 0, 1, 1, 0, 0, 1, 1, 2, 2, 3, 3, 2, 2, 3, 3,
                  0, 0, 1, 1, 0, 0, 1, 1, 2, 2, 3, 3, 2, 2, 3, 3,
                  4, 4, 5, 5, 4, 4, 5, 5, 6, 6, 7, 7, 6, 6, 7, 7,
                  4, 4, 5, 5, 4, 4, 5, 5, 6, 6, 7, 7, 6, 6, 7, 7,
                  0, 0, 1, 1, 0, 0, 1, 1, 2, 2, 3, 3, 2, 2, 3, 3,
                  0, 0, 1, 1, 0, 0, 1, 1, 2, 2, 3, 3, 2, 2, 3, 3,
                  4, 4, 5, 5, 4, 4, 5, 5, 6, 6, 7, 7, 6, 6, 7, 7,
                  4, 4, 5, 5, 4, 4, 5, 5, 6, 6, 7, 7, 6, 6, 7, 7,
                  8, 8, 9, 9, 8, 8, 9, 9,10,10,11,11,10,10,11,11,
                  8, 8, 9, 9, 8, 8, 9, 9,10,10,11,11,10,10,11,11,
                 12,12,13,13,12,12,13,13,14,14,15,15,14,14,15,15,
                 12,12,13,13,12,12,13,13,14,14,15,15,14,14,15,15,
                  8, 8, 9, 9, 8, 8, 9, 9,10,10,11,11,10,10,11,11,
                  8, 8, 9, 9, 8, 8, 9, 9,10,10,11,11,10,10,11,11,
                 12,12,13,13,12,12,13,13,14,14,15,15,14,14,15,15,
                 12,12,13,13,12,12,13,13,14,14,15,15,14,14,15,15};
```

```
int getx(addr, max_depth)
/* Return the x coordinate of the upper left hand corner of addr for a
   tree with maximum depth max_depth. */
 long *addr;
 int max_depth;
{
 register x;

 x = xval[(*addr >> 4) & 017];
 x |= xval[(*addr >> 8) & 0377] << 2;
 x |= xval[(*addr >> 16) & 0377] << 6;
 x |= xval[(*addr >> 24) & 0377] << 10;
 x >>= B_MAX_DEPTH - max_depth;
 return (x);
}




int QKy(addr, max_depth)
/* Return the y coordinate of the upper left hand corner of addr for a
   tree with maximum depth max_depth. */

 long *addr;
 int max_depth;
{
 register y;

 y = yval[(*addr >> 4) & 017];
 y |= yval[(*addr >> 8) & 0377] << 2;
 y |= yval[(*addr >> 16) & 0377] << 6;
 y |= yval[(*addr >> 24) & 0377] << 10;
 y >>= B_MAX_DEPTH - max_depth;
 return (y);
}

int getdepth(addr)
/* Return the depth of the node.  Simply return the bottom 4 bits. */

 long *addr;
{

 return(*addr & 017);
}
```

A FAST HSL-TO-RGB TRANSFORM

(page 448)

Ken Fishkin

```c
#include <math.h>
#include <stdio.h>

#define MIN(a,b) (((a) < (b)) ? (a) : (b))
#define MAX(a,b) (((a) > (b)) ? (a) : (b))

    /*
     * RGB-HSL transforms.
     * Ken Fishkin, Pixar Inc., January 1989.
     */


    /*
     * given r,g,b on [0 ... 1],
     * return (h,s,l) on [0 ... 1]
     */
void
RGB_to_HSL     (r,g,b,h,s,l)
double  r,g,b;
double *h, *s, *l;
{
    double v;
    double m;
    double vm;
    double r2, g2, b2;

    v = MAX(r,g);
    v = MAX(v,b);
    m = MIN(r,g);
    m = MIN(m,b);

    if ((*l = (m + v) / 2.0) <= 0.0) return;
    if ((*s = vm = v - m) > 0.0) {
            *s /= (*l <= 0.5)
            ? (v + m )
            : (2.0 - v - m)
            ;
    } else
    return;
```

```
        r2 = (v - r) / vm;
        g2 = (v - g) / vm;
        b2 = (v - b) / vm;

        if (r == v)
            *h = (g == m ? 5.0 + b2 : 1.0 - g2);
        else if (g == v)
            *h = (b == m ? 1.0 + r2 : 3.0 - b2);
        else
            *h = (r == m ? 3.0 + g2 : 5.0 - r2);

            *h /= 6;
    }


    /*
     * given h,s,l on [0..1],
     * return r,g,b on [0..1]
     */
void
HSL_to_RGB(h,sl,l,r,g,b)
double    h,sl,l;
double    *r, *g, *b;
{
    double v;

    v = (l <= 0.5) ? (l * (1.0 + sl)) : (l + sl - l * sl);
    if (v <= 0) {
        *r = *g = *b = 0.0;
    } else {
        double m;
        double sv;
        int sextant;
        double fract, vsf, mid1, mid2;

        m = l + l - v;
        sv = (v - m ) / v;
        h *= 6.0;
        sextant = h;
        fract = h - sextant;
        vsf = v * sv * fract;
        mid1 = m + vsf;
        mid2 = v - vsf;
        switch (sextant) {
            case 0: *r = v; *g = mid1; *b = m; break;
            case 1: *r = mid2; *g = v; *b = m; break;
            case 2: *r = m; *g = v; *b = mid1; break;
            case 3: *r = m; *g = mid2; *b = v; break;
            case 4: *r = mid1; *g = m; *b = v; break;
            case 5: *r = v; *g = m; *b = mid2; break;
        }
    }
}
```

MATRIX ORTHOGONALIZATION

(page 464)

Eric Raible

```
/*
 * Reorthogonalize matrix R - that is find an orthogonal matrix that is
 * "close" to R by computing an approximation to the orthogonal matrix
 *
 *            T  -1/2
 *    RC = R(R R)
 *
 *                             T        -1
 * [RC is orthogonal because (RC) = (RC) ]
 *                                                      -1/2
 * To compute C, we evaluate the Taylor expansion of F(x) = (I + x)
 * (where x = C - I) about x=0.
 * This gives C = I - (1/2)x + (3/8)x^2 - (5/16)x^3 + ...
 */

static float coef[10] =                   /* From mathematica */
   { 1, -1/2., 3/8., -5/16., 35/128., -63/256.,
     231/1024., -429/2048., 6435/32768., -12155/65536. };

MATRIX_reorthogonalize (R, limit)
     Matrix R;
{
  Matrix I, Temp, X, X_power, Sum;
  int power;

  limit = MAX(limit, 10);

  MATRIX_transpose (R, Temp);         /* Rt */
  MATRIX_multiply (Temp, R, Temp);    /* RtR */
  MATRIX_identify (I);
  MATRIX_subtract (Temp, I, X);       /* RtR - I */
  MATRIX_identify (X_power);          /* X^0 */
  MATRIX_identify (Sum);              /* coef[0] * X^0 */

  for (power = 1; power < limit; ++power)
    {
      MATRIX_multiply (X_power, X, X_power);
      MATRIX_constant_multiply (coef[power], X_power, Temp);
      MATRIX_add (Sum, Temp, Sum);
    }

  MATRIX_multiply (R, Sum, R);
}
```

MATRIX INVERSION

(page 470)

Richard Carling

```
/*
 *    inverse( original_matrix, inverse_matrix )
 *
 *    calculate the inverse of a 4x4 matrix
 *
 *      -1
 *     A  = ___1__  adjoint A
 *           det A
 */

inverse( in, out ) matrix4 *in, *out;
{
    int i, j;
    double det, det4x4();

    /* calculate the adjoint matrix */

    adjoint( in, out );

    /*  calculate the 4x4 determinent
     *  if the determinent is zero,
     *  then the inverse matrix is not unique.
     */

    det = det4x4( out );

    if ( fabs( det ) < SMALL_NUMBER) {
        printf("Non-singular matrix, no inverse!\n");
        exit();
    }

    /* scale the adjoint matrix to get the inverse */

    for (i=0; i<4; i++)
        for(j=0; j<4; j++)
        out->element[i][j] = out->element[i][j] / det;
}
```

```
/*
 *    adjoint( original_matrix, inverse_matrix )
 *
 *      calculate the adjoint of a 4x4 matrix
 *
 *      Let   a     denote the minor determinant of matrix A obtained by
 *             ij
 *
 *      deleting the ith row and jth column from A.
 *
 *                        i+j
 *      Let   b    = (-1)     a
 *             ij              ji
 *
 *      The matrix B = (b  ) is the adjoint of A
 *                       ij
 */

adjoint( in, out ) matrix4 *in; matrix4 *out;
{
    double a1, a2, a3, a4, b1, b2, b3, b4;
    double c1, c2, c3, c4, d1, d2, d3, d4;
    double det3x3();

    /* assign to individual variable names to aid  */
    /* selecting correct values  */

    a1 = in->element[0][0]; b1 = in->element[0][1];
    c1 = in->element[0][2]; d1 = in->element[0][3];

    a2 = in->element[1][0]; b2 = in->element[1][1];
    c2 = in->element[1][2]; d2 = in->element[1][3];

    a3 = in->element[2][0]; b3 = in->element[2][1];
    c3 = in->element[2][2]; d3 = in->element[2][3];

    a4 = in->element[3][0]; b4 = in->element[3][1];
    c4 = in->element[3][2]; d4 = in->element[3][3];
```

```c
    /* row column labeling reversed since we transpose rows & columns */

    out->element[0][0]  =    det3x3( b2, b3, b4, c2, c3, c4, d2, d3, d4);
    out->element[1][0]  =  - det3x3( a2, a3, a4, c2, c3, c4, d2, d3, d4);
    out->element[2][0]  =    det3x3( a2, a3, a4, b2, b3, b4, d2, d3, d4);
    out->element[3][0]  =  - det3x3( a2, a3, a4, b2, b3, b4, c2, c3, c4);

    out->element[0][1]  =  - det3x3( b1, b3, b4, c1, c3, c4, d1, d3, d4);
    out->element[1][1]  =    det3x3( a1, a3, a4, c1, c3, c4, d1, d3, d4);
    out->element[2][1]  =  - det3x3( a1, a3, a4, b1, b3, b4, d1, d3, d4);
    out->element[3][1]  =    det3x3( a1, a3, a4, b1, b3, b4, c1, c3, c4);

    out->element[0][2]  =    det3x3( b1, b2, b4, c1, c2, c4, d1, d2, d4);
    out->element[1][2]  =  - det3x3( a1, a2, a4, c1, c2, c4, d1, d2, d4);
    out->element[2][2]  =    det3x3( a1, a2, a4, b1, b2, b4, d1, d2, d4);
    out->element[3][2]  =  - det3x3( a1, a2, a4, b1, b2, b4, c1, c2, c4);

    out->element[0][3]  =  - det3x3( b1, b2, b3, c1, c2, c3, d1, d2, d3);
    out->element[1][3]  =    det3x3( a1, a2, a3, c1, c2, c3, d1, d2, d3);
    out->element[2][3]  =  - det3x3( a1, a2, a3, b1, b2, b3, d1, d2, d3);
    out->element[3][3]  =    det3x3( a1, a2, a3, b1, b2, b3, c1, c2, c3);
}
/*
 * double = det4x4( matrix )
 *
 * calculate the determinent of a 4x4 matrix.
 */
double det4x4( m ) matrix4 *m;
{
    double ans;
    double a1, a2, a3, a4, b1, b2, b3, b4, c1, c2, c3, c4, d1, d2, d3,
           d4;
    double det3x3();

    /* assign to individual variable names to aid selecting */
    /*   correct elements */

    a1 = m->element[0][0]; b1 = m->element[0][1];
    c1 = m->element[0][2]; d1 = m->element[0][3];

    a2 = m->element[1][0]; b2 = m->element[1][1];
    c2 = m->element[1][2]; d2 = m->element[1][3];

    a3 = m->element[2][0]; b3 = m->element[2][1];
    c3 = m->element[2][2]; d3 = m->element[2][3];

    a4 = m->element[3][0]; b4 = m->element[3][1];
    c4 = m->element[3][2]; d4 = m->element[3][3];

    ans = a1 * det3x3( b2, b3, b4, c2, c3, c4, d2, d3, d4)
        - b1 * det3x3( a2, a3, a4, c2, c3, c4, d2, d3, d4)
        + c1 * det3x3( a2, a3, a4, b2, b3, b4, d2, d3, d4)
        - d1 * det3x3( a2, a3, a4, b2, b3, b4, c2, c3, c4);
    return ans;
}
```

```
/*
 * double = det3x3(  a1, a2, a3, b1, b2, b3, c1, c2, c3 )
 *
 * calculate the determinent of a 3x3 matrix
 * in the form
 *
 *      | a1,  b1,  c1 |
 *      | a2,  b2,  c2 |
 *      | a3,  b3,  c3 |
 */

double det3x3( a1, a2, a3, b1, b2, b3, c1, c2, c3 )
double a1, a2, a3, b1, b2, b3, c1, c2, c3;
{
    double ans;
    double det2x2();

    ans = a1 * det2x2( b2, b3, c2, c3 )
        - b1 * det2x2( a2, a3, c2, c3 )
        + c1 * det2x2( a2, a3, b2, b3 );
    return ans;
}

/*
 * double = det2x2( double a, double b, double c, double d )
 *
 * calculate the determinent of a 2x2 matrix.
 */

double det2x2( a, b, c, d)
double a, b, c, d;
{
    double ans;
    ans = a * d - b * c;
    return ans;
}
```

EFFICIENT
POST-CONCATENATION
OF TRANSFORMATION
MATRICES

(page 476)

Joseph M. Cychosz

```
#include    <math.h>
#include    "graphics.h"


/*      M4xform.c - Basic 4x4 transformation package.
 *
 *  Description:
 *      M4xform.c contains a collection of routines used to perform
 *      direct post-concatenated transformation operations.
 *
 *
 *  Contents:
 *      M4RotateX           Post-concatenate a x-axis rotation.
 *      M4RotateY           Post-concatenate a y-axis rotation.
 *      M4RotateZ           Post-concatenate a z-axis rotation.
 *      M4Scale             Post-concatenate a scaling.
 *      M4Translate         Post-concatenate a translation.
 *      M4ZPerspective      Post-concatenate a z-axis perspective
 *                          transformation.
 *
 *  Externals:
 *      cos, sin.
 */




/*      M4RotateX - Post-concatenate a x-axis rotation matrix.  */

Matrix4  *M4RotateX    (m,a)
        Matrix4  *m;            /* Current transformation matrix*/
        double   a;             /* Rotation angle              */
{
        double   c, s;
        double   t;
        int      i;
```

```
        c = cos (a);  s = sin (a);

        for (i = 0 ; i < 4 ; i++) {
            t = m->element[i][1];
            m->element[i][1] = t*c - m->element[i][2]*s;
            m->element[i][2] = t*s + m->element[i][2]*c;
        }
        return (m);
}


/*   M4RotateY - Post-concatenate a y-axis rotation matrix.   */

Matrix4      *M4RotateY     (m,a)
        Matrix4  *m;            /* Current transformation matrix*/
        double  a;             /* Rotation angle         */
{
        double  c, s;
        double  t;
        int     i;

        c = cos (a);  s = sin (a);

        for (i = 0 ; i < 4 ; i++) {
            t = m->element[i][0];
            m->element[i][0] = t*c + m->element[i][2]*s;
            m->element[i][2] = m->element[i][2]*c - t*s;
        }
        return (m);
}


/*       M4RotateZ - Post-concatenate a z-axis rotation matrix.   */

Matrix4  *M4RotateZ     (m,a)
        Matrix4  *m;            /* Current transformation matrix*/
        double  a;             /* Rotation angle          */
{
        double  c, s;
        double  t;
        int     i;

        c = cos (a);  s = sin (a);

        for (i = 0 ; i < 4 ; i++) {
            t = m->element[i][0];
            m->element[i][0] = t*c - m->element[i][1]*s;
            m->element[i][1] = t*s + m->element[i][1]*c;
        }
        return (m);
}
```

771

```c
/*       M4Scale  - Post-concatenate a scaling.   */

Matrix4 *M4Scale (m,sx,sy,sz)
        Matrix4 *m;             /* Current transformation matrix */
        double  sx, sy, sz;   /* Scale factors about x,y,z */
{
        int     i;

        for (i = 0 ; i < 4 ; i++) {
             m->element[i][0] *= sx;
             m->element[i][1] *= sy;
             m->element[i][2] *= sz;
        }
        return (m);
}



/*       M4Translate - Post-concatenate a translation.   */

Matrix4 *M4Translate  (m,tx,ty,tz)
        Matrix4 *m;             /* Current transformation matrix */
        double  tx, ty, tz;   /* Translation distance */
{
        int     i;

        for (i = 0 ; i < 4 ; i++) {
             m->element[i][0] += m->element[i][3]*tx;
             m->element[i][1] += m->element[i][3]*ty;
             m->element[i][2] += m->element[i][3]*tz;
        }
        return (m);
}



/* M4ZPerspective  Post-concatenate a perspective        */
/*transformation.                                         */
/*                                                        */
/* Perspective is along the z-axis with the eye at +z.   */

Matrix4 *M4ZPerspective     (m,d)
        Matrix4 *m;             /* Current transformation matrix  */
        double  d;              /* Perspective distance           */
{
        int     i;
        double  f = 1. / d;

        for (i = 0 ; i < 4 ; i++) {
             m->element[i][3] += m->element[i][2]*f;
             m->element[i][2]  = 0.;
        }
        return (m);
}
```

FIXED-POINT
TRIGONOMETRY WITH
CORDIC ITERATIONS

(page 494)

Ken Turkowski

```c
#define COSCALE 0x22c2dd1c /* 0.271572 */
#define QUARTER ((int)(3.141592654 / 2.0 * (1 << 28)))
static long arctantab[32] = {   /* MS 4 integral bits for radians */
    297197971, 210828714, 124459457, 65760959, 33381290, 16755422,
    8385879, 4193963, 2097109, 1048571, 524287, 262144, 131072,
    65536, 32768, 16384, 8192, 4096, 2048, 1024, 512, 256, 128, 64, 32,
    16, 8, 4, 2, 1, 0, 0,
};

CordicRotate(px, py, theta)
long *px, *py;
register long theta;        /* Assume that abs(theta) <= pi */
{
    register int i;
    register long x = *px, y = *py, xtemp;
    register long *arctanptr = arctantab;

    /* The -1 may need to be pulled out and done as a left shift */
    for (i = -1; i <= 28; i++) {
        if (theta < 0) {
            xtemp = x + (y >> i);
            y     = y - (x >> i);
            x = xtemp;
            theta += *arctanptr++;
        } else {
            xtemp = x - (y >> i);
            y     = y + (x >> i);
            x = xtemp;
            theta -= *arctanptr++;
        }
    }

    *px = frmul(x, COSCALE); /* Compensate for CORDIC enlargement */
    *py = frmul(y, COSCALE); /* frmul(a,b)=(a*b)>>31, high part   */
                             /* of 64-bit product */
}
```

```
CordicPolarize(argx, argy)
long *argx, *argy      /* We assume these are already in the */
                       /*   right half plane */
{
    register long theta, yi, i;
    register long x = *argx, y = *argy;
    register long *arctanptr = arctantab;
    for (i = -1; i <= 28; i++) {
        if (y < 0) {          /* Rotate positive */
            yi = y + (x >> i);
            x  = x - (y >> i);
            y  = yi;
            theta -= *arctanptr++;
        } else {              /* Rotate negative */
            yi = y - (x >> i);
            x  = x + (y >> i);
            y  = yi;
            theta += *arctanptr++;
        }
    }

    *argx = frmul(x, COSCALE);
    *argy = theta;
}
```

USING QUATERNIONS
FOR CODING 3D
TRANSFORMATIONS

(page 498)

Patrick-Gilles Maillot

```c
set_obs_position(x,y,z)
float    x, y, z;
{
int i;

/*
 * Set the values of the eye's position.
 * The position here represents the position of the orthonormal base
 * in respect to the observer.
 */
    P[0] = -x;
    P[1] = -y;
    P[2] = -z;
/*
 * Set the visualization to be in the decreasing x axis
 */
    Q[0] = 1.;
    for (i = 1; i < 4; i++) Q[i] = 0.;
}

translate_quaternion(x,i,w)
float    x;
int i, w;
{
int j, k;
float    A, B, D, E, F;

    if (w < 0) {
/*
 * The observer moves in respect to the scene.
 */
    P[i - 1] -= x;
  } else {
```

```
/*
 * The scene moves in respect to the observer.
 * Compute the successor axis of i [1,2,3];
 * and then the successor axis of j [1,2,3];
 */
    if ((j = i + 1) > 3) j = 1;
    if ((k = j + 1) > 3) k = 1;
    A = Q[j]; B = Q[k]; F = Q[0]; E = Q[i];
    P[i - 1] += x * (E * E + F * F - A * A - B * B);
    D = x + x;
    P[j - 1] += D * (E * A + F * B);
    P[k - 1] += D * (E * B + F * A);
    }
}


rotate_quaternion(x,y,i,w)
float    x, y;
int i, w;
{
int j, k;
float    E, F, R1;
/*
 * Compute the successor axis of i [1,2,3] and   j [1,2,3];
 */
    if ((j = i + 1) > 3) j = 1;
    if ((k = j + 1) > 3) k = 1;
    E = Q[i];
    Q[i] = E * x + w * y * Q[0];
    Q[0] = Q[0] * x - w * y * E;
    E = Q[j];
    Q[j] = E * x + y * Q[k];
    Q[k] = Q[k] * x - y * E;
    if (w < 0) {
/* Compute a new position if the observer moves in respect to the scene
*/
        j -= 1; k -= 1;
        R1 = x * x - y * y;
        F = 2. * x * y;
        E = P[j];
        P[j] = E * R1 + F * P[k];
        P[k] = P[k] * R1 - F * E;
    }
}
```

776

```
Evaluate_matrix()
{
float    e, f, r[4];
int i, j, k;
/*
 * We will need some square values!
 */
    for (i = 0; i < 4; i++) r[i] = Q[i] * Q[i];
/*
 * Compute each element of the matrix.
 * j is the successor of i (in 1,2,3), while k is the successor of j.
 */
    for (i = 1; i < 4; i++) {
        if ((j = i + 1) > 3) j = 1;
        if ((k = j + 1) > 3) k = 1;
        e = 2. * Q[i] * Q[j];
        f = 2. * Q[k] * Q[0];
        M[j][i] = e - f;
        M[i][j] = e + f;
        M[i][i] = r[i] + r[0] - r[j] - r[k];
        M[0][i] = P[i - 1];
        M[i][0] = 0.;
    }
    M[0][0] = 1.;
}
```

3D VIEWING AND ROTATION USING ORTHONORMAL BASES

(page 516)

Steve Cunningham

```c
#include "GraphicsGems.h"

/*
 * Transformations are presented as 4 by 3 matrices, omitting the
 * fourth column to save memory.
 *
 * Functions are used from the Graphics Gems vector C library
 */

typedef float Transform[4][3];

void BuildViewTransform( VRP, EP, UP, T )
     Point3 VRP, EP, UP;
     Transform T;
{
    Vector3  U, V, N;
    float    dot;

    /*
     * Compute vector  N = EP - VRP  and normalize  N
     */
    N.x = EP.x - VRP.x; N.y = EP.y - VRP.y; N.z = EP.z - VRP.z;
    V3Normalize(&N);

    /*
     * Compute vector  V = VP - VRP
     * Make vector  V  orthogonal to  N  and normalize  V
     */
    V.x = UP.x - VRP.x; V.y = UP.y - VRP.y; V.z = UP.z - VRP.z;
    dot = V3Dot(&V,&N);
    V.x -= dot * N.x; V.y -= dot * N.y; V.z -= dot * N.z;
    V3Normalize(&V);
```

```
/*
 * Compute vector  U = V x N  (cross product)
 */
V3Cross(&V,&N,&U);

/*
 * Write the vectors U, V, and N as the first three rows of the
 *        first, second, and third columns of  T, respectively
 */
T[0][0] = U.x;          /* column 1 , vector U */
T[1][0] = U.y;
T[2][0] = U.z;
T[0][1] = V.x;          /* column 2 , vector V */
T[1][1] = V.y;
T[2][1] = V.z;
T[0][2] = N.x;          /* column 3 , vector N */
T[1][2] = N.y;
T[2][2] = N.z;

/*
 * Compute the fourth row of  T  to include the translation of
 *        VRP  to the origin
 */
T[3][0] = - U.x * VRP.x - U.y * VRP.y - U.z * VRP.z;
T[3][1] = - V.x * VRP.x - V.y * VRP.y - V.z * VRP.z;
T[3][2] = - N.x * VRP.x - N.y * VRP.y - N.z * VRP.z;

return;
```

FORMS, VECTORS,
AND TRANSFORMS

(page 533)

Bob Wallis

```
/*------------------------------------------------------------------
The main program below is set up to solve the Bezier subdivision problem
in "Forms, Vectors, and Transforms".  The subroutines are useful in
solving general problems which require manipulating matrices via exact
integer arithmetic.  The intended application is validating or avoiding
tedious algebraic calculations.  As such, no thought was given to
efficiency.
-----------------------------------------------------------------*/
#define ABS(x)  ((x)>(0)? (x):(-x))
#define N 4              /* size of matrices to deal with */
int     M[N][N] =            /* Bezier weights */
{
      1,    0,    0,    0,
     -3,    3,    0,    0,
      3,   -6,    3,    0,
     -1,    3,   -3,    1,
};
int     T[N][N] =        / re-parameterization xform for top half */
{
      1,   -1,    1,   -1,
      0,    2,   -4,    6,
      0,    0,    4,  -12,
      0,    0,    0,    8
};
main ()
{
    int     i,
            j,
            scale,
            gcd,
            C[N][N],
            S[N][N],
            Madj[N][N],
            Tadj[N][N],
            Mdet,
            Tdet;
```

```
        Tdet = adjoint (T, Tadj);       /* inverse without division by */
        Mdet = adjoint (M, Madj);       /* determinant of T and M */
        matmult (Madj, Tadj, C);
        matmult (C, M, S);              /* Madj*Tadj*M -> S */
        scale = gcd = Mdet * Tdet;      /* scale factors of both determinants */
        for (i = 0; i < N; i++)         /* find the greatest common */
        {                               /* demoninator of S and determinants */
                for (j = 0; j < N; j++)
                        gcd = Gcd (gcd, S[i][j]);
        }
        scale /= gcd;                   /* divide everything by gcd to get */
        for (i = 0; i < N; i++)         /* matrix and scale factor in lowest */
        {                               /* integer terms possible */
                for (j = 0; j < N; j++)
                        S[i][j] /= gcd;
        }
        printf ("scale factor = 1/%d  ", scale);
        print_mat ("M=", M, N);         /* display the results */
        print_mat ("T=", T, N);
        print_mat ("S=", S, N);         /* subdivision matrix */
        exit (0);
}
Gcd (a, b)                              /*returns greatest common demoninator */
int     a,                              /* of (a,b) */
        b;
{
        int     i,
                r;
        a = ABS (a);                    /* force positive */
        b = ABS (b);
        if (a < b)                      /* exchange so that a >= b */
        {
                i = b;
                b = a;
                a = i;
        }
        if   (b == 0)
                return (a);             /* finished */
        r = a % b;                      /* remainder */
        if (r == 0)
                return (b);             /* finished */
        else                            /* recursive call */
                return (Gcd (b, r));
}
```

```
adjoint (A, Aadj)                       /* returns determinant of A */
int        A[N][N],                     /* input matrix */
           Aadj[N][N];                  /* output = adjoint of A */
{                                       /* must have N >= 3 */
    int    i,
           j,
           I[N],                        /* arrays of row and column indices */
           J[N],
           Isub[N],                     /* sub-arrays of the above */
           Jsub[N],
           cofactor,
           det;
    if (N < 3)
    {
        printf ("must have N >= 3\n");
        exit (1);
    }
    for (i = 0; i < N; i++)
    {                                   /* lookup tables to select a */
        I[i] = i;                       /* particular subset of */
        J[i] = i;                       /* rows and columns */
    }
    det = 0;
    for (i = 0; i < N; i++)
    {                                   /* delete ith row */
        subarray (I, Isub, N, i);
        for (j = 0; j < N; j++)
        {                               /* delete jth column */
            subarray (J, Jsub, N, j);
            cofactor = determinant (A, Isub, Jsub, N - 1,(i + j) & 1);
            if (j == 0)        /* use 0th column for det */
                det += cofactor * A[i][0];
        Aadj[j][i] = cofactor;
        }
    }
    return (det);
}
determinant (A, I, J, n, parity)/* actually gets a sub-determinant */
int        A[N][N],                     /* input = entire matrix */
           I[N],                        /* row sub-array we want */
           J[N],                        /* col sub-array we want */
           parity,                      /* 1-> flip polarity */
           n;                           /* # elements in subarrays */
```

782

```c
{
    int     i,
            j,
            det,
            j_,
            Jsub[N];
    if (n <= 2)                     /* call ourselves till we get down to */
    {                               /* a 2x2 matrix */
        det =
            (A[I[0]][J[0]] * A[I[1]][J[1]]) -
            (A[I[1]][J[0]] * A[I[0]][J[1]]);
        if (parity)
        det = -det;
        return (det);
    }                               /* if (n <= 2) */
    det = 0;                        /* n > 2; call recursively */
    i = I[0];                       /* strike out 0th row */
    for (j_ = 0; j_ < n; j_++)
    {                               /* strike out jth column */
        subarray (J, Jsub, n, j_);
        j = J[j_];                  /* I + 1 => struck out 0th row */
        det += A[i][j] * determinant (A, I + 1, Jsub, n - 1, j_ & 1);
    }
    if (parity)
        det = -det;
    return (det);
}
subarray (src, dest, n, k)          /* strike out kth row/column */
int     *src,                       /*   source array of n indices */
        *dest,                      /* dest array formed by deleting k   */
        n,
        k;
{
    int     i;
    for (i = 0; i < n; i++, src++)
        if (i != k)                 /* skip over k */
            *dest++ = *src;
}
```

```
matmult (A, B, C)                          /* C = A*B */
int      A[N][N],
         B[N][N],
         C[N][N];
{
    int      i,
             j,
             k,
             sum;
    for (i = 0; i < N; i++)
    {
        for (k = 0; k < N; k++)
        {
            sum = 0;
            for (j = 0; j < N; j++)
                sum += A[i][j] * B[j][k];
            C[i][k] = sum;
        }
    }
}
print_mat (string, mat, n)
char    *string;
int      mat[N][N],
         n;
{
    int      i,
             j;
    printf ("%s\n", string);
    for (i = 0; i < n; i++)
    {
        for (j = 0; j < n; j++)
        printf (" %8ld", mat[i][j]);
    printf ("\n");
    }
}
```

TRANSFORMING
AXIS-ALIGNED
BOUNDING BOXES

(page 548)

Jim Arvo

```
/ * Transforms a 3D axis-aligned box via a 3x3 matrix and a translation
 * vector and returns an axis-aligned box enclosing the result. */

void Transform_Box( M, T, A, B )
Matrix3  M;        /* Transform matrix.                 */
Vector3  T;        /* Translation matrix.               */
Box3     A;        /* The original bounding box.        */
Box3     *B;       /* The transformed bounding box.     */
    {
    float    a, b;
    float    Amin[3], Amax[3];
    float    Bmin[3], Bmax[3];
    int      i, j;

    /*Copy box A into a min array and a max array for easy reference.*/

    Amin[0] = A.min.x;  Amax[0] = A.max.x;
    Amin[1] = A.min.y;  Amax[1] = A.max.y;
    Amin[2] = A.min.z;  Amax[2] = A.max.z;

    /* Take care of translation by beginning at T. */

    Bmin[0] = Bmax[0] = T.x;
    Bmin[1] = Bmax[1] = T.y;
    Bmin[2] = Bmax[2] = T.z;

    /* Now find the extreme points by considering the product of the */
    /* min and max with each component of M.   */

    for( i = 0; i < 3; i++ )
    for( j = 0; j < 3; j++ )
        {
        a = M.element[i][j] * Amin[j];
        b = M.element[i][j] * Amax[j];
        if( a < b )
```

```
            {
        Bmin[i] += a;
        Bmax[i] += b;
            }
        else
            {
        Bmin[i] += b;
        Bmax[i] += a;
            }
        }

    /* Copy the result into the new box. */

    B->min.x = Bmin[0];   B->max.x = Bmax[0];
    B->min.y = Bmin[1];   B->max.y = Bmax[1];
    B->min.z = Bmin[2];   B->max.z = Bmax[2];

    }
```

SOLVING THE NEAREST-POINT-ON-CURVE PROBLEM AND A BÉZIER CURVE-BASED ROOT-FINDER

(pages 607 and 408)

Philip J. Schneider

```c
/*  point_on_curve.c  */

#include <stdio.h>
#include <malloc.h>
#include <math.h>
#include "2d.h"


/*
 *  Forward declarations
 */
        Point2  NearestPointOnCurve();
static  int FindRoots();
static  Point2  *ConvertToBezierForm();
static  double  ComputeXIntercept();
static  int ControlPolygonFlatEnough();
static  int CrossingCount();
static  Point2  Bezier();
static  Vector2 *V2Sub();
static  Vector2 V2ScaleII();

        int     MAXDEPTH = 64;      /*  Maximum depth for recursion */
#define EPSILON (ldexp(1.0,-MAXDEPTH-1)) /*Flatness control value */
#define DEGREE  3               /*  Cubic Bezier curve             */
#define W_DEGREE 5              /*  Degree of eqn to find roots of */

#ifdef TESTMODE
/*
 *  main :
 *  Given a cubic Bezier curve (i.e., its control points), and some
 *  arbitrary point in the plane, find the point on the curve
 *  closest to that arbitrary point.
 */
main()
{
```

```
    static Point2 bezCurve[4] = {        /*  A cubic Bezier curve       */
        { 0.0, 0.0 },
        { 1.0, 2.0 },
        { 3.0, 3.0 },
        { 4.0, 2.0 },
    };
    static Point2 arbPoint = { 3.5, 2.0 }; /*Some arbitrary point*/
    Point2    pointOnCurve;               /*  Nearest point on the curve */

    /*  Find the closest point */
    pointOnCurve = NearestPointOnCurve(arbPoint, bezCurve);
    printf("pointOnCurve : (%4.4f, %4.4f)\n", pointOnCurve.x,
        pointOnCurve.y);
}
#endif /* TESTMODE */


/*
 *
 *  NearestPointOnCurve :
 *      Compute the parameter value of the point on a Bezier
 *      curve segment closest to some arbtitrary, user-input point.
 *      Return the point on the curve at that parameter value.
 *
 */
Point2 NearestPointOnCurve(P, V)
    Point2    P;               /* The user-supplied point   */
    Point2    *V;              /* Control points of cubic Bezier */
{
    Point2    *w;              /* Ctl pts for 5th-degree eqn    */
    double    t_candidate[W_DEGREE];        /* Possible roots       */
    int       n_solutions;     /* Number of roots found    */
    double    t;               /* Parameter value of closest pt*/

    /* Convert problem to 5th-degree Bezier form     */
    w = ConvertToBezierForm(P, V);

    /* Find all possible roots of 5th-degree equation */
    n_solutions = FindRoots(w, W_DEGREE, t_candidate, 0);
    free((char *)w);

    /* Compare distances of P to all candidates, and to t=0, and t=1 */
    {
        double    dist, new_dist;
        Point2    p;
        Vector2   v;
        int       i;
```

788

```
        /* Check distance to beginning of curve, where t = 0    */
            dist = V2SquaredLength(V2Sub(&P, &V[0], &v));
            t = 0.0;

        /* Find distances for candidate points    */
            for (i = 0; i < n_solutions; i++) {
                p = Bezier(V, DEGREE, t_candidate[i], NULL, NULL);
                new_dist = V2SquaredLength(V2Sub(&P, &p, &v));
                if (new_dist < dist) {
                    dist = new_dist;
                    t = t_candidate[i];
                }
            }

        /* Finally, look at distance to end point, where t = 1.0 */
            new_dist = V2SquaredLength(V2Sub(&P, &V[DEGREE], &v));
            if (new_dist < dist) {
                dist = new_dist;
                t = 1.0;
            }
        }

        /*  Return the point on the curve at parameter value t */
        printf("t : %4.12f\n", t);
        return (Bezier(V, DEGREE, t, NULL, NULL));
}


/*
 *  ConvertToBezierForm :
 *      Given a point and a Bezier curve, generate a 5th-degree
 *      Bezier-format equation whose solution finds the point on the
 *      curve nearest the user-defined point.
 */
static Point2 *ConvertToBezierForm(P, V)
    Point2      P;            /* The point to find t for */
    Point2      *V;           /* The control points          */
{
    int         i, j, k, m, n, ub, lb;
    double      t;            /* Value of t for point P  */
    int         row, column;     /* Table indices           */
    Vector2     c[DEGREE+1];     /* V(i)'s - P              */
    Vector2     d[DEGREE];       /* V(i+1) - V(i)           */
    Point2      *w;           /* Ctl pts of 5th-degree curve */
    double      cdTable[3][4];        /* Dot product of c, d         */
    static double z[3][4] = {    /* Precomputed "z" for cubics */
    {1.0, 0.6, 0.3, 0.1},
    {0.4, 0.6, 0.6, 0.4},
    {0.1, 0.3, 0.6, 1.0},
    };
```

```
/*Determine the c's -- these are vectors created by subtracting*/
/* point P from each of the control points                     */
for (i = 0; i <= DEGREE; i++) {
    V2Sub(&V[i], &P, &c[i]);
}
/* Determine the d's -- these are vectors created by subtracting*/
/* each control point from the next                            */
for (i = 0; i <= DEGREE - 1; i++) {
    d[i] = V2ScaleII(V2Sub(&V[i+1], &V[i], &d[i]), 3.0);
}


/* Create the c,d table -- this is a table of dot products of the */
/* c's and d's                                                    */
for (row = 0; row <= DEGREE - 1; row++) {
    for (column = 0; column <= DEGREE; column++) {
        cdTable[row][column] = V2Dot(&d[row], &c[column]);
    }
}


/* Now, apply the z's to the dot products, on the skew diagonal*/
/* Also, set up the x-values, making these "points"           */
w = (Point2 *)malloc((unsigned)(W_DEGREE+1) * sizeof(Point2));
for (i = 0; i <= W_DEGREE; i++) {
    w[i].y = 0.0;
    w[i].x = (double)(i) / W_DEGREE;
}

n = DEGREE;
m = DEGREE-1;
for (k = 0; k <= n + m; k++) {
    lb = MAX(0, k - m);
    ub = MIN(k, n);
    for (i = lb; i <= ub; i++) {
        j = k - i;
        w[i+j].y += cdTable[j][i] * z[j][i];
    }
}

    return (w);
}
```

```
/*
 *  FindRoots :
 *    Given a 5th-degree equation in Bernstein-Bezier form, find
 *    all of the roots in the interval [0, 1].   Return the number
 *    of roots found.
 */
static int FindRoots(w, degree, t, depth)
    Point2   *w;            /* The control points            */
    int      degree;        /* The degree of the polynomial  */
    double   *t;            /* RETURN candidate t-values     */
    int      depth;         /* The depth of the recursion    */
{
    int      i;
    Point2   Left[W_DEGREE+1],  /* New left and right          */
             Right[W_DEGREE+1];     /* control polygons        */
    int      left_count,        /* Solution count from         */
             right_count;       /* children                 */
    double   left_t[W_DEGREE+1],    /* Solutions from kids        */
             right_t[W_DEGREE+1];

    switch (CrossingCount(w, degree)) {
        case 0 : {   /* No solutions here       */
          return 0;
          break;
    }
    case 1 : {   /* Unique solution        */
        /* Stop recursion when the tree is deep enough      */
        /* if deep enough, return 1 solution at midpoint    */
        if (depth >= MAXDEPTH) {
            t[0] = (w[0].x + w[W_DEGREE].x) / 2.0;
            return 1;
        }
        if (ControlPolygonFlatEnough(w, degree)) {
            t[0] = ComputeXIntercept(w, degree);
            return 1;
        }
        break;
    }
}


    /* Otherwise, solve recursively after */
    /* subdividing control polygon        */
    Bezier(w, degree, 0.5, Left, Right);
    left_count  = FindRoots(Left,  degree, left_t, depth+1);
    right_count = FindRoots(Right, degree, right_t, depth+1);
```

```
      /* Gather solutions together    */
      for (i = 0; i < left_count; i++) {
          t[i] = left_t[i];
      }
      for (i = 0; i < right_count; i++) {
          t[i+left_count] = right_t[i];
      }

      /* Send back total number of solutions    */
      return (left_count+right_count);
}


/*
 * CrossingCount :
 *   Count the number of times a Bezier control polygon
 *   crosses the 0-axis. This number is >= the number of roots.
 *
 */
static int CrossingCount(V, degree)
    Point2    *V;              /*  Control pts of Bezier curve  */
    int       degree;          /*  Degreee of Bezier curve        */
{
    int       i;
    int       n_crossings = 0;  /*  Number of zero-crossings       */
    int       sign, old_sign;    /*  Sign of coefficients          */

    sign = old_sign = SGN(V[0].y);
    for (i = 1; i <= degree; i++) {
        sign = SGN(V[i].y);
        if (sign != old_sign) n_crossings++;
        old_sign = sign;
    }
    return n_crossings;
}
```

```
/*
 *  ControlPolygonFlatEnough :
 *  Check if the control polygon of a Bezier curve is flat enough
 *  for recursive subdivision to bottom out.
 *
 */
static int ControlPolygonFlatEnough(V, degree)
    Point2    *V;         /* Control points   */
    int       degree;         /* Degree of polynomial    */
{
    int       i;          /* Index variable          */
    double    *distance;         /* Distances from pts to line   */
    double    max_distance_above;    /* maximum of these        */
    double    max_distance_below;
    double    error;            /* Precision of root         */
    Vector2   t;            /* Vector from V[0] to V[degree]*/
    double    intercept_1,
              intercept_2,
              left_intercept,
              right_intercept;
    double    a, b, c;       /* Coefficients of implicit     */
                            /* eqn for line from V[0]-V[deg]*/

    /* Find the  perpendicular distance           */
    /* from each interior control point to        */
    /* line connecting V[0] and V[degree] */
    distance = (double *)malloc((unsigned)(degree + 1) *
                sizeof(double));
    {
    double  abSquared;

    /* Derive the implicit equation for line connecting first *'
    /*  and last control points */
    a = V[0].y - V[degree].y;
    b = V[degree].x - V[0].x;
    c = V[0].x * V[degree].y - V[degree].x * V[0].y;

    abSquared = (a * a) + (b * b);

        for (i = 1; i < degree; i++) {
        /* Compute distance from each of the points to that line */
            distance[i] = a * V[i].x + b * V[i].y + c;
            if (distance[i] > 0.0) {
                distance[i] = (distance[i] * distance[i]) / abSquared;
            }
            if (distance[i] < 0.0) {
                distance[i] = -((distance[i] * distance[i]) /
                    abSquared);
            }
        }
    }
}
```

```c
    /* Find the largest distance    */
    max_distance_above = 0.0;
    max_distance_below = 0.0;
    for (i = 1; i < degree; i++) {
        if (distance[i] < 0.0) {
            max_distance_below = MIN(max_distance_below, distance[i]);
        };
        if (distance[i] > 0.0) {
            max_distance_above = MAX(max_distance_above, distance[i]);
        }
    }
    free((char *)distance);

    {
    double  det, dInv;
    double  a1, b1, c1, a2, b2, c2;

    /*  Implicit equation for zero line */
    a1 = 0.0;
    b1 = 1.0;
    c1 = 0.0;

    /*  Implicit equation for "above" line */
    a2 = a;
    b2 = b;
    c2 = c + max_distance_above;

    det = a1 * b2 - a2 * b1;
    dInv = 1.0/det;

    intercept_1 = (b1 * c2 - b2 * c1) * dInv;

    /*  Implicit equation for "below" line */
    a2 = a;
    b2 = b;
    c2 = c + max_distance_below;

    det = a1 * b2 - a2 * b1;
    dInv = 1.0/det;

    intercept_2 = (b1 * c2 - b2 * c1) * dInv;
    }

    /* Compute intercepts of bounding box */
    left_intercept = MIN(intercept_1, intercept_2);
    right_intercept = MAX(intercept_1, intercept_2);

    error = 0.5 * (right_intercept-left_intercept);
    if (error < EPSILON) {
        return 1;
    }
    else {
        return 0;
    }
}
```

```
/*
 * ComputeXIntercept :
 * Compute intersection of chord from first control point to last
 *      with 0-axis.
 *
 */
static double ComputeXIntercept(V, degree)
    Point2      *V;             /* Control points    */
    int         degree;         /* Degree of curve   */
{
    double      XLK, YLK, XNM, YNM, XMK, YMK;
    double      det, detInv;
    double      S, T;
    double      X, Y;

    XLK = 1.0 - 0.0;
    YLK = 0.0 - 0.0;
    XNM = V[degree].x - V[0].x;
    YNM = V[degree].y - V[0].y;
    XMK = V[0].x - 0.0;
    YMK = V[0].y - 0.0;

    det = XNM*YLK - YNM*XLK;
    detInv = 1.0/det;

    S = (XNM*YMK - YNM*XMK) * detInv;
    T = (XLK*YMK - YLK*XMK) * detInv;

    X = 0.0 + XLK * S;
    Y = 0.0 + YLK * S;

    return X;
}


/*
 * Bezier :
 * Evaluate a Bezier curve at a particular parameter value
 *      Fill in control points for resulting sub-curves if "Left" and
 * "Right" are non-null.
 *
 */
static Point2 Bezier(V, degree, t, Left, Right)
    int         degree;         /* Degree of bezier curve  */
    Point2      *V;             /* Control pts             */
    double      t;              /* Parameter value         */
    Point2      *Left;          /* RETURN left half ctl pts    */
    Point2      *Right;         /* RETURN right half ctl pts   */
{
    int         i, j;           /* Index variables   */
    Point2      Vtemp[W_DEGREE+1][W_DEGREE+1];
```

```c
    /* Copy control points */
    for (j =0; j <= degree; j++) {
        Vtemp[0][j] = V[j];
    }

    /* Triangle computation     */
    for (i = 1; i <= degree; i++) {
        for (j =0 ; j <= degree - i; j++) {
            Vtemp[i][j].x =
                (1.0 - t) * Vtemp[i-1][j].x + t * Vtemp[i-1][j+1].x;
            Vtemp[i][j].y =
                (1.0 - t) * Vtemp[i-1][j].y + t * Vtemp[i-1][j+1].y;
        }
    }

    if (Left != NULL) {
        for (j = 0; j <= degree; j++) {
            Left[j]   = Vtemp[j][0];
        }
    }
    if (Right != NULL) {
        for (j = 0; j <= degree; j++) {
            Right[j] = Vtemp[degree-j][j];
        }
    }

    return (Vtemp[degree][0]);
}


static Vector2 *V2Sub(a, b, c)
    Vector2   *a, *b, *c;
{
    c->x = a->x - b->x;
    c->y = a->y - b->y;

    return (c);
}


static Vector2 V2ScaleII(v, s)
    Vector2   *v;
    double    s;
{
    Vector2 result;

    result.x = v->x * s; result.y = v->y * s;
    return (result);
}
```

796

AN ALGORITHM FOR
AUTOMATICALLY FITTING
DIGITIZED CURVES

(page 612)

Philip J. Schneider

```c
/*  fit_cubic.c   */
/*  Piecewise cubic fitting code    */


#include <stdio.h>
#include <malloc.h>
#include <math.h>
#include "2d.h"

typedef Point2 *BezierCurve;

/* Forward declarations */
        void            FitCurve();
static  void            FitCubic();
static  double          *Reparameterize();
static  double          NewtonRaphsonRootFind();
static  Point2          Bezier();
static  double          B0(), B1(), B2(), B3();
static  Vector2         ComputeLeftTangent();
static  Vector2         ComputeRightTangent();
static  Vector2         ComputeCenterTangent();
static  double          ComputeMaxError();
static  double          *ChordLengthParameterize();
static  BezierCurve     GenerateBezier();
static  Vector2         V2AddII();
static  Vector2         V2ScaleII();
static  Vector2         V2Sub();

#define MAXPOINTS       1000            /* The most points you can have */

#ifdef TESTMODE
```

```
/*
 * main:
 *   Example of how to use the curve-fitting code.  Given an array
 *    of points and a tolerance (squared error between points and
 *    fitted curve), the algorithm will generate a piecewise
 *    cubic Bezier representation that approximates the points.
 *   When a cubic is generated, the routine "DrawBezierCurve"
 *   is called, which outputs the Bezier curve just created
 *   (arguments are the degree and the control points, respectively).
 *   Users will have to implement this function themselves
 *    ascii output, etc.
 *
 */
main()
{
    static Point2 d[7] = {      /*  Digitized points */
        { 0.0, 0.0 },
        { 0.0, 0.5 },
        { 1.1, 1.4 },
        { 2.1, 1.6 },
        { 3.2, 1.1 },
        { 4.0, 0.2 },
        { 4.0, 0.0 },
    };
    double  error = 4.0;        /*  Squared error */
    FitCurve(d, 7, error);      /*  Fit the Bezier curves */
}
#endif                          /* TESTMODE */

/*
 * FitCurve :
 *      Fit a Bezier curve to a set of digitized points
 */
void FitCurve(d, nPts, error)
    Point2   *d;                /*  Array of digitized points   */
    int      nPts;             /*  Number of digitized points  */
    double   error;            /*  User-defined error squared  */
{
    Vector2   tHat1, tHat2;     /*  Unit tangent vectors at endpoints */

    tHat1 = ComputeLeftTangent(d, 0);
    tHat2 = ComputeRightTangent(d, nPts - 1);
    FitCubic(d, 0, nPts - 1, tHat1, tHat2, error);
}
```

798

```
/*
 * FitCubic :
 *      Fit a Bezier curve to a (sub)set of digitized points
 */
static void FitCubic(d, first, last, tHat1, tHat2, error)
    Point2    *d;          /* Array of digitized points */
    int       first, last; /* Indices of first and last pts in region */
    Vector2   tHat1, tHat2;    /* Unit tangent vectors at endpoints */
    double    error;       /* User-defined error squared      */
{
    BezierCurve   bezCurve; /*Control points of fitted Bezier curve*/
    double    *u;          /* Parameter values for point  */
    double    *uPrime;     /* Improved parameter values */
    double    maxError;    /* Maximum fitting error   */
    int       splitPoint;  /* Point to split point set at   */
    int       nPts;        /* Number of points in subset  */
    double    iterationError; /*Error below which you try iterating */
    int       maxIterations = 4; /* Max times to try iterating */
    Vector2   tHatCenter;      /* Unit tangent vector at splitPoint */
    int       i;

    iterationError = error * error;
    nPts = last - first + 1;

    /* Use heuristic if region only has two points in it */
    if (nPts == 2) {
        double dist = V2DistanceBetween2Points(&d[last], &d[first]) /
            3.0;

        bezCurve = (Point2 *)malloc(4 * sizeof(Point2));
        bezCurve[0] = d[first];
        bezCurve[3] = d[last];
        V2Add(&bezCurve[0], V2Scale(&tHat1, dist), &bezCurve[1]);
        V2Add(&bezCurve[3], V2Scale(&tHat2, dist), &bezCurve[2]);
        DrawBezierCurve(3, bezCurve);
        return;
    }

    /* Parameterize points, and attempt to fit curve */
    u = ChordLengthParameterize(d, first, last);
    bezCurve = GenerateBezier(d, first, last, u, tHat1, tHat2);

    /* Find max deviation of points to fitted curve */
    maxError = ComputeMaxError(d, first, last, bezCurve, u,
                &splitPoint);
    if (maxError < error) {
        DrawBezierCurve(3, bezCurve);
        return;
    }
```

```c
    /*  If error not too large, try some reparameterization  */
    /*  and iteration */
    if (maxError < iterationError) {
        for (i = 0; i < maxIterations; i++) {
            uPrime = Reparameterize(d, first, last, u, bezCurve);
            bezCurve = GenerateBezier(d, first, last, uPrime, tHat1,
                    tHat2);
            maxError = ComputeMaxError(d, first, last,
                        bezCurve, uPrime, &splitPoint);
            if (maxError < error) {
            DrawBezierCurve(3, bezCurve);
            return;
        }
        free((char *)u);
        u = uPrime;
    }
}


    /* Fitting failed -- split at max error point and fit recursively
    tHatCenter = ComputeCenterTangent(d, splitPoint);
    FitCubic(d, first, splitPoint, tHat1, tHatCenter, error);
    V2Negate(&tHatCenter);
    FitCubic(d, splitPoint, last, tHatCenter, tHat2, error);
}


/*
 *  GenerateBezier :
 *  Use least-squares method to find Bezier control points for region.
 *
 */
static BezierCurve  GenerateBezier(d, first, last, uPrime, tHat1,
                tHat2)
    Point2      *d;             /*  Array of digitized points     */
    int         first, last;      /*  Indices defining region */
    double      *uPrime;        /*  Parameter values for region */
    Vector2     tHat1, tHat2;      /*  Unit tangents at endpoints     */
{
    int         i;
    Vector2     A[MAXPOINTS][2];  /* Precomputed rhs for eqn    */
    int         nPts;             /* Number of pts in sub-curve */
    double      C[2][2];          /* Matrix C            */
    double      X[2];             /* Matrix X            */
    double      det_C0_C1,        /* Determinants of matrices */
                det_C0_X,
                det_X_C1;
    double      alpha_l,          /* Alpha values, left and right */
                alpha_r;
    Vector2     tmp;              /* Utility variable         */
    BezierCurve bezCurve;         /* RETURN bezier curve ctl pts     */

    bezCurve = (Point2 *)malloc(4 * sizeof(Point2));
    nPts = last - first + 1;
```

```
/* Compute the A's      */
for (i = 0; i < nPts; i++) {
    Vector2        v1, v2;
    v1 = tHat1;
    v2 = tHat2;
    V2Scale(&v1, B1(uPrime[i]));
    V2Scale(&v2, B2(uPrime[i]));
    A[i][0] = v1;
    A[i][1] = v2;
}

/* Create the C and X matrices  */
C[0][0] = 0.0;
C[0][1] = 0.0;
C[1][0] = 0.0;
C[1][1] = 0.0;
X[0]    = 0.0;
X[1]    = 0.0;

for (i = 0; i < nPts; i++) {
    C[0][0] += V2Dot(&A[i][0], &A[i][0]);
    C[0][1] += V2Dot(&A[i][0], &A[i][1]);
/*                  C[1][0] += V2Dot(&A[i][0], &A[i][1]);*/
    C[1][0] = C[0][1];
    C[1][1] += V2Dot(&A[i][1], &A[i][1]);

    tmp = V2Sub(d[first + i],
        V2AddII(
          V2ScaleII(d[first], B0(uPrime[i])),
             V2AddII(
                 V2ScaleII(d[first], B1(uPrime[i])),
                    V2AddII(
                        V2ScaleII(d[last], B2(uPrime[i])),
                        V2ScaleII(d[last], B3(uPrime[i]))))));


    X[0] += V2Dot(&A[i][0], &tmp);
    X[1] += V2Dot(&A[i][1], &tmp);
}

/* Compute the determinants of C and X       */
det_C0_C1 = C[0][0] * C[1][1] - C[1][0] * C[0][1];
det_C0_X  = C[0][0] * X[1]    - C[0][1] * X[0];
det_X_C1  = X[0]    * C[1][1] - X[1]    * C[0][1];

/* Finally, derive alpha values */
if (det_C0_C1 == 0.0) {
    det_C0_C1 = (C[0][0] * C[1][1]) * 10e-12;
}
alpha_l = det_X_C1 / det_C0_C1;
alpha_r = det_C0_X / det_C0_C1;
```

```
        /*  If alpha negative, use the Wu/Barsky heuristic (see text) */
        if (alpha_l < 0.0 || alpha_r < 0.0) {
            double  dist = V2DistanceBetween2Points(&d[last], &d[first])
                             3.0;

            bezCurve[0] = d[first];
            bezCurve[3] = d[last];
            V2Add(&bezCurve[0], V2Scale(&tHat1, dist), &bezCurve[1]);
            V2Add(&bezCurve[3], V2Scale(&tHat2, dist), &bezCurve[2]);
            return (bezCurve);
        }

        /*  First and last control points of the Bezier curve are */
        /*  positioned exactly at the first and last data points */
        /*  Control points 1 and 2 are positioned an alpha distance out */
        /*   on the tangent vectors, left and right, respectively */
        bezCurve[0] = d[first];
        bezCurve[3] = d[last];
        V2Add(&bezCurve[0], V2Scale(&tHat1, alpha_l), &bezCurve[1]);
        V2Add(&bezCurve[3], V2Scale(&tHat2, alpha_r), &bezCurve[2]);
        return (bezCurve);
}


/*
 *  Reparameterize:
 *  Given set of points and their parameterization, try to find
 *   a better parameterization.
 *
 */
static double *Reparameterize(d, first, last, u, bezCurve)
    Point2     *d;          /*  Array of digitized points    */
    int        first, last; /*  Indices defining region */
    double     *u;          /*  Current parameter values     */
    BezierCurve    bezCurve;   /*  Current fitted curve      */
{
    int        nPts = last-first+1;
    int        i;
    double     *uPrime;     /*  New parameter values     */

    uPrime = (double *)malloc(nPts * sizeof(double));
    for (i = first; i <= last; i++) {
        uPrime[i-first] = NewtonRaphsonRootFind(bezCurve, d[i], u[i-
                                    first]);
    }
    return (uPrime);
}
```

```
/*
 *  NewtonRaphsonRootFind :
 *  Use Newton-Raphson iteration to find better root.
 */
static double NewtonRaphsonRootFind(Q, P, u)
    BezierCurve    Q;              /*  Current fitted curve    */
    Point2         P;              /*  Digitized point         */
    double         u;              /*  Parameter value for "P" */
{
    double         numerator, denominator;
    Point2         Q1[3], Q2[2];   /*  Q' and Q''              */
    Point2         Q_u, Q1_u, Q2_u; /*u evaluated at Q, Q', & Q'' */
    double         uPrime;         /*  Improved u              */
    int            i;

    /* Compute Q(u)    */
    Q_u = Bezier(3, Q, u);

    /* Generate control vertices for Q'    */
    for (i = 0; i <= 2; i++) {
        Q1[i].x = (Q[i+1].x - Q[i].x) * 3.0;
        Q1[i].y = (Q[i+1].y - Q[i].y) * 3.0;
    }

    /* Generate control vertices for Q'' */
    for (i = 0; i <= 1; i++) {
        Q2[i].x = (Q1[i+1].x - Q1[i].x) * 2.0;
        Q2[i].y = (Q1[i+1].y - Q1[i].y) * 2.0;
    }

    /* Compute Q'(u) and Q''(u)        */
    Q1_u = Bezier(2, Q1, u);
    Q2_u = Bezier(1, Q2, u);

    /* Compute f(u)/f'(u) */
    numerator = (Q_u.x - P.x) * (Q1_u.x) + (Q_u.y - P.y) * (Q1_u.y);
    denominator = (Q1_u.x) * (Q1_u.x) + (Q1_u.y) * (Q1_u.y) +
                  (Q_u.x - P.x) * (Q2_u.x) + (Q_u.y - P.y) * (Q2_u.y);

    /* u = u - f(u)/f'(u) */
    uPrime = u - (numerator/denominator);
    return (uPrime);
}
```

```
/*
 * Bezier :
 *      Evaluate a Bezier curve at a particular parameter value
 *
 */
static Point2 Bezier(degree, V, t)
    int      degree;        /* The degree of the bezier curve     */
    Point2   *V;        /* Array of control points         */
    double   t;            /* Parametric value to find point for   */
{
    int      i, j;
    Point2   Q;                /* Point on curve at parameter t   */
    Point2   *Vtemp;            /* Local copy of control points        */

    /* Copy array */
    Vtemp = (Point2 *)malloc((unsigned)((degree+1)
                * sizeof (Point2)));
    for (i = 0; i <= degree; i++) {
        Vtemp[i] = V[i];
    }

    /* Triangle computation    */
    for (i = 1; i <= degree; i++) {
        for (j = 0; j <= degree-i; j++) {
            Vtemp[j].x = (1.0 - t) * Vtemp[j].x + t * Vtemp[j+1].x;
            Vtemp[j].y = (1.0 - t) * Vtemp[j].y + t * Vtemp[j+1].y;
        }
    }

    Q = Vtemp[0];
    free((char *)Vtemp);
    return Q;
}


/*
 * B0, B1, B2, B3 :
 *  Bezier multipliers
 */
static double B0(u)
    double   u;
{
    double tmp = 1.0 - u;
    return (tmp * tmp * tmp);
}
```

```
static double B1(u)
    double  u;
{
    double tmp = 1.0 - u;
    return (3 * u * (tmp * tmp));
}

static double B2(u)
    double  u;
{
    double tmp = 1.0 - u;
    return (3 * u * u * tmp);
}

static double B3(u)
    double  u;
{
    return (u * u * u);
}


/*
 * ComputeLeftTangent, ComputeRightTangent, ComputeCenterTangent :
 *Approximate unit tangents at endpoints and "center" of digitized curve
 */
static Vector2 ComputeLeftTangent(d, end)
    Point2    *d;            /* Digitized points*/
    int       end;           /* Index to "left" end of region */
{
    Vector2   tHat1;
    tHat1 = V2Sub(d[end+1], d[end]);
    tHat1 = *V2Normalize(&tHat1);
    return tHat1;
}

static Vector2 ComputeRightTangent(d, end)
    Point2    *d;            /* Digitized points        */
    int       end;           /* Index to "right" end of region */
{
    Vector2   tHat2;
    tHat2 = V2Sub(d[end-1], d[end]);
    tHat2 = *V2Normalize(&tHat2);
    return tHat2;
}
```

```
static Vector2 ComputeCenterTangent(d, center)
    Point2    *d;          /*  Digitized points            */
    int       center;      /*  Index to point inside region */
{
    Vector2  V1, V2, tHatCenter;

    V1 = V2Sub(d[center-1], d[center]);
    V2 = V2Sub(d[center], d[center+1]);
    tHatCenter.x = (V1.x + V2.x)/2.0;
    tHatCenter.y = (V1.y + V2.y)/2.0;
    tHatCenter = *V2Normalize(&tHatCenter);
    return tHatCenter;
}



/*
 *  ChordLengthParameterize :
 *  Assign parameter values to digitized points
 *  using relative distances between points.
 */
static double *ChordLengthParameterize(d, first, last)
    Point2    *d;                  /* Array of digitized points */
    int       first, last;         /*  Indices defining region */
{
    int       i;
    double    *u;                  /*  Parameterization          */

    u = (double *)malloc((unsigned)(last-first+1) *
            sizeof(double));

    u[0] = 0.0;
    for (i = first+1; i <= last; i++) {
        u[i-first] = u[i-first-1] +
                         V2DistanceBetween2Points(&d[i], &d[i-1])
    }

    for (i = first + 1; i <= last; i++) {
        u[i-first] = u[i-first] / u[last-first];
    }

    return(u);
}
```

```
/*
 *   ComputeMaxError :
 *   Find the maximum squared distance of digitized points
 *   to fitted curve.
 */
static double ComputeMaxError(d, first, last, bezCurve, u,
                    splitPoint)
    Point2      *d;             /*  Array of digitized points    */
    int         first, last;    /*   Indices defining region */
    BezierCurve   bezCurve;         /*   Fitted Bezier curve        */
    double      *u;             /*  Parameterization of points   */
    int         *splitPoint;        /*  Point of maximum error   */
{
    int         i;
    double      maxDist;        /*  Maximum error        */
    double      dist;          /*  Current error        */
    Point2      P;             /*  Point on curve       */
    Vector2     v;             /*  Vector from point to curve   */

    *splitPoint = (last - first + 1)/2;
    maxDist = 0.0;
    for (i = first + 1; i < last; i++) {
        P = Bezier(3, bezCurve, u[i-first]);
        v = V2Sub(P, d[i]);
        dist = V2SquaredLength(&v);
        if (dist >= maxDist) {
            maxDist = dist;
            *splitPoint = i;
        }
    }
    return (maxDist);
}
static Vector2 V2AddII(a, b)
    Vector2 a, b;
{
    Vector2   c;
    c.x = a.x + b.x;   c.y = a.y + b.y;
    return (c);
}
static Vector2 V2ScaleII(v, s)
    Vector2   v;
    double    s;
{
    Vector2 result;
    result.x = v.x * s; result.y = v.y * s;
    return (result);
}

static Vector2 V2Sub(a, b)
    Vector2   a, b;
{
    Vector2   c;
    c.x = a.x - b.x; c.y = a.y - b.y;
    return (c);
}
```

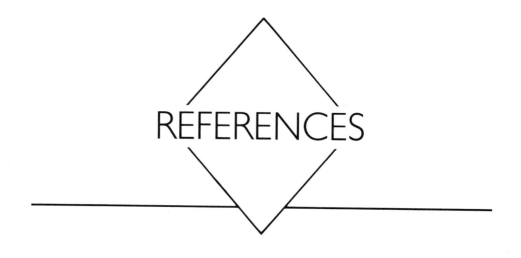

REFERENCES

ACM Transactions on Graphics (1987). Color Plates 15–18. **6**(3), 235. (Proper Treatment of Pixels as Integers)

Albano, A. (1974). "Representation of Digitized Contours in Terms of Conic Arcs and Straight-Line Segments," *Computer Graphics and Image Processing*. **3**, 23–33. (An Algorithm for Automatically Fitting Digitized Curves)

Anjyo, K., Ochi, T., and Usami, Y. (1987). "A Practical Method of Constructing Surfaces in Three-dimensional Digitized Space," *The Visual Computer*. **3**, 4–12. (Defining Surfaces from Contour Data)

Arvo, J. (1986). "Backward Ray Tracing," *SIGGRAPH Course Notes*, **12**. (Shadow Attenuation for Ray Tracing Transparent Objects)

Arvo, J., and Kirk, D. (1987). "Fair Play," SIGGRAPH '87 Film Show Contribution, Midnight Movie Group, Apollo Computer, Inc. (Efficient Generation of Sampling Jitter Using Look-up Tables)

Arvo, J., and Kirk, D. (1987). "Fast Ray Tracing by Ray Classification," *Computer Graphics*. **21**(4), 55–64. (Efficient Generation of Sampling Jitter Using Look-up Tables)

Bao, P. G., and Rokne, J. G. (1990). "Quadruple-Step Line Generation," *Computers and Graphics*. **13**(4). (Symmetric Double Step Line Algorithm)

Barry, C. D., Ellis, R. A., Graesser, S. M., and Marshall, G. R. (1971). "A Computer Program for Modelling Molecular Structures," *Proceedings 1991 IFIP*, 1552–1558. (Rotation Tools)

Bartels, R. H., Beatty, J. C., and Barsky, B. A. (1987). *An Introduction to Splines for Use in Computer Graphics and Geometric Modeling*. Morgan Kaufman, Los Altos, Calif. (Explicit Spline Interpolation Formulas; Fast Spline Drawing; An Algorithm for Automatically Fitting Digitized Curves)

Beeler, M., Gosper, R. W., and Schroppel, R. (1972). "HAKMEM," Massachusetts Institute of Technology Artificial Intelligence Laboratory Report AIM-239. (A Fast Algorithm for General Raster Rotation)

Berger, M. (1986). *Computer Graphics with Pascal*. Benjamin/Cummings, Menlo Park, Calif. (3D Viewing and Rotation Using Orthonormal Bases)

Bergman, L., Fuchs, H., Grant, E., and Spach, S. (1986). "Image Rendering by Adaptive Refinement," *Computer Graphics* (SIGGRAPH). **20**(4), 29–37. (Recording Animation in Binary Order for Progressive Temporal Refinement)

Blaker, J. W. (1971). *Geometric Optics—The Matrix Theory*. Marcel Dekker, New York. (A Fast Algorithm for General Raster Rotation)

Blinn, J. F. (1977). "Models of Light Reflection for Computer Synthesized Pictures," *Computer Graphics*. **11**(2). (Fast Dot Products for Shading)

Blinn, J. F. (1982). "A Generalization of Algebraic Surface Drawing," *ACM Transactions on Graphics*. **1**(3).

Blinn, J. F. (1982). "Light Reflections Functions for Simulation of Clouds and Dusty Surfaces," *Computer Graphics* (SIGGRAPH). **16**(3). (Simulating Fog and Haze)

Blinn, J. F. (1989). "Optimal Tubes–Jim Blinn's Corner," *IEEE Computer Graphics and Applications*. Sept., 8–13. (Matrix Inversion)

Bloch, N. J. (1987). *Abstract Algebra with Applications*. Prentice-Hall, Englewood Cliffs, N.J. (Periodic Tilings of the Plane on a Raster Grid)

Bloomenthal, J. (1985). "Modeling the Mighty Maple," *Proceedings of SIGGRAPH 1985, Computer Graphics* **19**(3), 305–311. (Calculation of Reference Frames along a Space Curve)

Bloomenthal, J. (1988). "Approximation of Sweep Surfaces by Tensor Product B-Splines," University of Utah Technical Report UUCS-88-008. (Calculation of Reference Frames along a Space Curve)

Bloomenthal, J. (1988). "Polygonalization of Implicit Surface," *Computer Aided Geometric Design*. **5**, 341–355. (Defining Surfaces from Sampled Data)

Boehm, W., Farin, G., and Kahman, J. (1984). "A Survey of Curve and Surface Methods in CAGD," *Computer-Aided Geometric Design*. **1**, 1–60 (A Bézier Curve–Based Root-Finder; An Algorithm for Automatically Fitting Digitized Curves)

Bookstein, F. L. (1979). "Fitting Conic Sections to Scattered Data," *Computer Graphics and Image Processing*. **9**, 56–71. (An Algorithm for Automatically Fitting Digitized Curves)

Bowyer, A., and Woodwark, J. (1983). *A Programmer's Geometry*. Butterworth's, London. (Useful 2D Geometry; Useful 3D Geometry)

Bresenham, J. E. (1965). "Algorithm for Computer Control of a Digital Plotter," *IBM Systems Journal*. **4**(1), 25–30. Reprinted in *Interactive Computer Graphics*, edited by H. Freeman, IEEE Computer Society, 1980. (Digital Line Drawing; Symmetric Double Step Line Algorithm)

Bresenham, J. E. (1977). "A Linear Algorithm for Incremental Digital Display of Circular Arcs," *CACM*. **20**, 100–106. (Spheres-to-Voxels Conversion)

Britton, E. G., Lipscomb, J. S., and Pique, M. E. (1978). "Making Nested Rotations

Convenient for the User," *Computer Graphics* (SIGGRAPH). **12**(3), 222–227. (Rotation Tools)

Bronsvoort, W. F., van Wijk, J. J., and Jansen, F. W. (1984). "Two Methods for Improving the Efficiency of Ray Casting in Solid Modelling," *Computer-Aided Design*. **16**(1), 51–55. (A Simple Ray Rejection Test)

Burn, R. P. (1982). *A Pathway into Number Theory*. Cambridge University Press, Cambridge, England. (Periodic Tilings of the Plane on a Raster Grid)

Burn, R. P. (1985). *Groups, A Path to Geometry*. Cambridge University Press, Cambridge, England. (Periodic Tilings of the Plane on a Raster Grid)

Campbell, G., De Fanti, T. A., *et al.* (1986). "Two Bit/Pixel Full Color Encoding," *Computer Graphics* (SIGGRAPH). **16**(3), 297–307. (A Simple Method for Color Quantization: Octree Quantization)

Carpenter, L. (1984). "The A-Buffer, an Antialiased Hidden Surface Method," *Computer Graphics*. (Fast Anti-Aliasing Polygon Scan Conversion)

Catmull, E. (1978). "A Hidden-Surface Algorithm with Anti-Aliasing," *Computer Graphics*. (Fast Anti-Aliasing Polygon Scan Conversion)

Catmull, E., and Smith, A. R. (1980). "3-D Transformations of Images in Scanline Order," *ACM Computer Graphics* (SIGGRAPH). **14**(3), 279–285. (A Fast Algorithm for General Raster Rotation)

Chang, S., Shantz, M., and Rocchetti, R. (1989). "Rendering Cubic Curves and Surfaces with Integer Adaptive Forward Differencing," *Computer Graphics* (SIGGRAPH). **23**(3). (Tutorial on Forward Differencing)

Chen, T. C. (1972). "Automatic Computation of Exponentials, Logarithms, Ratios and Square Roots," *IBM J. Res. Dev.* 380–388. (Trigonometry with CORDIC Iterations)

Cheng, F., and Jiaan, W. C. (1986). "Finding the Intersection Points of a Line with a Polygon and Its Applications," *Proceedings of 1986 ACM 14th Annual Computer Science Conference: CSC'86*. (Two-Dimensional Clipping: A Vector-Based Approach)

Chong, W. L. (1980). "Automatic Curve Fitting Using an Adaptive Local Algorithm," *ACM Transactions on Mathematical Software*. **6**(1), 45–57. (An Algorithm for Automatically Fitting Digitized Curves)

Clearly, J. G., Wyvill, B., Birtwistle, G. M., and Vatti, R. (1983). "Multiprocessor Ray Tracing," Technical Report No. 83/128/17, Dept. of Computer Science, University of Calgary. (Efficient Generation of Sampling Jitter Using Look-up Tables)

Cline, A. K. (1974). "Scalar- and Planar-Valued Curve Fitting Using Splines under Tension," *Communications of the ACM*. **17**, 218–223. (An Algorithm for Automatically Fitting Digitized Curves)

Collins, G. E., and Loos, R. (1976). "Polynomial Root Isolation by Differentiation," *ACM Symposium on Symbolic and Algebraic Computation*, 15–25. (A Bézier Curve–Based Root-Finder)

Conte, S. D., and deBoor, C. (1972). *Elementary Numerical Analysis*. McGraw-Hill. (An Algorithm for Automatically Fitting Digitized Curves)

Cook, R. L. (1983). "Antialiased Point Sampling," Technical Memo No. 94, Lucasfilm, Ltd. (Efficient Generation of Sampling Jitter Using Look-up Tables)

Cook, R. L. (1986). "Stochastic Sampling in Computer Graphics," *ACM Transactions on Graphics.* **5**(1), 51–72. (Efficient Generation of Sampling Jitter Using Look-up Tables)

Cook, R. L., Carpenter, L., and Catmull, E. (1987). "The Reyes Image Rendering Architecture," *Computer Graphics.* **21**(4), 95–102. (Efficient Generation of Sampling Jitter Using Look-up Tables)

Cook, R. L., Porter, T., and Carpenter, L. (1984). "Distributed Ray Tracing," *Computer Graphics.* **18**(3), 137–145. (Efficient Generation of Sampling Jitter Using Look-up Tables)

Cook, R. L., and Torrance, K. E. (1982). "A Reflectance Model for Computer Graphics," *ACM Trans. Graph.* **1**(1), 7–24. (Fast Dot Products for Shading)

Coxeter, H. S. M. *et al.* (1987). *M. C. Escher: Art and Science.* Elsevier Science. (Periodic Tilings of the Plane on a Raster Grid)

Coxeter, H. S. M. (1948). *Regular Polytropes.* Methuen and Co., Ltd., London. (A Digital "Dissolve" Effect)

Crow, F. C. (1977). "The Aliasing Problem in Computer-Generated Shaded Images," *Communications of the ACM.* (Fast Anti-Aliasing Polygon Scan Conversion)

Crow, F. C. (1984). "Summed-Area Tables for Texture Mapping," *Computer Graphics* (SIGGRAPH). **18**(3). (Interpretation of Texture Map Indices; Multidimensional Sum Tables)

Davis, P. J. (1975). *Interpolation and Approximation.* Dover Publications, New York. (An Algorithm for Automatically Fitting Digitized Curves)

DeRose, A. D. (1985). "Geometric Continuity: A Parameterization Independent Measure of Continuity of Computer Aided Geometric Design," Ph.D. thesis, University of California, Berkeley. (An Algorithm for Automatically Fitting Digitized Curves)

Despain, A. M. (1974). "Fourier Transform Computers Using CORDIC Iterations," *IEEE Trans. Comput.* **C-23**(10), 993–1001. (Trigonometry with CORDIC Iterations)

Dierckx, P. (1982). "Algorithms for Smoothing Data with Periodic and Parametric Splines," *Computer Graphics and Image Processing.* **20**, 171–184. (An Algorithm for Automatically Fitting Digitized Curves)

Dippé, M. A. Z., and Wold, E. H. (1985). "Antialiasing through Stochastic Sampling," *Computer Graphics.* **19**(3), 61–67. (Efficient Generation of Sampling Jitter Using Look-up Tables)

Dippé, M. E., and Swensen, J. (1984). "An Adaptive Subdivision Algorithm and Parallel Architecture for Realistic Image Synthesis," *Computer Graphics.* **18**(3), 149–158. (Efficient Generation of Sampling Jitter Using Look-up Tables)

Dube, R. P. (1987). "Preliminary Specifications of Spline Curves," *IEEE Transactions on Computers.* **C-28**(4), 286–290. (An Algorithm for Automatically Fitting Digitized Curves)

Duff, T. (1985). "Compositing 3D Rendered Images," *Computer Graphics.* (Fast Anti-Aliasing Polygon Scan Conversion)

Dürst, M. J. (1988). "Additional Reference to Marching Cubes," *Computer Graphics*. **22**(2), 72–73. (Defining Surfaces from Sampled Data)

Farin, G. (1988). *Curves and Surfaces for Computer Aided Geometric Design*. Academic Press. (A Bézier Curve–Based Root-Finder; Explicit Cubic Spline Interpolation Formulas)

Faux, I., and Pratt, M. (1979). *Computational Geometry for Design and Manufacture*. Ellis Horwood Ltd., Chichester, West Sussex, England. (Properties of Surface Normal Transformations)

Fishkin, K. P., and Barsky, B. A. (1985). "An Analysis and Algorithm for Filling Propagation," *Proc. Graphics Interface '85*, 203–212. (A Seed Fill Algorithm; Filling a Region in a Frame Buffer)

Floyd, R. W., and Steinberg, L. (1975). "An Adaptive Algorithm for Spatial Gray Scale," *Society for Information Displays*. International Symposium Digest of Technical Papers, p. 36. (A Digital "Dissolve" Effect)

Foley, J. D., and Van Dam, A. (1982). *Fundamentals of Interactive Computer Graphics*. Addison-Wesley, Reading, Mass. (Fast Scan Conversion of Arbitrary Polygons; A Digital "Dissolve" Effect; Efficient Post-Concatenation of Transformation Matrices; 3D Viewing and Rotation Using Orthonormal Bases)

Fuchs, H., Kedem, Z. M., and Uselton, S. P. (1977). "Optimal Surface Reconstruction from Planar Contours," *Communications of the ACM*. **20**(10), 693–702. (Defining Surfaces from Contour Data)

Ganapathy, S., and Dennehy, T. G. (1982). "A New General Triangulation Method for Planar Contours," *Computer Graphics*. **16**(3), 69–75. (Defining Surfaces from Contour Data)

Gasson, P. C. (1983). *Geometry of Spatial Forms*. Ellis Horwood Ltd., Chichester, West Sussex, England. (Efficient Post-Concatenation of Transformation Matrices)

Giloi, W. K. (1978). *Interactive Computer Graphics*. Prentice-Hall, Englewood Cliffs, N.J. (An Algorithm for Automatically Fitting Digitized Curves)

Glassner, A. S. (1984). "Adaptive Precision in Texture Mapping," *Computer Graphics* (SIGGRAPH). **20**(4). (Interpretation of Texture Map Indices)

Glassner, A. S., *et al.* (1989). *An Introduction to Ray Tracing*. Academic Press, London. (Fast Dot Products for Shading)

Goldman, R. N. (1985). "Illicit Expressions in Vector Algebra," *ACM Transactions on Graphics*. **4**(3). (Forms, Vectors, and Transforms)

Gouraud, H. (1971a). "Continuous Shading of Curved Surfaces," *IEEE Transactions on Computer*. (Reprinted in H. Freeman, ed., *Interactive Computer Graphics*, IEEE Computer Society.) (Computing Surface Normals for 3D Models)

Gouraud, H. (1971b). "Computer Display of Curved Surfaces," *IEEE Transactions* **C-20**(6), 623. (Computing Surface Normals for 3D Models)

Graham, R. L., Knuth, D. E., and Patashnik, O. (1989). *Concrete Mathematics*. Addison-Wesley, Reading, Mass. (Rendering Fat Lines on a Raster Grid; Tutorial on Forward Differencing)

Graphics Standards Planning Committee (1979). "Status Report of the Graphics Standards Committee," *Computer Graphics*. **13**(3). (A Fast HSL-to-RGB Transform)

Greene, N. (1983). "Transformation Identities," Technical Report No. 14, New York Institute of Technology Computer Graphics Lab. (Transformation Identities)

Greene, N. (1986). "Environment Mapping and Other Applications of World Projection," *IEEE Computer Graphics and Applications*. **6**(11), 21–29. (Digital Cartography for Computer Graphics)

Greene, N., and Heckbert, P. (1986). "Creating Raster Omnimax Images from Multiple Perspective Views Using the Elliptical Weighted Average Filter," *IEEE Computer Graphics & Applications*. (Interpretation of Texture Map Indices)

Grossman, M. (1970). "Parametric Curve Fitting," *The Computer Journal*. **14**(2), 169–172. (An Algorithm for Automatically Fitting Digitized Curves)

Gupta, S., and Sproull, R. F. (1981). "Filtering Edges for Gray-Scale Displays," *Computer Graphics*. **15**(3), 1–5. (Area of Intersection: Circle and a Half-Plane; Vertical Distance from a Point to a Line)

Hall, R. A. (1989). *Illumination and Color in Computer Generated Imagery*. Springer-Verlag, New York. (Fast Dot Products for Shading)

Hearn, D., and Baker, M. P. (1986). *Computer Graphics*. Prentice-Hall, Englewood Cliffs, N.J. (3D Viewing and Rotation Using Orthonormal Bases)

Heckbert, P. S. (to appear). "An Algorithm for In-Place Filtered Zoom." (A Fast Algorithm for General Raster Rotation)

Heckbert, P. S. (1982). "Color Image Quantization for Frame Buffer Display," *ACM Computer Graphics* (SIGGRAPH). **16**(3), 297–307. (A Digital "Dissolve" Effect; Proper Treatment of Pixels as Integers; A Simple Method for Color Quantization: Octree Quantization)

Heckbert, P. S. (1984). "Techniques for Real-Time Frame Buffer Animation," Computer FX '84 Conference, London. (Mapping RGB Triples onto Four Bits)

Heckbert, P. S. (1989). "Fundamentals of Texture Mapping and Image Warping," Master's thesis, UCB/CSD 89/516, Dept. of Computer Science, University of California at Berkeley. (Generic Convex Polygon Scan Conversion and Clipping)

Higgins, T. M., and Booth, K. S. (1986). "A Cell-Based Model for Paint Systems," *Proceedings, Graphics Interface, '86*, Canadian Information Processing Society, 82–90. (A Fast Algorithm for General Raster Rotation)

Hobby, J. D. (1985). "Digitized Brush Trajectories," Report No. STAN-CS-85-1070, Dept. of Computer Science, Stanford University. (Rendering Fat Lines on a Raster Grid)

Holden, A. (1971). *Shapes, Space, and Symmetry*. Columbia University Press, New York. (A Digital "Dissolve" Effect)

Holladay, T. M. (1980). "An Optimum Algorithm for Halftone Generation for Displays and Hard Copies," *Proc. Soc. Inf. Display*. **21**, 185–192. (Periodic Tilings of the Plane on a Raster Grid)

Huang, T. S., ed. (1980). "Two-Dimensional Digital Signal Processing II, Transforms and

Median Filters,'' in *Topics in Applied Physics* (*43*). Springer-Verlag, Berlin. (Median Findings on a 3×3 Grid)

Ichida, K., Kiyono, T., and Yoshimoto, F. (1977). "Curve Fitting by a One-Pass Method with a Piecewise Cubic Polynomial," *ACM Transactions on Mathematical Software.* **3**(2), 164–174. (An Algorithm for Automatically Fitting Digitized Curves)

Ingalls, D. H. H. (1978). "The Smalltalk-76 Programming System: Design and Implementation," *Fifth ACM Symp. Prin. Prog. Lang.*, 9–16. (A Fast Algorithm for General Raster Rotation)

Jakson, C. L., and Tanimoto, S. L. (1980). "Octrees and Their Use in Representing Three-Dimensional Objects," *Computer Graphics and Image Processing.* **14**(3), 249–270. (A Simple Method for Color Quantization: Octree Quantization)

Jarvis, J. F., Judice, N., and Nike, N. H. (1976). "A Survey of Techniques for the Display of Continuous Tone Pictures on Bilevel Displays," *Computer Graphics and Image Processing.* **5**(1), 13–40 (A Simple Method for Color Quantization: Octree Quantization)

Joblove, G. H., and Greenberg, D. (1978). "Color Spaces for Computer Graphics," *ACM Computer Graphics* (SIGGRAPH). **12**(3), 20–25. (A Digital "Dissolve" Effect)

Johnson, J. R. (1989). *Introduction to Digital Signal Processing.* Prentice Hall, Englewood Cliffs, N.J. (A Fast Algorithm for General Raster Rotation)

Kajiya, J., and Von Herzen, B. P. (1984). "Ray Tracing Volume Densities," *Computer Graphics* (SIGGRAPH). **18**(3). (Simulating Fog and Haze)

Kajiya, J. T. (1986). "The Rendering Equation," *Computer Graphics.* **20**(4), 269–278. (Efficient Generation of Sampling Jitter Using Look-up Tables)

Kaufman, A., and Bakalash, R. (1988). "Memory and Processing Architecture for 3D Voxel-Based Imagery," *IEEE Computer Graphics and Applications.* **18**(11), 10–23. (Spheres-to-Voxels Conversion)

Kindle, J. (1950). *Analytic Geometry.* Schaum's Outline Series, McGraw-Hill, New York. (Useful 2D Geometry)

Klok, F. (1986). "Two Moving Coordinate Frames for Sweeping along a 3D Trajectory," *Computer Aided Geometric Design.* **3**. (Calculation of Reference Frames along a Space Curve)

Knowlton, K. (1980). "Progressive Transmission of Grey-Scale and Binary Pictures by Simple, Efficient, and Lossless Encoding Schemes," *Proc. IEEE.* **68**(7), 885–896. (Recording Animation in Binary Order for Progressive Temporal Refinement)

Knuth, D. E. (1981). *The Art of Computer Programming—Seminumerical Algorithms, Vol. 2, (2nd ed.).* Addison-Wesley, Reading, Mass. (Efficient Generation of Sampling Jitter Using Look-up Tables)

Knuth, D. E. (1981). *Art of Computer Programming, Vol. 2, Fundamental Algorithms.* Addison-Wesley, Reading, Mass. (Periodic Tilings of the Plane on a Raster Grid)

Kornfeld, C. (1977). "The Image Prism: A Device for Rotating and Mirroring Bitmap Images," *IEEE Computer Graphics and Applications.* **7**(5), 25. (A Fast Algorithm for General Raster Rotation)

Kozak, J. (1986). "Shape Preserving Approximation," *Computers in Industry.* **7**, 435–440. (An Algorithm for Automatically Fitting Digitized Curves)

Krieger, R. A. (1984). "3-D Environments for 2-D Animation," Math Essay, University of Waterloo, Ontario. (A Fast Algorithm for General Raster Rotation)

Lane, J. (1989). Personal communication. (A Bézier Curve–Based Root-Finder)

Lawson, C. L., and Hanson, R. J. (1974). *Solving Least-Squares Problems.* Prentice-Hall, Englewood Cliffs, N.J. (Computing Surface Normals for 3D Models)

L'Ecuyer, P. (1988). "Efficient and Portable Combined Random Number Generators," *Communications of the ACM.* **31**(6), 742–749. (Efficient Generation of Sampling Jitter Using Look-up Tables)

Lee, M. E., Redner, R. A., and Uselton, S. P. (1985). "Statistically Optimized Sampling for Distributed Ray Tracing," *Computer Graphics.* **19**(3), 51–72. (Efficient Generation of Sampling Jitter Using Look-up Tables)

Levoy, M. S. (1981). "Area Flooding Algorithms," presented at SIGGRAPH '82 2D Animation Tutorial. (Filling a Region in a Frame Buffer)

Lien, S., Shantz, M., and Pratt, V. (1987). "Adaptive Forward Differencing for Rendering Curves and Surfaces," *Computer Graphics* (SIGGRAPH). **21**(4). (Tutorial on Forward Differencing)

Limb, J. O., Rubinstein, C. D., and Thompson, J. E. (1977). "Digital Coding of Color Video Signals—A Review," *IEEE Trans. Communication.* **25**(11), 1349–1385. (A Digital "Dissolve" Effect)

Lorenson, W., and Cline, H. (1987). "Marching Cubes: A High Resolution 3D Surface Construction Algorithm," *Computer Graphics.* **21**(4), 163–169. (Defining Surfaces from Sampled Data)

Lozover, O., and Preiss, K. (1981). "Automatic Generation of a Cubic B-Spline Representation for a General Digitized Curve." In Encarancao, J. L., ed., *Eurographics '81.* North-Holland. (An Algorithm for Automatically Fitting Digitized Curves)

Maillot, P.-G. (1983). *PATK3D: Logiciel interactif de visualisation d'objets en 3 dimensions,* Université Claude Bernard, Lyon I, Lyon, France. (Using Quaternions for Coding 3D Transformations)

Maillot, P.-G. (1986). *Contribution à l'étude des systèmes graphiques, architectures logicielle et matérielle,* Ph.D. Thesis. Université Claude Bernard, Lyon I, Lyon, France. (Using Quaternions for Coding 3D Transformations)

McKeown, K. R., and Badler, N. I. (1980). "Creating Polyhedral Stellations," *ACM Computer Graphics* (SIGGRAPH). **14**(3), 19–24. (A Digital "Dissolve" Effect)

Max, N. (1989). "Smooth Appearance for Polygonal Surfaces," *Visual Computer.* Vol. 5, 160–173. (Computing Surface Normals for 3D Models)

Meagher, D. (1982). "Geometric Modelling Using Octree Encoding," *Computer Graphics and Image Processing.* **19**(2), 129–147. (A Simple Method for Color Quantization: Octree Quantization; Spheres-to-Voxels Conversion)

Misner, C. W., Thorne, K. S., and Wheeler, J. A. (1973). *Gravitation.* Freeman. (Forms, Vectors, and Transforms)

Morton, (1986). "A Digital Dissolve for Bit-Mapped Graphics Screens," *Dr. Dobb's Journal*. (A Digital "Dissolve" Effect)

Newell, M. E., and Sequin, C. H. (1980). "The Inside Story on Self-Intersecting Polygons," *Lambda*. **1**(2), 20–24. (Fast Scan Conversion of Arbitrary Polygons)

Newman, W. M., and Sproull, R. F. (1979). *Principles of Interactive Computer Graphics*. McGraw-Hill, New York. (A Fast Algorithm for General Raster Rotation (first ed.); A Digital "Dissolve" Effect; 3D Viewing and Rotation Using Orthonormal Bases (second ed.); The Use of Coordinate Frames in Computer Graphics)

Nicholl, T. M., Nicholl, R. A., and Lee, D. T. (1987). "An Efficient New Algorithm for 2-D Line Clipping," *ACM Computer Graphics*. **21**(4), 253–261. (Two-Dimensional Clipping: A Vector-Based Approach)

Niimi, H., *et al.* (1984). "A Parallel Processor System for Three-Dimensional Color Graphics," *Computer Graphics* (SIGGRAPH). **20**(4), 95–101. (Scanline Depth Gradient of a Z-Buffered Triangle)

Nishimura, H., Ohno, H., Kawata, T., Shirakawa, I., and Omura, K. (1983). "LINKS-1: A Parallel Pipelined Multimicrocomputer System for Image Creation," *Conference Proceedings of the 10th Annual International Symposium on Computer Architecture*, SIGGARCH, 387–394. (Efficient Generation of Sampling Jitter Using Look-up Tables)

Oppenheim, A. V., and Schaeffer, R. W. (1975). *Digital Signal Processing*. Prentice-Hall, Englewood Cliffs, N.J. (Filters for Common Resampling Tasks)

Paeth, A. W. (1986). "Design and Experience with a Generalized Raster Toolkit," *Proceedings, Graphics Interface '86*, Canadian Information Processing Society, Vancouver. (Median Finding on a 3×3 Grid; A Digital "Dissolve" Effect; Proper Treatment of Pixels as Integers)

Paeth, A. W. (1986a). "A Fast Algorithm for General Raster Rotation," *Proceedings, Graphics Interface '86*, Canadian Information Processing Society, Vancouver. 77–81. (A Fast Algorithm for General Raster Rotation; Transformation Identities)

Paeth, A. W. (1986b). "The IM Raster Toolkit—Design, Implementation, and Use," University of Waterloo Technical Report CS-86-65. (Median Finding on a 3×3 Grid; A Fast Algorithm for General Raster Rotation; A Digital "Dissolve" Effect; Proper Treatment of Pixels as Integers)

Paeth, A. W. (1987). "The IM Raster Toolkit—Design, Implementation, and Use," Institute for Computer Research Report UW/ICR 87-03. (Median Finding on a 3×3 Grid; A Fast Algorithm for General Raster Rotation; A Digital "Dissolve" Effect; Proper Treatment of Pixels as Integers)

Paeth, A. W. (1988). "Lemming Editor," *IRIS Software Exchange*. Summer 1988 (1), 17. (A Fast 2D Point-on-Line Test; A Fast Approximation to the Hypotenuse)

Paeth, A. W. (1989a). "Algorithms for Fast Color Correction," *Proceedings of the SID* (Society for Information Display). **30**(3), 169–175. (Proper Treatment of Pixels as Integers)

Paeth, A. W. (1989b). "Algorithms for Fast Color Correction," University of Waterloo Technical Report CS-89-42. (Proper Treatment of Pixels as Integers)

Paeth, A. W. (to appear). "Color Cubes and Color Polyhedra and Color Mapping." (A Digital "Dissolve" Effect)

Paeth, A. W. (to appear). "Fast Median Finding Using Exchange Networks," University of Waterloo Technical Report CS-90. (Median Finding on a 3 × 3 Grid)

Pars, L. A. (1965). *A Treatise on Analytical Dynamics*. John Wiley and Sons, New York. (Rotation Tools)

Pavlidis, T. (1983). "Curve Fitting with Conic Splines," *ACM Transactions on Graphics*. **2**, 1–31. (An Algorithm for Automatically Fitting Digitized Curves)

PHIGS. (1987). *Programmer's Hierarchical Interactive Graphics System (PHIGS)* ISO, DIS 9592-1. (Using Quaternions for Coding 3D Transformations)

Piegl, L. (1986). "Curve Fitting Algorithm for Rough Cutting," *Computer-Aided Design*. **18**(2), 79–82. (An Algorithm for Automatically Fitting Digitized Curves)

Pinkert, J. R. (1976). "An Exact Method of Finding Roots of a Complex Polynomial," *ACM Transactions on Mathematics*. **2**(4). (Using Sturm Sequences to Bracket Real Roots of Polynomial Equations)

Pique, M. E. (1987). "Semantics of Interactive Rotations," *Proceedings of 1986 Workshop on 3D Graphics*, 259–269. (Rotation Tools)

Plass, M., and Stone, M. (1983). "Curve-Fitting with Piecewise Parametric Cubics," *Computer Graphics*. **17**(3), 229–239. (An Algorithm for Automatically Fitting Digitized Curves)

Phong, B.-T. (1973). "Illumination for Computer-Generated Images," Univ. of Utah Comput. Sci. Dept. UTEC-CSC **73**, 129. (Computing Surface Normals for 3D Models)

Porter, T., and Duff, T. (1984). "Composing Digital Images," *ACM Computer Graphics* (SIGGRAPH). **18**(3), 253–259. (A Fast Algorithm for General Raster Rotation; Alpha Blending)

Press, W. H. (1988). *Numerical Recipes in C: The Art of Scientific Computing*. Cambridge University Press. (Efficient Generation of Sampling Jitter Using Look-up Tables)

Ralston, A. (1965). *A First Course in Numerical Analysis*. McGraw-Hill. (Tutorial on Forward Differencing)

Reeves, W. T. (1981). "Quantitative Representations of Complex Dynamic Shapes for Motion Analysis," Ph.D. thesis, University of Toronto. (An Algorithm for Automatically Fitting Digitized Curves)

Reinsch, C. H. (1967). "Smoothing by Spline Functions," *Numerische Mathematik*. **10**, 177–183. (An Algorithm for Automatically Fitting Digitized Curves)

Rogers, D. F. (1985). *Procedural Elements for Computer Graphics*. McGraw-Hill, New York. (Spheres-to-Voxels Conversion; Concave Polygon Scan Conversion)

Rogers, D. F., and Adams, J. A. (1976). *Mathematical Elements for Computer Graphics*. McGraw-Hill, New York. (Rotation Tools)

Rokne, J. G., Wyvill, B., and Wu, X. (1990). "Fast Line Scan-Conversion," *ACM Transactions on Graphics*. In press. (Symmetric Double Step Line Algorithm)

Ross, S. (1976). *A First Course in Probability*. Macmillan. (Multidimensional Sum Tables)

Salmon, R., and Slater, M. (1987). *Computer Graphics: Systems and Concepts*. Addison-Wesley, Reading, Mass. (3D Viewing and Rotation Using Orthonormal Bases)

Scheid, F. (1968). *Schaum's Outline of Numerical Analysis*. McGraw-Hill. (Tutorial on Forward Differencing)

Schmitt, F. J. M., Barsky, B. A., and Du, W. H. (1986). "An Adaptive Subdivision Method for Surface-Fitting from Sampled Data," *Proceedings of SIGGRAPH '86*, 179–188. (An Algorithm for Automatically Fitting Digitized Curves)

Schneider, P. J. (1988). "Phoenix: An Interactive Curve Design System Based on the Automatic Fitting of Hand-Sketched Curves," Master's thesis, University of Washington. (A Bézier Curve–Based Root-Finder; Solving the Nearest-Point-on-Curve Problem; An Algorithm for Automatically Fitting Digitized Curves)

Schoenberg, I. J. (1973). *Cardinal Spline Interpolation*. SIAM. (Explicit Cubic Spline Interpolation Formulas)

Schumaker, R. A., Brand, R., Gilliland, M., and Sharp, W. "Study for Applying Computer Generated Images to Visual Stimulation," AFHRL-TR-69-14, U.S. Air Force Human Resources Laboratory. (A Digital "Dissolve" Effect)

Schweikert, D. G. (1966). "An Interpolation Curve Using a Spline in Tension," *J. Math. Phys.* **45**, 312–317. (An Algorithm for Automatically Fitting Digitized Curves)

Sedgewick, R. (1983). *Algorithms*. Addison-Wesley, Reading, Mass. (Two-Dimensional Clipping: A Vector-Based Approach)

Shani, U. (1980). "Filling Regions in Binary Raster Images: A Graph-Theoretic Approach," *SIGGRAPH '80 Conference Proceedings*, 321–327. (Filling a Region in a Frame Buffer)

Shani, U., and Ballard, D. H. (1984). "Splines as Embeddings for Generalized Cylinders," *Computer Vision, Graphics, and Image Processing*. **27**. (Calculation of Reference Frames along a Space Curve)

Shapira, A. (1990). "Source Code for Terrain Visibility Programs," *Computational Geometry Lab. Technical Report #90–0418*, ECSE Dept., Rensselaer Polytechnic Institute. (Fast Line–Edge Intersections on a Uniform Grid)

Shinya, M., Saito, T., and Takahashi, T. (1989). "Rendering Techniques for Transparent Objects," *Proc. Graphics Interface*, 173–182. (Shadow Attenuation for Ray Tracing Transparent Objects)

Shinya, M., Takahashi, T., and Naito, S. (1987). "Principles and Applications of Pencil Tracing," *Computer Graphics* (SIGGRAPH). **21**(4), 45–54. (Shadow Attenuation for Ray Tracing Transparent Objects)

Shoemake, K. (1985). "Animating Rotation with Quaternion Curves," *ACM, Siggraph '85*. **19**(3) 245–254. (Using Quaternions for Coding 3D Transformations)

Sloan, K. R., Jr., and Tanimoto, S. L. (1979). "Progressive Refinement of Raster Images," *IEEE Trans. on Computers*. **C-28**(11), 871–874. (Recording Animation in Binary Order for Progressive Temporal Refinement)

Sloan, K. R., Jr., and Brown, C. M. (1979). "Color Map Techniques," *Computer Graphics and Image Processing*. **10**(4), 297–317. (Mapping RGB Triples onto Four Bits)

Smith, A. R. (1978). "Color Gamut Transform Pairs," *ACM Computer Graphics* (SIGGRAPH). **12**(3), 12–19. (A Digital "Dissolve" Effect; Proper Treatment of Pixels as Integers; A Fast HSL-to-RGB Transform)

Smith, A. R. (1979). "Tint Fill," *SIGGRAPH '79 Proceedings*, 279–283. (A Seed Fill Algorithm)

Smith, A. R. (1982). "Fill Tutorial Notes," presented at SIGGRAPH '82 2D Animation Tutorial. (Filling a Region in a Frame Buffer)

Smith, A. R. (1987). "Planar 2-Pass Texture Mapping and Warping," *ACM Computer Graphics* (SIGGRAPH). **21**(4), 263–272. (A Fast Algorithm for General Raster Rotation)

Snyder, J. P. (1984). *Map Projections Used by the U.S. Geological Survey*. U.S. Government Printing Office, Washington, D.C. (Albers Equal-Area Conic Map Projection)

Snyder, J. M., and Barr, A. H. (1987). "Ray Tracing Complex Models Containing Surface Tessellations," *ACM Computer Graphics*. **21**(4). (An Efficient Ray–Polygon Intersection)

Sturm, C. (1835). "Mém. Présentés par Divers Savants," à l'Acad. Royale des Sciences de l'Institut de France, t. 6, Paris. (Using Sturm Sequences to Bracket Real Roots of Polynomial Equations)

Sutherland, I. E., and Hodgman, G. W. (1974). "Reentrant Polygon Clipping," *Communications of the ACM*. **17**(1), 32–42. (Generic Convex Polygon Scan Conversion and Clipping; Two-Dimensional Clipping: A Vector-Based Approach; Fast Anti-Aliasing Polygon Scan Conversion)

Swanson, R. W., and Thayer, L. J. (1986). "A Fast Shaded-Polygon Renderer," *Computer Graphics* (SIGGRAPH). **20**(4), 95–101. (Scanline Depth Gradient of a Z-Buffered Triangle)

Sweeney, M. (1984). "The Waterloo CGL Ray Tracing Package," Master's thesis, Dept. of Computer Science, University of Waterloo. (Shadow Attenuation for Ray Tracing Transparent Objects)

Tosan, E. (1982). *Quaternions et rotations dans l'espace*. Tutorial notes. Université Claude Bernard, Lyon I, Lyon, France. (Using Quaternions for Coding 3D Transformations)

Tountas, C., and Katz, L. (1971). "Interactive Graphics in Molecular Biology: Real-time Three-dimensional Rotations of Images and Image Fragments," Proceedings Summer Computer Simulation Conference. **1**, 241–247. (Rotation Tools)

Turkowski, K. E. (1982). "Anti-Aliasing through the Use of Coordinate Transformations," *ACM Trans. Graphics* **1**(3), 215–234. (Trigonometry with CORDIC Iterations)

Turkowski, K. E. (1986). "Anti-Aliasing in Topological Color Spaces," *ACM Computer Graphics*. (SIGGRAPH). **20**(3), 307–314. (A Digital "Dissolve" Effect)

Turnbull, M. A. (1957). *Theory of Equations*, fifth edition (reprint of original 1927 text).

Oliver and Boyd, Edinburgh. (Using Sturm Sequences to Bracket Real Roots of Polynomial Equations)

Van Wyck, C. J. (1984). "Clipping to the Boundary of a Circular-Arc Polygon," *Computer Vision, Graphics, and Image Processing.* **25**, 383–392. (Two-Dimensional Clipping: A Vector-Based Approach)

Vercken, C., Potier, C., and Vignes, S. (1987). "Spline Curve Fitting for an Interactive Design Environment," in *Theoretical Foundations of Computer Graphics and CAD.* NATO. (An Algorithm for Automatically Fitting Digitized Curves)

Volder, J. E. (1959). "The CORDIC Trigonometric Computing Technique," *IRE Trans. Electron. Comput.* **EC-8**(3), 330–334. (Trigonometry with CORDIC Iterations)

Walther, J. S. (1971). "A Unified Algorithm for Elementary Functions." In *Proceedings of AFIPS 1971 Spring Joint Computer Conference, Vol. 38,* pp. 379–385. AFIPS Press, Arlington, Virginia. (Trigonometry with CORDIC Iterations)

Watkins, M. A. (1987). "Degree Reduction of Bézier Curves and Surfaces," Master's thesis, University of Utah. (An Algorithm for Automatically Fitting Digitized Curves)

Weiman, C. F. R. (1989). "Continuous Anti-Aliased Rotation.and Zoom of Raster Images," *ACM Computer Graphics* (SIGGRAPH). **23**(3), 291. (A Fast Algorithm for General Raster Rotation)

Whitted, T., and Weimer, D. M. (1981). "A Software Testbed for the Development of 3D Raster Graphics Systems," **1**(1), 43–58. (Generic Convex Polygon Scan Conversion and Clipping)

Wilkinson, J. H. (1988). *The Algebraic Eigenvalue Problem* (reprint of original 1965 edition). Claredon Press, Oxford. (Using Sturm Sequences to Bracket Real Roots of Polynomial Equations)

Williams, L. (1978). "Casting Curved Shadows on Curved Surfaces," *Computer Graphics* (SIGGRAPH). **12**, 270–274. (Matrix Inversion)

Williams, L. (1983). "Pyramidal Parametrics," *Computer Graphics* (SIGGRAPH). **17**(3). (Interpretation of Texture Map Indices)

Wolberg, G., and Boult, T. E. (1989). "Separable Image Warping with Spatial Lookup Tables," *ACM Computer Graphics* (SIGGRAPH). **23**(3), 369–377. (A Fast Algorithm for General Raster Rotation)

Wu, S. C., Abel, J. F., and Greenburg, D. P. (1977). "An Interactive Computer Graphics Approach to Surface Representation," *Communications of the ACM.* **20**(10), 703–712. (An Algorithm for Automatically Fitting Digitized Curves)

Wu, X., and Rokne, J. G. (1987). "Double-Step Incremental Generation of Lines and Circles," *Computer Vision, Graphics and Image Processing.* **37**, 331–334. (Symmetric Double Step Line Algorithm)

Wyvill, G., McPheeters, C., and Wyvill, B. (1986). "Data Structure for *Soft* Objects," *The Visual Computer.* **2**, 227–234. (Defining Surfaces from Sampled Data)

Yamaguchi, F. (1978). "A New Curve Fitting Method Using a CRT Computer Display,"

Graphics and Image Processing, 425–437. (An Algorithm for Automatically Fitting Digitized Curves)

Yang, M., Kim, C., Cheng, K., Yang, C., and Liu, S. (1986). "Automatic Curve Fitting with Quadratic B-Spline Functions and Its Applications of Computer-Aided Animation," *Computer Vision, Graphics, and Image Processing*. **33**, 346–363. (An Algorithm for Automatically Fitting Digitized Curves)

Yellot, J. I., Jr. (1983). "Spectral Consequences of Photoreceptor Sampling in the Rhesus Retina," *Science*. No. 221, 382–385. (Efficient Generation of Sampling Jitter Using Look-up Tables)

Zwikker, C. (1963). *Advanced Geometry of Plane Curves*. Dover Publications, New York. (Useful 2D Geometry)

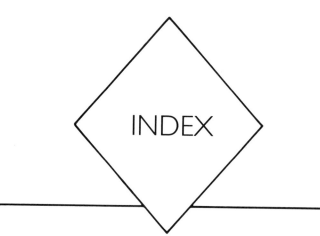

INDEX

GRAPHICS GEMS

Designed by Joni Hopkins McDonald.
Chapter opening graphics drawn by Andrew S. Glassner.
Composed by Science Typographers Incorporated
in Century School Book, Tegra Century 702
with display lines in Tegra Humanist 521.
Printed and bound by The Maple-Vail Book Manufacturing Group.